# Writing About Literature

## TWELFTH EDITION

## Edgar V. Roberts

*Professor Emeritus, Lehman College*
*The City University of New York*

**Longman**

Boston   Columbus   Indianapolis   New York   San Francisco   Upper Saddle River

Amsterdam   Cape Town   Dubai   London   Madrid   Milan   Munich   Paris   Montreal   Toronto

Delhi   Mexico City   Sao Paulo   Sydney   Hong Kong   Seoul   Singapore   Taipei   Tokyo

Senior Acquisitions Editor: Vivian Garcia
Executive Marketing Manager: Joyce Nilsen
Production Manager: Savoula Amanatidis
Project Coordination, Text Design, and Electronic Page Makeup: Nesbitt Graphics, Inc.
Cover Design Manager: Wendy Ann Fredericks
Cover and Chapter Opener Photo: Copyright © Mark Klein/Klein Photography
Senior Manufacturing Buyer: Dennis J. Para
Printer and Binder: Courier Corporation—Stoughton
Cover Printer: Courier Corporation—Stoughton

For permission to use copyrighted material, grateful acknowledgment is made to the copyright holders on p. 413, which are hereby made part of this copyright page.

**Library of Congress Cataloging-in-Publication Data**
Roberts, Edgar V.
    Writing about literature / Edgar V. Roberts. — 12th ed.
    p. cm.
    Includes bibliographical references and index.
    ISBN-13: 978-0-13-601456-0 (alk. paper)
    ISBN-10: 0-13-601456-9 (alk. paper)
  1.  English language—Rhetoric.  2.  Criticism—Authorship.  3.  Academic writing.  I. Title.
    PE1479.C7R59 2009
    808'.0668—dc22

                        2009034447

**Longman**
is an imprint of

www.pearsonhighered.com

3 4 5 6 7 8 9 10—CRS—12 11 10

ISBN-13: 978-0-13-601456-0
ISBN-10: 0-13-601456-9

## Part II   Writing Essays on Designated Literary Topics

### CHAPTER 2   WRITING ABOUT A CLOSE READING: ANALYZING ENTIRE SHORT POEMS OR SELECTED SHORT PASSAGES   52

### CHAPTER 3   WRITING ABOUT POINT OF VIEW: THE POSITION OR STANCE OF THE WORK'S NARRATOR OR SPEAKER   65

# Contents

## PART III    Writing about More General Literary Topics

### CHAPTER 14   WRITING ABOUT A PROBLEM: CHALLENGES TO OVERCOME IN READING      214

### CHAPTER 15   WRITING ESSAYS OF COMPARISON-CONTRAST AND EXTENDED COMPARISON-CONTRAST: LEARNING BY SEEING LITERARY WORKS TOGETHER      224

STORIES

*A woman is shocked by news of her husband's death, but there is still a greater shock in store for her.*

*Worthiness cannot rise when it is depressed by poverty and inequality.*

*Living in colonial Salem, Young Goodman Brown has a bewildering encounter that affects his outlook on life and his attitudes toward people.*

## POEMS

## PLAYS

# To Instructors

In the twelfth edition of *Writing About Literature*, I have kept and strengthened those features that you have valued over the years. While the constant emphasis in the book is on writing complete essays about literature, the chapters may be used as starting points for classroom study and discussion and may also be adapted for shorter writing assignments. In a one-semester course, the book offers selective choices for study and writing, whereas in a two- or three-semester sequence, it is extensive enough to offer the possibility of complete or close-to-complete use.

The various chapter discussions were originally developed as essay assignments. Many years ago, when I was just starting out as a teacher of literature and writing, I learned that there was a direct connection between the ways I made my assignments and the quality of student work. The more I described to my students what I wanted, and the longer I took in explaining things, the better their final essays turned out to be. Soon, however, I found myself spending close to entire periods in assigning essays, and it was then that I began to hand out my directions, thus saving much valuable classroom time. I tried and tested each assignment in a number of separate classes, and I made innumerable improvements based on both student questions and student writing. When I was able to put everything together, *Writing Themes About Literature*, now *Writing About Literature*, was the result, first published in 1964.

## Organization

An important alteration for the twelfth edition is that Chapter 1, the general introduction, is also numbered as Part I to emphasize its significance as a major introductory section. The arrangement of the major chapters is also new here, under the categories "Part II, Writing Essays on Designated Literary Topics" and "Part III, Writing about More General Literary Topics." Another new feature of the twelfth edition is an extra chapter-title line indicating which genres might be most suitable for the approach discussed in the chapter. Some of the topics—such as setting ("Fiction, Drama, and Narrative Poems"), point of view ("Fiction and Narrative Poetry"), and prosody ("Poetry")—lend themselves naturally to particular genres. Of course, for many of the assignments, all three genres are, and always have been, convenient. The comparison-contrast chapter in Part III (Chapter 15), for example, illustrates the ways in which the earlier techniques may be focused on any of the chapter-title topics in the book. This chapter also illustrates how a longer comparison-contrast essay may consider all the genres simultaneously, as a group.

As in past editions, each chapter on literary topics consists of two parts. The first part is a discussion of a particular writing approach—such as character, structure, or prosody—and the second part consists of suggestions for writing, together with an Illustrative Essay (or essays) showing how students might wish to adapt the approach for their own assignments. A major characteristic preserved in this edition is that, after the general introduction of Part I, the chapters of Parts II and III are arranged in a loose order of increasing difficulty. Thus, the chapters on prosody (Chapter 13) and research (Chapter 18) are increasingly detailed and complex, but they also build on the various techniques of analysis presented in the earlier chapters. Chapter 16, on literary works as they are related to their historical period, might work best if students acquire an introduction, either through study or discussion, to some of the issues that were important when particular works were published.

Part IV includes the appendices. Appendix A is a brief introduction to various critical approaches to literary study. Appendix B concerns the always essential topic of documentation. A brief collection of works used for references and Illustrative Essays is contained in Appendix C. This appendix is not intended as a full-scale anthology, but is intended to help make the discussions and the Illustrative Essays self-contained.

Although you might assign the chapters in sequence throughout your course, you may also choose them according to your objectives and needs. For example, you might wish to pass over the earlier chapters and go directly to the later ones. You might also choose the chapter on comparison-contrast (Chapter 15) as the basis of separate assignments such as symbolism, structure, character, or point of view. Or you might concentrate on just a few of the chapters, assigning them two or more times until students overcome initial difficulties. No matter how the chapters are used, the two parts—discussion and illustration—are designed to encourage students to improve their skills as readers and writers.

The Illustrative Essays concluding the chapters are offered in the belief that the word *imitation* need not be preceded by adjectives like *slavish* and *mere*. In the twelfth edition there are twelve Illustrative Essays that were not a part of the eleventh addition, including three that are entirely new. I emphasize that the purpose of these essays is to show what *might* be done—not what *must* be done—on particular assignments. It is clear that students writing about literary works are facing a complex task. First, they must read a new work for the first time; second, they must attempt to understand it; and third, they must then apply new or unfamiliar concepts to that work as they begin to write about it. By guiding them in developing a thematic form in which to express their ideas, the Illustrative Essays are intended to help them overcome the third difficulty. *Guidance* and *help* are keys here, *not* prescription. At first, of course, some students may want to follow the Illustrative Essays closely, whereas others may adapt them or else use them as points of departure. My hope is that students will free themselves to go their own ways as they gain more writing experience.

Following the Illustrative Essays are commentaries, something students recommended that I include in the fourth edition, and that I have kept ever since. These are designed to connect the principles in the first part of each chapter to the interpretive writing in the second part.

## Revisions, Additions, Other Changes, and Retentions

All changes in the twelfth edition of *Writing About Literature*, as in earlier editions, are designed to help students read, study, think, plan, organize, draft, and write. In making the many revisions, alterations, rearrangements, and additions (as well as subtractions), I have tried to clarify, improve, and freshen the underlying information and examples. In addition to the new essays, many of the titles, headings, and subheadings have been retained to make them encapsulate the discussions they precede. My hope is that these informative headings will assist students in their understanding of the various topics. In a number of the chapters, the writing sections headed "Raise Questions to Develop Ideas" are augmented, and to the various "Writing Topics about . . ." sections I have designed topics to help students when they go to the library or to search the Web. Questions in these sections are mainly keyed to the works anthologized in Appendix C ("Works Used for References and Illustrative Essays"), but I encourage you to adapt them to the selections in whatever anthologies you may be using. In a number of chapters, there are short related topics that are boxed and shaded to set them apart for emphasis. These discussions, such as "Referring to Authors' Names," "Vehicle and Tenor," and "Plagiarism: An Embarrassing but Vital Subject—and a Danger to Be Overcome," to name just a few, are designed as short notes to help students think about and develop their own writing. Users of previous editions have found these boxed discussions helpful.

Aside from the extensive revisions and improvements, the chapters are internally different because of a number of changes in Appendix C. The twelfth edition of *Writing About Literature* is not designed as a full-scale anthology, but even so the selections are intended to be as representative as possible. Additions to Appendix C are John Donne's "Death Be Not Proud," Shirley Jackson's "The Lottery," Edgar Allan Poe's "The Cask of Amontillado," Eudora Welty's "A Worn Path," and Walt Whitman's "Reconciliation." Also, a small number of works included in the eleventh edition have been omitted here. To accompany these changes, there are a number of changes in the topics of the Illustrative Essays. With all the changes, the twelfth edition of *Writing About Literature* remains a comprehensive guide for composition courses in which literature is introduced and for literature courses at any level.

An innovation of the sixth edition that has been retained in all subsequent editions is the glossary, which is based on the terms set in boldface in the text. The increasing number of students taking entrance examinations and the GRE has justified this continuation. To help students acquaint themselves with important literary terms and concepts, the glossary includes brief independent definitions together with text page numbers for further reference.

## Writing and Literature

The twelfth edition brings into focus something that has been true of *Writing About Literature* since it first appeared. The book is primarily a practical guide for writing; the stress throughout is on how thinking and writing skills may be improved through the reading of literature. This emphasis is made to help students not only in composition and literature but also in most of their other classes. In subjects such as biology, economics, history, political science, psychology, and sociology, instructors use texts and ask students to develop essays from raw data. Writing is based on external, written materials, not on the student's own experiences or on opinions. Writing is about reading.

Yet we instructors of writing and literature face the problems we have always faced. In our colleges and universities, the demand for good student writing has gone beyond a requirement and a goal and now has ascended to the degree of a clamor. The needs of other departments have been brought into strong focus by the creation of programs for writing across the curriculum. Such demands have correspondingly imposed a wide diversification of subject matter, straining the general knowledge of English department staffs and also creating topical and thematic pressure on composition and literature courses. Writing programs that stress internalized subject matter, such as personal experiences or occasional topic materials, have little bearing on writing for other courses. We, as English faculty with a background in literature, have the task of meeting the service needs of our institutions without compromising our own disciplinary commitment.

The approach in *Writing About Literature* is aimed at these problems. English teachers can work within their own discipline—literature—while also fulfilling a major and usually required responsibility of teaching writing that is externally, not internally, directed. The book thus keeps the following issues in perspective:

- The requirement by our institutions for thinking and writing skills
- The need of students to develop as writers through the study of written texts
- The responsibility of the English faculty to teach writing while still working within their own expertise

It is therefore gratifying to claim that, for the last four and a half decades, *Writing About Literature* has been offering assistance to meet these needs. The approach works but I believe it is still novel. It gives coherence to the sometimes  fragmented composition course. It also provides for adaptation and, as I have stressed, variety. Using the book, you can develop a virtually endless number of new topics for essays. One obvious benefit is the possibility of entirely eliminating not only the "theme barrels" of infamous memory but also the newer interference from "enterprises" that provide critical and research essays through the Internet. I do not have words to express my contempt for such "business" ventures.

Although *Writing About Literature* is designed as a rhetoric of practical criticism for students, it is based on profoundly held convictions. Simply to make assignments and let students do with them what they will is to invite student frustration. If students develop knowledge of specific approaches to literary subject material, however, they can begin to improve their expertise as readers. As Alexander Pope said so well and so wittily in *An Essay on Criticism* (lines 362–63),

> True Ease in Writing comes from Art, not Chance,
> As those move easiest who have learn'd to dance.

I have a concluding article of faith. We who are devoted to the teaching of literature are committed to our belief in its value. The study of literature, together with the lifelong love of literature, is valid in and for itself. But literature as an art form employs techniques that can be fully appreciated only through study, understanding, reflection, discussion, and analysis—in short, through systematic and disciplined effort. In the pursuit of a liberal education, no one can become mentally free without intensive intellectual discipline. It is axiomatic that the development of writing skills in one area (in this instance, the interpretation of literature) has an enabling and creative effect upon skills in other areas. The search for information with a particular goal in mind; the asking of pointed questions; the testing, rephrasing, and developing of ideas—all these and more are transferable skills for students to build on throughout their college years and beyond. Thus, my aim in *Writing About Literature* is to help students read and write systematically about individual literary works and thereby develop the confidence, power, and freedom that are the close bosom-friends of professional mastery in any and all subjects.

## Acknowledgments

As I complete the twelfth edition of *Writing About Literature*, I renew my deepest thanks to all of you who have been loyal to the earlier editions. Your approval of the book is a great honor. As I think about the revisions for this edition, I am impressed with how much *Writing About Literature* has been influenced by the collective wisdom of many students and teachers. Those who have been particularly helpful for the twelfth edition are Bethany Blankenship, University of Montana Western; Kerri Jordan, Mississippi College; William A. Davis, College of Notre Dame of Maryland; Carolee Ritter, Southeast Community College; Danny L. Delong, Southeast Community College; Rafeeq O. McGiveron, Lansing Community College; Vivian Gist Spencer, Anne Arundel Community College; and Dr. Booker T. Anthony, Fayetteville State University. Conversations and discussions with many others have influenced my changes in innumerable and immeasurable ways. I thank Vivian Garcia, senior literature editor, Pearson Longman, for her constant thoughtfulness, encouragement, and helpfulness. Phil Miller of Pearson Prentice Hall has given me firm and friendly support over a number of years. I also thank the Pearson Longman production team for the twelfth edition: Donna DeBenedictis, managing editor; Savoula Amanatidis, production manager; and Dennis J. Para, senior manufacturing buyer. In addition, I am especially grateful to Heather Vomero, editorial assistant; Joyce Nilsen, executive marketing manager; Jean-Pierre Dufresne, marketing assistant; and Jennifer Bevington, text permissions researcher. Special thanks go to Betty Duncan, who diligently copyedited the manuscript and offered many, many corrections and improvements. Additional thanks are due to Aaron Downey of Matrix Productions, whose efforts on behalf of the book have been extensive. I am also grateful to Brooke Mitchell and Diane Foster. I particularly thank Jonathan Roberts for his skilled and patient help in preparing the disks of the halting and tentative drafts leading to the final copy. Thank you each and every one.

Edgar V. Roberts

# Chapter 1

# The Process of Reading, Responding to, and Writing about Literature

Fiction, Poetry, and Drama

The following chapters introduce a number of analytical approaches important in the study of literature, along with guidance for writing informative and well-focused essays based on these approaches. The chapters will help you fulfill two goals of composition and English courses: (1) to write good essays; and (2) to understand and assimilate great works of literature.

The premise of the book is that no educational process is complete until you can *apply* what you study. That is, you have not learned something—really *learned* it—until you talk or write about it. This does not mean that you retell a story, state an undeveloped opinion, or describe an author's life, but rather that you deal directly with topical and artistic issues about individual works. The need to write requires that you strengthen your understanding and knowledge through the recognition of where your original study might have fallen short. Thus, it is easy for you to read the chapter on point of view (Chapter 3), and it is also easy to read Shirley Jackson's story "The Lottery." Your grasp of point of view as a concept will not be complete, however, nor will your appreciation of the technical artistry of this story be complete, until you have prepared yourself to write about the technique. As you do so, you will need to reread parts of the work, study your notes, and apply your knowledge to the problem at hand; you must check facts, grasp relationships, develop insights, and try to express yourself with as much exactness and certainty as possible.

Primarily, then, this book aims to help you improve your writing skills through the use of literature as subject matter. After you have finished a number of essays derived from the following chapters, you will be able to approach just about any literary work with the confidence that you can understand it and write about it.

## What is Literature, and Why Do We Study It?

We use the word **literature**, in a broad sense, to mean compositions that tell stories, dramatize situations, express emotions, and analyze and advocate ideas. Before the invention of writing thousands of years ago, literary works were necessarily spoken or sung, and they were retained only as long as living people continued to repeat them. In some societies, the oral tradition of literature still exists, with many poems and stories designed exclusively for spoken delivery. Even in our modern age of writing, printing, and electronic communication, much literature is still heard aloud rather than read silently. Parents delight their children with stories and poems read aloud; poets and storywriters read their works directly before live audiences; plays and scripts are interpreted on stages and before movie and television cameras for the benefit of a vast public.

No matter how we assimilate literature, we gain much from it. In truth, readers often cannot explain why they enjoy reading, for goals and ideals are not easily articulated. There are, however, areas of general agreement about the value of systematic and extensive reading.

Literature helps us grow, both personally and intellectually. It opens doors for us. It stretches our minds. It develops our imagination, increases our understanding, and enlarges our power of sympathy. It helps us see beauty in the world around us. It links us with the cultural, philosophical, and religious world of which we are a part. It enables us to recognize human dreams and struggles in different places and times. It helps us develop mature sensibility and compassion for all living beings. It nurtures our ability to appreciate the beauty of order and arrangement—gifts that are also bestowed by a well-structured song, a beautifully painted canvas, or a skillfully chiseled statue. It enables us to see worthiness in the aims of all people. It exercises our emotions through interest, concern, sympathy, tension, excitement, regret, fear, laughter, and hope. It encourages us to assist creative and talented people who need recognition and support. Through our cumulative experience in reading, literature shapes our goals and values by clarifying our own identities—both positively, through acceptance of the admirable in human beings, and negatively, through rejection of the sinister. It enables us to develop perspectives on events occurring locally and globally, and thereby it gives us understanding and control. It is one of the shaping influences of life. It makes us human.

## Types of Literature: The Genres

Literature may be classified into four categories or genres: (1) prose fiction, (2) poetry, (3) drama, and (4) nonfiction prose. Usually the first three are classified as **imaginative literature**.

The genres of imaginative literature not only have much in common but also distinguishing characteristics. **Prose fiction**, or **narrative fiction**, includes **myths, parables, romances, novels**, and **short stories**. Originally, fiction meant anything made up, crafted, or shaped, but today the word refers to prose stories based in the imaginations of authors. The essence of fiction is **narration**, the relating or recounting of a sequence of events or **actions**. Fictional works usually focus on one or a few major characters who change and grow (in their ability to make decisions, their awareness or insight, their intellect, their attitude toward others, their sensitivity, and their moral capacity) as a result of how they deal with other characters and how they attempt to solve their problems. Although fiction, like all imaginative literature, can introduce true historical details, it is not real history, for its main purpose is to interest, stimulate, instruct, and divert, not to create a precise historical record.

If prose is expansive, **poetry** tends toward brevity. It offers us high points of emotion, reflection, thought, and feeling in what the English poet Wordsworth called "narrow room[s]." Yet in this context, it expresses the most powerful and deeply felt experiences of human beings, often awakening deep **responses** of welcome recognition: "Yes, I know what that's like. I would feel the same way. That's exactly right." Poems make us think, make us reflect, and generally instruct us. They can also stimulate us, surprise us, make us laugh or cry, inspire us, exalt us. Many poems become our lifelong friends, and we visit them again and again for insight, understanding, laughter, or the quiet reflection of joy or sorrow.

Poetry's power lies not only in its words and thoughts but also its music, using rhyme and a variety of rhythms to intensify its emotional impact. Although poems themselves vary widely in length, individual lines are often short because poets distill the greatest meaning and imaginative power from their words through rhetorical devices such as **imagery** and **metaphor**. Though poetry often requires many formal and metrical restrictions, it is paradoxically the very restrictiveness of poetry that provides poets with great freedom. Traditionally important poetic forms include the fourteen-line **sonnet**, as well as **ballads**, **blank verse**, **couplets**, **elegies**, epigrams, **hymns**, limericks, **odes**, **quatrains**, **songs** or **lyrics**, **tercets** or **triplets**, **villanelles**, and the increasingly popular **haiku**. Many songs or lyrics have been set to music, and some were written expressly for that purpose. Some poems are long and discursive, like many poems by the American poet Walt Whitman. **Epic** poems, such as those by Homer and Milton, contain thousands of lines. Since the time of Whitman, many poets have abandoned rhymes and regular rhythms in favor of **free verse**, a far-ranging type of poetry growing out of content and the natural rhythms of spoken language.

**Drama** is literature designed for stage or film presentation by people—actors—for the benefit and delight of other people—an audience. The essence of drama is the development of **character** and situation through speech and action. Like fiction, drama may focus on a single character or a small number of characters, and it enacts fictional (and sometimes historical) events as if they were happening right before our eyes. The audience therefore is a direct witness to the ways in which characters are influenced and changed by events and by other characters. Although most modern plays use prose dialogue (the conversation of two or more characters), on the principle that the language of drama should resemble the language of ordinary people as much as possible, many plays from the past, such as those of ancient Greece and Renaissance England, are in poetic form.

**Nonfiction prose** consists of news reports, feature articles, essays, editorials, textbooks, historical and biographical works, and the like, all of which describe or interpret facts and present judgments and opinions. The goal of nonfiction prose is to present truths and conclusions about the factual world. Imaginative literature, although also grounded in facts, is less concerned with the factual record than with the revelation of truths about life and human nature. Recently another genre has been emphasized within the category of nonfiction prose. This is **creative nonfiction**, a type of literature that is technically nonfiction, such as essays, articles, diaries, and journals, but that nevertheless introduces carefully structured form, vivid examples, relevant quotations, and highly creative and imaginative insights.

## Reading Literature and Responding to It Actively

Sometimes we find it difficult, after we have finished reading a work, to express thoughts and to answer pointed questions about it. But more active and thoughtful reading gives us the understanding to develop well-considered answers. Obviously, we need to follow the work and to understand its details, but just as important, we need to respond to the words, get at the ideas, and understand the implications of what is happening. We rely on our own fund of knowledge and experience to verify the accuracy and truth of situations and incidents, and we try to articulate our own emotional responses to the characters and their problems.

To illustrate such active responding, let us consider "The Necklace" (1884), by the French writer Guy de Maupassant.[1] "The Necklace" is one of the best known of all stories, and it is included here with marginal notes like those that any reader might make during original and follow-up readings. Many notes, particularly at the beginning, are *assimilative*; that is, they record details about the action. But as the story progresses, the marginal comments are more concerned with conclusions about the story's meaning. Toward the end, the comments are full rather than minimal; they result not only from first responses but also from considered thought. Here, then, is Maupassant's "The Necklace."

---

[1]Henri-René-Albert-Guy de Maupassant (1850–1893) is considered one of the major nineteenth-century French naturalist writers. Scion of an aristocratic Norman family, he received his baccalaureate degree from a lycée at Le Havre, after which he began studying law. When the Franco-Prussian War broke out, he served in the French army, including battlefield duty. After leaving the military, he became a minor bureaucrat, first in the Ministry of Marine and then in the Ministry of Education (also the workplace of Loisel, the husband of "The Necklace").

As a youth, Maupassant was an energetic oarsman, swimmer, and boatman—a power that he also devoted to his career as a writer. During the 1870s in Paris, he had regularly submitted his literary efforts to the novelist Gustave Flaubert (1821–1880), a family friend who regarded him as a son and whose criticism both improved and encouraged him. In Maupassant's thirties, after the death of his mentor Flaubert, his career flourished. His first published volume was a collection of poems (*Des Vers*, 1880), which he had to withdraw after it created a scandal and a lawsuit because of its sexual openness. After this time, until his death in 1893, he produced thirty volumes—novels, poems, articles, travel books, and three hundred short stories. In addition to "The Necklace," a few of his better-known stories are "The Ball of Fat," "Mademoiselle Fifi," and "A Piece of String."

Maupassant was a meticulous writer, devoting much attention to the reality of everyday existence (hence his status as a naturalist writer). A number of his stories are about events occurring during the Franco-Prussian War. Some are about life among bureaucrats, some about peasant life in Normandy, and a large number, including "The Necklace," about Parisian life. His major stories are characterized by strong irony; human beings are influenced by forces they cannot control, and their wishes are often frustrated by their own defects. Under such circumstances, Maupassant's characters exhibit varying degrees of weakness, hypocrisy, vanity, insensitivity, callousness, and even cruelty, but those who are victimized are viewed with understanding and sympathy.

## Guy de Maupassant (1850–1893)

### *The Necklace* (1884)

Translated by Edgar V. Roberts

She was one of those pretty and charming women, born, as if by an error of destiny, into a family of clerks and copyists. She had no dowry, no prospects, no way of getting known, courted, loved, married by a rich and distinguished man. She finally settled for a marriage with a minor clerk in the Ministry of Education.

Without the money to dress well, she had to wear everyday clothes, and she was as unhappy as if she had really come down in the world, for women have neither rank nor race. In place of high birth or important family connections, they can rely only on their beauty, their grace, and their charm. Their inborn finesse, their elegant taste, their engaging personalities, which are their only power, make working-class women the equals of the grandest ladies.

She suffered constantly, feeling herself destined for all delicacies and luxuries. She suffered because of her grim apartment with its drab walls, threadbare furniture, ugly curtains. All such things, which most other women in her situation would not even have noticed, tortured her and filled her with despair. The sight of the young country girl who did her simple housework awakened in her only a sense of desolation and lost hopes. She daydreamed of large, silent anterooms, decorated with oriental tapestries and lighted by high bronze floor lamps, with two elegant valets in short culottes dozing in large armchairs under the effects of forced-air heaters. She imagined large drawing rooms draped in the most expensive silks, with fine end tables on which were placed knickknacks of inestimable value. She dreamed of the perfume of dainty private rooms, which were designed only for intimate tête-à-têtes with the closest friends, who because of their achievements and fame would make her the envy of all other women.

When she sat down to dinner at her round little table covered with a cloth that had not been washed for three days, in front of her husband who opened the kettle while declaring ecstatically, "Ah, good old beef stew! I don't know anything better," she dreamed of expensive banquets with shining place settings, and wall hangings portraying ancient heroes and exotic birds in an enchanted

*"She" is pretty but poor, and has no chance in life unless she marries. Without connections, she has no entry into high society, and she marries an insignificant clerk.*

*She is unhappy.*

*A view of women who have no chance for an independent life and a career. In 1884, women had nothing more than this. Sad.*

*She suffers because of her cheap belongings, wanting expensive things. She dreams of wealth and of how other women would envy her if she could display finery. But such luxuries are unrealistic and unattainable for her.*

*Her husband's taste is for plain things, while she dreams of expensive gourmet food. He has adjusted to his status. She has not.*

forest. She imagined a gourmet-prepared main course carried on the most exquisite trays and served on the most beautiful dishes, with whispered gallantries that she would hear with a sphinxlike smile as she dined on the pink meat of a trout or the delicate wing of a quail.

5    She had no decent dresses, no jewels, nothing. And she loved nothing but these; she believed herself born only for these. She burned with the desire to please, to be envied, to be attractive and sought after.

*She lives for her unrealistic dreams, and these increase her frustration.*

She had a rich friend, a comrade from convent days, whom she did not want to see anymore because she suffered so much when she returned home. She would weep for the entire day afterward with sorrow, regret, despair, and misery.

*She even thinks of giving up a rich friend because she is so depressed after visiting her.*

Well, one evening, her husband came home glowing and carrying a large envelope.

*A new section in the story.*

"Here," he said, "this is something for you."

She quickly tore open the envelope and took out a card engraved with these words:

*The Chancellor of Education
and Mrs. George Ramponneau
request that Mr. and Mrs. Loisel
do them the honor of coming to dinner
at the Ministry of Education
on the evening of January 8.*

*An invitation to dinner at the Ministry of Education. A big plum.*

10    Instead of being delighted, as her husband had hoped, she threw the invitation spitefully on the table, muttering:

"What do you expect me to do with this?"

"But Sweetie, I thought you'd be glad. You never get to go out, and this is a special occasion! I had a lot of trouble getting the invitation. The demand is high, and not many clerks get invited. Everyone important will be there."

*Loisel really doesn't understand her. He can't sympathize with her unhappiness.*

She looked at him angrily and stated impatiently:

"What do you expect me to wear to go there?"

15    He had not thought of that. He stammered:

"But your theater dress. That seems nice to me . . ."

*She declares that she hasn't anything to wear.*
*He tries to persuade her that her theater dress might do for the occasion.*

He stopped, amazed and bewildered, as his wife began to cry. Large tears fell slowly from the corners of her eyes to her mouth. He said falteringly:

"What's wrong? What's the matter?"

But with a strong effort she had recovered, and she answered calmly as she wiped her damp cheeks:

20    "Nothing, except that I have nothing to wear and therefore can't go to the party. Give your invitation to

someone else at the office whose wife will have nicer clothes than mine."

Distressed, he responded:

"Well, all right, Mathilde. How much would a new dress cost, something you could use at other times, but not anything fancy?"

*Her name is Mathilde. He volunteers to pay for a new dress. She is manipulating him.*

She thought for a few moments, adding things up and thinking also of an amount that she could ask without getting an immediate refusal and a frightened outcry from the frugal clerk.

Finally she responded tentatively:

"I don't know exactly, but it seems to me that I could get by on four hundred francs."

25

He blanched slightly at this because he had set aside just that amount to buy a shotgun for Sunday lark-hunts the next summer with a few friends in the Plain of Nanterre.

*The dress will cost him his next summer's vacation. (He doesn't seem to have included her in his plans.)*

However, he said:

"All right, you've got four hundred francs, but make it a pretty dress."

As the day of the party drew near, Mrs. Loisel seemed sad, uneasy, anxious, even though her gown was all ready. One evening her husband said to her:

*A new section, the third in the story. The day of the party is near. Tension is mounting.*

"What's the matter? You've been acting funny for several days."

30

She answered:

"It's awful, but I don't have any jewels to wear, not a single gem, nothing to dress up my outfit. I'll look like a beggar. I'd almost rather not go to the party."

*Now she complains that she doesn't have any nice jewelry. She is manipulating him again.*

He responded:

"You can wear a corsage of cut flowers. This year it's all the rage. For only ten francs you can get two or three gorgeous roses."

She was not convinced.

35

"No . . . there's nothing more humiliating than look-ing shabby in the company of rich women."

*She has a good point, but there seems to be no way out.*

But her husband exclaimed:

"God, but you're silly! Go to your friend Mrs. Forestier, and ask her to lend you some jewelry. You know her well enough to do that."

*He proposes a solution: Borrow jewelry from Mrs. Forestier, who is the rich friend mentioned earlier.*

She uttered a cry of joy:

"That's right. I hadn't thought of that."

40

The next day she went to her friend's house and de-scribed her problem.

Mrs. Forestier went to her mirrored wardrobe, took out a large jewel box, opened it, and said to Mrs. Loisel:

"Choose, my dear."

She saw bracelets, then a pearl necklace, then a

*Mathilde has her choice of her friend's jewels.*

Venetian cross of finely worked gold and gems. She tried on the jewelry in front of a mirror and hesitated, unable to make up her mind about each one. She kept asking:

45 "Do you have anything else?"

"Certainly. Look to your heart's content. I don't know what you'd like best."

Suddenly she found a superb diamond necklace in a black satin box, and her heart throbbed with desire for it. Her hands shook as she picked it up. She fastened it around her neck, watched it gleam at her throat, and looked at herself ecstatically.

*A "superb" diamond necklace. This is what the story has been building up to.*

Then she asked, haltingly and anxiously:

"Could you lend me this, nothing but this?"

*This is what she wants, just this.*

50 "Why yes, certainly."

She jumped up, hugged her friend joyfully, then hurried away with her treasure.

*She leaves with the "treasure." Things might be looking up for her.*

The day of the party came. Mrs. Loisel was a success. She was prettier than anyone else, stylish, graceful, smiling and wild with joy. All the men saw her, asked her name, sought to be introduced. All the important administrators stood in line to waltz with her. The Chancellor himself eyed her.

*A new section.*

*The party. Mathilde is a huge success.*

She danced joyfully, passionately, intoxicated with pleasure, thinking of nothing but the moment, in the triumph of her beauty, in the glory of her success, on Cloud Nine with happiness made up of all the admiration, of all the aroused desire, of this victory so complete and so sweet to the heart of any woman.

*Another judgment about women. Does the author mean that only women want to be admired? Don't men want to be admired too?*

She did not leave until four o'clock in the morning. Her husband, since midnight, had been sleeping in a little empty room with three other men whose wives had also been enjoying themselves.

*Loisel, with other husbands, is bored, while the wives are literally having a ball.*

55 He threw, over her shoulders, the shawl that he had brought for the trip home—a modest everyday wrap, the poverty of which contrasted sharply with the elegance of her evening gown. She felt it and hurried away to avoid being noticed by the other women who luxuriated in rich furs.

*Ashamed of her shabby everyday shawl, she rushes away to avoid being seen. She is forced back into the reality of her true situation. Her glamour is gone.*

Loisel tried to hold her back:

"Wait a minute. You'll catch cold outdoors. I'll call a cab."

But she paid no attention and hurried down the stairs. When they reached the street they found no carriages. They began to look for one, shouting at cabmen passing by at a distance.

They walked toward the Seine, desperate, shivering. Finally, on a quay, they found one of those old nightgoing buggies that are seen in Paris only after dark, as

*A comedown after the nice evening. They take a wretched-looking buggy home.*

if they were ashamed of their wretched appearance in daylight.

It took them to their door, on the Street of Martyrs, and they sadly climbed the stairs to their flat. For her, it was finished. As for him, he could think only that he had to begin work at the Ministry of Education at ten o'clock.

*"Street of Martyrs." Is this name significant?* 60

*Loisel is down-to-earth.*

She took the shawl off her shoulders, in front of the mirror, to see herself once more in her glory. But suddenly she cried out. The necklace was no longer around her neck!

*SHE HAS LOST THE NECK-LACE!*

Her husband, already half undressed, asked: "What's wrong?"

She turned toward him frantically: "I . . . I . . . I no longer have Mrs. Forestier's necklace." 65

He stood up, bewildered: "What! . . . How! . . . It's not possible!"

And they looked in the folds of the gown, in the folds of the shawl, in the pockets, everywhere. They found nothing.

*They can't locate it. It seems to be lost. What a horrible feeling. What a comedown.*

He asked: "You're sure you still had it when you left the party?" 70

"Yes. I checked it in the vestibule of the Ministry."

"But if you'd lost it in the street, we would've heard it fall. It must be in the cab."

"Yes, probably. Did you notice the number?"

"No. Did you see it?"

"No." 75

Overwhelmed, they looked at each other. Finally, Loisel got dressed again:

"I'm going out to retrace all our steps," he said, "to see if I can find the necklace that way."

And he went out. She stayed in her evening dress, without the energy to get ready for bed, stretched out in a chair, drained of strength and thought.

*He goes out to search for the necklace.*

Her husband came back at about seven o'clock. He had found nothing.

*But he is unsuccessful.*

He went to Police Headquarters and to the newspapers to announce a reward. He went to the small cab companies, and finally he followed up even the slightest hopeful lead.

*He really tries. He's doing his best.* 80

She waited the entire day, in the same enervated state, in the face of this frightful disaster.

Loisel came back in the evening, his face pale and haggard. He had found nothing.

"You'll have to write to your friend," he said, "that you broke a clasp on her necklace and that you're having it fixed. That'll give us time to look around."

She wrote as he dictated.

*Loisel's plan to explain delaying the return. He takes charge, is resourceful.*

85    By the end of the week they had lost all hope.

And Loisel, looking five years older, declared:

"We'll have to see about replacing the jewels."

The next day they took the case that had contained the necklace and went to the jeweler whose name was inside. He looked at his books:

"I wasn't the one, Madam, who sold the necklace. I only made the case."

90    Then they went from jeweler to jeweler, searching for a necklace like the other one, racking their memories, both of them sick with worry and anguish.

In a shop in the Palais-Royal, they found a necklace of diamonds that seemed to them exactly like the one they were looking for. It was priced at forty thousand francs. They could buy it for thirty-six thousand.

They got the jeweler to plouispromise not to sell it for three days. And they made an agreement that he would buy it back for thirty-four thousand francs if the original were recovered before the end of February.

Loisel had saved eighteen thousand francs that his father had left him. He would have to borrow the rest.

He borrowed, asking a thousand francs from one, five hundred from another, five louis° here, three louis there. He wrote promissory notes, undertook ruinous obligations, did business with finance companies and the whole tribe of loan sharks. He compromised himself for the remainder of his days, risked his signature without knowing whether he would be able to honor it; and, terrified by anguish over the future, by the black misery that was about to descend on him, by the prospect of all kinds of physical deprivations and moral tortures, he went to get the new necklace, and put down thirty-six thousand francs on the jeweler's counter.

95    Mrs. Loisel took the necklace back to Mrs. Forestier, who said with an offended tone:

"You should have brought it back sooner; I might have needed it."

She did not open the case, as her friend feared she might. If she had noticed the substitution, what would she have thought? What would she have said? Would she not have taken her for a thief?

Mrs. Loisel soon discovered the horrible life of the needy. She did her share, however, completely, heroically. That horrifying debt had to be paid. She would pay. They dismissed the maid; they changed their address; they rented an attic flat.

*Things are hopeless.*

*Note that Loisel does not even suggest that they explain things to Mrs. Forestier.*
*They hunt for a replacement.*

*A new diamond necklace will cost 36,000 francs, a monumental amount.*

*They make a deal with the jeweler. (Is Maupassant hinting that things might work out for them?)*

*It will take all of Loisel's inheritance. . .*
*. . . plus another eighteen thousand francs that must be borrowed at enormous rates of interest.*

*Mrs. Forestier is offended and complains about Mathilde's delay.*
*Is this enough justification for not telling the truth? It seems to be for the Loisels.*

*A new section, the fifth.*

---

°*louis*: a gold coin worth twenty francs.

She learned to do the heavy housework, dirty kitchen jobs. She washed the dishes, wearing away her manicured fingernails on greasy pots and encrusted baking dishes. She handwashed dirty linen, shirts, and dish towels that she hung out on the line to dry. Each morning, she took the garbage down to the street, and she carried up water, stopping at each floor to catch her breath. And, dressed in cheap housedresses, she went to the fruit dealer, the grocer, the butchers, with her basket under her arms, haggling, insulting, defending her measly cash penny by penny.

*They suffer to repay their debts. Loisel works late at night. Mathilde accepts a cheap attic flat and does all the heavy housework herself to save on domestic help.*

They had to make installment payments every month, and, to buy more time, to refinance loans.

*She pinches pennies, and haggles with the local tradesmen.*

The husband worked evenings to make fair copies of tradesmen's accounts, and late into the night he made copies at five cents a page.

*They struggle to meet payments.*        100

And this life lasted ten years.

*Mr. Loisel moonlights to make extra money.*

At the end of ten years, they had paid back everything—everything—including the extra charges imposed by loan sharks and the accumulation of compound interest.

*For ten years they struggle, but they endure.*

*Another new section, the sixth of the story.*

Mrs. Loisel looked old now. She had become the strong, hard, and rude woman of poor households. Her hair unkempt, with uneven skirts and rough, red hands, she spoke loudly, washed floors with large buckets of water. But sometimes, when her husband was at work, she sat down near the window, and she dreamed of that evening so long ago, of that party, where she had been so beautiful and so admired.

*The Loisels have successfully paid back the loans. They have been quite virtuous.*

*Mrs. Loisel (why does the narrator not say "Mathilde"?) is roughened and aged by the work. But she has behaved "heroically" (paragraph 98), and has shown her mettle.*

What would life have been like if she had not lost that necklace? Who knows? Who knows? Life is so peculiar, so uncertain. How little a thing it takes to destroy you or to save you!

*The point of the story? Small, uncertain things shape our lives; we hang by a thread.*        105

Well, one Sunday, when she had gone for a stroll along the Champs-Elysées to relax from the cares of the week, she suddenly noticed a woman walking with a child. It was Mrs. Forestier, still youthful, still beautiful, still attractive.

*The seventh part of the story, a scene on the Champs-Elysées. Mathilde sees Jeanne Forestier for the first time in the previous ten years.*

Mrs. Loisel felt moved. Would she speak to her? Yes, certainly. And now that she had paid, she could tell all. Why not?

She walked closer.

"Hello, Jeanne."

The other gave no sign of recognition and was astonished to be addressed so familiarly by this working-class woman. She stammered:

110

"But . . . Madam! . . . I don't know. . . . You must have made a mistake."

"No. I'm Mathilde Loisel."

Her friend cried out:

"Oh! . . . My poor Mathilde, you've changed so much."

115    "Yes. I've had some tough times since I saw you last; in fact hardships . . . and all because of you! . . ."

*Jeanne notes Mathilde's changed appearance.*

"Of me . . . how so?"

"You remember the diamond necklace that you lent me to go to the party at the Ministry of Education?"

"Yes. What then?"

"Well, I lost it."

*Mathilde tells Jeanne everything.*

120    "How, since you gave it back to me?"

"I returned another exactly like it. And for ten years we've been paying for it. You understand this wasn't easy for us, who have nothing. . . . Finally it's over, and I'm damn glad."

Mrs. Forestier stopp her.

"You say that you bought a diamond necklace to replace mine?"

"Yes, you didn't notice it, eh? It was exactly like yours."

125    And she smiled with proud and childish joy.

Mrs. Forestier, deeply moved, took both her hands.

"Oh, my poor Mathilde! But mine was only costume jewelry. At most, it was worth only five hundred francs! . . ."

*SURPRISE! The lost necklace was not made of real diamonds, and the Loisels have slaved for no reason at all. But hard work and sacrifice probably brought out better qualities in Mathilde than she otherwise might have shown. Is this the point of the story? Look again at paragraph 105.*

## Reading and Responding in a Computer File or Notebook

The marginal comments printed with "The Necklace" demonstrate the active reading-responding process you should apply to everything you read. Use the margins in your text similarly to record your comments and questions but plan also to record your more lengthy responses in a notebook, on note cards, on separate sheets of paper, or in a computer file. Be careful not to lose anything; keep all your notes. As you progress from work to work, you will find that your written or saved comments will be immensely important to you as your record, or journal, of your first impressions together with your more carefully considered and expanded thoughts.

In keeping your notebook, your objective should be to learn assigned works inside and out and then to say perceptive things about them. To achieve this goal, you need to read the work more than once. Develop a good note-taking system so that, as you read, you will create a "memory bank" of your own knowledge. You can make withdrawals from this fund of ideas when you begin to write. As an aid in developing your own procedures for reading and "depositing" your ideas, you may wish to begin with the following "Guidelines for Reading." Of course, you will want to modify these suggestions and add to them as you become a more experienced and disciplined reader.

### Guidelines for Reading

1. Observations for basic understanding
   a. Explain words, situations, and concepts. Write down words that are new or not immediately clear. Use your dictionary and record the relevant meanings in your notebook. Write down special difficulties so that you can ask your instructor about them.
   b. Determine what is happening in the work. For a story or play, where do the actions take place? What do they show? Who is involved? Who is the major figure? Why is he or she major? What relationships do the characters have with one another? What concerns do the characters have? What do they do? Who says what to whom? How do the speeches advance the action and reveal the characters? For a poem, what is the situation? Who is talking, and to whom? What does the speaker say about the situation? Why does the poem end as it does and where it does?
2. Notes on first impressions
   a. Make a record of your reactions and responses. What did you think was memorable, noteworthy, funny, or otherwise striking? Did you worry, get scared, laugh, smile, feel a thrill, learn a great deal, feel proud, find a lot to think about?
   b. Describe interesting characterizations, events, techniques, and ideas. If you like a character or an idea, explain what you like and do the same for characters and ideas you don't like. Is there anything else in the work that you especially like or dislike? Are parts easy or difficult to understand? Why? Are there any surprises? What was your reaction to them? Be sure to use your own words when writing your explanations.
3. Development of ideas and enlargement of responses
   a. Trace developing patterns. Make an outline or a scheme: What conflicts appear? Do these conflicts exist between people, groups, or ideas? How are the conflicts resolved? Is one force, idea, or side the winner? How do you respond to the winner or to the loser?
   b. Write expanded notes about characters, situations, and actions. What explanations need to be made about the characters? What is the nature of the situations (e.g., young people discover a damaged boat, and themselves, in the spring; a prisoner tries to hide her baby from cruel guards)? What is the nature of the actions (e.g., a mother and daughter go shopping; a series of strangers intrude upon the celebration of a Christening; a woman is told that her husband has been killed in a train wreck; a group of children are taken to a fashionable toy store)? What are the people like, and what are their habits and customs? What sort of language do they use?
   c. Memorize important, interesting, and well-written passages. Copy them in full on note cards and keep these in your pocket, purse, or backpack. When

walking to class, riding public transportation, or otherwise not occupying your time, learn them by heart. Please take memorization seriously.

d. Always write down questions that come up during your reading. You may raise these in class, and trying to write out your own answers will also aid your own study.

### Sample Notebook or Journal Entries on Maupassant's "The Necklace"

The following entries demonstrate how you can use the foregoing guidelines in your first thoughts about a work. You should try to develop enough observations and responses to be useful later, both for additional study and for developing essays. Notice that the entries are not only comments but also questions.

Early in the story, Mathilde seems to be spoiled. She and her husband are not well off, but she is unable to face her own situation.

She is a dreamer but seems harmless. Her daydreams about a fancy home, with all the expensive belongings, are not unusual. It would be unusual to find people who do not have such dreams.

She is embarrassed by her husband's taste for plain food. The storyteller contrasts her taste for trout and quail with Loisel's cheaper favorites.

When the Loisels get the invitation to the ball, Mathilde becomes difficult. Her wish for an expensive dress (the cost of Loisel's shotgun) creates a problem, and she creates another problem by wanting to wear fine jewelry.

Her change in character can be related to the places in the story: the Street of Martyrs, the dinner party scene, the attic flat. Also she fills the places she daydreams about with the most expensive things she can imagine.

Her success at the party shows that she has the charm the storyteller talks about in paragraph 2. She seems never to have had any other chance to exert her power.

The worst part of her personality is shown in rushing away from the party because she is ashamed of her ordinary and shabby shawl, which she had worn because the time of the story is January. It is Mathilde's unhappiness and unwillingness to adjust to her modest means that cause the financial downfall of the Loisels. This disaster is her fault.

Borrowing the money to replace the necklace shows that both Loisel and Mathilde have a strong sense of honor. Making up the loss is good, even if it destroys them financially.

There are some nice touches, like Loisel's seeming to be five years older (paragraph 86) and his staying with the other husbands of women enjoying themselves (paragraph 54). These are well done.

It's too bad that Loisel and Mathilde don't confess to Jeanne that the jewels are lost. Their pride or their honor stops them—or perhaps their fear of being accused of theft.

Their ten years of slavish work (paragraphs 98–102) show how they have come down in life. Mathilde does all her work by hand, so she really does pitch in and is, as the narrator says, heroic.

The attic flat is important. Mathilde becomes loud and frumpy when living there (paragraph 104), but she also develops strength. She does what she has to. The earlier apartment and the elegance of her imaginary rooms had brought out her limitations.

The narrator's statement "How little a thing it takes to destroy you or to save you!" (paragraph 105) is full of thought. The necklace is little, and it makes a gigantic problem. This creates the story's irony.

*Questions*: Is this story more about the surprise ending or about the character of Mathilde? Is she to be condemned or admired? Does the outcome stem from the little things that make us or break us, as the narrator suggests, or from the difficulty of rising above one's economic class, which seems true, or both? What do the speaker's remarks about women's status mean? (Remember, the story was published in 1884.) This probably isn't relevant, but wouldn't Jeanne, after hearing about the substitution, give the full value of the necklace to the Loisels (or at least return the necklace to them), and wouldn't they then be pretty well off?

These are reasonable—and also fairly full—remarks and observations about "The Necklace." Use your notebook or journal similarly for all reading assignments. If your assignment is simply to learn about a work, general notes like these should be enough. If you are preparing for a test, you might write pointed observations more in line with what is happening in your class, and also write and answer your own questions (see Chapter 19, "Writing Examinations on Literature"). If you have a writing assignment, observations like these can help you focus more closely on your topic—such as character, idea, or setting. Whatever your purpose, always take good notes and put in as many details and responses as you can. The notes will be invaluable to you as a mind refresher and as a wellspring of thought.

# Major Stages in Thinking and Writing about Literary Topics: Discovering Ideas, Preparing to Write, Making an Initial Draft, and Completing the Essay

Finished writing is the sharpened, focused expression of thought and study. It begins with the search for something to say—an idea. Not all ideas are equal; some are better than others, and getting good ideas is an ability that you will develop the more you think and write. As you discover ideas and explain them in words, you will also improve your perceptions and increase your critical faculties.

In addition, because literature itself contains the subject material (though not in a systematic way) of philosophy, religion, psychology, sociology, and politics, learning to analyze and write about literature will also improve your capacity to deal with these and other disciplines.

### Writing Does Not Come Easily—for Anyone

A major purpose of your being in college, of which your composition and literature course is a vital part, is to develop your capacity to think and to express your thoughts clearly and fully. However, the process of creating a successfully argued essay—the actual process itself of writing—is not automatic. Writing begins in uncertainty and hesitation, and it becomes certain and confident—accomplished—only as a result of great care, applied thought, a certain amount of experimentation, the passage of time, and much effort. When you read complete, polished, well-formed pieces of writing, you might assume, as many of us do, that the writers wrote their successful versions the first time they tried and never needed to make any changes and improvements at all. In an ideal world, perhaps, something like this could happen, but not in this one.

If you could see the early drafts of writing you admire, you would be surprised and startled—and also encouraged—to see that good writers are also human and that what they first write is often uncertain, vague, tangential, tentative, incomplete, and messy. Good writers do not always like their first drafts; nevertheless, they work with their efforts and build upon them. They reconsider their ideas and try to restate them, discard some details, add others, chop paragraphs in half and reassemble the parts elsewhere, throw out much (and then maybe recover some of it), revise or completely rewrite sentences, change words, correct misspellings, sharpen expressions, and add new material in the hope that they can tie all the parts together in a smooth, natural flow.

### The Goal of Writing: Show a Process of Thought

As you approach the task of writing, you should constantly realize that your goal should always be to *explain* the work you are analyzing. You should never be satisfied simply to restate the events in the work. Too often students fall easily into a pattern of retelling a story or play or of summarizing the details of a poem. But nothing could be further from what is expected from good writing. *Good writing should be the embodiment of your thought; it should show your thought in action.* Thinking is an active process that does not happen accidentally. Thinking requires that you develop ideas, draw conclusions, exemplify and support them with details, and connect everything in a coherent manner. Your goal should constantly be to explain the results of your thinking—your ideas, your play of mind over the materials of a work, your insights, your conclusions.

Approach each writing assignment in light of the following objectives: You should consider your reader as a person who has read the work, just as you have done. This person knows what is in the work and therefore does not need you to restate what she or he already knows. Instead, your reader wants to learn from you what to think about it. Therefore, always, your task as a writer is to explain something about the work, to describe the thoughts that you can develop about it. Let us consider again Maupassant's "The Necklace." We have recognized that the main character, Mathilde Loisel, is a young Parisian housewife who is married to a minor clerk in the Ministry of Education. We know this but if we are reading an essay about the story, we will want to learn more. Let us then suppose that a first goal of one of your paragraphs is to explain the deep dissatisfaction Mathilde feels in the early part of the story. Your paragraph might go as follows:

> In the early part of the story, Maupassant establishes that Mathilde is deeply dissatisfied with her life. Her threadbare furniture and drab walls are a cause of her unhappiness. Under these circumstances, her daydreams of beautiful rooms staffed by "elegant valets," together with a number of rooms for intimate conversations with friends, multiply her dissatisfaction. The meager meals that she shares with her husband make her imagine sumptuous banquets that she feels are rightfully hers by birth but that are denied her because of her circumstances. The emphasis in these early scenes of the story is always on Mathilde's discontentment and frustration.

Notice that this paragraph does not simply go over the story's events but refers to the events in order to explain to us, as readers, the causes for Mathilde's unhappiness. The paragraph illustrates your process of thought.

Here is another way in which you might use a thought to connect the same materials:

> In the early part of the story, Maupassant emphasizes the economic difficulty of Mathilde's life. The threadbare furniture and ugly curtains, for example, highlight that there is no money to purchase better things. The same sparseness of existence is shown by the meager meals that she shares with her husband. With the capacity to appreciate better things, Mathilde is forced by circumstances to make do with worse. Her dreams of sumptuous banquets are therefore natural, given her level of frustration with the life around her. In short, her unhappiness is an understandable consequence of her aversion to her plain and drab apartment and the tightness of money.

Here the details are substantially the same as in the first paragraph, but they are unified by a different idea—namely, the economic constraints of Mathilde's life. What is important is that neither paragraph retells only the details. Instead, the paragraphs illustrate the goal of writing with a purpose. *Whenever you write, you should always be trying, as in these examples, to use a governing thought or thoughts to shape the details in the work you are analyzing.*

For both practiced and beginning writers alike, there are four stages of thinking and writing, and in each of these there are characteristic activities. In the beginning stage, writers try to find the details and thoughts that seem to be right for eventual inclusion in what they are hoping to write. The next (or middle) stage is characterized by written drafts, or sketches—ideas, sentences, paragraphs. An advanced stage of writing is the forming and ordering of what has previously been done—the creation and determination of a final essay. Although these stages occur in a natural order, they are not separate and distinct but merge with each other and in effect are fused together. However, when you think you are close to finishing your essay, you may find that you are not as close as you might have thought. You are now in the finishing or completing stage when you need to include something else—something more, something different, something to make things complete. At this point, you can easily re-create an earlier stage to discover new details and ideas. You might say that your work is always tentative until you regard it as finished or until you need to turn it in.

## Discovering Ideas (Brainstorming)

With the foregoing general goal in mind, let us assume that you have read the work about which you are to write and have made notes and observations on which you are planning to base your thought. You are now ready to consider and plan what to include in your essay. This earliest stage of writing is unpredictable and somewhat frustrating because you are on a search. You do not know quite what you want, for you are reaching out for ideas and are not yet sure what they are and what you might say about them. This process of searching and discovery, sometimes also called **brainstorming**, requires you to examine any and every subject that your mind can produce.

Just as you are trying to reach for ideas, however, you also should try to introduce purpose and resolution into your thought. You have to zero in on something specific and develop your ideas through this process. Although what you first write may seem indefinite, the best way to help your thinking is to put your mind, figuratively, into specific channels or grooves, and then confine your thoughts within these boundaries. What matters is to get your mind going on a particular topic and to get your thoughts down on paper or onto a computer screen. Once you can see your thoughts in front of you, you can work with them and develop them. The drawing below can be helpful to you as an illustration of the various facets of a literary work or ways of talking about it.

Consider the work you have read—story, poem, or play—as the central circle, from which a number of points, like the rays of a star, shine out, some of them prominently, others less so. These points, or rays, are the various subjects, or topics, that you might decide to select in exploration, discovery, and discussion. Because some elements in a work may be more significant than others, the points are not all equal in size. Notice also that the points grow larger as they get nearer to the work, suggesting that once you select a point of discussion you may amplify that point with details and your own observations about the work.

You can consider literary works in many ways, but for now, as a way of getting started, you might choose to explore (1) the work's characters, (2) its historical period and background, (3) the social and economic conditions it depicts, (4) its major ideas, (5) any of its artistic qualities, or (6) any additional ideas that seem important to you.[2] These topics, of course, have many subtopics, but any one of them can help you in the concentration you will need for beginning your essay (and also for classroom discussion).

---

[2]Together with additional topics, these critical approaches are discussed in more detail in Appendix A.

All you need is one topic, just one; don't try everything at the same time. Let us see how our illustration can be revised to account for these topics. This time the number of points is reduced to illustrate the points or approaches we have just raised (with an additional and unnamed point to represent all the other approaches that might be used for other studies). These points represent your ways of discovering ideas about the work.

### Study the Characters in the Work

You do not need to be a professional psychologist to discuss the persons or characters that you find in a work (see also Chapter 4). You need to raise only issues about the characters and what they do and what they represent. What are the characters like at the beginning of the work? What happens to them? Do they do anything that causes them to change, and how are they changed? Are the changes for good or for bad? Why do the characters do the things they do? What do they do correctly? What do they do incorrectly? Why? For example, Mathilde is wrong not to tell Jeanne about the lost necklace. Such an immediate admission of truth would save her and her husband ten years of hardship and deprivation. But Mathilde does not tell the truth. Why not? What do we learn about her character because she avoids or ignores this admission?

In discussing character, you might also wish to raise the issue of whether the characters in the work do or do not do what might normally be expected from people in their circumstances. Do they correspond to type? The idea here is that certain attitudes and behaviors are typical of people at particular stages of life (e.g., children behaving like children, lovers dealing with their relationship, a young couple coping with difficult finances). Thus we might ask questions about whether the usual circumstances experienced by the characters affect them, either by limiting them in some way or by freeing them. What attitudes seem typical of the characters? How do these attitudes govern what the characters do, or do not do? For example, one of the most typical circumstances of life is marriage. According to the positive and ideal type of marriage, a husband and wife should be forthcoming with each other; they should tell each other things and should not conceal what is on their minds. If they have problems, they should discuss them and try to solve them together. In "The Necklace" we see that Mathilde and Loisel do not show

> ## THE NEED TO PRESENT AN ARGUMENT
> ## WHEN WRITING ESSAYS ABOUT LITERATURE
>
> As you write about literature, always keep trying to connect your explanations to a specific **argument**; that is, you are writing about a specific work, but you are trying to *prove*—or *demonstrate*—a point or idea about it. This book provides you with a number of separate subjects relating to the study of literature. As you select one of these and begin writing, however, you are not to explain just that such-and-such a story has a character who changes and grows or that such-and-such a poem contains the thought that nature creates great beauty. Rather, you should demonstrate the importance of your topic to the work as a whole in relation to a specific point or argument. One example of an argument might be that a story's first-person point of view permits readers to draw their own conclusions about the speaker's character. Another argument might be that the poet's thought is shown in a poem's details about the bustling sounds and sights of animals in springtime.
>
> Let us therefore repeat and stress that your writing should always have an argumentative edge—a goal of demonstrating the truth of your conclusions and clarifying and illuminating your idea about the topic *and* about the work. It is here that the accuracy of your choices of details from the work, the soundness of your conclusions, and the cumulative weight of your evidence are essential. You cannot allow your main ideas to rest on one detail alone but must support your conclusions by showing that the bulk of material leads to them and that they are linked in a reasonable chain of fact and logic. It is such clarification that is the goal of argumentation.

these desired qualities, and their absence of communication can be seen as an element in their financial catastrophe. However, during their long years of trouble they work together; they eventually exhibit the quality of honesty, and in this respect they fulfill their role, or type, as a married couple.

An analysis of typical attitudes themselves can also furnish you with material for discussion. For example, Mathilde, who is a member of the lower commercial class, has attitudes that are more appropriate to the upper or leisure class. She cannot bridge this gap, and her frustration causes her to nag her husband to give her enough money to live out her dream, if only for a moment.

### *Determine the Work's Historical Period and Background*

An obvious topic is the historical circumstances of the work. When was the work written? How well does it portray details about life at the time it appeared? What is historically unique about it? To what degree does it help you learn something about the past that you did not previously know? What actions in the work are like, or are unlike, actions going on at the present time? What truthfulness to life do you discover in the work? In "The Necklace," for example, which was published more than a century ago, Mathilde's duty is to stay at home as a housewife—a traditional role—while her husband is the family bread-winner. After the loss of the necklace, she can no longer afford domestic help, and she is compelled to do all her own housework and shopping. She has none of today's home conveniences—no dishwasher, microwave, refrigerator, or car. Her husband, a clerk or secretary-copyist, spends his workday copying business records by hand, for at the peri-od of the story there were few typewriters and absolutely no word processors. Discussing matters like these might also help you with works written during modern times because our own assumptions, artifacts, and habits will bear analysis and discussion.

### Analyze the Work's Social and Economic Conditions

Closely related to the historical period, an obvious topic to pursue in many works is the economic and social condition of the characters. To what level of life, economically, do the characters belong? How are events in the work related to their condition? How does their money, or lack of it, limit what they do? How do their economic circumstances ei-ther restrict or liberate their imaginations? How do their jobs and their apparent in-come determine their way of life? If we ask some of these questions about "The Necklace," as we have seen, we find that Mathilde and her husband are greatly burdened by their lack of money and that their obligation to repay their huge loan drives them into economic want and sacrifice.

An important part of the economic and social analysis of literature is the consider-ation of female characters and what it means to be a woman. This is the feminist analy-sis of literature, which asks questions like these: What role is Mathilde compelled to take as a result of her sex and family background? How does Jeanne's way of life contrast with that of Mathilde? What can Mathilde do with her life? To what degree is she limit-ed by her role as a housewife? Does she have any chance of an occupation outside the home? How does her economic condition cause her to yearn for better things? What causes her to borrow the necklace? What is her contribution, as a woman, to the repay-ment of the loans? Should Mathilde's limited life in "The Necklace" be considered as a political argument for greater freedom for women? Once you start asking questions like these, you will find that your thinking is developing along with your ideas for writing.

The feminist approach to the interpretation of literature has been well established, and it will usually provide you with a way to discuss a work. It is also possible, of course, to analyze what a work says about the condition of being a man or being a child. De-pending on the work, many of the questions important in a feminist approach are not dissimilar to those you might use if you are dealing with childhood or male adulthood.

One of the most important social and economic topics is that of race and eth-nicity. What happens in the work that seems to occur mainly because of the race of the characters? Is the author pointing out any deprivations, any absence of opportu-nity, any oppression? What do the characters do under such circumstances? Do they succeed or not? Are they negative? Are they angry? Are they resolute and determined? Your aim in an inquiry of this type should be to concentrate on actions and ideas in the work that are clearly related to race.

### Explain the Work's Major Ideas

One of the major ways of focusing on a work is to zero in on various ideas and values or issues to be discovered there. What ideas might we gain from the story of the lengthy but needless sacrifice and drudgery experienced by Mathilde and her husband? One obvious and acceptable idea is presented by the speaker, namely, that even the smallest, most accidental incident can cause immense consequences. This is an idea that we might expand and illustrate in an entire essay. Here are some other ideas that we might also pursue, all of them based on the story's details.

- Many actions have unforeseeable and uncontrollable consequences.
- Lack of communication is a major cause of hardship.
- Adversity brings out a character's good qualities.
- Mutual effort enables people to overcome difficulties.

These ideas are all to be found in Maupassant's story. In other works, of course, we may find comparable ideas in addition to other major ideas and issues.

### Describe the Work's Artistic Qualities

A work's artistic qualities provide many possible topics for studying, but basically here you may consider matters such as the work's plan or organization and the author's narrative method, writing style, or poetic techniques. Thus, in "The Necklace," we observe that almost the entire story develops with Mathilde at the center (narrative method; see also Chapter 3, on point of view). At first, the story brings us close to Mathilde, for we are told of her dissatisfaction and impatience with her surroundings. As the story progresses, the storyteller/speaker presents her person and actions more objectively and also more distantly. Another artistic approach would be to determine the story's pattern of development—how, chronologically, the loss of the necklace brings financial misfortune to the Loisels. We might also look for the author's inclusion of symbols in the story, such as the name of the street where the Loisels originally live, their move to an attic flat, or the roughness of Mathilde's hands as a result of her constant housework. There are many other ways to consider the formal aspects of a literary work.

### Explain Any Other Approaches That Seem Important

Additional ways of looking at a work such as "The Necklace" might occur to you beyond those just described. One reader might raise the issue that the story's speaker seems to exhibit a particularly patronizing attitude toward women. He draws attention to Mathilde's joy because of the party and generalizes about how her "victory" was so "sweet to the heart of any woman" (paragraph 53). A writer might want to make more of this attitude. Another aspect of the story might be the way in which Mathilde's physical appearance undergoes change as a result of her dismissing the maid and taking on the household chores herself. Still another aspect is the attitude of Loisel and his relationship with Mathilde, which seems rather distant. The story tells nothing about his reactions to the misfortune beyond how he pitches in to restore the borrowed money, almost to the point of enslaving himself to the task. Would he never have uttered any reproachful words toward his wife? The points here are that (1) additional ideas may suggest themselves to you and (2) you should keep yourself open to explore and discuss any of these other ways of seeing and thinking.

# Preparing to Write

By this time, you will already have been focusing on your topic and will have assembled much that you can put into your essay. You should now aim to develop paragraphs and sketches of what you will eventually include. You should think constantly of the point or argument you want to develop, but invariably digressions will occur, together with other difficulties—false starts, dead ends, total cessation of thought, digressions, despair, hopelessness, and general frustration. Remember, however, that it is important just to start. Jump right in and start writing anything at all—no matter how unacceptable your first efforts may seem—and force yourself to deal with the materials. The writing down of ideas does not commit you. You should not think that these first ideas are untouchable and holy just because you have written them on paper or on your computer screen. You can throw them out in favor of new ideas, you can make cross-outs and changes, and you can move paragraphs or even sections around as you wish. However, if you do not start writing, your first thoughts will remain locked in your mind, and you will have nothing to work with. You must learn to accept the uncertainties in the writing process and make them work *for* you rather than *against* you.

### Build Ideas from Your Original Notes

You need to get your mind going by mining your notebook or computer file for useful things you have already written. Thus, let us use an observation in our original set of notes—"The attic flat is important"—in reference to the poorer rooms where Mathilde and her husband live while they are paying back their creditors. With such a note as a start, you might develop a number of ideas to support an argument about Mathilde's character, as in the following:

> The attic flat is important. Early in the story, in her apartment, Mathilde is dreamy and impractical. She seems delicate, but after losing the necklace, she is delicate no longer. She becomes a worker after they move to the flat. She does a lot more when living there.
>
> In the flat, Mathilde has to sacrifice. She gives up her servant, washes greasy pots, climbs stairs carrying buckets of water, sloshes water around to clean floors, and does all the clothes washing by hand.
>
> When living in the flat she gets stronger, but she also becomes loud and common. She argues with shopkeepers to get the lowest prices. She stops caring for herself. There is a reversal here, from incapable and well groomed to capable but coarse.

In this way, even in an assertion as basic as "The attic flat is important," the process of putting together details is a form of concentrated thought that leads you creatively forward. You can express thoughts and conclusions that you could not express at the beginning.

Such an exercise in stretching your mind leads you to put elements of the work together in ways that create ideas for good essays.

### *Trace Patterns of Action and Thought*

You can also discover ideas by making a list or scheme for the story or main idea. What conflicts appear? Do these conflicts exist between people, groups, or ideas? How does the author resolve them? Is one force, idea, or side the winner? Why? How do you respond to the winner or to the loser? Using this method, you might make a list similar to this one:

> At the beginning, Mathilde is a fish out of water. She dreams of wealth, but her life is drab and her husband is dull.
>
> Fantasies make her even more dissatisfied; she punishes herself by thinking of a wealthy life.
>
> When the Loisels get the dinner invitation, Mathilde pouts and whines. Her husband feels discomfort when she manipulates him into buying her an expensive party dress.
>
> Her world of daydreams hurts her real life when her desire for wealth causes her to borrow the necklace. Losing the necklace is just plain bad luck.

These arguments all focus on Mathilde's character, but you may wish to trace other patterns you find in the story. If you start planning an essay about another pattern, be sure to account for all the actions and scenes that relate to your topic. Otherwise, you may miss a piece of evidence that could lead you to new conclusions.

### *Raise and Answer Your Own Questions*

A habit you should always cultivate is to raise your own questions and try to answer them yourself as you consider your reading. The "Guidelines for Reading" will help you formulate questions (pp. 13–14), but you can raise additional questions like these:

- What is happening as the work unfolds? How does an action at the beginning of the work bring about later actions and speeches?
- Who are the main characters? What seems unusual or different about what they do in the work?
- What conclusions can you draw about the work's actions, scenes, and situations? Explain these conclusions.
- What are the characters and speakers like? What do they do and say about themselves, their goals, the people around them, their families and friends, their work, and the general circumstances of their lives?
- What kinds of words do the characters use: formal or informal words, slang or profanity?
- What literary conventions and devices have you discovered, and how do these affect the work? (When an author addresses readers directly, for example, that is a convention; when a comparison is used, that is a device, which might be either a metaphor or a simile.)

## THE NEED FOR THE ACTUAL PHYSICAL PROCESS OF WRITING

Thinking and writing are interdependent processes. If you don't get your thoughts into words that are visible to you on a paper or computer screen, your thinking will be impeded. It is therefore vital for you to use the writing process as the most significant means of developing your ideas. If you are doing an assignment in class—tests or impromptu essays—write your initial responses on a single side of your paper. This strategy will enable you to spread your materials out to get an actual physical overview of them when you begin writing. Everything will be open to you; none of your ideas will be hidden on the other side of the paper.

Outside of class, however, when you are at home or otherwise able to use a computer/word processor, your machine is an indispensable tool for your writing. It will help you develop ideas, for it quickly enables you to eliminate unworkable thoughts and to replace them with others. You can move sentences and paragraphs into new contexts, test how they look, and move them somewhere else if you choose.

In addition, with the rapid printers now available, you can print even the initial and tentative stages of writing. Using the printed draft, you can make additional notes, corrections, and suggestions for further development. With the marked-up draft as a guide, you can go back to the word processor and fill in your changes and improvements, repeating this procedure as often as you can. This facility makes the machine an incentive for improvement, right up to your final draft.

Word processing also helps you in the final preparation of your essays. Studies have shown that errors and awkward sentences are frequently found at the bottoms of pages prepared by hand or with a conventional typewriter. The reason is that writers hesitate to make improvements when they get near the end of a page because they shun the dreariness of starting the page over. Word processors eliminate this difficulty completely. Changes can be made anywhere in the draft, at any time, without any ill effect on the final appearance of your essay.

Regardless of your writing method, you should always remember that unwritten thought is incomplete thought. You cannot lay everything out at once on the word processor's screen. You can see only a small part of what you are writing. Therefore, somewhere in your writing process, you need to prepare a complete draft of what you have written. A clean, readable draft permits you to gather everything together and to make even more improvements through revision.

---

Of course, you can raise other questions as you reread the piece, or you can be left with one or two major questions that you decide to pursue.

### Put Ideas Together Using a Plus-Minus, Pro-Con, or Either-Or Method

A common and very helpful method of discovering ideas is to develop a set of contrasts: plus-minus, pro-con, either-or. Let us suppose a plus-minus method of considering the following question about Mathilde: Should she be "admired" (plus) or "condemned" (minus)?

| Plus: Admired? | Minus: Condemned? |
|---|---|
| After she cries when they get the invitation, she recovers with a "strong effort"—maybe she doesn't want her husband to feel bad. | She wants to be envied and admired only for being attractive and intriguing, not for more important qualities. She seems spoiled and selfish. |
| She scores a great victory at the dance. She really does have the power to charm and captivate. | She wastes her time in daydreaming about things she can't have, and she whines because she is unhappy. |
| Once she loses the necklace, she and her husband become poor and deprived. But she does "her share . . . completely, heroically" (paragraph 98) to make up for the loss. | Even though the Loisels live poorly, Mathilde manipulates her husband into giving her more money than they can afford for a party dress. |
| Even when she is poor, she dreams about that marvelous, shining moment at the great ball. This is pathetic because Mathilde gets worse than she deserves. | She assumes that her friend Jeanne would think her a thief if she admitted losing the necklace. Shouldn't she have had more confidence in Jeanne? |
| At the end, after everything is paid back and her reputation is secure, Mathilde confesses the loss to Jeanne. | She becomes loud and coarse and haggles about pennies, thus undergoing a cheapening of her person and manner. |

By putting contrasting observations side by side in this way, you will find that ideas will start to come naturally and will be helpful to you when you begin writing, regardless of how you finally organize your essay. It is possible, for example, that you might develop either column as the argumentative basis of an essay, or you might use your notes to support the idea that Mathilde is too complex to be either wholly admired or wholly condemned. You might also want to introduce an entirely new topic of development, such as Mathilde should be pitied rather than condemned or admired. In short, arranging materials in the plus-minus pattern is a powerful way to discover ideas—a truly helpful habit of promoting thought—that can lead to ways of development that you do not at first realize.

### *Originate and Develop Your Thoughts through Writing*

You should always write down what you are thinking, for, as a principle, unwritten thought is incomplete thought. Make a practice of writing your observations about the work, in addition to any questions that occur to you. This is an exciting step in preliminary writing because it can be useful when you write later drafts. You will discover that looking at what you have written can not only enable you to correct and improve the writing you have done but also lead you to recognize that you need more. The process goes just about like this: "Something needs to be added here—important details that my reader will not have noticed, new support for my argument, a new idea that has just occurred to me, a significant connection to link my thoughts." If you follow such a process, you will be using your own written ideas to create new ideas. You will be advancing your own abilities as a thinker and writer.

The processes just described of searching for ideas, or brainstorming, are useful for you at any stage of composition. Even when you are fairly close to finishing your essay, you might suddenly recognize that you need to add something more (or subtract something you don't like). When that happens, you may return to the discovery or brainstorming process to initiate and develop new ideas and new arguments.

## Making an Initial Draft of Your Essay

As you use the brainstorming and focusing techniques, you are also in fact beginning your essay. You will need to revise your ideas as connections among them become clearer and as you reexamine the work to discover details to support the argument you are making. By this stage, however, you already have many of the raw materials you need for developing your topic.

### *Base Your Essay on a Central Idea, Argument, or Statement*

By definition, an essay *is an organized, connected, and fully developed set of paragraphs that expand on a* **central idea, central argument,** or **central statement.** All parts of an essay should contribute to the reader's understanding of the idea. To achieve unity and completeness, each paragraph refers to the argument and demonstrates how selected details from the work relate to it and support it. The central idea helps you control and shape your essay, just as it also provides guidance for your reader.

A successful essay about literature is a brief but thorough (not exhaustive) examination of a literary work in light of topics like those we have already raised—character, background, and economic conditions, to circumstances of gender, major ideas, artistic qualities, and any additional topic such as point of view and symbolism. Central ideas or arguments might be that (1) a character is strong and tenacious, (2) the story shows the unpredictability of action, (3) the point of view makes the action seem "distant and objective," or (4) a major symbol governs the actions and thoughts of the major characters. In essays on these topics, all materials must be tied to such central ideas or arguments. Thus, it is a fact that Mathilde in "The Necklace" endures ten years of slavish work and sacrifice as she and her husband accumulate enough money to repay their monumental debt. This we know but it is not relevant to an essay on her character unless you connect it by a central argument showing how it demonstrates one of her major traits—her growing strength and perseverance.

Look through all of your ideas for one or two that catch your eye for development. In all the early stages of preliminary writing, the chances are that you have already discovered at least a few ideas that are more thought provoking, or more important, than the others.

Once you choose an idea that you think you can work with, write it as a complete sentence that is essential to the argument of your essay. A simple phrase such as "setting and character" does not focus thought the way a sentence does. The following sentence moves the topic toward new exploration and discovery because it combines a topic with an outcome: "The setting of 'The Necklace' reflects Mathilde's character." You can choose to be even more specific: "Mathilde's strengths and weaknesses are reflected in the real and imaginary places in 'The Necklace.'"

Now that you have phrased a single, central idea or argument for your essay, you have also established a guide by which you can accept, reject, rearrange, and change the ideas you have been planning to develop. You can now draft a few paragraphs (which you may base on some of the sketches you have already made; always use as much as you can of your early observations) to see whether your idea seems valid, or you can decide that it would be more helpful to make an outline or a list before you do more writing. In either case, you should use your notes for evidence to connect to your central idea. If you need to bolster your argument with more supporting details and ideas, go once again to the techniques of discovery and brainstorming.

Using the central idea that the changes in the story's settings reflect Mathilde's character might produce a paragraph like the following, which presents an argument about her negative qualities:

> The original apartment in the Street of Martyrs and the dreamworld of wealthy places both show negative sides of Mathilde's character. The real-life apartment, though livable, is shabby. The furnishings all bring out her discontent. The shabbiness makes her think only of luxuriousness, and having one servant girl causes her to dream of having many servants. The luxury of her dream life heightens her unhappiness with what she actually has.

In such a preliminary draft, in which the purpose is to connect details and thoughts to the major idea, many details from the story are used in support. In the final draft, this kind of support is essential.

### Create a Thesis Sentence as Your Guide to Organization

With your central idea or argument as your focus, you can decide which of the earlier observations and ideas can be developed further. Your goal is to establish a number of major topics to support your argument and to express them in a **thesis sentence,** or **thesis statement**—an organizing sentence that contains the major topics you plan to treat in your essay. Suppose you choose three ideas from your discovery stage of development. If you put the central idea at the left and the list of topics at the right, you have the shape of the thesis sentence. Note that the first two topics below are taken from the discovery paragraph.

| **Central Idea** | **Topics** |
| --- | --- |
| The setting of "The Necklace" reflects Mathilde's character. | 1. First apartment |
|  | 2. Dream-life mansion rooms |
|  | 3. Attic flat |

This arrangement leads to the following thesis statement, or thesis sentence.

> Mathilde's character growth is connected to her first apartment, her dream-life mansion rooms, and her attic flat.

You can revise the thesis sentence at any stage of the writing process if you find that you do not have enough evidence from the work to support it. Perhaps a new topic will occur to you, and you can include it, appropriately, as a part of your thesis sentence.

As we have seen, the central idea or central argument is the *glue* of the essay. The thesis sentence lists the parts to be fastened together—that is, the topics in which the central idea is to be demonstrated and argued. To alert your readers to your essay's structure, the thesis sentence is usually placed at the end of the introductory paragraph, just before the body of the essay.

As you write your first draft, you need to support the points of your thesis sentence with your notes and discovery materials. You can alter, reject, and rearrange ideas and details as you wish, as long as you change your thesis sentence to account for the changes (a major reason why many writers write their introductions last). The thesis sentence just shown contains three topics (it could be two, or four, or more) to be used in forming the body of the essay.

### Begin Each Paragraph with a Topic Sentence

Just as the organization of the *entire essay* is based on the thesis, the form of each *paragraph* is based on its **topic sentence**—an assertion about how a topic from the predicate of the thesis statement supports the argument contained or implied in the central idea. The first topic in our example is the relationship of Mathilde's character to her first apartment, and the resulting paragraph should emphasize this relationship. If your topic is the coarsening of her character during the ten-year travail, you can then form a topic sentence by connecting the trait with the location, as follows:

> The attic flat reflects the coarsening of Mathilde's character.

Beginning with this sentence, the paragraph will present details that argue how Mathilde's rough, heavy housework changes her behavior, appearance, and general outlook.

### Use Your Topic Sentences as the Arguments for Your Paragraph Development

Once you create a topic sentence, you can use it to focus your observations and conclusions. Let us see how our topic about the attic flat can be developed in a paragraph of argument:

> The attic flat reflects the coarsening of Mathilde's character. Maupassant emphasizes the burdens Mathilde endures to save money, such as mopping floors, cleaning greasy and encrusted pots and pans, taking out the garbage, and washing

## Referring to Authors' Names

As a general principle, for both male and female writers, you should regularly include the author's *full name* in the *first sentence* of your essay. Here are examples of first sentences:

> Shirley Jackson's "The Lottery" is a story featuring both suspense and horror.
>
> "The Lottery," by Shirley Jackson, is a story featuring both suspense and horror.

For all later references, use only last names, such as Jackson, Maupassant, Lawrence, or Porter. However, for the "giants" of literature, you should use the last names exclusively. In referring to writers like Shakespeare and Dickinson, for example, there is no need to include William or Emily.

Despite today's informal standards, never use an author's first name alone, as in "Shirley skillfully creates suspense and horror in 'The Lottery.'" Also, do not use a courtesy title before the names of dead authors, such as "Ms. Jackson's 'The Lottery' is a suspenseful horror story" or "Mr. Shakespeare's idea is that information is uncertain." Use the last names alone.

As with all conventions, of course, there are exceptions. If you are referring to a childhood work of a writer, the first name might be appropriate, but be sure to shift to the last name when referring to the writer's mature works. If your writer has a professional or a noble title, such as Lord Byron or Queen Elizabeth, it is not improper to use the title. Even then, however, the titles are commonly omitted for males, so most references to Lord Byron and Alfred, Lord Tennyson, should be simply to Byron and Tennyson.

Referring to living authors is somewhat problematic. Some journals and newspapers often use the courtesy titles Mr. and Ms. in their reviews. However, scholarly journals, which are likely to remain on library shelves and Web sites for many decades, follow the general principle of beginning with the entire name and then using only the last name for later references.

clothes and dishes by hand. This work makes her rough and coarse, an effect also shown by her giving up care of her hair and hands, wearing the cheapest dresses possible, haggling with the local shopkeepers, and becoming loud and penny-pinching. If at the beginning she is delicate and attractive, at the end she is unpleasant and coarse.

Here, details from the story are introduced to provide support for the topic sentence. All the subjects—the hard work, the lack of personal care, the wearing of cheap dresses, and the haggling with the shopkeepers—are introduced not to retell the story but rather to exemplify the argument the writer is making about Mathilde's character.

### Select Only One Topic—No More—for Each Paragraph

You should treat each separate topic in a single paragraph—one topic, one paragraph. However, if a topic seems especially difficult, long, and heavily detailed, you can divide it into two or more subtopics, each receiving a separate paragraph of its own—two or more subtopics, two or more separate paragraphs. Should you make this division, your topic then is really a section, and each paragraph in the section should have its own topic sentence.

### Develop an Outline as the Means of Organizing Your Essay

So far we have been creating a de facto **outline**—that is, a skeletal plan of organization. Some writers never use an outline at all but prefer informal lists of ideas; others always rely on outlines; still others insist that they cannot make an outline until they have finished writing. And then there are those writers who simply hate outlines. Regardless of your preference, your final essay should have a tight structure. Therefore, you should use a guiding outline to develop and shape your essay.

   The outline we focus on here is the **analytical sentence outline.** This type is easier to create than it sounds. It consists of (1) an introduction, including the central idea and the thesis sentence, together with (2) topic sentences that are to be used in each paragraph of the body, followed by (3) a conclusion. When applied to the subject we have been developing, such an outline looks like this:

**Title: How Setting in "The Necklace" Is Connected to Mathilde's Character**

1. **Introduction**
   a. *Central idea:* Maupassant uses setting to show Mathilde's character.
   b. *Thesis statement:* Her character growth is brought out by her first apartment, her daydreams about elegant rooms in a mansion, and her attic flat.
2. **Body:** *Topic sentences* a, b, and c (and d, e, and f, if necessary)
   a. Details about her first apartment explain her dissatisfaction and depression.
   b. Her daydreams about mansion rooms are like the apartment because they too make her unhappy.
   c. The attic flat reflects the coarsening of her character.
3. **Conclusion**
   *Topic sentence:* All details in the story, particularly the setting, are focused on the character of Mathilde.

The *conclusion* may be a summary of the body; it may evaluate the main idea; it may briefly suggest further points of discussion; or it may be a reflection on the details of the body.

### *Use Your Outline When Developing Your Essay*

The illustrative essays included throughout this book are organized according to the principles of the analytical sentence outline. To emphasize the shaping effect of these outlines, all central ideas, thesis sentences, and topic sentences are shaded. In your own writing, you can underline or italicize these "skeletal" sentences as a check on your organization. Unless your instructor requires such markings, however, remove them in your final drafts.

---

## THE USE OF VERB TENSES IN THE DISCUSSION OF LITERARY WORKS

Literary works spring into life with each and every reading. You may thus assume that everything happening takes place in the present, and when writing about literature, you should use the *present tense* of verbs. It is correct to say, "Mathilde and her husband *work* and *economize* [not *worked* and *economized*] for ten years to pay off the 18,000-franc loan they *take out* [not *took out*] to pay for the lost necklace."

When you consider an author's ideas, the present tense is also proper, on the principle that the words of an author are just as alive and current today (and tomorrow) as they were at the moment of writing, even if this same author might have been dead for hundreds or even thousands of years.

Because it is incorrect to shift tenses inappropriately, however, you may encounter a problem when you refer to actions that have occurred prior to the time of the main action. An instance is Susan Glaspell's *Trifles*, in which the play's main character, Minnie Wright (never seen on stage), is imprisoned in a nearby town while the major onstage characters, in her farmhouse kitchen, search for and discover evidence that might implicate her as the killer of her husband. In writing about this situation, you can introduce the past tense as long as you make the relationship clear between past and present, as in this example: "The play's action *makes clear* [present tense] that Minnie Wright actually *murdered* [past tense] her husband. Despite developing this knowledge, the two women on stage *conclude* [present tense] that Minnie's years of life with this wretched man *caused* [past tense] the grief and anger that *drove* [past tense] her to strangle him in his sleep. Therefore the women *hide* [present tense] the evidence that *leads* [present tense] to the conclusion that Minnie *committed* [past tense] the murder." This intermingling of past and present tenses is correct because it corresponds to the pattern of time brought out in the play.

A problem also arises when you introduce historical or biographical details about a work or author. It is appropriate to use the *past tense* for such details if they genuinely do belong to the past. Thus, it is correct to state that "Shakespeare *lived* from 1564 to 1616" or that "Shakespeare *wrote* his tragedy *Hamlet* in about 1600–1601." It is also permissible to mix past and present tenses when you are discussing historical facts about a literary work and are also considering it as a living text. Of prime importance is to keep things straight. Here is an example showing how past tenses (in bold) and present tenses (in italic) may be used when appropriate:

> Because *Hamlet* **was** first **performed** in about 1601, Shakespeare most probably **wrote** it shortly before this time. In the play, a tragedy, Shakespeare *treats* an act of vengeance, but more important, he *demonstrates* the difficulty of ever learning the exact truth. The hero, Prince Hamlet, *is* the focus of this difficulty, for the task of revenge *is assigned* to him by the Ghost of his father. Though the Ghost *claims* that his brother, Claudius, *is* his murderer, Hamlet *is* not able to verify this claim.

Here, the historical details are in the past tense, while all details about the play *Hamlet*, including Shakespeare as the creating author whose ideas and words are still alive, in the present.

As a general principle, you will be right most if not all of the time if you make a thorough effort to distinguish past and present details and to use the verb tenses that make these distinctions clear. Above all, however, when in doubt, *consult your instructor*.

## Illustrative Essay (First Draft)

The following Illustrative Essay is a first draft of the subject we have been developing. It follows our outline, and it includes details from the story in support of the various topics. It is by no means, however, as good a piece of writing as it could be. The draft omits a topic, some additional details, and some new insights that are included in the second draft, which follows later (pp. 43–45). It therefore reveals the need to make improvements through additional brainstorming and discovery-prewriting techniques.

The central idea, thesis sentence, and topic sentences are shaded here to stress the goal of strong organization. As your instructor wishes, you might use this or a similar system in your own essays.

Shah 1

Pooja Shah
Professor Aaden
English 200
2 November 2010

How Setting in "The Necklace" Is Related to Mathilde's Character

[1]      In "The Necklace," Guy de Maupassant does not give much detail about the setting. He does not even describe the necklace itself, which is the central object in his plot, but he says only that it is "superb" (paragraph 47). Rather, he uses the setting to reflect the character of the central figure, Mathilde Loisel.° All his details are presented to bring out her traits. Her character growth is related to her first apartment, her dream-life mansion rooms, and her attic flat.[†]

[2]      Details about her first apartment explain her dissatisfaction and depression. The walls are "drab," the furniture "threadbare," and the curtains "ugly" (paragraph 3). There is only a simple country girl to do the housework. The tablecloth is not changed daily, and the best dinner dish is beef stew. Mathilde has no evening clothes, only a theater dress that she does not like. These details show her dissatisfaction about her life with her low-salaried husband.

[3]      Her dream-life images of wealth are like the apartment because they too make her unhappy. In her daydreams about life in a mansion, the rooms are large, filled with expensive furniture and bric-a-brac, and draped in silk. She imagines private rooms for intimate talks and big dinners with delicacies like trout and quail. With dreams of such a rich home, she feels even more despair about her modest apartment on the Street of Martyrs in Paris.

[4]      The attic flat reflects the coarsening of Mathilde's character. Maupassant emphasizes the burdens she endures to save money, such as mopping floors, cleaning greasy and encrusted pots and pans, taking out the garbage, and washing clothes and dishes by hand. This work makes her rough and coarse, a fact also shown by her giving up care of her hair

---

°Central idea.
[†]Thesis sentence.

Shah 2

and hands, wearing the cheapest dresses possible, haggling with local
shopkeepers, and becoming loud and penny-pinching. If at the beginning
she is delicate and attractive, at the end she is unpleasant and coarse.

Maupassant focuses everything in the story, including the setting, on    [5]
the character of Mathilde. He does not add anything extra. Thus, he says
little about the big party scene but emphasizes the necessary detail that
Mathilde was a great "success" (paragraph 52). It is this detail that
brings out some of her early attractiveness and charm, despite her more
usual frustration and unhappiness. Thus, in "The Necklace," Maupassant
uses setting as a means to his end—the story of Mathilde and her
unnecessary sacrifice.

Shah 3

Work Cited

Maupassant, Guy de. "The Necklace." *Writing About Literature.* By Edgar
V. Roberts. 12th ed. New York: Pearson, 2010. 5–12. Print.

## Completing the Essay: Developing and
## Strengthening Your Essay through Revision

After finishing your first draft, like this one, you may wonder what more you can do. Things
may seem to be complete as they are, and that's it. You have read the work several times,
have used discovering and brainstorming techniques to establish ideas to write about, have
made an outline of your ideas, and have written a full draft. How can you do better?

The best way to begin is to observe that a major mistake writers make when writing about literature is to do no more than retell a story or summarize an idea. Retelling
a story shows only that you have read it, not that you have thought about it. Writing a
good essay requires you to arrange a pattern of argument and thought.

### *Make Your Own Arrangement of Details and Ideas*

One way to escape the trap of summarizing stories and to set up a pattern of development is to stress your own order when referring to parts of a work. Rearrange details to suit your own central idea or argument. It is often important to write first about the conclusion or middle. Should you find that you have followed the chronological order of the work instead of stressing your own order, you can use one of the preliminary writing techniques to figure out new ways to connect your materials. The principle is that you should introduce details about the work *only* to support the points you wish to make. Details for the sake of detail are unnecessary.

### *Use Details from the Work as Evidence to Support Your Argument*

When you write, you are like a detective using clues as evidence for building a case, or a lawyer citing evidence to support an argument. Your goal is to convince your readers of your knowledge and the reasonableness of your conclusions. It is vital to use evidence convincingly so that your readers can follow your ideas. Let us look briefly at two drafts of a new example to see how writing can be improved by the pointed use of details. These are from drafts of an essay on the character of Mathilde.

**Paragraph 1**

The major flaw of Mathilde's character is that she seems to be isolated, locked away from other people. She and her husband do not talk to each other much, except about external things. He speaks about his liking for beef stew, and she states that she cannot accept the big invitation because she has no nice dresses. Once she gets the dress, she complains because she has no jewelry. Even when borrowing the necklace from Jeanne Forestier, she does not say much. When she and her husband discover that the necklace is lost, they simply go over the details, and Loisel dictates a letter of explanation, which Mathilde writes in her own hand. Even when she meets Jeanne on the Champs-Elysées, Mathilde does not say a great deal about her life but only goes through enough details about the loss and replacement of the necklace to make Jeanne exclaim about the needlessness of the ten-year sacrifice.

**Paragraph 2**

The major flaw of Mathilde's character is that she is withdrawn and uncommunicative, apparently unwilling or unable to form an intimate relationship. For example, she and her husband do not talk to each other much, except about external things such as his taste for beef stew and her lack of a party dress and jewelry. With such an uncommunicative marriage, one might suppose that she would be more open with her close friend, Jeanne Forestier, but Mathilde does not say much even to her. This flaw hurts her greatly, because if she were more open she might have explained the loss and avoided the horrible sacrifice. This lack of openness, along with her self-indulgent dreaminess, is her biggest defect.

A comparison of these paragraphs shows that the first has more words than the second (156 compared to 119 [computer count]) but that it is more appropriate for a rough than a final draft because the writer does little more than retell the story. Paragraph 1 is cluttered with details that do not support any conclusions. If you try to find what it says about Maupassant's actual use of Mathilde's solitary traits in "The Necklace," you will get little help. The writer needs to revise the paragraph by eliminating details that do not support the central idea.

On the other hand, the details in paragraph 2 actually do support the declared topic. Phrases such as "for example," "with such," and "this lack" show that the writer of paragraph 2 has assumed that the audience knows the story and now wants to read an argument in support of a particular interpretation. Paragraph 2 therefore guides readers by connecting the details to the topic. It uses these details as evidence, *not* as a retelling of actions. By contrast, paragraph 1 recounts a number of relevant actions *but does not connect them to the topic.* More details, of course, could have been added to the second paragraph, but they are unnecessary because the paragraph develops the argument with the details used. Good writing has many qualities, but one of the most important is shown in a comparison of the two paragraphs: *In good writing, no details are included unless they are used as supporting evidence in a pattern of thought and argument.*

### *Always Keep to Your Point; Stick to It Tenaciously*

To show another distinction between first- and second-draft writing, let us consider a third example. The following unrevised paragraph, in which the writer assumes an audience that is interested in the relationship of economics to literature, is drawn from an essay about the idea of economic determinism in Maupassant's "The Necklace." In this paragraph, the writer is trying to argue the point that economic circumstances underlie a number of incidents in the story. The idea is to assert that Mathilde's difficulties result not from her character traits but rather from her financial restrictions.

> More important than chance in governing life is the idea that people are controlled by economic circumstances. Mathilde, as is shown at the story's opening, is born poor. Therefore, she doesn't get the right doors opened for her, and she settles down to marriage with a minor clerk, Loisel. With a vivid imagination and a burning desire for luxury, seeming to be born only for a life of ease and wealth, she finds that her poor home brings out her daydreams of expensive surroundings. She taunts her husband when he brings the big invitation because she does not have a suitable (that is, "expensive") dress. Once she gets the dress, it is jewelry she lacks, and she borrows that and loses it. The loss of the necklace means great trouble because it forces the Loisels to borrow heavily and to struggle financially for ten years.

This paragraph begins with an effective topic sentence, indicating that the writer has a good plan. The remaining part, however, shows how easily writers can be diverted from their objective. The flaw is that the material of the paragraph, while accurate, is not clearly connected to the topic. Once the second sentence is under way, the paragraph gets lost in a retelling of events, and the promising topic sentence is forgotten. The paragraph therefore shows that the use of detail alone will not support an intended meaning or argument. *As a writer, you must do the connecting yourself and make sure that all relationships are explicitly clear.* This point cannot be overstressed.

Let us see how the problem can be treated. If the ideal paragraph can be schematized with line drawings, we might say that the paragraph's topic should be a straight line, moving toward and reaching a specific goal (the topic or argument of the paragraph), with an exemplifying line moving away from the straight line briefly to bring in evidence, but returning to the line to demonstrate the relevance of each new fact. Thus, the ideal scheme looks like this, with a straight line touched a number of times by an undulating line:

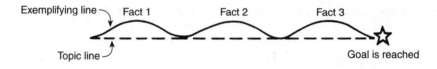

Notice that the exemplifying line, fluctuating to illustrate how documentation or exemplification is to be used, always returns to the topic line. A visual scheme for the faulty paragraph on "The Necklace," however, looks like this, with the line never returning but flying out into space.

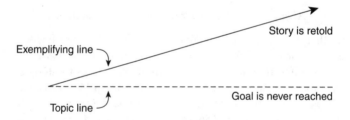

How might the faulty paragraph be improved? The best way is to remind the reader again and again of the topic and to use examples from the text in support.

As our model wavy-line diagram indicates, each time a topic is mentioned, the undulating line merges with the straight, or central-idea, line. This relationship of argument to illustrative examples should prevail no matter what subject you write about, and you have to be tenacious in forming these connecting relationships. If you are analyzing *point of view*, for example, you should keep connecting your material to the speaker, or narrator, and the same applies to topics such as character, idea, or setting. According to this principle, we might revise the paragraph on economic determinism in "The Necklace" as follows (parts of sentences stressing the relationship of the examples to the topic sentence are shaded):

> *More important than chance in governing life is the idea that people are controlled by economic circumstances.* As illustration, the speaker begins by emphasizing that Mathilde, the main character, is born poor. Therefore, she doesn't get the right doors opened for her, and she settles down to marriage with a minor clerk, Loisel. In keeping with the idea, her vivid imagination and burning desire for luxury feed on her weakness of

character as she feels deep unhappiness and depression because of the contrast between her daydreams of expensive surroundings and the poor home she actually has. These straitened economic circumstances inhibit her relationship with her husband, and she taunts him when he brings the big invitation because she does not have a suitable (that is, "expensive") dress. As a merging of her unrealistic dream life with actual reality, her borrowing of the necklace suggests the impossibility of overcoming economic restrictions. In the context of the idea, the ten-year sacrifice to pay for the lost necklace demonstrates that being poor keeps people down, destroying their dreams and their hopes for a better life.

The paragraph now successfully develops the argument promised by the topic sentence. While it has also been lengthened, the length has been caused not by inessential detail but by phrases and sentences that give form and direction. You might object that if you lengthened all your paragraphs in this way, your essays would grow too bulky. The answer is to reduce the number of major points and paragraphs, on the theory that *it is better to develop a few topics pointedly than to develop many pointlessly*. Revising for the purpose of strengthening central and topic ideas requires that you either throw out some topics or else incorporate them as subpoints in the topics you keep. To control your writing in this way can result only in improvement.

## Checking Your Development and Organization

It bears repeating over and over again that the first requirement of a good essay is to introduce a central idea or argument and then stick to it. Another major step toward excellence is to make your central idea expand and grow. The word *growth* is a metaphor describing the disclosure of ideas that were not at first noticeable, together with the expression of original, new, and fresh interpretations.

### *Try to Be Original*

In everything you write, now and in the future, you should always try to be original. You might claim that originality is impossible because you are writing about someone else's work. "The author has said everything," might be the argument, "and therefore I can do little more than follow the story." This claim rests on the mistaken assumption that you have no choice in selecting material and no opportunity to have individual thoughts and make original contributions.

But you do have choices and opportunities to be original. You really do. One obvious area of originality is the development and formulation of your central idea. For example, a natural first response to "The Necklace" is "The story is about a woman who loses a borrowed necklace and endures hardship to help pay for it." But this response does not promise an argument because it refers only to events in the story and not to any idea. You can point the sentence toward an argument, however, if you call the hardship "needless." Just this word alone demands that you explain the differences between needed and unneeded hardships, and your application of these differences to the heroine's plight would produce an original essay. Even better and more original insights could result if the topic of the budding essay were to connect the dreamy, withdrawn traits of the main character to her misfortunes. A resulting central idea might be "People themselves create their own difficulties." Such an argument would require you to define not only the personal but also the representative nature of Mathilde's experiences, an avenue of exploration that could produce much in the way of a fresh, original essay about "The Necklace."

You can also develop your ability to treat your subject originally if you plan the body of the essay to build up to what you think is your most important and incisive idea. As examples of such planning, the following brief outline suggests how a central idea can be widened and expanded:

### Argument: Mathilde Grows as a Character in "The Necklace"

1. She has normal daydreams about a better life.
2. In trying to make her daydreams seem real, she takes a risk but then loses.
3. She develops by facing her mistake and working hard to correct it.

The list shows how you can enlarge a subject if you treat your exemplifying details in an increasing order of importance. In this case, the order moves from Mathilde's habit of daydreaming to her growing strength of character. The pattern shows how you can meet two primary standards of excellence in writing—organization and growth.

Clearly, you should always try to develop your central idea or argument. Constantly adhere to your topic and constantly develop it. Nurture it and make it grow. Admittedly, in a short essay you will be able to move only a short distance with an idea or argument, but you should never be satisfied to leave the idea exactly where you found it. To the degree that you can learn to develop your ideas, you will receive recognition for increasingly original writing.

### Write with Specific Readers as Your Intended Audience

Whenever you write, you must decide how much detail to discuss. Usually you base this decision on your judgment of your readers. For example, if you assume that they have not read the work, you will need to include a short summary as background. Otherwise, they may not understand your argument.

Consider, too, whether your readers have any special interests or concerns. If they are particularly interested in politics, sociology, religion, or psychology, for example, you may need to select and develop your materials along one of these lines.

Your instructor will let you know who your audience is. Usually, it will be your instructor or your fellow students. They will be familiar with the work and will not expect you to retell a story or summarize an argument. Rather, they will want you to explain and interpret the work in the light of your main assertions about it. Thus, you can omit details that do not exemplify and support your argument, even if these details are important parts of the work. What you write should always be based on your developing idea together with your assessment of your readers.

### Use Exact, Comprehensive, and Forceful Language

In addition to being original, organized, and well developed, the best writing is exact, comprehensive, and forceful. At any stage of the composition process, you should try to correct and improve your earliest sentences and paragraphs, which usually need to be rethought, reworded, and rearranged.

Try to make your sentences meaningful. First, ask yourself whether your sentences mean what you really intend or whether you can make them more exact and therefore stronger. For example, consider these two sentences from essays about "The Necklace":

1. It seems as though the main character's dreams of luxury cause her to respond as she does in the story.
2. This incident, although it may seem trivial or unimportant, has substantial significance in the creation of the story. By this I mean that the incident that occurred is essentially what the story is all about.

These sentences are inexact and vague and therefore are unhelpful. Neither of them goes anywhere. Sentence 1 is satisfactory up to the verb *cause*, but then it falls apart because the writer has lost sight of an argumentative or thematic purpose. It would be better to describe what the response *is* rather than to say nothing more than that some kind of response *exists*. To make the sentence more exact, we might try the following revision.

Mathilde's dreams of luxury make her dissatisfied with her own possessions, and therefore she goes beyond her financial means to attend the big party.

With this revision, the writer could readily go on to consider the relationship of the early part of the story to the later parts. Without the revision, it is not clear where the writer might go.

Sentence 2 is vague because the writer has lost all contact with the main thread of argument. If we adopt the principle of trying to be exact, however, we can create more meaning and more promise:

The accidental loss of the necklace, which is trivial though costly, supports the narrator's claim that major turns in life are produced not by earthshaking events but rather by minor ones.

In addition to working for exactness, try to make sentences—all sentences, but particularly thesis and topic sentences—complete and comprehensive. Consider the following sentence:

The idea in "The Necklace" is that Mathilde and her husband work hard to pay for the lost necklace.

Although this sentence promises to describe an idea, it does no more than state the story's major action. It needs additional rethinking and rephrasing to make it more comprehensive, as in these two revisions:

1. In "The Necklace," Maupassant brings out the importance of overcoming mistakes through hard work and responsibility.
2. Maupassant's surprise ending in "The Necklace" emphasizes the need for always being truthful.

Both new sentences are connected to the action described by the original phrasing, "Mathilde and her husband work hard to pay for the lost necklace," although they point toward differing treatments. Sentence 1 concerns the virtue shown by the Loisels in their sacrifice. Because sentence 2 includes the word *symbolizes*, an essay stemming from it would stress the Loisels' mistake in not confessing the loss. In dealing with the symbolic meaning of their failure, an essay developed along the lines of sentence 2 would focus on the negative sides of their characters, and an essay developed from sentence 1 would stress their positive sides. Both of the revised sentences are therefore more comprehensive than the original sentence and thus would help a writer get on the track toward a thoughtful and analytical essay.

Of course, creating fine sentences is never easy, but as a mode of improvement, you might use some self-testing mechanisms:

- **For story materials.** Always relate the materials to a point or argument. Do not say simply, "Mathilde works constantly for ten years to help pay off the debt." Instead, blend the material into a point, like this: "Mathilde's ten-year effort shows her resolution to overcome the horror of indebtedness" or "Mathilde's ten-year effort brings out her strength of character."
- **For responses and impressions.** Do not say simply, "The story's ending left me with a definite impression." What are you telling your readers by writing a sentence like this? They want to know what your impression is, and therefore you need to describe it, as in the following: "The story's ending surprised me and also made me sympathetic to the major character" or "The story's ending struck me with the idea that life is unpredictable and unfair."
- **For ideas.** Make the idea clear and direct. Do not say, "Mathilde lives in a poor household," but rather refer to the story to bring out an idea, as follows: "Mathilde's story shows that being poor hurts a person's quality of life."
- **For critical commentary.** Do not be satisfied with a statement such as "I found 'The Necklace' interesting." All right, the story is interesting, but what does that tell us? Instead, try to describe *what* was interesting and *why* it was interesting, as in this sentence: "I found 'The Necklace' interesting because it shows how chance and bad luck may disrupt or even destroy people's lives."

Good writing begins with attempts, like these, to rephrase sentences to make them really say something. If you always name and pin down descriptions, responses, and judgments, no matter how difficult the task seems, your sentences can be strong and forceful because you will be making them exact and comprehensive.

## Illustrative Essay (Improved Draft)

If you refer again to the first draft of the essay about Maupassant's use of setting to illustrate Mathilde's character (pp. 34–35), you might notice that several parts of the draft need extensive reworking and revising. For example, paragraph 2 contains a series of short, unconnected comments, and the last sentence of that paragraph implies that Mathilde's dissatisfaction relates mainly to her husband rather than to her general circumstances. Paragraph 4 focuses too much on Mathilde's coarseness and not enough on her sacrifice and cooperation. The first draft also ignores the fact that the story ends in another location, the fashionable Parisian street the Champs-Elysées, where Maupassant continues to demonstrate the nature of Mathilde's character. Finally, there is not enough support in this draft for the contention (in paragraph 5) that everything in the story is related to the character of Mathilde.

To discover how these issues can be more fully considered, the following revision of the earlier draft creates more introductory detail, includes an additional paragraph, and reshapes each of the paragraphs to stress the relationship of the central idea or argument to the topics of the various paragraphs. Within the limits of a short assignment, the essay illustrates all the principles of organization and unity that we have been discussing here.

---

Shah 1

Pooja Shah

Professor Aaden

English 200

2 November 2010

How Maupassant Uses Setting in "The Necklace"

to Show Mathilde's Character                                                          [1]

In "The Necklace," Guy de Maupassant uses setting to reflect the character and development of the main character, Mathilde Loisel.° As a result, his setting is not particularly vivid or detailed. He does not even describe the ill-fated necklace—the central object in the story—but states only that it is "superb" (paragraph 47). In fact, he includes descriptions of setting only if they illuminate qualities about Mathilde. Her changing character can be connected to the first apartment, the dream-life mansion rooms, the attic flat, and a fashionable public street.†      [2]

Details about the modest apartment of the Loisels on the Street of Martyrs indicate Mathilde's peevish lack of adjustment to life. Though everything is serviceable, she is unhappy with the "drab" walls, "threadbare" furniture, and "ugly" curtains (paragraph 3). She has domestic help, but she wants more servants than the simple country girl who does the household chores in the apartment. Her embarrassment and dissatisfaction are shown by details of her irregularly cleaned tablecloth and the plain and inelegant beef stew that her husband adores. Even her best theater dress, which is appropriate for apartment life but inappropriate for more wealthy surroundings, makes her unhappy. All these details of the apartment establish that Mathilde's major trait at the story's beginning is maladjustment. She therefore seems unpleasant and unsympathetic.

---

°Central idea.
†Thesis sentence.

Shah 2

[3]      Like the real-life apartment, the impossibly wealthy setting of her daydreams about owning a mansion strengthens her unhappiness and her avoidance of reality. All the rooms of her fantasies are large and expensive, draped in silk and filled with nothing but the best furniture and bric-a-brac. Maupassant gives us the following description of her dream world:

> She imagined a gourmet-prepared main course carried on the most exquisite trays and served on the most beautiful dishes, with whispered gallantries that she would hear with a sphinxlike smile as she dined on the pink meat of a trout or the delicate wing of a quail. (paragraph 4)

With such impossible dreams, her despair is complete. Ironically, this despair, together with her inability to live with reality, brings about her undoing. It makes her agree to borrow the necklace (which is just as unreal as her daydreams of wealth), and losing the necklace drives her into the reality of giving up her apartment and moving into the attic flat.

[4]      Also ironically, the attic flat is related to the coarsening of her character while at the same time it brings out her best qualities of hard work and honesty. Maupassant emphasizes the drudgery of the work Mathilde endures to maintain the flat, such as walking up many stairs, washing floors with large buckets of water, cleaning greasy and encrusted pots and pans, taking out the garbage, washing clothes by hand, and haggling loudly with local shopkeepers. All this reflects her coarsening and loss of sensibility, also shown by her giving up hair and hand care and by wearing cheap dresses. The work she performs, however, makes her heroic (paragraph 98). As she cooperates to help her husband pay back the loans, her dreams of a mansion fade, and all she has left is the memory of her triumphant appearance at the Minister of Education's party. Thus, the attic flat brings out her physical change for the worse at the same time that it also brings out her psychological change for the better.

[5]      Her walk on the Champs-Elysées illustrates another combination of traits—self-indulgence and frankness. The Champs-Elysées is the most fashionable street in Paris, and her walk to it is similar to her earlier indulgences in her daydreams of upper-class wealth. But it is on this street where she meets Jeanne, and it is her frankness in confessing to Jeanne that

Shah 3

makes her completely honest. While the walk thus serves as the occasion for the story's concluding surprise and irony, Mathilde's being on the Champs-Elysées is totally in character, in keeping with her earlier reveries about luxury.

Other details in the story also have a similar bearing on Mathilde's [6] character. For example, the story presents little detail about the party scene beyond the statement that Mathilde is a great "success" (paragraph 52)—a judgment that shows her ability to shine if given the chance. After she and Loisel accept the fact that the necklace cannot be found, Maupassant includes details about the Parisian streets, about the visits to loan sharks, and about the jewelry shops, to bring out Mathilde's sense of honesty and pride as she "heroically" prepares to live her new life of poverty. Thus, in "The Necklace," Maupassant uses setting to highlight Mathilde's maladjustment, her needless misfortune, her loss of youth and beauty, and finally her growth as a responsible human being.

Shah 4

Work Cited

Maupassant, Guy de. "The Necklace." *Writing About Literature.* By Edgar V. Roberts. 12th ed. New York: Pearson, 2010. 5–12. Print.

## Commentary on the Essay

You will find here several improvements to the first draft. The language of paragraph 2 has been revised to show more clearly the inappropriateness of Mathilde's dissatisfaction. In paragraph 3, the irony of the story is brought out, and the writer has connected the details to the central idea in a richer pattern of ideas, showing the effects of Mathilde's despair. Paragraph 5—new in the improved draft—includes additional details about how Mathilde's walk on the Champs-Elysées is related to her character. In paragraph 6, the fact that Mathilde is able "to shine" at the dinner party is interpreted according to the central idea. Finally, the conclusion is now much more specific, summarizing the change in Mathilde's character rather than saying simply that the setting reveals "her needless misfortune." In short, the second draft reflects the complexity of "The Necklace" better than the first draft. Because the writer has revised the first-draft ideas about the story, the final essay is tightly structured, insightful, and forceful.

## Essay Commentaries

Throughout this book, the Illustrative Essays are followed by short commentaries that show how the essays embody the chapter instructions and guidelines. For each essay that has a number of possible approaches, the commentary points out which one is used, and when an essay uses two or more approaches, the commentary makes this fact clear. In addition, each commentary singles out one of the paragraphs for more detailed analysis of its argument and use of detail. The commentaries will hence help you develop the insights necessary to use the essays as aids in your own study and writing.

## Summary: Guidelines for Writing about Literature

To sum up, follow these guidelines whenever you write about a story or any kind of literature:

- Do not simply retell the story or summarize the work. Bring in story materials only when you can use them as support for your central idea or argument.
- Throughout your essay, keep reminding your reader of your central idea.
- Within each paragraph, make sure that you stress your topic idea.
- Develop your subject. Make it bigger than it was when you began.
- Always make your statements exact, comprehensive, and forceful.
- And this bears repeating: *Do not simply retell the story or summarize the work.*

## Writing Topics to Enhance the Writing Process

1. Write a brainstorming paragraph on the topic of anything in a literary work that you find especially good or interesting. Write as the thoughts occur to you; do not slow yourself down in an effort to make your writing seem perfect. You can make corrections and improvements later.
2. Using marginal and notebook notations, together with any additional thoughts, describe the way in which the author of a particular work has expressed important ideas and difficulties.
3. Create a plus-minus table to list your responses about a character or ideas in a work.
4. To determine the various customs and manners of the society out of which the work is derived, raise questions about the actions of characters in a story or play.
5. Analyze and explain the way in which the conflicts in a story or play are developed. What pattern or patterns do you find? Determine the relationship of the conflicts to the work's development and fashion your idea of this relationship as an argument for a potential essay.
6. Basing your ideas on your marginal and notebook notations, select an idea and develop a thesis sentence from it, using your idea and a list of possible topics for an argument or central idea for an essay.
7. Using the thesis sentence you write for exercise 6, develop a brief analytical sentence outline that could help you in writing a full essay.

# Chapter 1A

## A Short Guide to Using Quotations and Making References in Essays about Literature

In establishing evidence for the points you make in your essays and essay examinations, you constantly need to refer to various parts of stories, plays, and poems. You also need to include shorter and longer quotations and to keep the time sequences straight within the works you are writing about. In addition, you may need to refer to biographical and historical details that have a bearing on the work or works you are studying. So that your own writing may flow as accurately and naturally as possible, you must be able to integrate these references and distinctions of time clearly and easily.

### Integrate Passages and Ideas into Your Essay

Your essays should reflect your own thought as you study and analyze the characteristics, ideas, and qualities of an author's work. In a typical discussion of literature, you constantly need to introduce brief summaries, quotations, general interpretations, observations, and independent applications of everything you are discussing. It is not easy to keep these various elements integrated and to keep confusion from arising.

### Distinguish Your Own Thoughts from Those of Your Author

Often a major problem is that it is hard for your reader to figure out when *your* ideas have stopped and your *author's* have begun. You must therefore arrange your sentences to make the distinctions clear, but you must also blend your materials so that your reader may follow you easily. Let us see an example of how such problems may be handled. Here, the writer being discussed is the Victorian poet Matthew Arnold (1822–1888). The passage moves from reference to Arnold's ideas to the essay writer's independent application of the ideas.

[1] In his poem "Dover Beach," Arnold states that in past times religious faith was accepted as absolute truth. [2] To symbolize this idea, he refers to the ocean, which surrounds all land, and the surf, which constantly rushes onto the earth's shores.

[3] According to this symbolism, religious ideas are as vast as the ocean and as regular as the surf, and these ideas at one time constantly and irresistibly replenished people's lives. [4] Arnold's symbol of the flowing ocean changes, however, to a symbol of the ebbing ocean, thus illustrating his idea that belief and religious certainty were falling away. [5] It is this personal sense of spiritual emptiness that Arnold is associating with his own times because what he describes, in keeping with the symbolism, is that in the present time the "drear" shoreline has been left vacant by the "melancholy long withdrawing roar" of retreat and reduction (lines 25–27).

This specimen paragraph combines but also separates paraphrase, interpretation, and quotation, and it thereby eliminates any possible confusion about the origin of the ideas and also about who is saying what. In the first three sentences the writer uses the phrases "Arnold states," "To symbolize this idea," and "According to this symbolism," to show clearly that interpretation is to follow. Although the fourth sentence marks a new direction of Arnold's ideas, it continues to separate restatement from interpretation. The fifth sentence indicates, through the phrase "in keeping with the symbolism," what seems to the writer to be the major idea of "Dover Beach."

## Integrate Material by Using Quotation Marks

It is often necessary, and also interesting, to use short quotations from your author to illustrate and reinforce your ideas and interpretations. Here the problem of separating your thoughts from the author's is solved by quotation marks. In such an internal quotation, you may treat prose and poetry in the same way. If a poetic quotation extends from the end of one line to the beginning of another, however, use a capital letter to begin the next line, as in the following:

> In "Lines Written in Early Spring," Wordsworth describes a condition in which his speaker is united with the surrounding natural world. Nature is a combination of the "thousand blended notes" of joyful birds (line 1), the sights of "budding twigs" (line 17), and the "periwinkle" (line 10). In the exact words of the speaker, these "fair works" form a direct "link" to "The human soul that through me ran" (lines 5 and 6).

## Blend Quotations into Your Own Sentences

The use of internal quotations still creates the problem of blending materials, however, for quotations should never be brought in unless you prepare your reader for them in some way. Do *not*, for example, use quotations in the following manner:

> Wordsworth states that his woodland grove is filled with the sounds of birds, the sights of flowers, and the feeling of the light wind, making for the thought that creatures of the natural world take pleasure in life. "The birds around me hopped and played" (line 13).

This abrupt quotation throws the reader off balance because it is not blended into the previous sentence. It is necessary to prepare the reader to move from your discussion to the quotation, as in the following revision:

Wordsworth claims that his woodland scene is made joyful by the surrounding flowers and the gentle breeze, causing his speaker, who states that "The birds around me hopped and played," to conclude that the natural world has resulted from a "holy plan" created by Nature.

Here the quotation is made an actual part of the sentence. This sort of blending is satisfactory, provided that the quotation is brief.

## Indent and Block Long Quotations

You can follow a general rule for incorporating quotations in your writing: Do not quote within a sentence any passage longer than 20 or 25 words (but consult your instructor, for the allowable number of words may vary). Quotations of greater length demand so much separate attention that they interfere with your own sentence. It is possible but not desirable to conclude one of your sentences with a quotation, but you should never make an extensive quotation in the *middle* of a sentence. By the time you finish such an unwieldy sentence, your reader will have forgotten how it began, and how can that be clear writing? When your quotation is long, you should make a point of introducing it and setting it off separately as a block.

The physical layout of block quotations should be this: Leave three blank lines between your own discourse and the quotation. Double-space the quotation (like the rest of your essay), and indent it five spaces from your left margin to distinguish it from your own writing. You might use fewer spaces for longer lines of poetry, but the standard should always be to create a balanced, neat page. After the quotation, leave a three-line space again, and resume your own discourse. Here is a specimen, from an essay about Wordsworth's "Lines Written in Early Spring":

> In "Lines Written in Early Spring," Wordsworth develops an idea that the world of nature is linked directly to the moral human consciousness. He speaks of no religious systems or books of moral values. Instead, he derives his ideas directly from his experience, assuming that the world was made for the joy of the living creatures in it, including human beings ("man"), and that anyone disturbing that power of joy is violating "Nature's holy plan" itself. Wordsworth's moral criticism, in other words, is derived from his faith in the integrity of creation (lines 21–24):
>
> > If this belief from heaven be sent,
> > If such be Nature's holy plan,
> > Have I not reason to lament
> > What man has made of man?
>
> The concept that morality and life are joined is the most interesting and engaging aspect of the poem. It seems to encourage a live-and-let-live attitude toward others, however, not an active program of direct outreach and help.

When quoting lines of poetry, always remember to quote them as *lines*. Do not run them together as though they were continuous prose. When you create such block quotations, as in the preceding example, you do *not* need quotation marks.

Today, computer usage is becoming the established means of preparing papers, and therefore computer styling has become prominent in the handling of the matters discussed here. If you have style features in your menu, such as "Poem Text" or "Quotation," each of which sets block quotations apart from "Normal" text, you may certainly make use of the features. Be sure to explain to your instructor what you are doing, however, to make sure that your computer's features correspond to the styles that are required for your class.

## Use Ellipses to Show Omissions

Whether your quotation is long or short, you will often need to change some of the material in it to conform to your own sentence requirements. You might wish to omit something from the quotation that is not essential to your point or to the flow of your sentence. Indicate such omissions with ellipses (three spaced periods), as follows (from an essay about Eudara Welty's "A Worn Path"):

> Welty introduces Phoenix as an aging and impoverished but also lovely and delicate woman. Phoenix's dress, which reaches to "her shoe tops," is protected by a "long apron of bleached sugar sacks." Her skin has "a pattern all its own of numberless branching wrinkles, . . . but a golden color ran underneath." Nevertheless, her hair is shaped "in the frailest of ringlets, . . . with an odor like copper."

If your quotation is very brief, however, do not use ellipses because they might be more distracting than helpful. For example, do not use ellipses in a quotation like this:

> Keats asserts that ". . . a thing of beauty . . ." always gives joy.

Instead, make your quotation without the ellipses:

> Keats asserts that "a thing of beauty" always gives joy.

## Use Square Brackets to Enclose Words
## That You Add within Quotations

If you add words of your own to integrate the quotation into your own train of discourse or to explain words that may seem obscure, put square brackets around these words, as in the following passage:

> In "Lines Written in Early Spring," Wordsworth refers to a past experience of extreme happiness, in which Nature seemed to "link/The human soul that through . . . [him] ran" (lines 5–6). He is describing a state of mystical awareness in which "pleasant thoughts/Bring [him] sad thoughts" (lines 2–4) and make him "lament" (line 23) moral and political cruelty.

## Do Not Overquote

A word of caution: *Do not use too many quotations.* You will be judged on your own thought and on the continuity and development of your own essay. It is tempting to include many quotations on the theory that you need to use examples from the text to illustrate and support your ideas. Naturally, it is important to introduce examples, but realize that too many quotations can disturb the flow of your own thought. If your essay consists of many illustrations linked together by no more than your introductory sentences, how much thinking have you actually shown? Try therefore to create your own discussion, using appropriate examples to connect your thought to the text or texts you are analyzing.

## Preserve the Spellings in Your Sources

Always reproduce your source exactly. Sometimes the works of British authors may include words like *tyre, defence, honour,* and *labour.* Duplicate these as you find them. Although most anthologies modernize the spelling of older writers, you may often encounter "old-spelling" editions in which all words—such as *entring, Shew, beautie, ore* (for *over*), *witte* (for *wit*), *specifick, 'twas, guaranty* (for guarantee), or *determin'd*—are spelled and capitalized exactly as they were centuries ago. Your principle should be *to duplicate everything exactly as you find it,* even if this means spelling words like *achieve* as *atchieve, music* as *Musick,* or *joke* as *joak.* A student once changed the word *an* to *and* in the construction "an I were" in a Shakespeare play. The result was misleading because in introductory clauses of this type, *an* really meant *if* (or *and if*) and not *and.* Difficulties like this one are rare, but you can avoid them if you reproduce the text as you find it. Should you think that something is either misspelled or confusing as it stands, you may do one of two things:

1. Clarify or correct the confusing word or phrase within brackets, as in the following: In 1714, fencing was considered a "Gentlemany [i.e., gentlemanly] subject."
2. Use the word *sic* (Latin for *thus,* meaning "It is this way in the text") in brackets immediately after the problematic word or obvious mistake: He was just "finning [sic] his way back to health" when the next disaster struck.

# Chapter 2

# Writing about a Close Reading: Analyzing Entire Short Poems or Selected Short Passages

An essay based on a **close reading** is a detailed study of an entire short work, usually a poem, or else a passage of prose or verse that is part of a longer work. This type of essay is specific because it focuses on the selected poem or passage. It is also general because you do not consider only a single topic such as the nature of a character or the meaning of a particular idea but rather deal with all the elements you think are important. If the passage describes a person, for example, you might naturally want to discuss character. You might also want to stress the actions described in the passage, noteworthy ideas or expressions of emotion, or descriptions of the location of an action, if you decide that these matters are important. In other words, the content of a close-reading essay is variable. The passage you are studying governs what you write.

## The Purpose and Requirements of a Close-Reading Essay

Writing a close-reading essay magnifies your abilities and increases your skills. Think of these implications: If you can read and assimilate a single paragraph, you have then developed your power to read and assimilate an entire book. And if you can follow and appreciate a single poem, you will have acquired the skill to comprehend other poems. In addition, if you can understand a single speech by a dramatic character—any speech—you can go on to do the same for the entire play. This is not to say that writing a close-reading essay gives you the magic power instantly to understand every work you read, but what it does give you is the development of abilities on which you can build—an approach toward your comprehension and appreciation of other works.

The essay is designed as an explanation of what is in the assigned passage. General content is the objective, together with anything else that is noteworthy. To write the essay, you do not need to undertake a detailed analysis of diction, grammar, or style. Instead, analyze and discuss what you consider the most important aspects of the passage. Although you are free to consider special words and phrases, and should do so if you find them important, your aim is primarily to get at the content of your passage.

## The Location of the Passage in a Longer Work

Close-reading essays about portions of a work should demonstrate how the passage is connected to the rest of the work. The principle is that all parts are equally important and essential. Analyzing an individual part should therefore bring out not only the meaning but also the function within the larger structure of the work.

### *Expect an Early Passage to Get Things Going*

You may reasonably assume that—in the early portions of a poem, play, or story—the author is setting things in motion, introducing you to the characters and ideas, and explaining the situations and problems that are going to be dealt with in the work. Thus, you should try to discover how such early ideas, characterizations, insights, and descriptions are related to later developments. Always assume that everything you find there is connected to everything else in the work and then analyze and explain that connection.

### *Expect a Midpoint Passage to Include Anticipations of the Work's Conclusion*

In a passage at the work's midpoint, the story or idea usually takes a particular turn—either expected or unexpected. If the change is unexpected, you should explain how the passage focuses the various themes or ideas and then propels them toward the forthcoming conclusion or climax. It may be that the work features surprises, and the passage thus acquires a different meaning on second reading. It may be that the speaker has one set of assumptions while the readers have others and that the passage marks the speaker's increasing self-awareness. In short, your task is to determine the extent to which the passage (1) builds on what has happened previously and (2) prepares the way for the outcome.

### *Expect a Passage Near the End to Include Details about How Things Are Coming Together*

A passage at or near the work's end is designed to solve problems or be a focal point or climax for all the cumulative situations and ideas. You will thus need to show how the passage brings together all details, ideas, and themes. In a narrative work, what is happening? Is any action described in the passage a major action or a step leading to the major action? Has everything in the passage been prepared for earlier or are there any surprises? In a longer narrative poem, such as an epic, what is happening to the topics and ideas introduced earlier in the poem?

# Writing about the Close Reading of a Passage in a Prose Work, Drama, or Longer Poem

Focus on the general meaning and impact of the passage or poem. By raising and answering a number of specific questions, you can gather materials for shaping your essay. Once you create answers, write them into a form that you can adapt in your essay. Try to reach specific and focused conclusions.

### *Raise Questions to Discover Ideas*

- Does the passage (1) describe a scene, (2) develop a character, (3) present an action, (4) reveal a character's thoughts, (5) advance an argument, or (6) introduce an idea? How does all this work?
- What is the situation in the work? Who is the speaker? Who is being addressed? What does the speaker want? What ideas are contained in the work?
- What is the thematic content of the passage? How representative is it of the work as a whole? How does the passage relate to earlier and later parts of the entire text? (To deal with this question, you may assume that your reader is familiar with the entire work.)
- What noticeable aspects of diction and ideas are present in the passage? Do speeches or descriptions seem particularly related to any characterizations or ideas that appear elsewhere in the work?

### *Organize Your Essay on a Close Reading*

*Introduction*    Because the close-reading essay is concerned with details, you might have a problem developing a thematic structure. You can overcome this difficulty if you begin to work with either a generalization about the passage or a thesis based on the relationship of the passage to the work. Suppose, for example, that the passage is factually descriptive, introduces a major character, or raises a major idea. Any one of these observations may serve as a central idea.

*Body*    Develop the body of the essay according to what you find in the passage. For a passage of character description, analyze what is disclosed about the character, together with your analysis of what bearing this information has on the story or play as a whole. For a passage presenting an idea or ideas, analyze the idea and demonstrate how the idea is important for the rest of the work. In short, your aim in this kind of essay is double: (1) Discuss the passage itself; and (2) show how the passage functions within the entire work.

*Conclusion*    To conclude, stress the important details of your analysis. In addition, you may want to deal with secondary issues that arise in the passage but do not merit full consideration. The passage may contain specific phrases or underlying assumptions that you have not considered in the body of your essay. The conclusion is the place to mention these matters without developing them fully.

> ## NUMBER THE PASSAGE FOR EASY REFERENCE
>
> In preparing your essay, prepare a copy of the entire passage just as it appears in the text from which you are making your selection. Copy it exactly. Include your copy at the beginning of your essay, as in the following Illustrative Essays. For your reader's convenience, number the lines in poetry and the sentences in prose.

## Illustrative Essay

> The central idea, thesis sentence, and topic sentences are shaded here to stress the goal of strong organization. As your instructor wishes, you might use this or a similar system in your own essays.

---

Leland 1

Joshua Leland
Professor Rustelli
English 102
8 September 2010

A Close Reading of a Paragraph from Frank O'Connor's
"First Confession"°

[1] Nora's turn came, and I heard the sound of something slamming, and then her voice as if butter wouldn't melt in her mouth, and then another slam, and out she came. [2] God, the hypocrisy of women! [3] Her eyes were lowered, her head was bowed, and her hands were joined very low down on her stomach, and she walked up the aisle to the side altar looking like a saint. [4] You never saw such an exhibition of devotion, and I

---

°See pages 347–52 for this story.

remembered the devilish malice with which she had tormented me all the way from our door, and wondered were all religious people like that, really. [5] It was my turn now. [6] With the fear of damnation in my soul I went in, and the confessional door closed of itself behind me.

**[1]**    This paragraph from Frank O'Connor's "First Confession" appears midway in the story. It is transitional, coming between Jackie's "heartscalded" memories of family troubles and his happier memory of the confession itself. Though mainly narrative, the passage is punctuated by Jackie's recollections of disgust with his sister and fear of eternal punishment for his childhood "sins." It reflects geniality and good nature.* This mood is apparent in the comments of the narrator, his diction, the comic situation, and the narrator's apparent lack of self-awareness.†

**[2]**    More impressionistic than descriptive, the paragraph concentrates in a good-humored way on the direct but somewhat exaggerated responses of the narrator, Jackie. The first four sentences convey Jackie's reactions to Nora's confession. Sentence 1 describes his recollections of her voice in the confessional, and sentence 3 makes his judgment clear about the hypocrisy of her pious appearance when she leaves for the altar. Each of these descriptive sentences is followed by Jackie's angry reactions, at which readers smile if not laugh. This depth of feeling is transformed to "fear of damnation" at the beginning of sentence 6, which describes Jackie's own entry into the confessional, with the closing door suggesting that he is being shut off from the world and thrown into hell. In other words, the paragraph succinctly presents Jackie's sights, reactions, and confusion about the scene itself, all of which are part of the story's brief and comic family drama.

---

*Central idea.
†Thesis sentence.

Leland 3

The humorous action of the passage is augmented by Jackie's simple [3]
diction, which enables readers to concentrate fully on his responses. As
an adult telling the story, Jackie is recalling unpleasant childhood
memories, and his direct and descriptive choice of words enables readers
to be both amused and sympathetic at the same time. His words are
neither unusual nor difficult. What could be more ordinary, for example,
than *butter, slam, out, hands, joined, low, people*, and *closed*? Even
Jackie's moral and religious words fall within the vocabulary of ordinary
discussions about sin and punishment: *hypocrisy, exhibition, devilish*
*malice, tormented*, and *damnation*. In the passage, the diction therefore
accurately conveys Jackie's vision of the oppressive religious forces,
which he dislikes, fears, and exaggerates. Readers follow these words
easily and with amusement.

It is from Jackie's remarks that the comedy of the passage [4]
develops. Much of the humor rests on the inconsistency between
Nora's sisterly badgering and her saintly behavior at the confessional.
Since Jackie is careful here to stress her "devilish malice" against him
(sentence 4), readers might smile at the description of her worshipful
pose. But readers surely know that Nora is not unusual; she has been
behaving like any typical older sister or brother. So there is also a
comic contrast between her normal actions and Jackie's negative
opinions. The humor is thus directed more toward the narrator than the
sister.

In fact, it may be that the narrator's lack of self-awareness is the [5]
major cause of humor in the passage. Jackie is an adult telling a story
about his experience as a 7-year-old. Readers might expect him to be
mature and therefore to be amused and perhaps regretful about his
childhood annoyances and anger. But his child's-eye view seems still
to be controlling his responses. Comments about Nora such as
"looking like a saint" and "You never saw such an exhibition of
devotion" are not consistent with a person who has put childhood in
perspective. Hence readers may smile at not only the obvious comedy

Leland 4

of Nora's hypocrisy but also the narrator's lack of self-awareness. As he comments on his sister with his still jaundiced attitude, he shows his own limitations and, for this reason, directs amusement against himself.

[6]          Readers are more likely to smile at Jackie's remarks, however, than to object to his adult character. The thrust of the paragraph from "First Confession" is therefore on the good-natured comedy of the situation. For this reason, the paragraph is a successful turning point between Jackie's disturbing experiences with his sister, grandmother, and father, on the one hand, and the joyful confession with the kind and genial priest on the other. The child goes into the confession with the fear of damnation in his thoughts, but after the following farce, he finds the assurances that his fears are not justified and that his anger is normal and can be forgiven. Therefore, in retrospect, Jackie's anger and disgust were unnecessary, but they were important to him as a child—so much so that his exaggerations make him the center of the story's comedy. Jackie's bittersweet memories are successfully rendered and made comic in this exemplary passage from O'Connor's story.

Leland 5

Work Cited

O'Connor, Frank. "First Confession." *Writing About Literature*. By
    Edgar V. Roberts. 12th ed. New York: Pearson, 2010, 347–52. Print.

## Commentary on the Essay

A number of central ideas might have been made about the passage chosen for analysis: It is dramatic, it centers on the religious hypocrisy of Jackie's sister, it brings together the major themes of the story, or it creates a problem in the character of the narrator. The idea of the sample essay as brought out in paragraph 1, however, is that the passage reflects geniality and good nature. The essay does in fact deal with the sister's hypocrisy and also with the problem in the narrator's character, but these points are made in connection with the central idea.

In the body of the essay, paragraph 2 shows that the narrator's comments about his sister and his own spiritual condition add to the good nature of the passage. Paragraph 3 deals with the level of diction, noting that the words are appropriate both to the action and to Jackie's anger when recollecting it. Paragraph 4 explains the relationship between Jackie's remarks and the comedy being played out in the narration. In paragraph 5, the adult narrator's unwitting revelation of his own shortcomings is related to the good humor and comedy. The final paragraph (6) connects the passage to the latter half of the story, suggesting that the comedy that shines through the passage is, comparatively, like the forgiveness that is believed to follow the act of confession.

Because the essay is based on a close reading, its major feature is the use of many specific details. Thus, paragraph 2 stresses the actions and some of Jackie's comments upon it, while paragraph 3 provides many examples of his word choices. Paragraph 4 stresses the details about Nora's posturing and Jackie's comments about her. Paragraph 5 provides details of more of Jackie's comments and the limitations of character that they show. Finally, the concluding paragraph (6) includes the detail about Jackie's entering the confessional.

## Writing an Essay on the Close Reading of a Poem

The close reading of a poem does not mean that you need to explain everything you find in the poem. Theoretically, a complete or total explication would require you to explain the meaning and implications of each word and every line—a technique that obviously would be exhaustive (and exhausting). It would also be self-defeating, for writing about everything in great detail would prohibit you from using your judgment and deciding what is important.

A more manageable and desirable technique is therefore to devote attention to the meaning of individual parts in relationship to the entire work. You might think of your essay as your explanation, or "reading," of the poem. You will need to be selective and to consider only those details that you think are significant and vital to the thematic development of your essay.

### *Raise Questions to Discover Ideas*

- What does the title contribute to the reader's understanding?
- Who is speaking? Where is the speaker when the poem is happening or unfolding?
- What is the situation? What has happened in the past, or what is happening in the present, that has brought about the speech?
- What difficult, special, or unusual words does the poem contain? What references need explaining? How does an explanation assist in the understanding of the poem?

- How does the poem develop? Is it a personal statement? Is it a story?
- What is the main idea of the poem? What details make possible the formulation of the main idea?

### Organize Your Essay on the Close Reading of a Poem

In this close-reading essay you should plan to (1) follow the essential details of the poem, (2) understand the issues and the meaning the poem reveals, (3) explain some of the relationships of content to technique, and (4) note and discuss especially important or unique aspects of the poem.

*Introduction*   In your introduction, use your central idea to express a general view of the poem, which your essay will bear out. A close reading of Arnold's "Dover Beach," for example, might bring out the speaker's understanding that philosophical and religious certainty has been lost and that therefore people can find certainty only within individual relationships. In the following Illustrative Essay describing Thomas Hardy's "The Man He Killed," the central idea is that war is senseless.

*Body*   In the body of your essay, first explain the poem's content—not with a paraphrase but with a description of the poem's major organizing elements. Hence, if the speaker of the poem is a first-person "I," you do not need to reproduce this voice yourself in your description. Instead, describe the poem in your own words, with whatever brief introductory phrases you find necessary, as in paragraph 2 of the following Illustrative Essay.

Next, explain the poem's development or growth in relation to your central idea. Choose your own order of discussion, depending on your topics. You should, however, keep stressing your central idea with each new topic. Thus, you might wish to follow your description by discussing the poem's meaning or even by presenting two or more possible interpretations. You might also wish to refer to significant techniques. For example, in Dudley Randall's "Ballad of Birmingham," a noteworthy technique is the unintroduced quotations (i.e., quotations appearing without any "she said" or "he said" phrases) as the ballad writer's means of dramatizing the dialogue between mother and "baby."

You might also introduce unique topics, such as the understatements in stanza 2 of "Ballad of Birmingham" that instruments of violence "Aren't good for a little child." Such a reference to the mother's language underscores adult attempts to shield children from the potential violence of the outside world, and it therefore makes the event described in the poem's conclusion especially ironic. In short, discuss those aspects of meaning and technique that bear upon your central idea.

*Conclusion*   In your conclusion, you may repeat your major idea to reinforce your essay's thematic structure. Because your essay reflects a general but not an exhaustive reading, there will be parts of the poem that you will not have covered. You might therefore mention what might be gained from a more complete discussion of various parts of the poem (do not, however, begin an extensive discussion in your conclusion).

The last stanza of Hardy's "The Man He Killed," for example, contains the words "quaint and curious" in reference to war. These words are unusual, particularly because the speaker might have chosen hateful, senseless, destructive, or other similarly descriptive words. Why did Hardy have his speaker make such a choice? With brief attention to such a problem, you may conclude your essay.

## Illustrative Essay

Morales 1

Lindsey Morales

Professor Soloway

English 101

29 September 2010

A Close Reading of Thomas Hardy's "The Man He Killed"°

Hardy's "The Man He Killed" exposes the senselessness of war.* It                **[1]**
does this through a silent contrast between the needs of ordinary people, as
represented by a young man—the speaker—who has killed an enemy soldier
in battle, and the antihuman and unnatural deaths that happen in combat. Of
major note in this contrast are the speaker's circumstances, his language, his
sense of identity with the dead man, and his concerns and wishes.†

The speaker begins by contrasting the circumstances of warfare with          **[2]**
those of peace. He does not identify himself, but his speech reveals that
he is common and ordinary—a person, one of "the people"—who enjoys
drinking in a bar and who prefers friendship and helpfulness to violence.
If he and the man he killed had met in an inn, he says, they would have
shared many drinks together, but because they met on a battlefield, they
shot at each other, and he killed the other man. The speaker tries to
justify the killing but can produce no stronger reason than that the dead
man was his "foe." Once he states this reason, he again thinks of the
similarities between himself and the dead man, and then he concludes
that warfare is "quaint and curious" (line 17) because it forces a man to
kill another man whom he would have befriended if they had met during
peacetime.

---

°See page 372 for this poem.
*Central idea.
†Thesis sentence.

Morales 2

[3]     To make the irony of warfare clear, the poem uses easy, everyday language to bring out the speaker's ordinary qualities. His manner of speech is conversational, as in "We should have sat us down" (line 3), "'list" (for "enlist," line 13), and his use of "you" in the last stanza. Also, his word choices, shown in words like "nipperkin," "traps," and "fellow" (lines 4, 15, and 18), are common and informal, at least in British usage. This language is important because it establishes that the speaker is an average man who has been thrown by war into an unnatural role.

[4]     As another means of stressing the stupidity of war, the poem makes clear that the two men—the live soldier who killed and the dead soldier who was killed—were so alike that they could have been brothers or even twins. They had identical ways of life, identical troubles with money, identical wishes to help other people, and identical motives in enlisting in the army. Symbolically, the "man he killed" is so much like the speaker himself that the killing seems like a form of suicide. The poem thus raises the question of why two people who are so much like each other should be shoved into opposing battle lines in order to kill each other. This question is rhetorical, for the obvious answer is that there is no good reason.

[5]     Because the speaker (and also, very likely, the dead man) is shown as a person embodying the virtues of friendliness and helpfulness, Hardy's poem represents a strong disapproval of war. Clearly, political justifications for violence as a political policy are irrelevant to the characters and concerns of the men who fight. They, like the speaker, would prefer to follow their own needs rather than remote and vague ideals. The failure of complex but irrelevant political explanations is brought out most clearly in stanza 3, in which the speaker tries to give a reason for shooting the other man. Hardy's use of punctuation—the dashes—stresses the fact that the speaker has no commitment to the cause he served when killing. Thus the speaker stops at the word "because—" and gropes for a reason (line 9). Not being articulate, he can say only "Because he was my foe./Just so: my foe of course he was;/That's clear enough" (lines 10–12). These short bursts of words indicate that he cannot explain things to himself or to anyone else

Morales 3

except in the most obvious and trite terms, and in apparent embarrassment
he inserts "of course" as a way of emphasizing hostility even though he felt
none toward the man he killed.

A close reading thus shows the power of the poem's dramatic                [6]
argument. Hardy does not establish closely detailed reasons against
war as a policy but rather dramatizes the idea that all political
arguments are unimportant in view of the central and glaring brutality
of war—killing. Hardy's speaker is not able to express deep feelings;
rather he is confused because he is an average sort who wants only to
live and let live and to enjoy a drink in a bar with friends. But this very
commonness stresses the point that everyone is victimized by war—not
only those who die but also those who pull the triggers and push the
buttons.

Morales 4

Work Cited

Hardy, Thomas. "The Man He Killed." *Writing About Literature.* By
Edgar V. Roberts. 12th ed. New York: Pearson, 2010. 372. Print.

## Commentary on the Essay

This close-reading essay begins by stating a central idea about "The Man He Killed,"
then indicates the topics to follow that will develop the idea. Although nowhere does
the poem's speaker state that war is senseless, the essay takes the position that the poem
embodies this idea. A more detailed examination of the poem's themes might develop
the idea by discussing the ways in which individuals are caught up in social and political forces or the contrast between individuality and the state. In this essay, however, the
simple statement of the idea is enough.

Paragraph 2 describes the major details of the poem, with guiding phrases like "The
speaker begins," "he says," and "he again thinks." Thus, the paragraph explains how

things in the poem occur, as is appropriate for a close reading. Paragraph 3 is devoted to the speaker's words and idioms, with the idea that his conversational manner is part of the poem's contrasting method of argument.

Paragraph 4 extends paragraph 3 inasmuch as it points out the similarities of the speaker and the man he killed. If the situation were reversed, the dead man might say exactly the same things about the present speaker. This affinity underscores the suicidal nature of war. Paragraph 5 examines the style of the poem's fourth stanza. In this context, the treatment is brief. The last paragraph (6) reiterates the main idea and concludes with a tribute to the poem as an argument.

The entire essay therefore represents a reading and explanation of the poem's high points. It stresses a particular interpretation and briefly shows how various aspects of the poem bear it out.

### Writing Topics for a Close-Reading Essay

1. For an entire poem:
   a. William Blake's "The Tyger" or Robert Frost's "Desert Places." Try to establish how the poems bring out the speaker's ideas about evil or spiritual blankness.
   b. John Keats's "On First Looking into Chapman's Homer." How does Keats convey his sense of intellectual excitement and discovery?
2. For a paragraph from a story or play:
   a. Shirley Jackson's "The Lottery." Try to show how the passage connects the main character's imagination with his real death agony.
   b. Mark Twain's "Luck." Try to show how the passage indicates the speaker's thoughts about the story's major character, Scorseby.
3. For a single speech or a passage of dialogue from a play (you choose):
   a. Susan Glaspell's *Trifles*. Demonstrate how the speech (or speeches) shows the relationship between men and women.
   b. Anton Chekhov's *The Bear*. How does the speech or passage create character as it also conveys the play's humor?

# Chapter 3

## Writing about Point of View: The Position or Stance of the Work's Narrator or Speaker

The term **point of view** refers to the **speaker, narrator, persona,** or **voice** created by authors to tell stories, make observations, present arguments, and express personal attitudes and judgments. Literally, point of view deals with how action and dialogue have been seen and heard. How does the speaker learn about the situation? Is the speaker a participant in the situation or no more than a witness, either close or distant? How close to the action is she or he? How much does the speaker know? How accurate and complete are his or her reports? Is the speaker also involved in what happened? How thoroughly? Did he or she see everything, miss anything? How much did she or he understand? Point of view involves not only the speaker's actual position as an observer and recorder but also the ways in which the speaker's social, political, and mental circumstances affect the narrative. For this reason, point of view is one of the most complex and subtle aspects of literary study.

The underlying philosophical issue of point of view is epistemological: How do we acquire information? How can we verify its authenticity? How can we trust those who explain the world to us? What is their authority? Are they partial or impartial? What is their interest in telling us things? How reliable are their explanations? What physical and psychological positions might affect, or even distort, what they are saying? Do they have anything to hide? When they speak, are they trying to justify themselves to any degree?

It is important to recognize that authors try not only to make their works vital and interesting but also to bring their presentations alive. Their situation as writers is similar to a dramatic performance: In a play, the actors are always themselves, but in their roles they *impersonate* and temporarily *become* the characters they act. In fictional works, not only do authors impersonate or pretend to be characters who do the talking, but also they *create* these characters. One such character is Jackie, the narrator of Frank O'Connor's "First Confession," who is telling about events that occurred when he was a child. Because he is the subject as well as the narrator, he has firsthand knowledge of the actions, even though he also says things indicating that he, as an adult, has not fully assimilated his childhood experience. We may similarly note the unnamed narrator of Anita Scott Coleman's "Unfinished Masterpieces." Coleman arranges the narrative to make us sympathetic to her speaker's ideas about the strength of her major characters, but also about the suppression of their talents and the waste of their lives.

Because of the ramifications of creating a narrative voice, point of view may also be considered as the centralizing or guiding intelligence in a work—the mind that filters the fictional experience and presents only the most important details to create the maximum impact. It may be compared to the perspectives used by painters. In other words, the way we understand the reality presented in painted pictures— the point of view or guiding intelligence presented by the painter—determines our perceptions and understanding of the painter's ideas. Similarly, the point of view or guiding intelligence created by the author of a literary work determines how we read, understand, and respond, as with Montresor, the narrator of Edgar Allan Poe's "The Cask of Amontillado." As Montresor tells his story of revenge, we realize that the actions he describes are an unfolding record of his criminal insanity. We accept the accuracy of his tale, but we become repulsed by the madness of his confession. His concluding wish, that Fortunato rest in peace, is meaningless, perfunctory, and bizarre.

## An Exercise in Point of View:
## Reporting an Accident

As an exercise to show that point of view is derived from lifelike situations, let us imagine that there has been an auto accident. Two cars, driven by Alice and Bill, have collided, and the after-crash scene is represented in the drawing on the next page. How might this accident be described? What would Alice say? What would Bill say?

Now assume that Frank, who is Bill's best friend, and Mary, who knows neither Bill nor Alice, were witnesses. What might Frank say about who was responsible? What might Mary say? Additionally, assume that you are a reporter for a local newspaper and are sent to report on the accident. You know none of the people involved. How will your report differ from the other reports? Finally, to what degree are all the statements designed to persuade listeners and readers that the details and claims made in the respective reports are true?

The likely differences in the various reports may be explained by reference to point of view. Obviously, because both Alice and Bill are deeply involved—each of them is a major participant or what may be called a **major mover**—they will likely arrange their words to make themselves seem blameless. Frank, because he is Bill's best friend, will report things in Bill's favor. Mary will favor neither Alice nor Bill, but let us assume that she did not look up to see the colliding cars until she heard the crash. Thus, she did not see the accident happening but saw only the immediate aftereffects. Amid all this mixture of partial and impartial views of the action, to whom should we attribute the greatest reliability?

Each person's report will have the "hidden agenda" of making herself or himself seem honest, objective, intelligent, impartial, and thorough. Thus, although both

Alice and Bill may be truthful to the best of their abilities, their reports will not be reliable because they both have something to gain from avoiding responsibility for the accident. Also, Frank may be questionable as a witness because he is Bill's friend and may report things to Bill's advantage. Mary could be reliable, but she did not see everything; therefore, she is unreliable not because of motivation but rather because of her location as a witness. Most likely, *your* account as an impartial reporter will be the most reliable and objective of all because your major interest is to learn all the details and to report the truth accurately, with no concern about the personal interests of either Alice or Bill.

As you can see, the ramifications of describing actions are far-reaching, and the consideration of the various interests and situations is subtle. Indeed, of all the aspects of literature, point of view is the most complex because it is so much like life itself. On the one hand, point of view is intertwined with the many interests and wishes of humanity at large; on the other, it is linked to the enormous difficulty of uncovering and determining truth.

## Conditions That Affect Point of View

As this exercise in observation and expression demonstrates, point of view depends on two major details. The first is *the physical situation of the narrator, or speaker, as an observer.* How close to the action is the speaker? Is the speaker a major mover or major participant or no more than a witness, either close or distant? How much is he or she privileged to know? How accurate and complete are his or her reports? How do the speaker's characteristics emerge from the narration? What are his or her qualifications or limitations as an observer?

The second detail is *the speaker's intellectual and emotional position.* How might the speaker gain or lose from what takes place in the story? Do these interests color the speaker's observations and words? Does he or she have any persuasive purpose beyond being a straightforward recorder or observer? What values does the speaker impose upon the action?

In a story, as in many poems using narrative, authors take into account all these subtleties. For example, O'Connor's narrator, Jackie, in "First Confession" tells about boyhood family problems and his first experience with the sacrament of confession, but he has not yet fully separated himself from some of his childhood antagonisms. The narrator/speaker of Shelly Wagner's poem "The Boxes" is a mother describing the horror of searching for her lost son, who has drowned, and the anguish of her feelings in the years after the death. For these reasons, these narrators show their own involvement and concern about the events they describe. As readers, we need to determine how such varying modes of presentation determine the effects of these and all other stories and narrative poems.

## Determining a Work's Point of View

In your reading, you will encounter a wide variety of points of view. To begin your analysis, first determine the work's grammatical voice (i.e., first, second, or third person). Then study the ways in which the subject, characterization, dialogue, and form interact with the point of view.

### In the First-Person Point of View, the Narrator Tells about Events that He or She Has Personally Witnessed

If the voice of the work is an "I," the author is using the **first-person point of view**—the impersonation of a fictional narrator or speaker who may be named or unnamed. In our hypothetical accident reports, both Alice and Bill are first-person speakers who are named. Similarly, the narrator of O'Connor's "First Confession" is named and identified. By contrast, the first-person narrators of Matthew Arnold's "Dover Beach" and Samuel Taylor Coleridge's "Kubla Khan" are both unnamed, as are the speakers of Thomas Hardy's "Channel Firing" and Shakespeare's "Sonnet 30: When to the Sessions of Sweet Silent Thought." In Mark Twain's "Luck," there are two unnamed first-person speakers (the first "I" introduces the second "I").

## POINT OF VIEW AND OPINIONS

Because *point of view* is often popularly understood to mean ideas, opinions, or beliefs, it must be stressed that the term is not directly synonymous with any of these. Point of view refers to a work's mode of narration, comprising narrator, language, audience, and perceptions of events and characters, whereas opinions and beliefs are thoughts and ideas that may or may not have anything to do with a narration.

One may grant, however, that the position from which people see and understand things (e.g., established positions of political party, religion, social philosophy, and morality) has a most definite bearing on how they think and therefore on their opinions and beliefs. Opinions also affect how people view reality, and opinions affect, if not control, what they say about their perceptions of the world around them. Therefore, opinions stem out of point of view and at the same time have an influence on point of view. A four-star general and a buck private will have different things to say about what happens on a wartime battlefield.

For our purposes in this chapter, however, a discussion of point of view should emphasize how the narration and dramatic situation of a work create and shape the work. If ideas seem to be particularly important in a story, your objective should be not to analyze and discuss the ideas as ideas but rather to consider whether and how these ideas affect what the narrator concludes and says about the story's actions and situations.

First-person speakers report events as though they have acquired their knowledge in a number of ways:

- What they themselves have done, said, heard, and thought (firsthand experience).
- What they have observed others doing and saying (firsthand witness).
- What others have said to them or otherwise communicated to them (secondhand testimony and hearsay).
- What they are able to infer or deduce from the information they have discovered (inferential information).
- What they are able to conjecture about how a character or characters might think and act, given their knowledge of a situation (conjectural, imaginative, or intuitive information).

*First-Person Speakers Come in Many Varieties*    Of all the points of view, the first person is the most independent of the author because, as we have seen, the first-person speaker may have a unique identity, with name, job, and economic and social position. Often, however, the author creates a more anonymous but still independent first-person speaker, as with the unnamed speaker-narrator of Anita Scott Coleman's "Unfinished Masterpieces." The vistas of the first-person speaker may also be extended by the occasional use of the "we" personal pronoun. Such a first-person plural point of view lends additional reliability to the account, as in Shelly Wagner's poem "The Boxes" and Matthew Arnold's "Dover Beach," because the characters included as "we" and "us," even if they are unidentified by the speaker, may be considered as corroborating witnesses.

*Some First-Person Speakers Are Reliable, and Others Are Unreliable*   When you encounter a first-person narrative (whether a story or narrative poem), determine the narrator's position and ability, prejudices or self-interest, and judgment of his or her readers or listeners. Most first-person speakers describing their own experiences are to be accepted as authoritative. Such a speaker is a **reliable narrator**. But sometimes a first-person speaker may be an **unreliable narrator** because of limitations or vested interests that lead him or her to mislead, distort, or even lie. There is reason, for example, to question the reliability of the narrator of O'Connor's "First Confession." As an adult he is describing the events within his family and his after-school preparation sessions prior to his attending his first confession, but he is giving us his childhood memories and is not including the potential views of others about the ways in which things happened. Whether first-person speakers are reliable or unreliable, however, they are one of the means by which authors confer an authentic, lifelike aura to their works.

### In the Second-Person Point of View, the Narrator Is Speaking to Someone Else Who Is Addressed as "You"

The **second-person point of view**, the least common of the points of view and the most difficult for authors to manage, offers two major possibilities. In the first, a narrator (almost necessarily a first-person speaker) tells a listener what he or she has done and said at a past time. The actions might be a simple retelling of events, as when a parent tells a child about something the child did during infancy or when a doctor tells a patient with amnesia about events before the causative injury. Also, the actions might be subject to dispute and interpretation, as when a prosecuting attorney describes a crime for which a defendant is on trial or when a spouse lists grievances against an alienated spouse in a custody or divorce case. Still another situation of the second-person point of view might occur when an angry person accuses the listener of a betrayal or some other wrong. In such instances, it is worth bearing in mind that the point of view may be considered first person rather than second, for the speaker is likely to be speaking subjectively about his or her own perception or analysis of the listener's actions.

The second possibility is equally complex. Some narrators are obviously addressing a "you" but are instead referring mainly to themselves—and to listeners only tangentially—in preference to an "I," as in the last lines of Hardy's poem "The Man He Killed." In addition, some narrators follow the usage—not uncommon in colloquial speech—of the indefinite "you." In this use of point of view, the *you* (or *thou*) refers not to a specific listener but rather to anyone at all. In this way, the writer avoids the more formal use of such words as *one, a person,* or *people.* (Incidentally, the selection of *you* is nongender specific because it eliminates the need for the pronouns *he, she; she/he; he/she;* or *he or she.*)

It is not unusual for some narrators to address a listening audience as "you," and to this degree the situation may be categorized at least partially as second person. Anita Scott Coleman's "Unfinished Masterpieces" is such a work, in which the first-person narrator not only brings readers or listeners into her confidence but also speaks to the two major characters of the story as though they are still present. It is common in poetry for the speaker to include a "you" as a person being addressed. In addition to "The Man He Killed," we see the "you" listener in Arnold's "Dover Beach" (the "love"), John Keats's "Bright Star" (a distant star, likely the North Star), and Christina Rossetti's "Echo" (the "love"). Shakespeare imagines a listener in Sonnets 30 and 73. In these works, which are strongly dramatic, the mythical second-person listener is significantly involved in prompting and interacting with the speaker.

### In the Third-Person Point of View, the Speaker Emphasizes the Actions and Speeches of Others

If events in the work are described in the third person (*he, she, it, they*), the author is using the **third-person point of view**. It is not always easy to characterize the voice in this point of view. Sometimes the speaker uses an "I," as with the first narrator in Mark Twain's "Luck." Such a narrator may seem to be identical with the author, but at other times the author creates a distinct **authorial voice**, as in Katherine Mansfield's "Miss Brill." There are three variants of the third-person point of view: *dramatic* or *objective, omniscient,* and *limited omniscient.*

*The Dramatic or Objective Point of View Is the Most Basic Method of Narration* The most direct presentation of action and dialogue is the **dramatic** or **objective point of view** (also called **third-person objective**). It is the basic method of rendering action and speech that all the points of view share. The narrator of the dramatic point of view is an unidentified speaker who reports things in a way that is analogous to a hovering or tracking video camera or to what some critics have called "a fly on the wall (or tree)." Somehow, the narrator/ speaker is always on the spot—in rooms, forests, village squares, moving vehicles, or even in outer space—to tell us what is happening and what is being said.

The dramatic presentation is limited only to what is said and what happens. The writer does not overtly draw conclusions or make interpretations because the premise of the dramatic point of view is that readers, like a jury, can form their own judgments if they are shown the right evidence. Thus, Dudley Randall's "Ballad of Birmingham" is a short and powerful poem illustrating the dramatic point of view. It dramatizes a brief and poignant dialogue between a child and her mother, and it follows the mother to the scene of the bombed-out church to which the mother had sent the child. We, the readers, draw a number of conclusions about the situation (i.e., that racism is evil, that brutal violence is inexplicable, that innocent suffering is heart rending), but because of the dramatic point of view Randall does not *state* any of these conclusions for us.

*The Narrator of the Omniscient Point of View Can See All, Know All, and Potentially Disclose All*   The third-person point of view is **omniscient** (all-knowing) when the speaker not only presents action and dialogue but also reports the thoughts and reactions of the characters. In our everyday real world, we never know, nor can we ever know, what other people are thinking. For practical purposes, their minds are closed to us. However, we always make assumptions about the thoughts of others, and these assumptions are the basis of the omniscient point of view. Authors use it freely but judiciously to explain responses, thoughts, feelings, and plans—an additional dimension that aids in the development of character. For example, in Guy de Maupassant's "The Necklace," the speaker takes an omniscient stance to explain the responses and thoughts of the major character and also, though to a small degree, of her husband. However, even in an omniscient point of view story, relatively little description is actually devoted to the thoughts of the characters, for most of the narration must necessarily be taken up with objective descriptions.

*The Narrator or Speaker in the Limited or Limited-Omniscient Point of View Focuses on Thoughts and Deeds of a Major Character*   More common than the omniscient and dramatic points of view is the **limited third person** or **limited-omniscient third person**, in which the author concentrates on or *limits* the narration to the actions and thoughts of a major character. In our accident case, Frank, being Bill's friend, would be sympathetic to Bill. Thus, Frank's report of the collision would likely be third-person limited, with Bill as the center of interest. Depending on whether a narration focuses on action or motivation, the limited third-person narrator may explore the mentality of the major character either lightly or in depth. The name given to the central figure on whom the third-person omniscient point of view is focused is the **point-of-view character**. Thus, Mathilde Loisel in "The Necklace," Miss Brill in "Miss Brill," Louise in Kate Chopin's "The Story of an Hour," and Goodman Brown in Nathaniel Hawthorne's "Young Goodman Brown" are all point-of-view characters. Almost everything in these stories is there because the point-of-view characters see it, hear it, respond to it, think about it, imagine it entirely, do it or share in it, try to control it, or are controlled by it.

## Mixed Points of View

In some works, authors mix points of view in order to imitate reality. For example, many first-person narrators use various types of the third-person point of view during much of their narration. Authors may also vary points of view to sustain interest, create suspense, or put the burden of response entirely upon readers. Such shifting occurs at the end of Hawthorne's "Young Goodman Brown," where the narrator objectively and almost brutally summarizes Brown's loveless and morose life after his nightmare about evil. In poetry, the speaker of Arnold's "Dover Beach" speaks mainly for himself, but he also shifts to the "you" whom he is addressing and also to "we" in the concluding lines, in reference both to himself and the "you." There is a comparable shift in Hardy's "The Man He Killed," in which the speaker shifts from "I" to include the listener as "you," meaning "you" and "I" together.

## POINT OF VIEW AND VERB TENSE

As demonstrated in this chapter, point of view refers to the ways narrators and speakers perceive and report actions and speeches. In the broadest sense, however, point of view may be considered as a total way of rendering truth, and for this reason the **tense** chosen by the narrators is important. Most narratives rely on the past tense: The actions happened in the past, and they are now over.

The introduction of dialogue, however, even in a past-tense narration, dramatically brings the story into the present. Such dramatic rendering is accomplished by the dialogue concluding Maupassant's "The Necklace," for example, which emphasizes the immediacy of Mathilde's problems.

The narrator of a past-tense narrative may also introduce present-tense commentary during the narration—a strong means of signifying the importance of past events. Examples are in Frank O'Connor's "First Confession," in which the narrator, Jackie, makes personal comments about the events he is describing, and in Mark Twain's "Luck," a complex narrative in which the second first-person speaker both begins and ends his past-tense narrative in the present tense. It is also significant to note that the narrators of parables and fables use past-tense narratives as vehicles for teaching current lessons in philosophy and religion.

In recent years, a number of writers have used the present tense as their principal time reference. With the present tense, the narrative story or poem is rendered as a virtual drama that is unfolded moment by moment. In Wagner's "The Boxes," for instance, the speaker employs the present tense to emphasize that her pain is a constant part of her life.

Some writers intermingle tenses to show how time itself can be merged within the human mind because our consciousness never exists only in the present but instead is a composite made up of past memories cresting upon a present but never-ending wave sweeping us into the future. Thus, at the end of Coleman's "Unfinished Masterpieces," the past-tense narration shifts into the present to underscore the narrator's hopes that a time might yet come when the destiny of people may be commensurate with the power of their characters and talents. Matthew Arnold, in "Dover Beach," mingles the past, the present, and a hope for the future as he treats the difficulty of maintaining love and sincerity at a time of deteriorating faith and encroaching militarism.

# Summary: Guidelines for Point of View

The following guidelines summarize and further classify the types of points of view. Use them to distinguish differences and shades of variation in stories and poems.

1.  **First person** (*I, my, mine, me*, and sometimes *we, our*, and *us*). First-person speakers are involved to at least some degree in the actions of the work. Such narrators may have (a) complete understanding, (b) partial or incorrect understanding, (c) no understanding at all, or (d) complete understanding with the motive to mislead or lie. Although the narrators described in guidelines a through c are usually reliable and tell the truth, they may also sometimes be unreliable. The only way to tell is to study the story closely. Obviously, guideline d is by nature unreliable, but nevertheless the mode might possibly be accepted (although critically) on matters of detail.

    a.  *Major participant*
        i.   Who tells his or her own story and thoughts as a major mover
        ii.  Who tells a story about others and also about herself or himself as one of the major movers
        iii. Who tells a story mainly about others and about himself or herself only tangentially
    b.  *Minor participant*, who tells a story about events experienced and witnessed.
    c.  *Nonparticipating but identifiable speaker*, who learns about events in other ways (e.g., listening to participants through direct conversation, overhearing conversation, examining documents, hearing news reports, imagining what might have occurred). The narrative of such a speaker is a combination of fact and conjectural reconstruction.

2.  **Second person** (*you*, or possibly *thou*). This is a point of view that authors use often enough to justify our knowing about it. Its premise is that the speaker knows more about the actions of a character (the "you") than the character himself or herself. (a) It is used when the speaker (e.g., lawyer, spouse, friend, sports umpire, psychologist, parent, angry person) talks directly to the other person and explains that person's past actions and statements. More generally, and in a colloquial and informal style, the speaker may also use "you" to mean (b) himself or herself, (c) the reader, or (d) anyone at all.

3.  **Third person** (*she, he, it, they*). The speaker is outside the action and is mainly a reporter of actions and speeches. Some speakers may have unique and distinguishing traits even though no separate identity is claimed for them ("the unnamed third-person narrator"). Other third-person speakers who are not separately identifiable may represent the words and views of the authors themselves ("the authorial voice").

    a.  *Dramatic or third-person objective.* The narrator reports only what can be seen and heard. The thoughts of characters are included only if they are spoken or written (dialogue, reported or overheard conversation, letters, reports, etc.).
    b.  *Omniscient.* The omniscient speaker knows all, sees all, reports all, and when necessary, reveals the inner workings of the minds of any or all characters. Even an omniscient speaker, however, makes a mostly dramatic presentation.
    c.  *Limited, or limited omniscient.* The focus is on the actions, responses, thoughts, and feelings of a single major character. Although the narration may concentrate on the character's actions, it may simultaneously probe deep within the consciousness of the character.

# Writing about Point of View

In your essay on point of view, you should explain how point of view contributes to making the work exactly as it is. As you prepare to write, therefore, consider language, authority and opportunity for observation, the involvement or detachment of the speaker, the selection of detail, interpretive commentaries, and narrative development. The following questions will help you get started.

## *Raise Questions to Discover Ideas*

- How is the narration made to seem real or probable? Are the actions and speeches reported authentically, as they might be seen and reported in life?
- Is the narrator/speaker identifiable? What are the narrator's qualifications as an observer? How much of the story seems to result from the imaginative or creative powers of the narrator?
- How does the narrator/speaker perceive the time of the actions? If the predominant tense is the past, what relationship, if any, does the narrator establish between the past and the present (e.g., providing explanations, making conclusions)? If the tense is present, what effect does this tense have on your understanding of the story?
- To what extent does the point of view make the work interesting and effective?

## *First-Person Point of View*

- What situation prompts the speaker to tell the story or explain the situation? What does the story tell us about the experience and interests of the narrator/ speaker?
- Is the speaker talking to the reader, a listener, or herself? How does her audience affect what she is saying? Is the level of language appropriate to her and the situation? How much does she tell about herself?
- To what degree is the narrator involved in the action (i.e., as a major participant or major mover, minor participant, or nonparticipating observer)? Does he make himself the center of humor or admiration? How? Does he seem aware of changes he undergoes?
- Does the speaker criticize other characters? Why? Does she seem to report fairly and accurately what others have told her?
- How reliable is the speaker? Does the speaker seem to have anything to hide? Does it seem that he may be using the story for self-justification or exoneration? What effect does this complexity have on the story?

## *Second-Person Point of View*

- What situation prompts the use of the second person? How does the speaker acquire the authority to explain things to the listener? How directly involved is the listener? What is the relationship between the speaker and listener? If the listener is indefinite, why does the speaker choose to use "you" as the basis of the narration?

### Third-Person Point of View

- Does the author speak in an authorial voice, or does it seem that the author has adopted a special but unnamed voice for the work?
- What is the speaker's level of language (e.g., formal and grammatical, informal or intimate and ungrammatical)? Are actions, speeches, and explanations made fully or sparsely?
- From what apparent vantage point does the speaker report action and speeches? Does this vantage point make the characters seem distant or close? How much sympathy does the speaker express for the characters?
- To what degree is your interest centered on a particular character? Does the speaker give you thoughts and responses of this character (limited third person)?
- If the work is third-person omniscient, how extensive is this omniscience (e.g., all the characters or just a few)? Generally, what limitations or freedoms can be attributed to this point of view?
- What special kinds of knowledge does the narrator assume that the listeners or readers possess (e.g., familiarity with art, religion, politics, history, navigation, music, current or past social conditions)?
- How much dialogue is used in the story? Is the dialogue presented directly, as dramatic speech, or indirectly, as past-tense reports of speeches? What is your perception of the story's events as a result of the use of dialogue?

### Tense

- What tense is used predominantly throughout the story? If a single tense is used throughout (e.g., present, past), what is the effect of this constant use of tense?
- Does the story demonstrate a mixture of tenses? Why are the tenses mixed? What purpose is served by these variations? What is the effect of this mixture?
- Is any special use made of the future tense? What is the effect of this use on the present and past circumstances of the characters?

### Organize Your Essay about Point of View

Throughout your essay, you should develop your analysis of how the point of view determines such aspects as situation, form, general content, and language. The questions in the preceding section should help you decide how the point of view interacts with these other elements.

*Introduction*    Begin by briefly stating the major influence of the point of view on the work. (*Examples*: "The omniscient point of view permits many insights into the major character," or "The first-person point of view permits the work to resemble an exposé of back-room political deals.") How does the point of view make the work interesting and effective? How will your analysis support your central idea?

*Body*    An excellent way to build your argument is to explore how a different point of view might affect the presentation of the work. Hardy's poem "Channel Firing," for example, uses a first-person speaker—a skeleton long buried in a churchyard cemetery near the ocean. This speaker is awakened by the noise of nearby naval guns, a bizarre situation prompting ironic humor that could not be duplicated with a third-person point of view. Hardy's first-person point of view is essential because we learn, firsthand, about the speaker's feelings. Indeed, the poem is totally dependent on this speaker. Conversely, Mansfield's "Miss Brill" employs the third-person limited point of view, with the speaker presenting an intimate portrait of the major character while also preserving an objective and ironic distance. If Miss Brill herself were the narrator, we would get the intimacy that encourages us to sympathize with her, but we would lose the distance that permits us to see her objectively.

You can see that this approach requires creative imagination, for you must speculate about a point of view that is not present. Considering alternative points of view deeply, however, will greatly enhance your analytical and critical abilities.

*Conclusion*   In your conclusion, evaluate the success of the point of view. Is it consistent, effective, truthful? What does the writer gain or lose (if anything) by the selection of point of view?

## Illustrative Essay

The central idea, thesis sentence, and topic sentences are shaded here to stress the goal of strong organization. As your instructor wishes, you might use this or a similar system in your own essays.

Collins 1

Courtney Collins
Professor Thompson
English 101
4 October 2010

Shirley Jackson's Dramatic Point of View in "The Lottery"°

The dramatic point of view in Shirley Jackson's "The Lottery"   [1]
enables her to render horror in the midst of the ordinary. The story,
however, is not only one of horror, but it also may be called a surprise story,
an allegory, or a portrayal of human insensitivity and cruelty. But the
validity of all other claims for "The Lottery" hinges on the author's control

°See pages 338–43 for this story.

Collins 2

over point of view to make the events develop out of a seemingly everyday, matter-of-fact situation—a control that could not be easily maintained with another point of view.* The success of Jackson's point of view is achieved through her characterization, selection of details, and diction.†

[2]     Because of the dramatic point of view, Jackson succeeds in presenting the villagers as ordinary folks attending a normal, festive event—in contrast to the horror of their real purpose. The contrast depends on Jackson's speaker, who is emotionally uninvolved and who tells only enough about the three hundred townsfolk and their customs to permit the conclusion that they are ordinary, common people. The principal character is a local housewife, Tessie Hutchinson, but the speaker presents few details about her beyond the fact that she is just as ordinary and common as everyone else—an important characteristic when she, like any other ordinary person being singled out for punishment, objects not to the lottery itself but to the "unfairness" of the drawing. So it is also with the other characters, whose brief conversations are recorded but not analyzed. This detached, reportorial method of making the villagers seem common and one-dimensional is fundamental to Jackson's dramatic point of view, and the cruel twist of the ending depends on the method.

[3]     Although there could be much description, Jackson's speaker presents details only partially in order to conceal the lottery's horrible purpose. For example, the speaker presents enough information about the lottery to permit readers to understand its rules but does not disclose that the winning prize is instant death. The short saying "Lottery in June, corn be heavy soon" is mentioned as a remnant of a long-forgotten ritual, but the speaker does not explain anything more about this connection with scapegoats and human sacrifice (paragraph 32). All such references do not seem unusual as the narrator first presents them, and it is only the conclusion that reveals, in reconsideration, their shocking ghastliness.

[4]     Without doubt, a point of view other than the dramatic would spoil Jackson's concluding horror because it would require more

---

*Central idea.
†Thesis sentence.

explanatory detail. A first-person speaker, for example, would not be credible without explaining the situation and revealing feelings that would give away the ending. Such an "I" speaker would need to say something like "The little boys gathered rocks but seemed not to be thinking about their forthcoming use in the execution." But how would such detail affect the reader's response to the horrifying conclusion? Similarly, an omniscient narrator would need to include details about people's reactions (how could he or she be omniscient otherwise?). A more suitable alternative might be a limited omniscient point of view confined to, say, a stranger in town or to one of the local children. But any intelligent stranger would be asking "giveaway" questions, and any child but a tiny tot would know about the lottery's horrible purpose. Either point-of-view character would therefore require revealing the information too soon. The only possible conclusion is that the point of view that Jackson chose—the dramatic—is best for this story. Because it permits her naturally to hold back crucial details, it is essential for the suspenseful delay of horror.

Also, Jackson makes the narrator's language appropriate not only                    [5]
to the story's suspense but also to the simple character of the villagers. The words are accurate and descriptive but not elaborate. When Tessie Hutchinson appears, for example, she dries "her hands on her apron" (paragraph 8)—words that define her everyday household status. Most of these simple and straightforward words may be seen as part of Jackson's similar technique of withholding detail to delay the reader's understanding. A prime example is the pile of stones, which is in truth a brutal and cruel preparation for the stoning, yet this conclusion cannot be drawn from the easy words describing it (paragraph 2):

> Bobby Martin had already stuffed his pockets full of stones, and the other boys soon followed his example, selecting the smoothest and roundest stones; Bobby and Harry Jones and Dickie Delacroix—the villagers pronounced this name "Dellacroy"—eventually made a great pile of stones in one corner of the square and guarded it against the raids of the other boys.

Collins 4

Both the nicknames and the seeming description of childhood games divert attention and obscure the horrible purpose of the natives and their stones. Even at the end, the speaker uses the word "pebbles" to describe the stones given to Tessie's son Davy (paragraph 76). The implication is that Davy is playing a game, not participating in the killing of his own mother!

[6]    Such masterly control over point of view is a major cause of the creative strength of Jackson's "The Lottery." Her narrative method is to establish the appearance of everyday, harmless reality, which she maintains up to the beginning of the last ominous scene. She is so successful that a reader's first response to the stoning is that "such a killing could not take place among such common, earthy folks." Yet it is this reality that validates Jackson's vision. Horror is not to be found on moors and in haunted castles but among everyday people like Jackson's three hundred villagers. Without her control of the dramatic point of view, there could be little of this power of suggestion.

Collins 5

### Work Cited

Jackson, Shirley. "The Lottery." *Writing About Literature.* By Edgar V. Roberts. 12th ed. New York: Pearson, 2010, 338–43. Print.

## Commentary on the Essay

The strategy of this essay is to describe how Jackson's dramatic point of view is fundamental to her success in building up to the shocking horror of the ending. Words of tribute throughout the theme are "success," "control," "essential," "appropriate," and "masterly." The introductory paragraph sets out three areas for exploration in the body: character, detail, and diction. In your own essay on point of view, you might well devote all your analysis to any one of these points, but for illustration here they are all included.

The body begins with paragraph 2, in which the aim is *not* to present a full character study (since the essay is not about character but point of view), but rather to discuss the ways in which the dramatic point of view enables the characters to be rendered. The topic of the paragraph is that the villagers are to be judged not as complete human beings but as "ordinary folks." Once this idea is established, the thrust of the paragraph is to show how the point of view keeps readers at a distance sufficient to sustain this conclusion.

The second part of the body (paragraphs 3 and 4) emphasizes the sparseness of detail as an essential part of Jackson's purpose of delaying conclusions about the real horror of the drawing. Paragraph 4, which continues the topic of paragraph 3, shows how assertions about alternative points of view may reinforce ideas about the actual point of view that Jackson employs. The material for the paragraph is derived from notes speculating about whether Jackson's technique of withholding detail to build toward the concluding horror (the topic of paragraph 3) could be maintained if the author had used differing points of view. A combination of analysis, thought, and imagination is therefore at work in the paragraph. In effect, the supporting details in the paragraph demonstrate a negative: Other points of view would not allow for the withholding technique. (The first-person and the omniscient points of view would require giving away the ending. Even the more congenial limited omniscient point of view would be ineffective because most point-of-view characters would uncover information rather than withhold it.) In the light of the less suitable alternatives, therefore, paragraph 4 concludes by confirming the superiority of Jackson's use of the dramatic point of view.

The third section of the body (paragraph 5) emphasizes the idea that the flat, colorless diction defers awareness of what is happening; therefore the point of view is vital in the story's surprise and horror. The concluding paragraph (6) emphasizes the way in which general response to the story, and also its success, are conditioned by the detached, dramatic point of view.

## Writing Topics about Point of View

1. Write a short narrative from the first-person point of view of one of these characters:
   a. Mathilde Loisel in "The Necklace": How I ruined ten years of my life by not telling the truth.
   b. The baker in "Miss Brill": My favorite customer.
   c. Fortunato in "The Cask of Amontillado": Why is Montresor telling me about the special wine he keeps in the family vaults?
   d. Faith in "Young Goodman Brown": I don't understand why my husband is so sour and sullen all the time.
   e. Nora in "First Confession": My terrible younger brother.
2. How would Hawthorne's story "Young Goodman Brown" be affected if told by a narrator with a different point of view (different knowledge, different interests, different purposes for telling the story), such as the narrators of "The Lottery" or "The Story of an Hour"?
3. Recall a childhood occasion on which you were punished. Write an explanation of the punishment as though you were the adult who was in the position of punishing you. Be sure to consider your childhood self objectively, in the third person.

Present things from the viewpoint of the adult, and try to determine how the adult would have learned about your action, judged it, and decided on your punishment.

4. Write an essay about the proposition that people often have something to gain when they speak and that therefore we need to be critical about what others tell us. Are they trying to change our judgments and opinions? Are they telling the truth? Are they leaving out any important details? Are they trying to sell us something? In your discussion, you may strengthen your ideas by referring to stories that you have been reading.

5. In the reference section of your library, find two books on literary terms and concepts. How completely and clearly do these works explain the concept of point of view? With the aid of these books, together with the materials in this chapter, describe the interests and views of the narrators in "First Confession," "The Man He Killed," "On First Looking into Chapman's Homer," or another work of your choice.

# Chapter 4

## Writing about Character: The People in Literature

Writers of fiction create narratives that enhance and deepen our understanding of human character and human life. In our own day, under the influences of such pioneers as Freud, Jung, and Skinner, the science of psychology has influenced both the creation and the study of literature. It is well known that Freud buttressed some of his psychological conclusions by referring to literary works, especially plays by Shakespeare. Widely known films such as *Spellbound* (1945) and *The Snake Pit* (1948) have popularized the relationships between literary character and psychology. Without doubt, the presentation and understanding of character is a major aim of fiction (and literature generally).

In literature, a **character** is a verbal representation of a human being. Through action, speech, description, and commentary, authors portray characters who are worth caring about, cheering for, and even loving, although there are also characters you may laugh at, dislike, or even hate.

In a story or play emphasizing a major character, you may expect that each action or speech, no matter how small, is part of a total presentation of the complex combination of both the inner and the outer self that constitutes a human being. Whereas in life things may "just happen," in literature all actions, interactions, speeches, and observations are deliberate. Thus, you read about important actions like a young woman's long ordeal of work and sacrifice (Maupassant's "The Necklace" [Chapter 1]), a young man's convoluted pathway into mistrust and suspicion (Nathaniel Hawthorne's "Young Goodman Brown"), or a devoted grandmother's errand of mercy (Eudora Welty's "A Worn Path"). By making such actions interesting, authors help you understand and appreciate not only their major characters but also life itself.

## Character Traits

In studying a literary character, try to determine the character's outstanding traits. A **trait** is a quality of mind or habitual mode of behavior that is evident in both active and passive ways, such as never repaying borrowed money, supplying moral support to friends and loved ones, being a person on whom people always rely, listening to the thoughts and problems of others, avoiding eye contact, taking the biggest portions, or always thinking oneself the center of attention.

Sometimes, of course, the traits we encounter are minor and therefore negligible, but often a trait may be a person's *primary* characteristic (not only in fiction but also in life). Thus, characters may be ambitious or lazy, serene or anxious, aggressive or fearful, thoughtful or inconsiderate, open or secretive, confident or self-doubting, kind or cruel, quiet or noisy, visionary or practical, careful or careless, impartial or biased, straightforward or underhanded, "winners" or "losers," and so on.

With this sort of list, to which you may add at will, you can analyze and develop conclusions about character. For example, Mathilde in Maupassant's "The Necklace" indulges in dreams of unattainable wealth and comfort and is so swept up in her visions that she scorns her comparatively good life with her reliable but dull husband. It is fair to say that this denial of reality is her major trait. It is also a major weakness because Maupassant shows that her dream life harms her real life. A contrast is seen in the speaker of Amy Lowell's poem "Patterns," who is realistically facing the truth that her hopes for happiness have been destroyed because of her fiancé's battlefield death. By similarly analyzing the thoughts, actions, and speeches of the literary characters you encounter, you can also draw conclusions about their nature and their qualities.

### Distinguish between Circumstances and Character Traits

When you study a fictional person, distinguish between circumstances and character, for circumstances have value *only if you show that they demonstrate important traits*. Thus, if our friend Sam wins a lottery, let us congratulate him on his luck. His win does not say much about his *character*, however, unless you also point out that for years he has been regularly spending hundreds of dollars each week for lottery tickets. In other words, making an extraordinary effort to win the lottery *is* a character trait but winning (or losing) *is not*.

Or, let us suppose that an author stresses the neatness of one character and the sloppiness of another. If you accept the premise that people care for their appearance according to choice—and that choices develop from character—you can use these details to make conclusions about a person's self-esteem or the lack of it. In short, when reading about characters in literature, look beyond circumstances, actions, and appearances and attempt to determine what these things show about character. Always try to get from the outside to the inside, for it is the internal qualities of character that determine external behavior.

# How Authors Disclose Character in Literature

Basically, authors rely on five ways of bringing characters to life. Remember that you must use your own knowledge and experience to make judgments about the qualities of the characters.

### The Actions of Characters Reveal Their Qualities

What characters *do* is our best clue to understanding what they *are*. For example, walking in the woods is recreation for most people, and it shows little about their characters except a fondness for the outdoors (perhaps a significant trait). But Phoenix's walk through the woods in Eudora Welty's "A Worn Path" is difficult and dangerous for her. Her walk, seen within the context of her age and her mission, can be taken as the expression of her loving, responsible character. Often characters are unaware of the meanings and implications of their actions. Smirnov in Anton Chekhov's play *The Bear*, for example, would be a fool to teach Mrs. Popov to use her dueling pistol because she has threatened to kill him with it. Even before he recognizes his love for her, he is subconsciously aware of this love, and his potentially self-destructive action shows that his loving nature has overwhelmed his instinct for self-preservation.

Like ordinary human beings, fictional characters do not necessarily understand how they may be changing or why they do the things they do. The strong inner conflict experienced by the two women in Susan Glaspell's short play *Trifles* brings out their strength of character. Theoretically, they have an overriding obligation to the law, but they discover that they have an even stronger personal obligation to the accused killer, Minnie. Hence, they show their adaptability and their willingness to alter their behavior as a result of the things they discover in the farmhouse kitchen. In Katherine Mansfield's "Miss Brill," the major character is alone—always alone—and she goes to a public park to enjoy the passing crowd (her only weekly entertainment). She eavesdrops on people sitting nearby and draws silent conclusions about them, thus vicariously sharing in their lives. She even supposes that all those in the park are actors, along with herself, performing in a massive drama of life. Her unrealistic daydreams reveal her habitual solitude and pathetic vulnerability.

### The Author's Descriptions Tell Us about Characters

Appearance and environment reveal much about a character's social and economic status, and they also tell us about character traits. Mathilde in Maupassant's "The Necklace" dreams about wealth and unlimited purchasing power. Although her unrealizable desires destroy her way of life, they also cause her strength of character to emerge. The descriptions of the rural countryside in Eudora Welty's "A Worn Path" are independently unique and interesting, but beyond that they also bring out the determination of Phoenix, her loyalty and dedication to her grandson, and also her age and softening physical condition.

### What Characters Say Reveals What They Are Like

Although the speeches of most characters are functional—essential to keeping the action moving along—they provide material from which you may draw conclusions. When the second traveler of Nathaniel Hawthorne's "Young Goodman Brown" speaks, for example, he reveals his devious and deceptive nature even though ostensibly he appears friendly. The lawmen in *Trifles* speak straightforwardly but without much understanding of the women in the story. Their speeches suggest that their characters are similarly direct but unimaginative, although their constant belittling of the two women indicates their inability to understand others.

Often, characters use speech to hide their motives, although we as readers should see through such a ploy. The narrator Montresor in Poe's "The Cask of Amontillado," for example, is a vengeful schemer, and we can see this much from his indirect and manipulative language when he speaks to the equally unpleasant but gullible Fortunato. To Fortunato, Montresor seems friendly and sociable, perhaps unexpectedly so, but to us, he is clearly lurid and demonic.

### What Others Say Tells Us about a Character

By studying what characters say about each other, you can enhance your understanding of the character being discussed. For example, the major character in Glaspell's *Trifles* is the farmwoman Minnie Wright. But Minnie never appears as a character, and we learn about her only through the conversations between Mrs. Hale and Mrs. Peters. It is from them that her character is revealed as an oppressed woman who has finally snapped and turned on her oppressor, her husband.

Ironically, speeches often indicate something other than what the speakers intend, perhaps because of prejudice, stupidity, or foolishness. Nora, in Frank O'Connor's "First Confession" tells about Jackie's lashing out at her with a butter knife, but in effect she describes the boy's individuality just as she also discloses her own spitefulness.

### The Author, Speaking as a Storyteller or an Observer, May Present Judgments about Characters

What the author, speaking as a work's authorial voice, says about a character is usually accurate, and the authorial voice can be accepted factually. However, when the authorial voice interprets actions and characteristics, as in Hawthorne's "Young Goodman Brown," the author himself or herself assumes the role of a reader or critic, whose opinions are therefore open to question. For this reason, authors frequently avoid interpretations and devote their skill to arranging events and speeches so that readers can draw their own conclusions.

## Types of Characters: Round and Flat

No writer can present an entire life history of a protagonist, nor can each character in a story get "equal time" for development. Accordingly, some characters grow to be full and alive, while others remain shadowy. The British novelist and critic E. M. Forster, in *Aspects of the Novel*, calls the two major types "round" and "flat."

### Round Characters Are Three-Dimensional and Lifelike

The basic trait of **round characters** is that we are told enough about them to permit the conclusion that they are three-dimensional, rounded, authentic, memorable, original, and true to life. They are the centers of our attention in most works of fiction. Their roundness and fullness are characterized by both individuality and unpredictability. It is true that, like all human beings, round characters have inherent qualities that the circumstances of a story bring out, and therefore their full realization as characters is directly connected to the stories in which they live their lives. Jackie, of O'Connor's "First Confession," is round and dynamic. We learn from his adult narration that he has been a normal and typical child, trying to maintain his sense of individuality amid what he considers to be embarrassing family circumstances. His thoughts about "solutions" to his problems are of course greatly in excess, but when the time comes for him to confess his "sins," he does not evade them but dutifully states everything that he has been thinking. As amusing as his story is, his confession about the truth of his inner thoughts constitutes the type of adjustment that characterizes him as a round character.

A complementary quality of round characters is that they are often dynamic. **Dynamic characters** recognize, change with, or adjust to circumstances. The reverse side of this coin is that circumstances may also bring a dynamic character to ruin. Such changes may be shown in (1) an action or actions, (2) the realization of new strength and therefore the affirmation of previous decisions, (3) the acceptance of new conditions and the need for making changes, (4) the discovery of unrecognized truths, or (5) the reconciliation of the character with adverse conditions. We may consider Minnie, in Glaspell's *Trifles*, as dynamic. We learn that as a young woman she was happy and musical, though shy, but that she has been deprived and blighted by her 20-year marriage. Finally, however, a particularly cruel action by her husband so enrages her that she breaks out of her subservient role and commits an act of violence. In short, her action shows her as a dynamic character capable of radical and earthshaking change. This is not to say that only round characters are dynamic, for less significant characters in a story may also be altered because of circumstances.

Because a round character plays a major role in a story, he or she is often called the **hero** or **heroine**. Some round characters are not particularly heroic, however, so it is preferable to use the more neutral word **protagonist** (the "first actor"). The protagonist is central to the action, moves against an **antagonist** (the "opposing actor"), and exhibits the ability to adapt to new situations.

### Flat Characters Are Simple and One-Dimensional

In contrast with round characters, **flat characters** are simple and one-dimensional. They may have no more than a single role to perform in a story, or they may be associated with no more than a single dominating idea. Most flat characters end pretty much where they begin, and for this reason we may think of them as **static**, not dynamic. Often their absence of growth or development results from lack of knowledge or understanding, or even from stupidity or insensitivity. Flat characters are not worthless in fiction, however, for they highlight the development of the round characters, as with the lawmen in Glaspell's *Trifles* and the characters whom Goodman Brown meets in Hawthorne's "Young Goodman Brown."

Usually, flat characters are minor (e.g., relatives, acquaintances, functionaries), but not all minor characters are necessarily flat. Sometimes flat characters are prominent in certain types of literature, such as cowboy, police, and detective stories, where the focus is less on character than on performance. Such characters might be lively and engaging, even though they do not undergo significant change and development. They must be strong, tough, and clever enough to perform recurring tasks such as solving a crime, overcoming a villain, or finding a treasure. The term **stock character** is often used to describe characters in these repeating situations. To the degree that stock characters have many common traits, they are **representative** of their class or group. Such characters, with variations in names, ages, and sexes, have been constant in literature since the ancient Greeks. Some regular stock or representative characters are the insensitive father, the interfering mother, the sassy younger sister or brother, the greedy politician, the harassed boss, the resourceful cowboy or detective, the overbearing or henpecked husband, the submissive or nagging wife, the absent-minded professor, the angry police captain, the lovable drunk, and the town do-gooder.

Stock characters are usually also flat as long as they do no more than perform their roles and exhibit conventional and unindividual traits. When they possess no attitudes except those of their class, they are often called **stereotype** characters because they all seem to have been cast in the same mold.

When authors bring characters into focus, however, no matter what roles they perform, the characters emerge from flatness and move into roundness. For example, Louise Mallard of Kate Chopin's "The Story of an Hour" is a traditional housewife, and if she were no more than that she would be flat and stereotypical. After receiving the news that her husband has died, however, the roundness of her character is brought out by her sudden and unexpected exhilaration at the prospect of being widowed and free. One may compare Louise with the title character of Mansfield's "Miss Brill." At first Miss Brill seems dull. She almost literally has no life, and as a character she is flat. But the story demonstrates that she protects herself by indulging in her remarkable inner life of imagination and creativity, and for this reason she is to be judged as round. In sum, the ability to grow and develop and adjust to changing circumstances makes characters round and dynamic. Absence of these traits makes characters flat and static.

## Reality and Probability: Verisimilitude

Characters in fiction should be true to life. Therefore their actions, statements, and thoughts must all be what human beings are *likely* to do, say, and think under the conditions presented in the literary work. This is the standard of **verisimilitude**, **probability**, or **plausibility**. One may readily admit that there are people *in life* who perform tasks or exhibit characteristics that are difficult or seemingly impossible (such as always leading the team to victory, always getting A+'s on every test, always being cheerful and helpful, or always understanding the needs of others). However, such characters in fiction would not be true to life because they do not fit within normal or usual behavior.

You should therefore distinguish between what characters may *possibly* do and what they *most frequently* or *most usually* do. When we speak of character, we speak of a person's normal, not exceptional, behavior. Thus, in Maupassant's "The Necklace," it is possible that Mathilde could be truthful and tell her friend Jeanne Forestier about the lost necklace. In light of Mathilde's pride and sense of self-respect, however, it is more normal for her and her husband to hide the loss and borrow money for a replacement, even though they must endure the harsh financial consequences for ten years. Faced with these choices (either self-sacrifice or the admission of a fault or a possible crime), the decision she makes with her husband is the more *probable* one.

Nevertheless, probability does not rule out surprise or even exaggeration. The sudden and seemingly impossible changes concluding *The Bear*, for example, are not improbable because Chekhov early in the play shows that both Mrs. Popov and Smirnov are emotional, somewhat foolish, and impulsive. Even in the face of their unpredictable embraces closing the play, these qualities of character dominate their lives. For such individuals, surprise might be accepted as a probable, or normal, condition of life.

Writers render probability of character in many ways. Works that are more or less mirrors of life, such as Mansfield's "Miss Brill," set up a pattern of ordinary, everyday probability. Less realistic conditions establish different frameworks of probability, in which characters are *expected* to be unusual, as in Hawthorne's "Young Goodman Brown." Because a major way of explaining this story is that Brown is having a nightmarish psychotic trance, his bizarre and unnatural responses are probable. Equally probable is the way the doctors explain Louise Mallard's sudden death at the end of Chopin's "The Story of an Hour" even though their smug analysis is totally and comically wrong.

You might also encounter works containing *supernatural* figures such as the second traveler in "Young Goodman Brown." You may wonder whether such characters are probable or improbable. Usually, gods and goddesses embody qualities of the best and most moral human beings, and devils like Hawthorne's guide take on attributes of the worst. However, you might remember that the devil is often given dashing and engaging qualities so that he can deceive gullible sinners and then drag them screaming in fear into the fiery pits of hell. The friendliness of Brown's guide is therefore not an improbable trait. In judging characters of this or any other type, your best criteria are probability, consistency, and believability.

## Writing about Character

Usually, your topic will be a major character in a story or drama, although you might also study one or more minor characters. After your customary overview, begin taking notes. List as many traits as you can and determine how the author presents details about the character through actions, appearance, speeches, comments by others, or authorial explanations. If you discover unusual traits, determine what they show. The following suggestions and questions will help you get started.

### *Raise Questions to Discover Ideas*

- Who is the major character? What do you learn about this character from his or her actions and speeches? From the speeches and actions of other characters? How else do you learn about the character?
- How important is the character to the work's principal action? Which characters oppose the major character? How do the major character and the opposing character(s) interact? What effects do these interactions create?
- What actions bring out important traits of the main character? To what degree is the character creating events or just responding to them?
- Describe the main character's actions: Are they good or bad, intelligent or stupid, deliberate or spontaneous? How do they help you understand her or him? What do they show about the character as a person?

- Describe and explain the traits, both major and minor, of the character you plan to discuss. To what extent do the traits permit you to judge the character? What is your judgment?
- What descriptions (if any) of how the character looks do you discover in the story? What does this appearance demonstrate about him or her?
- In what ways is the character's major trait a strength—or a weakness? As the story progresses, to what degree does the trait become more (or less) prominent?
- Is the character round and dynamic? How does the character recognize, change with, or adjust to circumstances?
- If the character you are analyzing is flat or static, what function does he or she perform in the story (e.g., by doing a task or by bringing out qualities of the major character)?
- If the character is a stereotype, to what type does he or she belong? To what degree does the character stay in the stereotypical role or rise above it? How?
- What do any of the other characters do, say, or think to give you understanding of the character you are analyzing? What does the character say or think about himself or herself? What does the storyteller or narrator say? How valid are these comments and insights? How well do such comments and insights help you understand the character?
- Is the character lifelike or unreal? Consistent or inconsistent? Believable or not believable?

## Organize Your Essay about Character

*Introduction*    Identify the character you are studying and refer to noteworthy problems in determining this character's qualities.

*Body*    Use your central idea and thesis sentence to create the form for the body of your essay. Consider one of the following approaches to organize your ideas and form the basis for your essay.

1. **Develop a central trait or major characteristic,** such as "a single-minded dedication to vengeance" (Montresor of "The Cask of Amontillado") or "the habit of seeing the world only on one's own terms" (Miss Brill of "Miss Brill"). This kind of structure shows how the work embodies the trait. For example, in one part a trait may be brought out through speeches that characters make about the major character (as at the end of Welty's "A Worn Path"), and in another part through that character's own speeches and actions (also in Welty's "A Worn Path"). Studying the trait thus enables you to focus on the differing ways in which the author presents the character, and it also helps you focus on separate parts of the work.
2. **Explain a character's growth or change.** This type of essay describes a character's traits at the work's beginning and then analyzes changes or developments. It is important to stress the actual alterations as they emerge but at the same time to avoid retelling the story. Additionally, you should not only describe the changing traits but also analyze how they are brought out within the work, such as the dream of Goodman Brown or Minnie Wright's long ordeal.
3. **Organize your essay around central actions, objects, or quotations that reveal primary characteristics.** Key incidents may stand out (such as using a breadknife to strike out against a person), along with objects closely associated with the character

being analyzed (such as a broken birdcage). There may be important quotations spoken by the character or by someone else in the work. Show how such elements serve as signposts or guides to understanding the character. (See the following Illustrative Essay for an example of this type of development.)

4. **Develop qualities of a flat character or characters.** If the character is flat (such as the sheriff and county attorney in *Trifles* or the servants in *The Bear*), you might develop topics such as the function and relative significance of the character, the group the character represents, the relationship of the flat character to the round ones, the importance of this relationship, and any additional qualities or traits. For a flat character, you should explain the circumstances or defects that keep the character from being round, as well as the importance of these shortcomings in the author's presentation of character.

*Conclusion*    When bringing your essay to a close, show how the character's traits are related to the work as a whole. If the person was good but came to a bad end, does this misfortune make him or her seem especially worthy? If the person suffers, does the suffering suggest any attitudes about the class or type of which he or she is a part? Or does it illustrate the author's general view of human life? Or both? Do the characteristics explain why the person helps or hinders other characters? How does your essay help to clear up first-reading misunderstandings?

## Illustrative Essay

The central idea, thesis sentence, and topic sentences are shaded here to stress the goal of strong organization. As your instructor wishes, you might use this or a similar system in your own essays.

Weiner 1

Sam Weiner

Professor O'Hara

English 102

15 October 2010

The Character of Mathilde Loisel in Guy de

Maupassant's "The Necklace"°

Guy de Maupassant's Mathilde Loisel, the young Parisian housewife

in "The Necklace," is above all a dreamer. Her dreams are excessive, but                    [1]

---

°See pages 5–12 for this story.

Weiner 2

they also make her both weak and strong.* Her weakness is that she is
dissatisfied with her life because her dreams make her dissatisfied with
her life. Her strength is ultimately her ability to work in order to preserve
her conceptions of honor. Maupassant shows her qualities in the
introduction, the cover-up, and the poverty she and her husband endure.†

[2]          In the early part of the story, Mathilde is dreaming vainly about
wealth and social position. She thinks that money and a life of ease are
everything, and her highest aim in life is ease and luxury, which she
thinks she was somehow born to have as a matter of right. Her husband,
however, a lowly clerk, can afford only a small and spare household. It
is clear that she is made angry by the tension between her dreams and
the stark reality of her life. The result is that she is unable to appreciate
anything that she has. She does not treat her husband with love and
respect but whines at him instead about his shortcomings as a provider.
Her borrowing of the necklace for the big party is, in a way, her attempt
to escape her drab life and to live out her dream, if only for a single
night. Her character is limited by her unrealistic vision of any sort of
life beyond the moment of her great triumph at the party.

[3]          The cover-up of the loss of the borrowed necklace brings out the
worst in Mathilde. She believes more strongly in the real value of the
necklace than in her friendship with Jeanne Forestier. If she had
possessed the character strength to tell the truth to Jeanne about the loss,
she would never have had the trouble she and her husband actually
experience. But her character is too limited and weak to permit her to
endure the embarrassment, and perhaps the anger of her friend, that
telling the truth would bring. Thus, by covering up the loss, she loses
friendship, truth, and financial future all at the same time.

[4]          But her life of poverty and sacrifice to pay back the money lenders
brings out a strength of her character that was not previously clear.
She pitches in to work and to economize. She gives up her servant, her
good address on the Rue des Martyrs, and everything else connected

---

*Central idea.
†Thesis sentence.

Weiner 3

with her dreams of good living. Although her character is firm and strong
in this respect, her hard work makes her loud and coarse, just the opposite
of the wealthy, refined person she dreamed she might have been.

Thus, Mathilde is a character whose dream life keeps her from          [5]
seeing the truth until the truth hits her with a vengeance. It is this
weakness, not just bad luck, that is responsible for all her pain. This
same weakness of character, however, brings out her best quality of
sharing the work to preserve honor and good name. She may be dreamy,
unlucky, and foolish, but she is not bad. On balance, she actually
becomes a strong and deserving character, but she gets a life that is
much worse than she deserves.

Weiner 4

Work Cited

Maupassant, Guy de. "The Necklace." *Writing About Literature*. By Edgar
V. Roberts.12th ed. New York: Pearson, 2010. 5–12. Print.

## Commentary on the Essay

This essay is representative of the first type of organization described earlier—a central
trait or major characteristic (p. 90). The strategy of the essay is to support the central idea that Mathilde is excessively and harmfully a dreamer. The introduction asserts
that this quality produces a character of both weakness and strength. Paragraph 2 develops her weakness inasmuch as Mathilde's dreams make her too unhappy to adjust
to the life she shares with her husband. This paragraph relies for its details on the author's descriptions of Mathilde's dreams and on her complaints when her husband
comes home with the invitation to the big party. This judgment about her is based on
the essay writer's assumptions that dream life should not affect real life negatively.

Paragraph 3 continues with Mathilde's weak side, showing the disastrous effects of
her skewed values. The details of this paragraph are taken from of the activities by the
Loisels to hide their loss of the necklace, together with an implicit comparison of how a
frank admission of the loss might have avoided their cripplingly harmful indebtedness.

Paragraph 4 emphasizes Mathilde's strengths, which result, like her weakness, from her character as an unrealistic day-dreamer. The judgment is clearly based on the idea that hard work and cooperation are virtues.

The concluding paragraph (5) attempts to weigh Mathilde's character (one might wish to dispute the assertion that the bad luck of the Loisels is not the major cause of their troubles) and states that her endurance of the ten-year hardship makes her seem worthy of a better fate than she receives.

### Writing Topics about Character

1. Compare the ways in which actions and speeches are used to bring out the character traits of Jackie of O'Connor's "First Confession," Mrs. Popov of Chekhov's *The Bear*, and Goodman Brown of Hawthorne's "Young Goodman Brown."

2. Write a brief essay comparing the changes or developments of two major or round characters in stories or plays included in Appendix C. You might deal with issues such as what the characters are like at the beginning; what conflicts they confront, deal with, or avoid; or what qualities are brought out that signal the changes or developments.

3. Compare the qualities and functions of two or more flat characters (e.g., the men in Glaspell's *Trifles* or the secondary characters in Chopin's "The Story of an Hour"). How do they bring out qualities of the major characters? What do you discover about their own character traits?

4. Using Miss Brill (Mansfield's "Miss Brill"), Minnie Wright (Glaspell's *Trifles*), and Scoresby ("Twain's "Luck") as examples, describe the effects of circumstance on character. Under the rubric "circumstance" you may consider elements such as education, family, economic and social status, wartime conditions, and geographic isolation.

5. Write a brief story about an important decision you have made (e.g., picking a school, beginning or leaving a job, declaring a major, or ending a friendship). Show how your own qualities of character (to the extent that you understand them), together with your own experiences, have gone into the decision. You may write more comfortably if you give yourself another name and describe your actions in the third person.

6. Topics for paragraphs or short essays:
   a. What characteristics of the speaker are brought out by Lowell in "Patterns"? Should the classifications *round* and *flat* even apply to her? Why or why not?
   b. Why does the speaker of Arnold's "Dover Beach" philosophize about the darkness and the pounding surf nearby? What qualities of character do his thoughts reveal?
   c. Consider this proposition: To friends who haven't seen us for a time, we are round; but to ourselves and most other people, we are flat.

# Chapter 5

# Writing about Plot: The Development of Conflict and Tension in Literature

Fiction, Drama, and Narrative Poetry

## Plot: The Motivation and Causality of Literature

Stories, drama, narrative poetry, and films are made up mostly of actions or incidents that follow one another in **chronological** order. The same is also true of life, but there is a major difference: Fiction must make sense even though life itself does not always seem to make sense at all. Finding a sequential or narrative order is therefore only a first step in our consideration of fiction. What we depend on for the sense or meaning of fiction is **plot**—the elements governing the unfolding of the actions.

The English novelist E. M. Forster, in *Aspects of the Novel* (1927), presents a memorable illustration of plot. To illustrate a bare set of actions, he proposes the following: "The king died, and then the queen died." Forster points out, however, that this sequence does not form a plot because it lacks *motivation* and *causality*; it's too much like life itself to be fictional. Thus, he introduces motivation and causality in his next example: "The king died, and then the queen died of grief." The phrase "of grief" shows that one thing (grief) controls or overcomes another (the normal desire to live), and motivation and causation enter the sequence to form a plot. In a well-plotted story or play, one thing precedes or follows another not simply because time ticks away but more important, because *effects* follow *causes*. In a good work of fiction, nothing is irrelevant or accidental; everything is related and causative.

## Determining the Conflicts in a Story, Drama, or Narrative Poem

The controlling impulse in a connected pattern of causes and effects is **conflict**, which refers to people or circumstances that a character must face and try to overcome. Conflicts bring out extremes of human energy, causing characters to engage in the decisions, actions, responses, and interactions that make up fictional literature.

In its most elemental form, a conflict is the opposition of two people. Their conflict may take the shape of anger, hatred, envy, argument, avoidance, political or moral opposition, gossip, lies, fighting, and many other actions and attitudes. Conflicts may also exist between groups, although conflicts between individuals are more identifiable and therefore more suitable for stories. Conflicts may also be abstract—for example, when an individual opposes larger forces such as natural objects, ideas, modes of behavior, or public opinion. A difficult or even impossible *choice*—a **dilemma**—is a natural conflict for an individual person. A conflict may also be brought out in ideas and opinions that clash. In short, conflict shows itself in many ways.

*Relating Conflict Directly to Doubt, Tension, and Interest*    Conflict is the major element of plot because opposing forces arouse *curiosity*, cause *doubt*, create *tension*, and produce *interest*. The same responses are the lifeblood of athletic competition. Consider which kind of athletic event is more interesting: (1) One team gets so far ahead that the outcome is no longer in doubt, or (2) both teams are so evenly matched that the outcome is uncertain until the final seconds. Obviously, games are uninteresting—as games—unless they develop as contests between teams of comparable strength. The same principle applies to conflicts in stories and dramas. There should be uncertainty about a protagonist's success or failure. Unless there is doubt, there is no tension, and without tension there is no interest.

*Finding the Conflicts to Determine the Plot*    To see a plot in operation, let us build on Forster's description. Here is a simple plot for a story of our own: "John and Jane meet, fall in love, and get married." This sentence contains a plot because it shows cause and effect (they get married *because* they fall in love), but with no conflict, the plot is not interesting. However, let us introduce conflicting elements into this common "boy meets girl" story:

> John and Jane meet in college and fall in love. They go together for a number of years and plan to marry, but a problem arises. Jane first wants to establish herself in a career, and after marriage she wants to be an equal contributor to the family. John understands Jane's wishes for equality, but he wants to get married first and let her finish her studies and have her career after they have children. Jane believes that John's plan is unacceptable because she thinks of it as a trap from which she might not escape. As they discuss their options, they find themselves increasingly more irritated and unhappy with each other. Finally, they bring their plans to an end, and they part in both anger and sorrow. Their love is not dead, but both go on to marry someone else and build separate lives and careers. In their new lives, neither is totally happy even though they like and respect their spouses. The years pass, and, after children and grandchildren, Jane and John meet again. He is now divorced, and she is a widow. Because their earlier conflict is no longer a barrier, they rekindle their love, marry, and try to make up for the past. Their new happiness, however, is tinged with regret and reproach because of their earlier conflicts, their unhappy decision to part, their lost years, and their increasing age.

Here we find a true plot because our original "boy meets girl" topic now contains a major conflict from which a number of related complications develop. These complications embody disagreements, choices, arguments, and ill feelings that produce tension, uncertainty, separation, and regret. When we learn that John and Jane finally join together at the end, we might still find the story painful to contemplate because it does not give us a "happily ever after" ending. Nevertheless, the story makes sense—

as a story—because its plot brings out the plausible consequences of the understandable aims and hopes of John and Jane during their long relationship. It is the imposition of necessary causes and effects upon a series of events in time that creates the story's plot.

## Writing about the Plot of a Particular Work

An essay about plot is an analysis of the conflict and its developments in a story or play. The organization of your essay should not be modeled on sequential sections and principal events, however, because these invite only a retelling of the story. Instead, the organization is to be developed from the important elements of conflict. As you look for ideas about plot, try to answer the following questions.

### Questions for Discovering Ideas

- Who are the major and minor characters, and how do their characteristics put them in conflict? How can you describe the conflict or conflicts?
- How does the story's action grow out of the major conflict?
- If the conflict stems from contrasting ideas or values, what are these and how are they brought out?
- What problems do the major characters face? How do the characters deal with these problems?
- How do the major characters achieve (or not achieve) their major goal(s)? What obstacles do they overcome? What obstacles overcome them or alter them?
- At the end, are the characters successful or unsuccessful, happy or unhappy, satisfied or dissatisfied, changed or unchanged, enlightened or ignorant? How has the resolution of the major conflict produced these results?

## Organize Your Essay about Plot

### Strategies for Organizing Ideas

To keep your essay brief, you need to be selective. Rather than detailing everything a character does, for example, stress the major elements in his or her conflict. Such an essay on Eudora Welty's "A Worn Path" might emphasize Phoenix as she encounters the various obstacles both in the woods and in town. When there is a conflict between two major characters, the obvious approach is to focus equally on both. For brevity, however, emphasis might be placed on just one. Thus, an essay on the plot of Frank O'Connor's "First Confession" most likely might stress details about Jackie's responses but might also deal with the positions of the sister and the mother. It might also be possible to consider the position of the priest at the confessional.

In addition, the plot may be analyzed more broadly in terms of impulses, goals, values, issues, and historical perspectives. Thus, you might emphasize the elements of chance working against Mathilde in Guy de Maupassant's "The Necklace" (Chapter 1) as a contrast to her dreams about wealth. A discussion of the plot of Edgar Allan Poe's "The Cask of Amontillado" might stress the mysterious and cruel nature of Montresor, the narrator, because the plot could not develop without his apparently complex motivation.

The conclusion may contain a brief summary of the points you have made. It is also a fitting location for a brief consideration of the effect or *impact* produced by the conflict. Additional ideas might focus on whether the author has arranged actions and dialogue to direct your favor toward one side or the other or whether the plot is possible or impossible, serious or comic, fair or unfair, powerful or indifferent, and so on.

## Illustrative Essay

> The central idea, thesis sentence, and topic sentences are shaded here to stress the goal of strong organization. As your instructor wishes, you might use this or a similar system in your own essays.

Becks 1

Maria Becks

Professor Van Westen

English 101

18 December 2010

The Plot of Eudora Welty's "A Worn Path"°

[1]     At first, the complexity of Eudora Welty's plot in "A Worn Path" is not clear. The main character is Phoenix Jackson, an old, poor, and frail woman; the story seems to be no more than a record of her walk to Natchez through the woods from her rural home. By the story's end, however, the plot is clear: It consists of the brave attempts of a courageous, valiant woman to carry on against overwhelming forces.* Her determination despite the great odds against her gives the story its impact. The powers ranged against her are old age, poverty, environment, and illness.†

[2]     Old age as a silent but overpowering antagonist is shown in signs of Phoenix's increasing senility. Not her mind but her feet tell her where to

---

°See pages 359–64 for this story.
*Central idea.
†Thesis sentence.

Becks 2

find the medical office in Natchez. Despite her inner strength, she is unable to explain her errand when the nursing attendant asks her. Instead she sits dumbly and unknowingly for a time, until "a flame of comprehension" comes across her face (paragraph 87). Against the power of advancing age, Phoenix is slowly losing. The implication is that soon she will lose entirely.

Her grinding poverty, made evident by the narrator, emerges an [3] equally crushing opponent. Because she cannot afford a bus or taxi to take her to town, she must walk. She has no money and acquires her ten cents for the paper windmill by stealing and begging. The "soothing medicine" she gets for her grandson (paragraph 92) is given to her out of charity. Despite the boy's need for advanced medical care, she has no money to provide it, and the story therefore shows that her guardianship is doomed.

Closely connected to her poverty is the way through the woods, which [4] during her walk seems to be an almost active opponent. The long hill tires her, the thorn bush catches her clothes, the log endangers her balance as she crosses the creek, and the barbed-wire fence threatens to puncture her skin. Another danger on her way is the stray dog, which topples her over. Apparently not afraid, however, Phoenix carries on a cheerful monologue:

> "Out of my way, all you foxes, owls, beetles, jack rabbits, coons and wild animals! . . . Keep out from under these feet, little bobwhites. . . . Keep the big wild hogs out of my path. Don't let none of these come running my direction. I got a long way." (paragraph 3)

She prevails for the moment as she enters Natchez, but all the hazards of her walk are still there, waiting for her to return.

The force against Phoenix that shows her plight most clearly and [5] pathetically is her grandson's incurable illness. His condition highlights her helplessness, for she is his only support. Her difficulties would be enough for one person alone, but with the grandson the odds against her are doubled. Despite her care, there is nothing anyone can do for the grandson but take the long worn path to get something to help him endure his pain.

This brief description of the conflicts in "A Worn Path" only hints [6] at the story's power. Welty layers the details to bring out the full range of

Becks 3

the conditions against Phoenix, who cannot win despite her
determination and devotion. The most hopeless fact, the condition of
the invalid grandson, is not revealed until she reaches the medical
office, and this delayed final revelation makes one's heart go out to her.
The plot is strong because it is so real, and Phoenix is a pathetic but
memorable protagonist struggling against overwhelming odds.

Becks 4

Work Cited

Welty, Eudora. "A Worn Path." *Writing About Literature*. By Edgar V.
Roberts. 12th ed. New York: Pearson, 2010, 359–64. Print.

## Commentary on the Essay

The strategy of this essay is to explain the elements of plot in "A Worn Path" selectively, without duplicating the story's narrative order. Thus, the third aspect of conflict, the woods, might be introduced first if the story's narrative order were to be followed, but it is deferred while the more personal elements of old age and poverty are considered. It is important to note that the essay does not deal with the story's other characters as part of Phoenix's conflict. Rather, Phoenix's antagonist takes the shape of impersonal and unconquerable forces, like the grandson's illness.

Paragraph 1 briefly describes how one's first impressions are changed because of what happens at the end of the story. The thesis statement anticipates the body by listing the four topics about to be treated. Paragraph 2 concerns Phoenix's old age; paragraph 3, her poverty; paragraph 4, the woods; and paragraph 5, her grandson's illness. The concluding paragraph (6) points out that in this set of conflicts the protagonist cannot win, except as she lives out her duty and her devotion to help her grandson. Continuing the theme of the introduction, the last paragraph also accounts for the power of the plot: By building up to Phoenix's personal strength against unbeatable forces, the story evokes sympathy and admiration.

**Writing Topics about Plot**

1. Compare the use of interior scenes in Kate Chopin's "The Story of an Hour," O'Connor's "First Confession," Anton Chekhov's *The Bear*, or Susan Glaspell's *Trifles*. How do these scenes bring out the various conflicts in the works? How do characters in the interiors contribute to plot developments? What is the relationship of these characters to the major themes of the works?

2. Describe the plot of Shirley Jackson's "The Lottery." What is the principal conflict in the story? Who is the principal advocate of the custom of the lottery? How does the town's population enter into the plot as a collective character in support of the lottery?

3. Compare "The Story of an Hour" and Nathaniel Hawthorne's "Young Goodman Brown" as stories developing plots about clashing social or religious values and customs. In what ways are the plots similar and different?

4. Select a circumstance in your life that caused you doubt, difficulty, and conflict. Making yourself anonymous (give yourself a fictitious name and put yourself in a fictitious location), write a brief story about the occasion, stressing how your conflict began, how it affected you, and how you resolved it. You might describe the details in chronological order or you might begin the story in the present tense and then introduce details in flashback.

5. Write a brief episode or story that takes place in a historical period you believe you know well, being as factually accurate as you can. Introduce your own fictional characters as important "movers and shakers" and deal with their public or personal conflicts, or both. You may model your characters and episodes on historical persons, but you are free to exercise your imagination completely and construct your own characters.

# Chapter 6

# Writing about Structure: The Organization of Fiction, Poetry, and Drama

**Structure** refers to the ways in which writers arrange materials in accord with the general ideas and purposes of their works. Unlike plot, which is concerned with conflict or conflicts, structure defines the layouts of works—the ways the story, play, or poem is shaped. Structure is about matters such as placement, balance, recurring themes, true and misleading conclusions, suspense, and the imitation of models or forms such as reports, letters, conversations, or confessions. A work might be divided into numbered sections or parts, it might begin in a countryside (or one state) and conclude in a city (or another state), or it might develop a relationship between two people from their first introduction to their falling in love.

## Formal Categories of Structure

Many aspects of structure are common to all genres of literature. Particularly for stories and plays, however, the following aspects form a skeleton, a pattern of development.

### The Exposition Provides the Materials Necessary to Put the Plot into Operation

**Exposition** is the laying out, the putting forth, of the materials in the story—the main characters, their backgrounds, their characteristics, interests, goals, limitations, potentials, and basic assumptions. Exposition may not be limited to the beginning of the work, where it is most expected, but may be found anywhere. Thus, intricacies, twists, turns, false leads, blind alleys, surprises, and other quirks may be introduced to interest, intrigue, perplex, mystify, and please readers. Whenever something new arises, to the degree that it is new, it is a part of exposition.

### The Complication Marks the Beginning and the Growth of the Conflict

The **complication** is the onset and development of the major conflict—the plot. The major participants are the protagonist and antagonist, together with whatever ideas and values they represent, such as good or evil, freedom or oppression, independence or dependence, love or hate, intelligence or stupidity, or knowledge or ignorance.

### The Crisis Marks the Decisions Made to End the Conflict

The **crisis** (a separating, distinguishing, or turning point) marks that part of the action where the conflict reaches its greatest tension. During the crisis, a decision or an action to resolve the conflict is undertaken, and therefore the crisis is the point at which curiosity, uncertainty, and tension are greatest. Usually, the crisis is followed closely by the next stage, the climax. Often, in fact, the two are so close together that they are considered the same.

### The Climax Is the Conclusion of the Conflict

Because the **climax** (Greek for "ladder") is a consequence of the crisis, it is the story's *high point* and may take the shape of a decision, an action, an affirmation or denial, an illumination, a realization, or a reversal of expectations and intentions. It is the logical, even if sometimes improbable, conclusion of the preceding actions; no new major developments follow it. In most stories or plays, the climax occurs at or close to the end. In Anton Chekhov's play, *The Bear*, for example, the climax is that Smirnov suddenly holds and obviously touches the angry Mrs. Popov as he is instructing her in how to hold her dueling pistol, with which she is hoping to shoot him. Everything that happens prior to this situation leads to it. In this sudden embrace, he immediately loses all his anger toward her, and impetuously declares his love. This unexpected reversal is magnificently comic. Comparably, but with no such reversal, and no such comedy, the climax of Amy Lowell's poem "Patterns" is the very last sentence of the speaker's monologue: "Christ, what are patterns for?" This outburst crystallizes the speaker's developing sorrow, frustration, anger, and hurt.

### The Resolution or Dénouement Finishes the Work and Releases the Tension

The **resolution** (a releasing or an untying) or **dénouement** (untying) is the completing of the story or play after the climax; once the climax has occurred, the work's tension and uncertainty are finished, and most authors conclude quickly to avoid losing their readers' interest. For instance, the dénouement of Katherine Mansfield's "Miss Brill" comprises a few short details about the major character's returning home, sitting down, and putting away her muff. Edgar Allan Poe ends "The Cask of Amontillado" by the narrator's pointing out that all the events happened 50 years before. Shirley Jackson ends "The Lottery" quickly by pointing out the swiftness with which the townspeople award the "winning" prize. Frank O'Connor ends "First Confession" with a short conversation between the brother and sister. In other words, after the story's major conflicts are finished, the job of the dénouement is to tie things up as quickly as possible.

## Formal and Actual Structure

The structure just described is a *formal* one, an ideal pattern that moves directly from beginning to end. Few narratives and dramas follow this pattern exactly, however. Thus, a typical mystery story holds back crucial details of exposition (because the goal is to mystify); a suspense story keeps the protagonist ignorant but provides readers with abundant details in order to maximize concern and tension about the outcome.

More realistic and less "artificial" stories might also contain structural variations. For example, Welty's "A Worn Path" produces a *double take* because of unique structuring. During most of the story, Phoenix's conflicts seem to be primarily age, solitude, and poverty. Instead of being able to ride on public transportation, for example, she is taking an unaccompanied walk through difficult and dangerous terrain. At the end, however, we are introduced to an additional difficulty—a new conflict—that enlarges our responses to include not just concern but also heartfelt anguish, for what had appeared to be a difficult walk becomes a virtually insurmountable problem with illness. "A Worn Path" is just one example of how a structural variation maximizes the impact of a work.

There are many other possible variants in structure. One of these is called **flashback**, or **selective recollection**, in which present circumstances are explained by the selective introduction of past events. The moment at which the flashback is introduced may be a part of the resolution of the plot, and the flashback might lead you into a moment of climax but then go from there to develop the details that are more properly part of the exposition. Let us again consider our brief story about John and Jane (p. 96) and use the flashback method of structuring the story:

> Jane is now old, and a noise outside causes her to remember the argument that forced her to part with John many years before. They were deeply in love, but their disagreement about her wishes for a career and equality split them apart. Then she pictures in her mind the years she and John have spent happily together after they married. She then contrasts her present happiness with her memory of her earlier, less happy marriage, and from there she recalls her youthful years of courtship with John before their disastrous conflict developed. Then she looks over at John, reading in a chair, and smiles. John smiles back, and the two embrace. Even then, Jane realizes that she is crying.

In this little narrative the action begins and remains in the present. Important parts of the past flood the protagonist's memory in flashback, though not in the order in which they happened. Memory might be used structurally in other ways. An example is Shelly Wagner's poem "The Boxes," which is a narrative spoken by a mother to her dead son. The events of the poem are disclosed through the speaker's memories of the past, but the poem's conclusion depends on the speaker's temporary consideration that time has changed to a point before the death so that she can speak to her son as though he is still living. The poem thus searingly illustrates the poignancy and finality of the situation. In short, a technique like selective recollection permits a unique narrative that departs significantly from a strictly formal and chronological structural pattern.

Each narrative or drama has a unique structure. Some stories may be structured according to simple geography or room arrangements, as in Irving Layton's poem "Rhine Boat Trip" (a meditation upon castles observed by a tourist on the Rhine leading to thoughts of cattle cars during the World War II Holocaust), or in Guy de Maupassant's "The Necklace" (a movement from a modest apartment, to an attic flat, to a local street), or in Poe's "The Cask of Amontillado" (a progressive movement downward from the street level to the Montresor family vaults). A story may unfold in an apparently

accidental way, with the characters making vital discoveries about the major characters, as in Susan Glaspell's *Trifles*. Additionally, parts of a work may be set out as fragments of conversation, as in O'Connor's "First Confession, or as a ceremony, as in
Nathaniel Hawthorne's "Young Goodman Brown," or as an announcement of a party,
as in "The Necklace." The possible variations in structuring literary works are almost
literally infinite.

You might also aid yourself by drawing a scheme or plan to explain, graphically, the
structure of the work you are analyzing. Mansfield's story "Miss Brill," for example, may
be conveniently compared with a person running happily along a narrow path deep
within a dark forest and making a turn only to plunge suddenly and unexpectedly off a
steep cliff. You might draw this comparison like this:

In writing an essay about the structure of "Miss Brill," you could employ this scheme as
a guide. This is not to say that the structure of the story could not be profitably analyzed
in another way but that such a scheme might help you to give insight, meaning, and
form to your essay.

Sometimes the use of an illustration can create an insight or series of insights that
might at first not have been clear to you. For example, Shakespeare's Sonnet No. 73 has
three quatrains and a concluding rhymed couplet.

William Shakespeare (1564–1616)

*Sonnet 73: That Time of Year Thou Mayst in Me Behold* (1609)

**Quatrain I**

That time of year thou mayst in me behold,
  When yellow leaves, or none, or few do hang
Upon those boughs which shake against the cold,
  Bare ruined choirs, where late the sweet birds sang.

**Quatrain II**

In me thou seest the twilight of such day,
  As after sunset fadeth in the West,
Which by and by black night doth take away,
  Death's second self that seals up all in rest.

### Quatrain III

In me thou seest the glowing of such fire,
    That on the ashes of his youth doth lie,
As the death bed, whereon it must expire,
    Consumed with that which it was nourished by.

### Couplet

This thou perceiv'st, which makes thy love more strong.
To love that well, which thou must leave ere long.

We can see a number of links connecting the quatrains and the couplet. Each quatrain refers both to the speaker's present state and also to conditions that are passing or will pass—specifically, autumn, sunset, and a dying fire. In addition, the quatrains are grammatically parallel. Each one includes the phrase "in me," together with the parallel phrases "thou mayst behold," "thou seest," and "thou seest" again. In the couplet the phrase "thou perceiv'st" and the word "that" as a pronoun referring to the speaker appear, so that each major unit contains references to the speaker and his listener. In each of the quatrains, death is a common topic. It is spelled out specifically in quatrains II and III, and quatrain I refers to barren branches from which dying and yellowing leaves have fallen. The speaker states that he is in just such circumstances, so that his concluding statement "To love that well, which thou must leave ere long" in the concluding couplet is a fitting resumé of the poem.

We might make these links vivid through a graph, not unlike the well-known method of the Venn diagram that uses ellipses to show connections among sets (after John Venn [1834–1923], an English logician). Allowing for the fact that each part must be independent and distinct as well as connected, a plan or graph might be made of four overlapping triangles, with a list of common elements included within the triangles as a "key":

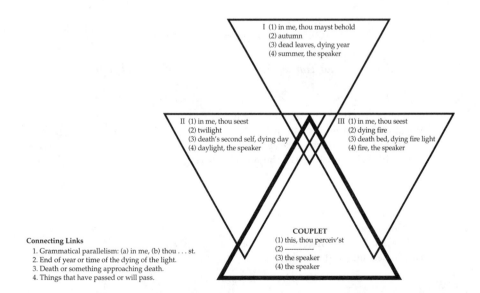

I (1) in me, thou mayst behold
(2) autumn
(3) dead leaves, dying year
(4) summer, the speaker

II (1) in me, thou seest
(2) twilight
(3) death's second self, dying day
(4) daylight, the speaker

III (1) in me, thou seest
(2) dying fire
(3) death bed, dying fire light
(4) fire, the speaker

**COUPLET**
(1) this, thou perceiv'st
(2) ------------
(3) the speaker
(4) the speaker

**Connecting Links**
1. Grammatical parallelism: (a) in me, (b) thou . . . st.
2. End of year or time of the dying of the light.
3. Death or something approaching death.
4. Things that have passed or will pass.

In our sketch, interconnecting triangles show the structure of parallels and common topics, but in analyzing another work you might prefer circles, lines, planes, other geometric figures, or a drawing like the poor fellow falling off the cliff. If you wish, you might make a list, and you always have the option of simply studying carefully and taking good notes. What is important is that you attempt to look at the work you are studying as a structure of some sort so that you may write an essay about this structure. Making a drawing or a graph has the virtue of giving you a visual grasp of the fact that the parts of a unified work are distinct and connected—important discoveries both for your understanding of the work and your writing of an essay.

## Writing about Structure in Fiction, Poetry, and Drama

Your essay should concern arrangement and shape. In form, the essay should not restate or summarize the part-by-part unfolding of the narrative or argument. Rather, it should explain why things are where they are: "Why is this here and not there?" is the fundamental question you need to answer. Thus, it is possible to begin with a consideration of a work's crisis and then to consider how the exposition and complication have built up to it. A vital piece of information, for example, might have been withheld in the earlier exposition, as in Eudora Welty's "A Worn Path" and Jackson's "The Lottery," and introduced only at or near the conclusion. Therefore, the crisis might be heightened because there would have been less suspense if the detail had been introduced earlier. Consider the following questions in planning to write about the story's structure.

### Raise Questions to Discover Ideas

- If spaces or numbers divide the story into sections or parts, what is the structural importance of these parts?
- If there are no marked divisions, what major sections can you find? (You might make divisions according to places where actions occur, various times of day, changing weather, or increasingly important events.)
- If the story departs in major ways from the formal structure of exposition, complication, crisis, climax, and resolution, what purpose do these departures serve?
- What variations in chronological order, if any, appear in the story (e.g., gaps in the time sequence, flashbacks or selective recollection)? What effects are achieved by these variations?
- Does the story delay any crucial details of exposition? Why? What effect is achieved by the delay?
- Where does an important action or a major section (such as the climax) begin? End? How is it related to the other formal structural elements, such as the crisis? Is the climax an action, a realization, or a decision? To what degree does it relieve the work's tension? What is the effect of the climax on your understanding of the characters involved in it? How is this effect related to the arrangement of the climax?

## Organize Your Essay about Structure

*Introduction*    Your essay should show why an entire narrative is arranged the way it is—to reveal the nature of a character's situation, to create surprise, or to evoke sympathy, reveal nobility (or depravity) of character, unravel apparently insoluble puzzles, express philosophical or political values, or bring out maximum humor. However, you might also explain the structure of no more than a part of the story, such as the climax or the complication.

*Body*    Your essay is best developed in concert or agreement with what the work contains. The location of scenes is an obvious organizing element. Thus, essays on the structure of Hawthorne's "Young Goodman Brown" and Mansfield's "Miss Brill" might be based on the fact that both take place outdoors (a dark forest for one and a sunny public park for the other). Similarly, an essay might explore the structure of Maupassant's "The Necklace" by contrasting the story's indoor and outdoor locations. In Glaspell's *Trifles*, much is made of the various parts of a kitchen in an early twentieth-century Iowa farmhouse, and an essay might trace the structural importance of these.

Other ways to consider structure may be derived from a work's notable aspects, such as the growing suspense and horrible conclusion of Poe's "The Cask of Amontillado" or the revelations about the "sinfulness" of Goodman Brown's father and neighbors in Hawthorne's "Young Goodman Brown."

*Conclusion*    The conclusion should highlight the main parts of your essay. You may also deal briefly with the relationship of structure to the plot. If the work you have analyzed departs from chronological order, you might explain the causes and effects of this departure. Your aim should be to focus on the success of the work as it has been brought about by the author's choices in development.

## Illustrative Essay

> The central idea, thesis sentence, and topic sentences are shaded here to stress the goal of strong organization. As your instructor wishes, you might use this or a similar system in your own essays.

Wu 1

Nancy Wu
Professor Lyles
English 100
1 December 2010

The Structure of Eudora Welty's "A Worn Path"°

[1]        On the surface, Eudora Welty's "A Worn Path" is structured simply. The narrative is not difficult to follow, and things go forward in straight

---

°See pages 359–64 for this story.

chronology. The main character is Phoenix Jackson, an old, poor black woman. She walks from her rural home in Mississippi through the woods to Natchez to get a free bottle of medicine for her grandson, who is a hopeless invalid. Everything takes place in just a few hours. This action is only the frame, however, for a skillfully structured plot.* The masterly control of structure is shown in the story's locations and in the way in which the delayed revelation produces both mystery and complexity.†

The locations in the story coincide with the increasing difficulties faced by Phoenix. The first and most obvious worn path is the rural woods with all its physical difficulties. For most people, the obstacles would not be especially challenging, but for an old woman they are formidable. In Natchez, the location of the final part of the story, Phoenix's inability to bend over to tie her shoe demonstrates the lack of flexibility of old age. In the medical office, where the last scene takes place, two major difficulties of the plot are brought out. One is Phoenix's increasing senility, and the other is the disclosure that her grandson is an incurable invalid. This set of oppositions, the major conflicts in the plot, thus coincide with locations or scenes and demonstrate the power against Phoenix.

[2]

The most powerful of these conditions, the revelation about the grandson, makes the story something like a mystery. Because this detail is withheld until the story's end, the reader wonders for most of the story what might happen next to Phoenix. In fact, some parts of the story are false leads. For example, the episode with the young hunter's dog is threatening, but it leads nowhere; Phoenix, with the aid of the hunter, is unharmed. That she picks up and keeps his nickel might seem at first to be cause for punishment. In fact, she thinks it does, as this scene with the hunter (paragraphs 55–58) shows:

[3]

> . . . he laughed and lifted his gun and pointed it at Phoenix.
>
> She stood straight and faced him.
>
> "Doesn't the gun scare you?" he said, still pointing it.

---

*Central idea.
†Thesis sentence.

Wu 3

"No, sir, I seen plenty go off closer by, in my day, and for less than what I done," she said, holding utterly still.

But the hunter does not notice that the coin is lost, and he does not accuse her. Right up to the moment of her entering the medical building, therefore, the reader is still wondering what might happen.

[4]     Hence, the details about the grandson, carefully concealed until the end, make the story more complex than it at first seems. Because of this concluding revelation, the reader must go through a double take, a reconsideration of what has gone on before. Phoenix's difficult walk into town is then seen not as an ordinary errand but as a hopeless mission of mercy. Her character also bears reevaluation: She is not just a funny old woman who speaks to the woods and animals, but she is a brave and pathetic woman carrying on against crushing odds. These conclusions are not apparent for most of the story, and the bringing out of the carefully concealed details makes "A Worn Path" especially powerful.

[5]     Thus, the parts of "A Worn Path," although seemingly simple, are skillfully arranged. The key to the double take and reevaluation is Welty's withholding of the crucial detail of exposition until the very end. The result is that parts of the exposition and complication, through the speeches of the attendant and the nurse, merge with the climax near the story's end. In some respects, the detail makes it seem as though Phoenix's entire existence is a crisis, although she is not aware of this condition as she leaves the office to buy the paper windmill. It is this complex buildup and emotional peak that make the structure of "A Worn Path" the creation of a master writer.

Wu 4

Work Cited

Welty, Eudora. "A Worn Path." *Writing About Literature.* By Edgar V. Roberts. 12th ed. New York: Pearson, 2010. 359–64. Print.

# Commentary on the Essay

To highlight the differences between essays on plot and structure, the topic of this Illustrative Essay is Welty's "A Worn Path," also the topic of the Illustrative Essay on plot (p. 98). Both essays are concerned with the conflicts of the story, but the essay on plot concentrates on the opposing forces, whereas the essay on structure focuses on the placement and arrangement of the plot elements. Note that neither essay retells the story, event by event. Instead, these are analytical essays that explain the conflict (for plot) and the arrangement and layout (for structure). In both essays, the assumption is that the reader has read "A Worn Path"; hence, there is no need in the essay to retell the story.

The introduction of the essay points out that Welty's masterly structure accounts for the story's power. Paragraph 2 develops the topic that the geographical locations are arranged climactically to demonstrate the forces opposing the major character.

In paragraph 3, the subject is how the exposition about the grandson creates uncertainty about the issues and direction of the story. The early absence of this detail is thus vital structurally. As supporting evidence for this topic, this paragraph cites two important details—the theft of the hunter's nickel and the danger from his dog—as structural false leads about Phoenix's troubles. Other structurally important but misleading details could also be used as evidence for the argument, such as the dangers of the woods and the height of the stairs (both of which might cause fatigue or illness). The two conflicts cited in the paragraph, however, are enough to make the point about Welty's control of structure, and further exemplification is not needed. The quoted passage shows how the reader's concern is pointed toward serious conflicts for Phoenix, but not the major conflict brought out at the end by the disclosure of the grandson's condition.

Paragraph 4 deals with the complexity brought about by the delayed information: the necessary reevaluation of Phoenix' character and her mission to town. The final paragraph (5) also considers this complexity, accounting for the story's power by pointing out how a number of plot elements merge near the end to bring things out swiftly and powerfully.

### Writing Topics about Structure

1. What kind of story might "A Worn Path" be, structurally, if readers were initially told about Phoenix's purpose as she struggles on her way to town? How might the early narration of this detail make the story different from the story as we have it?

2. Consider the surprises in Kate Chopin's "The Story of an Hour," Maupassant's "The Necklace," and Anton Chekhov's *The Bear*. How much preparation is made, structurally, for the surprises? In retrospect, to what degree are the surprises not surprises at all but rather necessary outcomes of the preceding parts of the works?

3. Compare the structuring of the interior scenes in Chopin's "The Story of an Hour" and Maupassant's "The Necklace." How do these scenes bring out the various conflicts of the stories? How does the presence of characters in the individual rooms contribute to the organization of the stories? What is the relationship of these characters to the major actions of the stories?

4. Compare Anita Scott Coleman's "Unfinished Masterpieces" and Dudley Randall's "Ballad of Birmingham" as stories about clashing racial and social values. How

do the narrators express the values and ideas that make their attitudes clear? How do the stories develop, structurally, as a result of their attitudes?

5. Compare the ways in which attitudes toward law and military actions are organized in Glaspell's *Trifles*, Robert Browning's "My Last Duchess," Mark Twain's "Luck," and Amy Lowell's "Patterns." How do these works structure your responses toward the people with power and those without power?

6. Write contrasting paragraphs about a character (whom you know or about whom you have read). In the first, try to make your reader like the character. In the second, try to create a hostile response to the character. Write an additional paragraph explaining the ways in which you tried to organize and shape these opposite responses.

# Chapter 7

# Writing about Setting: The Background of Place, Objects, and Culture in Literature

L ike all human beings, literary characters do not exist in isolation. Just as they become human by interacting with other characters, they gain identity because of their cultural and political allegiances, their possessions, their jobs, and where they live, move, and have their being. They are usually involved deeply with their environments, and their surroundings are causes of much of their motivation and many of their possible conflicts. Plays, stories, and many poems must therefore necessarily include descriptions of places, objects, and backgrounds—the **setting.**

## What Is Setting?

Setting is the natural, manufactured, political, cultural, and temporal environment, including everything that characters know and own. Characters may be either helped or hurt by their surroundings, and they may fight about possessions and goals. Further, as characters speak with each other, they reveal the degree to which they share the customs and ideas of their times.

### *Authors Use Three Basic Types of Settings*

1. **Private homes, public buildings, and various possessions are important in literature, as in life.** To reveal or highlight qualities of character and to make literature lifelike, authors include many details about objects of human manufacture and construction. Houses, both interiors and exteriors, are common, as are possessions such as walking sticks, garden paths, park benches, Christmas trees, necklaces, boxes, pistols, clocks, and hair ribbons. In Guy de Maupassant's "The Necklace," the loss of a comfortable home brings out the best in the major character by forcing her to adjust to her economic reversal. In Katherine Mansfield's "Miss Brill," the return of the major character to her shabby room brings out both the economic and emotional poverty of her life. The discovery of a quilt, still in the process of being sewed, explains the major character's feelings and actions in Susan Glaspell's *Trifles*.

   Objects also enter directly into literary action and character. A broken birdcage reveals the pathetic and abusive husband–wife relationship in *Trifles*. The dress worn by the speaker in Any Lowell's "Patterns" enters into her thoughts as she contemplates the sudden news of her bereavement.

2. **Outdoor places are scenes of many literary actions.** The natural world is an obvious location for the action of many narratives and plays. It is therefore important to note natural surroundings (hills, shorelines, valleys, mountains, meadows, fields, trees, lakes, streams), living creatures (birds, dogs, horses, snakes), and also the times, seasons, and conditions in which things happen (morning or night, summer or winter, sunlight or cloudiness, wind or calmness, rain or shine, sunlight or darkness, snowfall or blizzard, heat or cold)—any or all of which may influence and interact with character, motivation, and conduct. Without the forest in Nathaniel Hawthorne's "Young Goodman Brown," there could be no story, for the events in the story could not have taken place anywhere else just as Hawthorne presents them.

3. **Cultural and historical circumstances are often prominent in literature.** Just as physical setting influences characters, so do historical and cultural conditions and assumptions. Frank O'Connor's "First Confession" is written for readers who understand the role of the Catholic Church in twentieth-century Irish life. In Matthew Arnold's "Dover Beach," the speaker assumes an understanding of the religious skepticism that developed in the nineteenth century. In Anton Chekhov's *The Bear*, the action takes place on an isolated late nineteenth-century Russian estate, and the characters therefore see life that is vastly different from current circumstances. The broad cultural setting of Irving Layton's poem "Rhine Boat Trip" brings out the contrast between the beauty of German scenery and mythology, on the one hand, and the ugliness and depravity of German atrocities in World War II, on the other.

## The Importance of Setting in Literature

Authors use setting to create meaning, just as painters include backgrounds and objects to render ideas. Such a use of setting is seen in Hawthorne's "Young Goodman Brown," where a woodland path that is difficult to follow and that is filled with obstacles is a major topographical feature. The path is of course no more than ordinary, granted the time and conditions in the story, but it also conveys the idea that life is difficult, unpredictable, and mysterious. Similarly, in Glaspell's *Trifles*, the fixtures and utensils in the kitchen of the Wright farm indicate that midwestern homesteads early in the twentieth century were bleak and oppressive.

### Setting Is Often Essential and Vital in the Story

To study the setting in a narrative (or play), discover the important details and then try to explain their function. Depending on the author's purpose, the amount of detail may vary. Edgar Allan Poe provides many graphic and also impressionistic details in "The Cask of Amontillado" so that we can follow, almost visually, the bizarre action at the story's end. In some works the setting is so intensely present, like the country estate interior in Chekhov's *The Bear*, that it is a virtual participant in the story's outcome.

### Setting Augments a Work's Realism and Credibility

One of the major purposes of literary setting is to establish **realism**, or **verisimilitude**. As the description of location and objects becomes particular and detailed, the events of the work become more believable. Maupassant places "The Necklace" in real locations in late nineteenth-century Paris, and for this reason the story has all the semblance of having actually happened. Even futuristic, symbolic, and fantastic stories, as well as ghost stories, seem more believable if they include places and objects from everyday experience. Hawthorne's "Young Goodman Brown" and Poe's "The Cask of Amontillado" are such stories. Although these works make no pretense to portray everyday realism, their credibility is enhanced because they take place in settings that have a strong basis in reality.

### Setting May Accentuate Qualities of Character

Setting may intersect with character as a means by which authors underscore the influence of place, circumstance, and time on human growth and change. Glaspell's setting in *Trifles* is the kitchen of the lonely, dreary Wright farm. This kitchen is a place of such hard work, oppression, and unrelieved joylessness that it explains the loss of Minnie's early brightness and promise and also helps us understand her angry act. (A blending of setting and character as seen in Maupassant's "The Necklace" is explored in the two drafts of the illustrative essay in Chapter 1, pages 34, 43.)

The way characters respond and adjust to setting can reveal their strength or weakness. In Shirley Jackson's "The Lottery," for example, a number of townspeople have grave doubts about the custom of the yearly lottery, but even so, they participate in the concluding mob action. Their acquiescence shows their lack of sensitivity and their inconsistency of thought. In Nathaniel Hawthorne's "Young Goodman Brown," Goodman Brown's Calvinistic religious conviction that human beings are totally depraved, which is confirmed to him during his nightmarish encounter in the forest, indicates the weakness and gullibility of his character just as it alienates him from family and community.

### Setting Is a Means by Which Authors Structure and Shape Their Works

Authors often use setting as one of the means of organizing their stories, as in Maupassant's "The Necklace." The story's final scene is believable because Mathilde leaves her impoverished home to take a nostalgic stroll on the Champs-Elysées, the most fashionable street in Paris. Without this change of setting, she could not have encountered Jeanne Forestier again, for their usual ways of life would no longer bring them together. In short, the structure of the story depends on a normal, natural change of scene.

Another organizational application of place, time, and object is the **framing (enclosing) setting** when an author opens with a particular description or activity and then returns to the same topic at the end. An example is Eudora Welty's "A Worn Path," which both begins and ends with a description of the main character's taking a walk along a familiar route through the countryside and the nearby town. The use of objects as a frame is seen in Mansfield's "Miss Brill," which opens and closes with references to the heroine's shabby fur piece. In such ways, framing creates a formal completeness, just as it may underscore the author's depiction of the human condition.

### Various Settings May Be Symbolic

If the scenes and materials of setting are highlighted or emphasized, they also may be taken as symbols through which the author expresses ideas (see also Chapter 11). The horse Toby in Chekhov's *The Bear* is such a symbol. Mrs. Popov has made caring for the horse, which was her dead husband's favorite, a major part of her memorial obligations. When she tells the servants not to give oats to this horse, Chekhov is using this ordinary animal to indicate that new commitments replace old ones. In Arnold's poem "Dover Beach," the light gleaming from across the English Channel that is soon "gone" may be understood as a symbol of the extinguishing of intellectual and religious faith that Arnold believed had taken place during the nineteenth century.

### Setting Contributes to Atmosphere and Mood

Most actions *require* no more than a functional description of setting. Thus, taking a walk in a forest needs just the statement that there are trees. However, if you find descriptions of shapes, light and shadows, animals, wind, and sounds, you may be sure that the author is creating an **atmosphere**, or **mood**, for the action, as in Hawthorne's "Young Goodman Brown." There are many ways to develop moods. Descriptions of bright colors (red, orange, yellow) may contribute to a mood of happiness. Colors dimmed by weak light, like the vaults in Poe's "The Cask of Amontillado," invoke gloom or augment hysteria. References to smells and sounds bring the setting to life further by asking additional sensory responses from the reader. The setting of a story in a small town or large city, in green or snow-covered fields, or in middle-class or lower-class residences may evoke responses to these places that contribute to the work's atmosphere.

### Setting May Underscore a Work's Irony

Just as setting may reinforce character and theme, so it may establish expectations that are the opposite of what occurs, not only in fiction but also in plays and poems. The colorful and orderly garden described in Lowell's "Patterns" emphasizes the irony of the deeply sad and anguished speaker. The dueling pistols in Chekhov's *The Bear* bring out the irony of the developing relationship between the major characters. These guns, which are designed for death, in fact become the means that prompt the characters to fall in love. A heavily ironic situation is created by Thomas Hardy in the poem "Channel Firing," when the noise of large guns at sea wakens the skeletons buried in an English churchyard. The irony is that those engaged in the gunnery practice, if "red war" gets still redder, will soon join the skeletons in the graveyard.

## Writing about Setting

In preparing to write about setting, determine the number and importance of locations, artifacts, and customs. Ask questions such as the following.

### Raise Questions to Discover Ideas

- How extensive are the visual descriptions? Does the author provide such vivid and carefully arranged detail about surroundings that you could draw a map or plan? Or is the scenery vague and difficult to imagine?
- What connections, if any, are apparent between locations and characters? Do the locations bring characters together, separate them, facilitate their privacy, make intimacy and conversation difficult?
- How fully are objects described? How vital are they to the action? How important are they in the development of the plot or idea? How are they connected to the mental states of the characters?
- How important to plot and character are shapes, colors, times of day, clouds, storms, light and sun, seasons of the year, and conditions of vegetation?
- Are the characters poor, moderately well off, or rich? How does their economic condition affect what happens to them, and how does it affect their actions and attitudes?
- What cultural, religious, and political conditions are brought out in the story? How do the characters accept and adjust to these conditions? How do the conditions affect the characters' judgments and actions?
- What is the state of houses, furniture, and objects (e.g., new and polished, old and worn, ragged and torn)? What connections can you find between these conditions and the outlook and behavior of the characters?
- How important are sounds or silences? To what degree is music or other sound important in the development of character and action?
- Do characters respect or mistreat the environment? If there is an environmental connection, how central is it to the story?
- What conclusions do you think the author expects you to draw as a result of the neighborhood, culture, and larger world of the story?

## Organize Your Essay about Setting

*Introduction*   Begin by making a brief description of the setting or scenes of the work, specifying the amount and importance of detail. Continue by describing the topics you plan to develop.

*Body*   As you prepare the body of your essay, you may need to combine your major approach with one or more of the others. Whatever topics for development you choose, be sure to consider setting not as an end in itself but rather as illustration and evidence for claims you are making about the particular story.

1. **Setting and action.** Explore the importance of setting in the work. How extensively is the setting described? Are locations essential or incidental to the actions? Does the setting serve as part of the action (e.g., places of flight or concealment; public places where people meet openly, or hidden places where they meet privately; natural or environmental conditions; seasonal conditions such as searing heat or numbing cold; customs and conventions)? Do any objects cause inspiration, difficulty, or

conflict (e.g., a coffin, a walking stick, a necklace, a mailbox, a dismal room, a hair ribbon, an ordinary box, a dead bird)? How directly do these objects influence the action?

2. **Setting and organization.** How is the setting connected to the various parts of the work? Does it undergo any changes as the action develops? Why are some parts of the setting more important than others? Is the setting used as a structural frame or enclosure for the story? How do objects, such as money or property, influence the characters? How do descriptions made at the start become important in the action later on?

3. **Setting and character.** (For examples of this approach, see the two drafts of the Illustrative Essay in Chapter 1.) Analyze the degree to which setting influences and interacts with character. Are the characters happy or unhappy where they live? Do they get into discussions or arguments about their home environments? Do they want to stay or leave? Do the economic, philosophical, religious, or ethnic aspects of the setting make the characters undergo changes? What jobs do the characters perform because of their ways of life? What freedoms or restraints do these jobs cause? How does the setting influence their decisions, transportation, speech habits, eating habits, attitudes about love and honor, and general behavior?

4. **Setting and atmosphere.** To what extent does setting contribute to mood? Does the setting go beyond the minimum needed for action or character? How do descriptive words paint verbal pictures and evoke moods through references to colors, shapes, sounds, smells, or tastes? Does the setting establish a mood, say, of joy or hopelessness, plenty or scarcity? Do events happen in daylight or at night? Do the locations and activities of the characters suggest permanence or impermanence (like a return home, the creation of figures out of mud, the repair of a battered boat, the description of ocean currents, the building of a fence)? Are things warm and pleasant or cold and harsh? What connection do you find between the atmosphere and the author's expressed or apparent thoughts about existence?

5. **Setting and other aspects of the work.** Does the setting reinforce the story's meaning? Does it establish irony about the circumstances and ideas in the story? If you choose this approach, consult the section titled "The Importance of Setting in Literature" earlier in this chapter. If you want to write about the symbolic implications of a setting, consult Chapter 11.

*Conclusion*    To conclude, summarize your major points or write about related aspects of setting that you have not considered. Thus, if your essay treats the relationship of setting and action, your conclusion might mention connections of the setting with character or atmosphere. You might also point out whether your central idea about setting also applies to other major aspects of the work.

## Illustrative Essay

> The central idea, thesis sentence, and topic sentences are shaded here to stress the goal of strong organization. As your instructor wishes, you might use this or a similar system in your own essays.

Fitzgerald 1

Derrick Fitzgerald

Professor Kashman

English 200

4 November 2010

Poe's Use of Setting to Create a Mood of Horror and Repulsion

in "The Cask of Amontillado"°

In "The Cask of Amontillado," Edgar Allan Poe uses many details            [1]
of setting to create a mood of horror and repulsion.* The story is a
detailed narration of an act of premeditated and ghastly vengeance. Poe's
character Montresor is both the narrator and the principal creator of the
twisted act of murder. He believes that his vengeance must be known
by the victim, Fortunato, and that it must be threatening and irrevocable.
At the end he is successful, and the reader is both fascinated and repulsed
by the story's mood of ghastliness and heartlessness. The mood is
established through Poe's descriptions of underground rooms, space, and
sound.†

The height of Poe's graphic description is the story's evocation of            [2]
gloomy and threatening vaults. The journey into the hellish "catacombs
of the Montresors" (paragraph 25), which are also the area for the
storage of Montresor's wine collection, ends with a room "lined with
human remains, piled to the vault overhead" (paragraph 68). The walls in
the rooms leading to this last, horrible room are dark and damp, and they
drip moisture from the river above; they also become increasingly airless
and suffocating. The bones on the walls and floors are evidence of
generations of death. In addition, Montresor uses the bones first to hide
his bricks and mortar and then to disguise the wall within which he
entombs Fortunato. The mood is further fixed by the narrator's
observations that each of the catacomb rooms is progressively more
covered and shrouded by spiderlike white and ghostly films of nitre,
which gloomily suggest increasing death and decay.

---

°See pages 352–56 for this story.
*Central idea.
†Thesis sentence.

Fitzgerald 2

[3]     The most disturbing of the catacomb rooms is the last one, the "interior recess" which is to be Fortunato's vertical grave. It is an inauspicious area, which Poe indicates was built "for no especial use within itself" (paragraph 68), but its dimensions are ominous. It is no accident that Poe gives us the dimensions of the recess. It is 4 feet deep, 3 feet wide, and 6 or 7 feet high—exactly the size of a large coffin standing on end. The failure of the faltering torches to illuminate the area suggests the ending of breath and light and the beginning of death. What could be more appropriately sinister, distressing, and ghastly?

[4]     The rooms not only provoke horror, but they are spatially arranged to complement Montresor's horrible act of vengeance. To reach these increasingly dark areas, the characters must continually walk downward. A circular staircase begins the descent, followed by a first and then a second set of stairs that end in the last deep crypt. The downward direction is like an inevitable journey toward the grave, and it also suggests a journey into a bleak, cold, dark, and damp hell.

[5]     Within this interior of death, Poe adds the eeriness of fearsome sound. Fortunato has a terrible rasping cough, to which Poe devotes an entire paragraph (paragraph 32). The jingling of the bells on Fortunato's carnival cap appear at first ordinary (paragraph 26), then bizarre (paragraph 40), and finally sepulchral (paragraph 89). Fortunato's attempt to get free of the chains results in desperate clanking (paragraph 76). He also moans (paragraph 76), laughs in fear and disbelief (paragraph 78), speaks weakly and sadly (paragraph 78), and at the end is silent (paragraph 89). Perhaps the most grisly sounds described by Poe are those of Fortunato's screams of protest, which Montresor cruelly stifles by screaming even louder and longer (paragraph 77)—an action that was duplicated for the insane man in the film *The Silence of the Lambs*. These described sounds, having their source in Montresor's diabolical action, create a mood of uneasiness, anxiety, repulsion, and horror.

[6]     Thus, Poe's setting within the eerie catacombs is both descriptive and evocative. The major action takes place in the last room, in the gravelike recess, leading to the climax of the story's movement into darkness and the very walls of death. In this way, Poe uses his setting to

Fitzgerald 3

show the horror of a twisted mind prompting a diseased individual to create a cruel and pitiless act of revenge. The events of the story, the sustained mood, and the narrator's compulsion with vengeance are all tied together by Poe's masterly control of setting.

Fitzgerald 4

Work Cited

Poe, Edgar A. "The Cask of Amontillado." *Writing About Literature*. By Edgar V. Roberts. 12th ed. New York: Pearson, 2010. 352–56. Print.

## Commentary on the Essay

Because it treats the relationship of setting to mood or atmosphere, this essay illustrates the fourth approach described on page 118. The essay considers those aspects of setting needed for the story and then stresses how Poe's descriptions create the story's dominant mood of horror and repulsion.

In the body, paragraphs 2 and 3 form a unit describing the physical layout of the deathly catacombs and point out the exactness and evocativeness of Poe's descriptions. Paragraph 4 concentrates on Poe's description of downward movement, suggesting that this use of space is a visual accompaniment of the story's conclusion in Fortunato's death.

Paragraph 5 treats Poe's use of sound as an accompaniment to the descriptions of the deadly catacombs. The paragraph's topic idea is that the sounds move progressively toward silence, in keeping with Montresor's creation of death. The sounds are therefore one of Poe's major means of achieving an atmosphere complementary to the repulsive and horrible action.

The conclusion summarizes the central idea, stressing once again that Poe goes beyond simple description to heighten the twisted, macabre mood of his story.

### Writing Topics about Setting

1. Compare and contrast how details of setting are used to establish the qualities and traits of the following characters: Mrs. Popov of Chekhov's *The Bear*; Miss Brill of Mansfield's "Miss Brill"; or the speakers of Lowell's "Patterns," Layton's "Rhine Boat Trip," or Arnold's "Dover Beach."

2. In what ways might we say that the events of both Kate Chopin's "The Story of an Hour" and Poe's "The Cask of Amontillado" are governed by the settings of the stories? To answer this question, consider the relationship of character to place and circumstance. How could the actions of the stories happen without the locations in which they occur?

3. Compare and contrast how details of setting establish qualities and traits of the following female characters: Faith of Hawthorne's "Young Goodman Brown," Miss Brill of Mansfield's "Miss Brill," Nora of O'Connor's "First Confession," Mrs. Popov of Chekhov's *The Bear*, and Louise of Chopin's "The Story of an Hour." To add to your comparison, you might introduce details about women in paintings or works of sculpture that you know.

4. Choose a story included in Appendix C and rewrite a page or two, taking the characters out of their setting and placing them in an entirely new setting or in the setting of another story (you choose). Then write a brief analysis dealing with these questions: How were your characters affected by their new settings? Did you make them change slowly or rapidly? Why? As a result of your rewriting, what can you conclude about the uses of setting in fiction?

5. Write a short narrative as though it is part of a story (which you may also wish to write for the assignment), using options a and/or b.
   a. Relate a natural setting or type of day to a mood—for example, a nice day to happiness and satisfaction or a cold, cloudy, rainy day to sadness. Or create irony by relating the nice day to sadness or the rainy day to happiness.
   b. Indicate how an object or a circumstance becomes the cause of conflict or reconciliation (such as the lost necklace in Maupassant's "The Necklace," the dead canary in Glaspell's *Trifles*, or the trip through the forest in Hawthorne's "Young Goodman Brown").

6. In your library, locate two books on the career of Edgar Allan Poe. On the basis of the information you find in these sources, write a brief account of Poe's uses of setting and place to evoke atmosphere and to bring out qualities of human character.

# Chapter 8

# Writing about an Idea or Theme: The Meaning and the "Messages" in Literature

Not easily defined, **idea** is a word that broadly refers to the result or results of thought. Synonymous words are *concept, thought, opinion,* and *principle.* Other words sometimes used synonymously are **assertion**, *assumption, conclusion, conviction, creed, dogma, hypothesis, proposition,* and *supposition.* In short, many words refer to the results of thinking—all of them either tightly or loosely connected to the word *idea.* In literary study, the consideration of ideas relates to *meaning, interpretation, explanation,* and *significance.* Although ideas are usually extensive and complex (and often elusive), separate ideas can be named by single words, such as *right, good, love, piety, causality, wilderness,* and, not surprisingly, *idea* itself. President Abraham Lincoln stated that our nation was conceived in [the idea of] liberty and dedicated to the proposition [i.e., the idea] that all human beings are created equal. It would be difficult to overstate the power and importance of these ideas.

## Ideas and Assertions

Although single words alone can name ideas, we must put these words into operation in *sentences* or *assertions* before they can advance our understanding. Good operational sentences about ideas are not the same as ordinary conversational statements such as "It's a nice day." An observation of this sort can be true (depending on the weather), but it gives us no ideas and does not stimulate our minds. Rather, a sentence asserting an idea should initiate a thought or argument about the day's quality, such as "A nice day requires light breezes, blue sky, a warm sun, relaxation, and happiness." Because this sentence makes an assertion about the word *nice*, it allows us to consider and develop the idea of a nice day.

In studying literature, always express ideas as assertions. For example, you might state that an idea in Anton Chekhov's *The Bear* is "love," but it would be difficult to discuss anything more unless you make an assertion promising an argument, such as "This play demonstrates the idea that love is irrational and irresistible." This assertion could lead you to explain the unlikely love that bursts out in the play. Similarly, for Eudora Welty's "A Worn Path" you might express the following idea, which would require further explanation: "The story of Phoenix's mission on her walk to town embodies the idea that caring for others gives no reward but the continuation of the duty itself."

Although we have noted only one idea in these two works, most stories contain many ideas. When one of the ideas turns up over and over again throughout a work, it is called the **theme**. In practice, the words *theme* and *major idea* are the same.

## Ideas and Values

Literature embodies **values** along with ideas. *Value*, of course, commonly refers to the price of something, but in the realm of ideas and principles, it is a standard of what is desired, sought, esteemed, and treasured. For example, *democracy* refers to our political system, but it is also a complex idea of representative government that we esteem most highly, as we also esteem concepts like honor, cooperation, generosity, and love. A vital idea/value is *justice*, which, put most simply, involves equality before the law and the fair evaluation of conduct that is deemed unacceptable or illegal. Such an idea of justice is a major topic of Susan Glaspell's play *Trifles*. Glaspell dramatizes the story of a farmwife who for thirty years has endured her husband's intimidation and her abject circumstances of life but finally has risen up against him in his sleep. By a rigid concept of justice as guilt-conviction-punishment, the wife, Minnie Wright, is guilty and should be convicted and punished. But justice as an idea also involves a full and fair consideration of the circumstances and motivation of wrongdoing, and it is such a consideration that the two women in the play make during their examination of Minnie's kitchen. Many of their speeches showing their sympathy to Minnie are equivalent to a jurylike deliberation. Their final decision is like a verdict, and their final concealment of Minnie's guilt is evidence for the idea that justice, to be most highly valued, should be tempered with understanding—even if the women do not use these exact words in their discussions of Minnie's situation. In short, the idea of justice underlying Glaspell's *Trifles* also involves a deeply held value.

## The Place of Ideas in Literature

Because writers of poems, plays, and stories are usually not systematic philosophers, it is not appropriate to go "message hunting" as though their works contained nothing but ideas. Indeed, there is great benefit and pleasure to be derived from just savoring a work—following the patterns of narrative and conflict, getting to like the characters, understanding the work's implications and suggestions, and listening to the sounds of the author's words, to name only a few of the reasons for which literature is treasured.

Nevertheless, ideas are vital to understanding and appreciating literature, for writers have ideas and want to communicate them. For example, in *The Bear*, Chekhov directs laughter at two unlikely people suddenly and unpredictably falling in love. The play is funny, however, because it is not only preposterous but also based on the *idea* that love takes precedence over other resolutions that people might make. William Blake in "The Tyger" describes the "fearful symmetry" of a wild tiger in "the forests of the night," but the poem also embodies *ideas* about the inexplicable nature of evil, the mystery of life, and the unsearchability of divine purpose in the universe.

### *Distinguish between Ideas and Actions*

As you analyze works for ideas, it is important to avoid the trap of confusing ideas and actions. Such a trap is contained in the following sentence about Frank O'Connor's "First Confession": "The major character, Jackie, misbehaves at home and tries to slash his sister with a breadknife." This sentence successfully describes a major action in the story, but it does not express an *idea* that connects characters and events, and for this reason it obstructs understanding. Some possible connections might be achieved with sentences like these: "'First Confession' illustrates the idea that family life may produce anger and potential violence" or "'First Confession' shows that compelling children to accept authority may cause effects that are the opposite of adult intentions." A study based on these connecting formulations could be focused on ideas and would not be sidetracked into doing no more than retelling O'Connor's story.

### *Distinguish between Ideas and Situations*

You should also make a distinction between situations and ideas. For example, in Amy Lowell's poem "Patterns," the narrator describes what is happening to her as a result of her fiancé's death. Her plight is not an idea but a situation that brings out ideas, such as that future plans may be destroyed by uncontrollable circumstances, that fate strikes the fortunate as well as the unfortunate, or that human institutions often seem arbitrary, capricious, and cruel. If you are able in such ways to distinguish a work's various situations from the writer's major idea or ideas, you will be able to focus on ideas and therefore sharpen your own thinking.

## How to Locate Ideas

Ideas are not as obvious as characters or setting. To determine an idea, you need to consider the meaning of what you read and then to develop explanatory and comprehensive assertions. Your assertions need not be the same as those that others might make. People notice different things, and individual formulations vary. In Kate Chopin's "The Story of an Hour," for example, an initial expression of some of the story's ideas might take any of the following three forms: (1) Even in a good marriage, husbands and wives can have ambivalent feelings about their married life. (2) An accident can bring out negative but previously unrecognized thoughts in a wife or husband. (3) Even those closest to a person may never realize that person's innermost feelings. Although any one of these choices could be a basic idea for studying "The Story of an Hour," they all have in common the main character's unexpected feelings of release when she is told that her husband has been killed. In discovering ideas, you should follow a similar process—making a number of formulations for an idea and then selecting one for further development.

As you read, be alert to the different ways in which authors convey ideas. One author might prefer an indirect way through a character's speeches, whereas another may prefer direct statement. In practice, authors can employ any or all the following methods.

### Study the Authorial Voice

Although authors mainly render action, dialogue, and situation, they sometimes state ideas to guide us and deepen our understanding. In Guy de Maupassant's "The Necklace," for example, the speaker/storyteller presents the idea that women have no more than charm and beauty to get on in the world (paragraph 2). Ironically, Maupassant uses the story to show that for the major character, Mathilde, nothing is effective, for her charm cannot prevent disaster. Nathaniel Hawthorne, in "Young Goodman Brown," uses the following words to express a powerful idea: "The fiend in his own shape is less hideous than when he rages in the breast of man" (paragraph 53). This statement is made as authorial commentary just when the major character, Goodman Brown, is speeding through "the benighted wilderness" on his way to the satanic meeting. Although the idea is complex, its essential aspect is that the causes of evil originate within human beings themselves, with the implication that we alone are responsible for all our actions.

### Study the Character and the Words of the First-Person Speaker

First-person narrators or speakers frequently express ideas along with their depiction of actions and situations, and they also make statements from which you can make inferences about ideas. (See also Chapter 3, on point of view.) Because what they say is part of a dramatic presentation, their ideas can be right or wrong, well considered or thoughtless, good or bad, or brilliant or half-baked, depending on the speaker. The I/we (first-person) speaker of Matthew Arnold's "Dover Beach," for example, laments the diminution of vital ideas from the past, concluding that this loss is accompanied by increasing ignorance, uncertainty, and violence in today's world. In Thomas Hardy's "Channel Firing," the speaker—a skeleton suddenly awakened by the nearby noise of naval gunfire at sea—implies that warfare has been a constant menace from ancient days to the present. Even if the speaker has dubious characteristics or is making a confession about personal shortcomings—as the speaker of Robert Frost's "Desert Places" is doing—you may nevertheless study and evaluate the work's ideas.

### Study the Statements Made by Characters

In many stories, characters express their own views, which can be right or wrong, admirable or contemptible. When you consider such dramatic speeches, you need to do considerable interpreting and evaluating yourself. In Chekhov's *The Bear*, both Smirnov and Mrs. Popov express many silly ideas about love and duty as they begin speaking to each other, and it is the sudden force of their love that reveals to us how wrongheaded their previous ideas have been. Old Man Warner in Shirley Jackson's "The Lottery" states that the lottery is valuable even though we learn from the narrator that the beliefs underlying it have long been forgotten. Because Warner is a zealous and insistent person, however, his words show that outdated ideas continue to do harm even when there is strong reason to reevaluate and dismiss them.

### Study the Work's Figures of Speech

**Figurative language** is one of the major components of poetry, but it also abounds in prose fiction (see also Chapter 10). In the sonnet "Bright Star," for example, John Keats emphasizes the idea that constancy is necessary in love by referring to a fixed and bright star (probably the North Star). Much metaphorical language is also to be found in both narratives and drama, as at the opening of Katherine Mansfield's "Miss Brill" where a sunny day is compared to gold and white wine. This lovely comparison suggests the idea of the beauty of the earth—an idea that contrasts ironically with the indifference and cruelty that Miss Brill experiences later in the story. Another notable figure occurs in Glaspell's *Trifles*, when one of the characters compares John Wright, the murdered husband, with a "raw wind that gets to the bone" (speech 103). With this figurative language, Glaspell conveys the idea that bluntness, indifference, and cruelty create great personal damage.

### Study How Characters Represent Ideas

Characters and their actions can often be equated with certain ideas and values. The power of Mathilde's story in Maupassant's "The Necklace" enables us to explain that she represents the idea that unrealizable dreams can inhibit one's ability to function in the real world. Two diverse or opposed characters can embody contrasting ideas, as with Louise and Josephine of Chopin's "The Story of an Hour." Each woman can be taken to represent differing views about the role of women in marriage. In effect, characters who stand for ideas can assume symbolic status, as in Hawthorne's "Young Goodman Brown," where the protagonist symbolizes the alienation that inevitably accompanies zealousness. Because characters can be equated directly with particular ideas, talking about them should lead naturally to a discussion of the ideas they may be taken to represent.

### Study the Work Itself as an Embodiment of Ideas

One of the most important ways in which authors express ideas is to interlock them within all parts and aspects of the work. The art of painting is instructive here, for a painting can be taken in with a single view that comprehends all the aspects of color, form, action, and expression, each of which can also be considered separately. In the same way, when considered totally, the various parts of a work may clearly embody major ideas, as in "Negro" by Langston Hughes. In this poem, Hughes makes objective the idea that blacks have been cruelly exploited throughout history. In addition, implicit in the poem is the idea that the urgency of ending racial barriers overrides all socially and politically convenient reasons for which these barriers—and the cruelties they bring about— have been established. Most works represent ideas in a similar way. Even "escape literature," which ostensibly enables readers to forget immediate problems, contains conflicts between good and evil, love and hate, good spies and bad, earthlings and aliens, and so on. Such works thereby *do* embody ideas, even though their avowed intention is not to make readers think but rather to help them forget.

## Writing about a Major Idea in Literature

Most likely you will write about what you consider the work's major idea or theme, but you may also get interested in a less obvious idea. As you begin brainstorming and developing your first drafts, consider questions such as those that follow.

### Raise Questions to Discover Ideas

#### General Ideas

- What ideas do you discover in the work? How do you discover them (through action, character depiction, scenes, language)?
- To what do the ideas pertain? To the individuals themselves? To individuals and society? To religion? To social, political, or economic justice?
- How balanced are the ideas? If a particular idea is strongly presented, what conditions and qualifications are also presented (if any)? What contradictory ideas are presented?
- Are the ideas limited to members of any groups represented by the characters (age, race, nationality, personal status)? Or are the ideas applicable to general conditions of life? Explain.
- Which characters in their own right represent or embody ideas? How do their actions and speeches bring these ideas out?
- If characters state ideas directly, how persuasive is their expression, how intelligent and well considered? How applicable are the ideas to the work? How applicable to more general conditions?
- With children, young adults, or the old, how do the circumstances express or embody an idea?

#### A Specific Idea

- What idea seems particularly important in the work? Why? Is it asserted directly, indirectly, dramatically, ironically? Does any one method predominate? Why?
- How pervasive in the work is the idea (throughout or intermittent)? To what degree is it associated with a major character or action? How does the structure of the work affect or shape your understanding of the idea?
- What value or values are embodied in the idea? Of what importance are the values to the work's meaning?
- How compelling is the idea? How could the work be appreciated without reference to any idea at all?

## Organize Your Essay on a Major Idea or Theme

In well-written stories, poems, and plays, narrative and dramatic elements have a strong bearing on ideas. In this sense, an idea is like a key in music or a continuous thread tying together actions, characters, statements, symbols, and dialogue. As readers, we can trace such threads throughout the entire fabric of the work.

As you write about ideas, you may find yourself relying most heavily on the direct statements of the authorial voice or on a combination of these and your interpretation of characters and action, or you might focus exclusively on a first-person speaker and use his or her ideas to develop your analysis. Always make clear the sources of your details and distinguish the sources from your own commentary.

*Introduction*   As you begin, state your general goal of describing an idea and of showing its importance in the work. Your brief statement of the idea will be your central idea for your essay.

*Body*   Each separate work will invite its own approach, but here are a number of strategies you might use to organize your essay.

1. **Analyze the idea as it applies to characters.** *Example*: "Minnie Wright embodies the idea that living with cruelty and insensitivity leads to alienation, unhappiness, despair, and even to violence." (Glaspell's *Trifles*)
2. **Show how actions bring out the idea.** *Example*: "That Mrs. Popov and Smirnov fall in love rather than go their rather foolish and fruitless ways indicates Chekhov's idea that love literally rescues human lives." (*The Bear*)
3. **Show how dialogue and separate speeches bring out the idea.** *Example*: "The priest's responses to Jackie's confession embody the idea that kindness and understanding are the best means to encourage religious and philosophical commitment." (O'Connor's "First Confession")
4. **Show how the work's structure is determined by the idea.** *Example*: "The idea that horror can affect a nation's beauty and tradition leads Irving Layton to introduce and conclude the poem by referring to aspects of the World War II Holocaust." ("Rhine Boat Trip")
5. **Treat variations or differing manifestations of the idea.** *Example*: "The idea that zealousness leads to harm is shown in Brown's nightmarish distortion of reality, his rejection of others, and his dying gloom." (Hawthorne's "Young Goodman Brown")
6. **Deal with a combination of these (together with any other significant aspect).** *Example*: "Chekhov's idea in *The Bear* that love is complex and contradictory is shown in Smirnov's initial scorn of Mrs. Popov, his self-declared independence of character, and his concluding embrace." (Here the idea is traced through speech, character, and action.)

*Conclusion*   Your conclusion might begin with a summary, together with your evaluation of the validity or force of the idea. If you have been convinced by the author's ideas, you might say that the author has expressed the idea forcefully and convincingly, or else you might show the relevance of the idea to current conditions. If you are not persuaded by the idea, you should demonstrate the idea's shortcomings or limitations. If you wish to mention a related idea, whether in the story you have studied or in some other story, you might introduce that here, but be sure to stress the connections.

## Illustrative Essay

The central idea, thesis sentence, and topic sentences are shaded here to stress the goal of strong organization. As your instructor wishes, you might use this or a similar system in your own essays.

Dayton 1

Willow Dayton

Professor McLaughlin

English 201

18 November 2010

The Idea of the Importance of Minor and "Trifling" Details

in Susan Glaspell's *Trifles*°

[1]          A major idea in Glaspell's short play *Trifles*—and the idea that gives
the play its name—is that truth is to be found not through earthshaking
matters but rather through small, insignificant, everyday things.* The
two women onstage during the entire play, Mrs. Hale and Mrs. Peters,
wait patiently in the kitchen of the Wright farmhouse while their
husbands and the County Attorney search for evidence about the death
of John Wright, who has been strangled in his sleep. Wright's wife,
Minnie, is the principal suspect, and she has been imprisoned in the
nearby town. As the two women wait, they examine the ordinary and
small things they find in the kitchen, such as broken jars of preserves, an
unfinished quilt, a dirty hand towel, and a dead canary. Because of their
observations, they soon understand that Minnie is guilty of the murder
for which she has been arrested. Their discovery is a major phase of the
idea that truth is to be found in the buildup of many separate small
details. These are not only about the dead man and his wife, however,
but also about the lives of the two married couples who are there
because of the murder.[†] A number of little details about their lives are
discovered and revealed in the kitchen, and these both characterize the
play's strong portraits of the wives and lead to the play's unexpected and
startling conclusion.

[2]          An important aspect of the play that might easily be ignored is the
way of life of all three married couples, not just one of the couples
alone. We see two of the couples firsthand (Mr. and Mrs. Hale and Mr.
and Mrs. Peters) and learn about the third (John and Minnie Wright)
through the dialogue and the discoveries made by Mrs. Hale and

---

°See pages 391–400 for this play.
*Central idea.
†Thesis sentence.

Dayton 2

Mrs. Peters. It may be said that, in accord with the major idea, married life is not a series of huge and powerfully significant events but rather is a day-in, day-out progression of both shorter and lengthier experiences— many of them small and trifling—that continue for years, decades, and lifetimes. To form an idea about the nature of marital relationships, relationships, one should consider the nature of the off-hand, ordinary, off-guard talk of husbands and wives.

In the short scenes of the play when Mr. Hale and Mr. Peters are     [3]
actually present, their conversation is minor and trifling—a trading of platitudes. These men speak just to say something or anything, but in their small-minded banter they expose their generally negative feelings about women. To them, women are inferior, even though it is clear that both of them have been married a long while. Mr. Hale, a farmer, talks dismissively about the "trifles" that occupy women (speech 30). Mr. Peters, the local sheriff, disparages "kitchen things" (speech 25), and he also laughs at the knitting skills of the wives. This male insensitivity is reinforced by Mr. Henderson, the County Attorney, who late in the play states derisively to the other men: "you know juries when it comes to women," as though a woman, just because she is a woman, could never be convicted of a crime by a jury even if guilty (speech 139). It should be noted that the two women also hear these negative comments by their husbands. Henderson's patronizing compliment to women is obviously no praise at all. In speech 31, he says, "what would we do without the ladies?"

These banal and superficial remarks by the men—trifling speeches—     [4]
are much more significant than they seem. It is obvious that both wives have lived with similar condescension as long as they have been married, for such minor details contained in the men's speeches lead one to conclude that the two women, secretly at least, might believe that their marriages are far from ideal. The women do not complain, however, but it is this imperfect situation that lies at the root of the overwhelming decision upon which the women act at the play's end. One may speculate that if the women had felt totally approved and accepted, they would have made their decision more in line with the wishes of their husbands.

[5]     Just as the offhand comments by the men—trifling details—expose
the less than ideal marriages of Mrs. Hale and Mrs. Peters, so do similarly
small details reveal that the Wrights had by far the worst of all possible
marriages. As the two women examine the trifles in Minnie's kitchen, they
infer that Minnie endured bitter solitude and rejection during her entire
married life. It is fair to conclude that conversations between the Wrights
were not loving, but very likely scornful. Things were not always this way
for Minnie, however, as we learn from Mrs. Hale, who had known Minnie
when she was young, when she wore "pretty clothes," was "lively," and
sang in the choir (speech 56). And it is Mrs. Hale who points out that
Wright was "a hard man, . . . Like a raw wind that gets to the bone"
(speech 103). The ultimate small detail, which is actually immense in the
context of the play, is the discovery by the two women of Minnie's dead
canary. This canary had been the only thing of beauty she ever owned in
her married life, and certainly the only relief she ever knew from the
dreariness of life with Wright. Obviously, Wright had disliked the bird's
singing, and to show his contempt he had wrung the bird's neck (speech
114). This arbitrarily cruel act, the women infer, brought Minnie to total
grief and despair. Unable to endure things any longer, she murdered
Wright in his sleep by strangling him with a rope tied with a quilting knot.

[6]     In line with the major idea about the significance of trifling details,
the women form an unspoken alliance of sympathy for Minnie. Their
conversation reveals that both have experienced comparable though less
severe isolation and loneliness during their lives on early twentieth-
century farms. Mrs. Hale says, "I know how things can be—for women"
(speech 136). Mrs. Peters tells about the loneliness of life on a
homestead in Dakota, when she endured the extreme sorrow of losing a
child (speech 131). The implication is that her husband considered her
feelings as nothing more than "trifles." It seems clear that the loneliness
and hard life experienced by the two women, on the one hand, and by
Minnie, on the other, are only those of degree. Because the women
sympathize with Minnie's lonely plight so completely, however, they
reach an understanding that the wretched details of her life actually
extenuate her guilt.

Dayton 4

Above this understanding, Mrs. Hale, the stronger and more    [7]
independent of the two women, also recognizes that she herself, in effect,
committed a moral crime because she did not make a greater effort to see
and befriend Minnie before things got desperate for her (speech 134).
Mrs. Hale's sense of having fallen short suggests that explaining the
kitchen trifles to the men, and thus revealing Minnie's guilt, would also
be an implicit judgment against herself. And so she, along with Mrs.
Peters (who tends to be more deferential to the men and to the importance
of the law), withholds the conclusive evidence that would confirm the
case for murder that the men are trying to build. It is therefore Mrs. Hale
who sews and therefore hides the "trifle" of Minnie's disturbed stitching
on the quilt (speeches 77–81), and it is also she who conceals the tiny
dead bird in her coat pocket, the last action in the play (paragraph 147
S. D.°). By doing away with the evidence, Mrs. Hale, with the silent
consent of Mrs. Peters, illegally but justifiably covers up Minnie's guilt
and baffles the law. This immensely significant action is based on the
conclusion that the women have made about the idea that real truth—not
just legal truth, but human truth—is to be discovered in the trifling details
they have discovered in Minnie Wright's kitchen.

The two women are perceptive. They act on deeply felt ideas,    [8]
and they understand the meaning of individual details when they see
them. That is the key. Ironically, Mrs. Hale and Mrs. Peters do a
better job of detailed detective work than the lawmen—Mr. Peters
and Mr. Henderson. The men look everywhere in the house, but they
waste their time because they do not look in the kitchen, where the
real "clues" could be uncovered that would lead them to solving the
crime. And so they are in fact inept and do not learn anything to
confirm their suspicions. By contrast, the women correctly see the
true evidence, trifling as it may be, and they discover that their
interest is to take sides with Minnie. Glaspell's *Trifles* demonstrates
that a gap exists between the interests of men and women, and the
idea underlying this division is to be found in how women interpret
details and therefore discover truth.

---

°S. D.: Stage direction.

Dayton 5

Work Cited

Glaspell, Susan. *Trifles. Writing About Literature.* By Edgar V.
Roberts.12th ed. New York: Pearson, 2010. 391–400. Print.

## Commentary on the Essay

This essay follows strategy 6 (p. 129) by showing how various components of the play exhibit the principal idea about the importance of little things, both in the marriage of the Wrights and also in the marriages of the two women who have come to the Wright household with their husbands. Throughout, the essay points out that situations, dialogue, and actions are evidence for the various conclusions. Paragraph transitions are effected by phrases such as "These" (paragraph 4), "Just as" (paragraph 5), and "In line with" (paragraph 6). All these transitions emphasize the continuity of the topic.

Paragraph 1 introduces and stresses the major idea and points out some of the necessary plot detail to substantiate the essay's central idea.

As the operative aspect of Glaspell's principal idea, paragraphs 2 and 3 show how the play develops through the discussion of the contrasting marriage lives of the on-stage couples. The idea that truth is to be found in small details is shown in paragraph 2 to be an introduction to paragraph 3, which stresses the trifling conversations of the men. Continuing this development, paragraph 4 draws conclusions about the effect of the men's talk on Mrs. Hale and Mrs. Peters, both of whom are not endeared to the men because of what they have said. Paragraph 5 considers details about the Wright marriage, pointing out that Minnie Wright had reached the end of her endurance when Wright killed her bird. Paragraphs 6 and 7 concentrate on the two women, who develop sufficient sympathy for Minnie to sustain them when they in effect absolve her from guilt in her husband's strangulation. The thinking underlying these two paragraphs, and also the final one, paragraph 8, is that the women have established a silent bond in supporting Minnie and have seen no persuasive reason to prefer supporting the law, in this case, as represented by their husbands.

Paragraph 8 then, beyond being used for a brief summary, considers the detail that the urgency of the need to act forces the women to act almost reflexively in support of Minnie. The major new detail here is the tension between the duty to law of the two women, on the one hand, and their personal allegiance to Minnie and her plight, on the other.

### Writing Topics about Ideas

1. Compare the ideas in two works containing similar themes. *Examples*: Arnold's "Dover Beach" and Hardy's "Channel Firing," Keats's "Bright Star" and Shakespeare's "Let Me Not to the Marriage of True Minds," Frost's "Desert Places" and

Hawthorne's "Young Goodman Brown," Layton's "Rhine Boat Trip" and Edgar Allan Poe's "The Cask of Amontillado," Chopin's "The Story of an Hour," and Chekhov's *The Bear*. For help in developing your essay, consult Chapter 15 on the technique of comparison-contrast.

2. Consider Maupassant's "The Necklace" in the light of economic determinism. That is, to what degree are the circumstances and traits of the characters, particularly Mathilde, controlled and limited by their economic status? According to the idea, how likely is it that the characters could ever rise above their circumstances?

3. Write an essay criticizing the ideas in a work (see Appendix C) that you dislike or that you are indifferent to. What statements in the work do you disagree with? What actions? What characters? How do your own beliefs and values cause you to dislike the work's ideas? How might the work be changed to illustrate ideas that you would agree with?

4. Select an idea that particularly interests you and outline a brief story showing how characters may or may not live up to the idea. If you have difficulty getting started, try one of these ideas:
    - Interest and enthusiasm are hard to maintain for long.
    - Fortune has often given people an abundance of worldly things, but few people ever believe they have received enough.
    - When people reach adulthood, they leave childish things behind them.
    - It is awkward to confront another person about a grievance.
    - Making romantic or career decisions is difficult because they demand fundamental and complete changes in life's directions.

5. Using books that you discover in the card or computer catalog in your college or local library, search for discussions of only one of the following topics and write a brief report on what you find.
    - Hardy on the power of the working classes.
    - Hawthorne on the significance of religion, both good and bad.
    - Keats on the significance of intuition and imagination as creative power.
    - The ideas underlying Poe's concept of the short story.

# Chapter 9

## Writing about Imagery: The Literary Work's Link to the Senses

In literature, **imagery** refers to words that trigger your imagination to recall and re-combine **images**—memories or mental pictures of sights, sounds, tastes, smells, sensations of touch, and motions. The process is both active and mentally vigorous, for when words or descriptions produce images, you constantly use your personal experiences with life and language to help you give shape and understanding to the works you are reading. In effect, you are re-creating the work *in your own way* through the controlled stimulation produced by the writer's words. Imagery is therefore one of the strongest modes of literary expression because it provides a channel to your active imagination, and along this channel, writers bring their works directly to you and into your consciousness. Authors use words and, as you read them, you must draw on your own experience to re-create the life that they evoke.

For example, encountering the word *lake* may bring to your mind your literal memory of a particular lake. Your mental picture—or image—may be a distant view of calm waters reflecting blue sky, a nearby view of gentle waves rippling in the wind, a close-up view of the sandy lake bottom from a boat or a dock, or an overhead view of a sun-drenched shoreline. Similarly, the words *rose*, *apple*, *hot dog*, *malted milk*, and *pizza* all cause you to recollect these objects and may also cause you to recall their smells and tastes. Active and graphic words like *row*, *swim*, and *dive* stimulate you mentally to create moving images of someone performing these actions.

### Responses and the Writer's Use of Detail

In studying imagery, we try to comprehend and explain our imaginative perception of the pictures and impressions evoked by the work's images. We let the poet's words simmer and percolate in our minds. To get our imaginations stirring, we might follow Samuel Taylor Coleridge in this description from the poem "Kubla Khan"(lines 37–41):

> A damsel with a dulcimer
> In a vision once I saw:
> It was an Abyssinian maid,
> And on her dulcimer she played
> Singing of Mount Abora.

We do not read about the color of the young woman's clothing or anything else about her appearance except that she is playing a dulcimer—an exotic stringed instrument—and that she is singing a song about a mountain in a foreign, remote land. But Coleridge's image is enough. From it we can imagine a vivid, exotic picture of a young woman from a distant land, singing a song and accompanying herself on her dulcimer, together with the loveliness of her song (even though we never hear it or understand it). The image lives.

## The Relationship of Imagery to Ideas and Attitudes

Images do more than elicit impressions. By the authenticating effects of the vision and perceptions underlying them, they give you new ways of seeing the world and of strengthening your old ways of seeing it. Shakespeare's speaker in "Sonnet 73: That Time of Year Thou Mayst in Me Behold," for example, emphasizes that he is getting older and therefore closer to the time of his death. Rather than stating this idea so uninterestingly, however, Shakespeare dramatizes it through the introduction of images of autumn, evening, and a dying fire. In quatrain II, the speaker describes the approaching evening of life (lines 5–8):

> In me thou seest the twilight of such day
> 　As after sunset fadeth in the West,
> Which by and by black night doth take away,
> 　Death's second self that seals up all in rest.

This expanded image, like those in the other quatrains of this sonnet, forms an easily recognized and affirmable link with the experiences of readers, who have seen many sunsets and have known many elderly people. Such uses of imagery comprise one of the strongest means by which literature reinforces themes and interpretations of life.

## Types of Imagery

### *Visual Imagery Is the Language of Sight*

Our power of sight is the most significant of our senses, for it is a key to our remembrance of other sense impressions. Therefore, the most frequently occurring literary imagery is to things that we can visualize either exactly or approximately—**visual images,** which in fact often operate identically with images of action (see kinesthetic imagery, p. 139). In the poem "Cargoes," John Masefield asks us to recreate mental pictures or images of ocean-going merchant vessels from three periods of human history. He refers to a large ancient sailing vessel, a quinquereme, which he associates with the biblical King Solomon. Then he turns to a "stately Spanish galleon" of the Renaissance and finally refers to an early twentieth-century British ship caked with salt, carrying grubby and cheap freight over the English Channel.

His images are vivid as they stand and need no further amplification. For us to re-construct them imaginatively, we do not need ever to have seen the ancient bibli-cal lands or waters or ever to have seen or handled the cheap commodities delivered by a modern merchant ship. We have seen enough in our lives both in reality and in pictures to *imagine* places and objects like these, and hence Masefield is suc-cessful in fixing his visual images in our minds.

### Auditory Imagery Is the Language of Sound

**Auditory images** trigger our experiences with sound. For such images, let us con-sider Wilfred Owen's "Anthem for Doomed Youth," which is about the death of soldiers in warfare and the sorrow of their loved ones. The poem begins with the question of "what passing-bells" may be tolled for "those who die as cattle." Owen's speaker is referring to the traditional tolling of a church bell or a cemetery bell to announce that a new burial is to take place. Reference to the sounds of such a solemn ceremony suggests a period of peace and order, when there is time to pay respect to the dead. But the poem then points out contrastingly that the only sound for those who have fallen in battle is the "rapid rattle" of "stuttering" rifles—in other words, not the solemn and dignified sounds of peace but the bloodthirsty and horrifying noises of war. Owen's auditory images evoke corresponding sounds in our imaginations, and they help us experience the poem and hate the depravity of war.

### Olfactory, Gustatory, and Tactile Imagery Refers to Smell, Taste, and Touch

In addition to sight and sound, you will also find images from the other senses. An **olfactory image** refers to smell; a **gustatory image**, to taste; and a **tactile image**, to touch. A great deal of love poetry, for example, includes *olfactory images* about the fra-grances of flowers.

Images derived from and referring to taste—*gustatory images*—are also com-mon though less frequent than those referring to sight and sound. Lines 5 and 10 of Masefield's "Cargoes," for example, includes references to "sweet white wine" and "cinnamon." Although the poem refers to these commodities as cargoes, the words themselves also register in our minds as gustatory images because they refer to our sense of taste.

*Tactile images* of touch and texture are not as common because touch is difficult to render except in terms of effects. The speaker of Amy Lowell's "Patterns," for example, uses tactile imagery when imagining a never-to-happen embrace with her fiancé, who, we learn, has been killed on a wartime battlefield in Flanders. Her imagery records the effect of the embrace ("bruised"), whereas her internalized feelings are expressed in metaphors ("aching, melting, unafraid") (lines 51–52):

> And the buttons of his waistcoat bruised my body as he clasped me,
> Aching, melting, unafraid.

Tactile images are not uncommon in love poetry where references to touch and feeling are natural. Usually, however, love poetry deals with yearning and hope rather than sexual fulfillment (as in John Keats's "Bright Star").[1]

### Kinetic and Kinesthetic Imagery Refers to Motion and Activity

References to movement are also images. Images of general motion are **kinetic** (remember that *motion pictures* are called "cinema"; note the closeness of *kine* and *cine*), whereas the term **kinesthetic image** is applied to human or animal movement and effort. Imagery of motion is closely related to visual images, for motion is most often seen. Masefield's "British coaster" in "Cargoes," for example, is a visual image, but when it goes "Butting through the channel," the reference to motion makes it also kinetic. When Thomas Hardy's skeletons sit upright at the beginning of "Channel Firing," the image is kinesthetic, as is the action of Lowell's speaker walking in the garden alone after being informed of her fiancé's death.

The areas from which kinetic and kinesthetic imagery can be derived are varied and unpredictable. Occupations, trades, professions, businesses, recreational activities—all these might furnish images. One poet introduces references from gardening, another from money and banking, another from modern real estate developments, another from the falling of leaves in autumn, another from life in the jungle. The freshness, newness, and surprise of much poetry result from the many and varied areas from which writers draw their images.

# Writing about Imagery

### Raise Questions to Discover Ideas

In preparing to write, you should develop a set of thoughtful notes dealing with issues such as the following:

- What type or types of images prevail in the work? Visual (shapes, colors)? Auditory (sounds)? Olfactory (smells)? Tactile (touch and texture)? Gustatory (taste)? Kinetic or kinesthetic (motion)? Or is the imagery a combination of these?
- To what degree do the images reflect the writer's actual observation or the writer's reading and knowledge of fields such as science or history?
- How well do the images stand out? How vivid are they? How is this vividness achieved?
- Within a group of images—say, visual or auditory—do the images pertain to one location or area rather than another (e.g., natural scenes rather than interiors, snowy scenes rather than grassy ones, loud and harsh sounds rather than quiet and civilized ones)?

---

[1]But see David Lehman, ed. *The Best American Erotic Poems from 1800 to the Present*. New York: Scribner, 2008.

- What explanation is needed for the images? (Images might be derived from the classics or the Bible, the Revolutionary War or World War II, the behaviors of four-footed creatures or birds, etc.)
- What effect do the circumstances described in the work (e.g., conditions of brightness or darkness, warmth or cold, etc.) have upon your responses to the images? What poetic purpose do you think the poet achieves by controlling these responses?
- How well are the images integrated within the poem's argument or development?

Answering questions like these should provide you with a sizable body of ready-made material that you can convert directly to the body of your essay.

## Organize Your Essay about Imagery

*Introduction*　Connect a brief overview of the work to your plan of development, such as that the writer uses images to strengthen ideas about war, character, or love or that the writer relies predominantly on images of sight, sound, and action.

*Body*　You might deal exclusively with one of the following aspects, or, equally likely, you may combine your approaches, as you wish.

1. **Images suggesting ideas and/or moods.** Such an essay should emphasize the effects of the imagery. What ideas or moods are evoked by the images? (The auditory images beginning Owen's "Anthem for Doomed Youth," for example, all point toward a condemnation of war's brutal cruelty.) Do the images promote approval or disapproval? Cheerfulness? Melancholy? Are the images drab, exciting, vivid? How? Why? Are they conducive to humor or surprise? How does the writer achieve these effects? Are the images consistent, or are they ambiguous? (For example, the images in the first two stanzas of Masefield's "Cargoes" indicate approval, but in the third stanza the images unambiguously indicate disapproval.)
2. **The types of images.** Here the emphasis is on the categories of images themselves. Is there a predominance of a particular type of image (e.g., visual or auditory images), or is there a blending? Is there a bunching of types at particular points in the poem or story? If so, why? Is there any shifting as the work develops (as, for example, in Owen's "Anthem for Doomed Youth," where the auditory images first describe loudness and harshness, but later images describe quietness and sorrow)? Are the images appropriate, granting the nature and apparent intent of the work? Do they assist in making the ideas seem convincing? If there seems to be any inappropriateness, what is its effect?
3. **Systems of images.** Here the emphasis should be on the areas from which the images are drawn. This is another way of considering the appropriateness of the imagery. Is there a pattern of similar or consistent images, such as brightness changing to darkness (Katherine Mansfield's story "Miss Brill") or pride in military triumph changing to repentance (Dickinson's "My Triumph Lasted Till the Drums"—see the Illustrative Essay on page 141)? Do all the images adhere consistently to a particular frame of reference, such as a sunlit garden (Lowell's "Patterns"), an extensive recreational forest and garden (Coleridge's "Kubla Khan"), a church graveyard (Hardy's "Channel Firing"), the sea in various stages of light (Masefield's "Cargoes"), or a darkened forest (William Blake's "The Tyger")? What is unusual or unique about the sets of images? What unexpected or new responses do they produce?

*Conclusion*   Your conclusion, in addition to recapitulating your major points, is the place for additional insights. It is not advisable to strike out in new directions here, but you might briefly take up one or more of the ideas that you have not developed in the body. In short, what have you learned from your study of imagery in the work?

## Illustrative Essay

The central idea, thesis sentence, and topic sentences are shaded here to stress the goal of strong organization. As your instructor wishes, you might use this or a similar system in your own essays.

Korpoulus 1

Mia Korpoulus

Professor Rolands

English 202

6 September 2010

Dickinson's Kinesthetic Imagery in "My Triumph Lasted

Till the Drums" (J1227, F1212)

My triumph lasted till the Drums
Had left the Dead alone
And then I dropped my Victory
And chastened stole along
To where the finished Faces                                      5
Conclusion turned on me
And then I hated Glory
And wished myself were They.

What is to be is best descried
When it has also been—                                          10
Could Prospect taste of Retrospect
The Tyrannies of Men
Were Tenderer, diviner
The Transitive toward—
A Bayonet's contrition                                          15
Is nothing to the Dead.

Dickinson's "My Triumph Lasted Till the Drums"—written in          [1]
approximately 1871, six years after the Civil War—deals with the tragic
slowness of human beings to benefit from experience. As applied to

Korpoulus 2

warfare, the lessons of horror, misery, and death always come too late. Militarists may think themselves exempt from the deaths of the battlefield, and so they go to war. Ironically, many such people become contrite as a result of their experience, but they are too late, always, for they do not apply their conversions in time to avoid the next battles. Such ideas underlie the mainly kinesthetic imagery of this profound and sensitive poem.° The images are focused on a fabric of past actions, leading to speculation about the future.*

[2]     Beginning the poem's first stanza is a combined kinesthetic and auditory image of a past military triumph, characterized by drum rolls and other obvious fanfare—the pomp of military victory. The speaker created by Dickinson for this stanza, the "I," is a person of power, a military leader who talks of the triumph celebrated by the drums. The image continues with the drummers going away, leaving "the Dead alone" on the field (line 2). The speaker says that he then faced his own personal reactions and that he became "chastened" (line 4) and regretful when seeing the "finished Faces" of the fallen dead.

[3]     Images suggesting the speaker's shame complete this first stanza. The speaker states that he "stole along," in quiet self-reproach, virtually hiding himself as he left the scene of triumph. Emphasizing his reactions, he continues his brief narrative, which becomes increasingly negative. A vital image of motion is that he drops "[his] Victory" once the Dead have been "left alone." Not only does he regret the victory of battle, but the "finished Faces" of the Dead make him hate whatever "Glory" accrued from victory. His regret goes so far as to make him wish to become one of those who are dead. In eight lines the quietness of the "finished Faces" has driven all satisfaction and exhilaration from the speaker's consciousness. His contrition is complete.

[4]     Stanza 2 marks not only a change in tense but also a separate and new speaker more in keeping with Dickinson's own voice. The kinesthetic imagery in this stanza points to the need for the past to change the future for the better. The speaker, deeply concerned with

---

°Central idea.
*Thesis sentence.

Korpoulus 3

preventing future death, states that "What is to be is best descried/When it has also been" (lines 9 and 10). Past actions, in other words, must be used to transform future goals and circumstances, for if what is to become is to be changed fully and completely, it can only undergo that change based on past experience.

Dickinson's speaker restates this idea again in line 11: "Could Prospect taste of Retrospect." The gustatory image of "taste" is important here, for it suggests that experience should be thoroughgoing if it is to influence the future. As an action, tasting implies an active alteration of past errors of conflict, a systematic change that alone could act as a brake on future military adventurism. To go a little further with the image of taste, the speaker implies that experience would perhaps not eliminate "The Tyrannies of Men" but would make such tyrannies more humane. The speaker here is not necessarily recommending any new type of government but instead offers the possibility that even a tyranny could become "Tenderer, diviner" (line 13) if it could only allow "Prospect [to] taste of Retrospect." Dickinson's concluding two lines constitute a blunt commentary on military might by introducing the active image of a bayonet, personified as though it is the soldier who holds it, which develops a contrite spirit too late to do anything to save the dead victims of war.

[5]

Because stanza 1 is clearly voiced by a speaker who renounces war and wartime death and because stanza 2 shifts to a totally different speaker who makes more general pronouncements, the poem might seem disunified. Actually, however, stanza 2 is a critique of stanza 1, and through it, the poem is unified. Stanza 2 deals with the issue that the moral transformation of military persons, such as the speaker of the first stanza, must happen not after but before the bayonet is ever used. As things are at present, however, if such moral or religious contrition ever occurs, it always does so after the fact. The image of repentance in lines 15 and 16, "A Bayonet's contrition/Is nothing to the Dead," creates a powerful climax to the poem and provides a strong appeal for altering personal and collective military action.

[6]

Korpoulus 4

Work Cited

Dickinson, Emily. "My Triumph Lasted Till the Drums." *Writing About Literature.* By Edgar V. Roberts. 12th ed. New York: Pearson, 2010. 141. Print.

## Commentary on the Essay

This essay treats the mainly kinesthetic military images that Dickinson introduces in "My Triumph Lasted Till the Drums." It thus is illustrative of the third approach (p. 140). The aim of the discussion is to show how the poem and the speaker change attitudes about military glory. Thus, the opening image of triumphal pomp is followed quickly by the speaker's confessing to actions showing his overwhelming regret because of the "finished Faces" of those who have died in battle.

The introductory paragraph (1) provides a brief general discussion of the poem, followed by the central idea and the thesis sentence. Paragraphs 2 and 3 deal with images that develop to reveal the transformation of the speaker of the first half of the poem. In paragraphs 4 and 5, the change in the nature of the poem is discussed, stressing how the second half of the poem, with a different speaker, is in effect a critique of the first half. A different kind of image, that of taste (a gustatory image), is discussed in paragraph 5 because of how Dickinson stresses the deeply basic need for changed attitudes about military might.

Paragraph 6, the last in the essay, points out that the second speaker unifies the poem. This paragraph also reiterates the idea that the poem is unified by the speaker's concluding image of the "Bayonet's contrition."

### Writing Topics about Imagery

1. Compare the images of home in Owen's "Anthem for Doomed Youth" (p. 377) and Kate Chopin's "The Story of an Hour" (p. 326) or Guy de Maupassant's "The Necklace" (p. 5). Describe the differing effects of the images. How are the images used? How effectively do these images aid in the development of the principal actions described in each poem?
2. On the basis of the poems in Appendix C by Matthew Arnold, Blake, Coleridge, Robert Frost, and Irving Layton, write an essay discussing the poetic use of images drawn from the natural world. What sorts of references do the poets make? What attitudes do they express about the details they select? What is the relationship between the images and religious views? What judgments about God and nature do the poets show by their images?
3. Write an essay considering the imagery in Hardy's "Channel Firing," Shakespeare's "Sonnet 73: That Time of Year Thou Mayst in Me Behold" (Chapter 6, p. 105), or

Blake's "The Tyger." As you develop your thoughts, be sure to consider the dramatic function of the images in the poem you choose and to account for the impressions and ideas that they create. You may also wish to introduce references to images from other poems that are relevant at various parts of your essay.

4. Write a short poem describing one of the following:
   - Athletes who have just completed an exhausting run
   - Children getting out of school for the day
   - The antics of your dog, cat, horse, llama, or other pet
   - A cat that always sits down on your schoolwork and then purrs when you try to shoo him/her off
   - A particularly good meal you had recently
   - The best concert that you ever attended
   - Driving to work/school on a cloudy/rainy/snowy/sunny day

   Then write an analysis of the images you selected for your poem and explain your choices. What details stand out in your mind? What do you recall best—sight, smell, sound, action? What is the relationship between your images and the ideas you attempt to express in your poem?

5. Write an essay considering the graphic or pictorial nature of the imagery in Coleridge's "Kubla Khan" and Keats's "On First Looking into Chapman's Homer" (Chapter 10 p. 148), along with other works that you may wish to discuss. What similarities and differences do you find in subject matter, treatment, arrangement, and general ideas? On the basis of your comparison, what relationships do you perceive between sight and literary imagery?

6. Use the retrieval system (computer or card catalog) in your library to research the topic of imagery in Shakespeare (see *Shakespeare: imagery*; *Shakespeare: style and imagery*). You might also determine what you can find online. How many titles do you discover? Over how many years have these works been published? Take out one of the works and write a brief report on any of the chapters. What topics are discussed? What types of imagery are introduced? What relationship does the author make between imagery and content?

# Chapter 10

# Writing about Metaphor and Simile: A Source of Depth and Range in Literature

Figures of speech, metaphorical language, figurative language, figurative devices, and rhetorical figures are terms describing organized patterns of comparison that deepen, broaden, extend, illuminate, and emphasize meaning. First and foremost, the use of figures of speech is a major characteristic by which great literature provides us with fresh and original ways of thinking, feeling, and understanding. Although metaphorical language is sometimes called "ornate," as though it were somehow inessential and unnecessarily decorative, it is not uncommon in conversational speech, and it is vitally important in literary thought and expression.

Unlike the writing of the social and "hard" sciences, imaginative literature does not purport to offer a direct correspondence of words and things. Yes, literature often presents specific and accurate descriptions and explanations, but it also moves in areas of implication and suggestiveness through the use of metaphorical language, which enables writers to amplify their ideas while still employing a relatively small number of words. Such language is therefore a sine qua non in imaginative literature, particularly poetry, where it compresses thought, deepens understanding, and shapes response.

There are many metaphorical figures, some of which are *paradox, anaphora, apostrophe, personification, synecdoche* and *metonymy, pun* (or *paronomasia*), *synesthesia, overstatement,* and *understatement*. All these figures are modes of comparison, and they may be expressed in single words, phrases, clauses, or entire structures. The two most important and easily recognized figures of speech, with which we will be concerned here, are metaphors and similes.

## Metaphors and Similes: The Major Figures of Speech

### *A Metaphor Shows That Something Unknown Can Be Understood Because It Is Identical to Something Known*

A **metaphor** (a "carrying out [*phor*] of change [*meta*]") *equates* known objects or actions with something that is unknown or to be explained (e.g., "Your words are *music* to my ears," "You are the *sunshine* of my life," "My life is *a squirrel cage*"). The equation of the metaphor not only explains and illuminates the thing—let us choose John

Keats's star in the poem "Bright Star"—but also offers distinctive and original ways of seeing it, applying it, and thinking about it. Thus, Keats draws his metaphor of the star because of its constancy in the heavens, for in human history the star has kept its identical location from century to century. Keats applies this quality to his speaker's wish for love that is unchanging and permanent—both a natural and an appropriate equation of celestial star and human desire.

Metaphors are inseparable from language. In a heavy storm, for example, trees may be said to *bow* constantly as the wind blows against them. *Bow* is a metaphor because the word commonly refers to performers bending forward to acknowledge the applause of an audience and to indicate their gratitude for the audience's approval. The metaphor therefore asks us to equate our knowledge of theater life (something known) to a weather occurrence (something to be explained). A comparable reference to theater life creates one of the best-known metaphors to appear in Shakespeare's plays: "All the world's a stage,/And all the men and women merely players." Here, Shakespeare's character Jacques (*JAY-queez*) from Act 2, scene 7 of *As You Like It,* equates human life directly with stage life. In other words, the things said and done by stage actors are also said and done by living people in real life. It is important to recognize that Shakespeare's metaphor does not state that the world is *like* a stage but that it literally *is* a stage.

### *A Simile Shows That Something Unknown Can Be Understood Because It Is Similar to Something Known*

A **simile** (a "showing of likeness or resemblance") illustrates the *similarity* or *comparability* of the known to something unknown or to be explained. Whereas a metaphor merges identities, a simile focuses on resemblances (e.g., "Your words are *like music* to me," "You are *like sunshine* in my life," "I feel *like a squirrel in a cage*"). Similes are distinguishable from metaphors because they are introduced by *like* with nouns and *as* (also *as if* and *as though*) with clauses. If Keats had written that his speaker's desire for steadfastness is *like* the bright star, his comparison would have been a simile.

Let us consider one of the best-known similes in poetry, from "A Valediction: Forbidding Mourning" by the seventeenth-century poet John Donne. This is a dramatic poem spoken by a lover about to go on a trip. His loved one is presumably sorrowful, and he attempts to console her by claiming that even when he is gone, he will remain with her in spirit. The following stanza contains a famous simile embodying this idea.

> Our two souls therefore, which are one,
>     Though I must go, endure not yet
> A breach,° but an expansion
>     Like gold to airy thinness beat.

The simile compares the souls of the speaker and his loved one to gold, a metal both valuable and malleable. By the simile, the speaker asserts that the impending departure

---

°*breach*: break, separation.

will not be a separation but rather a thinning out so that the relationship of the lovers will remain constant and rich even as the distance between them increases. Because the comparison is introduced by "Like," the emphasis of the figurative language is on the *similarity* of the lovers' love to gold (which is always gold even when it is thinned out by the goldsmith's hammer), not on the *identification* of the two.

## Characteristics of Metaphors and Similes

Metaphors and similes are based in imagery, the means by which literature is made graphic and vivid (see Chapter 9). That is, by using words that convey images, the writer prompts us to recall memories (images) of sights, sounds, tastes, smells, sensations, and motions. Metaphors and similes go beyond literal imagery to introduce perceptions and comparisons that can be unusual, unpredictable, and surprising, as in Donne's simile comparing the lovers' relationship to gold. The comparison emphasizes the bond between the two lovers; the reference to gold shows how valuable the bond is; the unusual and original comparison is a major element that makes the poem striking and memorable.

To see metaphorical language in further operation, let us take a commonly described condition—happiness. In everyday speech, we might use the sentence "She was happy" to state that a particular character was experiencing joy and excitement. The sentence is of course accurate, but it is not interesting. A more vivid way of saying the same thing is to use an image of action, such as "She jumped for joy." But another and better way of communicating joy is the following simile: "She felt as if she had just won the lottery." Because readers easily understand the disbelief, excitement, exhilaration, and delight that such an event would bring, they also understand—and feel—the character's happiness. It is the *simile* that evokes this perception and enables each reader to personalize the experience, for no simple description could help a reader comprehend the same degree of emotion.

As a parallel poetic example, let us look at Keats's famous sonnet "On First Looking into Chapman's Homer," which Keats wrote soon after reading Homer's great epics *The Iliad* and *The Odyssey* in the translations by the Renaissance poet George Chapman. Keats, one of the greatest of all poets himself, describes his enthusiasm about Chapman's successful and exciting work.

John Keats (1795–1821)

*On First Looking into Chapman's Homer°* (1816)

Much have I travell'd in the realms of gold,*
And many goodly states and kingdoms seen:
Round many western islands† have I been

---

°"On First Looking into Chapman's Homer": George Chapman (c. 1560–1634) published his translations of Homer's *The Iliad* in 1612 and *The Odyssey* in 1614–1615.
*realms of gold*: the world of great art.   †*islands*: ancient literature.

> Which bards in fealty to Apollo°° hold.
> Oft of one wide expanse** had I been told
>     That deep-brow'd Homer ruled as his demesne;†† 5
>     Yet did I never breathe its pure serene°°°
> Till I heard Chapman speak out loud and bold:
> Then felt I like some watcher of the skies
>     When a new planet swims into his ken;***
> Or like stout Cortez††† when with eagle eyes 10
>     He star'd at the Pacific—and all his men
> Look'd at each other with a wild surmise°°°°—
>     Silent, upon a peak in Darien.

As a first step in understanding the power of metaphorical language, we can briefly paraphrase the sonnet's content.

> I have enjoyed much art and read much poetry, and I have been told that Homer is the best writer of all. However, I did not appreciate his works until I first read them in Chapman's loud and bold translation. This discovery was exciting and awe-inspiring.

If all Keats had written had been a paragraph like this one, we would pay little attention to it because it is bland and gives us no sense of the exploration and wonder that the poem itself provides for us. On the other hand, the poem itself presents us with two indelibly memorable similes ("like some watcher of the skies" and "like stout Cortez"), which stand out and demand a special effort of imagination. To appreciate these similes fully, we need to imagine what it would be like to be an astronomer as he or she discovers a previously unknown planet and what it would have been like to be one of the first European explorers to see the Pacific Ocean. As we imagine ourselves in these roles, we get a sense of the amazement, excitement, exhilaration, and joy that would accompany such discoveries. With that experience comes the realization that the world—the universe—is far bigger and more astonishing than we had ever dreamed.

In this way, metaphorical language makes strong demands on our creative imaginations. It bears repeating that as we develop our own mental pictures under the stimulation of metaphors and similes, we also develop appropriately associated attitudes and feelings. Let us consider once more Keats's metaphor "realms of gold," which invites us both to imagine brilliant and shining kingdoms and also to join Keats in valuing and loving not just poetry but all literature. The metaphorical "realms of gold" acts upon our minds, liberating our imaginations, directing our understanding, and evoking our feelings. In such a way, reading and responding to the works of writers like Keats produces both mental and emotional experiences that were previously hidden to us. Writers constantly give us something new, widening our comprehension, increasing our knowledge, and deepening our imagination.

---

°°*bards . . . Apollo*: writers who are sworn subjects of Apollo, the Greek god of light, music, poetry, prophecy, and the sun.    **expanse*: epic poetry.    ††*demesne*: realm, estate.    °°°*serene*: a clear expanse of air; also grandeur, clarity; rulers were also called "serene majesty."    ****ken*: range of vision.    †††*Cortez*: Hernando Cortés (1485–1547), a Spanish general and the conqueror of Mexico. Keats confuses him with Vasco de Balboa (c. 1475–1519), the first European to see the Pacific Ocean (in 1510) from Darien, an early name for the Isthmus of Panama.    °°°°*surmise*: conjecture, supposition.

---

### VEHICLE AND TENOR

To describe the relationship between a writer's ideas and the metaphors and similes chosen to objectify them, two useful terms have been coined by I. A. Richards (in *The Philosophy of Rhetoric*, 1929). First is the **vehicle**, or the specific words of the metaphor or simile. Second is the **tenor**, which is the totality of ideas and attitudes of not only the literary speaker but also the author. For example, the tenor of Donne's simile in "A Valediction: Forbidding Mourning" is the inseparable love and unbreakable connection of the two lovers; the vehicle is the hammering of gold "to airy thinness." Similarly, the tenor of the similes in the sestet of Keats's sonnet is awe and wonder; the vehicle is the description of astronomical and geographical discovery.

---

## Writing about Metaphors and Similes

Begin by determining the use, line by line, of metaphors or similes. Obviously, similes are the easiest figures to recognize because they introduce comparisons with *like* or *as*. Metaphors can be recognized because the topics are discussed not as themselves but as other topics. If the poems speak of falling leaves or law courts but the subjects are memory or increasing age, you are looking at metaphors.

### *Raise Questions to Discover Ideas*

- What metaphors and/or similes does the work contain? Where do they occur? Under what circumstances? How extensive are they?
- How do you recognize them? Are they signaled by a single word or phrase, such as "desert places" in Robert Frost's "Desert Places" (p. 369), or are they more extensively detailed, as in Shakespeare's "Sonnet 30: When to the Sessions of Sweet Silent Thought" (p. 152)?
- How vivid are the metaphors and similes? How obvious? How unusual? What kind of effort is needed to understand them in context?
- Structurally, how are the metaphors and similes developed? How do they rise out of the situation envisioned in the work? To what degree are they integrated into the work's development of ideas? How do they relate to other aspects of the work?
- Is one type of figure used in a particular section while another type predominates in another section? Why?
- If you have discovered a number of metaphors, what relationships can you find among them, such as the judicial and financial connections in Shakespeare's "When to the Sessions of Sweet Silent Thought" (p. 152)?
- How do the metaphors or similes broaden, deepen, or otherwise assist in making the ideas in the poem forceful?
- In general, how appropriate and meaningful is the metaphorical language in the poem? What effect does this language have on the poem's tone and on your understanding and appreciation of the poem?

### Organize Your Essay about Metaphors and Similes

*Introduction*   In your introduction, relate the quality of the figures of speech to the general nature of the work. Thus, metaphors and similes of suffering might be appropriate to a religious, redemptive work, while those of sunshine and cheer might be right for a romantic one. If there is any discrepancy between the metaphorical language and the topic, you could consider that contrast as a possible central idea, for it would clearly indicate the writer's ironic perspective. Suppose that the topic of the poem is love, but the figures put you in mind of darkness and cold. What would the writer be saying about the quality of love? You should also try to justify any claims that you make about the figures. For example, the major metaphor of Amy Lowell's "Patterns" is that people are virtually compelled to live their lives controlled by many habits, restrictions, customs, expectations, duties, roles, and services—"patterns." How is this metaphor to be taken? As an outcry for personal freedom? As an expression of rage against restrictions? As a suggestion that customs that restrict may also be customs that provide solace? How do you explain your answer or answers? Your introduction is the place to establish ideas and justifications of this sort.

*Body*   The following approaches for discussing rhetorical figures are not mutually exclusive, and you may combine them as you wish. Most likely, your essay will bring in most of the following classifications.

1. **Interpret the meaning and effect of the metaphorical language.** Here you explain how the metaphors and/or similes enable you to make an interpretation. In lines 17–19 of "Kubla Khan," for example (p. 368), Samuel Taylor Coleridge introduces the following simile:

   > And from this chasm, with ceaseless turmoil seething,
   > As if this earth in fast thick pants were breathing,
   > A mighty fountain momently was forced:

   Coleridge's simile of "fast thick pants" almost literally animates the earth as a moving, working power, panting as it forces the fountain out of the chasm. The idea is that the phenomena of nature are not dead but vigorously alive. A directly explanatory approach, such as this, requires that metaphors and similes be expanded and interpreted, including the explanation of necessary references and allusions.

2. **Analyze the frames of reference and their appropriateness to the subject matter.** Here you classify and locate the sources and types of references and determine the appropriateness of these to the poem's subject matter. Ask questions similar to these: Does the writer refer extensively to nature, science, warfare, politics, business, reading (e.g., Shakespeare's metaphor equating personal reverie with courtroom proceedings in Sonnet 30)? Does the metaphor seem appropriate? How? Why?

3. **Focus on the interests and sensibilities of the poet.** In a way, this approach is like strategy 2, but the emphasis here is on what the selectivity of the writer might show about his or her vision and interests. You might begin by listing the figures in the work and then determining the sources. But then you should raise questions like the following: Does the writer use figures derived from one sense rather than another (i.e., sight, hearing, taste, smell, touch)? Does he or she record color, brightness, shadow, shape, depth, height,

number, size, slowness, speed, emptiness, fullness, richness, drabness? Has the writer re-lied on the associations of figures of sense? Do metaphors and similes referring to green plants and trees, to red roses, or to rich fabrics, for example, suggest that life is full and beautiful, or do references to touch suggest amorous warmth? This approach is designed to help you draw conclusions about the author's taste or sensibility.

4. **Examine the relationship of one figure to the other figures and ideas of the work.** The assumption of this approach is that each literary work is unified and organically whole so that each part is closely related and inseparable from everything else. Usu-ally, it is best to pick a figure that occurs at the beginning of the work and then deter-mine how this figure influences your perception of the remainder. Your aim is to consider the relationship of part to parts and part to whole. The beginning of Frost's poem "Desert Places," for example, describes "snow falling and night falling." What is the effect of this opening on the poem's metaphor of human "desert places"? To help you with questions like this, you might substitute a totally different detail such as, for this poem, the rising sun on a beautiful day or playing with a kitten, rather than the onset of cold and night. Such suppositions, which would clearly be out of place, may help you understand and then explain the poet's figures of speech.

*Conclusion*   In your conclusion, summarize your main points, describe your general impressions, try to describe the impact of the figures, indicate your personal respons-es, or show what might further be done along the lines you have been developing. If you know other works by the same writer or other works by other writers who use comparable or contrasting figures, you might explain the relationship of the other work or works to your present analysis.

## Illustrative Essay

The central idea, thesis sentence, and topic sentences are shaded here to stress the goal of strong organization. As your instructor wishes, you might use this or a similar system in your own essays.

Capra 1

Robert Capra

Professor Estevez

English 201

4 September 2010

Shakespeare's Metaphors in "Sonnet 30: When
to the Sessions of Sweet Silent Thought"

When to the sessions° of sweet silent thought
I summon* up remembrance of things past,
I sigh the lack of many a thing I sought,

---

°*sessions*: courtroom sessions.   *_summon:_ give notice to appear in court.

Capra 2

And with old woes new wail my dear time's waste:
Then can I drown an eye, unused to flow,                                5
For precious friends hid in death's dateless° night,
And weep afresh love's long since canceled woe,
And moan th'expense of many a vanished sight.
Then can I grieve at grievances foregone,
And heavily* from woe to woe tell† o'er                                 10
The sad account of fore-bemoanéd moan,
Which I new pay,°° as if not paid before.
    But if the while I think on thee, dear friend,
    All losses are restored, and sorrows end.

In this sonnet, Shakespeare stresses the sadness of remembering [1]
past regrets and misfortunes. He says, however, through his speaker, that
a person with such heavyheartedness may be cheered by present
thoughts about a good friend. His metaphors present original and unique
ways of seeing personal life in this perspective.** He creates metaphors
drawn from the public and business world of law courts, money and
value, and banking and money handling.††

    In the first quatrain, Shakespeare presents a metaphor of law and the [2]
courtroom to show that memories of past experience are constantly
present and influential over a person's present life. Like a judge issuing a
subpoena to compel defendants to appear in court, Shakespeare's speaker
"summon[s]" his memory of "things past" to stand trial before him. In
the context of the sonnet, this courtroom metaphor suggests that people
are their own judges and that their ideals and morals are actual laws by
which they measure themselves. The speaker finds himself guilty of
wasting his time in the past. Removing himself, however, from the strict
punishment that a real judge might require, he does not condemn himself
for his "dear time's waste" but instead laments it (line 4). The metaphor is
thus used to indicate that a person's consciousness is made up just as
much of self-doubt and reproach as of more positive qualities.

    By introducing a closely related metaphor of money and value in [3]
the second quatrain, Shakespeare implies that living is a lifelong process
of continued investment. According to this metaphor, living requires the

---

°*dateless:* endless, eternal.   *\**heavily*: sadly.   †*tell:* count or tally.   °°*pay:* a double-jeopardy payment.
**Central idea.
††Thesis sentence.

constant spending of emotions and commitment to others. In other words, friendship and love need regular effort to keep them alive. When friends invariably move away and loved ones die, however, it is as though the emotional payments continue in memory though not in actuality. The absent people were prized in life, and they continue to be prized even though they are dead. In addition, the speaker's dead friends are "precious" because of the time and love he gave to them, and his remembered "sight" of those who have "vanished" causes him to "moan" because of his great "expense" and continued emotional expenditure for them (line 8).

[4]      Like the money and value metaphor, the metaphor of banking and money handling of the third quatrain emphasizes that memory is a bank in which life's experiences are deposited. All the emotions stimulated by remembered experience are present there, and they may be withdrawn and experienced again in moments of "sweet silent thought," just as a depositor may withdraw money. Interestingly, in the three quatrains, the speaker recalls somber memories of loss rather than things that were joyful. Thus, he counts the melancholy aspect of his experience—his woe—just as a merchant or banker counts money: "And heavily from woe to woe tell o'er" (line 10). Because strong emotions still accompany his memories of past mistakes, the metaphor extends to borrowing and the payment of interest. The speaker goes on to say that he pays again with "new" woe the accounts that he had already paid with old woe. In such a way, the speaker implies, the recollection of his memories puts him in double emotional jeopardy. The metaphor implies that the past is so much a part of the present that a person never stops feeling pain and regret.

[5]      The courtroom, money-and-value, and money-handling metaphors combine in the sonnet's concluding couplet to show how a happy present life may overcome past regrets. The "dear friend" being addressed in these lines has the resources (financial) to settle all the emotional judgments that the speaker as a self-judge has made against himself (legal). It is as though the friend is a rich patron who rescues him from emotional bankruptcy (legal and financial) and the doom resulting from a sentence of emotional misery and depression (legal).

Capra 4

In these metaphors, therefore, Shakespeare's references are drawn [6]
from ordinary public and financial actions, but his use of them is creative
and entirely new, and it will always be new. In particular, the idea of line 8
("And moan th'expense of many a vanished sight") stresses that people, as
a necessary part of their lives, spend much emotional energy on others.
Without such personal investment, one cannot have precious friends and
loved ones. In keeping with this metaphor of money and investment, one
could measure life not in months or years but in the spending of emotion
and involvement in personal relationship with others. By inviting readers to
explore his metaphors of love and friendship, Shakespeare has added
original and powerful insights into the value of life.

Capra 5

Work Cited

Shakespeare, William. "Sonnet 30: When to the Sessions of Sweet Silent
Thought." *Writing About Literature.* By Edgar V. Roberts. 12th ed.
New York: Pearson, 2010. 152. Print.

## Commentary on the Essay

This essay treats the three classes of metaphors that Shakespeare introduces in Sonnet 30. It thus illustrates strategy 2 (p. 151). But the aim of the discussion is not to explore the extent and nature of the comparison between the metaphors and the personal situations described in the sonnet. Instead, the goal is to explain how the metaphors develop Shakespeare's meaning. This essay therefore also illustrates strategy 1 (p. 151).

In addition to presenting a brief description of the sonnet, the introduction (paragraph 1) brings out the central idea and the thesis sentence. Paragraph 2 deals with the meaning of Shakespeare's law and courtroom metaphor. His money metaphor is explained in paragraph 3. Paragraph 4 considers the banking or money-handling metaphor. Paragraph 5 shows how Shakespeare's concluding couplet, by emphasizing the reference to the reader or listener, focuses the three strands of metaphor derived from the past. The essay's conclusion comments generally on the creativity of Shakespeare's metaphors, and it also amplifies the way in which the money metaphor leads toward an increased understanding of life.

Throughout the essay, transitions are brought about by the linking words in the topic sentences. In paragraph 3, for example, the words "closely related" and "in the second quatrain" move the reader from paragraph 2 to the new content. In paragraph 4, the words effecting the transition are "Like the money-and-value metaphor" and "of the third quatrain." The opening sentence of paragraph 5 refers collectively to the subjects of paragraphs 2, 3, and 4, thereby concentrating them on the new topic of paragraph 5.

### Writing Topics about Metaphors and Similes

1. Consider some of the metaphors and similes in the works (poems, stories, plays) included in Appendix C and elsewhere in the book. Write an essay that deals with the following questions. How effective are the figures you select? What insights do the figures provide within the contexts of their respective poems? How appropriate are they? Might they be expanded more fully, and if they were, what would be the effect? You might choose any of the following topics, or any others, depending on your wishes:

   - The "darkling plain" simile in Matthew Arnold's "Dover Beach"
   - The metaphor of autumn in Shakespeare's "That Time of Year Thou Mayst in Me Behold."
   - The metaphor of the quilting knot in Susan Glaspell's *Trifles*
   - The metaphorical use of the black box in Shirley Jackson's "The Lottery"
   - The metaphor of the shabby fur piece in Katherine Mansfield's "Miss Brill"
   - The metaphor in William Blake's "The Tyger"
   - The metaphor of the Rhine River in Irving Layton's "Rhine Boat Trip"
   - Similes in Wilfred Owen's "Anthem for Doomed Youth" or Coleridge's "Kubla Khan"
   - The metaphor of "red war" in Thomas Hardy's "Channel Firing"
   - The use of similes in Langston Hughes's "Negro"
   - The horse Toby as a metaphor in Anton Chekhov's *The Bear*

2. Write a poem in which you create a governing metaphor or simile. An example might be: My girlfriend/boyfriend is like (a) an opening flower, (b) a difficult book, (c) an insoluble mathematical problem, (d) a bill that cannot be paid, (e) a slow-moving chess game. Another example: Teaching a person how to do a particular job is like (a) shoveling heavy snow, (b) climbing a mountain during a landslide, (c) having someone force you underwater when you're gasping for breath. When you finish, describe the relationship between your comparison and the development and structure of your poem.

3. In your library's reference section, find the third edition of J. A. Cuddon's *A Dictionary of Literary Terms and Literary Theory* (1991) or some other dictionary of literary terms that you find on the shelves. Study the entries for *metaphor* and *simile* and write a brief report on these sections.

# Chapter 11

# Writing about Symbolism and Allegory: Keys to Extended Meaning

Symbolism and allegory, like metaphors and similes (see Chapter 10), are modes that expand meaning. They are literary devices developed from the connections that real-life people make between their own existence and particular objects, places, or occurrences, through experience, reading, and memory. By highlighting details as symbols and stories or parts of stories as allegories, writers expand their meaning while keeping their works within reasonable lengths. As examples, let us realize that a bereaved mother may associate personal grief with household boxes and containers. A young man may, upon seeing the North Star, dedicate himself to constant love. A beloved animal may cause a widow to remember her love for her departed husband. A distant view of a vanishing light may cause a man to think that traditional ideas are being lost. The significance of details like these can be meaningful not only at the time they occur but also throughout life. It is as though the memory of such things alone can be the same as pages of explanation and analysis, for merely bringing them to mind or speaking about them unlocks their meanings, implications, and consequences. They become symbols, as they in fact are in Shelly Wagner's "The Boxes," John Keats's "Bright Star," Anton Chekhov's *The Bear*, and Matthew Arnold's "Dover Beach."

## Symbolism and Meaning

The words *symbol* and *symbolism* are derived from the Greek word meaning "to throw together" (*syn*, "together," and *ballein*, "to throw"). A symbol creates a direct meaningful equation between (1) a specific object, scene, character, or action and (2) ideas, values, persons, or ways of life. In effect, a **symbol** is a *substitute* for the elements being signified, much as the flag stands for the ideals of our nation. For this reason, symbolism goes beyond the close referral of word to thing; it is more like a window through which one can glimpse the extensive world outside. **Symbolism** is a shorthand way of referring to extensive ideas or attitudes that otherwise would bog down a story, divert the attention of the audience in a theater, or unreasonably lengthen a poem.

The use of symbols is a way of moving outward, a means of extending and crystallizing information and ideas. For example, at the time of William Blake (1757–1827), the word *tiger* meant both a large, wild cat and also the specific animal we know today as a tiger. The word's connotation therefore links it with wildness and predation. As a symbol in "The Tyger" (p. 365), however, Blake uses the animal as a stand-in for what he considers cosmic negativism—the savage, wild forces that undermine the progress of civilization. Thus, the tiger as a symbol is more meaningful than either the denotation or the connotation of the word would indicate.

When we first see a symbol in literature, it may seem to carry no more weight than its surface or obvious meaning. It can be a description of a character, an object, a place, an action, or a situation, and it may function normally and usefully in this capacity. What makes a symbol symbolic, however, is its capacity to signify additional levels of meaning—major ideas, simple or complex emotions, or philosophical or religious qualities or values. There are two types of symbols—cultural and contextual.

### Cultural Symbols Are Derived from Our Cultural and Historical Heritage

Many symbols are *generally* or *universally* recognized and are therefore **cultural** (also called **universal**). They embody ideas and emotions that writers and readers share as heirs of the same historical and cultural tradition. When using cultural symbols, a writer assumes that readers already know what the symbols represent. An example is the character Sisyphus of ancient Greek myth. As a punishment for trying to overcome death not just once but twice, Sisyphus is doomed by the underworld gods to roll a large boulder up a high hill forever. Just as he gets the boulder to the top, it rolls down, and then he is fated to roll it up again—and again—and again—because the boulder always rolls back. The plight of Sisyphus has been interpreted as a symbol of the human condition: Despite constant struggle, a person rarely if ever completes anything. Work must always be done over and over from day to day and from generation to generation, and the same problems plague humanity throughout all time. Because of such fruitless effort, life seems to have little or no meaning. Nevertheless, there is hope: People who confront their tasks, as Sisyphus does, stay involved and active, and their tasks make their lives meaningful. A writer referring to Sisyphus would expect us to understand that this ancient mythological figure symbolizes these conditions.

Similarly, ordinary water, because living creatures cannot live without it, is recognized as a symbol of life. It has this meaning in the ceremony of baptism, and it conveys this meaning and dimension in a variety of literary contexts. Thus, a spouting fountain might symbolize optimism (as upwelling, bubbling life), and a stagnant pool might symbolize the pollution and diminution of life. Water is also a universal symbol of sexuality, and its condition or state can symbolize various romantic relationships. For instance, stories in which lovers meet near a turbulent stream, a roaring waterfall, a mud puddle, a beach with high breakers, a stormy sea, a calm lake, or a wide and gently flowing river symbolically represent love relationships that range from uncertainty to serenity.

### Contextual Symbols Are Symbolic Only in Individual Works

Objects and descriptions that are not universal symbols can be symbols *only if they are made so within individual works.* These are **contextual symbols,** also sometimes called **private**, or **authorial**, **symbols**. Unlike cultural symbols, contextual symbols derive their meanings from the context and circumstances of individual works. As an example, the "shady seat" mentioned in Amy Lowell's "Patterns" (line 86) takes on powerful symbolic value, for we learn that it was where the speaker and her fiancé had planned, before he was sent off to war, to make love in the open air. As a symbol, the shady seat suggests a wished-for liberation from confining and stultifying cultural expectations and for a total union of love and a desire for personal freedom. A symbolic object in a story is the never-seen cask of Amontillado wine in Edgar Allan Poe's "The Cask of Amontillado." It is the promise of trying out the wine that enables Montresor to lure Fortunato into the subterranean wine cellar and is therefore symbolic of Montresor's deceit and lurid ruthlessness.

Like Lowell's shady seat, Poe's invisible wine is a major contextual symbol. But there is not necessarily any carryover from one work to the next. In other works, a shady seat and case of wine are not symbolic unless the authors who include them deliberately give them symbolic meaning. Further, if such objects actually are introduced as symbols, they can be given meanings that are different from those in the works by Lowell and Poe.

### Determine What Is Symbolic (and Not Symbolic)

In determining whether a particular object, action, or character is a symbol, you need to judge the importance that the author gives to it. If the element is prominent and also maintains a consistency of meaning, you can justify interpreting it as a symbol. For example, the jug of porter (beer) carried by Jackie's grandmother in Frank O'Connor's story "First Confession" is one of the things that symbolizes for Jackie the grandmother's peasantlike and boorish habits. The porter is symbolic, however, only within the story. In another context, a reference to porter would not carry the symbolic meaning with which Jackie invests it in "First Confession." Comparably, at the beginning of Wagner's "The Boxes," the speaker refers to "boxes in the house," including footlockers, hampers, and a trunk. Readers will note that such large containers could easily conceal a small boy. At the story's end, however, the speaker states that she still visits the cemetery where her son is buried. The box she mentions at the end is thus a coffin, and for this reason the "Boxes" of the poem's title may be construed as a contextual symbol of death.

## Allegory

An **allegory** is like a symbol because it transfers and broadens meaning. The term is derived from the Greek word *allegorein*, which means "to say something beyond what is commonly understood" (from *allos*, "other" and *agoreuein*, "to speak in public"). Allegory, however, is more sustained than symbolism. An allegory is to a symbol as a motion picture is to a still picture. In form, an allegory is a complete and self-sufficient narrative, but it also signifies another series of conditions or events. Although some stories are allegories from beginning to end, many stories that are not allegories can nevertheless contain brief sections or episodes that are *allegorical*. Allegories are often concerned with morality and especially with religion, but we may also find political and social allegories. To the degree that literary works are true not only because of the lives of their main characters but also because of life generally, one might maintain that much literature may be considered allegorical even though the authors did not plan their works as allegories.

## Understand the Applications and Meaning of Allegory

Allegories and the allegorical method are more than literary exercises. Without question, readers and listeners learn and memorize stories and tales more easily than moral lessons, and therefore allegory is a favorite method of teaching morality. In addition, thought and expression have not always been free and safe. The threat of censorship and the danger of political or economic reprisal have often caused authors to express their views indirectly in the form of allegory rather than to name names and write openly, thereby risking political prosecution, accusations of libel, or even bodily harm. Hence, the double meanings of many allegories are based not just in the literary form but also in the reality of circumstances in our difficult world.

In considering allegory, determine whether all or part of a work can have an extended, allegorical meaning. The popularity of George Lucas's movie *Star Wars* and its sequels (in videotape and newly refurbished rereleases on DVD) and also its "prequels" (*The Phantom Menace, Attack of the Clones,* and *Revenge of the Sith*), for example, is attributable at least partly to its being an allegory about the conflict between good and evil. Obi-Wan Kenobi (intelligence) assists Luke Skywalker (heroism, boldness) and instructs him in "the Force" (moral or religious faith). Thus armed and guided, Skywalker opposes the powers of Darth Vader (evil) to rescue Princess Leia (purity and goodness) with the aid of the latest spaceships and weaponry (technology). The story has produced a set of popular adventure films, accompanied by dramatic music and ingenious visual and sound effects. With the obvious allegorical overtones, however, it stands for any person's quest for self-fulfillment.

To apply a part of the allegory more specifically, consider that for a time the evil Vader imprisons Skywalker and that Skywalker must exert all his skill and strength to get free and overcome Vader. In the allegorical application of the episode, this imprisonment signifies those moments of doubt, discouragement, and depression that people experience while trying to better themselves through education, work, self-improvement, friendship, marriage, and so on.

Almost from the beginning of recorded literature, similar heroic deeds have been represented in allegorical forms. From ancient Greece, the allegorical hero Jason sails the *Argo* to distant lands to gain the Golden Fleece (those who take risks are rewarded). From Anglo-Saxon England, the hero Beowulf saves King Hrothgar's throne by killing the monster Grendel and his even more monstrous mother (victory comes to those who rely on the forces of good). From seventeenth-century England, Bunyan's *The Pilgrim's Progress* tells how the hero Christian overcomes difficulties and temptations while traveling from this world to the next (belief, perseverance, and resistance to temptation save the faithful). As long as the parallel connections are close and consistent, such as those mentioned here, an allegorical interpretation is valid.

# Fable, Parable, and Myth

Closely related to symbolism and allegory in the ability to extend and expand meaning are three additional forms—fable, parable, and myth.

### A Fable Is a Short Tale with a Pointed Moral

The **fable** (from Latin *fabula*, a story or narration) is an old, brief, and popular form. Often but not always, fables are about animals that possess human traits (such fables are called **beast fables**). Past collectors and editors of fables have attached "morals" or explanations to the brief stories, as is the case with Aesop, the most enduringly popular of fable writers. Tradition has it that Aesop was a slave who composed fables in ancient Greece. His fable "The Fox and the Grapes" signifies the trait of belittling things we cannot have. More recent popular contributions to the fable tradition include Walt Disney's "Mickey Mouse," Walt Kelly's "Pogo," and Berke Breathed's "Bloom County." The adjective *fabulous* refers to the collective body of fables of all sorts, even though the word is often used as little more than a vague term of approval.

### A Parable Is a Short Narrative Illustrating a Religious Concept

A **parable** (from Greek *parabolé*, a "setting beside" or comparison) is a short, simple story with a moral or religious bent. Parables are most often associated with Jesus, who used them to embody unique religious insights and truths. For example, his parables "The Prodigal Son" and "The Good Samaritan," as recorded by Luke, are interpreted to show God's understanding, forgiveness, concern, and love.

### A Myth Is a Tale with Social, Political, Religious, or Philosophical Meanings

A **myth** (from Greek *muthos*, a "story" or "plot") is a traditional story that embodies and codifies the religious, philosophical, and cultural values of the civilization in which it is composed. Usually the central figures of mythical stories are heroes, gods, and demigods, such as the ancient figures Aeneas, Atalanta, Athena, Hera, Hercules, Oedipus, Pandora, Prometheus, Sisyphus, Venus, and Zeus. Although most myths are fictional, many are remotely based in historical truth. They are by no means confined to the past, for the word *myth* can also refer to abstractions and ideas that people today hold collectively, such as the concept of perpetual military supremacy or the idea that future problems can be deferred indefinitely. Sometimes the words *myth* and *mythical* are used with the meaning "fanciful" or "untrue." Such disparagement is misleading because the truths of mythology are not to be found literally in the mythical stories themselves but rather in their symbolic and allegorical interpretations.

# Allusion in Symbolism and Allegory

Cultural or universal symbols and allegories often allude to other works from our cultural heritage, such as the Bible, ancient history and literature, and works of the British and American traditions. Sometimes understanding a story may require knowledge of history and current politics.

If the meaning of a symbol is not immediately clear to you, you will need a dictionary or other reference work. The scope of your college dictionary will surprise you. If you cannot find an entry there, however, try one of the major encyclopedias or ask your reference librarian, who can direct you to shelves loaded with helpful books. A few excellent guides are *The Oxford Companion to Classical Literature* (ed. M. C. Howatson and Ian Chilvers), *The Oxford Companion to English Literature* (ed. Margaret Drabble), *Merriam Webster's Encyclopedia of Literature*, Timothy Gantz's *Early Greek Myth: A Guide to Literary and Artistic Sources*, and Richmond Y. Hathorn's *Greek Mythology*.

Useful aids in finding biblical references are *Cruden's Complete Concordance*, which in various editions has been a reliable guide since 1737, and *The Strongest Strong's Exhaustive Concordance of the Bible* (2001), which has been revised and expanded regularly since it was first published in 1890. These concordances list all the major words used in the Bible (King James version), so you can easily locate the chapter and verse of any and all biblical passages. If you still have trouble after using sources like these, see your instructor.

# Writing about Symbolism and Allegory

As you read, take notes and make all the observations you can about the presence of symbols or **allusions** or both. Explanatory notes will help you establish basic information, but you also need to explain meanings and create interpretations in your own words. Use a dictionary for understanding words or phrases that require further study. For allusions, you might check out original sources to determine original contexts. Try to determine the ways in which your poem is similar to or different from the original work or source and then determine the purpose served by the allusion.

### *Raise Questions to Discover Ideas*

#### Cultural or Universal Symbols

- What symbols that you consider cultural or universal can you discover in names, objects, places, situations, or actions in the work (e.g., the character Faith and the walking stick in Nathaniel Hawthorne's "Young Goodman Brown," the funeral bells in Wilfred Owen's "Anthem for Doomed Youth," the snow in Robert Frost's "Desert Places," and Bethlehem in William Butler Yeats's "The Second Coming")?

- How are these symbols used? What do they mean, both specifically, in the poem, and universally, in a broader context? What would the poem be like without the symbolic meaning?

### Contextual Symbols

- What contextual symbols can you locate in the work (e.g., boxes, children singing in the choir, yellow leaves in autumn)? How is the symbolism used specifically in the poem? What would the poem be like if the symbols were not taken to be symbolic?
- What causes you to conclude that the symbols are truly symbolic? What is being symbolized? What do the symbols mean? How definite or direct is the symbolism?
- Is the symbolism used systematically throughout the work, or is it used only once? How does the symbolism affect the work's ideas or emotions?

### Other Forms

- What enables you to identify the story as a parable or fable? What lesson or moral is either clearly stated or implicit?
- What mythological identification is established in the work? What do you find in the story (names, situations, etc.) that enables you to determine its mythological significance? How is the myth to be interpreted? What symbolic value does the myth have? What current and timeless application does it have?

## Organize Your Essay about Symbolism or Allegory

*Introduction*    Relate the central idea of your essay to the meaning of the major symbols or allegorical thrust of the story. An idea about Hawthorne's "Young Goodman Brown," for example, is that fanaticism darkens and limits the human soul. An early incident in the story provides symbolic support for this idea. Specifically, when Goodman Brown enters the woods, he resolves "to stand firm against the devil," and he then looks up toward "Heaven above him." As he looks, a "black mass of cloud" appears to hide the "brightening stars" (paragraph 47). Within the limits of our central idea, the cloud can be seen as a symbol, just like the widening path or the night walk itself. Look for ways to make solid connections like this when you designate something as a symbol or allegory.

Also, your essay will need to include justifications for your symbols or allegorical parallels. In Poe's "The Cask of Amontillado," for example, Montresor's underground vaults may be taken as an image of his unexpressed hatred and evil wishes. When Fortunato ventures with him into the vaults, we may understand that Fortunato will never be able to free himself from Montresor's diabolical clutches. If you treat the vaults as a symbol, it is important to apply it to the festering hatreds and secret schemes that characterize many people who on the surface may seem calm and in control of their lives. In the same way, in describing the allegorical elements in "Young Goodman Brown," you need to establish a comprehensive statement such as the following: People lose ideals and forsake principles not because they are evil but because they misunderstand the people around them (see the second illustrative essay in this chapter, p. 168).

*Body*  For the body of your essay, there are a number of strategies for discussing symbolism and allegory. You might use one exclusively or a combination.

### Symbolism

1.  **The meaning of a major symbol.** Identify the symbol and what it stands for. Then answer questions such as these: Is the symbol cultural or contextual? How do you decide? How do you derive your interpretation of the symbolic meaning? What is the extent of the meaning? Does the symbol undergo modification or new applications if it reappears in the work? How does the symbol affect your understanding of the work? Does the symbol bring out any ironies? How does the symbol add strength and depth to the work?

2.  **The development and relationship of symbols.** A good approach is to determine how symbolism is related to the work's narrative structure. Where does the symbol occur? If it is early, how do the following parts relate to the ideas borne by the symbol? What logical or chronological function does the symbol serve in the work's development? Is the symbol repeated, and if so, to what effect? If the symbol is introduced later, has it been anticipated earlier? How do you know? Can the symbol be considered climactic? What might the structure of the work have been like if the symbolism had not been used?

3.  **Two or more symbols.** When considering two or more symbols, deal with issues such as these: How do the symbols connect with each other (like night and the cloud in "Young Goodman Brown" as symbols of a darkening mind)? What additional meanings do the symbols provide? What is the function of the symbols in the work's narrative? If the symbol is a person, object, or setting, what physical aspects are described? Why? Are colors included? Shapes? Sizes? Sounds? In light of this description, how applicable is the symbol to the ideas it embodies? How appropriate is the literal condition to the symbolic condition? The answers to questions like these should lead not so much to a detailed account of the meaning of the symbols but rather to an account of their appropriateness to the topics and ideas expressed or implicit in the work.

### Allegory

1.  **The application and meaning of the allegory.** What is the subject of the story (allegory, fable, parable, myth)? How can it be more generally applied to ideas or to qualities of human character, not only of its own time but also of our own? What other versions of the story do you know, if any? Does it illustrate, either closely or loosely, particular philosophies or religious views? If so, what are these? How do you know?

2.  **The consistency of the allegory.** Is the allegory used consistently throughout the story, or is it used intermittently? Explain and illustrate this use. Would it be correct to call your story *allegorical* rather than an *allegory*? Can you determine how parts of the story are introduced for their allegorical importance? Examples are the events that occur in the darkened church in O'Connor's "First Confession; the Parisian street (Rue des Martyrs) on which the Loisels first live in Guy de Maupassant's "The Necklace" (in Chapter 1), which may correspond to the temptation to live beyond one's means; and the frozen preserves in Susan Glaspell's *Trifles*, which we may take as allegorical equivalents of life's sometimes destructive difficulties.

*Conclusion*   You might summarize main points, describe general impressions, explain the impact of the symbolic or allegorical methods, indicate personal responses, or suggest further lines of thought and application. You might also assess the quality and appropriateness of the symbolism or allegory (such as Hawthorne's "Young Goodman Brown" opening in darkness and closing in gloom). If your poem is rich in symbols or allusions, you might also consider some of the elements that you have not discussed in the body and try to tie these together with those you have already discussed. It would also be appropriate to introduce any new ideas you developed as a result of your study.

## Illustrative Essay (Symbolism in a Poem)

> The central idea, thesis sentence, and topic sentences are shaded here to stress the goal of strong organization. As your instructor wishes, you might use this or a similar system in your own essays.

Murray 1

Jessica Murray

Professor Stein

English 100

16 October 2010

Symbolism in William Butler Yeats's

"The Second Coming"°

William Butler Yeats's "The Second Coming" is a prophetic poem that   [1]

lays out reasons for being scared about the future. The poem's symbolism

combines traditional materials from ancient history and literature

together with Yeats's own scheme for visualizing the rise and fall of

civilizations. This scheme is designed to explain both the disruption of

our present but old culture and the installation of a frightening new one.*

To make his prophecies clear, Yeats uses his symbolism as a reflection of

the horrors of the twentieth century.[†]

Yeats's first major symbol, the gyre, or spiral—or rather two   [2]

interconnecting gyres—pervades the poem visually, for it outlines the

cyclical nature of moral and political changes. Flying outward at the

---

°See the text for this poem, pages 382–83.
*Central idea.
[†]Thesis sentence.

widest point of the gyre, symbolizing our present era, a falcon is used by Yeats to introduce the idea that "the center cannot hold." The "desert birds," hovering around the "lion body and the head of a man" (the sphinxlike figure) show a tighter circle in a second gyre, symbolizing a new stage of history. Thus, the widening symbolic gyre in line 1 is interpenetrating with the narrowing gyre pointing at the "rough beast." This intersecting and blending show that new things both emerge and separate from old things. The spatial symbolism thus illustrates that the past is breaking up while the future is about to take the shape of the past—but at its worst, not at its best.

[3]     Embodying this horror-to-be, the second major symbol is the sphinxlike creature moving its "slow thighs" in the sands of the desert. The attributes of the monstrous creature are blankness and pitilessness. Yeats describes it as a "rough beast" (line 21), with the "indignant desert birds" flying in circles above it like vultures. This description symbolizes the brutal nature of the new age. Yeats wrote the poem in 1919, right after the conclusion of World War I, which had seen both the viciousness and mindlessness of trench warfare. The disruption of life caused by this war was a disturbing indicator of the repressiveness and brutality to come.

[4]     It is this brutality that makes ironic another of the poem's major symbol—the long-awaited "second coming" of Jesus. Yeats alludes to the second coming in the poem's title and also in lines 9 and 10:

> Surely some revelation is at hand;
>
> Surely the Second Coming is at hand.

The reference is to New Testament prophecies about the return of Christ at the end of historical time. In the Bible, war and rumors of war are claimed as being the signs indicating that the return, or "Second Coming," is near. Thus far, both the biblical signs and the observations of Yeats coincide. The twist, however, is that Yeats is suggesting through the symbol that after the breakup of the present age, the new age will be marked not by God's kingdom but by the "rough beast." Because Yeats visualizes the beast as a sphinx, his model is the kind of despotism known in ancient Egypt when power was held absolutely by the pharaoh.

Murray 3

A unique aspect of Yeats's symbolism is that he fuses his own          [5]
symbolism with symbolism of paganism and Christianity. The
"ceremony of innocence," for example (line 6), uses the language of
Christian communion. By indicating that it is being drowned, however,
Yeats asserts that the tradition is being lost and brutalized. The *Spiritus
Mundi* (line 12) is an abstract allusion to a common human bond of
images and characteristics, but because of the image of brutality it
produces, as a symbol it demonstrates that horror is now and ever will be
a normal condition of human life. In addition, the "blood-dimmed tide"
(line 5) is an allusion to Shakespeare's Macbeth, who symbolically has
stained the ocean red with King Duncan's blood. The "blood-dimmed
tide" therefore both allusively and symbolically indicates the global
scope of the evil age being born.

"The Second Coming" is rich in symbols that are both traditional          [6]
and personal, and there are additional symbols. The most easily
visualized of these is the falcon out of control, flying higher and higher
and farther away from the falconer, to symbolize the anarchy that Yeats
mentions in line 4 as being "loosed" in the world. An example of a
symbol being used ironically is the reference to Bethlehem where,
according to the Gospels of Matthew and Luke, Jesus, the "Prince of
Peace," was born. In "The Second Coming," Yeats asserts instead that the
new birth will not lead to peace, but instead will bring about a future age
of repression and brutality. Yeats's poem thus offers a complex and
disturbing fabric of symbolism.

Murray 4

Work Cited

Yeats, William Butler. "The Second Coming." *Writing About Literature.*
By Edgar V. Roberts. 12th ed. New York: Pearson, 2010, 382–83. Print.

## Commentary on the Essay

The introduction of this essay (paragraph 1) briefly characterizes Yeats's poem and asserts that the arguments are made through the use of symbols. The central idea is about the replacement of the old by the new, and the thesis sentence states that Yeats combines major symbols to achieve an effect of horror. Paragraph 2 describes the shape of the symbol as a complex and interconnected set of "gyres," or spirals. Paragraph 3 considers the "rough beast" as a symbol of emerging brutality. Paragraph 4 treats the title's use of New Testament prophetic symbolism, showing that Yeats makes his point by reversing the outcome that tradition had predicted. Paragraph 5 demonstrates the complexity of Yeats's poem by stressing how he fuses symbolism and allusion. The last paragraph (6) contains a brief summary and then proceeds to illustrate the richness of "The Second Coming" with brief references to additional symbols.

## Illustrative Essay (Allegory in a Story)

Oppelt 1

Ty Oppelt

Professor Griffin

English 101

3 October 2010

The Allegory of Nathaniel Hawthorne's

"Young Goodman Brown"°

[1]      Nathaniel Hawthorne's "Young Goodman Brown" is a nightmarish narrative. It allegorizes the process by which something good— religion—becomes a justification for intolerance and prejudice. The major character, Young Goodman Brown of Salem during colonial times, begins as a pious and holy person, but he takes a walk into a nearby darkening forest of both suspicion and sanctimoniousness. The process is portrayed by Hawthorne as being originated by the devil himself, who leads Goodman Brown into the night. By the end of the allegory, Brown is transformed into an unforgiving, antisocial, dour, and dreary misanthrope.

[2]      Hawthorne's choice of location for the story reminds us that it was in historical Salem, in the late seventeenth century, that religious zealousness became so extreme that a number of witch trials and public

°For the text of this story, see pages 330–38.

Oppelt 2

hangings took place solely on the basis of suspicion and false accusation. This setting indicates that Hawthorne's immediate allegorical target is the overzealous pursuit of religious principles. And so Goodman Brown's trip not only takes him into the gloom of night but also marks a descent into the darkest dungeon of his soul.*

Although the story directly details elements in the growth of [3] religious zealotry, Hawthorne's allegory may also be applied more generally to the ways in which people uncritically follow *any* ideal that leads them to distrust and suspect others. The allegory is thus relevant to those who swallow political slogans, who believe in their own racial or ethnic superiority, or who justify super patriotism and super nationalism. As such persons persuade themselves of their own supremacy, they ignore the greater need for love, understanding, toleration, cooperation, and forgiveness. Hawthorne's allegory is a realistic portrait of how people get into such a mental state, with Goodman Brown as the example of the attitude. Such people push ahead even against their own good nature and background, and they develop their prejudices through delusion and suspicion.†

Young Goodman Brown's pathway into the night is not a direct [4] plunge into evil, but Hawthorne shows that Brown is not without good nature because he has misgivings about what he is doing. Many times early in the story, we learn that he has doubts about the "evil purpose" of his allegorical walk. At the very beginning, Faith calls him back and pleads with him to stay the night with her (paragraph 2), but even so, he leaves her. As he walks away he thinks of himself as "a wretch" for doing so (paragraph 7). He excuses himself with a promise that once the evening is over he will stick with Faith forever after, an "excellent resolve for the future," as the narrator ironically states (paragraph 8). When Goodman Brown is reproached by the devil for being late—we conclude that Brown's purpose was to keep this diabolical appointment—he gives the excuse "Faith kept me back a while" (paragraph 12), a sentence of ironic double meaning. Once he has kept his appointment with the devil, he states his

---

*Central idea.
†Thesis sentence.

Oppelt 3

intention to go no farther because he has "scruples" which remind him that "it is my purpose now to return whence I came" (paragraph 15). Even when Goodman Brown is standing before the altar of profanation deep within the forest, he appeals to Faith, "Look up to Heaven, and resist the Wicked One!" (paragraph 68). All this hesitation represents a true conscience in Goodman Brown even though he ignores it as he progresses deeper into the forest of sin. His failure is his inability or unwillingness to make his own insight and conscience his guides of conduct.

[5]     It is important to remember that Goodman Brown is favored by his background, which might reasonably be expected to have kept him on a true path of goodness. Almost as a claim of entitlement he cries out, "With Heaven above, and Faith below, I will yet stand firm against the devil" (paragraph 46). He also cries out for Faith even when he hears a voice resembling hers that is "uttering lamentations" within the darkening woods (paragraph 47). When he sees Faith's pink ribbon mysteriously flutter down, he exclaims, "My Faith is gone!" (paragraph 50). These instances show allegorically that Goodman Brown's previous way of life has given him the right paths to follow and the right persons in whom to believe. Even as he is tempted when he is standing before the "unhallowed altar" (paragraph 64), he asks the question "But, where is Faith?" as though he could reclaim the innocence that he has previously known (paragraph 57). Just as he ignores his conscience, he also ignores the power of his background, and it is this neglect that fuels his change into the "demoniac" who abandons himself to "the instinct that guides mortal man to evil" (paragraph 51).

[6]     Another major element in Goodman Brown's allegorical path into darkness is that he develops the assumption that virtually all the people he knows have yielded their lives to sin and are therefore unworthy. In the grips of this distorted view of others, he believes not what he sees but what he thinks he is seeing. Thus, he witnesses the encounter between the devil and Goody Cloyse shortly after he enters the forest, but what he sees is not the good woman who taught him his catechism but rather a witch who is bent on evil and who is friendly with the devil. He ignores the fact that he too is friendly with the devil (the image of his own

Oppelt 4

father) and therefore, while ignoring the log in his own eye, he condemns Goody Cloyse for the speck in hers. After his transformation, when he walks back into his village from his allegorical walk into evil, he "snatche[s] away" a child from Goody as though she were preaching the words of the devil and not God (paragraph 70). He cannot believe that others possess goodness as long he is convinced by the devil's words that "the whole earth [is] one stain of guilt, one mighty blood-spot" (paragraph 63). For this reason, he condemns both his minister and Deacon Gookin, whose conspiratorial voices he thinks he overhears on the pathway through the forest. In short, the process of Hawthorne's allegory about the growth of harmful pietism demonstrates that travelers on the pathway to prejudice accept suspicion and mistrust without trying to get at the whole truth and without recognizing that judgment is not in human but rather is in divine hands.

[7]

As Hawthorne allegorizes the development of religious discrimination he makes clear that, like any kind of discrimination, mistrust and suspicion form its basis. Certainly, as the devil claims, human beings commit many criminal and depraved sins (paragraph 63), but this does not mean that all human beings are equally at fault and that they are beyond love and redemption. The key for Goodman Brown is that he exceeds his judgmental role and bases his condemnation of others solely on his own hasty and mistrustful conclusions. As long as he has faith he will not falter, but when he leaves his faith or believes that he has lost his faith, he is adrift and will see only evil wherever he looks. For this reason, he falls victim to suspicion and loathing, and he becomes harsh and desperate forever after, as Hawthorne shows happened to him after the fateful night. The story's conclusion completes the allegorical cycle beginning with Brown's initiation into evil and extending to his "dying hour" of "gloom" and his unhopeful tombstone (paragraph 72).

[8]

Hawthorne's "Young Goodman Brown" allegorizes the paradox of how noble beliefs become ignoble. Goodman Brown dies in gloom because he believes that his wrong vision is true. His form of evil is the hardest to stop because wrongdoers who are convinced of their own goodness are beyond reach. In view of such self-righteous evil, whether cloaked in the apparent virtues of Puritanism or of some other blindly

Oppelt 5

rigorous doctrine, Hawthorne writes, "the fiend in his own shape is less hideous than when he rages in the breast of man" (paragraph 53). As Hawthorne presents the allegory of Young Goodman Brown, the "hero" is one of the many who convince themselves that they alone walk in light but who actually create darkness.

Oppelt 6

Work Cited

Hawthorne, Nathaniel. "Young Goodman Brown." *Writing About Literature.* By Edgar V. Roberts. 12th ed. New York: Pearson, 2010. 330–38. Print.

## Commentary on the Essay

Unity in the essay is achieved by a number of means. For example, paragraph 2 extends a topic in paragraph 1. Also, a phrase in sentence 2 of paragraph 1 is echoed in sentence 1 of paragraph 8. Making additional connections within the essay are individual words such as "another," "while," "therefore," and the repetition of words throughout the essay that are contained in the thesis sentence.

The first three paragraphs of the essay constitute an extended introduction to the topics of paragraphs 4 through 8, for they establish "Young Goodman Brown" as an allegory. Paragraph 1 briefly considers the allegorical nature of the narrative. Paragraph 2 relates the historical basis of the topic to Hawthorne's purpose in writing the story, and it concludes with the essay's central idea. Paragraph 3 broadens the scope of Hawthorne's allegory by showing that it includes zealousness wherever it might appear. Paragraph 3 also concludes with the essay's thesis sentence.

Paragraph 4 deals with an important aspect of the allegory, one that makes it particularly relevant and timely even today—namely, people of basically good nature may fall into suspicious error under the pretense of goodness. Similarly, paragraph 5 points out that such people usually come from good backgrounds and have benefited from good influences during their lives.

Paragraphs 6 and 7 locate the origins of evil in two major human qualities—first, the belief in one's own delusions; and second, the mental confusion that results from the conviction that appearance is more real and believable than reality itself. Paragraph 8 concludes the essay on the note that the finished "product"—a person who has become suspicious and misguided—demonstrates how good ideas, when pushed to the extreme by false imagination, can backfire.

### Writing Topics about Symbolism and Allegory

1. Compare and contrast the symbolism in Blake's "The Tyger," Arnold's "Dover Beach," Langston Hughes's "Negro," and Poe's "The Cask of Amontillado." To what degree do the works rely on contextual symbols? On universal symbols? On the basis of your comparison, what is the case for asserting that realism and fantasy are directly related to the nature of the symbolism presented in these works?

2. Why do writers who advocate moral, philosophical, or religious issues frequently use symbolism or allegory? In treating this question, you might introduce references from Hawthorne's "Young Goodman Brown," Thomas Hardy's "Channel Firing," and Arnold's "Dover Beach."

3. Write an essay on the allegorical method of one or more of the parables included in the Gospel of St. Luke, such as "The Bridegroom" (5:34–35), "The Garments and the Wineskins" (5:36–39), "The Sower" (8:4–15), "The Good Samaritan" (10:25–37), "The Prodigal Son" (15:11–32), "The Ox in the Well" (14:5–6), "The Watering of Animals on the Sabbath" (13:15–17), "The Rich Fool" (12:16–21), "Lazarus" (16:19–31), "The Widow and the Judge" (18:1–8), and "The Pharisee and the Publican" (18:9–14).

4. What is the nature of the symbols pertaining to the role of single and married women in Katherine Mansfield's "Miss Brill," Chekhov's *The Bear*, Glaspell's *Trifles*, Kate Chopin's "The Story of an Hour," and Robert Browning's "My Last Duchess"?

5. Consider the meaning of the symbols of war in Arnold's "Dover Beach," Hardy's "The Man He Killed," Irving Layton's "Rhine Boat Trip," Lowell's "Patterns," and Owen's "Anthem for Doomed Youth."

6. Compare the use of religious symbols in Dudley Randall's "The Ballad of Birmingham," Yeats's "The Second Coming," and Hawthorne's "Young Goodman Brown." What are the locations from which the poets draw their symbols? How do the symbols figure into the ideas and actions of the works?

7. Write a poem in which you develop a major symbol, as Maupassant does in "The Necklace" (with the necklace) and Layton does in "Rhine Boat Trip" (with the cattle cars). To get yourself started, you might think about the meaning of symbols like these:

   - A littered street or sidewalk
   - Coffee hour after church
   - An athletic competition
   - A computer
   - The checkout counter at the neighborhood supermarket
   - The family dog looking out a window as the children leave for school

8. Write your own brief story using a widely recognized cultural symbol such as the flag (patriotism, love of country, a certain type of politics), water (life, sexuality, regeneration), or the population explosion (the end of life on earth). By arranging actions and dialogue, make clear the issues conveyed by your symbol and try to resolve conflicts the symbol might raise among your characters.

9. Using the card or computer catalog of your library or online searches, discover a recent critical-biographical work about Hawthorne. Explain what the book says about Hawthorne's uses of symbolism. To what extent does the book relate Hawthorne's symbolism to his religious and family heritage?

# Chapter 12

# Writing about Tone: The Writer's Control over Attitudes and Feelings

Tone refers to the methods by which writers and speakers reveal attitudes or feelings. It is an aspect of all spoken and written statements, whether earnest declarations of love, requests to pass a dinner dish, letters from students asking parents for money, or official government notices threatening penalties if taxes and fines are not paid. Because tone is often equated with *attitude*, it is important to realize that tone refers not so much to attitudes themselves but rather to those techniques and modes of presentation that reveal or create attitudes.

As a literary concept, *tone* is adapted from the phrase *tone of voice* in speech. Tone of voice reflects attitudes toward a particular object or situation and toward listeners. Let us suppose that our good friend Mary has a difficult assignment on which she expects to work all day. Things go well and she finishes quickly. She happily tells her friend Anne, "I'm so pleased. I needed only two hours for that." Then she decides to buy tickets for a popular concert and must wait through a long and slow line. After getting her tickets, she tells the people at the end of the line, "I'm so pleased. I needed only two hours for that." The sentences are exactly the same, but by changing her emphasis and vocal inflection, Mary indicates her disgust and impatience with her long wait, just as she shows her sympathy with the people still in line. By controlling the *tone* of her statements, in other words, Mary conveys satisfaction at one time and indignation at another.

As this example indicates, an attitude itself may be summarized with a word or phrase (satisfaction or indignation, love or contempt, interest or indifference, deference or command, etc.), but the study of tone examines those aspects of situation, language, action, and background that bring out the attitude. In the last two lines of Wilfred Owen's "Anthem for Doomed Youth" (p. 377), for example, the speaker refers to the reactions of those at home for the young men who have died in battle:

Their flowers [shall be] the tenderness of patient minds,
And each slow dusk a drawing-down of blinds.

These words suggest that the anguish of immediate sorrow is past and those left at home must endure unending, lifelong, quiet sorrow, indicated by the "drawing-down of blinds," which by shutting out light also suggests an end of hope, expectation, and love.

# Tone and Attitudes

In most literary works, attitudes point in a number of directions so that tone becomes a highly complex matter. The following things to look for, however, should help you in understanding and describing literary tone.

### Determine the Writer's Attitude toward the Material

By reading a work carefully, we may deduce the author's attitude or attitudes toward the subject matter. In "The Story of an Hour," for example, Kate Chopin sympathetically portrays a young wife's secret wishes for freedom, just as she also humorously reveals the unwitting smugness that often pervades the married lives of men and women. In "Echo," Christina Rossetti's speaker addresses a lover who is long dead, and by this means, Rossetti renders attitudes of yearning and sorrow. In a broader perspective, authors may view human beings with amused affection, as in Anton Chekhov's *The Bear*, or with amused resignation, as in Thomas Hardy's "Channel Firing." All these works exhibit various degrees of irony, which is one of the most significant aspects of authorial tone.

### Discover the Writer's Attitude toward Readers

Authors recognize that readers participate in the creative act and that all elements of a story—word choice, characterization, allusions, levels of reality—must take readers' responses into account (note the discussion of reader- response criticism in Appendix A). When Nathaniel Hawthorne's woodland guide in "Young Goodman Brown" refers to "King Philip's War," for example, Hawthorne assumes that his readers know that this war was inhumane, greedy, and cruel. By allowing this assumption to stand, he indicates respect for the knowledge of his readers, and he also assumes their essential agreement with him. Chekhov in *The Bear* assumes that readers understand that Smirnov's speeches reveal him as irascible and petulant, but they also show him as both generous and funny. Authors always make such considerations about readers by implicitly complimenting them on their knowledge and also by satisfying their curiosity and desire to be interested, stimulated, and pleased.

### Determine Other Dominant Attitudes

Beyond general authorial tone, there are many internal and dramatically rendered expressions of attitude. For example, the speaker of Amy Lowell's "Patterns" is a decent and proper upper-class young woman. Yet at the news of her fiancé's death, her sorrowful meditation brings out that she had made a promise to him to make love outside, on a "shady seat" in the garden (lines 86–89). This personal confession symbolically reveals an inner warmth that her social situation does not suggest, and it also makes the poem pathetically poignant.

In addition, as characters interact, their tone dramatically shows their judgments about other characters and situations. A complicated control of tone occurs at the end of Susan Glaspell's *Trifles* when the two major characters, Mrs. Hale and Mrs. Peters, cover up incriminating evidence about Minnie Wright. When the two women are examining the things in the kitchen, however, before they actually do the covering up, Mrs. Peters speaks not about illegality, but rather about the possible embarrassment of the action:

> MRS. PETERS. [*Takes the bottle, looks about for something to wrap it in; takes petticoat from the clothes brought from the other room, very nervously begins winding this around the bottle. In a false voice.*] My, it's a good thing the men couldn't hear us. Wouldn't they just laugh! Getting all stirred up over a little thing like a—dead canary. As if that could have anything to do with—with—wouldn't they *laugh*! (speech 137)

Notice that her words reveal her knowledge that men scoff at feminine concerns, like Minnie's quilting knots, and therefore she openly anticipates the men's amusement. The reader, however, knows that Mrs. Peters will actually join Mrs. Hale in hiding and covering up the incriminating evidence about Minnie.

## Tone and Humor

A major aspect of tone is humor. Everyone likes to laugh, and shared laughter is part of good human relationships; but not everyone can explain why things are funny. Laughter resists close analysis; it is often unplanned, personal, idiosyncratic, and usually unpredictable. Nonetheless, there are a number of common elements:

1. **There must be an object to laugh at.** There must be something at which to laugh—a person, a thing, a situation, a custom, a habit of speech or dialect, an arrangement of words, and so on.
2. **Laughter usually stems out of disproportion or incongruity.** People normally know what to expect under given conditions, and anything contrary to these expectations is *incongruous* and may therefore generate laughter. When the temperature is 100°F, you expect people to dress lightly, but if you were to see a man wearing a heavy overcoat, a warm hat, a muffler, and large gloves and waving his arms and stamping his feet as though to keep warm, he would violate your expectations. Because his garments and behavior are *inappropriate* or *incongruous*, you would think he was funny. A student in a basic English class once wrote about a "*congregation* of verbs" and about parts of speech as "nouns, verbs, and *proverbs*." The student meant the *conjugation* of verbs, of course, and also (maybe) either *adverbs* or *pronouns*, but somehow his understanding slipped, and he created a comic incongruity. Such inadvertent verbal errors are called **malapropisms**, after Mrs. Malaprop, a character in Richard Brinsley Sheridan's eighteenth-century play *The Rivals* (1775). In the literary creation of malapropisms, the tone is directed against the speaker, for the amusement of both readers and author alike.
3. **Safety and/or goodwill prevents harm and ensures laughter.** Seeing a person slip on a banana peel and hurtle through the air may cause laughter, but only if we ourselves are not that person, for laughter depends on insulation from danger and pain. In comic situations that involve physical abuse—falling down stairs

or being hit in the face by cream pies—the abuse never harms the participants. The incongruity of such situations causes laughter, and the immunity from pain and injury prevents responses of horror. Goodwill enters into humor in romantic comedy or in any other work where we are drawn into general sympathy with the major figures, such as Smirnov and Mrs. Popov in Chekhov's *The Bear*. As the author leads the characters toward their unexpected outburst of love at the play's end, our involvement produces happiness, smiles, and sympathetic laughter.

4. **Unfamiliarity, newness, and uniqueness are needed to produce the spontaneity of laughter.** Laughter depends on seeing something new or unique or on experiencing something familiar in a new light. Because laughter is prompted by flashes of insight or sudden revelations, it is always spontaneous, even when readers already know and understand the object of their laughter. Indeed, the task of the comic writer is to develop ordinary materials to that point when spontaneity frees readers to laugh. Thus, you can read and reread Chekhov's *The Bear* and laugh each time because, even though you know what will happen, the play shapes your acceptance of how reconciliation penetrates a wall of anger and guilt. The concluding embraces by Smirnov and Mrs. Popov are now and always will be comic because they are so spontaneous and incongruous.

## Tone and Irony

The capacity to have more than one attitude toward someone or something is a uniquely human trait. We know that people are not perfect, but we love a number of them anyway. Therefore, we speak to them not only with love and praise but also with banter and criticism. On occasion, you may have given mildly insulting greeting cards to your loved ones, not to affront them but to amuse them. You share smiles and laughs, and at the same time you also remind them of your affection.

The word **irony** describes such contradictory statements or situations. Irony is natural to human beings who are aware of life's ambiguities and complexities. It develops from the realization that life does not always measure up to promise, that friends and loved ones are sometimes angry at each other, that the universe contains incomprehensible mysteries, that the social and political structure is often oppressive rather than liberating, that even those with great love and the best of intentions are frequently imposed upon, that doubt exists even in the certainty of knowledge and faith, and that human character is built through chagrin, regret, and pain as much as through emulation and praise. In expressing an idea ironically, writers pay the greatest compliment to their audience, for they assume that readers have sufficient intelligence and skill to discover the real meaning of quizzical or ambiguous statements and situations.

### Understand the Four Major Kinds of Irony:
### Verbal, Situational, Cosmic, and Dramatic

*Verbal Irony Depends on the Interplay of Words*     In **verbal irony,** one thing is said, but the opposite is meant. In the example opening this chapter, Mary's ironic expression of pleasure after her two-hour wait for tickets really means that she is disgusted. There are important types of verbal irony. In **understatement**, the expression does not fully describe the importance of a situation and for this reason it makes the point strongly through indirection and implication. During the early days of the American space program, an astronaut was asked what he would think if all his reentry safety equipment failed as he was returning to earth after a space exploration, thus dooming him and all aboard to certain death. His answer was this, "A thing like that could ruin your whole day." Such words—adequate for a minor mishap during ordinary daily living, but totally inadequate for a major disaster—demonstrate the nature of understatement, which emphasizes by describing the minimum rather than maximum situation.

By contrast, in **hyperbole**, or **overstatement**, the words are obviously and inappropriately excessive, and readers or listeners therefore understand that the true meaning is considerably less than what is said. An example is Smirnov's exaggerated dialogue with Mrs. Popov in Chekhov's *The Bear* (speech 69). Though Smirnov tells about the number of times he has jilted women and women have jilted him, readers understand that he is exaggerating his past romantic life to impress Mrs. Popov. The gulf between his exaggeration and the (probably) more modest reality creates smiles and chuckles.

Often verbal irony is ambiguous, having double meaning, or **double entendre**. Midway through Hawthorne's "Young Goodman Brown," for example, the woodland guide leaves Brown alone while stating, "when you feel like moving again, there is my staff to help you along" (paragraph 40). The word "staff" is ambiguous, for it refers to the staff that resembles a serpent (paragraph 13). The word therefore suggests that the devilish guide is leaving Brown not only with a real staff but also with the spirit of evil, unlike the divine "staff" of Psalm 23:4 that gives comfort. Ambiguity, of course, may be used in relation to any topic. Quite often double entendre is used in statements about sexuality for the amusement of listeners or readers.

*Situational Irony Fills the Gap Between Hope and Reality*     **Situational irony**, or **irony of situation**, refers to the chasm between what we hope for or expect and what actually happens. It is often pessimistic because it emphasizes that human beings usually have little or no control over their lives or anything else. The forces of opposition may be psychological, social, cultural, political, or environmental. The situation is not temporary, one might add, but permanent and universal, as in Hardy's "Channel Firing" in which the topic is the omnipresence of war in the past, present, and future. Although situational irony often involves disaster, it need not always do so. For example, a happier occurrence of situational irony is in Chekhov's *The Bear*, for the two characters shift from anger to love as they fall into the grips of emotions that, as the saying goes, are "bigger than both of them."

*Cosmic Irony Stems from the Power of Fate, Chance, Kings, and Desperate Men*     A special kind of situational irony that emphasizes the pessimistic and fatalistic side of life is **cosmic irony**, or **irony of fate**. By the standard of cosmic irony, the universe is indifferent to individuals, who are subject to blind chance, accident, uncontrollable emotions, perpetual misfortune, and misery. Even if things temporarily go well, people's lives end badly, and their best efforts do not rescue them or make them happy. A work illustrating cosmic irony is Glaspell's *Trifles*, which develops out of the stultifying conditions of farm life that Minnie Wright endured for many years while living with her dreary and abusive husband. She has no profession, no other hope, no other life except the lonely, dreary farm—nothing. After thirty years of wretchedness, she buys a canary that warbles for her to make her life somewhat more beautiful. Within a year, her insensitive and boorish husband wrings the bird's neck, and she in turn has an ultimate reaction against him. Her situation is cosmically ironic, for the implication of *Trifles* is that human beings are caught in a web of adverse circumstances from which there is no escape.

*Dramatic Irony Results from Misunderstanding and Lack of Knowledge*    Like cosmic irony, **dramatic irony** is a special kind of situational irony. It happens when a character either has no information about a situation or else misjudges it, but readers (and often some of the other characters) see everything completely and correctly. The classic model of dramatic irony is found in Sophocles' ancient Greek play *Oedipus the King*. In this play, everyone—other characters and readers alike—knows the truth long before Oedipus knows it. Writers of nondramatic works also make use of dramatic irony, as is seen in Chopin's "The Story of an Hour" in which the doctors are ignorant of Louise's secret response to the report of her husband's death. We readers, however, do indeed know and understand her feelings, and therefore we conclude rightly that the medical diagnosis by the doctors of her sudden death shows not their skill but rather their masculine vanity.

# Writing about Tone

Begin with a careful reading, noting those elements of the work that convey attitudes. Consider whether the work genuinely creates the attitudes it is designed to evoke. In Langston Hughes's "Negro," for example, are the references to real slavery and wage slavery, together with atrocities committed in the Belgian Congo, sufficiently real to support the poem's underlying sense of rage and threat? In Edgar Allan Poe's "The Cask of Amontillado," does the claim by Montresor that Fortunato insulted him explain in any way why Montresor carries out his twisted act of revenge? Depending on the work, your devising and answering such questions will help you understand an author's control over tone. Similar questions apply when you study internal qualities such as style and characterization.

### Raise Questions to Discover Ideas

- How strongly do you respond to the work? What attitudes can you identify and characterize? What elements in the story elicit your concern, indignation, fearfulness, anguish, amusement, or sense of affirmation?

- What causes you to sympathize or not to sympathize with characters, situations, or ideas? What makes the circumstances in the work admirable or understandable (or deplorable)?
- In fiction and drama, what does the dialogue suggest about the author's attitudes toward the characters? How does it influence your attitudes? What qualities of diction permit and encourage your responses?
- To what degree, if any, does the work supersede any previous ideas you might have had about the same or similar subject matter? What do you think changed your attitude?
- What role does the narrator or speaker play in your attitudes toward the dramatic or fictional material? Does the speaker seem intelligent or stupid, friendly or unfriendly, sane or insane, idealistic or pragmatic?
- In an amusing or comic story, what elements of plot, character, and diction are particularly comic? How strongly do you respond to humor-producing situations? Why?
- What ironies do you find in the work (verbal, situational, cosmic)? How is the irony connected to philosophies of marriage, family, society, politics, religion, or morality?
- To what extent are characters controlled by fate, social or racial discrimination, limitations of intelligence, economic and political inequality, and limited opportunity?
- Do any words seem unusual or noteworthy, such as words in dialect, polysyllabic words, or foreign words or phrases that the author assumes you know? Are there any especially connotative or emotive words? What authorial assumptions about the readers do these words suggest?

## Organize Your Essay About Tone

*Introduction*   Your introduction should describe the general situation of the work and its dominant moods or impressions, such as that the work leads to cynicism, as in Hardy's "Channel Firing," or to laughter and delight, as in Chekhov's *The Bear*. Problems connected with describing the work's tone should also be introduced here.

*Body*   Your goal is to show how the author establishes the dominant mood or moods of the work, such as the poignancy of Lowell's "Patterns" or the hilarity of Chekhov's *The Bear*. Some possibilities are the use or misuse of language, the exposé of a pretentious speaker, the use of exact and specific descriptions, the isolation of a major character, the failure of plans, and the continuance of naiveté in a disillusioned world. You might find a convenient approach in one of these:

1. **Audience, situation, and characters.** Is any person or group directly addressed by the speaker? What attitude is expressed (love, respect, condescension, confidentiality, confidence, etc.)? What is the basic situation in the story? Do you find irony? If so, what kind is it? What does the irony show (e.g., optimism or pessimism)? How is the situation controlled to shape your responses? That is, can actions, situations, or characters be seen as expressions of attitude or as embodiments of certain favorable or unfavorable ideas or positions? What is the nature of the speaker or persona? Why does the persona speak exactly as he or she does? How is the persona's character manipulated to show apparent authorial attitude and to elicit your responses? Does

the story promote respect, admiration, dislike, or other feelings about character or situation? How?

2. **Descriptions and diction.** Descriptions or diction in the work should not be analyzed for themselves alone but should be related to attitude. *For descriptions*: To what degree do descriptions of natural scenery and conditions (snowstorms, cold, rain, ice, intense sunlight) convey an attitude that complements or opposes the circumstances of the characters? Are there any systematic references to colors, sounds, or noises that collectively reflect an attitude? *For diction*: Do connotative meanings of words control response in any way? Does the range of vocabulary require readers to have a large or technical vocabulary? Do speech patterns or the use of dialect evoke attitudes about speakers or their condition of life? Is the level of diction normal, slang, standard, or substandard? What is the effect of such a level? Are there unusual or particularly noteworthy expressions? If so, what attitudes do these show? Does the author use verbal irony? To what effect?

3. **Humor.** Is the work funny? How funny, how intense? How is the humor achieved? Does the humor develop out of incongruous situations or language, or both? Is there an underlying basis of attack in the humor, or are the objects of laughter still respected or even loved even though they cause amusement?

4. **Ideas.** Are any ideas advocated, defended mildly, or attacked? How does the author clarify his or her attitude toward these ideas—directly, by statement, or indirectly, through understatement, overstatement, or a character's speeches? In what ways does the story assume a common ground of assent between author and reader? That is, what common assumptions do you find about history, religion, politics, morality, behavioral standards, and so on? Is it easy to give assent (temporary or permanent) to these ideas, or is any concession needed by the reader to approach the work? (For example, a major subject of Glaspell's *Trifles* is the negative effects on a farmwife caused by the isolation and bleakness of an early twentieth-century farm. Things have changed since the time of the play, and the life of such women is certainly better, but sympathetic modern readers can readily understand the psychological situation of the play and can therefore understand Minnie Wright's reaction to her circumstances.)

5. **Unique characteristics of the work.** Each work has unique properties that contribute to the tone. Hardy's "Channel Firing," for example, develops from the comic idea that guns being fired at sea are so loud that they waken the dead in their coffins. In other works, there might be some recurring word or phrase that seems special, as in Rossetti's "Echo." In this poem, the speaker's anguished memory of her dead lover and her yearning are emphasized through the repetitions of the words "Come," "Dream," and "long ago."

*Conclusion*    In your conclusion, first summarize your main points and then go on to redefinitions, explanations, or afterthoughts, together with ideas reinforcing earlier points. You might also mention some other major aspect of the story's tone that you did not develop in the body.

## Illustrative Essay

The central idea, thesis sentence, and topic sentences are shaded here to stress the goal of strong organization. As your instructor wishes, you might use this or a similar system in your own essays.

Lawson 1

Annabelle Lawson

Professor Wilkie

English 100

3 October 2010

Kate Chopin's Irony in "The Story of an Hour"°

"The Story of an Hour" is a remarkably short short story that        [1]
exhibits Kate Chopin's complex control over tone. There are many
ironies in the story, which grow out of error, misunderstanding,
incorrect expectation, and pompous pride.* In addition, the story raises
an ironic question about the nature of marriage as an institution. All this
is a great deal for so brief a story, yet it is all there. The story contains a
rich mixture of situational, cosmic, and dramatic irony.†

The center of the story's situational irony is Louise Mallard, the        [2]
central character. Not much is disclosed about her character, her major
circumstances being that she has been a faithful and dedicated housewife
and that she suffers from heart disease. Her situation reaches a crisis at
the story's beginning when she is given the information that her husband
has died. As a loving wife, she weeps convulsively at the news and then
retreats to her room, presumably to grieve in solitude. A previously
unknown and unsuspected feeling then comes to her—the realization that
she is now "free." In other words, she understands that her marriage has
put her in bondage, even though at the same time she recognizes that her
husband "had never looked save with love upon her" (paragraph 13). For
the first time in her life, she recognizes the gap between her life and her
hidden hopes and expectations, virtually a definition of situational irony.

Both situational and cosmic ironies are focused on the people closest        [3]
to Louise—namely, her sister, Josephine, and Brently Mallard's friend,
Richards. They are kindly and have the best intentions toward her.
Richards verifies the truth of the train wreck before coming to the
Mallard household with the news and then tells Josephine. In turn,
Josephine breaks the news gently to Louise, in "veiled hints that revealed

---

°See pages 326–28 for this story.
*Central idea.
†Thesis sentence.

Lawson 2

in half concealing" (paragraph 2), so as to forestall the shock that would bring on a fatal heart attack. Josephine is successful and her concern causes her to beg Louise to come out of her room, for Josephine believes that Louise will make herself ill with grief (paragraph 17). With these best intentions, of course, Josephine becomes the inadvertent cause of bringing Louise in sight of the front door just as Brently Mallard, safe all along, enters it, and the shock of seeing him brings about Louise's fatal heart attack. Thus, through no fault of her own, Josephine brings about the blow of fate that she and Richards have tried to avoid.

[4]        Another major cosmic irony in the story results from the inaccuracy and unreliability of information. At the time of the story (1894), the best and most modern method of sending information over distances was by telegraph. Richards is in the newspaper office "when intelligence of the railroad disaster was received, with Brently Mallard's name leading the list of 'killed'" (paragraph 2). Since the news could never have come so rapidly in the days before telegraphy was common, we may suppose that Louise would never have had the news of the death in the days before telegraphy and therefore would never have experienced the emotional crisis brought about by the inaccurate news. The error of information may be caused by human mistake, but the consequences are cosmic for Louise—and, one might add, for her unsuspecting husband, who enters the house only to witness his wife's sudden death.

[5]        This irony-filled story also contains dramatic irony that may be found in two details. None of the characters understands what Louise begins feeling as she sits upstairs. Their experience and their imagination make it impossible for them to comprehend her feelings. This failure of understanding is particularly sad with regard to Josephine and Richards, for these two are the closest ones to her. Thus, in effect, Louise dies alone even though she is surrounded by the people who love her most. In the case of the doctors who diagnose the cause of Louise's death, the lack of understanding is bitterly ironic:

> When the doctors came they said she had died of heart disease—of
> joy that kills. (paragraph 23)

The somewhat pompous doctors find it impossible to imagine the true reason for Louise's shock, for, they obviously think, what other reason

Lawson 3

than joy at seeing her restored husband could bring about such a powerful assault on her system? "The Story of an Hour," of course, ends on this grim but also somewhat comic note.

The story's crowning situational irony is the discrepancy between normal and conventional ideas of marriage as ideal and the reality of marriage as fact. One senses the authorial voice insisting strongly on uncomfortable reality when Louise contemplates a future life free of the need for satisfying anyone else: [6]

> There would be no powerful will bending hers in that blind
> persistence with which men and women believe they have a right
> to impose a private will upon a fellow-creature. (paragraph 14)

Louise's marriage has not been bad, but the story at this point straightforwardly goes to the heart of the conflict between personal freedom and marital obligation. Chopin's words "blind persistence" are particularly effective here in establishing an attitude of disapproval if not of protest.

Even though "The Story of an Hour" might be considered as a tract against traditional marriage, it is above all a superbly crafted story. In just twenty-three paragraphs it introduces a complex number of ironies revolving about the crisis created by the mistakes and misunderstandings of a single hour. It is the sudden coming together of all these ironies that crash in on Louise Mallard and destroy her. These ironies come into full focus only when she suddenly believes that her husband has been killed, only to learn just as suddenly that he is still alive. In life, for most people, such a crisis may never happen. As a general principle, the story's major irony is that even the best and most enviable circumstances of life contain inherent imperfections, unarticulated frustration, and potential unhappiness. [7]

Lawson 4

## Work Cited

Chopin, Kate. "The Story of an Hour." *Writing About Literature.* By
    Edgar V. Roberts. 12th ed. New York: Pearson, 2010. 326–28. Print.

# Commentary on the Essay

The topic of this essay on tone is Chopin's complex use of irony in "The Story of an Hour." Throughout the essay, a good deal of the story's action is used to exemplify the sorts of irony being discussed. Links and connections within the essay are brought out by phrases like "even though," "also," "the crowning situational irony," "another," and "both."

Paragraph 1, the introduction, contains the central idea that announces the causes producing irony. The thesis sentence indicates that the combination of situational, cosmic, and dramatic irony will be explored in the body. Paragraph 2 demonstrates how situational irony applies to the circumstances of the major character, Louise. Paragraph 3 shows how both situational and cosmic irony enter into the story through Louise's sister, Josephine, and Brently's friend, Richards.

An additional element of cosmic irony is discussed in paragraph 4. This irony is made to seem particularly unfortunate because the telegraphic errors are totally modern and could never have occurred in a pre-technological age.

In paragraph 5, the story's dramatic irony is introduced. This irony results from the lack of understanding by those closest to Louise and from the pompous intellectual blindness of the examining physicians. Paragraph 6 introduces Chopin's major idea criticizing marriage as an institution. Connected to the thematic purpose of the essay, however, this idea is shown to be integrated with the story's major situational irony. The final paragraph, 7, pays tribute to the story as a story and speculates about how Chopin deals truthfully with difficult issues of life and marriage.

### Writing Topics about Tone

1.  Consider a story or poem in which the speaker is the central character (for example, Matthew Arnold's "Dover Beach," Robert Frost's "Desert Places," Hardy's "The Man He Killed," John Keats's "Bright Star," Lowell's "Patterns," and Rossetti's "Echo." Write an essay showing how the language of the speaker affects your attitudes toward him or her (i.e., your sympathy for the speaker, your interest in the story or the situation).

2.  Write an essay comparing and contrasting attitudes toward two or more of the following female characters: Louise in Chopin's "The Story of an Hour," Mathilde in Guy de Maupassant's "The Necklace," Mrs. Popov in Chekhov's *The Bear*, and Minnie Wright in Glaspell's *Trifles*. How does the author's presentation control your understanding of them? What details of tone might be important in a feminist approach to these works?

3.  In Frank Connor's "First Confession," the adult narrator, Jackie, is describing events that happened to him as a child. What are your attitudes toward Jackie? What do you think are O'Connor's attitudes toward him? To what degree has Jackie separated himself from his childhood emotions? What does he say that might be considered residual childhood responses? What effect, if any, do such comments create?

4.  Write a fragment of a story or drama of your own about, for example, a student, a supervisor, or a politician. Treat your main character with dramatic irony; that is, your character thinks he or she knows all the details about a situation but really does not (e.g., a male student declares interest in a female student without

realizing that she is already engaged; a supervisor expresses distrust of one of the best workers in the firm; a politician accuses an opponent of actions that were done not by the opponent but by a supporter). What action, words, and situations do you think you should choose to make your irony clear, and why?

5. Write either (a) two character sketches or (b) two descriptions of an action, as though you were planning to include them as part of a story. For either your sketches or your descriptions, make the first favorable and the second negative. Describe your word choices in the contrasting accounts: What kinds of words do you select, and on what principles? What words might you select if you wanted a neutral account? On the basis of your answers, what can you conclude about the development of a fiction writer's style?

# Chapter 13

# Writing about Prosody: Sound, Rhythm, and Rhyme in Poetry

Poetry

**P**rosody (the pronunciation or accent of a song or poem, a song set to music) is the general word describing the study of poetic sounds and rhythms. Common alternative words are **metrics, versification, mechanics of verse**, and the **music of poetry**. Most readers, when reading poetry aloud, interpret the lines and develop an appropriate speed and expressiveness of delivery—a proper *rhythm*. Indeed, some people think of rhythm and sound as the *music* of poetry because they convey musical rhythms and tempos. Like music, poetry often requires a regular beat. The tempo and loudness of poetry may vary freely, however, and a reader may stop at any time to repeat the sounds and to think about the words and ideas. It is the music of poetry that makes the speaking and hearing of poetry dramatic, exciting, and inspiring.

In considering prosody, we should recognize that poets, being especially attuned to language, blend words and ideas together so that "the sound" becomes "an echo to the sense" (Pope, *An Essay on Criticism*, 1711, line 365). The consequence of this idea is that *prosodic technique cannot be separated from a poem's content.* For this reason, the study of prosody determines how poets control their words so that the sound of a poem complements its expression of emotions and ideas.

## Important Definitions for Studying Prosody

To understand and discuss prosody, you need to explain the various sounds of both speech and poetry. Let us grant that the subject is technical, detailed, and subtle, and as a result, the study of vocal production can take and has taken entire careers. A basic knowledge of spoken sound, however, will enable you to analyze that aspect of the poet's craft that pertains to qualities of pronunciation and rhythm.

### Vowel Sounds Create the Flow of Poetic Speech

A continuous stream of speech, whether conversation, oratory, or poetry, is provided mainly by **vowel sounds**. A vowel (from the Latin word *vox*, or "voice") results from vibrations resonating in the space between the tongue and the top of the mouth. As our tongues go up or down or forward or backward, as they curl or flatten out, and as our lips move synchronously with our tongues, we form vowels. Some vowels are "long," such as *ee* (fl*ee*), *ay* (st*ay*), *oh* (*o*pen), and *oo* (f*oo*d). Others are "short," such as *i* (f*i*t), *u* (f*u*n), and *e* (s*e*t). Some vowels are called "front" (e.g., s*ee*, pl*ay*) and some are called "back" (kn*o*wing, m*oo*n), depending on the position of the tongue in the production of the sound. Some are rounded (h*o*pe, h*oo*p) because their production requires pursed lips, but more are unrounded (gr*ee*n, sw*i*m).

Many of our English vowel sounds are pronounced as a *schwa*, or minimal vowel sound, despite their spellings (e.g., the *e* in "th*e* boy," the *a* in "*a*lone"). Thus, "*a*bout," "stag*e*s," "rap*i*d," "nati*o*n," and "circ*u*s" contain the vowels *a, e, i, o,* and *u,* but all the italicized letters make the same *schwa* sound.

Of special importance is the *diphthong* (two voices, two sounds)—that is, a meaningful sound that begins with one vowel sound and then is completed by the movement to another vowel sound. The three English diphthongs are *i* (tr*y*, appl*i*ance), *ou* (h*ou*se, sh*ou*t), and *oi* (f*oi*l, empl*oy*).

### *Consonant Sounds Are Meaningful Sounds Produced through the Creation of Vocal Obstructions in the Mouth*

**Consonant sounds** ("sounds made at the same time as vowels") result from the touching and near touching of various parts of the mouth (lips, tongue, teeth, hard palate, and soft palate), thus producing meaningful sounds that are made at the same time as the flow of vowel sound. Some consonants might theoretically be prolonged (e.g., *m, h, sh*), while others are by nature only momentary (*t, k*). In combination, consonants and vowels make for understandable speech. Making exact descriptions of the consonants of English speech is quite detailed and complex. Basically, however, consonant sounds are classified into three major groups.

1. **Stop sounds, also called *plosives,* are percussive and abrupt.** There are six *stop sounds*, which are made by the momentary stoppage and release of breath either when the lips touch each other (*p* and *b*, called "labial" consonants) or when the tongue touches the hard palate (the *k* and *g* in *keep* and *gear*, called "alveo-palatal" or "hard-palatal" consonants) or soft palate (the *k* and *g* in *cool* and *goal*, called "velar" or "soft-palatal" consonants), or when the tongue touches the alveolar ridge immediately above the upper teeth (*t* and *d*, called "dental" consonants).

2. **Continuant sounds are smooth and flowing.** *Continuant sounds* are produced by the steady release of the breath in conjunction with various positions of the tongue in relation to the lips, teeth, and palate, as in *n, ng, l, r, th* (as in *th*orn), *th* (as in *th*e), *f, v, s, z, sh* (as in *sh*arp), and *zh* (as in plea*s*ure); or with the touching of the lower lip and upper teeth for the sounds *f* and *v*; or with the touching of both lips for the sound *m*. Two special sounds called *affricates* begin with the stops *t* and *d* and then become the continuants *sh* and *zh* (as in *ch*ew and *j*udge).

3. **Semivowel sounds are more like consonants than vowels.** *Semivowel sounds* are midway between vowels and consonants, and they have in common that they move from an originating sound and then move to another vowel sound. They are *w* (*w*agon, *w*in, *w*eather), *y* (*y*es, *y*oung, un*i*on), and *h* (*h*ope, *h*eap).

*Consonant sounds may be either voiced or voiceless*    *Voiced consonants* are produced with the vibration of the vocal chords (e.g., *b, d, g, v, z, zh*), and *voiceless consonants* are produced by the breath alone, for this reason being whispered sounds (e.g., *p, t, k, f, s, sh*). Among the semivowels, *w* and *y* are voiced, but *h* is voiceless.

*Nasal Consonants result from the release of sound through the nose*     Three consonants require the stoppage of the breath in the mouth so that the sound can be released through the nose. The consonants, called *nasals*, are *n, m,* and *ng* (as in su*n*, su*m*, and su*ng*). In English, the *n* and *m* sounds may begin and end words or may appear in the middle of a word, whereas the *ng* sound appears in the middle or end of a word but does not begin a word. The nasals affect the pronunciation of adjoining consonants, as in words like *mountain* and *student*, in which the *t* and *d* sounds are released nasally by many speakers of English. Adjoining consonants also affect the pronunciation of the nasal, as in words like *sink* and *think*, in which the concluding *k* sound causes the preceding nasal to be an *ng* sound, as in *sing* and *thing*, even though the sound is spelled with an *n* alone.

## Segments: Individually Meaningful Sounds

Individual sounds in combination make up syllables and words, and separate words in combination make up lines of poetry. Syllables and words are made up of **segments**, or individually meaningful sounds (that linguists call *segmental phonemes*). In the word *top*, there are three meaningful segments: *t, o,* and *p*. When you hear these three sounds in order, you recognize the word *top*, as distinguished from *tape, tap, type,* and *taupe*. It takes three alphabetical letters—*t, o,* and *p*—to spell (or *graph*) *top* because each letter is identical with a segment. Quite often, however, English uses more than one letter to spell a segment. For example, in the word *enough*, there are four segments (*e, n, u, f* ), although six letters are required for the correct spelling: *e, n, ou,* and *gh*. The last two segments (*u* and *f* ) require two letters each (two letters forming one segment are called a *digraph*). In the word *through,* there are three segments but *seven* letters. To be spelled correctly in this word, the *oo* segment must have four letters (*ough*). Note, however, that in the word *flute* the *oo* segment requires only one letter, *u*. When we study the effects of various segments in relationship to poetic rhythm, we deal with **sound**; usually our concern is with prosodic devices such as alliteration, assonance, and rhyme.

   When segments are meaningfully combined, they make up syllables and words. A **syllable**, in both prose and poetry, consists of a single meaningful strand of sound such as the article *a* in "*a* table," the stem *lin* in "*lin*en," and the entire word *screech*. The article *a*, which is both a syllable and a word, has only one segment; *lin*, the first syllable of a two-syllable word, contains three segments (*lin* does not occur alone in English but is used in combinations such as *line* (or *lining*), *lingerie, linoleum, crinoline,* and *linnet*); *screech* is a complete word of one syllable consisting of the five segments *s, k, r, ee,* and *tch*. The past tense of *screech* (*screeched*) adds one meaningful sound, *t*, and two letters, *ed*, but this additional sound does not create a new syllable. The understanding of what constitutes syllables is important because poetic rhythm is determined by the positions of heavily stressed and lightly stressed syllables.

### Distinguish Between Spellings and the Actual Sounds of Words

It is important—vital—to understand the differences between spelling, or **graphics**, and pronunciation, or **phonetics**. Not all English sounds are spelled and pronounced in the same way, as with *top*. Thus the letter *s* has three very different sounds in the words *sweet, sugar,* and *flows: s, sh* (as in "*sharp*"), and *z*. On the other hand, the words *Fuchsia, ocean, nation, sure, fissure, Eschscholzia,* and *machine* use different combinations of letters to spell the *sh* sound. These combinations are *chsi, ce, ti, s* followed by *u, ss* followed by *u, schsch,* and *ch*. In the word *business,* the *si* spells a *z* segment; curiously, in some American dialects the *ss* also spells a *z* segment.

Vowel sounds may also be spelled in different ways. The *ee* sound, for example, can be spelled *i* in *machine, ee* in *speed, ea* in *eat, e* in *even,* and *y* in *funny,* yet the vowel sounds in *eat, break,* and *bear* are not the same even though they are spelled the same. Contrastingly, a beginning *w* sound in English may be spelled with a *w,* as in *win* and *wine,* but it is also spelled with an *o* in the word *one.* Once again in the word *business,* the *u* spells a short *i* (as in *trip*), and the *e* also spells a short *i.* Remember this: In English, with both consonants and vowel sounds, *do not confuse spellings with sounds.*

## Poetic Rhythm

Rhythm in speech is a combination of vocal speeds, rises and falls, starts and stops, vigor and slackness, and relaxation and tension. In ordinary speech and in prose, rhythm is not as important as the flow of ideas. In poetry, rhythm is significant because poetry is emotionally charged, compact, and intense. Poets invite us to change speeds while reading— to slow down and linger over some words and sounds and to pass rapidly over others. They also invite us to give more-than-ordinary vocal stress or emphasis to certain syllables and less stress to others. The more intense syllables are called **heavy stress** syllables, and it is the heavy stresses that determine the **accent** or **beat** of a poetic **line**. The less intense syllables receive **light stress**. In traditional verse, poets select patterns called **feet**, which consist of a regularized relationship of heavy stresses to light stresses.

### Scansion is the Systematic Study of Poetic Rhythm

To study the patterns of versification in any poem, you **scan** the poem. The act of scanning—**scansion**—enables you to discover not only how the poem establishes a prevailing metrical pattern but also how and why there are variations in the pattern.

*Determine Stresses, or Beats*    In the scansion of a poem, it is important to use a commonly recognized notational system to record stresses or accents. A *heavy* or *primary stress* (also called an **accented syllable**) may be indicated by capital letters, as in "To BE or NOT to BE," or it may also be indicated by a prime mark or **acute accent** (´). A *light stress* (also sometimes called an **unaccented syllable**) has often been indicated by a bowl-like half circle called a **breve** (˘) or sometimes by a raised circle or degree sign (°). If you are using capital letters to indicate a heavy stress, use lowercase letters alone, without any marks over the letters, to indicate the light stress, as in John Milton's

"When I con-SID-er HOW my LIGHT is SPENT." To separate one foot from another, a **virgule** or slash (/) may be used. Thus, the following line, from Samuel Taylor Coleridge's "The Rime of the Ancient Mariner," may be schematized formally in this way:

WA – ter, / WA - ter, / EV - ery WHERE

Here the virgules or slashes show that the line contains two two-syllable feet followed by a single three-syllable foot.

*Determine the Meter or Measure*    A major part of scansion is the determination of a poem's **meter**, or the number of feet in its lines. Lines containing five feet are **pentameter**, four are **tetrameter**, three are **trimeter**, two are **dimeter**, and one is **monometer**. (To these may be added the less common line lengths **hexameter**, a six-foot line; **heptameter** or **septenary**, seven feet; and **octameter**, eight feet.) In terms of accent or beat, a trimeter line has three beats (heavy stresses), a pentameter line five beats, and so on.

# The Major Metrical Feet

You are now ready to scan poems and to determine the patterns of metrical feet, which measure the relationships of syllables and stresses. In English the names of the feet are derived from Greek poetry. We may classify them as feet of two syllables, three syllables, and one syllable (or imperfect).

### *The Two-Syllable Foot*

1. **Iamb** (*Light/Heavy*). The most important poetic foot in English is the iamb (a word of unknown origin), which contains a light stress followed by a heavy stress:

the WINDS

The iamb is the most important and most common foot because it most nearly duplicates natural speech while it also elevates speech to poetry. It is the most versatile of English poetic feet, and it is capable of great variation. Even within the same line, iambic feet vary in intensity, thus supporting the shades of meaning designed by the poet. For example, in this line of iambic pentameter from William Wordsworth's sonnet "The World Is Too Much with Us," each foot is unique;

The WINDS / that WILL / be HOWL - / ing AT / all HOURS, /

Even though "will" and "at" technically are heavily stressed in their individual iambic positions, they are not as strongly emphasized as "winds," "howl-," and "hours" (indeed, they are also less strong than "all," which is in the light-stress position in the concluding iamb). Such variability, approximating the stresses and rhythms of actual speech, makes the iambic foot suitable for both serious and light verse, and it therefore helps poets to focus attention on ideas and emotions. If they use it with skill, it never becomes monotonous, for it does not distract readers by drawing attention to its own rhythm.

2. **Trochee** *(Heavy/Light)*. The trochee (*"running"*), sometimes called the **choree** (*"dancing"*), consists of a heavy accent followed by a light one:

FLOW – er

Rhythmically, most two-syllable English words are **trochaic** (tro-KAY-ick), as may be seen in words like *author, early, follow, major, morning, often, singing, snowfall, something, story, water, walking, willow,* and *window.* A major exception is seen in many two-syllable words beginning with prefixes, such as *sublime, because,* and *impel.* Another exception is found in two-syllable words that are borrowed from another language but are still pronounced as in the original language, as with *antique, chemise, garage, machine,* and *technique,* all of which are importations from French, a language in which an iambic structure prevails. Illustrating the characteristic trochaic rhythm of English, however, the final stresses in many French words borrowed many years ago now regularly accent the next-to-last syllable, as shown by *apartment, castle, cherry, denim, expression, incoherence, language, lesson, nation,* and *very.*

Because trochaic rhythm has often been called *falling, dying, light,* or *anticlimactic* and because iambic rhythm has been called *rising, elevating, serious,* and *climactic,* poets have preferred the iambic foot. They therefore have arranged various placements of single- and multiple-syllable words, and have also used a variety of other means so that the heavy-stress syllable is at the end of the foot, as in Shakespeare's

With - IN / his BEND - / ing SICK - / le's COM - / pass COME, /

in which three successive trochaic words (*bending, sickle's,* and *compass*) are arranged to match the iambic meter.

3. **Spondee** *(Heavy/Heavy)*. The spondee (originally two long notes played at the pouring of an offering)—also called a **hovering accent**—consists of two successive, equally heavy accents, as in "men's eyes" in Shakespeare's line

When IN / dis - GRACE / with FOR - /tune AND / MEN'S EYES

The spondee is mainly a substitute foot in English verse because successive spondees usually are resolved into iambs or trochees. An entire poem written in spondees would be unlikely within traditional metrical patterns and ordinary English syntax. As a substitute, however, the spondee creates emphasis, very often because the two stressed syllables of the spondee are next to a stressed syllable in a previous or following foot, thus in practice creating three successive strong stresses and in some instances four. The effect is that in reading the voice lingers on or hovers over the stressed words, and the mind dwells on the ideas expressed in the words. This kind of emphasis is seen in the first two iambic foot positions in line 9 of John Keats's "Bright Star":

NO—YET / STILL STEAD - / fast, STILL / un - CHANGE - / a - BLE

4. **PYRRHIC** *(Light/Light)*. The pyrrhic (a *"foot,"* a *"war dance"*) consists of two unstressed syllables, even though one of them may be in a normally stressed position, as in "on their" in this line from Alexander Pope's *Pastorals* (4.5):

Now SLEEP - / ing FLOCKS / on their / SOFT FLEEC - / es LIE. /

The pyrrhic is usually made up of weakly accented words such as prepositions (e.g., *on, to*) and articles (*the, a*). Like the spondee, it is a substitute foot for an iamb or a trochee. An entire poem could not be in pyrrhics because most of the pyrrhics, like spondees, would be resolved as trochees and iambs. As a substitute foot, however, the pyrrhic acts as a rhythmic catapult to move the reader swiftly to the next heavy-stress syllable, and therefore it undergirds the ideas conveyed by more significant words.

### The Three-Syllable Foot

1. **Dactyl** (*Heavy/Light/Light*). The dactyl (originally Greek for "a finger" because a finger has a long joint and two shorter joints) begins with a heavy stress followed by two lights:

   > GREEN as our / HOPE in it, /WHITE as our
   > / FAITH in it. / (Swinburne)

2. **Anapest** (*Light/Light/Heavy*). The **anapest** (*beaten back* or *turned around*; the reverse of a dactyl) consists of two light accents followed by a heavy accent:

   > by the DAWN'S / ear - ly LIGHT. / (Key)

### The Imperfect Foot

A single stressed syllable by itself or an unstressed syllable by itself creates an **imperfect foot**. There is nothing "imperfect" about an imperfect foot. Instead, the imperfect foot is a variant or substitute occurring in a poem in which one of the major feet forms the metrical pattern. Most often, the imperfect foot is designed to make the poem sound more natural, less like poetry and more like ordinary speech. The second line of our national anthem, Francis Scott Key's "The Star-Spangled Banner," for example, is anapestic, but it contains an imperfect foot at the end:

> What so PROUD - / ly we HAILED /
> at the TWI- /light's last GLEAM- / ing. /

## Substitution

Most regular poems (that is, poems written according to the "rules" of prosody) follow a formal pattern that may be analyzed according to the feet we have been describing here. Too much formal regularity, however, sometimes makes for monotony, and so for interest and emphasis (and also, especially, because of the natural rhythms of English speech), poets frequently alter and enlarge the regular patterns through the **substitution** of a dominant foot by a variant foot. Thus, in an iambic line the poet may insert a spondee or an anapest and by this means provide a wider and more conversational rhythmical range than the unvarying use of the poem's chosen pattern. As an example, the pattern of Jonathan Swift's "A Description of the Morning" is iambic pentameter

> ### SPECIAL METERS
>
> Many poems contain meters other than those described above. Poets like Robert Browning; Alfred, Lord Tennyson; Edgar Allan Poe; and Algernon Charles Swinburne introduce special or unusual meters. Other poets manipulate pauses, or caesurae (discussed later), to create the effects of unusual meters. For these reasons, you should know about metrical feet such as the following:
>
> 1. **Amphibrach** ("short at both ends"). A light, heavy, and light:
>
>    Ah FEED me / and FILL me / with PLEAS - ure / (Swinburne)
>
> 2. **Amphimacer** ("long at both ends"), or **cretic** (a song from the Island of Crete). A heavy, light, and heavy:
>
>    LOVE is BEST. / (Browning)
>
> 3. **Bacchius** or **Bacchic** (pertaining to Bacchus, the Ancient Greek god of wine and conviviality). A light stress followed by two heavy stresses:
>
>    Some LATE LARK / (William Ernest Henley)
>
> 4. **Dipody, dipodic foot** (literally, "two feet" combining to make one), or **syzygy** (a "yoking together"), or *double duple* meter. Dipodic measure develops in longer lines when a poet submerges two regular feet under a stronger beat so that a "galloping" or "rollicking" rhythm results. The following line from John Masefield's "Cargoes," for example, may be scanned as trochaic hexameter, with the concluding foot being an iamb:
>
>    QUIN - que / REME of / NIN- e- /
>    VEH from / DIS-tant / o - PHIR, /
>
> In reading, however, a stronger beat is superimposed, which makes one foot out of two—*dipodic measure,* or *syzygy:*
>
> QUIN - quer - eme of / NIN - e - veh from / DIS – tant o –PHIR,

(i.e., five iambs per line). However, Swift introduces a formal substitution at the beginning of the following line:

DUNS at / his LORD- / ship's GATE / be - GAN / to MEET;

The first foot is a trochee, and the strong accent on *Duns* enables Swift to stress his comic assertion that even a member of the nobility, who supposedly has the money to pay his bills, does not do so and therefore is dunned by bill collectors. Note also that the light accent on *at* enables the voice to move rapidly through *at his lord*. Thus, although the first two feet are a trochee and an iamb, the rhythmical effect is that of an imperfect foot followed by an anapest:

DUNS at / his LORD- /

This fairly common substitution helps Swift emphasize and satirize the unglamorous side of London life early in the eighteenth century.

When studying rhythm, your main concern in noting substitutions is to determine the formal metrical pattern and then to analyze the variations on this pattern and their principal techniques and effects. Always try to show how these variations have enabled the poet to get points across and to achieve emphasis.

## Accentual, Strong-Stress, and "Sprung" Rhythms

The foregoing descriptions of poetic feet will enable the analysis of most so-called traditional poetry. A number of poets, however, stretch the bounds of traditional feet, and use often unmeasured rhythms derived from accentual or strong stresses. Such lines are historically linked to English poetry as our language existed a thousand years ago. At that time, each line was divided in two, with two major alliterated stresses occurring in each half. In the nineteenth century, Gerard Manley Hopkins (1844–1889) developed what he called "sprung" rhythm, a rhythm in which the major stresses would be released or "sprung" from the line. The method is complex, but one of the primary characteristics is the placement together of one-syllable stressed words, as in second of these lines from his poem "God's Grandeur":

> It gathers to a greatness, like the ooze of oil
> Crushed. Why do MEN THEN NOW NOT RECK his ROD°?

Here we find five successive heavy stresses. Many of Hopkins's lines combine alliteration and strong stresses in this way to create the same powerful emphasis.

## The Caesura: The Pause That Aims for Variety and Natural Rhythms in Poetry

Whenever we speak, we run words together rapidly without apparent pauses, but we do stop briefly and almost unnoticeably between significant units or phrases. Intelligible conversation could not take place without these pauses, which, both grammatically and rhythmically, create separate units of meaning called **cadence groups**. In poetry using a regular meter, the cadence groups operate just as they do in prose to make ideas

---

°rod: royal scepter.

clear. That is, as we follow the poetic measures, we also pause briefly at the ends of phrases, and we pause longer, for emphasis, at the ends of sentences. In scansion, the name of these pauses, which linguists call *junctures*, is **caesura** (a "cutting off"), pluralized as **caesurae**. When writing out our scansion of a line, we use two diagonal slashes or virgules (//) to indicate a caesura so that the caesura can be distinguished from the single virgule separating feet. Often the caesura coincides with the end of a foot, as at the end of the second iamb in line 4 of Robert Frost's "Desert Places":

> But a / FEW WEEDS // and STUB - / ble SHOW - / ing LAST. /

The caesura, however, may fall within a foot, and there may be more than one in a line, as within the second and fourth iambs in line 1 of "Desert Places":

> Snow FALL - / ing // and / NIGHT FALL - / ing // FAST / oh, FAST /

When a caesura ends a line, usually marked by a comma, semicolon, or period, that line is **end-stopped**, as in this famous line opening Keats's "Endymion":

> a THING / of BEAU - / ty // is / a JOY / for - EV - er. /

If a line has no punctuation at the end and the thought carries over to the next line, it is called **run-on**. A term also used to indicate run-on lines is **enjambement** ("straddling"). The following passage, a continuation of the poem by Keats, contains three run-on lines. Incidentally, Keats was widely criticized in his time for this use of enjambement.

> Its loveliness increases; // it will never
> Pass into nothingness; // but still will keep
> A bower quiet for us, // and a sleep
> Full of sweet dreams, // . . .

It is important to recognize that the formal rhythms of poetry are superimposed on the rhythms of natural speech, creating a tension between the two. By manipulating the placement of caesurae—the pauses that fall randomly in speech—poets create many of the variant rhythms that are provided by formal substitution. If the poet ends a cadence group within a foot, the pause, or caesura, may cause us actually to *hear* trochees, amphibrachs, and other variant feet even though the line may scan correctly and regularly in the established meter. This type of de facto variation is **rhetorical substitution.** A noteworthy example in an iambic pentameter line is this one from the first Epistle of Pope's *Essay on Man* (Epistle I, line 66):

> His AC- / tions', // PAS-/sions', // BE-/ing's, // USE /and END; /

This is the second line in a "heroic" couplet, which theoretically requires that there should be only a single caesura following the fourth syllable. In this line, however, Pope provides us with great rhythmical variety. He uses not one but rather three caesurae, each of them producing an emphatic pause or juncture. Pope's line is regularly iambic, but the effect is different in actual reading or speaking. Because of the caesurae after the third, fifth, and seventh syllables, the rhythm produces an amphibrach, a trochee, another trochee, and an amphimacer. The effect is a skillful line containing two inner two-syllable feet, framed by two three-syllable feet, thus:

> His AC-tions', // PAS-sions', // BE-ing's, // USE and END;
> AMPHIBRACH          TROCHEE          TROCHEE          AMPHIMACER

The spoken substitutions brought about by the caesurae in this regular line produce the effect of substitution—rhetorical substitution—and therefore tension and interest. Never believe for even a moment that Pope did not know exactly what he was doing with words and rhythms.

## Segmental Poetic Devices

Once you have completed your analysis of rhythms, you should consider the segmental poetic devices in the poem. Usually, these devices are used to create emphasis, but sometimes in context they may echo or imitate actions and objects. The segmental devices most common in poetry are assonance, alliteration, onomatopoeia, euphony, and cacophony.

### Identical Vowel Sounds Create Assonance

**Assonance** (response *to a sound*) is the repetition of identical *vowel* sounds in different words—for example, the short *i* in "swift Camilla skims" (Pope). It is a strong means of emphasis, as in the following line by Edmund Spenser, where the *u* sound connects the two words *lull* and *slumber*, and the short *i* connects *him*, *in*, and *his*:

> And more, to lull him in his slumber soft.

### Identical Consonant Sounds Create Alliteration

Like assonance, **alliteration** (response *to a letter*) is a means of highlighting ideas by words containing the same consonant sound—for example, the repeated *m* in Spenser's "Mixed with a murmuring wind," or the *s* sound in Edmund Waller's praise of Oliver Cromwell, "Your never-failing sword made war to cease" (*A Panegyric to My Lord Protector, 1655 line 109*), which emphasizes the connection between the words *sword* and *cease*.

There are two kinds of alliteration. Most commonly, alliteration is regarded as the repetition of identical consonant sounds that usually (but not necessarily) begin syllables in close patterns—for example, in Pope's lines "Laborious, heavy, busy, bold, and blind," "While pensive poets painful vigils keep," and "brazen brainless brothers." When used judiciously, alliteration gives strength to ideas by emphasizing key words, but too much can cause comic and catastrophic consequences.

The second form of alliteration occurs when a poet repeats identical or similar consonant sounds that do not begin syllables but nevertheless create a pattern—for example, the *z* segment in the line "In these places freezing breezes easily cause sneezes," or the *m*, *b*, and *p* segments (all of which are made *bilabially*—that is, with both lips) in "The *m*iserably *m*umbling and *m*omentously *m*urmuring *b*umpkin *p*ropels *p*egs and *p*ebbles in the *bubb*ling *p*ool." Such clearly designed patterns are hard to overlook.

### Verbal Imitation of Real Sounds Is Onomatopoeia, or "Poetic Sound Effects"

**Onomatopoeia** ("the coining or creating of names") is a blend of consonant and vowel sounds designed to *imitate* or *suggest* a situation or an action. It is made possible in poetry because many English words are **echoic** in origin; that is, they are verbal echoes of the actions they describe, such as *buzz, bump, slap*, and so on. In "Anthem for Doomed Youth," Wilfred Owen uses such words to create onomatopoeia. Through the combined use of assonance and alliteration, he imitates the repeating sounds of rifles in combat in the passage "Only the stuttering rifles' rapid rattle / Can patter out their hasty orisons." Here, Owen's use of the *t, r*, and *k* sounds, together with the short *a* vowel, accounts for his successful control of onomatopoeia.

### Pleasing Sounds Create Euphony, and Harsh Sounds Create Cacophony

Words describing smooth or jarring sounds, particularly those resulting from consonants, are euphony and cacophony. **Euphony** ("good sound") refers to words containing consonants that permit an easy and smooth flow of spoken sound. Although there is no rule that some consonants are inherently more pleasant than others, students of poetry often cite sounds like *m, n, ng, l, v*, and *z*, together with *w* and *y*, as being especially easy on the ears. The opposite of euphony is **cacophony** ("bad sound"), in which percussive and choppy sounds make for vigorous and noisy pronunciation, as in tongue twisters like "black bug's blood" and "shuffling shellfish fashioned by a selfish sushi chef." Obviously, unintentional cacophony is a mark of imperfect control. When a poet deliberately creates it for effect, however, as in Pope's "The hoarse, rough verse should like the torrent roar" (*An Essay on Criticism*, line 369) and in Coleridge's "Huge fragments vaulted like rebounding hail, / Or chaffy grain beneath the thresher's flail" ("Kubla Khan," lines 21–22), cacophony is a mark of poetic skill. Although poets generally aim at easily flowing, euphonious lines, cacophony does have a place, always depending on the poet's intention and subject matter.

## Rhyme: The Duplication and Similarity of Sounds

**Rhyme** refers to words containing identical final syllables. One type of rhyme involves words with identical concluding vowel sounds, or assonance, as in *day, weigh, hey, bouquet, fiancé*, and *matinee*. A second type of rhyme is created by assonance combined with identical consonant sounds, as in *ache, bake, break*, and *opaque*; or *turn, yearn, fern, spurn*, and *adjourn*; or *double* and *trouble*, or *slippery* and *frippery*. Rhymes like these, because their rhyming sounds are identical, are called **exact rhymes.** It is important to note that rhymes result from *sound* rather than from spelling; words do not have to be spelled the same way or look alike to rhyme. All the words rhyming with *day*, for example, are spelled differently, but because they all contain the same "long ay" sound, they rhyme.

Rhyme, above all, gives delight and sustains interest, and it strengthens a poem's psychological impact. Through its network of identical sounds that echo and resonate in our minds, it promotes memory by clinching feelings and ideas. It has been an important aspect of poetry for hundreds of years, and, although many poets have shunned it because they find it restrictive and artificial, it is closely connected with how well particular poems move us or leave us flat. There are few restrictions on the types of words that poets may choose in making rhymes. Nouns may be rhymed with verbs, adjectives, adverbs, and other nouns or with any other rhyming word, regardless of part of speech.

Most often, rhymes are placed at the ends of lines. Two successive lines may rhyme, for example, or rhymes may appear in alternating lines. It is also possible to introduce rhyming words at intervals of four, five, or more lines. If rhyming sounds are too far away from each other, however, it is difficult for readers to recall them and they therefore lose their effectiveness. Sometimes poets use rhyme within individual lines—**internal rhyme.** Amy Lowell uses internal rhyme effectively in "Patterns," a poem about the grief and sorrow of war. In lines 2 and 3 she rhymes *daffodils* and *squills*, a rhyme she repeats internally in line 22 ("daffodils and squills") and also in line 95 ("squills and daffodils"), thus emphasizing these flowers, which might have been part of a wedding bouquet that is never to be. Internal rhyme is not common, but you should be alert for it and make note of it when it occurs.

Poets who are skillful and original rhymers are able to create fresh, unusual, and surprising turns of thought. We can therefore judge poets on their use of rhyme. Often poets are truly creative rhymers, putting together words like *bent 'em* and *Tarentum* or *masterly* and *dastardly*. Some rhymers, whom an anonymous sixteenth-century critic called a "rakehelly rout of ragged rhymers," are satisfied with easy rhymes, or **cliché rhymes,** like *trees* and *breeze*, a rhyme that Pope criticized in 1711 in *An Essay on Criticism* (lines 350–351):

> Where-e'er you find the *cooling Western Breeze,*
> In the next Line, it *whispers thro' the Trees;*

But good rhymes and good poets go together, in creative cooperation. The seventeenth-century poet John Dryden, who wrote volumes of rhyming couplets, acknowledged that the need to find rhyming words inspired ideas he had not anticipated. In this sense, rhyme has been—and still is—a vital element of poetic creativity.

## Rhyme and Meter

The effects of rhyme are closely bound to rhythm and meter. There is general agreement that rhymes coinciding with a strong accent are conducive to serious subjects. Commensurately, rhymes coinciding with syllables of light stress are appropriate for light and comic subject matter. There is no hard-and-fast rule about such matters, for the effects of rhyme always result from the poet's skill, regardless of rhymes. There is enough truth in the observations, however, to warrant considering the relationship of rhyme and accent.

### Rising Rhymes Form the Climaxing Syllables
### of Iambs and Anapests

The most significant type of **rising rhyme** is **iambic rhyme**, which utilizes one-syllable words in an iambic foot (like *the west* and *in rest, more strong* and *ere long*) and two-syllable words in which the accent falls on the second syllable (like *away* and *today, demand* and *command.* Such rhymes are also called **heavy-stress rhyme**, or **accented rhyme**. Iambic rhyme is illustrated in the concluding lines of Keats's "Bright Star" (the rhymes are capitalized):

> Still, still to hear her tender-taken BREATH,
> And so live ever—or else swoon to DEATH.

Here, the rhyming sounds are produced by one-syllable words—*breath* and *death*—that occur in the final heavy-stress positions of the lines. The rhyme climaxing a final syllable can also involve spondees, as in lines 9–12 of Shakespeare's "Sonnet 18: Shall I Compare Thee to a Summer's Day?" (capitalized to show stress):

> But thy eternal summer shall NOT FADE,
> Nor lose possession of that fair THOU OWEST;
> Nor shall Death brag thou wander'st in HIS SHADE,
> When in eternal lines to time THOU GROWEST.

### Falling Rhymes Conclude with One or Two
### or More Lightly Stressed Syllables.

Rhymes using words of two or more syllables in which the heavy stress is followed by light syllables are **trochaic rhyme** or **double rhyme** for two-syllable rhymes and **dactylic rhyme** or **triple rhyme** for three-syllable rhymes. Less technically, these types of rhymes are also called **falling rhymes** or, sometimes, **dying rhymes** because the intensity of pronunciation decreases on the light accent or accents following the heavy accent. Coleridge's "Kubla Khan" (lines 17 and 18) furnishes us with an example of trochaic rhyme (capitalized here):

> And from this chasm, with ceaseless turmoil SEETHING,
> As if this earth in fast thick pants were BREATHING

Here, the rhyme almost pictorially describes the "fountain" that is bursting upward and then falling downward from the chasm in the scene that Coleridge makes verbally for us here.

Double rhymes can also be used to stress irony, as in *measure* and *pleasure* in Wordsworth's "Lines Written in Early Spring" (lines 13–16, capitalized here):

> The birds around me hopped and played,
>> Their thoughts I cannot MEASURE—
> But the least motion which they made,
>> It seemed a thrill of PLEASURE.

In this poem, Wordsworth contrasts the beauty and innocence of a natural scene with the inequality and injustice of the human scene. The effect of his trochaic rhyme is to complement his lamentation of the fact that human beings fail to make their own relationships as beautiful as the world that nature has given us.

Dactylic, or triple, rhyme, even more than trochaic rhyme, is light or humorous because it tends to minimize the subject matter and maximize the rhythm. A poet noted for his cleverness in this regard is Ogden Nash (1902–1971), who created many comic triple rhymes. In "Very Like a Whale," for example, we find *better for* rhymed with *metaphor*, and *experience* with *Assyrians*. How many of us could be clever enough to create rhymes like these?

### Variations in Rhyme Extend the Boundaries of Rhyming Poetry

Unlike poets writing in other languages (such as Italian, which offers virtually endless rhyming possibilities because most Italian words end in vowel sounds), English poets are limited in selecting rhymes because our language is short in identical word terminations. To compensate for this shortfall of English rhymes, a tradition has grown that many English words may be rhymed even if their sounds do not duplicate each other exactly.

Rhymes may therefore be created out of words with similar but not identical sounds—**inexact rhyme**. In most inexact rhymes, either the vowel segments are different while the consonants are the same or vice versa. In addition to *inexact rhyme,* this type of rhyme is variously called **slant rhyme, near rhyme, half rhyme, off rhyme, analyzed rhyme**, or **suspended rhyme**. In employing slant rhyme, a poet can pair *bleak* with *broke* or *could* with *solitude*. We find slant rhymes in Coleridge's "Kubla Khan," where he rhymes *haunted* with *enchanted*, *ever* and *river*, and *forced* and *burst*.

Another common variation is **eye rhyme**, or **sight rhyme**. In eye rhyme, the sounds to be eye-rhymed are *identical in spelling* but *different in pronunciation*. Entire words may be eye-rhymed, so that *wind* (verb) may be joined to *wind* (noun), and *cóntest* (noun) may be used with *contest́* (verb). In most eye rhymes, however, it is only the relevant parts of words that must be spelled identically. Thus, *stove* may pair with *prove* and *above* and *bough* may match *cough, dough, enough,* and *through*, despite all the differing pronunciations. The following lines contain eye rhyme:

> Although his claim was not to praise but *bury*,
> His speech for Caesar roused the crowd to *fury*.

The different pronunciations of *bury* and *fury* make clear the contrast between exact rhyme and eye rhyme. In exact rhyme, *identical sound is crucial*; spelling is usually the same but may be different as long as the sounds remain identical. In eye rhyme, the *eye-rhyming patterns must be spelled identically, but the sounds must be different*.

An additional variation is **identical rhyme**; that is, the same words are placed into rhyming positions, such as *veil* and *veil* or *stone* and *stone*. Perhaps the most extreme variation is *vowel rhyme*, in which poets put words ending in vowels into rhyming positions, as in *day* and *sky* or *key* and *play*.

# Rhyme Schemes

A **rhyme scheme** refers to a poem's pattern of rhyming sounds, which can be schematized by alphabetical letters. The first rhyming sounds, such as *love* and *dove*, are marked with an *a*; the next rhyming sounds, such as *swell* and *fell*, receive a *b*; the next sounds, such as *first* and *burst*, receive a *c*; and so on. Thus, a pattern of lines ending with the words *love, moon, thicket; dove, June, picket;* and *above, croon, wicket* can be schematized as a b c, a b c, a b c.

To formulate a rhyme scheme or pattern, you include the meter and the number of feet in each line as well as the letters indicating rhymes. Here is such a formulation:

Iambic pentameter:  a b a b, c d c d, e f e f

This scheme shows that all the lines in the poem are iambic, with five feet in each line. Commas are used here to mark a stanzaic pattern of three 4-line units, or **quatrains,** with the rhymes falling on the first and third, and the second and fourth, lines of each quatrain.

Should the number of feet in the lines of a poem or **stanza** vary, as in odes and songs, you show this fact by using a number in front of each letter:

Iambic:  4a 3b 4a 3b 5a 5a 4b

This formulation shows an intricate pattern of rhymes and line lengths in a stanza of seven lines. The first, third, fifth, and sixth lines rhyme and vary from four to five feet. The second, fourth, and seventh lines also rhyme and vary from three to four feet.

The absence of a rhyme sound is indicated by an *x*. Thus, you formulate the rhyme scheme of **ballad measure,** as in Dudley Randall's "Ballad of Birmingham," like this:

Iambic:  4x 3a 4x 3a

The formulation shows that the quatrain alternates iambic tetrameter (four feet) with iambic trimeter (three feet). In this ballad quatrain, only lines 2 and 4 rhyme; there is no end rhyme in lines 1 and 3.

# Writing about Prosody

Because studying prosody requires a good deal of specific detail and description, it is best to limit your study to a short poem or to a short passage from a long poem (as with the illustrative essay). A sonnet, a stanza of a lyric poem, or a fragment from a long poem will often be sufficient. If you choose a fragment, it should be self-contained, such as an entire speech or a short episode or scene.

The analysis of even a short poem, however, can grow long because of the need to describe word positions and stresses and also to determine the various effects. For this reason, you do not have to exhaust your topic. Try to make your discussion representative of the prosody of your poem or passage.

Your first reading in preparation for your essay should be for comprehension. On second and third readings, make notes of sounds, accents, and rhymes by reading the poem aloud. To perceive sounds, one student assisted herself by reading aloud in an exaggerated way in front of a mirror. If you have privacy or are not self-conscious, you might do the same. Let yourself go a bit. As you dramatize your reading (maybe even in front of fellow students), you will find that heightened levels of reading also accompany the poet's expression of important ideas. Mark these spots for later analysis so that you will be able to make strong assertions about the relationship of sound to sense.

As a goal, you might try to determine whether and how the prosody of a poem may be used as an organizational element. In an Italian or Petrarchan sonnet, for example, the rhymes are important in tying together the development of ideas. In a Shakespearean sonnet, there are three 4-line groups (quatrains), each containing the development of a particular idea or image or symbol, and the concluding two lines rhyme and at the same time create a "cap," or idea, tying the previous ideas together.

Carry out your study of the passage in the following way. What counts in this preliminary study of prosody is that your analyses be clear enough to provide help in developing your actual discussion.

- Prepare a working copy of the poem or passage and duplicate it three or four times. Triple space your copy so that you will have plenty of room to mark your observations.
- Determine the formal pattern of metrical feet. You may wish to use lowercase letters for light stresses and capital letters for heavy stresses, as in Tennyson's "And ON / a SUD - /den, LO! / the LEV - / el LAKE." Capital letters bring out the strong accents and are especially graphic in the indication of spondees. If your poem is spoken by an "I," for analytical purposes you may write the capital *I* as a small letter, as in "i SAID." [There are other ways to mark the feet. A traditional way is to use a short acute accent or stress mark for heavily stressed syllables (´) and either a breve or a degree sign for unaccented or lightly stressed syllables ( ˘ or °), as in "And ón / a súd / den Ló! / the lév - / el Láke." Capital letters, however, are more noticeable and are more easily managed.]
- Indicate the separate feet by a diagonal slash or virgule (/). Indicate caesurae and end-of-line pauses by double virgules (//).
- Use colored pencils or some other clear system of marking to underline, circle, make boxes, or otherwise mark the formal and rhetorical substitutions that you discover. Students have actually enjoyed the discovery of metrics and versification that the colored pencil system brings out.
- Do the same for alliteration, assonance, onomatopoeia, and rhyme. The use of a separate color for each separate effect is helpful, for different colors make prosodic distinctions stand out clearly. Any easily recognized system that is convenient for you is acceptable. It is also a good idea to circle clear variations in regular and substitute metrical patterns. (Thus, anapests and trochees might be circled or underlined to help you in identifying them when you begin writing your essay.)
- It is good to use a standard pronunciation guide for your discussion of sounds. You may employ one of the standard collegiate dictionaries. If you have had formal linguistic study, by all means use the phonemic or phonetic systems if you have these as symbols or special characters on your computer. If you have difficulty in using these systems when you are typing your essay or preparing it on the computer, you may wish to create your own method of indicating sounds,

but try the computer first. That may not be an easy task, and if you still have trouble, you might use any workable system. Thus, to indicate the vowel sound in "yes," you might use *eh* and then use *sh* for the consonant sound in "shake" or "nation," *uh* for the vowel sound in "up," and so on.

Once you have analyzed the various effects in your poem and have recorded these on your work sheets and in your notes, you will be ready to formulate a central idea and organization. The focus of your essay should reflect the most significant features of prosody in relationship to some other element of the poem, such as speaker, tone, or ideas.

## Organize Your Essay about Prosody

Depending on your assignment, you might wish to discuss all aspects of rhythm or sound, or perhaps just one, such as the poet's use of regular meter, a particular substitution, or alliteration or assonance. It is possible, for example, to devote an entire essay to (1) regular meter; (2) one particular variation in meter, such as the anapest or spondee; (3) the caesura; (4) assonance; (5) alliteration; (6) onomatopoeia; or (7) rhyme.

*Introduction*    After a brief description of the poem (such as that it is a sonnet, a two-stanza lyric, a ballad, etc.), establish the scope of your essay. Your central idea will outline the thought that you wish to carry out through your prosodic analysis, such as that regularity of meter is consistent with a happy, firm vision of love or life, that frequent spondees emphasize the solidity of the speaker's wish to love, or that particular sounds echo some of the poem's actions.

*Body*    The body may include all the following elements or just one, depending on your instructor's assignment.

1. **Rhythm.** Establish the formal metrical pattern. What is the dominant metrical foot and line length? Are some lines shorter than the pattern? What relationship do the variable lengths have with the subject matter? If the poem is a lyric or a sonnet, are important words and syllables successfully placed in stressed positions in order to achieve emphasis? Try to relate line lengths to exposition, development of ideas, and rising or falling emotions. It is also important to look for either repeating or varying metrical patterns as the subject matter reaches peaks or climaxes. Generally, deal with the relationship between the formal rhythmical pattern and the poet's ideas and attitudes.

   When noting substitutions, analyze the formal variations and the principal effects of these. If you concentrate on only one substitution, describe any apparent pattern in its use—that is, its locations, recurrences, and effects on meaning.

   For caesurae, treat the effectiveness of the poet's control. Can you see any pattern of use? Are the pauses regular or random? Describe noticeable principles of placement, such as (1) the creation of rhythmical similarities in various parts of the poem, (2) the development of particular rhetorical effects, or (3) the creation of interest through rhythmical variety. Do the caesurae lead to important ideas and attitudes? Are the lines all end-stopped, or do you discover enjambement? How do these rhythmical characteristics aid in descriptions and in the expressions of ideas?

---

### REFERRING TO SOUNDS IN POETRY

To make illustrations clear, emphasize the sounds that you are calling attention to. If you use an entire word to illustrate a sound, underline or italicize only the sound, not the entire word, and put the word within quotation marks (e.g., "The poet uses a t sound ['tip,' 'top,' and 'terrific' or '*tip*,' '*top*,' and '*terrific*']"). When you refer to entire words containing particular segments, however, underline or italicize these words (e.g, "The poet uses a t in tip, top, and terrific," or "The poet uses a *t* in *tip*, *top*, and *terrific*). Refer all questions to your instructor.

---

2. **Segmental effects.** Here you might be discussing, collectively or separately, the use and effects of assonance, alliteration, onomatopoeia, and cacophony and euphony. Be sure to establish that the instances you choose have really occurred systematically enough within the poem to form a pattern. Illustrate sounds by some means of highlighting, circling, italicizing, or otherwise noting relevant words. You might make separate paragraphs on alliteration, assonance, and any other seemingly important pattern. Also, depending on the length of your assignment, you might concentrate on only one noteworthy effect, like a representative pattern of assonance, rather than on everything. Throughout your discussion, always keep foremost the relationship between content and sound.

3. **Rhyme.** Your discussion of rhyme should describe the major features of the poem's rhymes, the basic scheme, the variants, the lengths and rhythms of the rhyming words, and anything else that is noteworthy. If you can discuss the grammar of the rhymes, note the kinds of words (verbs, nouns, etc.) used for rhymes: Are they all the same? Does one form predominate? Is there variety? Can you determine the grammatical positions of the rhyming words? How may these characteristics be related to the idea or theme of the poem?

   You might also discuss the qualities of the rhyming words. Are the words specific? Concrete? Abstract? Are there any striking rhymes? Any surprises? Any rhymes that are particularly clever and witty? Do any rhymes give unique comparisons or contrasts? How?

   Generally, note any striking or unique rhyming effects. Without becoming overly subtle or far-fetched, you can make valid and interesting conclusions. Do any sounds in the rhyming words appear in patterns of assonance or alliteration elsewhere in the poem? Do the rhymes enter into any onomatopoeic effects? Broadly, what aspects of rhyme are uniquely effective because they blend so fully with the poem's thought and mood?

*Conclusion*   In your conclusion, try to develop a short evaluation of the poet's prosodic performance. If we accept the premise that poetry is designed not only to stimulate emotions but also to provide information and transfer attitudes, to what degree do the prosodic techniques of your poem contribute to these goals? Without going into excessive detail (and writing another essay), what more can you say here? What has been the value of your study to your understanding and appreciating the poem? If you think your analysis has helped you to develop new awareness of the poet's craft, it would be appropriate to state what you have learned.

## Illustrative Essay

> The central idea, thesis sentence, and topic sentences are shaded here to stress the goal of strong organization. As your instructor wishes, you might use this or a similar system in your own essays.

Muhammad 1

Aisha Muhammad

Professor Singer

English 101

17 November 2010

Alfred, Lord Tennyson's Control of Rhythm and Segments in

"The Passing of Arthur" (Lines 349–360)[1]

Alfred, Lord Tennyson, "The Passing of Arthur"

(Lines 349–360)°

| | |
|---|---|
| But the other swiftly strode from ridge to ridge, | 1 |
| Clothed with his breath, and looking, as he walked | 2 |
| Larger than human on the frozen hills. | 3 |
| He heard the deep behind him, and a cry | 4 |
| Before. His own thought drove him like a goad. | 5 |
| Dry clashed his harness in the icy caves | 6 |
| And barren chasms, and all to left and right | 7 |
| The bare black cliff clanged round him, as he based | 8 |
| His feet on juts of slippery crag than rang | 9 |
| Sharp-smitten with the dint of armed heels— | 10 |
| And on a sudden, lo! The level lake, | 11 |
| And the long glories of the winter moon. | 12 |

---

[1]For illustration, this essay analyzes a passage from Tennyson's "The Passing of Arthur," which is part of *Idylls of the King*. Containing 469 lines, "The Passing of Arthur" describes the last battle and death of Arthur, legendary king of early Britain. After the fight, in which Arthur has been mortally wounded by the traitor Mordred, only Arthur and his follower Sir Bedivere remain alive. Arthur commands Bedivere to throw the royal sword Excalibur into the lake from which Arthur had originally received it. After great hesitation and false claims, Bedivere does throw the sword into the lake, and a hand rises out of the water to catch it. Bedivere then carries Arthur to the lake shore, where the dying king is taken aboard a mysterious funeral barge. In the passage selected for analysis (lines 349–360), Tennyson describes Bedivere carrying Arthur down the hills and cliffs from the battlefield to the lake below.

°Lines 349–360 are numbered here as 1–12.

Muhammad 2

[1]          In this twelve-line selection, Tennyson describes the ordeal of
Sir Bedivere as he carries the dying King Arthur down from the
mountainous heights, where he was wounded, to the lake, where he will
be sent to his final rest. Tennyson emphasizes the bleakness and hostility
of this ghostly and deserted landscape. The metrical pattern he uses is
unrhymed iambic pentameter—blank verse—which is suitable for lengthy
narrative poetry. Appropriately, the verse augments the natural
descriptions and echoes, first, Bedivere's tenseness, and then his
relaxation.* Tennyson's control enables a true blending of sound and
sense, as may be seen in his use of rhythm and in his manipulation of
segmental devices, including onomatopoeia.†

[2]          Tennyson controls his meter to emphasize exertions and moods.
In line 1, the meter is regular, except for an anapast in the first foot.
This regularity may be interpreted as emphasizing the swiftness and
surefootedness of Bedivere. However, Bedivere is about to undergo a
severe test, and Tennyson's rhythm quickly becomes irregular, as
though to strain the pentameter verse in illustration of the knight's
exertions. Tennyson therefore uses variations to highlight key words.
For example, he uses the effect of anapests in a number of lines. In
line 2, he emphasizes the chill air and Bedivere's vitality in the
following way:

CLOTHED with/ his BREATH

The image is one of being surrounded by one's own breath, which
vaporizes on hitting cold air; and the rhythmical variation—a trochaic
substitution in the first foot—enables the voice to build up to the word
*breath*, a most effective internal climax.

[3]          Tennyson uses the same kind of rhythmical effect in line 3. He
emphasizes the "frozen hills" in the line "Larger than human on the
frozen hills" by creating a caesura after the fifth syllable. The heavy
stress of the third foot falls on the preposition "on" usually a lightly
stressed word, which with the article "the" creates the effect of an

---

*Central idea.
†Thesis sentence.

anapest consisting of two unstressed syllables leading up to the first, stressed, syllable of "frozen." The effect is that the voice builds up to the word and thus emphasizes the extreme conditions in which Bedivere is walking:

on / the FRO - / zen HILLS.//

Tennyson uses this rhythmical effect twelve times in the passage. It is one of his major means of rhetorical emphasis.

Tennyson's most effective metrical variation is the spondee, which appears in lines 5, 6, 8 (twice), 10, and 12. These substitutions, occurring mainly in the section describing how Bedivere forces his way down the frozen hills, permits the descriptive lines to ring out, as in:

[4]

The BARE / BLACK CLIFF/ CLANGED ROUND /

and

DRY CLASHED / his HAR - / ness

These substitutions are so strong that they seem deliberately designed to remind readers of the actual sounds of Bedivere's exertions. In addition to this use of the spondee as a sound effect, a remarkable use of the spondee for psychological effect occurs in line 5, where there are in effect three successive heavy stresses. These internalize Bedivere's efforts and determination, reaching a high point on the word *drove*:

His OWN / THOUGHT DROVE / him //

There are other substitutions, too, both formal and rhetorical, and the tension that these variations create keeps the responsive reader alert to Bedivere's tasks. One type of variation is the appearance of amphibrachic rhythm, which is produced in lines 2, 3, 4, 6, 7, and 11. The effect is achieved by a pattern that complements the rhetorical anapests. A caesura in the middle of a foot leaves the three preceding syllables as a light, heavy, and light, the rhythmical form of the amphibrach. In line 2, for example, it appears thus:

[5]

// and LOOK - / ing //

Muhammad 4

In line 6, it takes this form:

/ his HAR - / ness //

[6]     Still another related variation is that of the apparently imperfect feet in lines 5, 8, 11, and 12. These imperfect feet are produced by a caesura, which isolates the syllable, as "him" is in line 8:

The bare / black cliff / clang'd round / him. //

It is not stretching the quality of Tennyson's poetic skill to suggest that the word "him" in solitude at the end of this line may be designed to emphasize Bedivere's isolation in the midst of the lonely landscape through which he is walking. An additional imperfect foot occurs in line 11, where the syllable (on the word "lo!") is surrounded by two caesurae and is therefore thrust into a position of great stress:

And on / a sud - / den // LO! // the lev - / el lake

Other, less significant substitutions are the trochees in lines 3 and 7 and the pyrrhic in line 12. All the described variations suggest the energy that Bedivere expends during his heroic action.

[7]     Many of the variations are produced by Tennyson's sentence structure, which results in a free placement of the caesurae and in a free use of end-stopping and enjambement. Four of the first five lines are end-stopped (two by commas, two by periods). Bedivere is exerting himself during these lines, and he is making short tests to gather strength. His dangerous descent is described during the next four lines, and none of these lines is end-stopped. Bedivere is disturbed (being goaded by "his own thought"), but he must keep going; and the free sentence structure and free metrical variation underscore his physical and mental difficulties. In the last two lines, however, when he has reached the lake, the lines "relax" with the caesuras falling exactly after the fifth syllable. In other words, the sentence structure of the last two lines is regular, an effect suggesting the return to order and beauty after the previous, rugged chaos.

[8]     This rhythmical virtuosity is accompanied by a similarly brilliant control over segmental devices. Alliteration is the most obvious,

Muhammad 5

permitting Tennyson to tie key words and their signifying actions
together, as in the *s*'s in *swiftly strode* in line 1 or the *b*'s in *barren, bare,
black,* and *based* in lines 7 and 8. Other notable examples are the
aspirated *h*'s in lines 2–6 (*he*, *human*, *hills*, *heard*, be*h*ind, *h*im, *h*is,
*h*arness), the *k*'s in lines 6–9 (*c*lashed, *c*aves, *c*hasms, *c*liff, *c*langed,
*c*rag) and the *l*'s in lines 11 and 12 (*l*o, *l*evel, *l*ake, *l*ong, g*l*ories). One
might compare these *l*'s with the *l*'s in the more anguished context of
lines 8 and 9, where the sounds appear as the second segment in the
heavy, ringing words there (b*l*ack, c*l*iff, c*l*anged, s*l*ippery). The sounds
are the same, and the emphasis is similar, but the effects are different.

Tennyson also skillfully uses assonance throughout the passage. In         [9]
the first five lines, for example, the long *o* appears in six words. The first
three *o*'s are in descriptive or metaphoric words (str*o*de, cl*o*thed, fr*o*zen),
and the last three are in words suggesting Bedivere's pain and anguish
(*o*wn, dr*o*ve, g*o*ad). These assonantal *o* sounds tie the physical to the
psychological. Other patterns of assonance are the short *a* in lines 7–9
(ch*a*sms, cl*a*nged, bl*a*ck, cr*a*g, r*a*ng), the *ä* of line 10 (sh*ä*rp, *ä*rmed), the
long *i* of lines 4–7 (beh*i*nd, cr*y*, l*i*ke, dr*y*, *i*cy, r*i*ght), and the short *i* of
lines 1, 2, 9, and 10 (sw*i*ftly, r*i*dge, w*i*th, h*i*s, sl*i*ppery, sm*i*tten, w*i*th,
d*i*nt). One might remark also that in the last two lines, which describe
the level lake and the moon, Tennyson introduces a number of
comparatively less strenuous vowel sounds on words like "on",
"sudden," "lo," "level," "long," "glories," and "moon." The sounds of
these words complement the tranquility of the lakeside scene.

> And *o*n a s*u*dden, l*o*! the level lake,
> And the l*o*ng gl*o*ries of the winter m*oo*n.

The last two lines are examples of onomatopoeia, since the liquid          [10]
*l* sounds recall the gentle lapping of waves on a lake shore. There are
other examples of onomatopoeia, too. The explosive stop sounds *b*, *k*,
*d*, and *t* in lines 6–10 are like the sounds of Sir Bedivere's feet on the
"juts of slippery crag." In line 2, Tennyson describes Bedivere in the
cold air as being "Clothed with his breath," and in the entire passage,
Tennyson employs many words with the aspirate *h* (*h*e, *h*is, *h*e, *h*uman,
*h*ills, He *h*eard, be*h*ind, *h*is *h*arness, *h*im). In the descriptive context,

Muhammad 6

the sounds of such words skillfully complement the exertions that Bedivere makes as he carries King Arthur from the heights to the level lake.

[11]      This short passage is filled with many examples of Tennyson's technical poetic skill. His sounds and rhythms bring the language alive to speak along with the meaning. They emphasize the grandeur of Arthur and his faithful follower, and for one brief moment, they bear out the vitality that Tennyson associated with the heroic past.

Muhammad 7

Work Cited

Tennyson, Alfred, Lord. Fragment from *Idylls of the King*: "The Passing of Arthur." *Writing About Literature*. By Edgar V. Roberts. 12th ed. New York: Pearson, 2010. 207. Print.

## Commentary on the Essay

This essay presents a full treatment of the prosody of the passage from Tennyson. Paragraphs 2–7 deal with the relationship of the rhythm to the content. Note that prosody is not discussed in isolation but as it augments Tennyson's descriptions of action and scenes. Thus, paragraph 4 refers to the use of the spondee as a substitute foot to reinforce ideas. Also in this paragraph, there is a short comparison of alternative ways of saying what Tennyson says so well. Such a speculative comparison should not be attempted often, but it is effective here in bringing out the quality of Tennyson's use of the spondee as a means of emphasis.

Paragraphs 8 and 9 present a discussion of the alliteration and assonance of the passage, and paragraph 10 considers onomatopoeia.

Of greatest importance for the clarity of the essay, there are many supporting examples, spaced, centered, accurately marked, and numbered by line. In any essay about prosody, readers are likely to be unsure of the validity of the writer's observation unless such examples are provided and located within the poem being discussed.

### Writing Topics about Rhythm and Rhyme in Poetry

1. For Shakespeare's Sonnet 73, "That Time of Year Thou Mayst in Me Behold" (see Chapter 6, p.105), analyze the ways in which Shakespeare creates his iambics. That is, what is the relationship of lightly accented syllables to the heavily accented ones? Where does Shakespeare use articles (*the*), pronouns (*this, his*), prepositions (*upon, against, of*), relative clause markers (*which, that*), and adverb clause markers (*as, when*) in relation to syllables of heavy stress? On the basis of this study, how would you characterize Shakespeare's control of the iambic foot?

2. Analyze the rhymes in one of the Shakespeare sonnets, or else the rhymes in Coleridge's "Kubla Khan" or Matthew Arnold's "Dover Beach," or another poem of your choice. What is interesting or unique about the various rhyming words? What relationships can you discover between the rhymes and the topics of the poems?

3. Compare one of the rhyming poems with one of the nonrhyming poems included in this book. What differences in reading and sound can you discover as a result of the use or nonuse of rhyme? What benefits does rhyme give to the poem? What benefits does nonrhyme give?

4. Analyze Thomas Hardy's use of rhymes in "Channel Firing." What effects does he create by rhyming words with trochaic rhythm, like *hatters* and *matters*, and also by rhyming three-syllable words (dactylic rhythms) *saner be* and *century*? What is the relationship of such rhymes to the rhymes that fall on heavy stresses in the poem?

5. Write a short poem of your own using rhymes with trochaic words or dactylic words such as *computer, emetic, scholastic, remarkable, along with me, inedible, moron, anxiously, emotion, fishing,* and so on. If you have trouble with exact rhymes, see what you can do with slant rhymes and eye rhymes. The idea is to use your ingenuity.

6. Using the topical index in your library, take out a book on prosody, such as Harvey Gross's *Sound and Form in Modern Poetry* (1968) or *The Structure of Verse* (1966), or Gay Wilson Allen's *American Prosody* (1935, reprinted 1966). Select a topic (e.g., formal or experimental prosody) or a poet (e.g., Frost, Arnold, Shakespeare, Blake) and write a summary of the ideas and observations that the writers make on your subject. What relationship do the writers make about prosody and the poet's ideas? How does prosody enter into the writer's thought? Into the ways in which the poets emphasize ideas and images? If you go online, you will be able to sift through hundreds of thousands of entries. Be very selective.

# Chapter 14

## Writing about a Problem: Challenges to Overcome in Reading

Fiction, Poetry, and Drama

A **problem** is a question that you cannot answer correctly and easily about a body of material that you are considering. Like many of our English words, *problem* came to us in a circuitous route from the ancient Greeks, and it originally referred to an obstacle—something thrown in our way. You may thus think of it as a difficulty to our understanding and accomplishment, to be considered and, if possible, overcome. Ironically, problems are not always easy to recognize and describe, for we may not always be aware that problems exist. Therefore, we need to identify the existence of a problem, to determine what it is, to describe its boundaries and significance, and to deal with it satisfactorily.

Indeed, it is true that the first step in solving a problem, or in dealing with an issue, is to explain its dimensions and its extent. It is also true that if we can clearly describe the nature and extent of a problem, we have gone a good distance down the road toward a solution. Even so, problems are often hard both to see and to explain—in intellectual pursuits generally, not just in literature. Determining the nature of problems occupies much attention and energy of researchers in scientific, social, political, and humanistic fields. The development of solutions and answers must be preceded by an often long and painstaking analysis of why some things are not happening and why other things are not working. When such insights can be developed, then solutions to problems may well be near, looming on the intellectual horizon, ready to shed the light of understanding on us. In short, the attempt to deal with problems is a common effort in literally all human endeavors. One of the most important techniques that you can acquire is therefore to be able to identify problems, to describe them accurately, and then to determine and explain solutions.

Not all questions, of course, are problems. The question "Who is the major character in Shakespeare's tragedy *Hamlet*?" is not a problem because the obvious answer is Hamlet. Let us go a little further, however, and ask another question: "Why is it *correct* to say that Hamlet is the major character?" This question is not as easy as the first, and for this reason it is a problem. It requires that we think about our answer, even though we do not need to search very far. Hamlet is the title character. He is involved in most of the actions of the play. He is so much the center of our interest, concern, and liking that his death causes sadness and regret. To "solve" this problem has required a number of responses, all of which provide answers to the question "why?"

More complex, however, and more typical of most problems are questions such as these: "Why does Hamlet talk of suicide during his first major speech in the play?" "Why does he treat Ophelia so coarsely and insultingly?" "Why does he delay in avenging his father's death?" Essays on literary problems are normally concerned with such questions because they require a good deal of thought, together with a number of interpretations knitted together into an entire essay.

## Strategies for Developing an Essay about a Problem

Your major purpose is to convince your reader that your solution is a good one. This you do by using evidence correctly in making sound conclusions. In nonscientific subjects like literature, you seldom or never find absolute proofs, so your conclusions will not be *proved* in the way you prove triangles congruent in geometry. But your organization, your use of facts from the text, your interpretations, and your application of general or specific knowledge should all make your conclusions convincing. Thus, your basic strategy is *persuasion*. Here are some strategies for developing an essay designed to persuade a reader to accept your solution to a problem.

### Strategy 1: Demonstrate That Conditions for a Solution Are Fulfilled

Suppose that you are writing on the frequently raised problem of why Hamlet delays revenge against his stepfather, King Claudius. Many times, readers claim that Hamlet is dilatory and simply prefers to delay engaging in action. But let us suppose that you take a different tack—namely, Hamlet delays because he is never sure that Claudius is guilty. This point then is the beginning of your "solution" to the problem. In your essay, you support your answer by challenging the credibility of the information that Hamlet receives about the crime (i.e., the visits from the Ghost and Claudius's distress at the play within the play). Once you have "attacked" these sources of data on the grounds that they are unreliable, you have been persuasive because your solution is consistent with the details of the play.

### Strategy 2: Analyze Significant Words in the Phrasing of the Problem

Your object in this approach is to clarify important words in the statement of the problem and then to determine if they are applicable or not. This kind of attention to words might in fact give you enough material for all or part of your essay. Thus, an essay on the problem of Hamlet's delay might focus in part on a treatment of the word *delay*: What, really, does *delay* mean? For Hamlet, is there a difference between delay that is reasonable and delay that is unreasonable? Does Hamlet delay unreasonably? Is his delay the result of a psychological fault? Would speedy revenge be more or less reasonable than the delay? By the time that you have answered such pointed questions, you will also have sufficient material for your full essay.

### Strategy 3: Refer to Literary Conventions or Expectations

The theory of this aspect of **argument** is that literary problems can be solved by reference either to the literary mode or conventions of a work, or to other characteristics of the work itself. In other words, what appears to be a problem is really no more than a normal characteristic. For example, a question might be raised about why Mathilde in Guy de Maupassant's "The Necklace" (Chapter 1) does not tell her friend Jeanne Forestier about the loss of the necklace. A plausible answer is that, all motivation aside, the story builds up to a surprise (at least for first-time readers) that could be spoiled by an early disclosure. To solve the problem, in other words, one has recourse to the structure of the story—to the literary convention that Maupassant observes in "The Necklace." Similarly, a student once raised a problem about the impossibility of skeletons speaking in Thomas Hardy's "Channel Firing" (page 370). The answer to this problem is that Hardy is playing and joking with the idea that the noise of naval gunnery blasting away at sea is loud enough to waken the dead. Once this given circumstance is accepted, whatever problem there was actually vanishes.

### Strategy 4: Argue against Possible Objections

With this strategy, you raise your own objections and then argue against them. Called **procatalepsis** ("to consider beforehand"), or **anticipation**, this approach helps you sharpen your arguments because *anticipating* and dealing with objections forces you to make analyses and to use facts that you might otherwise overlook. Although procatalepsis can be used point by point throughout your essay, you may find it most useful at the end.

The situation to imagine is that someone is raising objections to your solution to the problem. It is then your task to show that the objections (1) are not accurate or valid, (2) are not strong or convincing, or (3) are based on unusual rather than usual conditions (on an exception and not the rule). Here are some examples of these approaches.

*A. The Objection is Not Accurate or Valid*     You reject this objection by showing that either the interpretation or the conclusions are wrong and by emphasizing that the evidence supports your solution.

> Although Hamlet's delay is reasonable, the claim might be made that his duty is to kill Claudius in revenge immediately after the Ghost's accusations. This claim is not persuasive because it assumes that Hamlet knows everything the audience knows. The audience accepts the Ghost's word that Claudius is guilty, but Hamlet has no reason to believe the Ghost. Would it not seem insane for Hamlet to kill Claudius, who reigns legally, and then to claim he did it because of the Ghost's words? The argument for speedy revenge is not good because it is based on an incorrect view of Hamlet's situation.

*B. The Objection is Not Strong or Convincing*     You *concede* that the objection has some truth or validity, but you then try to show that it is weak and that your own solution is stronger.

> One might claim that Claudius's distress at the play within the play is evidence for his guilt and that therefore Hamlet should carry out his revenge right away. This argument

has merit, and Hamlet's speech after Claudius has fled the scene ("I'll take the Ghost's word for a thousand pound") shows that the "conscience of the king" has been caught. But the King's guilty behavior is not a strong cause for killing him. Hamlet could justifiably ask for an investigation of his father's death on these grounds, but he could not justify a revenge killing. Claudius could not be convicted in any court on the testimony that he was disturbed at seeing "the Murder of Gonzago." Even after the play within the play, the reasons for delay are stronger than for action.

*C. The Objection Depends on Unusual Rather than Usual Conditions*   You reject the objection on the grounds that it could be valid only if normal conditions were suspended. The objection depends on an exception, not a rule.

> The case for quick action is simple: Hamlet should kill Claudius right after seeing the Ghost (I.3), or else after seeing the King's reaction to the stage murder of Gonzago (III.2), or else after seeing the Ghost again in the Queen's room (III.4). Redress under these circumstances, goes the argument, must be both personal and extralegal. This argument wrongly assumes that due process does not exist in the Denmark of Hamlet and Claudius. Nothing in the play indicates that the Danes, even though they carouse a bit, do not value legality and the rules of evidence. Thus, Hamlet cannot rush out to kill Claudius because he knows that the king has not had anything close to due process. The argument for quick action is poor because it rests on an exception being made from civilized law.

# Writing about a Problem

You may not always be able to launch your writing directly into a "solution" of the problem at hand but instead may need to devote much attention to considering the nature of the problem. In other words, the various aspects and dimensions of the problem may not be immediately apparent, and it will be necessary to explain just why and how a particular situation is problematic. The first step in your essay is therefore to clarify things. A situation may need to be explained. There may be a word or phrase that needs clarification or discussion. Certain characters in the work may do things for reasons that are not immediately clear. Whatever the case, it may prove necessary for you to devote a paragraph, or more, to consider the nature of the problem.

Remember that writing an essay on a problem requires you to argue in favor of a position: Either there is a solution or there is not. To develop your position requires that you show the steps to your conclusion. Your general thematic form is thus (1) to describe the conditions that need to be met for the solution you propose and then (2) to demonstrate that these conditions exist. If you assert that there is no solution, then your form would be the same for the first part, but your second part—the development—would show that these conditions have *not* been met.

# Organize Your Essay about a Problem

*Introduction*   Begin with a statement of the problem, presenting as much detail as seems to be needed, and describe the conditions that a solution requires. Your central idea is a brief statement of your answer, or your solution. You may probably not find it possible to describe the problem in a single sentence and in fact may need to go into detail to explain the problematic situation. You will also need to explain the importance of the problem to an understanding of the work: Without a knowledge of the problem, a reader's comprehension may be limited. With a knowledge of the problem and a solution, however, this comprehension will be enhanced, thus permitting a deeper understanding of the work at hand.

*Body*    In developing your essay, use one or more of the strategies described in this chapter. These again are (1) to demonstrate that conditions for a solution are fulfilled, (2) to analyze the words in the phrasing of the problem; (3) to refer to literary expectations or limitations, and (4) to argue against possible objections. You might combine these. Thus, if we assume that your argument is that Hamlet's delay is reasonable, you might first consider the word *delay* (strategy 2); then you might use strategy 1 to explain the reasons for Hamlet's delay. Finally, to answer objections to your argument, you might show that he acts promptly when he believes he is justified (strategy 4). Whatever your topic, the important thing is to use the method or methods that best help you make a good argument for your solution.

*Conclusion*    In your conclusion, try to affirm the validity of your solution in view of the supporting evidence. You might do this by reemphasizing your strongest points by presenting a brief summary or by thinking of your argument as still continuing and thus using the strategy of procatalepsis to raise and answer possible objections to your solution.

## Illustrative Essay

The central idea, thesis sentence, and topic sentences are shaded here to stress the goal of strong organization. As your instructor wishes, you might use this or a similar system in your own essays.

Waller 1

Jesse Waller

Professor Clark

English 102

6 November 2010

The Problem of Historical Time

and Reference in Amy Lowell's "Patterns"°

[1]          In Amy Lowell's "Patterns," the unnamed speaker is a young British

woman who talks the poem alive as a personal and private monologue.

---

°See pages 373–76 for this poem.

Waller 2

At first she is meditating on her basic situation—namely, that she feels unhappily restricted by social patterns. This situation seems to be her main difficulty. She is alone, walking on the pathways of her very elaborate garden, and she dreams that she would prefer to be with her lover. It is not until more than halfway through the poem, however, that she reveals the grimness of her situation. She has just received a letter telling her that her lover has been killed in a war in Flanders, fighting with "the Duke." The remaining half of the poem is much more serious and more moving than the first half, as we follow the speaker's thoughts about how her lover's death has ended all her hopes for happiness and fulfillment. With this information, in fact, the poem undergoes a shift in focus, which does not constitute a problem in reading. There is another problem, however, and that concerns the apparent time of the poem. The time frame first seems relevant to World War I, at the time when the poem was published (1916), but it appears that the speaker is referring to events that went on far earlier in history. Whether Lowell created this problem deliberately, it is clear that "Patterns" invites readers to think about such an apparent anachronism.* An examination of the historical situation of the poem, together with a consideration of how the speaker's situation may have general application, points toward a solution to the problem.†

    The date of "Patterns," 1916, makes it seem that the imagined time of the speaker's reflection is World War I. This war was fierce enough. Bloody and costly fighting between allied armies and the Germans actually did really take place in Flanders, where the speaker says that her fiancé was killed. Just a year before "Patterns" appeared, for example, the German Army had used chlorine gas as a military weapon at Ypres, in Flanders. Thus, the circumstances of "Patterns" might be considered a symbol of the huge numbers of deaths that justified the claims that the greater part of an entire generation of young men had been killed. Consistent with this reading is the letter of notification that the speaker has just received. She states that the letters in the words seemed to squirm "like snakes" (line 66), and in her grief, she sank "on a seat in the shade"

[2]

---

*Central idea.
†Thesis sentence.

Waller 3

(line 19), where she had hoped that she and Lord Hartwell might one day have made love together. The poem works well here if one takes things just as they seem—as an interior monologue spoken by a woman in deep grief and anguish because of the loss of her sweetheart during World War I.

[3]     The problem intervenes, however, because the poem seems to concern not events of World War I but rather those of an earlier time in history. In fact, the time of the poem seems to be the eighteenth century. This is especially noticeable when the speaker refers to "the Duke in Flanders" (line 105), a reference that calls to mind John Churchill, First Duke of Marlborough (1650–1722). Historically, he was the leader of forces allied against France and Louis XIV during the War of the Spanish Succession, or "Queen Anne's War," in Europe. This war lasted from 1701 to 1713. Marlborough was the guiding force in a number of famous battles then, and in particular, he led the allied armies to their success. Thus, the reference to "the Duke" suggests that Flanders was the place where the speaker's lover was killed, two hundred years before the imagined time of the poem.

[4]     Other details support this conclusion about time. The speaker describes her clothing, which clearly puts her in the fashion of the eighteenth century. She is corseted in "whalebone" (line 18), wears a "pink and silver" stiffened gown of heavy brocade that sweeps to the ground (lines, 5, 12, 18, 40–43), has hair that is powdered (line 6), and carries a "jewelled fan" (line 6). Her dress is "richly figured" (line 10), and she is wearing ribboned shoes (line 16). She is, she says, "a plate of current fashion" (line 15).

[5]     Additionally, when the speaker recalls and considers the appearance of her fiancé, Lord Hartwell, she imagines that he would be wearing a waistcoat (line 51), heavy boots with buckles, and a sword (lines 46–49). She makes no references to twentieth-century clothing, and she does not make any statements that refer to the twentieth century. Without doubt, her words—private and secret as they are—are those of an aristocratic woman living in the eighteenth century. This is indeed problematic.

[6]     Rather than being anachronistic, however, the eighteenth-century references suggest a solution to the problem of how the speaker's personal tragedy should be understood. The many details relevant to the eighteenth century suggest that the fighting in Flanders of "Patterns"

Waller 4

may indeed refer to the War of the Spanish Succession, which really did
happen two hundred years before "Patterns" was published. In addition,
along this avenue of thought, one might also consider that almost exactly
another hundred years after that war, a different war took place, much of
it also in Flanders. This was the war against Napoleon Bonaparte and his
attempt to create a French empire in Europe. The war is best known
because of the final Battle of Waterloo in 1815. Waterloo was and still is
in Flanders, south of modern Brussels, and it ended Napoleon's military
power and drove him into exile. The leader of the forces against
Napoleon was another well-known Duke, the Duke of Wellington
(1769–1852), and therefore Lowell's reference to "the Duke" could
possibly refer to him, for he was actually more famous than
Marlborough. And finally, there was the bitter Flanders fighting of
World War I, during the time when Lowell published "Patterns." These
three separate wars, of course, were each separated by a century, but it
appears that Lowell is using Flanders and the reference to "the Duke"—
who could be taken as any military leader—to symbolize a seemingly
permanent pattern of endless battles and battle deaths and, presumably,
an endless pattern of grief for the loving people back home.

    The point of "Patterns"—and a plausible solution to the problem    [7]
about the vagueness of the poem's time period—is therefore that military
fighting and dying are still going on, with the conclusion being that such
conditions will not end no matter what the century may be. Deaths are
deaths. They are happening now; they have happened regularly in the past;
they will continue to happen regularly in the future. Lowell's speaker,
walking in her garden and carrying the official notification of her fiancé's
death in her bosom, establishes the pattern of deep sorrow and ruined
hope.

    Thus, because of the permanence of death and grief, Lowell's    [8]
"Patterns" is timely for the early eighteenth century; for the early
nineteenth century; for Lowell's time; by extension, for our own time;
and, regrettably, for the future. The problem—the apparent anachronism
in the poem—is not accidental and a flaw but is rather an aspect of
Lowell's design to emphasize the permanent nature of military

Waller 5

catastrophe. The speaker's agonized question—"Christ! What are
patterns for?"—could be said by anyone who has ever received an
official notice like the one received by Lowell's speaker. The problem of
time and reference in the poem, then, is only incidental and is not a
problem, for the main issue of "Patterns" is the anguish of those, like the
speaker, who have fruitlessly waited for a loved one to return home. The
situation of Lowell's speaker is fictitious, but the comparable situation of
many women and families, in three centuries, was totally real. Their
grief transcends any time and place.

Waller 6

Work Cited

Lowell, Amy. "Patterns." *Writing About Literature.* By Edgar V.
Roberts. 12th ed. New York: Pearson, 2010. 373–76. Print.

## Commentary on the Essay

This essay combines strategies 1 and 3 described on pages 215 and 216. After briefly
considering one apparent problem in Lowell's "Patterns," the writer demonstrates that
there are aspects of the poem that create an additional problem about the poem's time
frame but that these aspects themselves are to be taken as the major details supporting a solution.

The development of the essay takes the form of observing, analyzing, and solving.
At first, the concession is made that the problem is not immediately apparent, and therefore paragraphs 1–3 explain the central idea and the thesis sentence as topics to develop
in considering the nature of the problem. Paragraphs 4 and 5 are devoted to a description of the historical details that underlie the problem and that anticipate a solution. Such
a need frequently occurs in the analysis of problems, for it is necessary to phrase the
problem clearly. In other words, to define the problem well and completely also points
toward a solution.

Paragraphs 6–8 describe the solution—namely, the problem about the anachronism in the poem is no more than apparent, and therefore the problem, when seen in

this perspective, is no longer a problem. The paragraphs also point out that the differing time frames that are present in the poem actually create one of the poem's major strengths.

### Writing Topics about Literary Problems

1. In Matthew Arnold's "Dover Beach," the lines "Ah, love, let us be true/To one another!" (lines 29 and 30) have been read to refer not so much to the need for love as to the need for fidelity in all relationships. Which choice seems more correct? Explain.
2. Samuel Taylor Coleridge was planning a much longer poem when he began writing "Kubla Khan," but he was interrupted and could write no more. Some critics, however, are satisfied that the poem is complete as it stands. Defend the judgment that the poem may be considered finished.
3. Even though Anton Chekhov's *The Bear* is a farce, some observers have claimed that the passionate embraces of Smirnov and Mrs. Popov at the end happen suddenly and unexpectedly. Does this outcome spoil the play by making it too unrealistic, too arbitrary, too unnatural?
4. To what degree would more details describing the horrors of war make Wilfred Owen's "Anthem for Doomed Youth" a more or less effective poem?
5. Because Edgar Allan Poe often writes about lurid and sensational subjects, some critics have stated that his works do not embody ideas. Consider whether this observation is true of "The Cask of Amontillado."
6. A view that is sometimes expressed about Shakespeare's sonnets is that the "systems" that Shakespeare introduces, such as comparing the aging speaker to various times of the year and times of day in "Sonnet 73: That Time of Year Thou Mayst in Me Behold" (Chapter 6) are so affected and pretentious that they detract from the ideas. With reference to this sonnet and to Shakespeare's "Sonnet 30" (Chapter 10), how valid is this judgment? Do the comparisons add to or detract from the poems?
7. Why is the presumed listener of Shelly Wagner's "Boxes" the speaker's dead son? Why does Wagner create this situation of speaker–listener?
8. Why do you think that Susan Glaspell, in *Trifles*, places Mrs. Hale and Mrs. Peters on stage continuously throughout the play, rather than two or more of the men?

# Chapter 15

# Writing Essays of Comparison-Contrast and Extended Comparison-Contrast: Learning by Seeing Literary Works Together

Comparison-contrast analysis is the act of putting things side by side—juxtaposing them, looking at them together—for a variety of purposes such as description, enhanced understanding, evaluation, and decision making. The technique underlies other important techniques, specifically (1) the analysis of causes and effects and (2) the scientific method of constant-and-variable analysis. Significant questions of these methods are, How is *A* both like and unlike *B*? What are the causes of *A*? How does a change in *A* affect *B*? These are all questions that call into play the technique of comparison and contrast.

The educational significance of the technique is to encourage you to make connections—one of the major aspects of productive thought and one of the most important characteristics, generally speaking, of leadership. As long as things *seem* different and disconnected, they in fact *are* different and disconnected. In practice, they are two separate and distinct entities. But when you discover that they have similarities and connections, then you can make relationships clear. You are in a position both to stress points of likeness and also to demonstrate just what makes things distinct and unique. For all these reasons, it is vital for you to find similarities and differences through the technique of comparison and contrast.

The immediate goal of a comparison-contrast essay on literary works is to compare and contrast different authors; two or more works by the same author; different drafts of the same work; or characters, incidents, techniques, and ideas in the same work or in a number of separate works. Developing and writing a comparison-contrast essay enables you to study works in perspective. No matter what works you consider together, the method helps you get at the essence of a work or writer. Similarities are brought out by comparison; differences, by contrast. In other words, you can enhance your understanding of what a thing *is* by using comparison-contrast to determine what it *is not*.

For example, our understanding of Shakespeare's "Sonnet 30: When to the Sessions of Sweet Silent Thought" (Chapter 10) may be enhanced if we compare it with

Christina Rossetti's poem "Echo." Both poems treat personal recollections of past experiences, told by a speaker to a listener who is not intended to be the reader. Both also refer to persons, now dead, with whom the speakers were closely involved. In these respects, the poems are comparable. In addition to these similarities, there are important differences. Shakespeare's speaker numbers the dead persons as friends whom he laments generally, whereas Rossetti refers specifically to one person with whom the speaker was in love. Rossetti's topic is the sorrow of dead love, the irrevocability of the past, and the present loneliness of the speaker. Shakespeare includes the references to dead friends as a way of accounting for present sorrows, but then his speaker turns to the present and asserts that thinking about the "dear friend," the poem's listener, enables him to restore past "losses" and end all "sorrows." In Rossetti's poem, there is no reconciliation of past and present; instead the speaker focuses entirely upon the sadness of the present moment. Although both poems are retrospective in nature, Shakespeare's poem looks toward the present, whereas Rossetti's looks mainly toward the past. The technique of comparison-contrast, in short, unlocks our understanding of the uniqueness of each poem.

## Guidelines for the Comparison-Contrast Essay

The preceding example, although brief, shows how the use of comparison-contrast makes it possible to identify leading similarities and distinguishing differences in two works. Frequently you can overcome the difficulties you might encounter in understanding one work by comparing and contrasting it with another work on a comparable subject. A few guidelines will help direct your efforts in writing comparison-contrast essays.

### *Clarify Your Intention*

When planning a comparison-contrast essay, first decide on your goal, for you can use the method in a number of ways. One objective is the equal and mutual illumination of two (or more) works. For example, an essay comparing Anita Scott Coleman's "Unfinished Masterpieces" with Nathaniel Hawthorne's "Young Goodman Brown" might compare ideas, characters, or methods in these stories equally, without stressing or favoring either. For most purposes, this method will prove most useful. If you wish to emphasize just one of the works, you might also use the comparison-contrast technique. Thus, you might highlight "Young Goodman Brown" by using comparable material in "Unfinished Masterpieces" (and vice versa). You might also show your preference for a particular story, poem, or play at the expense of another or emphasize a method or idea in one work that you do not find in the other work. The Illustrative Essay on two works beginning on page 230 shows how the essayist brings out the superiority of one work over the other, at least in certain chosen qualities.

### *Find Common Grounds for Comparison*

The second stage in preparing a comparison-contrast essay is to select and articulate a common ground for discussion. It is pointless to compare dissimilar things, for the resulting conclusions will not have much value. Instead, compare like with like: idea with idea, characterization with characterization, setting with setting, point of view with point of view, tone with tone. Nothing much can be learned from a comparison of Robert Frost's view of individuality and Anton Chekhov's view of love; but a comparison of the relationship of individuality with identity and character in Frost's "Desert Places" and Chekhov's *The Bear* suggests common ground, with the promise of significant ideas to be developed through the examination of similarities and differences.

In seeking common ground, you will need to be inventive and creative. For instance, if you compare Guy de Maupassant's "The Necklace" (Chapter 1) and Chekhov's *The Bear*, these two works at first may seem dissimilar. Yet common ground can be discovered, such as the treatment of self-deceit, the effects of chance on human affairs, and the authors' views of women. Although other works may seem even more dissimilar than these, it is usually possible to find a common ground for comparison and contrast. Much of your success in an essay of this type depends on your success in finding a workable basis—a common denominator—for comparison.

### *Integrate the Bases of Comparison*

Let us assume that you have decided on your rhetorical purpose and on the basis of your comparison. You have done your reading and taken notes, and you have a rough idea of what you want to say. The remaining problem is the treatment of your material.

One method that writers sometimes choose is to make your points first about one work and then about the other. Unfortunately, such a comparison makes your paper seem like two separate lumps. ("Work 1" takes up one-half of your paper to make one lump, and "Work 2" takes up the other half to make a second lump.) Also, the method involves repetition because you must repeat many points when you treat the second subject.

Therefore, a better method is to treat the major aspects of your main idea and to refer to the two (or more) works as they support your arguments. Thus, you refer constantly to *both* works, sometimes within the same sentence, and remind your reader of the point of your discussion. There are reasons for the superiority of this method: (1) You do not repeat your points needlessly, for you develop them as you raise them; (2) by constantly referring to the two works, you make your points without requiring a reader with a poor memory to reread previous sections.

As a model, here is a paragraph on "Natural References as a Basis of Comparison in Frost's 'Desert Places' and Shakespeare's 'Sonnet 73: That Time of Year Thou Mayst in Me Behold'" (Frost's poem is in Appendix C, and Sonnet 73 is in Chapter 6). The virtue of the paragraph is that it uses material from each of the poems simultaneously as the substance for the development of the ideas, as nearly as the time sequence of sentences allows. In this illustration, each sentence is numbered for easy reference.

(1) Both Shakespeare and Frost link their ideas to events occurring in the natural world. (2) Night as a parallel with death is common to both poems, with Frost speaking about it in his first line and Shakespeare introducing it in his seventh. (3) Along with night, Frost emphasizes the onset of winter and snow as a time of death and desolation. (4) With this natural description, Frost also symbolically refers to empty, secret, dead places

in the inner spirit—crannies of the soul where bleak winter snowfalls correspond to self-ishness and indifference. (5) By contrast, Shakespeare uses the fall season, with the yellowing and dropping of leaves and the migrations of birds, to stress the closeness of real death and therefore the need to love fully during the time remaining. (6) Both poems thus share a sense of gloom because both present death as inevitable and final, just like the emptiness of winter. (7) Because Shakespeare's sonnet is addressed to a listener who is also a loved one, however, it is more outgoing than the more introspective poem of Frost. (8) Frost turns the snow, the night, and the emptiness of the universe inward in order to show the speaker's inner bleakness, and by extension, the bleakness of many human spirits. (9) Shakespeare instead uses the bleakness of season, night, and dying fire to state the need for loving "well." (10) The poems thus use common references for differing purposes.

This paragraph links Shakespeare's references to nature to those of Frost. Five sentences speak of both authors together; three speak of Frost alone and two of Shakespeare alone, but all the sentences are unified topically. This interweaving of references indicates that the writer has learned both poems well enough to consider them together, and it also enables the writing to be more pointed and succinct than if the works were separately treated.

You can learn from this example: If you develop your essay by putting your two subjects constantly together, you will write economically and pointedly (not only for essays but also for tests). Beyond that, if you digest the material as successfully as this method indicates, you demonstrate that you are fulfilling a major educational goal—the assimilation and *use* of material. Too often, because you learn things separately (in separate works and courses, at separate times), you tend also to compartmentalize them. Instead, you should always try to relate them, to *synthesize* them. Comparison and contrast help in this process of putting together, of seeing things not as fragments but as parts of wholes.

### Avoid the Tennis-Ball Method

As you make your comparison, do not confuse an interlocking method with a "tennis-ball" method, in which you bounce your subject back and forth constantly and repetitively, almost as though you were hitting observations back and forth over a net. The tennis-ball method is shown in the following example from a comparison of the characters Mathilde (Maupassant's "The Necklace") and Mrs. Popov (Chekhov's *The Bear*).

> Mathilde is a young married woman; Mrs. Popov is also young but a widow. Mathilde has a limited social life, and she doesn't have more than one friend. Mrs. Popov chooses to lead a life of solitude. Mathilde's daydreams about wealth are responsible for her misfortune, and Mrs. Popov's dedication to the memory of her husband is actually limiting her life. Mathilde is made unhappy because of her shortcomings, but Mrs. Popov is rescued despite her shortcomings. In Mathilde's case, the focus is on adversity not only causing trouble but also strengthening character. Similarly, in Mrs. Popov's case, the focus is on a strong person realizing her strength regardless of her conscious decision to weaken herself.

Imagine the effect of an entire essay written in this invariable 1–2, 1–2, 1–2 order. Aside from the inflexible patterning of subjects, the tennis-ball method does not permit much illustrative development. You should not feel so constrained that you cannot take two or more sentences to develop a point about one writer or subject before you include comparative references to another. If you remember to interlock the two subjects of comparison, however, as in the paragraph about Frost and Shakespeare, your method will give you the freedom to develop your topics fully.

## The Extended Comparison-Contrast Essay

For a longer essay about a number of works—such as a limited research paper, comprehensive exam questions, and the sort of extended essay required at the end of a semester—comparison-contrast is an essential method. You may wish to compare the works on the basis of elements such as ideas, plot, language, structure, character, metaphor, point of view, or setting. Because of the larger number of works, however, you will need to modify the way in which you employ comparison-contrast. Suppose you are considering not just two works but rather six, seven, or more. You need first to find a common ground to use as your central, unifying idea, just as you do for a comparison of only two works. Once you establish the common ground, you can classify or group your works on the basis of the similarities and differences they exemplify with regard to the topic. The idea is to get two *groups* for comparison and contrast, not just two works.

Let us assume that three or four works treat a topic in one way but that two or three do it in another (e.g., either criticism or praise of wealth and trade, the joys or sorrows of love, the enthusiasm of youth, gratitude for life, or the disillusionment of age). In writing about these works, you might treat the topic itself in a straightforward comparison-contrast method but use details from the works within the groupings as the material that you use for illustration and argument.

To make your essay as specific as possible, it is best to stress only a small number of works with each of your subpoints. Once you have established these points, there is no need to go into details about all the other works. Instead, you need to make no more than brief references to the other works, for your purpose should be to strengthen your points without bulking up your essay with more and more examples. Once you go to another subpoint, you might then use different works for illustration so that by the end of your essay you will have given due attention to each work in your assignment. In this way—by treating many works in small comparative groups—you can keep your essay reasonably free of excessive detail.

The Illustrative Essay beginning on page 234 shows how this grouping may be done. In the first part of the body of this essay, six works are used comparatively to show how private needs conflict with social, public demands. A second section shows how three works can be compared and contrasted on the basis of how they treat the topic of public concerns as expressed through law. Finally, three additional works are cited to indicate contrasts between personal demands and the demands upon individuals in time of war.

# Writing a Comparison-Contrast Essay

In planning your essay, you should first narrow and simplify your topic so that you can handle it conveniently. If your subject is a comparison of two poets (as in the comparison-contrast essay on Amy Lowell and Wilfred Owen beginning on page 230), choose one or two of each poet's poems on the same or a similar topic and write your essay about these.

Once you have found an organizing principle, along with the relevant works, begin to refine and focus the direction of your essay. As you study each work, note common or contrasting elements and use these to form your central idea. At the same time, you can select the most illustrative works and classify them according to your topic, such as war, love, work, faithfulness, or self-analysis.

## Organize Your Comparison-Contrast Essay

*Introduction*    Begin by stating the works, authors, characters, or ideas that you are considering; then show that you have narrowed the topic for purposes of comparison and contrast. Your central idea should briefly highlight the principal grounds of discussion, such as that both works treat a common topic, exhibit a similar idea, use a similar form, or develop an identical attitude and that major or minor differences help make the works unique. You may also assert that one work is superior to the other, if you wish to make this judgment and expand on it.

*Body*    The body of your essay is governed by the works and your basis of comparison (presentations of ideas, depictions of character, uses of setting, qualities of style and tone, uses of poetic form, uses of comparable imagery or symbols, uses of point of view, etc.). For a comparison-contrast treatment on such a basis, your goal should be to shed light on both (or more) of the works you are treating. For example, you might examine stories written from a first-person point of view. An essay on this topic might compare the ways in which each author uses point of view to achieve similar or distinct effects; or it might compare poems that employ similar images, symbols, or ironic methods. Sometimes, the process can be as simple as identifying female or male protagonists and comparing the ways in which their characters are developed. Another obvious approach is to compare the *subjects*, as opposed to the *idea*. You might identify works dealing with general subjects such as love, death, youth, race, or war. Such groupings provide a basis for excellent comparisons and contrasts.

As you develop your essay, remember to keep comparison-contrast foremost. That is, your discussions of point of view, figurative language, or whatever should not so much explain these topics *as topics* but rather should explore *similarities and differences* of the works you are comparing. If your topic is an idea, for example, you need to explain the idea but just enough to establish points of similarity or difference. As you develop such an essay, you might illustrate your arguments by referring to related uses of elements such as setting, characterization, symbolism, point of view, or metaphor. When you introduce these new subjects, you will be on target as long as you use them in the context of comparison-contrast.

*Conclusion*     In concluding, you might reflect on other ideas or techniques in the works you have compared, make observations about similar qualities, or summarize briefly the grounds of your comparison. If there is a point you have considered especially important, you might stress that point again in your conclusion. Also, your comparison might have led you to conclude that one work—or group of works—is superior to another. Stressing that point again would make an effective conclusion.

## Illustrative Essay (Comparing and Contrasting Two Works)

The central idea, thesis sentence, and topic sentences are shaded here to stress the goal of strong organization. As your instructor wishes, you might use this or a similar system in your own essays.

Sanchez 1

Natalie Sanchez

Professor McKinley

English 100

16 October 2010

The Views of War in Amy Lowell's "Patterns"

and Wilfred Owen's "Anthem for Doomed Youth"°

[1]      Amy Lowell's "Patterns" and Wilfred Owen's "Anthem for Doomed Youth" are both powerful condemnations of war.* Owen's short poem speaks generally about the ugliness of war and about large groups of sorrowful people. Lowell's longer poem focuses on the personal grief of just one person. In a sense, Lowell's poem begins where Owen's ends, a fact that accounts for both the similarities and the differences between the two works. The antiwar themes can be compared on the basis of their subjects, their lengths, their concreteness, and their use of a common metaphor.†

[2]      "Anthem for Doomed Youth" attacks war more directly than "Patterns." Owen's opening line, "What passing-bells for these who die as

°See pages 373–76 and 377 for these poems.
*Central idea.
†Thesis sentence.

Sanchez 2

cattle?" suggests that in war human beings are depersonalized before they are slaughtered, like so much meat, and his observations about the "monstrous" guns and the "shrill, demented" shells unambiguously condemn the horrors of war. By contrast, in "Patterns," warfare is far away, on another continent, intruding only when the messenger delivers the letter stating that the speaker's fiancé has been killed (lines 63–64). A comparable situation governs the last six lines of Owen's poem, quietly describing how those at home respond to the loss of their loved ones. Thus, the antiwar focus in "Patterns" is the contrast between the calm, peaceful life of the speaker's garden and the anguish of her responses. In "Anthem for Doomed Youth," the stress is more on the external horrors of war that bring about the need for ceremonies honoring the dead.

    Another major difference between the poems is their wide discrepancy in length. "Patterns" is an interior monologue, or meditation, of 107 lines, but it could not be shorter and still be convincing. Lowell's speaker thinks of the past and contemplates her future loneliness. Her final outburst, "Christ! What are patterns for?" (line 107) would make no sense if she did not explain her situation as extensively as she does. "Anthem for Doomed Youth," however, is brief—a fourteen-line sonnet—because it is more general and less personal than "Patterns." Although Owen's speaker shows great sympathy, he or she views the sorrows of others distantly, unlike Lowell, who goes right into the mind and spirit of the grieving speaker. In the last six lines of "Anthem for Doomed Youth," Owen's use of phrases such as "tenderness of patient minds" and "drawing-down of blinds" is a powerful representation of deep grief. He gives no further details even though thousands of individual stories might be told. In contrast, Lowell tells just one of these stories as she focuses on her solitary speaker's ruined hopes and dreams. Thus, the contrasting lengths of the poems are determined by the specific or more general consideration of the effects of war.

[3]

    Despite these differences of approach and length, both poems are similarly concrete and real. Owen moves from the real scenes and sounds of far-off battlefields to the homes of the many soldiers who have been killed in battle, but Lowell's scene is a single place—the garden of

[4]

Sanchez 3

her speaker's estate. The speaker walks on real gravel along garden paths that contain daffodils, squills, a fountain, and a lime tree. She thinks of her clothing and her ribboned shoes and of her fiancé's boots, sword hilts, and buttons. The images in Owen's poem are equally real but are not about specific individuals, as in "Patterns." Thus, Owen's images are those of cattle, bells, rifle shots, shells, bugles, candles, and window blinds. Both poems reflect reality, but Owen's details are more general and public, whereas Lowell's are more personal and intimate.

[5]          Along with this concreteness, the poems share the major metaphor that cultural patterns both control and frustrate human wishes and hopes. In "Patterns," this metaphor is shown in warfare itself (line 106), which is the pinnacle of organized human patterns of destruction. Further examples of the metaphor are found in details about clothing (particularly the speaker's stiff, confining gown in lines 5, 18, 21, 73, and 101 and the lover's military boots in lines 46 and 49); the orderly, formal garden paths in which the speaker is walking (lines 1 and 93); her restraint at hearing about her lover's death; and her courtesy, despite her grief, in ordering refreshment for the messenger (line 69). Within such rigid patterns, her hopes for happiness have vanished, along with the sensuous spontaneity symbolized by her lover's hope to make love to her on a "shady seat" in the garden (lines 85–89). The metaphor of the constricting pattern is also seen in "Anthem for Doomed Youth," except that in this poem, the pattern is the funeral, not love or marriage. Owen's speaker contrasts the calm, peaceful tolling of "passing-bells" (line 1) to the frightening sounds of war represented by the "monstrous anger of the guns," "the stuttering rifles' rapid rattle," and "the demented choirs of wailing shells" (lines 2, 3, and 7). Thus, whereas Lowell uses the metaphor to reveal the irony of hope and desire being destroyed by war, Owen uses it to reveal the irony of war's negation of peaceful ceremonies.

[6]          Although in these ways the poems share topics and some aspects of treatment, they are distinct and individual. "Patterns" includes many references to visible things, whereas "Anthem for Doomed Youth" emphasizes sound (and silence). Both poems conclude on powerfully emotional although different notes. Owen's poem dwells on the pathos and sadness that war brings to many unnamed people, and Lowell's

Sanchez 4

expresses the most intimate thoughts of a woman who is alone in the
first agony of her grief. Although neither poem attacks the usual political
justifications for war (the needs to mobilize, to sacrifice, to achieve
peace through fighting, and so on), the attack is there by implication, for
both poems make their appeal by stressing how war destroys the
relationships that make life worth living. For this reason, despite their
differences, both "Patterns" and "Anthem for Doomed Youth" are
parallel antiwar poems, and both are expressions of deeply felt emotions.

Sanchez 5

### Works Cited

Lowell, Amy, "Patterns," *Writing About Literature.* By Edgar V. Roberts.
    12th ed. New York: Pearson, 2010. 373–76. Print.

Owen, Wilfred. "Anthem for Doomed Youth." *Writing About Literature.* By
    Edgar V. Roberts. 12th ed. New York: Pearson, 2010. 377. Print.

## Commentary on the Essay

This essay shows how approximately equal attention can be given to the two works being
studied. Words stressing similarity are *common, share, equally, parallel, both, similar,* and
*also*. Contrasts are stressed by *while, whereas, different, dissimilar, contrast, although,* and
*except*. Transitions from paragraph to paragraph are not different in this type of essay
from those in other essays. Thus, the phrases *despite, along with this,* and *in these ways,*
which are used here, could be used anywhere for the same transitional purpose.

The central idea—that the poems mutually condemn war—is brought out in paragraph 1, together with the supporting idea that the poems blend into each other because
both show responses to news of battle casualties.

Paragraph 2, the first in the body, discusses how each poem brings out its attack on
warfare. Paragraph 3 explains the differing lengths of the poems as a function of differences in perspective. Because Owen's sonnet views war and its effects at a distance, it is
brief; but because Lowell's interior monologue views death intimately, it needs more detail and greater length.

Paragraph 4, on the topic of concreteness and reality, shows that the two works can receive equal attention without the bouncing back and forth of the tennis-ball method. Three of the sentences in this paragraph (3, 4, and 6) are devoted exclusively to details in one poem or the other; but sentences 1, 2, 5, and 7 refer to both works, stressing points of broad or specific comparison. The scheme demonstrates that the two works are, in effect, interlocked within the paragraph.

Paragraph 5, the last in the body, considers the similar and dissimilar ways in which the poems treat the common metaphor of cultural patterns.

The conclusion, paragraph 6, summarizes the central idea and stresses the ways in which the two poems, although similar, are distinct and unique.

## Illustrative Essay (Extended Comparison-Contrast)

Wolinsky 1

Jared Wolinsky

Professor Dufresne

English 100

9 October 2010

Literary Treatments of the Tension

between Private and Public Life

[1]     The tension and conflict between private or personal life, on the one hand, and public or civic and national life, on the other, is a topic common to many literary works.° Authors show that individuals try to maintain their personal lives and commitments even though they are tested and stressed by public and external forces. Ideally, individuals should have the freedom to follow their own wishes independently of the outside world. It is a fact, however, that living itself causes people to venture into the public world and therefore to encounter conflicts. Taking a walk, going to school, finding a job, attending a concert, getting married, following a profession—just living—all draw people into the public world in which rules, regulations, and laws compete with private wishes. To greater and lesser degrees, such conflicts are found in Matthew Arnold's "Dover Beach," Chekhov's *The Bear*, Glaspell's *Trifles*, Chopin's "The Story of an Hour," Thomas Hardy's "Channel Firing," Hawthorne's "Young Goodman Brown," John Keats's "Bright Star," Irving Layton's

---

°Central idea.

Wolinsky 2

"Rhine Boat Trip," Lowell's "Patterns," Shakespeare's Sonnet 73: "That Time of Year Thou Mayst in Me Behold," Walt Whitman's "Reconciliation," and William Wordsworth's "Lines Written in Early Spring."* In these works, clashes are shown between the interests of individuals and those of the social, legal, and military public.†

[2] One of the major private–public conflicts is created by the way in which characters respond to social conventions and expectations. In Chekhov's *The Bear*, for example, Mrs. Popov has given up her personal life to spend her time in remembering her dead husband. She wears black, stays in her house for a whole year, and swears eternal fidelity; and she does all this to fulfill what she considers her public role as a grieving widow. Fortunately for her, Smirnov arrives on the scene and arouses her enough to make her give up this deadly but also silly pose. Not as fortunate is Hawthorne's Goodman Brown in "Young Goodman Brown." Brown's obligation is much less public and also more philosophical than Mrs. Popov's because his religiously inspired vision of evil fills him with lifelong gloom. Although Mrs. Popov is easily moved away from her position by the prospect of immediate life and vitality, Brown's mindless distrust locks him into a fear of evil from which not even his own faithful wife can shake him. Brown and Mrs. Popov therefore go in entirely different directions—one toward personal fulfillment, the other toward personal destruction.

[3] A major idea in the various works is that philosophical or religious difficulties such as those of Goodman Brown force a crisis in an individual life. In Arnold's "Dover Beach," the speaker expresses regret about uncertainty and the loss of religious faith that symbolically wear away civilization just like the surf that beats on the shores of Dover Beach. This situation might be expected to make a person as dreary and depressed as Goodman Brown actually is. Arnold's speaker, however, in the lines "Ah, love, let us be true / To one another," finds power in personal fidelity and commitment (lines 29 and 30). In other words, the public world of "human misery" and the diminishing "Sea of Faith" are

---

*See Chapter 6 for Shakespeare's Sonnet 73 and Appendix C for all other works.
†Thesis sentence.

Wolinsky 3

beyond control, and therefore all that is left is personal commitment. This is not to say that "Young Goodman Brown," as a story, is negative, for Hawthorne implies that a positive personal life lies in the denial of choices like those made by Brown and in the acceptance of choices like those made by Mrs. Popov and Arnold's speaker.

[4]     To deny or to ignore the public world is a possible option that, under some circumstances, can be chosen. For example, "Dover Beach" reflects a conscious decision to ignore the philosophic and religious uncertainty that the speaker finds in the intellectual and public world. Even more independent of such a public world, Shakespeare's "That Time of Year" and Keats's "Bright Star" bring out their ideas as reflections on purely personal situations. Shakespeare's speaker deals with the love between himself and the listener, whereas Keats's speaker, addressing a distant star, considers his need for comparable steadfastness in his relationship with his "fair love." Louise, the major character in Chopin's "The Story of an Hour," embodies an interesting variation on the personal matters brought up in these two sonnets. At first, Louise is prostrated by the news coming from the public world, through the medium of telegraph, that her husband has been killed in a train wreck. Her first vision of herself is that of a grieving, private widow. As she thinks about things, however, she quickly begins to anticipate the liberation and freedom—to become free to explore her newly anticipated personal world—that widowhood will give her. Ironically, it is the reappearance of her husband, who moves freely in the public world, that shocks her into her sudden heart failure and death. What she looks forward to as the free choice to do what she wants and to go where she wishes has suddenly been withdrawn from her by her renewed status within the publicly sanctioned system of marriage, and it is her recognition of her abrupt loss of this private possibility that ends her life.

[5]     The complexity of the conflict between private and public life is brought out in the way in which governments secure their power through law and legality. With immense power, the law often acts as an arbitrary form of public judgment that disregards personal needs and circumstances. This idea is brought out on the most personal level in Glaspell's *Trifles* in

Wolinsky 4

which the two major characters, both women, urgently confront the conflict between their personal identification with the accused woman, Minnie, and their public obligation to the law. One of the women, Mrs. Peters, is reminded that she is "married to the law," but she and Mrs. Hale suppress the evidence that they know would condemn Minnie, even though technically—by law, that is—their knowledge is public property. Their way of resolving the conflict is therefore to accept personal obligations to the self rather than to the public.

The legal conflict is also treated more generally and philosophically [6] in some works. For example, William Wordsworth deals with the morality—or immorality—of the conflict in "Lines Written in Early Spring" when he says, "Have I not reason to lament / What man has made of man?" (lines 23 and 24). This question in its most extreme form refers to legalized suppression and persecution, but Wordsworth does little more with the topic than to say that he laments it. Layton, however, in "Rhine Boat Trip," deals with the extremity of human cruelty. In this poem, Layton condemns the Nazi exterminations of "Jewish mothers" and "murdered rabbis" during the Holocaust of World War II. Ironically, the exterminations were carried out legally, for it has commonly been observed that the Nazis created laws to justify all their moral atrocities.

Works that deal with war especially highlight the conflict [7] between personal and public concerns. It is a fact that individuals must take up arms when the public demands their wartime service, but the conflict between personal and public values reaches its most disturbing height when persons and families go through the consequent difficulties in all phases of their lives. A character who is personally caught up by the public demands of war is the speaker of Lowell's "Patterns." Because her fiancé has been killed fighting abroad, her extreme grief leads her to question those military "patterns" that have destroyed her personal plans for life (line 107). A comparable but also comic contrast is dramatized by Hardy in "Channel Firing." In this poem, set in a church graveyard, the skeleton of "Parson Thirdly" views "gunnery practice out at sea" (line 10) as

Wolinsky 5

evidence that his "forty year" dedication to serving his church—in other words, serving in public life—was a total waste. His conclusion is that he would have been better off ignoring his public role and instead following personal interests of "pipes and beer" (line 32). Whereas Parson Thirdly is disturbed by the noises of the publicly approved naval gunfire, Whitman's speaker in "Reconciliation" is moved to final and personal pity by the actual contact with the dead. As the speaker sees his dead enemy, lying "still in the coffin," he touches "lightly" with his lips "the white face in the coffin" in an act of personal reconciliation. Here, as in Lowell's "Patterns," whatever public value warfare might possess is insignificant in the face of the permanence of death. On the subject of warfare, writers inevitably contrast personal and public values, and without the slightest hesitation they assert that public things are negligible when compared with the importance of personal lives and concerns.

[8]     The works discussed here show varied and powerful conflicts between public demands and personal interests, and are in general agreement that, under ideal conditions, private life should be supreme. They also demonstrate that in many ways, the public world invades the private world with a wide range of demands and expectations, from making people behave foolishly to destroying them utterly. Naturally, the tone of the works is shaped by the degree of seriousness of the conflict. Chekhov's *The Bear* is good-humored and farcical because the characters overcome the social roles in which they are cast. More sober are works such as "Dover Beach" and "Young Goodman Brown," in which characters either are overcome by public commitments or deliberately turn their backs on them. In the highest range of seriousness are works such as "Rhine Boat Trip," "Patterns," and "Reconciliation" in which individuals have been crushed by irresistible public forces.

Wolinsky 6

Works Cited

Arnold, Matthew. "Dover Beach." *Writing About Literature*. By Edgar V.
　　Roberts. 12th ed. New York: Pearson, 2010. 364–65. Print.

Chekhov, Anton. *The Bear: A Joke in One Act. Writing About Literature*. By
　　Edgar V. Roberts. 12th ed. New York: Pearson, 2010. 383–91. Print.

Chopin, Kate. "The Story of an Hour." *Writing About Literature*. By
　　Edgar V. Roberts. 12th ed. New York: Pearson, 2010. 326–28. Print.

Glaspell, Susan. *Trifles. Writing About Literature*. By Edgar V. Roberts.
　　12th ed. New York: Pearson, 2010. 391–400. Print.

Hardy, Thomas. "Channel Firing." *Writing About Literature*. By Edgar V.
　　Roberts. 12th ed. New York: Pearson, 2010. 370–71. Print.

Hawthorne, Nathaniel. "Young Goodman Brown." *Writing About
　　Literature*. By Edgar V. Roberts. 12th ed. New York: Pearson, 2010.
　　330–38. Print.

Keats, John. "Bright Star." *Writing About Literature*. By Edgar V.
　　Roberts. 12th ed. New York: Pearson, 2010. 372–73. Print.

Layton, Irving. "Rhine Boat Trip." *Writing About Literature*. By Edgar
　　V. Roberts. 12th ed. New York: Pearson, 2010. 373. Print.

Lowell, Amy. "Patterns." *Writing About Literature*. By Edgar V. Roberts.
　　12th ed. New York: Pearson, 2010. 373–76. Print.

Shakespeare, William. "Sonnet 73: That Time of Year Thou Mayst in Me
　　Behold." *Writing About Literature*. By Edgar V. Roberts. 12th ed.
　　New York: Pearson, 2010. 105–106. Print.

Whitman, Walt. "Reconciliation." *Writing About Literature*. By Edgar V.
　　Roberts. 12th ed. New York: Pearson, 2010. 381. Print.

Wordsworth, William. "Lines Written in Early Spring." *Writing About
　　Literature*. By Edgar V. Roberts. 12th ed. New York: Pearson, 2010.
　　381–82. Print.

## Commentary on the Essay

This extended comparison-contrast essay, combining for discussion all three genres of fiction, poetry, and drama, is visualized as an assignment climaxing a unit of study. The expectation prompting the assignment is that a fairly large number of literary works can be profitably compared on the basis of a unifying subject, idea, or technique. For this essay, the works—eight poems, two stories, and two short plays—are compared and contrasted on the common topic of private-public conflicts. It is obviously impossible in a short essay to discuss all the works in detail in every paragraph. The essay therefore demonstrates that a writer may introduce a large number of works in a straightforward comparison-contrast method without a need for detailed comparison of each work with every other work on each of the major subtopics (social, legal, military).

Thus, the first section, consisting of paragraphs 2–4, treats six of the works. In paragraph 2, however, only two works are discussed, and in paragraph 3 one of these works is carried over for comparison with only one additional work. Paragraph 4 springs out of the third, utilizing one of the works discussed there and then bringing out comparisons with three additional works.

The same technique is used in the rest of the essay. Paragraph 5 introduces only one work; paragraph 6 introduces two additional works; and paragraph 7 introduces three works for comparison and contrast. Each of the twelve works has then been discussed at least once in terms of how it contributes to the major topic. One might note that the essay concentrates on a relatively small number of the works, such as Chekhov's *The Bear* and Hawthorne's "Young Goodman Brown," but that as newer topics are introduced, the essay goes on to works that are more closely connected to these topics.

The technique of extended comparison-contrast used in this way shows how the various works can be defined and distinguished in relation to the common idea—the contrast between personal and public life. The concluding paragraph summarizes these distinctions by suggesting a continuous line along which each of the works may be placed.

Even so, the treatment of so many texts might easily cause crowding and confusion. The division of the major topic into subtopics, as noted, is a major means of trying to make the essay easy to follow. An additional means is the introduction of transitional words and phrases such as *also, choose,* and *one of the major conflicts.*

An extended comparison-contrast essay cannot present a full treatment of each of the works. The works are unique, and they deal independently with many things that are outside the topic of an extended comparison-contrast essay. Ideas that are independently important in Hardy's "Channel Firing," for example, are that (1) human beings need eternal rest and not eternal life, (2) God is amused by—or indifferent to—human affairs, (3) religious callings or vocations may be futile, and (4) war itself is the supreme form of cruelty. All these topics could be treated in another essay, but they do not pertain to the goals of this particular essay. A topic compatible with the general private-public topic is needed, and the connection is readily made (paragraph 7) through the character of Hardy's Parson Thirdly. Because the essay deals with the conflicts brought out by Thirdly's comments, Hardy's poem is linked to all the other works for comparative purposes. So it is with the other works, each of which could also be the subject of analysis from many standpoints other than comparison-contrast. The effect of the comparison of all the works collectively, however, is the enhanced understanding of each of the works separately. To achieve such an understanding and to explain it are the major goals of the extended comparison-contrast method.

### Writing Topics Based on Comparison and Contrast

1. The use of the speaker in Arnold's "Dover Beach" and Wordsworth's "Lines Written in Early Spring"
2. The description of fidelity to love in Keats's "Bright Star" and Shakespeare's Sonnet 73: "That Time of Year Thou Mayst in Me Behold" or in Arnold's "Dover Beach" and Lowell's "Patterns"
3. The view of women in Chekhov's *The Bear* and Maupassant's "The Necklace" or in Glaspell's *Trifles* and Katherine Mansfield's "Miss Brill"
4. The use of descriptive scenery in Hawthorne's "Young Goodman Brown" and Lowell's "Patterns" or in Edgar Allan Poe's "The Cask of Amontillado" and Coleman's "Unfinished Masterpieces"
5. Symbols of disapproval in Hardy's "Channel Firing" and Frost's "Desert Places"
6. The treatment of loss in Shakespeare's "Sonnet 30: When to the Sessions of Sweet Silent Thought" and Shelly Wagner's "The Boxes"
7. Treatments of racial prejudice and hate crime in Dudley Randall's "Ballad of Birmingham" and Langston Hughes's "Negro"
8. For an extended comparison-contrast essay, any of the foregoing topics applied to a number of separate works

# Chapter 16

## Writing about a Work in Its Historical, Intellectual, and Cultural Context

Fiction, Poetry, and Drama

Everything written, spoken, painted, or composed reflects the period of its composition—its **historical**, **intellectual**, and **cultural context**, or milieu. Putting literature aside for the moment, we cannot open our mouths to speak without consciously or subconsciously taking into account the conditions in which we live, our ways of life, our intellectual goals, and our aims and aspirations. We are always a part of our greater culture, and our observations and thoughts are a constant function of the attitudes, idioms, ideas, and customs of our time and place. All things emerge from their own era, whether as a revolutionary idea, reaction, or synthesis; and one of the major tasks of the disciplined reader is to understand the relationship of historical times and artistic works. To study a work of literature in historical and cultural perspective is to determine the degree to which the work belongs in, and perhaps transcends, its period.

To carry out such a study, you need to develop thoughts about the connections of literature to life. You might consider the obvious fact that as circumstances change, writers express attitudes reflecting these changes. You might also consider that artists themselves want to create new ideas from existing ones and also to suggest improvements and reforms in government and society. A permanent standard of judging art is therefore its newness—that is, its status of being different—and artists are always trying to meet this standard. To the degree that writers of the past (and present) have been successful, it is possible to place their works in the light of historical perspective—if not of definite progress.

The idea of reading works in historical and sociological perspective is not to file them away in a historical pigeonhole but to improve understanding of the entire work. The aim is to produce accuracy of reading and of judgments, and to avoid errors that result from failure to see that writers, and artists generally, respond to their own times, either by embracing the present or by probing idealistically into the past. An interesting example is Samuel Taylor Coleridge's poem "Kubla Khan." It was published in 1816, a time when it was an accepted fact that scientists could explore the heavens with telescopes and everyday matter with microscopes. Absolutely new descriptions of the elements and their properties had been made, and the known world was appearing to be less awesome and more regular than it had ever seemed previously. But not everything was yielding to scientific discovery, and Coleridge was interested in evoking a less detailed but more mysterious past. And thus he based his poem "Kubla Khan" on the distant, almost magical time of the great emperor Kublai Khan, who had ruled China in the thirteenth century. It is as though Coleridge deliberately created his poem as an antithesis of the increasing scientism of his times.

## History, Culture, and Multiculturalism

It is such connections that are formative in literary history, which is in effect the chronicling of the interaction of ideas, events, social and political conditions, and literary modes. Of particularly increasing interest has been the consideration of literature as it reflects the society from which the writers of literature have come and on which they have based their work. Recently, great attention has been devoted to multicultural studies and literary works—that is, works that are based in the stories of people who for the greater portion of modern history have been suppressed and also ignored. The United States is a unique place in the world because during its relatively short existence it has seen a virtually constant immigration of national groups and cultures.

The process is by no means over. The census of 1940 recorded about 130 million Americans. Our population is now more than 305 million, and it is increasing daily. In addition to the massive numbers of African Americans, Chinese Americans, Central Europeans, and Scandinavians, much of whose immigration occurred before the twentieth century, new waves of people today have come from Asia, the Caribbean Islands, and Central and South America. As with all immigrants, many have arrived here with little or no knowledge of English but with strong memories of their native cultures. The second generations of these people have learned English but have experienced many of the traditional difficulties of integrating themselves into American life. They have encountered prejudice, hostility, segregation, and violence, for even though they were born on American soil they had much to overcome. A good deal of twentieth and early twenty-first century literature concerns the struggles of immigrants and their descendants as they have lived and worked and found a home in the United States.

As one might expect, this process of movement has stirred a not inconsiderable controversy. Politically, a traditional idea of long duration is that America is a "melting pot" of people of differing races and cultures, involving the blending and merging of the old world to create something entirely new. A contrary concept is that of multiculturalism: the idea that the members of each incoming group—on the basis of race, ethnicity, national origin, and culture—do not shed their unique qualities even though they have become American residents and citizens. Each group seeks to preserve its identity in the new land, and our culture is pluralistic. It is therefore diversity that should be celebrated, not assimilationism. Although there are profound political implications of this idea, including many possible divisions, our present focus is with the literature that has risen along with the many changes brought about by our unique nation of immigrants and their descendants.

## Literature in Its Time and Place

Analyzing a literary work as a product of cultural and intellectual history is the task of (1) determining what can be clearly deducible as coming directly out of the major issues existing at the time it was written and (2) deciding what is new and permanent—that is, of determining what has been created by the author of the work from ideas prevalent at the time of composition. The concern is to see both the similarity and dissimilarity of a work and its period.

Such a study of literature is valuable because it promotes the realization that ideas and ways of seeing the universe change with time and place. Too often it is easy to read texts as though they were all written last week and to attribute to writers ideas that they never had. Shakespeare, for example, had a number of political ideas, but he had no experience with representative government as we know it today. Therefore, in considering works of his that touch the subject of politics, such as the *Henry IV* plays, *Richard II*, and *Henry V*, you should understand why he dramatizes the importance of a just and strong monarch or the necessity of a moral aristocracy. We can enthusiastically accept his idea that wise rulers and moral people are necessary in the creation of successful government, even though we today apply the principle not to monarchy—the form that Shakespeare knew—but to democracy.

## Writing about a Work in Its Historical and Cultural Context

The first part of your task is to decide what is topical about the work on which you are going to write. Usually, there is enough in a work's descriptions, actions, locations, customs, and cultural assumptions to find something there that is unique. Irving Layton's "Rhine Boat Trip," for example, is derived from reflections about the unspeakable German atrocities and concentration camps during World War II.

Some works, however, may seem to offer a special challenge because of their apparent lack of references; that is, they seem to be so closely connected with our own contemporary ideas and assumptions that you may not readily see them in historical and cultural perspective. At first, Matthew Arnold's poem "Dover Beach" might give this impression. But "Dover Beach" provides abundant symbolism about the loss of religious certainty in the nineteenth century, and this idea, which many people today also feel, would provide you with sufficient material on which to begin the thoughts for an essay.

Another problem might arise when the work assigned is remote either in history or in place. In such works, however, the subject matter brings out ideals and attitudes of the writer, and these can then be related to the time in which the work was written, just as it may also be related to our own times. Robert Browning's poem "My Last Duchess" is such a work. It was published in 1842, but its subject is a Renaissance Italian nobleman who is callous and self-centered and who wields despotic power. Thus, it is apparent that Browning is providing a timely idea that absolute power produces destructive results both on the individual wielding it and on those around him. This is an idea that is certainly up to date—in fact, it is up to the minute. Browning's presentation of the duke can therefore be analyzed as a good deal more than a dramatic study of a powerful eccentric of past times.

### Raise Questions to Discover Ideas

It is important to realize that the major source of your information is the work itself. In your reading, you will discover a great deal about the period of the author—even our own period—and, more important, about the place of the work in that period. You need to ask and answer a number of questions.

- Are historical circumstances specifically mentioned? What are they? What does the author say about them?
- Does the writer describe conditions with photographic detail, or is he less concerned with pictorial details and more with human and political issues?
- To what national, ethnic, social, and economic class do the principal characters belong? What is their background? What values do they hold or represent?
- Are the characters religious or not? To what degree do religious or philosophical thoughts govern the actions of the characters?
- Is the principal character (or any character) an important part of the prevailing social and economic system as outlined in the work, or is she an outsider? If she is outside the system, what conditions have put and now keep her there? Are you made to feel pleased or angry with these conditions?
- Does the character eventually win a place in the system, is she left out of the system, or is she broken by it?
- What assumptions do you think the author had about the literary interests of his audience? That is, does it seem that the author wrote for a sophisticated audience, a simple-minded one, or a sensation-seeking one?
- What conclusions can you draw, on the basis of your answers to these and like questions, about the author's attitudes toward his times? Does he attempt to give a complete view or a partial view? Does he seem to be recommending values that are similar, or contrary, to those held during his era?

From questions such as these, you will soon discover a suitable topic, for there is need here, as always, for narrowing the focus of your discussion. For example, a question about the fortunes of particular characters can lead to an avenue of inquiry like the following: How can the unrealized talents of the characters in Anita Scott Coleman's story "Unfinished Masterpieces" be shown to reflect Coleman's views about American racial politics in the early twentieth century? Events or situations themselves can be focused in the same way. The details about Jackie's home life in Frank O'Connor's "First Confession" might suggest a topic like "The Negative Effect of Home Life on the Individual." Your creation of topics like these should enable you to develop an interesting and relevant essay.

This use of the work of literature itself as an authority for your remarks in the essay may seem open to the objection that literary works are often not reliable as actual source material for history. Sometimes works contain exaggerations made for comic or satiric effect, and sometimes they develop out of improbable circumstances. As history, therefore, the close study of a literary work is a weak substitute for more accurate documentation.

The answer to this objection—and also an important realization—is that the focus of this assignment *is* the work itself. Your essay is about the historical period only as it is reflected in the work. Your concern is not to use the work for evidence in writing history but rather as evidence of a literary reaction to historical and cultural circumstances. Even if there are exaggerations and caricatures or if conditions reported are brighter or darker than life, these very aspects of the work become an important part of the material you bring to your essay. Your aim should not be to use the work as a filter through which you attempt to acquire historical data, but to determine to what use such observable data have been put within the work.

Some types of literature are more readily approached from the historical, intellectual, and cultural point of view than others. Usually novels, short stories, narrative poems, dramas, and essays are fairly obviously rooted in customs and ideas of their time. Many of these works can be discussed without extensive reading in secondary historical sources. By contrast, many short lyric poems are not obviously connected with their respective periods, and to write about these works may require more inferential efforts.

## Organize Your Essay about a Work and Its Context

In the following plan, the introduction might be proportionately longer than usual because of the need for presenting detailed information about the work and what you know about its historical period.

*Introduction*      In addition to defining your central idea and thesis sentence, your aim here should be to place the work in its context. You should identify the work, state the time of its publication and, if known, its composition. You should also include any biographical data relevant to an understanding of the work and its background. You should also state whether there are any special problems in discussing the work, such as that it is a historical novel, or a work remote in time, or that there is some controversy about it.

You should also state the pertinent historical facts concerning the events and ideas that you have selected for discussion. There is no need for extensive explication but only for those details that are relevant. If your work was written during or shortly after a recent war, for example, you may assume that your readers know as much generally about this war as you do and need only those details that will remind them of their knowledge. Thus, if you are discussing Hardy's "The Man He Killed," you might state that the poem is probably based on a soldier's view stemming out of the trench warfare on the Western front during World War I. You might then go on to state that this war was immensely complex, for it had implications for all European nations and the United States; that it was fought on not only land but also the sea; that it was sometimes called the "Great War" and also "the war to end all wars"; that it was also seen as an ideological war in which nations felt their prestige to be at stake; that the war highlighted for many the idea that life and love were impermanent and fleeting; that the war was immensely wasteful and destructive; and that it was difficult to pinpoint the causes of the war and to explain the reasons for which opposing nations took sides. There is nothing unusual about these conclusions: The point about them is that they are general statements about the period rather than detailed descriptions.

*Body*    After dealing with introductory details, you should aim to show how they apply to the work you are studying. You may wish to include both of the following or just one or the other.

1. **A discussion of how the work embodies the facts or of how the facts shape the work.** Thus, Hardy's "The Man He Killed" not only demonstrates the commonsense quality of the speaker but also exposes the sham of theoretical warfare when contrasted with the ordinary needs and wants of an average human being. The poem can be seen as an assertion that international political concerns, in human terms, are valueless. Similarly, in discussing Browning's "My Last Duchess," you might show that the duke's conversational manners (his pre-empting the discussion of marriage details by reflecting on the portrait of his former duchess and his stating that his "just pretense" for a dowry will be acceptable) can be related to the assertion that the poem is an effective counterargument against nineteenth-century claims that "great men" are needed to perform the great tasks that are required in public and political life. Browning's "great man" is so preoccupied with his own power that he listens to no one and abandons all human decency.

2. **A discussion of literary matters—that is, style, structure, tone, point of view, and imagery—that can be related to the period.**    Thus, ideas about the need for personal freedom may be related to poems written in free verse. An awareness of the horror of discrimination may be related to the ballad structure of Dudley Randall's "Ballad of Birmingham," in which the simple poetic structure emphasizes the extreme to which such cruelty can go. The modern stress on psychology may account for the limited point of view story, Katherine Mansfield's "Miss Brill," in which we as readers directly follow the thoughts and responses of the major character. The compact, brief stanzas of Langston Hughes's "Negro" enables the poet to express a brief world history of the exploitation of blacks. What is important here is to apply the context of the work to its literary characteristics.

*Conclusion*    To conclude, you should try to determine which elements you have discussed seem out of date and which ones are still relevant and important. For purposes of your conclusion, you may assume that your own point of view is modern and up to date, although on this issue you should perhaps assert yourself humbly and emphasize your broadmindedness. Thus, in this section you might attempt to determine whether Browning's exposé of the ruthless duke in "My Last Duchess" is still applicable, granted that many people in various nations have invented the title "President for Life," and continue to fill that role. Does Young Goodman Brown's (in Nathaniel Hawthorne's "Young Goodman Brown") preoccupation with the evil of others seem to be relevant today, or should we regard his ideas as having passed their time? What should be our responses to those young men described by Gwendolyn Brooks who claim that they are "real cool"? It is questions such as these that you might ask and attempt to answer in your conclusion.

# Illustrative Essay

The central idea, thesis sentence, and topic sentences are shaded here to stress the goal of strong organization. As your instructor wishes, you might use this or a similar system in your own essays.

Larkin 1

Barry Larkin

Professor Decker

English 101

23 September 2010

Langston Hughes's References to Black Servitude

and Black Pride in "Negro"

Negro (1958)

I am a Negro:
  Black as the night is black.
  Black like the depths of my Africa.
I've been a slave:
  Caesar told me to keep his door-steps clean.       5
  I brushed the boots of Washington.
I've been a worker:
  Under my hand the pyramids arose.
  I made mortar for the Woolworth Building.
I've been a singer:       10
  All the way from Africa to Georgia
  I carried my sorrow songs.
  I made ragtime.
I've been a victim:
  The Belgians cut off my hands in the Congo.       15
  They lynch me still in Mississippi.
I am a Negro:
  Black as the night is black,
  Black like the depths of my Africa.

[1]      Langston Hughes was a strong voice of the Harlem Renaissance, a twentieth-century movement that declared that the time had come to recognize the significance of African Americans in all phases of life. In "Negro," Hughes propels this argument by showing that oppression

Larkin 2

against blacks is as old as human history.° He might have chosen to develop his idea in a lengthy book study, with many supportive details and many references. Instead, his interest is to be brief and memorable—almost as though he is providing details for a political agenda—and he chooses to create a poem of six brief stanzas. The poem demonstrates how eloquent a spokesman and leader Hughes was for his people. The poem is built on the contrast between what the heritage of blacks should be—the entitlement to equality and freedom—and what in fact it is and has been—the indignity of slavery and oppression.*

The form of "Negro" is both simple and direct. There are six    [2]
stanzas in the poem, each beginning with the pronoun "I" followed by a grammatical form of the verb *to be*. The total number of lines is nineteen. Stanzas 1 and 6 identify the speaker as a representative Negro whose identity is the same as his race—black—"Black like the depths of my Africa" (lines 3 and 19). These opening and concluding stanzas are current in scope, for they are in the present tense and they define the speaker's racial identity and pride in the color of his African heritage.

Stanzas 2, 3, and 5 are historical, however, briefly referring to the    [3]
servitude and suffering that blacks have experienced. The emphasis in these stanzas is on the past, and Hughes's use of the present-perfect tense bears out his continuing historical emphasis. These comprehensive stanzas jump time and place, from the slavery and oppression of ancient Rome and ancient Egypt, on the one hand, to Revolutionary War times and modern industrial times of the United States, on the other. Symbolically, the speaker says that in the palace of Caesar, he was a slave who kept the doorsteps clean, just as he cleaned the boots as a personal servant of America's first president, George Washington. The idea is that the heights that these men (and others like them) reached were achieved by their dependence on the slavery of blacks. Similarly, the Belgian colonial regime in Africa was sustained by oppressive cruelty against blacks, which is symbolized by the cutting off of the hands of slaves in the Congo (line 15). Hughes goes on to state that such

---

°Central idea.
*Thesis sentence.

Larkin 3

colonial oppression is by no means over, for his speaker refers to the neocolonial oppression of life in Mississippi (in 1958, the date of the poem), where lynching still occurred.

[4]        The most positive section of the poem is stanza 4, where Hughes tells us that the narrator has sung his "sorrow songs" during the entire history of displacement from "Africa to Georgia" (lines 11 and 12). This stanza is comparable to stanzas 1 and 6, for in all three stanzas Hughes declares the positive identity and value of African Americans. In stanza 4, the idea is that there is a vast human talent among blacks that has already been realized, with the implication that there is much more to come. Here, Hughes is emphasizing black pride because the power of making music and providing musical beauty is a capacity that can never be suppressed, even through the long centuries of black oppression that date from the origin of history. The possibility of continued high achievement, Hughes implies, is endless.

[5]        As we have seen, "Negro" concludes and ends on the importance of realizing the promises of history for the present time. The tenses of the verbs bring this out, for everything implies a current condition. The past has had its day, with its oppression, and is now over or should be over. The present is now the greatest concern. The time has come for African Americans to appreciate their own blackness, "like the depths of my Africa" (lines 3 and 19). Things are in some respects the same, yet they are changed because the time has come for liberation, for freedom. The idea is that it is time for the end of oppression—a time when African Americans can listen to themselves and their "sorrow songs" and can be themselves as they were meant to be when they were in their original homes in Africa.

[6]        "Negro" is therefore a thoroughly modern poem. It recognizes the past but emphasizes the significance of the present. In three of the poem's stanzas, Hughes refers to the past. The final stanza indicates that the present is the same as the past but that African Americans have moved up from slavery and oppression and can build their new identity out of their past history. Even though this last stanza is identical to the first, word for word, it suggests that it is time to move, to claim a new movement of history, a new direction. Hughes's argument is that this direction is forward.

Larkin 4

Work Cited

Hughes, Langston. "Negro." *Writing About Literature*. By Edgar V. Roberts. 12th ed. New York: Pearson, 2010. 248. Print.

## Commentary on the Essay

As an essay about a literary work as it pertains to its historical period, this essay deals with the issues of African American identity and liberation that have become a major idea in American life during the preceding generations of Americans. All the descriptions and interpretations of "Negro" are based on this connection. Because the issues of African American life have such strongly political overtones, the essay treats the poem as a work of exhortation as well as description. The essay makes transitions with the key words *however* (paragraph 3), *most positive* (4), *as we have seen* (5), and *therefore* (6).

In the body of this essay, paragraph 2 deals with the poem's shape and its essential simplicity. Of special interest is the poet's use of the present tense to sustain the argument that the poem is directed at current readers, who can translate their attitudes and interpretations of life into direct political action.

Paragraphs 3 and 4 are the most extensive in the essay, for they concern Hughes's interpretation of history and his emphasis on the indignities and horrors of black oppression from ancient times to the present. The unique analysis here is that the grammar of stanzas 2–5 is a major means by which Hughes sustains his argument. The idea in the essay here is to show that the past lives on in the present. Paragraph 4 follows Hughes's argument that the musical nature of African Americans is a positive symbol of their inherent human worthiness.

Paragraphs 5 and 6 emphasize once again the present implications of "Negro." Paragraph 5 especially emphasizes the present, while the concluding paragraph, 6, asserts that the poem is particularly modern. In this way, the essay demonstrates how Hughes's poem has a place in the historical times when it was written. The essay's analysis and its central idea both emphasize this connection.

### Writing Topics about Works in Their Historical, Intellectual, and Cultural Context

1. Consider a story or poem in which the topics are connected with philosophy or politics—for example, Arnold's "Dover Beach" (religion, philosophy), Robert Frost's "Desert Places" (the cosmos), Hardy's "The Man He Killed" (politics and war), and Amy Lowell's "Patterns" (war and human relationships). Write an essay about just one of these works, showing how the topic reflects ideas and concerns of the time it was written and also of today's times.

2. Consider William Blake's use of the image of the "Tyger" in "The Tyger." To what degree is the Tyger a symbol of what Blake considered to be evil? How does he seem to define evil? How current is his use of what today is considered an endangered animal? How does his poem speak to today's concerns?

3. In the context of current relationship of human beings to the natural world, how significant is William Wordsworth's "Lines Written in Early Spring"? Does the poem meet the same need for today's readers that it probably met for Wordsworth's readers?

4. The circumstances of farm life in the early twentieth century are reflected in Susan Glaspell's *Trifles*. Consider the circumstances of loneliness, isolation, lack of communication, and marital abuse that are treated in this play. To what degree are these issues still significant in today's world?

5. Describe the timeliness of the issues that Layton brings out in "Rhine Boat Trip."

6. Coleman's "Unfinished Masterpieces" deals with the issue of the inadequacy of opportunity. Specifically, her topic is that ability is meaningless when there is no chance to develop it. Write an essay attempting to demonstrate that her idea is as vital now as it was in the 1920s when she wrote her story.

7. The speaker of Luis Omar Salinas's "In a Farmhouse" is an eight-year-old boy who has been put to work picking cotton. What current issues are suggested by the speaker's plight?

8. Browning's "My Last Duchess" and Randall's "Ballad of Birmingham" touch upon the issue of political power. How do the works reflect what you take to have been the political concerns of their times, and what contrasts between the works are you able to make?

# Chapter 17

## Writing a Review Essay: Developing Ideas and Evaluating Literary Works for General Audiences

The **review** is a general essay on a literary work. It may also be thought of as a "critique," a "critical review," an "evaluation," or simply an "essay." It is a free form, for in a review virtually everything is relevant—subject matter, technique, social and intellectual background, biographical facts, relationship to other works by the same author or by different authors, historical importance, personal ideas and interpretations, and everything else. Unless you become a professional writer in the future, a review is the most likely kind of writing about literature that you may ever be called upon to do. Many businesses, associations, guilds, and other organizations issue regular newsletters or have meetings in which members are asked to discuss various subjects. Often, members of such groups are interested in learning about various works (including films) and authors—not only recent ones but also well-known and well-established ones—and hence there is a need for good reviews.

A major aim of review writing is to provide a general overview of the work, especially including an evaluation of the author's performance, together with other elements of the work that you should mention, special difficulties that you explain, and special features that you note.

Since the review provides for freedom of topics and development, it is also a challenge to the skills you have acquired thus far as a disciplined reader. Much of your experience has been *assimilation*—acquiring information and applying skills. Your tasks have been mainly fulfilling assignments that you are given in your classes. But with a review, you are left to your own devices. Freedom of choice should be a constant goal, and it is important to realize that your experience is equipping you more and more to know what to do with this freedom. You should not only know how to answer questions but should also decide on the questions to be asked. You should be able to synthesize the knowledge you are acquiring.

### Writing a Review Essay

Because reviews can be personal as well as objective, you may experiment with form and development. If you choose to write about only a single topic, be sure to emphasize the various aspects with clear transitions. If you decide to select a number of topics, as in the Illustrative Essay, be sure that your thesis sentence lists these topics.

### Raise Questions to Discover Ideas

- Who are the people for whom you intend your review? Are they a general audience or part of a particular group? What are the special interests of the group? What general interests do people in the group have in common?
- How much detail, special or general, do you think you should include about the work itself? How much knowledge does your audience expect you to demonstrate in your review? Should you introduce references to comparable works by the same author or by different authors?
- Have the people who make up your audience read the work? Should you design your review to be a substitute for their reading the work? Should your review aim at interesting your readers to read the work themselves?
- When was the work written? Just recently or a long time ago? What is the nationality of the author (if he or she is of another nationality)? What kind of background knowledge is needed for an understanding of the work, or what kind, and how much, is supplied by the author (e.g., a knowledge of military circumstances, of "old time" religion, of conditions in rural England or rural America)?
- To what genre does the work belong? What general issues need explaining before you begin your discussion of the work?
- What parts of the work are significant enough to warrant discussion in your review? What issues does the work bring out? What are the author's thoughts about these issues? How important are these thoughts? How timely is the work for today's readers?
- Do any particular characters, situations, or ideas stand out in the work that you are reviewing? What are these? Why are they significant?
- What aspects of the writer's style and presentation are worthy of mention? How fully do you think you can refer to these without losing your audience's interest?

## Organize Your Review Essay

*Introduction*    In your introduction, you should place the work in perspective. Although most frequently you will be asked to review a play or novel, it is good to bear in mind that you may also be writing a review about acting techniques or play production. If you are reviewing a new edition of an old work, you may be reconsidering the relevance of the past to the present, and you may also be judging the apparatus supplied by the editor. Always try to show that your work has relevance to the present group of readers.

*Body*    In the body, you should try either to arouse interest in the work or to discourage readers from reading it if it seems to dictate this conclusion.

Beyond providing introductory information, your principal objective is to describe the strengths and weaknesses of the work. To write such a description, you must call into play just about everything you have learned about analyzing literature for ideas, form, and style. In a sense, the review can be as specific as you wish to make it because the greatest part of the body should be given to analysis. In this analysis, you should try to bring out your own strengths and interests as a critical reader. It may be, for example, that you have become proficient in discussing ideas. Suppose that you observe intricately developed ideas in the work. You might choose to discuss that element in the body of your review, thereby appealing to your reader's interest in thought and ideas. You should always recognize, however, that your discussion should be of limited extent. There is no need for a detailed, word-by-word analysis. It is not an essay on ideas, style, or artistic qualities that you want but a review emphasizing such elements.

For specialized reviews, you might call into play those disciplines that have interested you thus far in your college career. For example, you may feel competent in handling ideas connected with sociology. Hence, in your review of a novel you might bring your sociological awareness to bear on the work. Or you may have developed an interest in psychology and might treat the characters in a work according to your understanding of psychological problems. Many reviewers use the opportunity of the review to include details that they consider particularly important or interesting. It may be that you are reminded of facts that might help you enhance the understanding of your readers.

Whatever your personal interests and specialties may be, however, your best guide for subject matter is the work itself, which will channel your thinking along definite lines. For example, you might connect the obvious character flaw of the hero of Nathaniel Hawthorne's "Young Goodman Brown" to religious concerns (for an audience of people who might be interested in religion). Or you might take the position that the same story might interest readers in considering the psychological importance of personal certainty and security. In the work you are assigned, you may similarly find that certain features will point you in a specific direction (humor, a connection with a particular philosophy, reflections on economic or social conditions, the nature of life on the frontier, etc.).

*Conclusion*   Your conclusion should be an attempt to evaluate the work, certainly not extensively, but at least you should give an outline of your responses and a suggestion to your readers of how they might respond—assuming that you have shown that your interests coincide approximately with theirs. If the body of your review has emphasized evaluation, you should close your essay with a simple résumé of your points. If you are ever asked to review a work in, say, no more than 150 words, the greatest part of the review should be devoted to evaluation.

## Illustrative Essay

The central idea, thesis sentence, and topic sentences are shaded here to stress the goal of strong organization. As your instructor wishes, you might use this or a similar system in your own essays.

Annie Braxton

Professor Winger

English 100

17 December 2010

Nathaniel Hawthorne's Story "Young Goodman Brown":°

A View of Mistaken Zeal

[1]      "Young Goodman Brown" is an allegorical story by Nathaniel Hawthorne (1804–1864), the classic nineteenth-century writer who probed deeply into the relationships between religion and guilt. Hawthorne sets the story in colonial Salem during the days of religious Puritanism. His major aim is to expose the weakness in the religious view that stresses the shortcomings and sins of human life.* Although this concern may seem narrow, the story itself is timely, presenting a dreamlike narrative, a realistic analysis of the growth of intolerance, and a number of questions of permanent importance.[†]

[2]      On the surface, the apparent vagueness and dreamlike nature of Hawthorne's details may leave at least a few readers puzzled. The action is a nighttime trip by Young Goodman Brown to a mysterious satanic gathering in a deep forest just outside the village of Salem. Brown begins his walk as a friendly youth, just three months married to a young woman named Faith. But the midnight cult-gathering leaves him disillusioned and embittered. He spends the rest of his life in pessimism and gloom. This much is clear, but the precise nature of Brown's experience is not. Does he really make a trip into the woods? It would seem so, but by the story's end, Hawthorne states that the whole episode may have been no more than a dream or nightmare, and he speaks about it as such. Yet when the morning comes, Brown walks back into town as though he is returning from an overnight trip, and he recoils in horror from a number of his fellow villagers, including his wife. Just as uncertain is the identity of the stranger whom Brown encounters on the path. The man resembles

---

°See pages 330–38 for this story.

*Central idea.

[†]Thesis sentence.

Braxton 2

Brown's father, but his serpentlike walking stick suggests the devil, who
later presides at the satanic ritual deep within the forest.

The fact is, however, that Hawthorne was clearly not interested in                    **[3]**
producing a realistic imitation of life in detail. Rather he wanted to get at
the inward, psychological reality of persons like Goodman Brown, who
mistakenly build a wall of anger and bitterness between themselves and
the people around them. From this perspective, Brown's walk into the
forest is a symbol of one of the ways in which people may turn sour. In
Brown's case, he falls under the spell of finding evil everywhere he
turns. So strong is his view that he rejects anyone not measuring up,
even if he must spend the rest of his life in spiritual isolation. Although
he is at the extreme edge, he is like many who cannot forgive and get
along with anyone who is different.

Brown is thus anything but heroic, even if he is the story's major                    **[4]**
character. Nevertheless, the story is provocative and compelling, and it
raises many timely questions. For example, how can something that is
designed for human salvation, like the religious system that Brown
inherited, lead its followers into disastrous mistakes? Does the failure result
from the people who misunderstand the basic message of the system or
from the system itself? To what degree can the religious structure of the
story be related to political and social institutions? Should any religious or
political philosophy be given greater importance than goodwill for others
and confidence in their integrity? Could any free society survive for long if
it were composed of persons like Goodman Brown after his dream, or
would it turn into some form of absolutism or despotism and soon be
reduced to persecution on moral, religious, or political grounds?

Although Hawthorne's story belongs to Salem village during the                       **[5]**
late seventeenth century—the location, one might remember, of the
infamous witchcraft trials—it has many layers. It is a memorable study
in spiritual deterioration and a vivid example of the need for trust and
goodwill in human relationships. Without such a spirit of trust, life itself
would soon resemble the life lived by Goodman Brown, whose vision
makes his world bleak and forbidding—a place controlled by negation
and death rather than understanding and acceptance.

# Commentary on the Essay

This review essay follows a normal pattern of exposition. The introduction (paragraph 1) briefly presents essential background, and it states a central idea about the timeliness of Hawthorne's ideas. Paragraph 2 deals with the problem of the dreamlike vagueness of the narrative. Paragraph 3 contains an explanation of the vagueness inasmuch as Hawthorne's point is to dramatize the way in which people become intolerant. Paragraph 4 describes the timeliness of this analysis in terms of important questions raised by the story. Paragraph 5 is a short tribute to the quality of Hawthorne's insights.

Throughout this Illustrative Essay, the purpose is not to examine any of the points in great depth but to interest readers in topics that they might like to consider when they themselves read the work.

### Writing Topics for Review Essays

Write on any of the following topics, each of which is accompanied by a suggestion of the audience for whom you might wish to intend your review.

1. A review of Susan Glaspell's *Trifles* (readers interested in law and the sentencing of offenders)
2. A review of Shelly Wagner's "The Boxes" (readers primarily composed of young mothers)
3. A review of Amy Lowell's "Patterns" (readers whose wives, husbands, sons, or daughters have been killed in war or police work)
4. A review of Anton Chekhov's *The Bear* (readers who want to enjoy humorous and farcical situations)
5. A review of Edgar Allan Poe's "The Cask of Amontillado" (readers who like stories of mystery, horror, and the bizarre)
6. A review of Matthew Arnold's "Dover Beach" (readers interested in the loss of ideals and how to compensate for this loss)
7. A review of William Blake's "The Tyger" (readers interested in definitions of evil and its origins)
8. A review of Robert Frost's "Desert Places" (readers interested in puzzles of personal philosophy)
9. A review of Irving Layton's "Rhine Boat Trip" (readers interested in World War II and the Holocaust)
10. A review of Dudley Randall's "Ballad of Birmingham" or Langston Hughes's "Negro" (readers particularly concerned about racial issues)
11. A review of Mark Twain's "Luck" (readers interested in the reputations of public figures)

# Chapter 18

# Writing and Documenting the Research Essay: Using Extra Resources for Understanding

Broadly, **research** is the act of systematic investigation, examination, and experimentation. It is the basic tool of intellectual inquiry for anyone engaged in any discipline—physics, chemistry, biology, psychology, anthropology, history, and literature, to name just a few disciplines. With research, our understanding and our civilization grow; without it, they die.

The major assumption of doing research is that the researcher is reaching out into new areas of knowledge. With each assignment, the researcher acquires not only the knowledge gained from the particular task but also the skills needed to undertake further research and thereby to gain further knowledge. Some research tasks are elementary, such as using a dictionary to discover the meaning of a word and thereby enhancing the understanding of an important passage. More involved research uses an array of resources: encyclopedias, biographies, introductions, critical studies, bibliographies, old newspapers, and histories. When you begin a research task, you usually have little or no knowledge about your topic, but with such resources, you can acquire expert knowledge in a relatively short time.

Although research is the animating spark of all disciplines, our topic here is **literary research**—the systematic use of primary and secondary sources in studying a literary problem. In doing literary research, you consult not only individual works themselves (*primary sources*) but many other works that shed light on them and interpret them (*secondary sources*). Typical research tasks are to learn important facts about a work and about the period in which it was written; to learn about the lives, careers, and other works of authors; to discover and apply the comments and judgments of modern or earlier critics; to learn details that help explain the meaning of works; and to learn about critical and artistic taste.

## Selecting a Topic

In most instances, your instructor assigns a research essay on a specific topic. Sometimes, however, the choice of a topic will be left in your hands. For such assignments, it is helpful to know the types of research essays that you might find most congenial. Here are some possibilities.

1. **A particular work.** You might treat character (e.g., "The Character of Louise in Kate Chopin's 'The Story of an Hour'" or "The Question of Whether Young Goodman Brown Is a Hero or a Dupe in Nathaniel Hawthorne's 'Young Goodman Brown'") or tone, ideas, structure, form, and the like. A research paper on a single work is similar to an essay on the same work, except that the research paper takes into account more views and facts than those you are likely to have without the research.

2. **A particular author.** A project might focus on an idea or some facet of style, imagery, setting, or tone of the author, tracing the origins and development of the topic through a number of different stories, poems, or plays. Examples are "Edgar Allan Poe's Treatment of the Speaker in His Short Stories" and "Robert Frost's Selections of Topics in His Early Poetry." This type of essay is suitable for a number of shorter works, although it is also applicable for a single major work, such as a longer story, novel, or play.

3. **Comparison and contrast** (see Chapter 15). There are two types.
    a. *An idea or quality common to two or more authors.* Here you show points of similarity or contrast, or you show how one author's work can be taken to criticize another's. A possible subject is "Contrasting Uses of Dialogue in Anton Chekhov and Susan Glaspell" or "The Theme of Male–Female Relations in Amy Lowell, Anton Chekhov, and Christina Rossetti."
    b. *Different critical views of a particular work or body of works.* Sometimes much is to be gained from an examination of differing critical opinions on topics like "The Meaning of Edgar Allan Poe's 'The Cask of Amontillado'" or "Various Views of Nathaniel Hawthorne's 'Young Goodman Brown.'" Such a study would attempt to determine the critical opinion and taste to which a work did or did not appeal, and it might also aim at conclusions about whether the work was in the advance or rear guard of its time.

4. **The influence of an idea, author, philosophy, political situation, or artistic movement on specific works of an author or authors.** An essay on influences can be specific and to the point, as in "Details of Black American Life as Reflected in Langston Hughes's 'Negro,'" or it can be more abstract and critical, as in "The Influence of Racial Oppression and the Goal of Racial Equality on the Speaker of Langston Hughes's 'Negro.'"

5. **The origin of a particular work or type of work.** Such an essay might examine an author's biography to discover the germination and development of a work—for example, "'Kubla Khan' as an Outgrowth of Samuel Taylor Coleridge's Reading." Another way of discovering origins might be to relate a work to a particular type or tradition: "'The Cask of Amontillado' and Edgar Allan Poe's Theory of the Short Story" or "Amy Lowell's 'Patterns' and Its Relationship to Antiwar Literature."

If you consider these types, an idea of what to write may come to you. Perhaps you have particularly liked one author or several authors. If so, you might start to think along the lines of types 1, 2, or 3. If you are interested in influences or origins, then type 4 or 5 may suit you better.

   If you still cannot decide on a topic after rereading the works you have liked, then you should carry your search for a topic into your school library. Look up your author or authors in the computer or card catalog. Your first goal should be to find a relatively recent book-length critical study published by a university press. Look for a title indicating that the book is a general one dealing with the author's major works rather than just one work. Study those chapters relevant to the work or works you have chosen. Most writers of critical studies describe their purpose and plan in their introductions or first chapters, so begin with the first part of the book. If there is no separate chapter on the primary text, use the index as your guide to the relevant pages. Reading in this way will give you enough knowledge about the issues and ideas raised by the work to enable you to select a promising topic. Once you make your decision, you are ready to develop a working bibliography.

# Setting Up a Bibliography

The best way to develop a working bibliography of books and articles is to begin with major critical studies of the writer or writers. Again, go to the computer or card catalog and find books that have been published by university presses. These books always contain comprehensive bibliographies. Be careful to read the chapters on your primary work or works and to look for the footnotes or endnotes, for often you can save time if you record the names of books and articles listed in these notes. Then refer to the bibliographies included at the ends of the books and select likely looking titles. Now, look at the dates of publication of the scholarly books. Let us suppose that you have been looking at three, published in 2002, 2004, and 2006. Unless you are planning an extensive research assignment, you can safely assume that the writers of critical works will have done the selecting for you of important works published before the date of publication. These bibliographies will be reliable, and you can use them with confidence. Thus, the bibliography in a book published in 2002 will be complete up through about 2000–2001, for the writer will have finished the manuscript a year or two before the book was published. But such bibliographies will not go up to the present. For that, you will need to search for works published after the most recent of the books.

### *Consult Bibliographical Guides*

Fortunately for students doing literary research, the Modern Language Association (MLA) of America has been providing a complete bibliography of literary studies for years, not only in English and American literatures but also in the literatures of many foreign languages. This is the *MLA International Bibliography of Books and Articles on the Modern Languages and Literatures* (*MLA Bibliography*). The *MLA Bibliography* started achieving completeness in the late 1950s. By 1969 the project had grown so large that it was published in several parts, which are bound together in library editions. University and college libraries have sets of this bibliography on open shelves or tables. At the present writing, the most recent of these bibliographies is the *2007 MLA Bibliography*, published in 2008. The *MLA Bibliography* is also published on CD-ROM and on the Internet, formats accessible to you through your college library facilities. You will need to consult with a librarian about Internet access so that you will have the proper identifying name and password.

There are many other bibliographies useful for students doing literary research, such as the *Essay and General Literature Index;* the *International Index;* the *Reader's Guide to Periodical Literature; A Bibliography of Literary Theory, Criticism and Philology,* 14th edition (2009; available on the Internet through Google); and various specific indexes. The *MLA Bibliography* is more than adequate, however, for most purposes in the study of literature. Remember that as you progress in your reading, the notes and bibliographies in the works you consult will also constitute an unfolding selective bibliography. For the Illustrative Research Essay in this chapter, a number of entries were discovered not only from bibliographies like those just listed but also from the reference lists in critical books.

The *MLA Bibliography*, in the traditional book format, is conveniently organized by period and author. Should you be doing research about Gwendolyn Brooks, look her up in *Volume I: British and Irish, Commonwealth, English, Caribbean, and American Literatures,* where you will also find references to most other authors of English and American literature, such as Shakespeare, William Wordsworth, Matthew Arnold, Amy Lowell, and Robert Frost, under the author's last name. In the *MLA Bibliography,* journal references are abbreviated, but a lengthy list explaining abbreviations appears at the beginning of the volume. Using the *MLA Bibliography* in the book format, begin with the most recent one and then go backward to your stopping point. If your library has machines dedicated to the electronic versions of the bibliography, you can do your searching by typing in the name of your author or subject. By whatever means you gain access to the bibliography, be sure to get the complete information, especially volume numbers and years of publication, for each article and book. You are now ready to find your sources and to take notes.

## Online Library Services

Through computer access, many college and university libraries are instantaneously connected to a vast array of local, national, and even international libraries so that, by using various online services, you can extend your research far beyond the capacities of your own library. You can use a personal computer to gain access to the catalogs of large research libraries, provided that you punch in the correct entry information.

### *Gaining Access to Books and Articles through the Internet*

Up until just a short time ago, many smaller schools did not have copies of all the books and scholarly periodicals containing the results and reports of research. Many students were therefore frustrated in their attempts to find all the works that they had included on their working bibliographies. Times, however, have changed. You may now gain access to many sources that are not in your library because many of the works you want to read are now directly available to you through computer, page by page. A major source is *Questia*, an electronic depository of books and articles, which is likely available to you through your college library. In total, *Questia* contains 72,000 "full text" books, and more than 2 million articles. For students doing research on Nathaniel Hawthorne's short stories, for example, *Questia* claims to have several thousand books and in excess of 1,500 scholarly articles. *EBSCOhost* is a multidisciplinary database that includes "MagillOnLiteraturePlus," which has plot summaries and analysis of fictional works. *EBSCOhost* also has "Book Index with Reviews" that includes excerpts of book reviews along with book summaries. *WilsonWeb* has databases in many disciplines and includes "Book Review Digest Plus," which has summaries of books as well as complete book reviews. *WilsonWeb* also has "Short Story Index," which indexes stories appearing in collections and periodicals since 1984. *Columbia Grangers World of Poetry* has references to many types of poetry.

Another major electronic source is JSTOR (i.e., *Journal Storage*), the scholarly journal archive. Most college and university libraries, and many high schools, subscribe to this service, and it is available to you as a registered student. It includes computerized copies of complete sets of hundreds of scholarly journals in arts and sciences. By gaining the proper credentials available to you as a student, you will have access to virtually any item that you have entered in your bibliography.

Still another vital research source is Google Scholar, which is in the process of duplicating the pages of many thousands of scholarly works. The service is available, like *Questia* and JSTOR, through your school library. In other words, these electronic book and article services are available right now to provide you with abundant materials that previously were not readily available to most students at American colleges and universities.

In addition, by using search engines to gain access to sites on the Web, you can also discover special topics directly related to your subject—for example, organizations devoted to making awards, clubs or other organizations that have been established in the home cities of particular authors, or works on topics inspired by various authors. The well-known Google search engine yields startling and overwhelming results. Presently, it has been estimated that as many as eight billion Web pages are available through the regular Google service. This is a gross figure, of course, and refers to the entire range of all intellectual and scholarly disciplines, of which literature is only a part. The result is that more and more references are presently available, and thousands of pages are being added each day. The numbers of possible Google references are literally beyond comprehension.

The Google entry for Shakespeare, for example, yields 53.4 million "hits." The numbers for other writers are not as staggering, but they are staggering enough. Google lists 4.26 million entries for Dickinson, and more than 4.5 million entries for Frost. For Langston Hughes, the number of entries is 1.28 million. Obviously, the figures cited here are too massive for ordinary classroom purposes, and your principal task in the face of these overwhelming figures is to narrow your search. Look through a limited number of the titles and pick out only those that you think will be most useful to you. You can also narrow your search by listing particular years of publication. For example, the year 2003 for Shakespeare's *Hamlet* in Google gives nine entries published that year on *Hamlet*, a number that facilitates the task of selection.

You can also connect with many major libraries, although the ease with which you can gain access through a computer search is variable. Some library catalogs are friendly, whereas others require a certain amount of trial and error on your part.[1] In many cases,

---

[1] Libraries generally encourage access to their resources, so proper entry instructions are often attached to computer terminals, particularly for internal use. When you are hooked into catalogs of distant libraries, you will find that the computer screen itself contains instructions about what you need to do to continue your search.

you will need several tries to learn how to find what you are looking for because the words that some libraries use to categorize holdings are not immediately apparent. In all cases, practice with the various systems is essential, for you cannot expect to get the most out of an electronic search the first time you try. You will be richly rewarded for spending a number of afternoons in experimenting with what can be gained through these references.

After you have gained access, you can look up books by specific authors or can select books about particular topics. A recent search for critical and interpretive works about Shakespeare in one of the major university libraries in the United States produced a list of more than four thousand titles (not just in English but also in other languages). The same library listed six hundred works (including videos) specifically about *Hamlet*. Another major university library produced more than seven thousand titles on Shakespeare biography and interpretation and close to five hundred titles exclusively on *Hamlet*. Obviously, a number of the titles are held in both libraries.

Once you have spent some time in looking up likely entries, your list will make up a fairly comprehensive search bibliography, which you can use when you physically enter the library to begin collecting and using materials. A major convenience is that many associated libraries, such as state colleges and urban public libraries, have pooled their resources. Thus, if you use the services of a network of nearby county libraries, you can go to another library to use materials that are not accessible at your own college or branch. If distances are great, however, and your own library does not have a book that you think is important to your project, you can ask a librarian to get the book for you through the Interlibrary Loan Service. Usually, given time, the libraries will accommodate as many of your needs as they can.

A promising new feature in computer research became available in 2004. This is the Google Scholar site (scholar.google.com), which contains general scholarly listings for the hard and social sciences as well as for literature. The listings refer to books, articles, and abstracts. One must hasten to add that Google Scholar provides a listing of works, not a collection. The articles themselves are only haphazardly available through the search engine, and you will often find a restriction on your right to access some of the listed materials. A particular convenience is that Google Scholar lists state libraries where particular books are part of the collection so that, if time is available, you can go to the libraries or request interlibrary loans. As yet, however, Google Scholar is not comprehensive for literary topics.

## Taking Notes and Paraphrasing Material

There are many ways of taking notes, but the consensus is that the best method is to use note cards.[2] If you have never used cards before, you might profit from consulting any one of a number of handbooks and special workbooks on research. The principal

---

[2]See Muriel Harris, *Prentice Hall Reference Guide to Grammar and Usage*, 5th ed. (Upper Saddle River: Prentice Hall, 2003) 283–301.

---

### AN IMPORTANT CONSIDERATION ABOUT COMPUTER-AIDED RESEARCH

Just a few years ago, the broadness of scope that electronic searches provide for most undergraduate students doing research assignments was not possible; today, it is commonplace. Even with the astounding possibilities of electronic resources, however, it is still necessary to take out actual books and articles—and read them and take notes on them—before you can begin and complete a research essay. The electronic services can help you locate materials, but they cannot do your reading, note taking, and writing. All that is still up to you, as it always has been.

---

advantage of cards is that you can see them all together when you lay them out on a desk or other large surface. As a result, cards may be easily classified; numbered and renumbered; shuffled; tried out in one place, rejected, and then used in another place (or thrown away); and arranged in order when you start to write.

### *Take Complete and Accurate Notes*

*Write the Source on Each Card*    As you take notes, write the source of your information on each card. This may seem bothersome, but it is easier than going back to the library to locate the correct source after you have begun your essay. You can save time if you take the complete data on one card—a "master card" for that source—and then create an abbreviation for the separate note cards you take from the source. Here is an example, which also includes the location where the reference was originally found (e.g., card catalog, computer search, bibliography in a book, the *MLA Bibliography*). Observe that the author's last name goes first.

---

Donovan, Josephine, ed. <u>Feminist</u>                    PN
    <u>Literary Criticism: Explorations</u>              98
    <u>in Theory</u>. 2nd ed. Lexington:                W64
    UP of Kentucky. 1989                          F4

DONOVAN

Library Catalog, "Women"

---

If you take many notes from this book, the name *Donovan* will serve as identification. Be sure not to lose your master cards because you will need them when you prepare your list of works cited. If possible, record the complete bibliographical data in a computer file.

*Record the Page Number for Each Note*    It would be hard to guess how much exasperation has been caused by the failure to record page numbers in notes. Be sure to write the page number down first, *before* you begin to take your note, and, to be doubly sure, write the page number again at the end of your note. If the detail goes from one page to the next in your source, record the exact spot where the page changes, as in this example:

---

Heilbrun and Stimson, in DONOVAN, pp. 63–64

[63] After the raising of the feminist consciousness it is necessary to develop/[64] "the growth of moral perception" through anger and the "amelioration of social inequities."

---

The reason for such care is that you may wish to use only a part of a note you have taken, and when there are two pages you will need to be accurate in locating what goes where.

*Record Only One Fact or Opinion on a Card*    Record only one major detail on each card—one quotation, one paraphrase, one observation—*never two or more*. You might be tempted to fill up the entire card with many separate but unrelated details, but such a try at economy often gets you in trouble because you might want to use some of the details in other places. If you have only one entry per card, you will avoid such problems and also retain the freedom you need.

*Use Quotation Marks for All Quoted Material*    In taking notes, it is extremely important—vitally important—to distinguish copied material from your own words. *Always put quotation marks around every direct quotation you copy verbatim from a source.* Make the quotation marks *immediately, before you forget,* so that you will always know that the words of your notes within quotation marks are the words of another writer.

Often, as you take a note, you may use some of your own words and some of the words from your source. In cases like this, be even more cautious. Put quotation marks around *every word* that you take directly from the source, even if your note looks like a picket fence. Later, when you begin writing your essay, your memory of what is yours and not yours will be dim, and *if you use another's words in your own essay without proper acknowledgment, you are risking the charge of plagiarism.* Much of the time, plagiarism is caused not by deliberate deception but rather by sloppy note taking.

### If Your Source Is Long, Make a Brief and Accurate Paraphrase

When you take notes, it is best to paraphrase the sources. A paraphrase is a restatement in your own words, and because of this, it is actually a first step in the writing of your essay. A big problem in paraphrasing is to capture the idea in the source without copying the words verbatim. The best way is to read and reread the passage you are noting. Turn over the book or journal—or put your computer screen to sleep—and write out the idea *in your own words* as accurately as you can. Once you have completed this note, compare it with the original and make corrections to improve your thought and emphasis. Add a short quotation if you believe it is needed, but be sure to use quotation marks. If your paraphrase is too close to the original, *throw out the note and write another one.* This effort may have its own reward because often you may be able to transfer some or even all of your note, word for word, directly to the appropriate place in your research essay.

To see the problems of paraphrasing, let us look at a paragraph of criticism and then see how a student doing research might take notes on it. The paragraph is by Richard F. Peterson, from an essay entitled "The Circle of Truth: The Stories of Katherine Mansfield and Mary Lavin," published in *Modern Fiction Studies* 24 (1978): 383–94. In the passage to be quoted, Peterson is considering the structures of two Mansfield stories, "Bliss" and "Miss Brill":

> "Bliss" and "Miss Brill" are flawed stories, but not because the truth they reveal about their protagonists is too brutal or painful for the tastes of the common reader. In each story, the climax of the narrative suggests an arranged reality that leaves a lasting impression, not of life, but of the author's cleverness. This strategy of arrangement for dramatic effect or revelation, unfortunately, is common in Katherine Mansfield's fiction. Too often in her stories a dropped remark at the right or wrong moment, a chance meeting or discovery, an intrusive figure in the shape of a fat man at a ball or in the Cafe de Madrid, a convenient death of a hired man or a stranger dying aboard a ship, or a *deus ex machina* in the form of two doves, a dill pickle, or a fly plays too much of a role in/[386] creating a character's dilemma or deciding the outcome of the narrative. 385–86

Because taking notes forces a shortening of this or any criticism, it also requires you to discriminate, judge, interpret, and select; good note taking is not easy. There are some things to guide you, however, when you go through the many sources you uncover.

*Think about the Purpose of Your Research*    You may not know exactly what you are "fishing for" when you start to take notes, for you cannot prejudge what your essay will contain. Research is a form of discovery. But soon you will notice subjects and issues that your sources constantly explore. If you can accept one of these as your major topic, or focus of interest, you can use that as your guide in all further note taking.

For example, suppose you start to take notes on criticism about Katherine Mansfield's "Miss Brill," and after a certain amount of reading, you decide to focus on the story's structure. This decision guides your further research and note taking. Thus, for example, Richard Peterson criticizes Mansfield's technique of arranging climaxes in her stories. With your topic being structure, it would therefore be appropriate to take a note on Peterson's judgment. The following note is adequate as a brief reminder of the content in the passage:

> Peterson 385                                    structure: negative
>
> Peterson claims that Mansfield creates climaxes
> that are too artificial, too unlifelike, giving the
> impression not of reality but of Mansfield's own
> "cleverness." 385

Let us now suppose that you want a fuller note, in the expectation that you need not just Peterson's general idea but also some of his supporting detail. Such a note might look like this:

> Peterson 385                                    structure: negative
>
> Peterson thinks that "Bliss" and "Miss Brill" are "flawed"
> because they have contrived endings that give the impres-
> sion "not of life but of" Mansfield's "cleverness." She
> arranges things artificially, according to Peterson, to cause
> the endings in many other stories. Some of these things are
> chance remarks, discoveries, or meetings, together with
> other unexpected or chance incidents and objects. These
> contrivances make their stories imperfect. 385

In an actual research essay, any part of this note would be useful. The words are almost all the note taker's own, and the few quotations are within quotation marks. Note that Peterson, the critic, is properly recognized as the source of the criticism, so you could adapt the note easily when you are doing your writing. The key here is that your note taking should be guided by your developing plan for your essay.

Note taking is part of your thinking and composing process. You may not always know whether you will be able to use each note that you take, and you will always exclude many notes when you write your essay. You will always find, however, that taking notes is easier once you have determined your purpose.

*Give Your Notes Titles*    To help plan and develop the various parts of your essay, write a title for each of your notes, as in the examples in this chapter. This practice is a form of outlining. Let us continue discussing the structure of Mansfield's "Miss Brill," the actual subject of the Illustrative Research Essay (p. 279). As you do your research, you discover that there is a divergence of critical thought about how the ending of the story should be understood. Here is a note about one of the diverging interpretations:

> Daly 90                          Last sentence of the story
>
> Miss Brill's "complete" "identification" with the shabby fur
> piece at the very end may cause readers to conclude that she is
> the one in tears but bravely does not recognize this fact, and
> also to conclude that she may never use the fur in public again
> because of her complete defeat. Everything may be for "per-
> haps the very last time."

Notice that the title classifies the topic of the note. If you use such classifications, a number of like-titled cards could underlie a section in your essay about how to understand
the concluding sentence of "Miss Brill." In addition, once you decide to explore the last
sentence, the topic itself will guide you in further study and note taking. (See the Illustrative Research Essay, in which paragraphs 15–20 concern this topic.)

*Write Down Your Own Original Thoughts and Mark Them as Your Own*     As you take
notes, you will be acquiring your own observations and thoughts. Do not push these
aside in your mind, on the chance of remembering them later, but write them down
immediately. Often you may notice a detail that your source does not mention, or you
may get a hint for an idea that the critic does not develop. Often, too, you may get
thoughts that can serve as "bridges" between details in your notes or as introductions
or concluding observations. Be sure to title your comments and to mark them as
your own thought. Here is such a note, which is on the emphasis on character as opposed to action in "Miss Brill":

> My Own                          Last sentence of the story
>
> Mansfield's letter of Jan. 17, 1921, indicates that action as
> such was less significant in her scheme for the story than
> the sympathetic evocation of Miss Brill's observations, im-
> pressions, and moods. She wanted to reveal character.

Observe that in paragraph 4 of the illustrative research essay, the substance of this note
(also a good deal of the language) is used to introduce new material once the passage
from the Mansfield letter has been quoted.

## Classify Your Cards and Group Them Accordingly

If you do a careful and thorough job of taking notes, your essay will already have been
forming in your mind. The titles of your cards will suggest areas to be developed as you

do your planning and initial drafting. Once you have assembled a stack of note cards derived from a reasonable number of sources (your instructor may have assigned an approximate number or a minimum number), you can sort them into groups according to the topics and titles. For the Illustrative Research Essay, after some shuffling and retitling, the cards were assembled in the following groups:

1. Writing and publication
2. General structure
3. Seasons and time of day as structure
4. Insensitive or cruel actions as structure
5. Concluding paragraphs; conclusion

If you look at the major sections of the Illustrative Research Essay, you will see that the topics are closely adapted from these groups of cards. In other words, *the arrangement of the cards is an effective means of outlining and organizing a research essay.*

*Make Logical Arrangements of the Cards in Each Group*    There is still much to do with each group of cards. You cannot use the details as they happen to fall randomly in your stack. You need to decide which notes are relevant. You might also need to retitle some cards and use them elsewhere. Those that remain will have to be arranged in a logical order for you to find use for them in your essay.

Once you have your cards in order, you can write whatever comments or transitions are needed to move from detail to detail. Write this material directly on the cards and be sure to use a different color ink so that you can distinguish later between the original note and what you add. Here is an example of such a "developed" note card:

---

Magalaner 39                          Structure, general

Speaking of Mansfield's sense of form and referring to "Miss Brill" as an example, Magalaner states that Mansfield has power to put together stories from "a myriad of threads into a rigidly patterned whole." 39

Some of these "threads" are the fall season, the time of day, examples of unkindness, the park bench sitters from the cupboards, and Miss Brill's stages of unreality (see Thorpe 661). Each of these is separate, but all work together to unify the story.

---

By adding such commentary to your note cards, you are also simplifying the writing of your first draft. In many instances, the note and the comment may be moved directly into the paper with minor adjustments (some of the content of this note appears in paragraph 5 of the illustrative essay, and almost all the topics introduced here are developed in paragraphs 8 to 13).

### *Be Creative and Original Even Though You Are Doing Research*

The major trap to avoid in a research paper is that your use of sources can become an end in itself and therefore a shortcut for your own thinking and writing. Often, students make the mistake of introducing details the way a master of ceremonies introduces performers in a variety show. This is unfortunate because it is the *student* whose essay will be judged, even though the sources, like the performers, do all the work. Thus, it is important to be creative and original in a research essay and to do your own thinking and writing, even though you are relying heavily on your sources. Here are five ways in which research essays may be original.

1. **Your selection of material is original with you.** In each major part of your essay you will include many details from your sources. To be creative, you should select different but related details and avoid overlapping or repetition. Your completed essay will be judged on the basis of the thoroughness with which you make your points with different details (which in turn will represent the completeness of your research). Even though you are relying on published materials and cannot be original on that score, your selection can be original because you bring these materials together for the first time and because you emphasize some details and minimize others. Inevitably, your assemblage of details from your sources will be unique and therefore original.
2. **Your development of your essay is yours alone.** Your arrangement of your various points is an obvious area of originality: One detail seems naturally to precede another, and certain conclusions stem from certain details. As you present the details, conclusions, and arguments from your sources, you can also add an original stamp by introducing supporting details different from those in the source material. You can also add your own emphasis to particular points—an emphasis that you do not find in your sources.
3. **Your words are yours and yours alone.** Naturally, the words that you use will be original because they are yours. Your topic sentences, for example, will all be your own. As you introduce details and conclusions, you will need to write "bridges" to get yourself from point to point. These can be introductory remarks or transitions. In other words, as you write, you are not just stringing your notes together but actively assembling and arranging your notes and thoughts in creative and unique ways.
4. **Explaining and contrasting controversial views is an original presentation of material.** Closely related to your selection is that in your research you may have found conflicting or differing views on a topic. If you make a point to describe and distinguish these views and explain the reasons for the differences, you are presenting material originally. To see how differing views can be handled, see paragraphs 15–17 of the Illustrative Research Essay.
5. **Your own insights and positions are uniquely your own.** There are three possibilities here, all related to how well you have learned the primary texts on which your research in secondary sources is based.
   a. *Weave your own interpretations and ideas into your essay.* An important part of taking notes is to make your own points *precisely when they occur to you.* Often you

can expand these as truly original parts of your essay. Your originality does not need to be extensive; it may consist of no more than a single insight. Here is such a card, which was written during research on the structure of "Miss Brill."

---

My Own                                    Miss Brill's unreality

It is ironic that the boy and girl sit down on the bench next to Miss Brill just when she is at the height of her fancies. By allowing her to overhear their insults, they almost slap her with the harshness of reality. She is then plunged instantly from the height of rapture to the depth of pain.

---

The originality here is built around the contrast between Miss Brill's exhilaration and her rapid and cruel deflation. This observation is not unusual or startling, but it nevertheless represents original thought about the story. When modified and adapted, much of this card is used as an important part of paragraph 14 of the Illustrative Research Essay. You can see that your writing a "My Own" note card can be immeasurably vital to you in the development of your own thoughts.

b. *Filling gaps in the sources enables you to present original thoughts and insights.* As you read your secondary sources, you may realize that an obvious conclusion is not being made or that an important detail is not being stressed. Here is an area that you can develop on your own. Your conclusions may involve a particular interpretation or major point of comparison, or they may rest on a particularly important but understressed word or fact. For example, paragraphs 17–20 in the Illustrative Research Essay form an argument based on observations that critics have overlooked, or have neglected to mention, about the conclusion of "Miss Brill." In your research, whenever you find such a critical "vacuum" (assuming that you cannot read all the articles about some of your topics, where your discovery may already have been made a number of times), it is right to include whatever is necessary to fill it.

c. *By disputing your sources, you are being original.* Your sources may present arguments that you wish to dispute. As you develop your disagreement, you will be arguing originally, for you will be using details in a different way from that of the critic or critics whom you are disputing, and your conclusions will be your own. This area of originality is similar to the laying out of controversial critical views, except that you furnish one of the opposing views yourself. The approach is limited because it is difficult to find many substantive points of interpretation on which there are not already clearly delineated opposing views. Paragraph 12 of the Illustrative Research Essay shows how a disagreement can lead to a different, if not original, interpretation.

## Documenting Your Work

It is necessary and essential to acknowledge—to *document*—all sources from which you have *quoted or paraphrased* factual and interpretive information. This point cannot be overemphasized because of the need to avoid being challenged for plagiarism. As the means of **documentation**, various reference systems use parenthetical references, footnotes, or endnotes. Whatever system is used, documentation almost always includes a carefully prepared bibliography, or list of works cited.

We will first discuss the list of works cited and then review the two major reference systems for use in a research paper. Parenthetical references, preferred by the Modern Language Association (MLA) since 1984, are described in the *MLA Handbook for Writers of Research Papers*, 7th edition, 2009. Footnotes or endnotes, recommended by the MLA before 1984, are still required by many instructors.

### *A List of Works Cited (Bibliography) Is a List of the Works You Have Used*

The key to any reference system is a carefully prepared list of works cited that is included at the end of the essay. "Works cited" means exactly that; the list should include just those books and articles you have actually *used* in your essay. If, however, your instructor requires that you use footnotes or endnotes, you can extend your concluding list to be a complete bibliography both of works cited and also of works consulted but not actually used. *Always, always, always, follow your instructor's directions.*

The list of works cited should include the following information, in each entry, in the form indicated. If you are using a word processor with the capacity to make italics, you can italicize book and article titles rather than underline them.

#### For a Book

1. The author's name: last name first, followed by first name and middle name or initial. Period.
2. The title, italicized or underlined. Period.
3. The city of publication (not state or nation), colon; publisher (easily recognized abbreviations or key words can be used unless they seem awkward or strange; see the *MLA Handbook*, pp. 247–49), comma; year of publication. Period.

#### For an Article

1. The author's name: last name first, followed by first name and middle name or initial. Period.
2. The title of the article in quotation marks. Period.
3. The title of the journal or periodical, italicized or underlined, followed by the volume number in Arabic (*not* Roman) numbers with no punctuation, then the year of publication within parentheses. Colon. For a daily paper or weekly magazine, omit the parentheses and cite the date in the British style followed by a colon (day, month, year, as in *2 Feb. 2005*:). Inclusive page numbers (without any preceding *p.* or *pp.*). Period.

The works cited should be listed alphabetically according to the last names of authors, with unsigned articles included in the list alphabetically by titles. Bibliographical lists are begun at the left margin, with subsequent lines in hanging indentation so that the key locating word—the author's last name or the first title word of an unsigned article—can be easily seen. Many unpredictable and complex combinations—including ways to describe works of art, musical or other performances, and films—are detailed extensively in the *MLA Handbook* (126–212). Here are two model entries.

> **BOOK:** Alpers, Antony. *The Life of Katherine Mansfield*. New York: Viking, 1980.
>
> **ARTICLE:** Hankin, Cheryl. "Fantasy and the Sense of an Ending in the Work of Katherine Mansfield." *Modern Fiction Studies* 24 (1978): 465–74.

### Refer to Works Parenthetically as You Draw Details from Them

Within your research essay, use parentheses in referring to works from which you are using facts and conclusions. This parenthetical citation system is recommended in the *MLA Handbook*, 7th edition (214–32), and its principle is to provide documentation without asking readers to interrupt their reading to find footnotes or endnotes. Readers wanting to see the complete reference can easily find it in your list of works cited. With this system, you incorporate the author's last name and the relevant page number or numbers directly, whenever possible, into the body of your essay. If the author's name is mentioned in your discussion, you need to give only the page number or numbers in parentheses. Here are two examples.

> Alexander Pope believed in the idea that the universe is a whole, a totally unified body, which provides a "viable benevolent system for the salvation of everyone who does good" (Kallich 24).

> Martin Kallich draws attention to Alexander Pope's belief in the idea that the universe is a whole, a totally unified body, which provides a "viable benevolent system for the salvation of everyone who does good" (24).

### Footnotes and Endnotes Are Formal and Traditional Reference Formats

The most formal system of documentation still widely used is that of *footnotes* (references at the bottom of each page) or *endnotes* (references listed numerically at the end of the essay). If your instructor wants you to use one of these formats, do the following: Make a note the first time you quote or refer to a source, with the details ordered as outlined below.

#### For a Book

1. The author's name: first name or initials first, followed by middle name or initial, then last name. Comma.
2. The title, underlined or italicized for a book, no punctuation. If you are referring to a work in a collection (article, story, poem) use quotation marks for that, but italicize or underline the title of the book. No punctuation, but use a comma after the title if an editor, translator, or edition number follows.
3. The name of the editor or translator, if relevant. Abbreviate "editor" or "edited by" as *ed.*, "editors" as *eds.* Use *trans.* for "translator" or "translated by." No punctuation, but use a comma if an edition number follows.

4. The edition (if indicated), abbreviated thus: *2nd ed.*, *3rd ed.*, and so on. No punctuation.
5. The publication facts, within parentheses, without any preceding or following punctuation, in the following order:
   a. City (but not the state or nation) of publication, colon.
   b. Publisher (clear abbreviations are acceptable and desirable), comma.
   c. Year of publication.
6. The page number(s) with no *p.* or *pp.*, for example, 5, 6–10, 15–19, 295–307, 311–16. Period. If you are referring to longer works, such as novels or longer stories with division or chapter numbers, include these numbers for readers who may be using an edition different from yours.

### For a Journal or Magazine Article

1. The author: first name or initials first, followed by middle name or initial, then last name. Comma.
2. The title of the article, in quotation marks. Comma.
3. The name of the journal, italicized or underlined. No punctuation.
4. The volume number, in Arabic numerals. No punctuation.
5. The year of publication within parentheses. Colon. For newspaper and journal articles, omit the parentheses and include day, month, and year (in the British style: *21 May 2005*). Colon.
6. The page number(s) with no *p.* or *pp.*: 5, 6–10, 34–36, 98–102, 345–47. Period.

For later notes to the same work, use the last name of the author as the reference unless you are referring to two or more works by the same author. Thus, if you refer to only one work by, say, Thomas Hardy, the name *Hardy* will be enough for all later references. Should you be referring to other works by Hardy, however, you will also need to make a short reference to the specific works to distinguish them, such as *Hardy*, *"The Three Strangers,"* and *Hardy*, *"The Man He Killed."*

Footnotes are placed at the bottom of each page, and endnotes are included on separate page(s) at the end of the essay. The first lines of both footnotes and endnotes should be paragraph indented, and continuing lines should be flush with the left margin. Both endnote and footnote numbers are set in a smaller font and positioned slightly above the line (as superior numbers) like this: [12]. You can single-space footnotes and endnotes and leave a line of space between them. Most computer programs have specially designed and consecutively numbered footnote formats. These are generally acceptable, but be sure to consult your instructor. (For a limited coverage of footnoting practices, see the *MLA Handbook*, 230–32, 181–84.)

*Sample Footnotes*    In the examples below, book titles and periodicals are shown *italicized*, as they would be in an essay prepared on the computer. If the essay is typewritten or handwritten, these titles should be <u>underlined</u>.

[1]Blanche H. Gelfant, *Women Writing in America: Voices in Collage* (Hanover: UP of New England, for Dartmouth College, 1984) 110.

²Günter Grass, "Losses," *Granta* 42 (Winter 1992): 99.

³John O'Meara, "*Hamlet* and the Fortunes of Sorrowful Imagination: A Re-examination of the Genesis and Fate of the Ghost," *Cahiers Elisabéthains* 35 (1989): 21.

⁴Grass 104.

⁵Gelfant 141.

⁶O'Meara 17.

As a principle, you do not need to repeat in a footnote or endnote any material that you have already mentioned in your own discourse. For example, if you recognize the author and title of your source, then the footnote or endnote should give no more than the data about publication. Here is an example:

> In *The Fiction of Katherine Mansfield,* Marvin Magalaner points out that Mansfield was as skillful in the development of epiphanies (that is, the use of highly significant though perhaps unobtrusive actions or statements to reveal the depths of a particular character) as James Joyce himself, the "inventor" of the technique.⁹
>
> ---
>
> ⁹(Carbondale: Southern Illinois UP, 1971) 130.

### *Many Academic Disciplines Set Their Own Requirements for Documentation*

Other reference systems and style manuals have been adopted by various disciplines (e.g., mathematics, medicine, psychology) to serve their own special needs. If you receive no instructions from your instructors in other courses, you can adapt the systems described here. If you need to use the documentation methods of other fields, however, use the *MLA Handbook*, pages 261–63 for guidance about which style manual to select.

## When in Doubt, Consult Your Instructor

As long as all you want from a reference is the page number of a quotation or paraphrase, the parenthetical system described briefly here—and detailed fully in the *MLA Handbook*—is the most suitable and convenient one you can use. However, you may wish to use footnotes or endnotes if you need to add more details, provide additional explanations, or refer your readers to other materials that you are not using.

Whatever method you follow, *you must always acknowledge sources properly.* Remember that whenever you begin to write and cite references, you might forget a number of specific details about documentation, and you will certainly discover that you have many questions. Be sure, then, to ask your instructor, who is your final authority.

## Organize Your Research Essay

*Introduction*    In your research essay, you may wish to expand your introduction more than usual because of the need to relate the problem of research to your topic. You may wish to bring in relevant historical or biographical information (see, for example, the introduction of the Illustrative Research Essay on pp. 280–81). You may also wish to summarize critical opinion or describe critical problems about your topic. The idea is to lead your reader into your topic by providing interesting and significant materials that you have found.

Because of the length of most research essays, some instructors require a topic outline, which is in effect a brief table of contents. This pattern is observed in the Illustrative Research Essay. *Because the inclusion of an outline is a matter of the instructor's choice, be sure to learn whether your instructor requires it.*

*Body and Conclusion*    As you write the body and conclusion of your research essay, your development will be governed by your choice of topic. Consult the relevant chapters in this book about what to include for whatever approach or approaches you select (setting, ideas, point of view, character, tone, or any other).

In length, the research essay can be anywhere from five to fifteen or more pages, depending on your instructor's assignment. Obviously, an essay on a single work will be shorter than one based on several. If you narrow the scope of your topic, as suggested in the approaches described at the beginning of this chapter, you can readily keep your essay within the assigned length. The following Illustrative Research Essay, for example, illustrates approach 1 (p. 260) by being limited to only one character in one story. Were you to write on characters in a number of other stories by Mansfield or any other writer (approach 2), you could limit your total number of pages by stressing comparative treatments and by avoiding excessive detail about problems pertaining to only one work.

Although you limit your topic yourself in consultation with your instructor, you may encounter problems because you will deal not with one source alone but with many. Naturally, the sources will provide you with details and also trigger many of your ideas. The problem is to handle the many strands without piling on too many details and without being led into digressions. It is therefore important to keep your central idea foremost; the constant stressing of your central idea will help you not only to select relevant materials but also reject irrelevant ones.

## Plagiarism: An Embarrassing but Vital Subject—and a Danger to Be Overcome

When you are using sources as the substance of many of the details in your essay, you run the risk of **plagiarism:** Using the words and ideas of other writers without their consent and without acknowledgment. Recognizing the source means being clear about the identity of other authors, together with the name or names of the works from which one gets details and ideas. When there is no recognition, readers, and the intellectual world generally, are deceived. They assume that the material they are reading is the original work and the intellectual possession of the writer. When there is no recognition, the plagiarizing author is committing intellectual theft.

This is no small matter. In the world of publications, many people who have committed plagiarism have suffered irreparable damage to their credibility and reputations as writers and authorities. Some well-known writers have found it hard if not impossible to continue their careers, all because of the wide knowledge of their plagiarism. It does not end there. A plagiarist might be open to legal actions, and might, if the situation is grave enough, be required to supply financial restitution to the author or authors whose work has been illegally appropriated. In schools and colleges, students who plagiarize may face academic discipline. Often the discipline is a failure for the course, but it might also include suspension and expulsion. It is not possible to predict all the ill consequences of committing an act of plagiarism.

It therefore bears constant awareness and emphasis that you need to distinguish between the sources you are using and your own work. Your readers will assume that everything you write is your own unless you indicate otherwise. Therefore, when blending your words with the ideas from sources, *be clear about proper acknowledgments.* Most commonly, if you are simply presenting details and facts, you can write straightforwardly and let parenthetical references suffice as your authority, as in the following sentence from the Illustrative Research Essay:

> Marvin Magalaner, using "Miss Brill" as an example, speaks of Mansfield's weaving of "a myriad of threads into a rigidly patterned whole" (39). Also noting Mansfield's control over form, Cheryl Hankin suggests that Mansfield's structuring is perhaps more "instinctive" than deliberate (474).

Here, there can be no question about plagiarism, for the names of the authors of the critical sources are fully acknowledged, the page numbers are specific, and the quotation marks clearly distinguish the words of the critics from the words of the essay writer. If you grant recognition as recommended here, no confusion can result about the authority underlying your essay. The linking

*(continued)*

words obviously belong to the writer of the essay, but the parenthetical references clearly indicate that the sentence is based on two sources.

If you use an interpretation unique to a particular writer, or if you rely on a significant quotation from your source, you should make your acknowledgment an essential part of your discussion, as in this sentence.

> Saralyn Daly, referring to Miss Brill as one of Mansfield's "isolatoes"—that is, solitary persons cut off from normal human contacts—fears that the couple's callous insults have caused Miss Brill to face the outside world with her fur piece "perhaps for the very last time" (88, 90).

Here, the idea of the critic is singled out for special acknowledgment. If you recognize your sources in this way, no confusion can arise about how you have used them.

Please, always keep foremost in your mind that the purpose of research is to acquire knowledge and details from which to advance your own thoughts and interpretations. You should consider your research discoveries as a springboard from which you can launch yourself into your own written work. In this way, research should be creative. A test of how you use research is to determine how well you move from the details you are using to the development of your own ideas. Once you have gone forth in this way, you are using research correctly and creatively. Plagiarism will then not even be a remote issue for you.

## Illustrative Research Essay

The central idea, thesis sentence, and topic sentences are shaded here to stress the goal of strong organization. As your instructor wishes, you might use this or a similar system in your own essays.

Peter Greenly

Professor Douglas

English 201

16 December 2010

The Structure of Katherine Mansfield's "Miss Brill"°

  I.  Introduction: The Writing of "Miss Brill"

 II.  The Structure of "Miss Brill"

---

°See pages 344–46 for this story.

    A. Season and Time of Day as Structure

    B. Insensitive or Cruel Actions as Structure

III. The Conclusion of "Miss Brill"

IV. Conclusion

**I. Introduction: The Writing of "Miss Brill"**

[1]     Katherine Mansfield wrote "Miss Brill"—one of the eighty-eight short stories and fragments she wrote in her brief life (Magalaner 5)—on the evening of November 11, 1920, when she was staying at Isola Bella, an island retreat in northern Italy where she had gone in her desperate attempt to overcome tuberculosis. In her own words, she describes the night of composition:

> Last night I walked about and saw the new moon with the old moon in her arms and the lights in the water and the hollow pools filled with stars—and lamented there was no God. But I came in and wrote Miss Brill instead; which is my insect Magnificat now and always. (Letters 594)

Her husband, J. Middleton Murry, who had remained in London, published the story in the November 26, 1920, issue of the journal *Athenaeum*, which he was then editing. In 1922, Mansfield included "Miss Brill" in her collection entitled *The Garden Party and Other Stories* (Daly 134).

[2]     She was particularly productive at the time of "Miss Brill" despite her illness, for she wrote a number of excellent stories then. The others, as reported by her biographer Antony Alpers, were "The Lady's Maid," "The Young Girl," "The Daughters of the Late Colonel," and "The Life of Ma Parker" (304–305). All these stories share the common bond of "love and pity" rather than the "harshness or satire" that typifies a number of her earlier stories (Alpers 305). As with the later stories, "Miss Brill," in the words of Angela Smith, possesses a "tantalizing power to puzzle the reader" (150).

[3]     Because the story is also both touching and powerful, it has become well known and also has been frequently anthologized (Gargano). Mansfield's title character is portrayed as a woman who has been

Greenly 3

excluded from "public history" (Gubar 31) because she lives exclusively in the "feminine world" (Maurois 337). Miss Brill's main concern, in other words, is not power and greatness but the privacy of personal moments, which may be upset by no more than a contemptuous giggle (Gubar 38). The story's poignancy stems from the heroine's eagerness to be "part of a scene that ruthlessly excludes her" and thus makes her "the loneliest of all . . . [characters in] Katherine Mansfield's stories about lonely women" (Fullbrook 103). The power of the story results from the feeling with which Mansfield renders the "inarticulate longings and the tumultuous feelings that lie beneath the surface of daily life" (McLaughlin 381). A mark of her skill is the way in which she enters the consciousness of the heroine, so much so that Claire Tomalin declares that the story is "conceived virtually as [a] dramatic" monologue (213). Mansfield's description in writing "Miss Brill" bears out these claims, for it shows how deeply she tried to create the pathetic inner life of her character:

> In *Miss Brill* I choose not only the length of every sentence, but
> even the sound of every sentence. I choose the rise and fall
> of every paragraph to fit her, and to fit her on that day at
> that very moment. After I'd written it I read it aloud—numbers
> of times—just as one would *play over* a musical composition—
> trying to get it nearer to the expression of Miss Brill—until it fitted
> her. (Letter to Richard Murry of January 17, 1921, qtd. in
> Sewell, 5–6)

## II. The Structure of "Miss Brill"

Mansfield's description strongly indicates that action in the story was less significant in her narrative aim than the sympathetic evocation of Miss Brill's responses and impressions. Such a design might lead readers to conclude that the story is not so much formed as forming—a free rather than planned development. In reference to Mansfield's talent generally, Edward Wagenknecht observes that the stories, including "Miss Brill," are "hardly even episodes or anecdotes. They offer reflections [instead] of some aspect of experience or express a mood" (163). This

[4]

Greenly 4

observation is true of "Miss Brill." The story grows from within the
character, and it leaves the impression of an individual who experiences a
"crisis in miniature," a "deep cut into time" in which life changes and all
hopes and expectations are reversed (Hankin 465). This concentration on
such important cuts is a significant part of Mansfield's narrative skill.
When writing in her journal, she called such moments "glimpses," which
one may think of as insights into the mysterious core of human character:

> And yet one has these "glimpses" . . . The waves, as I drove home
> this afternoon, and the high foam, how it was suspended in the air
> before it fell, . . . What is it that happens in that moment of
> suspension? It is timeless. In that moment (what *do* I mean?) the
> whole life of the soul is contained [Sandley 71].

[5]      It follows that Mansfield's achievement in "Miss Brill" is to
fashion—to glimpse—a credible character in an extreme of vulnerability.
The story embodies an intricate set of structures that complement this
downward movement.° Whatever the source of Mansfield's control over
form, critics agree that her power was great. Marvin Magalaner, using
"Miss Brill" as an example, speaks of Mansfield's weaving of "a myriad
of threads into a rigidly patterned whole" (39). Noting the same control
over form, Cheryl Hankin suggests that her structuring is perhaps more
"instinctive" than deliberate (474). These complementary threads,
stages, or "levels" of "unequal length" (Harmat uses the terms "niveaux"
and "longueur inégale," 49, 51) are the fall season, the time of day,
insensitive or cruel actions, and the final section or dénouement.*

*A. Season and Time of Day as Structure*

[6]      A significant aspect of structure in "Miss Brill" is Mansfield's use
of the season of the year. Autumn and its movement toward winter is
integral to the deteriorating circumstances of the heroine. In the first
paragraph, the narrator says that there is a "faint chill" in the air, and
this phrase is repeated in paragraph 10 of the story. Thus, the author

---

°Central idea.
*Thesis sentence.

Greenly 5

establishes autumn and the approaching end of the year as the beginning of the movement toward dashed hopes. This seasonal reference is also carried out when we read that "yellow leaves" are "down drooping" in the local *Jardins Publiques* (story, paragraph 6) and that leaves are drifting "now and again" from almost "nowhere, from the sky" (story, paragraph 1). It is the autumn cold that has caused Miss Brill to take out her bedraggled fur piece which later amuses the young girl. The chill, together with the fur, forms a structural setting integrated with the action and mood of the story. The story both begins and ends with the fur (Sewell 25), which is the direct cause of Miss Brill's deep hurt at the conclusion.

Like this seasonal structuring, the times of day parallel Miss Brill's darkening existence. At the beginning, the day is "brilliantly fine—the blue sky powdered with gold," and the light is "like white wine" (paragraph 1). This figurative language suggests the brightness and crispness of full sunlight. In paragraph 6, where we also learn of the yellow leaves, "the blue sky with gold-veined clouds" indicates that time has been passing as clouds accumulate during late afternoon. By the story's end, Miss Brill has returned in sadness to her "little dark room" (story, paragraph 18). In other words, the time moves from day to evening, from light to darkness, as an accompaniment to Miss Brill's mental pain.    [7]

*B. Insensitive or Cruel Actions as Structure*

Mansfield's most significant structural device, which is not emphasized by critics, is the introduction of insensitive or cruel actions. It is as though the hurt felt by Miss Brill on the bright Sunday afternoon is also being felt by many others. Because she is the spectator who is closely related to Mansfield's narrative voice, Miss Brill is the filter through whom these negative examples reach the reader. Considering the patterns that emerge, one may conclude that Mansfield intends the beauty of the day and the joyousness of the band as an ironic contrast to the pettiness and insensitivity of the people in the park.    [8]

The first characters are the silent couple on Miss Brill's bench (story, paragraph 3) and the incompatible couple (story, paragraph 4).    [9]

Greenly 6

Because the couples are no more than ordinary, they do not seem at first
to be part of a pattern of cruelty and rejection. But their incompatibility,
suggested by their silence and one-way complaining, establishes a
structural parallel with the young and insensitive couple who insult
Miss Brill later in the story. Thus, the first two couples prepare the way
for the third, and all show increasing insensitivity and cruelty.

[10]          Almost unnoticed as a second level of negation is the vast group of
"odd, silent, nearly all old" people filling "the benches and green chairs"
(story, paragraph 5). They seem to be no more than a normal part of the
Sunday afternoon landscape. But these people are significant structurally
because the "dark little rooms or even—even cupboards" that Miss Brill
associates with them describe her own circumstances at the story's end
(story, paragraphs 5, 18). The reader may conclude from Miss Brill's
quiet eavesdropping that she herself is one of these nameless and
faceless ones, all of whom lead similarly drab lives.

[11]          Once Mansfield has set these levels for her heroine, she introduces
examples—glimpses—of more active rejection and cruelty. The
beautiful woman who throws down the bunch of violets is the first of
these (story, paragraph 8). The causes of this woman's scorn are not
made clear, and Miss Brill does not know what to make of the incident;
but the woman's actions suggest that she has been involved in a
relationship that has ended bitterly.

[12]          The major figure involved in rejection, who is important enough to
be considered a structural double of Miss Brill, is the woman wearing
the ermine toque (story, paragraph 8). It is clear that she, like Miss Brill,
is one of "the lonely and isolated women in a hostile world" that
Mansfield is so skillful in portraying (Gordon, 926). This woman tries to
please the "gentleman in grey," but this man insults her by blowing
smoke in her face. It could be, as Peter Thorpe observes, that she is
"obviously a prostitute" (661). More likely, from the conversation
overheard by Miss Brill, the "ermine toque" has had a broken
relationship with the gentleman. Being familiar with his Sunday habits,
she deliberately comes to the park to meet him, as though by accident, to
attempt a reconciliation. After her rejection, her hurrying off to meet

Greenly 7

someone "much nicer" (there is no such person, for Mansfield uses the phrase "as though" to introduce the ermine toque's departure) is her way of masking her hurt. Regardless of the exact situation, however, Mansfield makes it plain that the encounter demonstrates vulnerability and unkindness.

Once Mansfield establishes this major incident, she introduces                    **[13]**
additional examples of insensitivity. At the end of paragraph 8, the hobbling old man "with long whiskers" is nearly knocked over by the group of four girls, who show arrogance if not contempt. The final examples involve Miss Brill herself. These are her shyness with her English pupils and the indifference of the old invalid who habitually falls asleep when she reads to him (story, paragraph 9).

Although "Miss Brill" is a brief story, Mansfield creates a large                    **[14]**
number of structural parallels to the sudden climax brought about by the insulting young couple. It is ironic that the boy and girl sit down on the bench next to Miss Brill just when she is most vulnerable and at the height of her fancies. By overhearing their insults, she is virtually slapped with the harshness of reality, and she is plunged from the height of rapture to the depth of pain. The boy and girl do not appear until the very end (story, paragraphs 11–14), but cruel actions like theirs have been fully anticipated in all the story's earlier parts. Mansfield's speaker does not take us to the homes of the other victims, as she does when we follow Miss Brill into her poor lodgings, but the narrative leads to the conclusion that the silent couple, the complaining wife and her husband, the unseen man rejected by the young woman, the ermine toque, and the funny gentleman, not to mention the many silent and withdrawn people sitting like statues in the park, all return to isolation and personal pain.

### III. The Conclusion of "Miss Brill"

Of unique importance in the structure of "Miss Brill" are the final                    **[15]**
two paragraphs, in which Miss Brill, all alone, returns to her tiny room. Saralyn Daly, referring to Miss Brill as one of Mansfield's "isolatoes"—that is, solitary persons cut off from normal human contacts—fears that the couple's insults have caused Miss Brill to face the outside world

"perhaps for the very last time" (88, 90). Sydney Kaplan adds a political dimension to Miss Brill's rejection, asserting that here and in other stories Mansfield is expressing "outrage" against "a society in which privilege is marked by indifference" to persons like Miss Brill (192). Her pathetic experience exemplifies a personal pattern in which the old are destroyed "by loneliness and sickness, by fear of death, by the thoughtless energy of the younger world around them" (Zinman 457). Mansfield herself considered such a negative situation more generally as "the snail under the leaf," which also implies that disaster is waiting for everyone, not just those who are old (Meyers, 213). With such a crushing experience for the major character, "Miss Brill" may be fitted to the structuring of Mansfield stories described by André Maurois: "moments of beauty suddenly broken by contact with ugliness, cruelty, or death" (342–43).

[16]          Because some critics have stated that Miss Brill's downfall is sudden, they have criticized the conclusion. Richard Peterson complains that the ending is artificial and contrived because of the improbability that the young couple would appear at just that moment to make their insults (385). On much the same ground, Sylvia Berkman declares that the ending is excessive, mechanical, and obvious (162, 175).

[17]          Hankin, however, hints at another way in which the conclusion may be taken, a way that makes the story seem deeply ironic. In describing patterns to be found in Mansfield's stories, Hankin notes the following situation, which may account for the story's ending:

> [A]n impending disillusionment or change in expectations may be deflected by the central character's transmutation of the experience into something positive. (466)

There is no question that the ending indicates the deep hurt that Miss Brill has experienced. Her dejection seems complete when she returns to her small "cupboard" room.

[18]          The story's very last sentence, however, may be read as a way of indicating that Miss Brill is going back to her regularly established habit of reconstructing reality, in this respect indicating the "something positive" described by Hankin: "But when she put the lid on she thought

she heard something crying" (story, paragraph 18). It is hard to read
this last sentence without finding irony and pathos there. By hearing
"something crying," Miss Brill is likely imagining that the fur piece,
and not she, has been hurt. One might remember that the thoughtless
young girl has laughed at the fur because it resembles a "fried whiting"
(story, paragraph 14). The irony here is that Miss Brill forgets about
the pain she has just experienced and now slips back into her life of
fantasy.

This pattern of evasion is consistent with Miss Brill's character.      **[19]**
Despite her loneliness, she has been holding a job (as a teacher of
English, presumably to French pupils) and has been voluntarily reading
to the aged invalid. Her life has been restricted, but her Sunday
afternoons of eavesdropping have enabled her, through "the power of her
imagination," to share the lives of many others (Hanson and Gurr 81).
Mansfield establishes this vicarious sociability as Miss Brill's major
strength, which Hanson and Gurr call "the saving grace of her life" (81).
Her method makes her strange and pathetic, but nevertheless she has
been functioning. Within such a framework, the deflating insults of
paragraphs 13 and 14 (story) may be seen as another incentive for her to
strengthen her fancy, not to abandon it.

This is not to interpret the story's conclusion as an indication that    **[20]**
Miss Brill has shaken off the couple's insults. She is foremost a "victim"
(Zinman 457), if not of others, then of her own powerful imagination.
But she is presented as a character with positive qualities. Indeed,
Mansfield herself expressed her own personal liking of Miss Brill. Her
husband, J. Middleton Murry, shortly after receiving the story from her
for publication, sent her a letter in which he expressed his fondness for
the protagonist. In a return letter to him of November 21, 1920,
Mansfield wrote that she shared this fondness. She went on in the same
letter to say:

> One writes (<u>one</u> reason why is) because one does care so
> passionately that one <u>must show</u> it—one must declare one's love.
> (qtd. in Magalaner 17)

Greenly 10

Surely Mansfield could love her creation out of pity alone, but if she had
added an element of strength, such as the brave but sad ability to adjust
to "impossible and intolerable conditions" (Zinman 457), then her love
would have an additional cause. Therefore, it is plausible that the last
sentence of "Miss Brill" shows the heroine's characteristic way of
surviving through the power of her own fantasies.

## IV. Conclusion

[21]        The greater structure of "Miss Brill" may therefore be taken as a
hard, disillusioned view of life itself in which those who are lonely,
closed out, and hurt are wounded even more. This pattern of exclusion
and hurt not only affects the restricted lives of the lonely but also reaches
directly into their minds and souls. Miss Brill's response is to retreat
further and further into an inner world of unreality but also to continue
life, even if it is at an almost totally subdued level. It is Mansfield's
"almost uncanny psychological insight" into the operation of this
characteristic response that gives "Miss Brill" both its form and also its
excellence (Hankin 467).

Greenly 11

## Works Cited

Alpers, Antony. *Katherine Mansfield: A Biography*. New York: Knopf,
     1953. Print.

Berkman, Sylvia. *Katherine Mansfield: A Critical Study*. New Haven:
     Yale UP (for Wellesley College), 1951. Print.

Daly, Saralyn R. *Katherine Mansfield*. New York: Twayne, 1965. Print.

Fullbrook, Kate. *Katherine Mansfield*. Bloomington and Indianapolis:
     Indiana UP, 1986. Print.

Greenly 12

Gargano, James W. "Mansfield's Miss Brill." *Explicator* 19. 2 (1960):
item 10 (one page, unpaginated). Print.

Gordon, Ian A. "Katherine Mansfield." D. L. Kirkpatrick, ed., *Reference
Guide to English Literature*. 2nd ed. Chicago and London: St.
James Press, 1991. II, 924–26. Print.

Gubar, Susan. "The Birth of the Artist as Heroine: (Re)production, the
*Kunstler-Roman* Tradition, and the Fiction of Katherine Mansfield."
*The Representation of Women in Fiction*. Ed. Carolyn Heilbrun and
Margaret R. Higonnet. Selected Papers from the English Institute,
1981. Baltimore: Johns Hopkins UP, 1983. 19–58. Print.

Hankin, Cheryl. "Fantasy and the Sense of an Ending in the Work of
Katherine Mansfield." *Modern Fiction Studies* 24 (1978): 465–74.
Print.

Hanson, Clare, and Andrew Gurr. *Katherine Mansfield*. New York:
St. Martin's, 1981. Print.

Harmat, Andrée-Marie. "Essai D'Analyse Structurale d'une Nouvelle
Lyrique Anglaise: 'Miss Brill' de Katherine Mansfield." *Les
Cahiers de la Nouvelle* 1 (1983): 49–74. Print.

Kaplan, Sydney Janet. *Katherine Mansfield and the Origins of
Modernist Fiction*. Ithaca and London: Cornell UP, 1991. Print.

Magalaner, Marvin. *The Fiction of Katherine Mansfield*. Carbondale:
Southern Illinois UP, 1971. Print.

Mansfield, Katherine. *Katherine Mansfield's Letters to John Middleton
Murry, 1913–1922*. Ed. John Middleton Murry. New York: Knopf,
1951. Print. Cited as "Letters."

———. *The Short Stories of Katherine Mansfield*. New York: Knopf,
1967. Print.

Maurois, André. *Points of View from Kipling to Graham Greene*. 1935.
New York: Ungar, 1968. Print.

Greenly 13

McLaughlin, Ann L. "The Same Job: The Shared Writing Aims of
Katherine Mansfield and Virginia Woolf." *Modern Fiction Studies*
24 (1978): 369–82. Print.

Meyers, Jeffrey. *Katherine Mansfield: A Darker View.* 1978. New York:
Cooper Square Press, 2002. Print.

Peterson, Richard F. "The Circle of Truth: The Stories of Katherine
Mansfield and Mary Lavin." *Modern Fiction Studies* 24 (1978):
383–94. Print.

Sandley, Sarah. "The Middle of the Note: Katherine Mansfield's
'Glimpses.'" *Katherine Mansfield: In from the Margin.* Ed. Roger
Robinson. Baton Rouge: Louisiana State UP, 1994. 70–89. Print.

Sewell, Arthur. *Katherine Mansfield: A Critical Essay.* Auckland:
Unicorn, 1936. Print.

Smith, Angela. *Katherine Mansfield: A Literary Life.* Houndmills,
Basingstoke: Palgrave, 2000. Print.

Thorpe, Peter. "Teaching 'Miss Brill.'" *College English* 23 (1962):
661–63. Print.

Tomalin, Claire. *Katherine Mansfield: A Secret Life.* New York: Knopf,
1988. Print.

Wagenknecht, Edward. *A Preface to Literature.* New York: Holt, 1954.
Print.

Zinman, Toby Silverman. "The Snail Under the Leaf: Katherine
Mansfield's Imagery." *Modern Fiction Studies* 24 (1978): 457–64.
Print.

# Commentary on the Essay

This essay fulfills an assignment of 2,500 to 3,000 words, with twenty to thirty sources. (There are actually twenty-five, not counting a dictionary reference.) The bibliography was developed from a college library card catalog; references in books of criticism

(Magalaner, Daly, Berkman); the *MLA International Bibliography*; the *Essay and General Literature Index*; and the Literature Resource Center available through Netscape and a county library system. The sources themselves were found in a college library with selective holdings, in a local public library, and in online resources. There is only one rare source, an article (Harmat) obtained in photocopy through interlibrary loan from one of only two United States libraries holding the journal in which it appears. The location was made through the national OCLS online service. For most semester-long or quarter-long courses, you will likely not have time to add to your sources by this method, but the article in question refers specifically to "Miss Brill," and it was therefore desirable to examine it.

The sources consist of books, articles, and chapters or portions of books. One article (Sewell) has been published as a separate short monograph. Also, one of the sources is the story "Miss Brill" itself (with locations made by paragraph number) together with editions of Mansfield's letters and a collection of her stories. The sources are used for facts, interpretations, reinforcement of conclusions, and general guidance and authority. All necessary thematic devices, including overall organization and transitions, are unique to the Illustrative Research Essay. The essay also contains passages taking issue with certain conclusions in a few of the sources. Additional particulars about the handling of sources and developing a research essay are included in the discussion of note taking and related matters in this chapter.

The introduction to the Illustrative Research Essay contains essential details about the writing of the story and the title as well as a pointed summary of critical appraisals of the story itself. The idea explored here is that the story dramatizes Miss Brill's emotional responses first to exhilaration and then to pain. The central idea (paragraph 5) is built out of this idea, explaining that the movement of emotions in the story is accompanied by an intricate and complementary set of structures.

Sections II and III examine various elements of the story for their structural relationship to Miss Brill's emotions. Section IIA details the structural uses of the settings of autumn and times of day, pointing out how they parallel her experiences. The longest part, section IIB (paragraphs 8–14), is based on an idea not found in the sources—that a number of characters are experiencing difficulties and cruelties such as those that befall Miss Brill. Paragraph 8 speaks of the hurts felt by others; paragraph 9 describes two obviously sad couples; paragraph 10 cites the old folks on the benches; paragraph 11 implies the scorn felt by the woman throwing down the violets; and paragraph 12 introduces the "ermine toque" and her attempt to ignore the hurt she experiences. Paragraph 13 contains brief descriptions of additional examples of insensitivity, two of them involving Miss Brill herself in her life outside the park. Paragraph 14 relates the foregoing instances of insensitivity and cruelty, emphasizing again the parallels to Miss Brill's situation.

Section III (paragraphs 15–20) is devoted to the story's conclusion. In paragraph 17, a hint found in a source (Hankin) is used to bring out the meaning of the story's final sentence and, therefore, of the story. An argument in support of this original interpretation is developed in paragraphs 18–20, which conclude with a reference to Mansfield's own personal approval of the main character.

Section IV (paragraph 21), the conclusion of the essay, relates the central idea to Mansfield's achievement in the story.

The list of works cited is the basis of all references in the essay, in accord with the *MLA Handbook for Writers of Research Papers,* 7th edition. By locating these references, a reader might readily examine, verify, and study any of the ideas and details drawn from the sources and developed in the essay.

**Writing Topics for Research Essays**

In beginning research on any of the following topics, follow the steps described in this chapter:

1.  Common themes in a number of stories by Hawthorne, Edgar Allan Poe, Thomas Hardy, or Mansfield
2.  Various critical views of Anton Chekhov's *The Bear*
3.  Susan Glaspell's use of the narrative material in *Trifles*
4.  Hawthorne's use of religious and moral topic material
5.  Shakespeare's imagery in the sonnets
6.  Views about women in Kate Chopin, Glaspell, Mansfield, and John Keats
7.  Poe's view of the short story as represented in "The Cask of Amontillado" and a number of other stories

# Chapter 19

## Writing Examinations on Literature

Fiction, Poetry, and Drama

Getting a good grade on a literature examination, or on any exam, is largely a result of intelligent and skillful preparation. Preparation means that you (1) study the material assigned, in conjunction with the comments made in class by your instructor and by fellow students in discussion; (2) develop and reinforce your own thoughts; (3) anticipate exam questions by creating and answering your own practice questions; and (4) understand the precise function of the test in your education.

First, realize that the test is not designed either to trap you or to hold down your grade. The grade you receive is a reflection of your achievement in the course. If your grades are high, congratulations; keep doing what you have been doing. If your grades are low, however, you can improve them through diligent and systematic study. Those students who can easily do satisfactory work might do superior work if they improved their habits of study and preparation. From whatever level you begin, *you can increase your achievement by improving your study methods*.

Your instructor has three major concerns in evaluating your tests (assuming the correct use of English): (1) to assess the extent of your command over the subject material of the course (How good is your retention?); (2) to assess how well you respond to a question or deal with an issue (How well do you separate the important from the unimportant? That is, how well do you think?); and (3) to assess how well you draw conclusions about the material (How well are you educating yourself?).

### Answer the Questions That Are Asked

Many elements go into writing good answers on tests, but *responsiveness* is the most important. A major cause of low exam grades is that students *often do not answer the questions asked*. Does a lack of responsiveness seem surprising? The problem is that some students do no more than retell a story or restate an argument, and they do not zero in on the issues in the question. This problem is not uncommon. Therefore, if you are asked, "Why does . . . ?," be sure to emphasize the *why* and use the *does* primarily to exemplify the *why*. If the question is about *organization*, focus on organization. If the question is about the *interpretation* of an idea, deal with the interpretation of the idea. In short, *always respond directly to the question or instruction*. Answer what is asked. Compare the following two answers to the same question.

**Question:**  How is the setting of Shirley Jackson's "The Lottery" important in the story's development?

**Answer A**

The setting of Shirley Jackson's "The Lottery" is a major element in the development of the story. The scene is laid in the town square of an unnamed American village, between the bank and the post office. There are many flowers blooming, and the grass is green. A pile of stones is set up in the square. Into this place, just before ten o'clock in the morning, come the villagers to hold their annual lottery. There are three hundred of them—children, men, and housewives. In the center of the square, the black lottery box is set up on a three-legged stool. This box has been around for years and looks broken and shabby. The setting requires that the villagers gather around the box and that the male head representing each family draw a slip of paper for his family. Once they have all drawn, it is discovered that Bill Hutchinson and his family are the "winners." He is not a lucky winner, however, because his family of five has to draw again individually. Bill's wife Tessie draws the black spot that Bill had drawn before for the entire family. Then all the villagers in the square fall upon her to stone her to death because that is the fate of the "winner." The setting here is therefore all important in the development of the story.

**Answer B**

The setting of Shirley Jackson's "The Lottery" is a major element in the development of the story. As a setting for the action, the town square of an unnamed American village is large enough to contain all three hundred citizens, a black lottery box, and also piles of stones, which the people can pick up and hurl. As a setting in time, the entire action takes place within a two-hour period between ten in the morning and noon. As a seasonal setting, the date of June 27, specifically mentioned as the day of the lottery, suggests a thoughtless and cruel early summer ritual of some sort. As a setting in character and society, the ordinary lifestyle of the people suggests only limited intelligence. It is not unlikely that such people would preserve a cruel and meaningless custom without thinking about its ghastly and horribly cruel effects. In all respects, the setting in place, time, season, and culture is all important in the development of the story.

Although answer A introduces important elements of the story's setting, it does not stress the importance of these elements in the story itself. It is also cluttered with details that have no bearing on the question. Indeed, it does not answer the question at all. On the other hand, answer B focuses directly on the connection, stressing how four aspects of setting relate to the story's development. Because of this emphasis, B is shorter than A by sixty words (225 words to 164, computer count). That is, with the focus directly on the issue of the question, there is no need for irrelevant narrative details. Thus, answer A is unresponsive and unnecessarily long, whereas answer B is responsive and includes only enough detail to exemplify the major points. Answer B succeeds in answering the question.

## Systematic Preparation

Your challenge is how best to prepare yourself to have a knowledgeable and ready mind at examination time. If you simply cram facts into your head for the test in the hope that you can adjust to the questions, you will likely flounder. You need a systematic approach.

### Read and Reread the Material on Which You Are to Be Examined

Above all, recognize that your preparation should begin as soon as the course begins, not on the night before the exam. Complete each assignment by the due date, for you will understand the classroom discussion only if you know the material (see also the guides for study in Chapter 1, pp. 13–14). Then, about a week before the exam, review each assignment, preferably rereading everything completely. If particular passages were read and discussed in class, make a special point of studying those passages and referring to the notes you took at the time of the discussions. With this preparation, your study on the night before the exam will be fruitful because it is the climax of your preparation, not your entire preparation.

### Construct Your Own Questions: Go on the Attack

To prepare yourself well for an exam, plan to read *actively*, not passively. Read with a goal and *go on the attack* by anticipating test conditions: Create and then answer your own practice questions. Yes, make up your own questions. Don't waste time, however, in trying to guess the questions you think your instructor might ask. Guessing correctly might happen (and wouldn't you be happy if it did?), but do not turn your study into a game of chance. Instead, arrange the subject matter by asking yourself questions that help you get things straight.

How can you construct your own questions? It is not as hard as you might think. Your instructor may have announced certain topics or ideas to be tested on the exam, and you might develop questions from these, or you might apply general questions to the specifics of your assignments, as in the following examples.

1. **Ideas about a character and the interactions of characters** (see also Chapter 4). What is character A like? How does A grow or change in the work? What does A learn or not learn that brings about the conclusion? To what degree does A represent a type or an idea? How does character B influence A? Does a change in character C bring about any corresponding change in A?
2. **Ideas about technical and structural questions.** These can be broad, covering everything from point of view (Chapter 3) to the meter of poetry (Chapter 13). The best guide here is to study those technical aspects that have been discussed in class, for it is unlikely that you will be asked to go beyond the levels considered in classroom discussion.

3. **Ideas about events or situations.** What relationship does episode A have to situation B? Does C's thinking about situation D have any influence on the outcome of event E?

4. **Ideas about a problem** (see also Chapter 14, p. 214). Why is character A or situation X this way and not that way? Is the conclusion justified by the ideas and events leading up to it?

### *Rephrase Your Notes as Questions*

Because your classroom notes are the fullest record you have about your instructor's views, one of the best ways to construct questions is to develop them from these notes. As you select topics and phrase questions, refer to passages from the texts that were studied by the class and stressed by your instructor. If there is time, memorize as many important phrases or lines as you can from the studied works. Plan to incorporate these into your answers as evidence to support the points you make. Remember that it is useful to work not only with main ideas from your notes but also with matters such as character, setting, imagery, symbolism, ideas, and organization.

Obviously, you cannot make questions from all your notes, and you will therefore need to select from those that seem most important. As an example, here is a short note written by a student during a classroom discussion of Shakespeare's *Hamlet*: "A study in how private problems get public, how a court conspiracy can produce disastrous national and international consequences." Notice that you can devise practice questions from this note:

1. In what ways is *Hamlet* not only about private problems but also about public ones?

2. Why should the political consequences of Claudius's murder of Hamlet's father be considered disastrous?

The principle here is that most exam questions do not ask just about *what* but rather get into the issues of *why*. Observe that the first question therefore introduces the words "in what ways" to the phrasing of the note. For the second question, the word "Why" has been used. Either qualification creates the need for you to study pointedly, and neither asks you merely to describe events from the play. Question 1 requires you to consider the wider political effects of Hamlet's hostility toward Claudius, including Hamlet's murder of Polonius and the subsequent madness of Ophelia. Question 2, with its emphasis on disaster, leads you to consider not only the ruination of the hopes and lives of those in the play but also the importance of young Fortinbras and the eventual establishment of Norwegian control over Denmark after Claudius and Hamlet have died. If you were to spend fifteen or twenty minutes writing practice answers to questions such as these, you could be confident in taking an examination on the material, for you could likely adapt or even partially duplicate your study answers to any exam question about the personal and political results of Claudius's murder of his brother, King Hamlet.

## Make Up and Answer Your Own Questions
## Even When Time Is Short

Whatever your subject, spend as much study time as possible making and answering your own questions. *Writing practice answers is one of the most important things you can do in preparing for your exam.* Remember also to work with your own remarks and the ideas you develop in the notebook or journal entries that you make when doing your regular assignments (see Chapter 1, pp. 14–15). Many of these will give you additional ideas for your own questions, which you can practice along with the questions you develop from your classroom notes.

Obviously, with limited study time, you will not be able to create your own questions and answers indefinitely. Even so, don't neglect asking and answering your own questions. If time is too short for full practice answers, write out the main heads, or topics, of an answer. When the press of time (or the need for sleep) no longer permits you to make even such a brief outline answer, keep thinking of questions and their answers as you go to the exam. *Never read passively or unresponsively; always read with a creative, question-and-answer goal.* Think of studying as a preliminary step leading to writing.

The time you spend in this way will be valuable, for as you practice, you will develop control and therefore confidence. Often those who have difficulty with tests or claim a phobia about them prepare passively rather than actively. Your instructor's test questions compel responsiveness, organization, thought, and insight. But a passively prepared student is not ready for this challenge and therefore writes answers that are unresponsive and filled with summary. The grade for such a performance is low, and the student's fear of tests is reinforced. The best way to break such long-standing patterns of fear or uncertainty is to study actively and creatively.

### Study with a Classmate

Often the thoughts of another person can help you understand the material to be tested. Find a fellow student with whom you can work comfortably but also productively, for both of you together can help each other individually. In view of the need for steady preparation throughout a course, regular discussions about the material are a good idea. You might also make your joint study systematic by setting aside a specific evening or afternoon for work sessions. Many students have said that they encounter problems in taking examinations because they are unfamiliar with the ways in which questions are phrased. Consequently, they waste time in understanding and interpreting the questions before they begin their answers, and sometimes they kill all their time because they misunderstand the questions entirely. If you work with a fellow student, however, and trade questions, you will be gaining experience (and confidence) in dealing with this basic difficulty about exams.[1] Working with someone else can be extremely rewarding, just as it can also be stimulating and instructive. Make the effort, and you'll never regret it.

---

[1] If you study with a fellow student, it might be advisable to tell your instructor about this and at the time of the exam to sit as far away as possible from each other.

# Two Basic Types of Questions about Literature

Generally, there are two types of questions on literature exams. Keep them in mind as you prepare. The first type is *factual*, or *mainly objective*; and the second is *general, comprehensive, broad*, or *mainly subjective*. Except for multiple-choice questions, very few questions are purely objective in a literature course.

### Anticipate the Kinds of Factual Questions That Might Be Asked

*Multiple-Choice Questions Ask You to Pick the Most Accurate and Likely Answers* Multiple-choice questions are almost necessarily factual. Your instructor will most likely use them for short quizzes, usually on days when an assignment is due, to make sure that you are keeping up with the reading. Multiple-choice questions test your knowledge of facts and your ingenuity in perceiving subtleties of phrasing. On literature exams, however, this type of question is rare.

*Identification Questions Ask for Accuracy, Explanation, and a Certain Amount of Interpretation*    Identification questions are interesting and challenging because they require you both to know details and also to develop thoughts about them. This type of question is frequently used as a check on the depth and scope of your reading. In fact, an entire exam could be composed of only identification questions, each requiring perhaps five minutes for you to answer. Here are some typical examples of what you might be asked to identify:

1. **A character.** To identify a character, it is necessary to describe briefly the character's position, main activity, and significance. Let us assume that "Fortunato" is the character to be identified. Our answer should state that he is the unsuspecting victim whom Montresor leads to death by live imprisonment in the underground vaults of Montresor's family estate in Edgar Allan Poe's "The Cask of Amontillado" (main activity). Fortunato's pride and gullibility are the major causes of the story's action, and he embodies the story's theme that human pride often leads not to success but rather to doom (significance) and, if you wish, that offending others may cause them to retaliate secretly and hurtfully. Under the category of "significance," of course, you might develop as many ideas as you have time for, but the short example here is a general model for most identification questions.
2. **Incidents or situations.** In identifying an incident or a situation (e.g., "A woman mourns the death of her husband"), first describe the circumstances and the principal character involved in them (Mrs. Popov's reaction to her widowhood in Anton Chekhov's play *The Bear*). Then, describe the importance of this incident or situation in the work. For example, in *The Bear*, Mrs. Popov is mourning the death of her husband, and in the course of the play, Chekhov uses her feelings to show amusingly that life and love with real emotion are stronger than allegiance to the dead.
3. **Things, places, and dates.** Your instructor may ask you to identify a hair ribbon (Nathaniel Hawthorne's "Young Goodman Brown"), a beach (Matthew Arnold's "Dover Beach"), or the date of Amy Lowell's "Patterns" (1916). For dates, you may be given a leeway of five or ten years. What is important about a date is not so much exactness as historical and intellectual perspective. The date of Lowell's "Patterns," for

example, was the third year of World War I, and the poem consequently reflects a re-action against the protracted and senseless loss of life in war (even though details of the poem itself suggest an eighteenth-century war; see pp. 218–222). To claim "World War I" as the date of the poem would be acceptable as an answer if it happens that you cannot remember the exact date.

4. **Quotations.** You should remember enough of the text to identify a passage taken from it or at least to make an informed guess. Generally, you should (1) locate the quo-tation, if you remember it, or else describe what you think is the probable location; (2) show the ways in which the quotation is typical of the content and style of the work you have read; and (3) describe the importance of the passage. If you suffer a lapse of memory, write a reasoned and careful explanation of your guess. Even if your guess is not actually correct, the knowledge and cogency of your explanation should give you points.

*Technical and Analytical Questions and Problems Require You to Relate Knowledge and Technical Understanding to the Issue*    In a scale of ascending importance, the third and most difficult type of factual question relates to those matters of writing that much of this book is concerned with: technique and analysis. You might be asked to analyze the *setting, images, point of view,* or *important idea* of a work; you might be asked about the *tone and style* of a story or poem; or you might be asked to *explicate* a poem that may or may not be duplicated for your benefit (if it is not duplicated, woe to students who have not studied their assignments). Questions like these assume that you have technical knowledge, and they also ask you to examine the text within the limitations imposed by the directions.

Obviously, technical questions occur more frequently in advanced courses than in introductory ones, and the questions become more subtle as the courses become more advanced. Instructors of introductory courses may ask about ideas and problems but will likely not use many of the others unless they state their intentions to do so in advance or unless technical terms have been studied in class.

Questions of this type are fairly long, perhaps allowing from fifteen to twenty-five minutes apiece. If you have two or more of these questions, try to space your time sensibly; do not devote eighty percent of your time to one question and leave only twenty percent for the rest.

### Understand How Your Responses Will Be Judged and Graded

*Identification Questions Probe Your Understanding and Application of Facts*    In all factual questions, your instructor is testing (1) your factual command and (2) your quick-ness in relating a part to the whole. Thus, suppose you are identifying the incident "A man kills a canary." It is correct to say that Susan Glaspell's play *Trifles* is the location of the incident, that the murdered farmer John Wright killed the bird, and that the canary belonged to his wife, Minnie. Knowledge of these details clearly establishes that you know the facts. But a strong answer must go further. Even in the brief time you have for short answers, you should always connect the facts (1) to major causality in the work, (2) to an important idea or ideas, (3) to the development of the work, and (4) for a quotation, to the style. Time is short and you must be selective, but if you can make your answer move from facts to significance, you will always fashion superior responses. Along these lines, let us look at an answer identifying the action from *Trifles*:

> The action is from Glaspell's *Trifles*. The man who kills the bird is John Wright, the dead man, and the owner is his wife, Minnie, who, before the story begins, has been jailed on suspicion of murder. The wringing of the little bird's neck is important because it is shown as an indignity and outrage in Minnie Wright's desperate life, and it obviously made her angry enough to put a rope around Wright's neck to strangle him in his sleep. It is thus the cause not only of the murder but also of the investigation bringing the two lawmen and their wives to the Wright kitchen. In fact, the killing of the bird makes the story possible because it is the wives who discover the dead bird's remains, and this discovery is the means by which Glaspell highlights them as the major characters of the action. Because the husband's senselessly brutal act shows how bleak the married life of Minnie Wright actually was, it dramatizes the lonely and victimized plight of women in a male-dominated way of life like that on the Wright farm. The discovery also raises the issue of legality and morality because the women decide to conceal the evidence, therefore protecting Minnie Wright from conviction and punishment.

Any of the points in this answer could be developed as a separate essay, but the paragraph is successful as a short answer because it goes beyond fact to deal with significance. Clearly, such answers are possible at the time of an exam only if you have devoted considerable thought beforehand to the works on which you are tested. The more thinking and practicing you do before an exam, the better your answers will be. Remember this advice as an axiom: *You cannot write superior answers if you do not think extensively before the exam.* By ambitious advance study, you will be able to reduce surprise to a minimum.

*Longer Factual Questions Probe Your Knowledge and Your Ability to Organize Your Thoughts*   More extended factual questions also require more thoroughly developed organization. Remember that for these questions your skill in writing essays is important because the quality of your composition will determine a major share of your instructor's evaluation of your answers. It is therefore best to take several minutes to gather your thoughts before you begin to write. Remember, *a ten-minute planned answer is preferable to a twenty-five-minute unplanned answer.* You do not need to write every possible fact on each particular question. Of greater importance is the use to which you put the facts that you know and the organization and development of your answer. Use a sheet of scratch paper to jot down important facts and your ideas about them in relation to the question. Then put them together, phrase a thesis sentence, and use your facts to exemplify and support your thesis.

It is always necessary to begin your answer pointedly, using key words or phrases from the question or direction if possible, so that your answer will have thematic shape. You should *never* begin an answer with "Because" and then go on from there without referring again to the question. To be most responsive during the short time available for an exam, you should use the question as your guide for your answer. Let us suppose that you have the following question on your test: "How does Glaspell use details in *Trifles* to reveal the character of Minnie Wright?" The most common way to go astray on such a question—and the easiest thing to do also—is to concentrate on Minnie Wright's character rather than on how Glaspell uses detail to bring out her character. The word *how* makes a vast difference in the nature of the final answer, and hence a good method on the exam is to duplicate key phrases in the question to ensure that you make your major points clear. Here is an opening sentence that uses the key words and phrases (italicized here) from the question to organize thought and provide focus.

> Glaspell *uses details* of setting, marital relationships, and personal habits *to reveal the character of Minnie Wright* as a person of great but unfulfilled potential whom anger has finally overcome.

Because this sentence repeats the key phrases from the question and because it promises to show *how* the details are to be focused on the character, it suggests that the answer to follow will be responsive.

### General, or Comprehensive, Questions Require You to Connect a Number of Works to Broader Matters of Idea and Technique

General, or comprehensive, questions are particularly important on final examinations, when your instructor is testing your total comprehension of the course material. Considerable time is usually allowed for answering this type of question, which can be phrased in a number of ways.

1. A *direct question* asking about philosophy, underlying attitudes, main ideas, characteristics of style, backgrounds, and so on. Here are some possible questions in this category.
   What use do _____, _____, and _____ make of the topic of _____?
   Define and characterize the short story as a genre of literature, using examples from the stories of _____, _____, and _____.
   Describe the use of dialogue by _____, _____, and _____.
   Contrast the technique of point of view as used by _____, _____, and _____.
2. A *"comment" question*, often based on an extensive quotation, borrowed from a critic or written by your instructor for the occasion, asking about a broad class of writers, a literary movement, or the like. Your instructor may ask you to treat this question broadly (taking in many writers) or else to apply the quotation to a specific writer.
3. A *"suppose" question*, such as "What advice might Minnie Wright of Glaspell's *Trifles* give the speakers of Lowell's 'Patterns' and Keats's 'Bright Star'?" or "What might the speaker of Rossetti's poem 'Echo' say if she were told that her dead lover was actually a person like Goodman Brown of Hawthorne's 'Young Goodman Brown'?" Although "suppose" questions seem whimsical at first sight, they have a serious design and should prompt original and radical thinking. The first question, for example, might cause a test writer to bring out, from Minnie Wright's perspective, that the love expressed by both speakers overlooks the possibilities of changes in character over a long period. She would likely sympathize with the speaker of "Patterns," a woman, but she might also say that the speaker's enthusiasm would need to be augmented by the constant exertion of kindness and mutual understanding. For the speaker of "Bright Star," a man, Mrs. Wright might say that the steadfast love he seeks should be linked to thoughtfulness and constant communication as well as passion.

Although "suppose" questions (and answers) are speculative, the need to respond to them requires a detailed consideration of the works involved, and in this respect the "suppose" question is a salutary means of learning. It is of course difficult to prepare for a "suppose" question, which you can therefore regard as a test not only of your knowledge but also of your adaptability, inventiveness, and ingenuity.

### Understand How Your Responses to General and Comprehensive Questions Will Be Judged and Graded

When answering broad, general questions, you are dealing with an unstructured situation, and you must not only supply an answer but—equally important—also must create a *structure* within which your answer can have meaning. You might say that you make up your own specific question out of the original general question. If you were asked to consider the role of women as seen in works by Lowell, Guy de Maupassant, and Glaspell, for example, you would structure the question by focusing a number of clearly defined topics. A possible way to begin answering such a question might be this:

> Lowell, Maupassant, and Glaspell present a view of female resilience by demonstrating the inner control, endurance, and power of adaptation of their major characters.

With this sort of focus, you would be able to proceed point by point, introducing supporting data as you form your answer.

As a general rule, the best method for answering a comprehensive question is comparison-contrast (see also Chapter 15). The reason is that in dealing with, say, a general question on Christina Rossetti, Chekhov, and John Keats, it is too easy to write *three* separate essays rather than *one*. Thus, you should try to create a topic such as "the treatment of real or idealized love" or "the difficulties in male-female relationships" and then develop your answer point by point rather than writer by writer. By creating your answer in this way, you can bring in references to each or all of the writers as they become relevant. If you were to treat each writer separately, your comprehensive answer would lose focus and effectiveness, and it would also be repetitive.

Remember that in judging your response to a general question, your instructor is interested in seeing (1) how effectively you perceive and explain the significant issues in the question, (2) how intelligently and clearly you organize your answer, and (3) how persuasively you link your answer to materials from the work as supporting evidence.

Bear in mind that in answering comprehensive questions, you do not have the freedom or license to write about anything at all. You must stick to the questions and must first of all directly answer the questions. The freedom you do have is the freedom to create your own organization and development in response to the questions that your instructor has asked you. The underlying idea of the comprehensive, general question is that you possess special knowledge and insight that cannot be discovered by more factual questions. You must therefore demonstrate your power of thinking and of perceiving relationships. You need to formulate your own responses to the material and introduce evidence that reflects your own insights and command of information.

A final thought: Try to enjoy the learning experience that preparing for an exam offers you. You will surprise yourself, and, hopefully, discover yourself. Good luck.

# Appendix A

## Critical Approaches Important in the Study of Literature

A number of critical theories or approaches for understanding and interpreting litera-ture are available to critics and students alike.[1] Many of these were developed during the twentieth century to create a discipline of literary studies comparable with disciplines in the natural and social sciences. Literary critics have often borrowed liberally from other disciplines (e.g., history, psychology, politics, anthropology) but have primarily aimed at developing literature as a study in its own right.

At the heart of the various critical approaches are many fundamental questions: What is literature? What does it do? Is its concern primarily to tell stories, to divert at-tention, to entertain, to communicate ideas, to persuade, and to teach, or is it to describe and interpret reality, or to explore and explain emotions—or is it all of these? To what degree is literature an art, as opposed to a medium for imparting knowledge? What more does it do than express ideas? How does it get its ideas across? What can it contribute to intellectual, artistic, political, and social thought and history? How is literature used, and how and why is it misused? Is it private? Public? What theoretical and technical exper-tise may be invoked to enhance literary studies? How valuable was literature in the past, and how valuable is it now? To what degree should literature be in the vanguard of so-cial and political change?

Questions such as these indicate that criticism is concerned not only with reading and interpreting stories, poems, and plays but also with establishing theoretical un-derstanding. Because of such extensive aims, a full explanation and illustration of the approaches would fill the pages of a long book. The following descriptions are there-fore intended as no more than brief introductions. Bear in mind that in the hands of skilled critics, the approaches are so subtle, sophisticated, and complex that they are not only critical stances but also philosophies.

Although the various approaches provide widely divergent ways to study literature and literary problems, they reflect major tendencies rather than absolute straitjack-eting. Not every approach is appropriate for every work, nor are the approaches always mutually exclusive. Even the most devoted practitioners of the methods do not pursue them rigidly. In addition, some of the approaches are more "user friendly" than others

---

[1]Some of the approaches described in this chapter are presented in Chapter 1 as basic study techniques for writing about literary works.

for certain types of discovery. To a degree at least, most critics therefore take a particular approach but use methods that technically belong to one or more of the other approaches. A critic stressing the topical/historical approach, for example, might introduce the close study of a work that is associated with the method of the New Criticism. Similarly, a psychoanalytical critic might include details about imagery. In short, a great deal of criticism is *pragmatic* or *eclectic* rather than rigid.

The approaches to be considered here are these: *moral/intellectual*; *topical/historical*; *New Critical/formalist*; *structuralist*; *feminist/gender studies/queer theory*; *economic determinist/Marxist*; *psychological/psychoanalytic*; *archetypal/symbolic/mythic*; *deconstructionist*; and *reader-response*.

The object of learning about these approaches, like everything else in this book, is to help you develop your own capacities as a reader and writer. Accordingly, following each of the descriptions is a brief paragraph showing how Nathaniel Hawthorne's story "Young Goodman Brown" (Appendix C) might be considered in the light of the particular approach. The illustrative paragraphs following the discussion of structuralism, for example, shows an application of the structuralist approach to Goodman Brown and his story, and so also with the feminist approach, the economic-determinist approach, and the others. These paragraphs are followed by additional paragraphs illustrating the same approaches based on other literary works. Whenever you are doing your own writing about literature, you are free to use the various approaches as part or all of your assignment, if you believe the approach may help you.

## Moral/Intellectual

The **moral/intellectual critical approach** is concerned with content, ideas, and values. The approach is as old as literature itself, for literature is a traditional mode of inculcating thought, morality, philosophy, and religion. The concern in moral/intellectual criticism is not only to discover meaning but also to determine whether works of literature are both *true* and *significant*.

To study literature from the moral/intellectual perspective is therefore to determine whether a work conveys a lesson or a message and whether it can help readers lead better lives and improve their understanding of the world. What ideas does the work contain? How strongly does the work bring forth its ideas? What application do the ideas have to the work's characters and situations? How may the ideas be evaluated intellectually? Morally? Discussions based on such questions do not imply that literature is primarily a medium of moral and intellectual exhortation. Ideally, moral/intellectual criticism should differ from sermonizing to the degree that readers should always be left with their own decisions about whether to assimilate the ideas of a work and about whether the ideas—and values—are personally or morally acceptable.

Sophisticated critics have sometimes demeaned the moral/intellectual approach on the grounds that "message hunting" reduces a work's artistic value by treating it like a sermon or political speech; but the approach will be valuable as long as readers expect literature to be applicable to their own lives.

**Example: Hawthorne's "Young Goodman Brown"**

"Young Goodman Brown" raises the issue of how an institution designed for human elevation, such as the religious system of colonial Salem, can be so ruinous. Does the failure result from the system itself or from the people who misunderstand it? Is what is true of religion as practiced by Brown also true of social and political institutions? Should any religious or political philosophy be given greater significance than goodwill and mutual trust? One of the major virtues of "Young Goodman Brown" is that it provokes questions like these but at the same time provides a number of satisfying answers. A particularly important one is that religious and moral beliefs should not be used to justify the condemnation of others. Another important answer is that attacks made from the refuge of a religion or group, such as Brown's Puritanism, are dangerous because the judge may condemn without thought and without personal responsibility.

# Topical/Historical

The **topical/historical critical approach** stresses the relationship of literature to its historical period, and for this reason it has had a long life. Although much literature may be applicable to many places and times, much of it also directly reflects the intellectual and social worlds of the authors. When was the work written? What were the circumstances that produced it? What major issues does it deal with? How does it fit into the author's career? John Keats's poem "On First Looking into Chapman's Homer" (see Chapter 10), for example, is his excited response to his reading of one of the major literary works of Western civilization. Thomas Hardy's "Channel Firing" (Appendix C) is an ironically acerbic response to continued armament and preparation for war in the past, in the present, and in the future.

The topical/historical approach investigates relationships of this sort, including the elucidation of words and concepts that today's readers may not immediately understand. Obviously, the approach may require the assistance of footnotes, dictionaries, library catalogs, histories, online searches, and handbooks.

A common criticism of the topical/historical approach is that, in the extreme, it deals with background knowledge rather than with literature itself. It is possible, for example, for a topical/historical critic to describe a writer's life, the period of the writer's work, and the social and intellectual ideas of the time—all without ever considering the meaning, importance, and value of any of that writer's works themselves.

A reaction against such an unconnected use of historical details is the so-called **New Historicism**. This approach justifies the parallel reading of both literary and nonliterary works in order to bring an informed understanding of the context of a literary work. The New Historicist assumes that history is not a "fixed" essence but a literary construction. As such, history is a prism through which a society views itself; a work of literature is given resonance by seeing the nonobjective context in which it was produced. This approach justifies the introduction of historical knowledge by integrating it with the understanding of particular texts. Readers of Matthew Arnold's "Dover Beach" (Appendix C), for example, sometimes find it difficult to follow the meaning of Arnold's statement "The Sea of Faith/Was once, too, at the full" (lines 21 and 22). Historical background has a definite role to play here. In Arnold's time there developed a method of treating the Bible as a historical document rather than a divinely inspired revelation. This approach has been called the "Higher Criticism" of the Bible, and to many thoughtful people, the Higher Criticism undermined the concept that the Bible was divine, infallible, and inerrant. Therefore, Arnold's idea is that the "Sea of Faith" is no longer at full tide but is now at an ebb. Because the introduction of such historical material is designed to facilitate the reading of the poem—and also the reading of other literature of the period—the New Historicism represents an integration of knowledge and interpretation. As a principle, New Historicism entails the acquisition of as much historical information as possible because our knowledge of the relationship of literature to its historical period can never be complete. The practitioner of Historical Criticism must always seek new information on the grounds that it may prove relevant to the understanding of various literary works.

### Example: Hawthorne's "Young Goodman Brown"

"Young Goodman Brown" is an allegorical story by Nathaniel Hawthorne (1804–1864), the major New England writer who probed deeply into the relationship between religion and guilt. His ancestors had been involved in religious persecutions, including the Salem witch trials, and he, living 150 years afterward, wanted to analyze the weaknesses and uncertainties of the sin-dominated religion of the earlier period, a tradition of which he was a resentful heir. Not surprisingly, therefore, the story about "Young Goodman Brown" takes place in Salem during Puritan times, and Hawthorne's implied judgments are those of a severe critic of how the harsh old religion destroyed personal and family relationships. Although the immediate concerns of the story belong to a vanished age, Hawthorne's treatment is still valuable because it is still timely.

# New Critical/Formalist

The New Criticism (the **New Critical/formalist critical approach**) has been a dominant force in modern literary studies. It focuses on literary texts as formal works of art, and for this reason, it can be seen as a reaction against the topical/historical approach. The objection raised by New Critics is that, as topical/historical critics consider literary history, they evade direct contact with actual texts.

The inspiration for the New Critical/formalist approach was the French practice of *explication de texte*, a method that emphasizes detailed examination and explanation. The New Criticism is at its most brilliant in the formal analysis of smaller units such as entire poems and short passages. For the analysis of larger structures, the New Criticism also uses a number of techniques that have been selected as the basis of chapters in this book. Discussions of point of view, tone, plot, character, and structure, for example, are formal ways of looking at literature that are derived from the New Criticism.

The aim of the formalist study of literature is to provide readers with not only the means of explaining the content of works (what, specifically, does a work say?) but also the insights needed for evaluating the artistic quality of individual works and writers (how well is it said?). A major aspect of New Critical thought is that content and form—including all ideas, ambiguities, subtleties, and even apparent contradictions—were originally within the conscious or subconscious control of the author. There are no accidents. It does not necessarily follow, however, that today's critic is able to define the author's intentions exactly, for such intentions require knowledge of biographical details that are irretrievably lost. Each literary work therefore takes on its own existence and identity, and the critic's work is to discover a reading or readings that explain the facts of the text. Please note that the New Critic does not claim infallible interpretations and does not exclude the validity of multiple readings of the same work.

Dissenters from the New Criticism have noted a tendency by New Critics to ignore relevant knowledge that history and biography can bring to literary studies. In addition, the approach has been subject to the charge that stressing the explication of texts alone fails to deal with literary value and appreciation. In other words, the formalist critic, in explaining the meaning of literature, sometimes neglects the reasons for which readers find literature interesting, stimulating, and valuable.

### Example: Hawthorne's "Young Goodman Brown"

A major aspect of Hawthorne's "Young Goodman Brown" is that the details are so vague and dreamlike that many readers are uncertain about what is happening. The action is a nighttime walk by the protagonist, Young Goodman Brown, into a deep forest where he encounters a mysterious satanic ritual that leaves him bitter and misanthropic. This much seems clear, but the precise nature of Brown's experience is not clear, nor is the identity of the stranger (father, village elder, devil) who accompanies Brown as he begins his walk. At the story's end, Hawthorne's narrator states that the whole episode may have been no more than a dream or nightmare. Yet when morning comes, Brown walks back into town as though returning from an overnight trip, and he recoils in horror from his fellow villagers, including his wife Faith (paragraph 70). Could his attitude result from nothing more than a nightmare?

Even at the story's end, these uncertainties remain. For this reason, one may conclude that Hawthorne deliberately creates the uncertainties to reveal how people like Brown build defensive walls of judgment around themselves. The story thus implies that the real source of Brown's anger is as vague as his nocturnal walk, but he doesn't understand it in this way. Because Brown's vision and judgment are absolute, he rejects everyone around him, even if the cost is a life of bitter suspicion and spiritual isolation.

## Structuralist

The principle of the **stucturalist critical approach** stems from the attempt to find relationships and connections among elements that appear to be separate and unique. Just as physical science reveals unifying and universal principles of matter such as gravity and the forces of electromagnetism (and is constantly searching for a "unified field theory"), the structuralist critic attempts to discover the forms unifying all literature. Thus, a structuralist description of Guy de Maupassant's "The Necklace" (Chapter 1) stresses that the main character, Mathilde, is an *active* protagonist who undergoes a *test* (or series of tests) and emerges with a victory, though not the kind she had originally hoped for. The same might be said of Smirnov and Mrs. Popov in Anton Chekhov's play *The Bear* (Appendix C). If this same kind of structural view is applied to Hawthorne's "Young Goodman Brown" (Appendix C), the protagonist is defeated in the test. Generally, the structuralist approach applies such patterns to other works of literature to determine that certain protagonists are active or submissive, that they pass or fail their tests, that they succeed or fail at other encounters, or that they might fail one kind of test but are victorious in another. The key is that many apparently unrelated works reveal many common patterns or contain similar structures with important variations.

The structuralist approach is important because it enables critics to discuss works from widely separate cultures and historical periods. In this respect, critics have followed the leads of modern anthropologists, most notably Claude Lévi-Strauss (1908–1990). Along such lines, critics have undertaken the serious examination of folktales and fairy tales. Some of the groundbreaking structuralist criticism, for example, was devoted to the structural analysis of themes, actions, and characters found in Russian folktales. The method also bridges popular and serious literature, making little distinction between the two insofar as the description of the structures is concerned. Indeed, structuralism furnishes an ideal approach for comparative literature, and the method also enables critics to consolidate genres such as modern romances, detective tales, soap operas, and "sitcoms."

Like the New Criticism, structuralism aims at comprehensiveness of description, and many critics would insist that the two are complementary and not separate. A distinction is that New Criticism is at its best in dealing with smaller units of literature, whereas structuralist criticism is best in the analysis of narratives and therefore larger units such as novels, myths, stories, plays, and films. Because structuralism shows how fiction is organized into various typical situations, the approach merges with the *archetypal* approach (see p. 313), and at times it is difficult to find any distinctions between structuralist and archetypal criticism.

Structuralism, however, deals not just with narrative structures but also with structures of any type, wherever they occur. For example, structuralism makes considerable use of linguistics. Modern linguistic scholars have determined that there is a difference between "deep structures" and "surface structures" in language. A structuralist analysis of style, therefore, emphasizes how writers utilize such structures. The structuralist interpretation of language also perceives distinguishing types or "grammars" of language that are recurrent in various types of literature. Suppose, for example, that you encounter opening passages like the following:

> Once upon a time, a young prince fell in love with a young princess. He was in love so deeply that he wanted to declare his love for her, and early one morning, he left his castle on his white charger, along with his retainers and servants, riding toward her castle home high in the distant and cloud-topped mountains.

> Early that morning, Alan found himself thinking about Anne. He had thought that she was being ambiguous when she said she loved him, and his feelings about her were not certain. His further thought left him still unsure.

The words of these two passages create different and distinct frames of reference. One is a fairy tale of the past, the other a modern internalized reflection of feeling. The passages therefore demonstrate how language itself fits into predetermined patterns or structures. Similar uses of language structures can be associated with other types of literature.

### Example: Hawthorne's "Young Goodman Brown"

Young Goodman Brown is a hero who is passive, not active. He is a *witness*, a *receiver* rather than a *doer*. His only action—taking his trip in the forest—occurs at the story's beginning. After that point, he no longer acts but instead is acted upon, and his reactions to what he sees around him put his life's beliefs to a test. Of course, many protagonists undergo similar testing (such as rescuing victims or overcoming particularly terrible dragons), and they emerge as heroes or conquerors. Not so with Goodman Brown. He is a responder who allows himself to be victimized by his own perceptions—or misperceptions. Despite all his previous experiences with his wife and with the good people of his village, he generalizes too hastily. He lets the single disillusioning experience of his nightmare govern his entire outlook on others, and thus he fails his test and turns his entire life into darkness.

## Feminist Criticism/Gender Studies/Queer Theory

*Feminism/Gender Studies/Queer Theory* displays divergent interests drawing insights from many disciplines. It is a still evolving and rich field of inquiry. The **feminist critical approach** had its genesis in the women's movement of the 1960s, shares many of its concerns, and has applied them to the study of literature. One of the early aims of feminist critics was to question the traditional canon and claim a place in it for neglected women writers. Writers such as Mary Shelley, Elizabeth Gaskell, Christina Rossetti, Kate Chopin, Charlotte Perkins Gillman, and Anita Scott Coleman have been given great critical attention as a result. Feminist critics also delineate the ways both male and female characters are portrayed in literature, looking at how societal norms about sexual difference are either enforced or subverted, and focusing partly on patriarchal structures and institutions such as marriage. As early as the beginning of the twentieth century, Virginia Woolf questioned whether there was a feminine/masculine divide in writing styles, a contentious subject among feminist critics to this day. Feminist critics are also interested in how interpreting texts differs between the sexes. For instance, in *A Map for Rereading* (New York: Pantheon, 1985), the critic Annette Kolodny analyzes how men and women read the same stories differently.

*Gender Studies*, a more recent critical approach, brings attention to gender rather than to sexual differences. Gender studies critics see the masculine/feminine divide as socially constructed and not innate. Drawing partly on the works of the French philosopher Michel Foucault (1926–1984) such as *The History of Sexuality* (New York: Vintage, 1990) and *Madness and Civilization* (New York: Vintage, 1988), which explore the way powerful institutions organize our society and way of thinking, Gender Studies critics apply Foucault's ideas to understanding patriarchal structures and their representations in literature. Many studies have also built on the insights of psychoanalysis and deconstruction, questioning Freud's male-oriented categories and seeking insights into the way language is constructed and the way it affects our thinking. In the essay, *Laugh of the Medusa* (1975), Hélène Cixous applies deconstructionist insights about binary oppositions to a study of discourse about women, showing how it disparages women.[2]

A more recent critical orientation, which came to prominence in the early 1990s is *Queer Theory*, which also appropriates many of the insights of deconstruction, particularly its understanding that binary oppositions are relative and that thinking about matters such as sexual orientation is partly ideological and partly social. Many Queer Theorists see the heterosexual/homosexual divide as less distinct than has been believed. Queer Theorists are interested in how homosexuals are portrayed in literature, and whether they write or read literature differently than heterosexuals. Queer theory has brought attention to recent literary works dealing explicitly with lesbian and gay themes, along with attention to sometimes "veiled" references to the same themes in writers whose works make up the standard canon.

### Example: Hawthorne's "Young Goodman Brown"

At the beginning of "Young Goodman Brown," Brown's wife, Faith, is seen only peripherally. In the traditional patriarchal spirit of wife-as-adjunct, she tells her new husband of her fears and then asks him to stay at home and take his journey at some other time. Hawthorne does not grant her the intelligence or dignity, however, to let her explain her concern (or might he not have been interested in what she had to say?), and she therefore remains in the background with her pink hair ribbon as her distinguishing symbol of submissive inferiority. During the midforest satanic ritual, she appears again and is given power, but only the power to cause her husband to go astray. Once she is led in as a novice in the practice of demonism, her husband falls right in step. Unfortunately, by following her, Brown can conveniently excuse himself from guilt by claiming that "she" had made him do it, just as Eve, in some traditional views of the fall of humankind, compelled Adam to eat the apple (Genesis 3:16–17). Hawthorne's attention to the male protagonist, in other words, permits him to neglect the independence and integrity of a female protagonist.

## Economic Determinist/Marxist

The concept of cultural and economic determinism is one of the major political ideas of the nineteenth century. Karl Marx (1818–1883) emphasized that the primary influence on life was economic, and he saw society enmeshed in a continuous conflict between capitalist oppressors and oppressed working people. The literature that emerged from this kind of analysis often features individuals who are coping with the ill effects of economic disadvantage. Sometimes called "proletarian" literature, it focuses on persons of the lower class—the poor and oppressed who spend their

---

[2]See Hélène Cixous, "The Laugh of the Medusa," trans. Keith Cohen and Paula Cohen, *Signs* 1, No. 4 (1976): 875–93.

lives in endless drudgery and misery and whose attempts to rise to the top usually result in renewed oppression.

Marx's political ideas were never widely accepted in the United States and have faded still more after the breakup of the Soviet Union, but the idea of economic determinism (and the related term *Social Darwinism*) is still credible. As a result, much literature can be judged from an economic perspective even though the economic critics may not be Marxian: What is the economic status of the characters? What happens to them as a result of this status? How do they fare against economic and political odds? What other conditions stemming from their class does the writer emphasize (e.g., poor education, poor nutrition, poor health care, inadequate opportunity)? To what extent does the work fail by overlooking the economic, social, and political implications of its material? In what other ways does economic determinism affect the work? How should readers consider the story in today's developed or underdeveloped world? Seemingly, Hawthorne's story "Young Goodman Brown," which we have used for analysis in these discussions, has no major economic implications, but an **economic determinist/ Marxist critical approach** might take the following turns.

### Example: Hawthorne's "Young Goodman Brown"

"Young Goodman Brown" is a fine story just as it is. It deals with the false values instilled by the skewed acceptance of sin-dominated religion, but it overlooks the economic implications of this situation. One might suspect that the real story in Goodman Brown's Salem should be about the disruption caused by an alienated member of a small society. In other words, after Brown's condemnation and distrust of others forces him into his own shell of sick imagination, Hawthorne does not deal with how such a disaffected character would injure the economic and public life of the town. Consider this, just for a moment: Why would the people from whom Brown recoils in disgust want to deal with him in business or personal matters? In town meetings, would they want to follow his opinions on crucial issues of public concern and investment? Would his preoccupation with sin and damnation make him anything more than a horror in his domestic life? Would his wife, Faith, be able to discuss household management with him or ask him about methods of caring for the children? All these questions of course are pointed toward another story—a story that Hawthorne did not write. They also indicate the shortcomings of Hawthorne's approach because it is clear that the major result of Young Goodman Brown's selfish preoccupation with evil would be a serious disruption of the economic and political affairs of his small community.

## Psychological/Psychoanalytic

The scientific study of the mind is a product of psychodynamic theory as established by Sigmund Freud (1856–1939) and of the psychoanalytic method practiced by his followers. Psychoanalysis provided a new key to the understanding of character by claiming that behavior is caused by hidden and unconscious motives. It was greeted as a revelation with far-reaching implications for all intellectual pursuits. Not surprisingly it has had a profound and continuing effect on post-Freudian literature.

In addition, its popularity produced the **psychological/psychoanalytic approach** to criticism.[3] Some critics use the approach to explain fictional characters, as in the landmark interpretation by Freud and Ernest Jones that Shakespeare's Hamlet suffers from an Oedipus complex. Still other critics use it as a way of analyzing authors and the artistic process. For example, John Livingston Lowes's study *The Road to Xanadu* presents a detailed examination of the mind, reading, and neuroses of Samual Taylor Coleridge, the author of "Kubla Khan" (Appendix C).

Critics using the psychoanalytic approach treat literature somewhat like information about patients in therapy. In the work itself, what are the obvious and hidden motives that cause a character's behavior and speech? How much background (e.g., repressed childhood trauma, adolescent memories) does the author reveal about a character? How purposeful is this information with regard to the character's psychological condition? How much is important in the analysis and understanding of the character?

In the consideration of authors, critics using the psychoanalytic model consider questions like these: What particular life experiences explain characteristic subjects or preoccupations? Was the author's life happy? Miserable? Upsetting? Solitary? Social? Can the death of someone in the author's family be associated with melancholy situations in that author's work? All eleven brothers and sisters of the English poet Thomas Gray, for example, died before reaching adulthood. Gray was the only one of the twelve to survive. In his poetry, Gray often deals with death, and he is therefore considered one of the "Graveyard School" of eighteenth-century poets. A psychoanalytical critic might make much of this connection.

### Example: Hawthorne's "Young Goodman Brown"

At the end of "Young Goodman Brown," Hawthorne's major character is no longer capable of normal existence. His nightmare should be read as a symbol of what in reality would have been lifelong mental subjection to the type of puritanical religion that emphasizes sin and guilt. Such preoccupation with sin is no hindrance to psychological health if the preoccupied people are convinced that God forgives them and grants them mercy. In their dealings with others, they remain healthy as long as they believe that other people have the same sincere trust in divine forgiveness. If their own faith is weak and uncertain, however, and if they cannot believe in forgiveness, then they are likely to transfer their own guilt—really a form of personal terror—to others. They remain conscious of their own sins, but they find it easy to claim that others are sinful—even those who are spiritually spotless and even their own family, who should be dearest to them. When this process of projection or transference occurs, such people have created the rationale of condemning others because of their own guilt. The price that they pay is a life of gloom, a fate that Hawthorne designates for Goodman Brown after his nightmare about demons in human form.

---

[3]See Chapter 4, "Writing about Character: The People in Literature."

## Archetypal/Symbolic/Mythic

The **archetypal/symbolic/mythic critical approach**, derived from the work of the Swiss psychoanalyst Carl Jung (1875–1961), presupposes that human life is built up out of patterns, or *archetypes* ("first molds," or "first patterns") that are similar throughout various cultures and historical times.[4] The approach is similar to the structuralist analysis of literature, for both approaches stress the connections that may be discovered in literature written in different times and in vastly different locations in the world.

In literary evaluation, the archetypal approach is used to support the claim that the very best literature is grounded in archetypal patterns. The archetypal critic therefore looks for archetypes such as God's creation of human beings, the sacrifice of a hero, or the search for paradise. How does an individual story, poem, or play fit into any of the archetypal patterns? What truths does this correlation provide (particularly truths that cross historical, national, and cultural lines)? How closely does the work fit the archetype? What variations can be seen? What meaning or meanings do the connections have?

The most tenuous aspect of archetypal criticism is Jung's assertion that the recurring patterns provide evidence for a "universal human consciousness" that all of us, by virtue of our humanity, still retain in our minds and in our very blood.

Not all critics accept the hypothesis of a universal human consciousness, but they nevertheless consider the approach important for comparisons and contrasts (see Chapter 15). Many human situations—such as adolescence, dawning love, the search for success, the reconciliation with one's mother and father, and the encroachment of age and death—are similar in structure and can be analyzed as archetypes. For example, the following situations can be seen as a pattern, or archetype, of initiation: A young man discovers the power of literature and understanding (Keats's "On First Looking into Chapman's Homer"); a man determines the importance of truth and fidelity amid uncertainty (Arnold's "Dover Beach"); a man and woman fall in love despite their wishes to remain independent (Chekhov's *The Bear*); a woman gains strength and integrity because of previously unrealized inner resources (Maupassant's "The Necklace"). The archetypal approach encourages the analysis of variations on the same theme, as in Susan Glaspell's *Trifles* (Appendix C) and Frank O'Connor's "First Confession" (Appendix C) when characters ignore the imposition of a particular moral (or legal) standard (one sort of initiation) and instead assert their own individuality and freedom (another sort of initiation).

### Example: Hawthorne's "Young Goodman Brown"

In the sense that Young Goodman Brown undergoes a change from psychological normality to rigidity, the story is a reverse archetype of the initiation ritual. According to the archetype of successful initiation, initiates seek to demonstrate their worthiness to become full-fledged members of society. Telemachus in Homer's *The Odyssey*, for

---

[4]Symbolism is also considered in Chapter 11.

example, is a young man who in the course of the epic goes through the initiation rit-
uals of travel, discussion, and battle. But in "Young Goodman Brown" we see initiation
in reverse, for just as there is an archetype of successful initiation, Brown's initiation
leads him into failure. In the private areas of life on which happiness depends, he falls
short. He sees evil in his fellow villagers, condemns his minister, and shrinks even from
his own family. His life therefore becomes filled with despair and gloom. His suspicions
are those of a Puritan of long ago, but the timeliness of Hawthorne's story is that the
archetype of misunderstanding and condemnation has not changed. Today's headlines
of misery and war are produced by the same kind of intolerance that is exhibited by
Goodman Brown.

## Deconstructionist

The **deconstructionist critical approach**—which deconstructionists explain not as an
approach but rather as a performance or as a strategy of reading—was developed by the
French philosopher Jacques Derrida (1930–2004). In the 1970s and 1980s it became a
major mode of criticism by critiquing the logocentric Western philosophical tradition.
*Logocentrism* is the belief that speech is a direct expression of a speaker's intention, that
it has a direct correspondence to reality, and that it is therefore the privileged arbiter of
interpretation. Derrida, by exposing what he saw as the fallacious assumptions of logocentrism, sought to undermine the basis of stable meanings derivable from language. The
implications for reading and therefore for literary studies were far-reaching.

Deconstructionist critics begin literary analysis by assuming the instability of language
and the impossibility of arriving at a fixed standard to anchor interpretation. The dic-
tum, in Derrida's *Of Grammatology*, that "there is nothing outside the text" indicates the
denial of any authoritative referent outside of words. Texts are always self-contradictory
because they can always be reread to undermine an apparently stable interpretation.
In part, this is due to how meaning is derived from binary oppositions such as
speech/writing, male/ female, good/evil. Each word of a pair obtains its significance by
contrast with the other, so that its meaning is relative, not absolute. A female may therefore be defined as lacking male features or a male as lacking female traits. In addition,
each set of opposites has been arranged hierarchically; speech, for instance, is considered
more immediate and therefore closer to reality than writing and therefore speech is the
privileged member of the set of speech/writing. These pairings are social constructs and
form part of our way of thinking, even if they do not necessarily reflect reality.

Other strategies for undermining the stability of texts are to see how they have
"gaps," missing pieces of information, or words with several meanings and connotations
that therefore "de-center" the meaning of the texts. Although a poem may seem to mean
one thing when our habitual, formalistic reading strategies are applied to it, it can be
shown to have a completely different meaning as well. Additional readings will yield still
other meanings. The text is therefore said to deconstruct itself as the reading strategies
applied to it are merely pointing out contradictory elements that inhere in the nature of
language itself.

Whereas formalist critics aim at resolving contradictions and ambiguities to form
a unified literary work, deconstructionists aim to find disunity and disruptions in

the language of a text. The typical deconstructionist strategy is to start with a standard formalistic reading of a text and then undermine that interpretation in order to yield a new one. The deconstructionist does not deny that interpretations are possible, only that there is no basis for appealing to final, absolute ones. Deconstruction has yielded some new, imaginative readings of canonical literature. Some critics of deconstruction argue that the "initial" formalistic readings of the deconstructionist strategy are the most rewarding and that often deconstructionist interpretations are incoherent.

### Example: Hawthorne's "Young Goodman Brown"

There are many uncertainties in the details of "Young Goodman Brown." If one starts with the stranger on the path, one might conclude that he could be Brown's father because he recognizes Brown immediately and speaks to him jovially. On the other hand, the stranger could be the devil (he is recognized as such by Goody Cloyse) because of his wriggling walking stick. After disappearing, the stranger also takes on the characteristics of an omniscient cult leader and seer because at the satanic celebration he knows all the secret sins committed by Brown's neighbors and the community of greater New England. Additionally, he might represent a perverted conscience whose aim is to mislead and befuddle people by steering them into the holier-than-thou judgmental attitude that Brown adopts. This method would be truly diabolical—to use religion in order to bring people to their own damnation. That the stranger is an evil force is therefore clear, but the pathways of his evil are not as clear. He seems to work his mission of damnation by reaching the souls of persons like Goodman Brown through means ordinarily attributed to conscience. If the stranger represents a satanic conscience, what are we to suppose that Hawthorne is asserting about what is considered real conscience?

## Reader-Response

The **reader-response critical approach** is rooted in *phenomenology*, a branch of philosophy that deals with the understanding of how things appear. The phenomenological idea of knowledge is based on the separation of the reality of our thoughts from the reality of the world. Our quest for truth is to be found not in the external world itself but rather in our mental *perception* and interpretation of externals. All that we human beings can know—actual *knowledge*—is our collective and personal understanding of the world and our conclusions about it.

As a consequence of the phenomenological concept, reader-response theory holds that the reader is a necessary third party in the author-text-reader relationship that constitutes the literary work. The work, in other words, is not fully created until readers make a *transaction* with it by assimilating it and *actualizing* it in the light of their own knowledge and experience. The representative questions of the theory are these: What does this work mean to me, in my present intellectual and moral makeup? How can the work improve my understanding and widen my insights? How can my increasing understanding help me understand the work more deeply? The theory is that the free interchange or transaction that such questions bring about leads toward interest and growth so that readers can assimilate literary works and accept them as parts of their lives and as parts of the civilization in which they live.

As an initial way of reading, the reader-response method may be personal and anecdotal. In addition, by stressing response rather than interpretation, one of the leading exponents of the method (Stanley Fish) has raised the extreme question about whether texts, by themselves, have objective identity. These aspects have been cited as both a shortcoming and an inconsequentiality of the method.

It is therefore important to stress that the reader-response theory is *open*. It permits beginning readers to bring their own personal reactions to literature, but it also aims to increase their discipline and skill. The more that readers bring to literature through their interests and disciplined studies, the more "competent" and comprehensive their "transactions" will be. It is possible, for example, to explain the structure of a work not according to commonly recognized categories such as exposition and climax but rather according to the personal reactions of disciplined readers. The contention is that structure, like other topics of study such as tone or the comprehension of figurative language, refers to the clearly definable responses of readers "transacting" with works. By such means, literature is subject not only to outward and objective analysis but also to inward and psychological responses.

The reader-response approach thus lends an additional dimension to the critical awareness of literature. If literary works imply that readers should possess special knowledge in fields such as art, politics, science, philosophy, religion, or morality, then disciplined readers will seek out such knowledge and use it in developing their responses. Also, because students experience many similar intellectual and cultural disciplines, it is logical to conclude that responses will tend not to diverge but to coalesce; agreements result not from personal but from cultural similarities. The reader-response theory, then, can and should be an avenue toward informed and detailed understanding of literature, but the initial emphasis is the *transaction* that readers make with literary works.

### Example: Hawthorne's "Young Goodman Brown"

"Young Goodman Brown" is worrisome because it shows so disturbingly that good intentions may cause harmful results. I think that a person with too high a set of expectations is ripe for disillusionment, just as Goodman Brown is. When people don't measure up to this person's standard of perfection, they can be thrown aside as though they are worthless. They may be good people, but whatever past mistakes they have made make it impossible for the person with high expectations to endure them. Goodman Brown makes the same kind of misjudgment, expecting perfection and turning sour when he learns about flaws. It is not that he is not a good man, because he is shown at the start as a person of belief and stability. He uncritically accepts his nightmare revelation that everyone else is evil, however (including his parents), and he finally distrusts everyone because of this baseless suspicion. He cannot look at his neighbors without avoiding them like an "anathema," and he turns away from his own wife "without a greeting" (paragraph 70). Brown's problem is that he equates being human with being unworthy. By such a distorted standard of judgment, all of us fail, and that is what makes the story so disturbing.

# Appendix B

## MLA Recommendations for Documenting Sources

Fiction, Poetry, and Drama

This appendix provides general guidelines for making source citations. For general information on citation recommendations by the Modern Language Association (MLA), see the *MLA Handbook for Writers of Research Papers*, 7th ed. (New York: MLA, 2009).

The following examples show the formats you are likely to use most often, both for nonelectronic (print) and electronic references.

### Citing Nonelectronic (Print) Sources

**Book by One author**

Fitzgerald, F. Scott. *The Great Gatsby*. New York: Scribners, 1925. Print.

**Book with No Author Listed**

*The Pictorial History of the Guitar*. New York: Random, 1992. Print.

**Book by Two (or Three) Authors**

Clemens, Samuel L., and Charles Dudley Warner. *The Gilded Age: A Tale of Today*. Hartford: American, 1874. Print.

**Book by Four or More Authors**

Guerin, Wilfred L., Earle Labor, Lee Morgan, Jeanne C. Reesman, and John R. Willingham. *A Handbook of Critical Approaches to Literature*. New York: Oxford UP, 2004. Print

or

Guerin, Wilfred L., et al. *A Handbook of Critical Approaches to Literature*. New York: Oxford UP, 2004. Print.

## Citing a Work in an Anthology

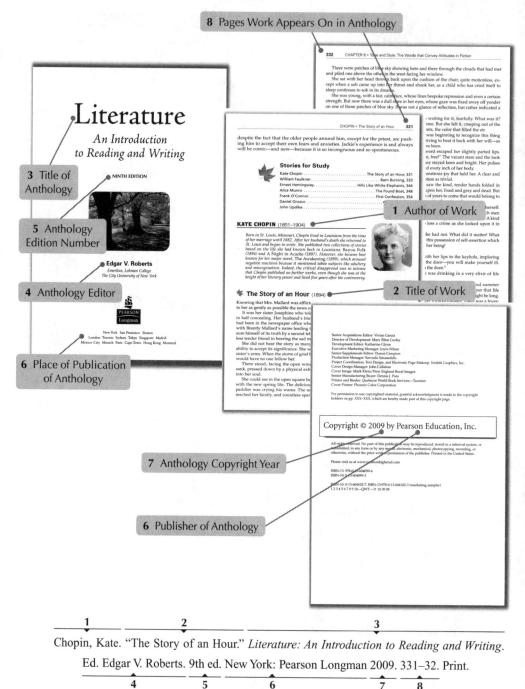

**8** Pages Work Appears On in Anthology

**3** Title of Anthology

**5** Anthology Edition Number

**4** Anthology Editor

**6** Place of Publication of Anthology

**7** Anthology Copyright Year

**6** Publisher of Anthology

**1** Author of Work

**2** Title of Work

Chopin, Kate. "The Story of an Hour." *Literature: An Introduction to Reading and Writing*. Ed. Edgar V. Roberts. 9th ed. New York: Pearson Longman 2009. 331–32. Print.

### Two Books by the Same Author

Reynolds, David S. *Beneath the American Renaissance.* Cambridge: Harvard UP, 1988. Print.

———. *Walt Whitman's America: A Cultural Biography.* New York: Knopf, 1995. Print.

### Book with an Editor

Scharnhorst, Gary, ed. *Selected Letters of Bret Harte.* Norman: U of Oklahoma P, 1997. Print.

### Book with Two Editors

Dionne, Craig, and Steve Mentz, eds. *Rogues and Early Modern English Culture.* Ann Arbor: U of Michigan P, 2004. Print.

### Book with an Author and an Editor

De Quille, Dan. *The Fighting Horse of the Stanislaus: Stories and Essays by Dan De Quille.* Ed. Lawrence I. Berkove. Iowa City: U of Iowa P, 1990. Print.

### Translated Book

Cervantes Saavedra, Miguel de. *Don Quixote de la Mancha.* Trans. Charles Jarvis. New York: Oxford UP, 1999. Print.

### Long Poem Published as a Book

Homer. *The Odyssey.* Trans. Robert Fitzgerald. New York: Vintage, 1990. Print.

### Collection of Poetry Published as a Book

Mueller, Lisel. *Alive Together: New and Selected Poems.* Baton Rouge: Louisiana State UP, 1996. Print.

### Literary Work in an Anthology

Chopin, Kate. "The Storm." *Fiction 100: An Anthology of Short Fiction.* 10th ed. Ed. James H. Pickering. Upper Saddle River: Pearson, 2004. 226–29. Print.

### Introduction, Preface, Foreword, or Afterword in a Book

Pryse, Marjorie. Introduction. *The Country of the Pointed Firs and Other Stories.* By Sarah Orne Jewett. New York: Norton, 1981. v–xix. Print.

**Article in a Reference Book**

Gerber, Phillip. "Naturalism." *The Encyclopedia of American Literature.* Ed.
Steven Serafin. New York: Continuum, 1999. 808–809. Print.

**Article in a Journal with Continuous Paging**

Rhodes, Chip. "Satire in Romanian Literature." *Humor* 8 (1995): 275–86.
Print.

**Article in a Journal That Pages Each Issue Separately**

Kruse, Horst. "The Motif of the Flattened Corpse." *Studies in American Humor*
4 (Spring, 1997): 47–53. Print.

**Signed Book Review**

Bird, John. Rev. of *The Singular Mark Twain*, by Fred Kaplan. *Mark Twain
Annual* 2 (2004): 57–61. Print.

**Unsigned Book Review**

Rev. of *Canons by Consensus: Critical Trends and American Literature
Anthologies*, by Joseph Csicsila. *Essays in Arts and Sciences* 24 (2000):
69–74. Print.

**Article in a Newspaper**

Albom, Mitch. "Longing for Another Slice of Dorm Pizza." *Detroit Free Press* 3
Apr. 2005: C1. Print.

**Editorial**

"Death Penalty Debate Finally Produces Useful Result." Editorial. *USA Today* 22
June, 2005: A15. Print.

**Letter to the Editor**

Mulder, Sara. Letter. *New York Times* 27 Sept. 2005, late ed., sec. 2: 5. Print.

**Article in a Magazine**

McDermott, John R. "The Famous Moustache That Was." *Life* 20 Dec. 1968:
53–56. Print.

### Article in an Encyclopedia

"Afghanistan." *Encyclopaedia Britannica. 2009 Student and Home Edition.* Chicago: Encyclopaedia Britannica. 2009. Print.

### Dictionary Entry

"Apricot." *The American Heritage Dictionary of the English Language.* 4th ed. 2000. Print.

### Government Publication

United States. Cong. Joint Committee on the Investigation of Land Use in the Midwest. *Hearings.* 105th Cong., 2nd sess. 4 vols. Washington GPO, 1997. Print.

### Lecture

Kaston Tange, Andrea. "The Importance of American Literature." Literature 100 class lecture. Eastern Michigan University, 5 Nov. 2002. Lecture.

### Letter

Hosko, John. Letter to the author. 23 Sept. 2000.

### Email

Judd, Jacob. Message to the author. 19 May 2009. E-mail.

### Interview

Stipe, Michael. Personal interview. 10 Nov. 2004.

### Film

*Napoleon Dynamite.* Dir. Jared Hess. Fox Searchlight, 2004. Film.

### Television Program

"The Parking Garage." *Seinfeld.* NBC. WDIV, Detroit, 23 July 1994. Television.

### Sound Recording

Strauss, Richard. *Vier letzte Lieder (Four Last Songs). Tod und Verklärung. Metamorphosen.* Cond. Herbert von Karajan. Perf. Gundula Janowitz. Rec. Nov. 1972, Aug. 1969. Musical Heritage Society, 1997. CD.

**Song on a Recording**

Graham, Susan. "Le spectre de la rose." By Hector Berlioz. *Susan Graham,*
*Berlioz, Les Nuits D'été.* London, 1997. CD.

**Music Video**

Outkast. "Hey Ya." *Speakerboxxx/The Love Below.* Dir. Bryan Barber. La Face,
2003. Music video.

## Citing Electronic Sources

Both students and instructors can now take advantage of the technology available
to assist in research. While many libraries offer varied databases that enable researchers to locate information easily, the main thrust of technology is now the
World Wide Web. At one time it was necessary, in the search of electronic sources,
to type the letters, numbers, symbols, dots, underlines, and spaces. That is no longer
true. Through the use of various search engines, such as Google and Yahoo!, you
simply need to enter the name of an author, a title, or a topic, upon which you will
be linked to a host of resources from all over the world—home pages of specific authors, literary organizations, and works on various topics by contemporary writers.
You'll find a good deal of what you're searching for at the touch of your keys. As you
perform your search, electronic references will appear on your screen with the proper
uniform resource locators (URL) intact, and as a result you may conveniently ignore
the basically unreadable collections of letters, periods, and signs contained in each
URL. Often, you may rely on entering just a few words in your search, and your
search engine will turn up an entire address, with all the dots and other symbols in the
correct order.

   An important caveat is that many sources still remain in printed journals and mag-
azines that may be or, more probably, may not be on the Web. To make your searches
thorough, therefore, *you must never neglect to search for printed information.*

### *MLA Style Guidelines for Electronic Sources*

Many of the guidelines that the MLA has authorized for the citation of electronic sources
overlap with the MLA recommendations for printed sources, but to avoid ambiguity, a
number of recommendations bear repetition. Electronic materials are to be document-
ed in basically the same style as printed sources. According to the seventh edition of the
*MLA Handbook,* which illustrates virtually all the situations you could ever possibly encounter, the following items need to be included if they are available. Because a number
of word-processing programs now support the use of italics, you can routinely use italics in your citations of electronic sources.

   1. The name of the author, editor, compiler, or translator of the source (if available and
      relevant), last name first, followed by an abbreviation, such as *ed.,* if appropriate.

2. If there is no author listed in the source, you should list the title first: the title of a poem, short story, article, or similar short work within a scholarly project, database, or periodical (in quotation marks); or the title of a posting to a discussion list or forum (taken from the subject line and enclosed by quotation marks), concluded by the phrase "Online posting."

3. The title of a book, italicized.

4. The name of the editor, compiler, or translator of the text (if relevant and if not cited earlier), preceded by (not followed by) any necessary abbreviations, such as *Ed.*

5. Publication information for any printed version of the source.

6. The title of the scholarly project, database, periodical, or professional or personal site, italicized; or, for a professional or personal site with no title, a description such as "Home Page."

7. The name of the editor of the scholarly project or database (if available).

8. The version number of the source (if not part of the title) or, for a journal, the volume number, issue number, or other identifying number. All numbers should be in Arabic, not Roman, numerals.

9. The date of publication or posting that you find in your source. Sometimes the original date is no longer available because it has been replaced with an update; if so, cite that. Dates should be arranged by (a) day of the month, (b) month (the names of longer months may be abbreviated), and (c) year.

10. For a work from a subscription service, the name of the service (and name, city, and state abbreviation if the subscriber is a library).

11. For a posting to a discussion list or forum, the name of the list or forum.

12. The number range or total number of pages, paragraphs, or other sections, if they are numbered. If you do your own numbering, include your numbers within square brackets [ ], and be sure to indicate what you have numbered.

13. The name of any institution or organization sponsoring or associated with the Web site.

14. The date when you consulted the source. If you have looked at the site a number of times, include the most recent date of use. The principle here is that the date immediately before the uniform resource locator (URL) will mark the last time you used the source.

15. The electronic address or URL of the source in angle brackets < >. Many programs now automatically include the angle brackets. If the URL is too long to fit on one line, it should be divided at a slash (/) if possible—do not introduce hyphenations into the URL as these may be mistaken for actual significant characters in that address.

## Book

Shaw, Bernard. *Pygmalion*. 1916, 1999. Bartleby Archive. Web. 10 July 2009.
<http://www.bartleby.com/138/>

## Poem

Carroll, Lewis. *The Hunting of the Snark*. 1876. *Literature.org*. Web. 10 July 2009.
< http://www.literature.org/authors/carroll-lewis/the-hunting-of-the-snark/>

**Play**

Shakespeare, William. *Hamlet*. ca. 1601. Project Gutenberg. Web. 10 July 2009.
<http://www.gutenberg.org/etext/1524>

**Journal Article**

Hart, D. Alexis. "Creating a Canvas of Knowledge: An Interview with Larry
Sanger." *Kairos* 13.2 (Spring 2009). Multiple Sections. Web. 10 July 2009.
<http://kairos.technorhetoric.net/13.2/interviews/hart/ index.html >

**Magazine Article**

Playbill Arts Staff. "Photo Update: DiDonato and Wheelchair Go On With the
Show." *Playbillarts.com* July 8, 2009. Web. 10 July 2009.
<http://www.playbillarts.com/features/article/8048.html>

**Posting to a Discussion List**

van Veen, Johan. "North German Music of the 17th Century." Online posting.
Google Groups. 8 June 2009. Web. 10 July 2009. <http://groups.google
.com/group/alt.music.j-s-bach/ browse_thread/thread/e6469cd684b3747d#>

**Scholarly Project**

*Voice of the Shuttle: Web Site for Humanities Research*. Ed. Alan Liu. 10 July 2009.
U of California Santa Barbara. Web. 10 July 2009. < http://vos.ucsb.edu/>

**Professional Site**

*NobelMuseum*. The Nobel Foundation. 2009. Web. 10 July 2009.
<http://www.nobelmuseum.se/zino.aspx?lan=en-us>

**Personal Site**

Barrett, Dan. *The Gentle Giant Home Page*. 25 April 2009. Web. 10 July 2009.
<http://blazemonger.com/GG/Gentle_Giant_Home_Page>

# Appendix C

## Works Used for References and Illustrative Essays

## Plays

## STORIES

## Kate Chopin (1851–1904)

### *The Story of an Hour* (1894)

Knowing that Mrs. Mallard was afflicted with a heart trouble, great care was taken to break to her as gently as possible the news of her husband's death.

It was her sister Josephine who told her, in broken sentences: veiled hints that revealed in half concealing. Her husband's friend Richards was there, too, near her. It was he who had been in the newspaper office when intelligence of the railroad disaster was received, with Brently Mallard's name leading the list of "killed." He had only taken the time to assure himself of its truth by a second telegram, and had hastened to forestall any less careful, less tender friend in bearing the sad message.

She did not hear the story as many women have heard the same, with a paralyzed inability to accept its significance. She wept at once, with sudden, wild abandonment, in her sister's arms. When the storm of grief had spent itself she went away to her room alone. She would have no one follow her.

There stood, facing the open window, a comfortable, roomy armchair. Into this she sank, pressed down by a physical exhaustion that haunted her body and seemed to reach into her soul.

5 She could see in the open square before her house the tops of trees that were all aquiver with the new spring life. The delicious breath of rain was in the air. In the street below a

peddler was crying his wares. The notes of a distant song which some one was singing reached her faintly, and countless sparrows were twittering in the eaves.

There were patches of blue sky showing here and there through the clouds that had met and piled one above the other in the west facing her window.

She sat with her head thrown back upon the cushion of the chair, quite motionless, except when a sob came up into her throat and shook her, as a child who has cried itself to sleep continues to sob in its dreams.

She was young, with a fair, calm face, whose lines bespoke repression and even a certain strength. But now there was a dull stare in her eyes, whose gaze was fixed away off yonder on one of those patches of blue sky. It was not a glance of reflection, but rather indicated a suspension of intelligent thought.

There was something coming to her and she was waiting for it, fearfully. What was it? She did not know; it was too subtle and elusive to name. But she felt it, creeping out of the sky, reaching toward her through the sounds, the scents, the color that filled the air.

Now her bosom rose and fell tumultuously. She was beginning to recognize this thing     10
that was approaching to possess her, and she was striving to beat it back with her will—as powerless as her two white slender hands would have been.

When she abandoned herself a little whispered word escaped her slightly parted lips. She said it over and over under her breath: "free, free, free!" The vacant stare and the look of terror that had followed it went from her eyes. They stayed keen and bright. Her pulses beat fast, and the coursing blood warmed and relaxed every inch of her body.

She did not stop to ask if it were or were not a monstrous joy that held her. A clear and exalted perception enabled her to dismiss the suggestion as trivial.

She knew that she would weep again when she saw the kind, tender hands folded in death; the face that had never looked save with love upon her, fixed and gray and dead. But she saw beyond that bitter moment a long procession of years to come that would belong to her absolutely. And she opened and spread her arms out to them in welcome.

There would be no one to live for during those coming years; she would live for herself. There would be no powerful will bending hers in that blind persistence with which men and women believe they have a right to impose a private will upon a fellow-creature. A kind intention or a cruel intention made the act seem no less a crime as she looked upon it in that brief moment of illumination.

And yet she had loved him—sometimes. Often she had not. What did it matter! What     15
could love, the unsolved mystery, count for in face of this possession of self assertion which she suddenly recognized as the strongest impulse of her being!

"Free! Body and soul free!" she kept whispering.

Josephine was kneeling before the closed door with her lips to the keyhole, imploring for admission. "Louise, open the door! I beg; open the door—you will make yourself ill. What are you doing, Louise? For heaven's sake open the door."

"Go away. I am not making myself ill." No; she was drinking in a very elixir of life through that open window.

Her fancy was running riot along those days ahead of her. Spring days, and summer days, and all sorts of days that would be her own. She breathed a quick prayer that life might be long. It was only yesterday she had thought with a shudder that life might be long.

She arose at length and opened the door to her sister's importunities. There was a fever-     20
ish triumph in her eyes, and she carried herself unwittingly like a goddess of Victory. She clasped her sister's waist, and together they descended the stairs. Richards stood waiting for them at the bottom.

Some one was opening the front door with a latchkey. It was Brently Mallard who entered, a little travel-stained, composedly carrying his grip-sack and umbrella. He had been far from the scene of accident, and did not even know there had been one. He stood amazed at Josephine's piercing cry: at Richards' quick motion to screen him from the view of his wife.

But Richards was too late.

When the doctors came they said she had died of heart disease—of joy that kills.

## Anita Scott Coleman (1890–1960)

### *Unfinished Masterpieces* (1927)

There are days which stand out clearly like limpid pools beside the dusty road; when your thoughts, crystal clear as water, are pinioned in loveliness like star-points. Solitary days, which come often, if you are given to browsing in fields of past adventure; or rarely, if you are seldom retrospective; and not at all, if you are too greatly concerned with rushing onward to a nebulous future. Days whereupon your experiences glimmer before you waveringly like motion-pictures and the people you have known stroll through the lanes of memory, arrayed in vari-colored splendor or in amusing disarray. Days like these are to be revered, for they have their humors and their whimsicalities. Hurry your thoughts and the gathering imageries take flight. Perplexity but makes the lens of introspection blur. And of annoyance beware, for it is an evil vapor that disseminates and drowns the visions in the sea of grim realities. Such days must be cultivated. Scenes for their reception must be set. Cushions perhaps, and warmth of fire. Above all, the warmth of sweet content. Ease and comfort, comfort and ease and moods of receptivity. Then hither, come hither the places and the people we have known, the associations that withstand time's effacements. Backward ho, through the mazes of the past.

STOP! "Why howdy, Dora Johns." Darling playmate of my child-years. With wooly hair a length too short for even pigtails. Mudspatters upon your funny black face. Mudspatters all over your dress and your little black hands mud-spattered too.

Why? What? Come on and see. And lo! I am a child again.

Hand in hand, unmindful of her muddy ones, we skip around the old ramshackle house, back to the furthest corner of an unkempt yard, impervious to the tin cans, the ash-heap, the litter, the clutter that impedes our way, our eyes upon, our thoughts bent upon one small clean-swept corner, where there is mud. More mud and water in a battered tin can. And row after row of mud. No, not mud—not merely mud, but things made out of mud. Row on row, drying in the sun.

5      Carefully, I sit down, doubling up, to be as small as possible, for only this corner where mud things are drying is clean and corners are seldom, if ever, quite large enough. Besides, I must not touch the things made out of mud. If the dried ones fall, they break. If the moist ones are molested, be it with ever so gentle a finger, they lose their shape. Moreover I must not disturb Dora.

Her little hands are busied with the mud. Little molder's fingers are deftly plying their skill. Her child's face is alight. What has splashed her grave child's face with such a light? I wondered. I wonder now. The glitter of brittle talent, a gleam of sterling genius or the glow from artistic fires burning within the soul of a little black child?

Little Dora shaping figures out of mud. Vases and urns, dolls and toys, flying birds and trotting horses, frisking dogs and playing kittens, marvelous things out of mud. Crying aloud as though dealt a blow if one of the dried mud-figures is broken. Working in mud for endless hours, while the neighbor children play. Their hilarious merriment dropping like bombs into the quiet of our clean-swept corner. Deadly missiles seeking to find a mark. The insistent halloes of futile mirth forever bubbling on the other side of a highboard fence. The dividing fence and upon one side the clean-swept corner and the row on row of mud things drying in the sun. And Dora seeming not to heed the seething bubbles upon the other side, shaping, shaping marvelous things out of mud.

Yet, Oh Dora, now that the day is ours, will you not say, "When did the bombs of futile mirth strike their target? When did the tin-cans and the rags and the old ash-heap crowd you out from your clean-swept corner? What rude hand caused the dried mud shapes to fall and break? Who set a ruthless foot in the midst of your damp mud things?" Or were you too plastic, as plastic as your mud? You dare not tell. Only this you can whisper into the mists of our today. You are one of the Master's unfinished shapes which He will some day gather to mold anew into the finished masterpiece.

A lump of mud. Now, there is a sobriquet for you—you funny, funny man. Mr. William Williams. I saw you but once. We chanced to meet in the home of a mutual friend. I thought you so very funny then. Uncouth and very boorish, but ever, when these pageants of the past, these dumb shows of inarticulate folks arise before me upon retrospective days, you appear garbed in the tatters of pathos.

"I am fifty-one years old," you kept repeating. How pitiful those fifty-one years are. You 10 wear a child's simplicity, the sort that is so sad to see upon a man. Fifty-one and penniless. Fifty-one and possessed of naught else but the clothing you wore. Fifty-one and no place on earth you might call home. You confessed to being a vagabond though "bum" was the term you used and you were very proud of your one accomplishment, an ability to avoid all labor.                                                                    •

"I've given no man a full day's honest work in all my fifty-one years," you boasted. "I gambles. I ain't no cotton-pickin' nigger." Your one and only boast after holding life, the fathomless fountain of eternal possibilities, in your possession for fifty-one priceless years.

Nevertheless you have lived and so intensely. You held us against our will. Clustered around you, listening to you talk. Relating clippings as it were from the scrap-book of your life.

Tales of the road, of the only places you knew. Roads leading away from plantations where the cotton waited to be picked by numberless "cotton-pickin' niggers." Roads leading to pool halls and gambling dens. Roads beginning and roads ending in "riding the roads," carrying backward and forward, here and yon through the weird goblin land of the South's black belt.

With a hardened casualness you told stories that revolted and at the same time cheered us with an all sufficing glow of thankfulness that life had spared us the sordidness of yours. Offhandily, you gave us humorous skits that tempered our laughter with wishes that we might know at least a bit of such a droll existence as had been yours. With magical words you painted pictures so sharply they cut scars upon our hearts. You drew others so filled with rollicking delight their gladsomeness was contagious. With the nonchalance of a player shuffling cards you flipped your characters before us, drawn directly from the cesspool of your contacts, and spellbound we listened.

Someone remarked how wonderful you talked and you replied, "Once, I sorter wanted 15 to write books. Once, I uster read a heaps. See times when I was broke and nobody would stake me for a game. I'd lay around and read. I've read the Bible through and through and every Police Gazette I could lay my hands on. Yes, suh, I've read a heap. And I've wished a lot'er times I'd sense enough to write a book."

Lump of mud. Containing the you, the splendid artist in you, the soul of you, the unfinished you in the ungainly lump of you, awaiting the gathering-up to be molded anew into the finished masterpiece.

What a day! Here is my friend at whose fire-side I have lingered beholding Mr. William Williams, great lump of mud. To be sure, she also is an unfinished production. Though it is apparent that the Master had all but done when she slipped from his hands and dropped to earth to lie groping like the rest of us thereon.

Let us sit here together, friend, and enjoy this day.

I shall try to discover what recent gift you have given to the poor the while you are quietly stitching upon the garments, linens and scarlet, with which to clothe your household. Sit here and smile with the welcoming light in your eyes, knowing that your door is open to such as William Williams and Dora Johns, the Dora who is become as the mud beneath one's feet. Kind mistress of the widely opened door where white and black, rich and poor, of whatever caste or creed may enter and find comfort and ease and food and drink.

## Nathaniel Hawthorne (1804–1864)

### *Young Goodman Brown* (1835)

Young Goodman Brown came forth at sunset, into the street of Salem village,° but put his head back, after crossing the threshold, to exchange a parting kiss with his young wife. And Faith, as the wife was aptly named, thrust her own pretty head into the street, letting the wind play with the pink ribbons of her cap, while she called to Goodman Brown.

"Dearest heart," whispered she, softly and rather sadly, when her lips were close to his ear, "prithee, put off your journey until sunrise, and sleep in your own bed tonight. A lone woman is troubled with such dreams and such thoughts, that she's afeared of herself, sometimes. Pray, tarry with me this night, dear husband, of all nights in the year!"

"My love and my Faith," replied young Goodman Brown, "of all nights in the year; this one night must I tarry away from thee. My journey, as thou callest it, forth and back again, must needs be done 'twixt now and sunrise. What, my sweet, pretty wife, dost thou doubt me already, and we but three months married!"

"Then God bless you!" said Faith with the pink ribbons, "and may you find all well, when you come back."

5　"Amen!" cried Goodman Brown. "Say thy prayers, dear Faith, and go to bed at dusk, and no harm will come to thee."

So they parted; and the young man pursued his way, until, being about to turn the corner by the meeting-house, he looked back and saw the head of Faith still peeping after him, with a melancholy air, in spite of her pink ribbons.

---

°*Salem village:* in Massachusetts, about fifteen miles north of Boston. The time of the story is the seventeenth or early eighteenth century.

"Poor little Faith!" thought he, for his heart smote him. "What a wretch am I, to leave her on such an errand! She talks of dreams, too. Methought, as she spoke, there was trouble in her face, as if a dream had warned her what work is to be done tonight. But no, no! 'twould kill her to think it. Well, she's a blessed angel on earth; and after this one night, I'll cling to her skirts and follow her to Heaven."

With this excellent resolve for the future, Goodman Brown felt himself justified in making more haste on his present evil purpose. He had taken a dreary road, darkened by all the gloomiest trees of the forest, which barely stood aside to let the narrow path creep through, and closed immediately behind. It was all as lonely as could be; and there is this peculiarity in such a solitude, that the traveller knows not who may be concealed by the innumerable trunks and the thick boughs overhead; so that, with lonely footsteps, he may yet be passing through an unseen multitude.

"There may be a devilish Indian behind every tree," said Goodman Brown to himself; and he glanced fearfully behind him, as he added, "What if the devil himself should be at my very elbow!"

His head being turned back, he passed a crook of the road, and looking forward 10 again, beheld the figure of a man, in grave and decent attire, seated at the foot of an old tree. He arose at Goodman Brown's approach, and walked onward, side by side with him.

"You are late, Goodman Brown," said he. "The clock of the Old South° was striking, as I came through Boston; and that is full fifteen minutes agone."

"Faith kept me back a while," replied the young man, with a tremor in his voice, caused by the sudden appearance of his companion, though not wholly unexpected.

It was now deep dusk in the forest, and deepest in that part of it where these two were journeying. As nearly as could be discerned, the second traveller was about fifty years old, apparently in the same rank of life as Goodman Brown, and bearing a considerable resemblance to him, though perhaps more in expression than features. Still, they might have been taken for father and son. And yet, though the elder person was as simply clad as the younger, and as simple in manner too, he had an indescribable air of one who knew the world, and would not have felt abashed at the governor's dinner-table, or in King William's* court, were it possible that his affairs should call him thither. But the only thing about him that could be fixed upon as remarkable, was his staff, which bore the likeness of a great black snake, so curiously wrought, that it might almost be seen to twist and wriggle itself like a living serpent. This, of course, must have been an ocular deception, assisted by the uncertain light.

"Come, Goodman Brown!" cried his fellow-traveller, "this is a dull pace for the beginning of a journey. Take my staff, if you are so soon weary."

"Friend," said the other, exchanging his slow pace for a full stop, "having kept covenant 15 by meeting thee here, it is my purpose now to return whence I came. I have scruples, touching the matter thou wot'st of." †

"Sayest thou so?" replied he of the serpent, smiling apart. "Let us walk on, nevertheless, reasoning as we go, and if I convince thee not, thou shalt turn back. We are but a little way in the forest, yet."

---

°*Old South:* The Old South Church, in Boston, is still there.   \*King William: William III was king of England from 1688 to 1701 (the time of the story). William IV was king from 1830 to 1837 (the period when Hawthorne wrote the story).   †*thou wot'st:* you know (thou knowest).

"Too far, too far!" exclaimed the goodman, unconsciously resuming his walk. "My father never went into the woods on such an errand, nor his father before him. We have been a race of honest men and good Christians, since the days of the martyrs.° And shall I be the first of the name of Brown that ever took this path and kept—"

"Such company, thou wouldst say," observed the elder person, interrupting his pause. "Well said, Goodman Brown! I have been as well acquainted with your family as ever a one among the Puritans; and that's no trifle to say. I helped your grandfather, the constable, when he lashed the Quaker woman so smartly through the streets of Salem. And it was I that brought your father a pitch-pine knot, kindled at my own hearth, to set fire to an Indian village, in King Philip's war.* They were my good friends, both; and many a pleasant walk have we had along this path, and returned merrily after midnight. I would fain be friends with you, for their sake."

"If it be as thou sayest," replied Goodman Brown, "I marvel they never spoke of these matters. Or, verily, I marvel not, seeing that the least rumor of the sort would have driven them from New England. We are a people of prayer, and good works to boot, and abide no such wickedness."

20    "Wickedness or not," said the traveller with twisted staff, "I have a very general acquaintance here in New England. The deacons of many a church have drunk the communion wine with me; the selectmen, of divers towns, make me their chairman; and a majority of the Great and General Court are firm supporters of my interest. The governor and I, too—but these are state secrets."

"Can this be so!" cried Goodman Brown, with a stare of amazement at his undisturbed companion. "Howbeit, I have nothing to do with the governor and council; they have their own ways, and are no rule for a simple husbandman like me. But, were I to go on with thee, how should I meet the eye of that good old man, our minister, at Salem village? Oh, his voice would make me tremble, both Sabbath-day and lecture-day!"

Thus far, the elder traveller had listened with due gravity, but now burst into a fit of irrepressible mirth, shaking himself so violently, that his snakelike staff actually seemed to wriggle in sympathy.

"Ha! ha! ha!" shouted he, again and again; then composing himself, "Well, go on, Goodman Brown, go on; but, prithee, don't kill me with laughing!"

"Well, then, to end the matter at once," said Goodman Brown, considerably nettled, "there is my wife, Faith. It would break her dear little heart; and I'd rather break my own!"

25    "Nay, if that be the case," answered the other, "e'en go thy ways, Goodman Brown. I would not, for twenty old women like the one hobbling before us, that Faith should come to any harm."

As he spoke, he pointed his staff at a female figure on the path, in whom Goodman Brown recognized a very pious and exemplary dame, who had taught him his catechism in youth, and was still his moral and spiritual adviser, jointly with the minister and Deacon Gookin.

---

°*days of the martyrs:* the period of martyrdom of Protestants in England during the reign of Queen Mary (1553–1558).    *King Philip's war:* This war (1675–1676), infamous for the atrocities committed by the New England settlers, resulted in the suppression of Indian tribal life and prepared the way for unlimited settlement of New England by European immigrants. "Philip" was the English name of Chief Metacomet of the Wampanoag tribe.

"A marvel, truly, that Goody° Cloyse should be so far in the wilderness, at nightfall!" said he. "But, with your leave, friend, I shall take a cut through the woods, until we have left this Christian woman behind. Being a stranger to you, she might ask whom I was consorting with, and whither I was going."

"Be it so," said his fellow-traveller. "Betake you to the woods, and let me keep the path."

Accordingly, the young man turned aside, but took care to watch his companion, who advanced softly along the road, until he had come within a staff's length of the old dame. She, meanwhile, was making the best of her way, with singular speed for so aged a woman, and mumbling some indistinct words, a prayer, doubtless, as she went. The traveller put forth his staff, and touched her withered neck with what seemed the serpent's tail.

"The devil!" screamed the pious old lady.                                         30

"Then Goody Cloyse knows her old friend?" observed the traveller, confronting her, and leaning on his writhing stick.

"Ah, forsooth, and is it your worship, indeed?" cried the good dame. "Yea, truly is it, and in the very image of my old gossip,* Goodman Brown, the grandfather of the silly fellow that now is. But, would your worship believe it? My broomstick hath strangely disappeared, stolen, as I suspect, by that unhanged witch, Goody Cory,† and that, too, when I was all anointed with the juice of smallage and cinquefoil and wolf's-bane—"°°

"Mingled with fine wheat and the fat of a new-born babe," said the shape of old Goodman Brown.

"Ah, your worship knows the recipe," cried the old lady, cackling aloud. "So, as I was saying, being all ready for the meeting, and no horse to ride on, I made up my mind to foot it; for they tell me there is a nice young man to be taken into communion tonight. But now your good worship will lend me your arm, and we shall be there in a twinkling."

"That can hardly be," answered her friend. "I will not spare you my arm, Goody Cloyse,  35 but here is my staff, if you will."

So saying, he threw it down at her feet, where, perhaps, it assumed life, being one of the rods which its owner had formerly lent to the Egyptian Magi.** Of this fact, however, Goodman Brown could not take cognizance. He had cast up his eyes in astonishment, and looking down again, beheld neither Goody Cloyse nor the serpentine staff, but his fellow-traveller alone, who waited for him as calmly as if nothing had happened.

"That old woman taught me my catechism!" said the young man; and there was a world of meaning in this simple comment.

They continued to walk onward, while the elder traveller exhorted his companion to make good speed and persevere in the path, discoursing so aptly, that his arguments seemed rather to spring up in the bosom of his auditor, than to be suggested by himself. As they went he plucked a branch of maple, to serve for a walking-stick, and began to strip it of the twigs and little boughs, which were wet with evening dew. The moment his fingers touched them, they became strangely withered and dried up, as with a week's sunshine. Thus the pair proceeded, at a good free pace, until suddenly, in a gloomy hollow of the road, Goodman Brown sat himself down on the stump of a tree, and refused to go any farther.

---

°*Goody:* shortened form of "goodwife," a respectful name for a married woman of low rank. "Goody Cloyse" was one of the women sentenced to execution by Hawthorne's great-grandfather, Judge John Hawthorne. *gossip:* from "good sib" or "good relative." †*Goody Cory:* the name of a woman who was also sentenced to execution by Judge John Hawthorne. °°*smallage and cinquefoil and wolf's-bane:* plants commonly used by witches to make ointments. **lent to the Egyptian Magi:* See Exodus 7:10–12.

"Friend," said he, stubbornly, "my mind is made up. Not another step will I budge on this errand. What if a wretched old woman do choose to go to the devil, when I thought she was going to Heaven! Is that any reason why I should quit my dear Faith, and go after her?"

40          "You will think better of this by and by," said his acquaintance, composedly. "Sit here and rest yourself a while; and when you feel like moving again, there is my staff to help you along."

Without more words, he threw his companion the maple stick, and was as speedily out of sight as if he had vanished into the deepening gloom. The young man sat a few moments by the roadside, applauding himself greatly, and thinking with how clear a conscience he should meet the minister, in his morning walk, nor shrink from the eye of good old Deacon Gookin. And what calm sleep would be his, that very night, which was to have been spent so wickedly, but purely and sweetly now, in the arms of Faith! Amidst these pleasant and praiseworthy meditations, Goodman Brown heard the tramp of horses along the road, and deemed it advisable to conceal himself within the verge of the forest, conscious of the guilty purpose that had brought him thither, though now so happily turned from it.

On came the hoof-tramps and the voices of the riders, two grave old voices, conversing soberly as they drew near. These mingled sounds appeared to pass along the road, within a few yards of the young man's hiding-place; but owing, doubtless, to the depth of the gloom, at that particular spot, neither the travellers nor their steeds were visible. Though their figures brushed the small boughs by the wayside, it could not be seen that they intercepted, even for a moment, the faint gleam from the strip of bright sky, athwart which they must have passed. Goodman Brown alternately crouched and stood on tiptoe, pulling aside the branches, and thrusting forth his head as far as he durst, without discerning so much as a shadow. It vexed him the more, because he could have sworn, were such a thing possible, that he recognized the voices of the minister and Deacon Gookin, jogging° along quietly, as they were wont to do, when bound to some ordination or ecclesiastical council. While yet within hearing, one of the riders stopped to pluck a switch.

"Of the two, reverend Sir," said the voice like the deacon's, "I had rather miss an ordination dinner than tonight's meeting. They tell me that some of our community are to be here from Falmouth and beyond, and others from Connecticut and Rhode Island; besides several of the Indian powwows,* who, after their fashion, know almost as much deviltry as the best of us. Moreover, there is a goodly young woman to be taken into communion."

"Mighty well, Deacon Gookin" replied the solemn old tones of the minister. "Spur up, or we shall be late. Nothing can be done, you know, until I get on the ground."

45          The hoofs clattered again, and the voices, talking so strangely in the empty air, passed on through the forest, where no church had ever been gathered, nor solitary Christian prayed. Whither, then, could these holy men be journeying, so deep into the heathen wilderness? Young Goodman Brown caught hold of a tree, for support, being ready to sink down on the ground, faint and over-burthened with the heavy sickness of his heart. He looked up to the sky, doubting whether there really was a Heaven above him. Yet, there was the blue arch, and the stars brightening in it.

---

°*jogging:* riding a horse at a slow trot; not to be confused with the current meaning of "jogging," which refers to running slowly on foot.    *powwows:* a Narragansett Indian word describing a ritual ceremony of dancing, incantation, and magic.

"With Heaven above, and Faith below, I will yet stand firm against the devil!" cried Goodman Brown.

While he still gazed upward, into the deep arch of the firmament, and had lifted his hands to pray, a cloud, though no wind was stirring, hurried across the zenith, and hid the brightening stars. The blue sky was still visible, except directly overhead, where this black mass of cloud was sweeping swiftly northward. Aloft in the air, as if from the depths of the cloud, came a confused and doubtful sound of voices. Once, the listener fancied that he could distinguish the accents of town's people of his own, men and women, both pious and ungodly, many of whom he had met at the communion-table, and had seen others rioting at the tavern. The next moment, so indistinct were the sounds, he doubted whether he had heard aught but the murmur of the old forest, whispering without a wind. Then came a stronger swell of those familiar tones, heard daily in the sunshine, at Salem village, but never, until now, from a cloud at night. There was one voice, of a young woman, uttering lamentations, yet with an uncertain sorrow, and entreating for some favor, which, perhaps, it would grieve her to obtain. And all the unseen multitude, both saints and sinners, seemed to encourage her onward.

"Faith!" shouted Goodman Brown, in a voice of agony and desperation; and the echoes of the forest mocked him, crying—"Faith! Faith!" as if bewildered wretches were seeking her, all through the wilderness.

The cry of grief, rage, and terror was yet piercing the night, when the unhappy husband held his breath for a response. There was a scream, drowned immediately in a louder murmur of voices fading into far-off laughter, as the dark cloud swept away, leaving the clear and silent sky above Goodman Brown. But something fluttered lightly down through the air, and caught on the branch of a tree. The young man seized it and beheld a pink ribbon.

"My Faith is gone!" cried he, after one stupefied moment. "There is no good on earth, 50 and sin is but a name. Come, devil! for to thee is this world given."

And maddened with despair, so that he laughed loud and long, did Goodman Brown grasp his staff and set forth again, at such a rate, that he seemed to fly along the forest path, rather than to walk or run. The road grew wilder and drearier, and more faintly traced, and vanished at length, leaving him in the heart of the dark wilderness, still rushing onward, with the instinct that guides mortal man to evil. The whole forest was peopled with frightful sounds; the creaking of the trees, the howling of wild beasts, and the yell of Indians; while, sometimes, the wind tolled like a distant church bell, and sometimes gave a broad roar around the traveller, as if all Nature were laughing him to scorn. But he was himself the chief horror of the scene, and shrank not from its other horrors.

"Ha! ha! ha!" roared Goodman Brown, when the wind laughed at him. "Let us hear which will laugh loudest! Think not to frighten me with your deviltry! Come witch, come wizard, come Indian powwow, come devil himself! and here comes Goodman Brown. You may as well fear him as he fear you!"

In truth, all through the haunted forest, there could be nothing more frightful than the figure of Goodman Brown. On he flew, among the black pines, brandishing his staff with frenzied gestures, now giving vent to an inspiration of horrid blasphemy, and now shouting forth such laughter, as set all the echoes of the forest laughing like demons around him. The fiend in his own shape is less hideous than when he rages in the breast of man. Thus sped the demoniac on his course, until, quivering among the trees, he saw a red light before him, as when the felled trunks and branches of a clearing have been set on fire, and throw up their lurid blaze against the sky, at the hour of midnight. He paused, in a lull of the tempest that had driven him onward, and heard the swell of what seemed a hymn, rolling solemnly from a distance, with the weight of many voices. He knew the tune. It was a familiar one in the choir of the village meeting-house. The verse died heavily away, and was lengthened by a chorus, not of human voices, but of all the sounds of the benighted wilderness, pealing in awful harmony together. Goodman Brown cried out; and his cry was lost to his own ear, by its unison with the cry of the desert.

In the interval of silence, he stole forward, until the light glared full upon his eyes. At one extremity of an open space, hemmed in by the dark wall of the forest, arose a rock, bearing some rude, natural resemblance either to an altar or a pulpit, and surrounded by four blazing pines, their tops aflame, their stems untouched, like candles at an evening meeting. The mass of foliage, that had overgrown the summit of the rock, was all on fire, blazing high into the night, and fitfully illuminating the whole field. Each pendent twig and leafy festoon was in a blaze. As the red light arose and fell, a numerous congregation alternately shone forth, then disappeared in shadow, and again grew, as it were, out of the darkness, peopling the heart of the solitary woods at once.

55   "A grave and dark-clad company!" quoth Goodman Brown.

In truth, they were such. Among them, quivering to-and-fro, between gloom and splendor, appeared faces that would be seen, next day, at the council-board of the province, and others which, Sabbath after Sabbath, looked devoutly heavenward, and benignantly over the crowded pews, from the holiest pulpits in the land. Some affirm that the lady of the governor was there. At least, there were high dames well known to her, and wives of honored husbands, and widows a great multitude, and ancient maidens, all of excellent repute, and fair young girls, who trembled lest their mothers should espy them. Either the sudden gleams of light, flashing over the obscure field, bedazzled Goodman Brown, or he recognized a score of the church members of Salem village, famous for their especial sanctity. Good old Deacon Gookin had arrived, and waited at the skirts of that venerable saint, his reverend pastor. But, irreverently consorting with these grave, reputable, and pious people, these elders of the church, these chaste dames and dewy virgins, there were men of dissolute lives and women of spotted fame, wretches given over to all mean and filthy vice, and suspected even of horrid crimes. It was strange to see, that the good shrank not from the wicked, nor were the sinners abashed by the saints. Scattered, also, among their pale-faced enemies, were the Indian priests, or powwows, who had often scared their native forest with more hideous incantations than any known to English witchcraft.

"But, where is Faith?" thought Goodman Brown; and, as hope came into his heart, he trembled.

Another verse of the hymn arose, a slow and mournful strain, such as the pious love, but joined to words which expressed all that our nature can conceive of sin, and darkly hinted at far more. Unfathomable to mere mortals is the lore of fiends. Verse after verse was sung, and still the chorus of the desert swelled between, like the deepest tone of a mighty organ. And, with the final peal of that dreadful anthem, there came a sound, as if the roaring wind, the rushing streams, the howling beasts, and every other voice of the unconverted wilderness were mingling and according with the voice of guilty man, in homage to the prince of all. The four blazing pines threw up a loftier flame, and obscurely discovered shapes and visages of horror on the smoke-wreaths, above the impious assembly. At the same moment, the fire on the rock shot redly forth, and formed a glowing arch above its base, where now appeared a figure. With reverence be it spoken, the apparition bore no slight similitude, both in garb and manner, to some grave divine of the New England churches.

"Bring forth the converts!" cried a voice, that echoed through the field and rolled into the forest.

At the word, Goodman Brown stepped forth from the shadow of the trees, and ap-  60
proached the congregation, with whom he felt a loathful brotherhood, by the sympathy of
all that was wicked in his heart. He could have well-nigh sworn, that the shape of his own
dead father beckoned him to advance, looking downward from a smoke-wreath, while a
woman, with dim features of despair, threw out her hand to warn him back. Was it his
mother? But he had no power to retreat one step, nor to resist, even in thought, when the
minister and good old Deacon Gookin seized his arms, and led him to the blazing rock.
Thither came also the slender form of a veiled female, led between Goody Cloyse, that
pious teacher of the catechism, and Martha Carrier, who had received the devil's promise
to be queen of hell. A rampant hag was she! And there stood the proselytes, beneath the
canopy of fire.

"Welcome, my children," said the dark figure, "to the communion of your race! Ye have
found, thus young, your nature and your destiny. My children, look behind you!"

They turned; and flashing forth, as it were, in a sheet of flame, the fiend-worshippers were
seen; the smile of welcome gleamed darkly on every visage.

"There," resumed the sable form, "are all whom ye have reverenced from youth. Ye
deemed them holier than yourselves, and shrank from your own sin, contrasting it with their
lives of righteousness and prayerful aspirations heavenward. Yet, here are they all, in my wor-
shipping assembly! This night it shall be granted you to know their secret deeds; how hoary-
bearded elders of the church have whispered wanton words to the young maids of their
households; how many a woman, eager for widow's weeds, has given her husband a drink
at bedtime, and let him sleep his last sleep in her bosom; how beardless youths have made
haste to inherit their father's wealth; and how fair damsels—blush not, sweet ones!—have
dug little graves in the garden, and bidden me, the sole guest, to an infant's funeral. By the
sympathy of your human hearts for sin, ye shall scent out all the places—whether in church,
bed-chamber, street, field, or forest—where crime has been committed, and shall exult to
behold the whole earth one stain of guilt, one mighty blood-spot. Far more than this! It shall
be yours to penetrate, in every bosom, the deep mystery of sin, the fountain of all wicked
arts, and which inexhaustibly supplies more evil impulses than human power—than my
power, at its utmost!—can make manifest in deeds. And now, my children, look upon each
other."

They did so; and, by the blaze of the hell-kindled torches, the wretched man beheld his
Faith, and the wife her husband, trembling before that unhallowed altar.

"Lo! there ye stand, my children," said the figure, in a deep and solemn tone, almost  65
sad, with its despairing awfulness, as if his once angelic nature° could yet mourn for our
miserable race. Depending upon one another's hearts, ye had still hoped that virtue were
not all a dream! Now are ye undeceived!—Evil is the nature of mankind. Evil must be your
only happiness. Welcome, again, my children, to the communion of your race!"

"Welcome!" repeated the fiend-worshippers, in one cry of despair and triumph.

And there they stood, the only pair, as it seemed, who were yet hesitating on the verge
of wickedness, in this dark world. A basin was hollowed, naturally, in the rock. Did it contain water, reddened by the lurid light? or was it blood? or, perchance, a liquid flame?
Herein did the Shape of Evil dip his hand, and prepare to lay the mark of baptism upon
their foreheads, that they might be partakers of the mystery of sin, more conscious of the
secret guilt of others, both in deed and thought, than they could now be of their own.

---

°*once angelic nature:* Lucifer ("light carrier"), another name for the Devil, led the traditional revolt of the
angels and was thrown into hell as his punishment. See Isaiah 14:12–15.

The husband cast one look at his pale wife, and Faith at him. What polluted wretches would the next glance show them to each other, shuddering alike at what they disclosed and what they saw!

"Faith! Faith!" cried the husband. "Look up to Heaven, and resist the Wicked One!"

Whether Faith obeyed, he knew not. Hardly had he spoken, when he found himself amid calm night and solitude, listening to a roar of the wind, which died heavily away through the forest. He staggered against the rock, and felt it chill and damp, while a hanging twig, that had been all on fire, besprinkled his cheek with the coldest dew.

70    The next morning, young Goodman Brown came slowly into the street of Salem village staring around him like a bewildered man. The good old minister was taking a walk along the grave-yard, to get an appetite for breakfast and meditate his sermon, and bestowed a blessing, as he passed, on Goodman Brown. He shrank from the venerable saint, as if to avoid an anathema. Old Deacon Gookin was at domestic worship, and the holy words of his prayer were heard through the open window. "What God doth the wizard pray to?" quoth Goodman Brown. Goody Cloyse, that excellent old Christian, stood in the early sunshine, at her own lattice, catechising a little girl, who had brought her a pint of morning's milk. Goodman Brown snatched away the child, as from the grasp of the fiend himself. Turning the corner by the meetinghouse, he spied the head of Faith, with the pink ribbons, gazing anxiously forth, and bursting into such joy at the sight of him that she skipt along the street, and almost kissed her husband before the whole village. But Goodman Brown looked sternly and sadly into her face, and passed on without a greeting.

Had Goodman Brown fallen asleep in the forest, and only dreamed a wild dream of a witch-meeting?

Be it so, if you will. But, alas! it was a dream of evil omen for young Goodman Brown. A stern, a sad, a darkly meditative, a distrustful, if not a desperate man did he become, from the night of that fearful dream. On the Sabbath day, when the congregation were singing a holy psalm, he could not listen, because an anthem of sin rushed loudly upon his ear, and drowned all the blessed strain. When the minister spoke from the pulpit, with power and fervid eloquence, and with his hand on the open Bible, of the sacred truths of our religion, and of saint-like lives and triumphant deaths, and of future bliss or misery unutterable, then did Goodman Brown turn pale, dreading lest the roof should thunder down upon the gray blasphemer and his hearers. Often, awaking suddenly at midnight, he shrank from the bosom of Faith, and at morning or eventide, when the family knelt down in prayer, he scowled, and muttered to himself, and gazed sternly at his wife, and turned away. And when he had lived long, and was borne to his grave, a hoary corpse, followed by Faith, an aged woman, and children and grandchildren, a goodly procession, besides neighbors not a few, they carved no hopeful verse upon his tombstone; for his dying hour was gloom.

Shirley Jackson (1919–1965)

*The Lottery* (1948)

The morning of June 27th was clear and sunny, with the fresh warmth of a full summer day; the flowers were blossoming profusely and the grass was richly green. The people of the village began to gather in the square, between the post office and the bank, around ten o'clock; in some towns there were so many people that the lottery took two days and had to be started on June 26th, but in this village, where there were only about three hundred people, the whole lottery took less than two hours, so it could begin at ten o'clock in the morning and still be through in time to allow the villagers to get home for noon dinner.

The children assembled first, of course. School was recently over for the summer, and the feeling of liberty sat uneasily on most of them; they tended to gather together quietly for a while before they broke into boisterous play, and their talk was still of the classroom and the teacher, of books and reprimands. Bobby Martin had already stuffed his pockets full of stones, and the other boys soon followed his example, selecting the smoothest and roundest stones; Bobby and Harry Jones and Dickie Delacroix—the villagers pronounced this name "Dellacroy"—eventually made a great pile of stones in one corner of the square and guarded it against the raids of the other boys. The girls stood aside, talking among themselves, looking over their shoulders at the boys, and the very small children rolled in the dust or clung to the hands of their older brothers or sisters.

Soon the men began to gather, surveying their own children, speaking of planting and rain, tractors and taxes. They stood together, away from the pile of stones in the corner, and their jokes were quiet and they smiled rather than laughed. The women, wearing faded house dresses and sweaters, came shortly after their menfolk. They greeted one another and exchanged bits of gossip as they went to join their husbands. Soon the women, standing by their husbands, began to call to their children, and the children came reluctantly, having to be called four or five times. Bobby Martin ducked under his mother's grasping hand and ran, laughing, back to the pile of stones. His father spoke up sharply, and Bobby came quickly and took his place between his father and his oldest brother.

The lottery was conducted—as were the square dances, the teen-age club, the Halloween program—by Mr. Summers, who had time and energy to devote to civic activities. He was a round-faced, jovial man and he ran the coal business, and people were sorry for him, because he had no children and his wife was a scold. When he arrived in the square, carrying the black wooden box, there was a murmur of conversation among the villagers, and he waved and called, "Little late today, folks." The postmaster, Mr. Graves, followed him, carrying a three-legged stool, and the stool was put in the center of the square and Mr. Summers set the black box down on it. The villagers kept their distance, leaving a space between themselves and the stool, and when Mr. Summers said, "Some of you fellows want to give me a hand?" there was a hesitation before two men, Mr. Martin and his oldest son, Baxter, came forward to hold the box steady on the stool while Mr. Summers stirred up the papers inside it.

The original paraphernalia for the lottery had been lost long ago, and the black box now resting on the stool had been put into use even before Old Man Warner, the oldest man in town, was born. Mr. Summers spoke frequently to the villagers about making a new box, but no one liked to upset even as much tradition as was represented by the black box. There was a story that the present box had been made with some pieces of the box that had preceded it, the one that had been constructed when the first people settled down to make a village here. Every year, after the lottery, Mr. Summers began talking again about a new box, but every year the subject was allowed to fade off without anything's being done. The black box grew shabbier each year; by now it was no longer completely black but splintered badly along one side to show the original wood color, and in some places faded or stained.

Mr. Martin and his oldest son, Baxter, held the black box securely on the stool until Mr. Summers had stirred the papers thoroughly with his hand. Because so much of the ritual had been forgotten or discarded, Mr. Summers had been successful in having slips of paper substituted for the chips of wood that had been used for generations. Chips of wood,

5

Mr. Summers had argued, had been all very well when the village was tiny, but now that the population was more than three hundred and likely to keep on growing, it was necessary to use something that would fit more easily into the black box. The night before the lottery, Mr. Summers and Mr. Graves made up the slips of paper and put them in the box, and it was then taken to the safe of Mr. Summers' coal company and locked up until Mr. Summers was ready to take it to the square next morning. The rest of the year, the box was put away, sometimes one place, sometimes another; it had spent one year in Mr. Graves's barn and another year underfoot in the post office, and sometimes it was set on a shelf in the Martin grocery and left there.

There was a great deal of fussing to be done before Mr. Summers declared the lottery open. There were the lists to make up—of heads of families, heads of households in each family, members of each household in each family. There was the proper swearing-in of Mr. Summers by the postmaster, as the official of the lottery; at one time, some people remembered, there had been a recital of some sort, performed by the official of the lottery, a perfunctory, tuneless chant that had been rattled off duly each year; some people believed that the official of the lottery used to stand just so when he said or sang it, others believed that he was supposed to walk among the people, but years and years ago this part of the ritual had been allowed to lapse. There had been, also, a ritual salute, which the official of the lottery had had to use in addressing each person who came up to draw from the box, but this also had changed with time, until now it was felt necessary only for the official to speak to each person approaching. Mr. Summers was very good at all this; in his clean white shirt and blue jeans, with one hand resting carelessly on the black box, he seemed very proper and important as he talked interminably to Mr. Graves and the Martins.

Just as Mr. Summers finally left off talking and turned to the assembled villagers, Mrs. Hutchinson came hurriedly along the path to the square, her sweater thrown over her shoulders, and slid into place in the back of the crowd. "Clean forgot what day it was," she said to Mrs. Delacroix, who stood next to her, and they both laughed softly. "Thought my old man was out back stacking wood," Mrs. Hutchinson went on, "and then I looked out the window and the kids was gone, and then I remembered it was the twenty-seventh and came a-running." She dried her hands on her apron, and Mrs. Delacroix said, "You're in time, though. They're still talking away up there."

Mrs. Hutchinson craned her neck to see through the crowd and found her husband and children standing near the front. She tapped Mrs. Delacroix on the arm as a farewell and began to make her way through the crowd. The people separated good-humoredly to let her through; two or three people said, in voices just loud enough to be heard across the crowd, "Here comes your Missus, Hutchinson," and "Bill, she made it after all." Mrs. Hutchinson reached her husband, and Mr. Summers, who had been waiting, said cheerfully, "Thought we were going to have to get on without you, Tessie." Mrs. Hutchinson said, grinning, "Wouldn't have me leave m'dishes in the sink, now, would you, Joe?," and soft laughter ran through the crowd as the people stirred back into position after Mrs. Hutchinson's arrival.

10    "Well, now," Mr. Summers said soberly, "guess we better get started, get this over with, so's we can go back to work. Anybody ain't here?"

"Dunbar," several people said. "Dunbar, Dunbar."

Mr. Summers consulted his list. "Clyde Dunbar," he said. "That's right. He's broke his leg, hasn't he? Who's drawing for him?"

"Me, I guess," a woman said, and Mr. Summers turned to look at her. "Wife draws for her husband," Mr. Summers said. "Don't you have a grown boy to do it for you, Janey?"

Although Mr. Summers and everyone else in the village knew the answer perfectly well, it was the business of the official of the lottery to ask such questions formally. Mr. Summers waited with an expression of polite interest while Mrs. Dunbar answered.

"Horace's not but sixteen yet," Mrs. Dunbar said regretfully. "Guess I gotta fill in for the old man this year."

"Right," Mr. Summers said. He made a note on the list he was holding. Then he asked, "Watson boy drawing this year?"           15

A tall boy in the crowd raised his hand. "Here," he said. "I'm drawing for m'mother and me." He blinked his eyes nervously and ducked his head as several voices in the crowd said things like "Good fellow, Jack," and "Glad to see your mother's got a man to do it."

"Well," Mr. Summers said, "guess that's everyone. Old Man Warner make it?"

"Here," a voice said, and Mr. Summers nodded.

A sudden hush fell on the crowd as Mr. Summers cleared his throat and looked at the list. "All ready?" he called. "Now, I'll read the names—heads of families first—and the men come up and take a paper out of the box. Keep the paper folded in your hand without looking at it until everyone has had a turn. Everything clear?"

The people had done it so many times that they only half listened to the directions;   20
most of them were quiet, wetting their lips, not looking around. Then Mr. Summers raised one hand high and said, "Adams." A man disengaged himself from the crowd and came forward. "Hi, Steve," Mr. Summers said, and Mr. Adams said, "Hi, Joe." They grinned at one another humorlessly and nervously. Then Mr. Adams reached into the black box and took out a folded paper. He held it firmly by one corner as he turned and went hastily back to his place in the crowd, where he stood a little apart from his family, not looking down at his hand.

"Allen," Mr. Summers said. "Anderson. . . . Bentham."

"Seems like there's no time at all between lotteries any more," Mrs. Delacroix said to Mrs. Graves in the back row. "Seems like we got through with the last one only last week."

"Time sure goes fast," Mrs. Graves said.

"Clark . . . Delacroix."

"There goes my old man," Mrs. Delacroix said. She held her breath while her husband   25
went forward.

"Dunbar," Mr. Summers said, and Mrs. Dunbar went steadily to the box while one of the women said, "Go on, Janey," and another said, "There she goes."

"We're next," Mrs. Graves said. She watched while Mr. Graves came around from the side of the box, greeted Mr. Summers gravely, and selected a slip of paper from the box. By now, all through the crowd there were men holding the small folded papers in their large hands, turning them over and over nervously. Mrs. Dunbar and her two sons stood together, Mrs. Dunbar holding the slip of paper.

"Harburt. . . . Hutchinson."

"Get up there, Bill," Mrs. Hutchinson said, and the people near her laughed.

"Jones."           30

"They do say," Mr. Adams said to Old Man Warner, who stood next to him, "that over in the north village they're talking of giving up the lottery."

Old Man Warner snorted. "Pack of crazy fools," he said. "Listening to the young folks, nothing's good enough for *them*. Next thing you know, they'll be wanting to go back to living in caves, nobody work any more, live *that* way for a while. Used to be a saying about 'Lottery in June, corn be heavy soon.' First thing you know, we'd all be eating stewed chickweed and acorns. There's *always* been a lottery," he added petulantly. "Bad enough to see young Joe Summers up there joking with everybody."

"Some places have already quit lotteries," Mrs. Adams said.

"Nothing but trouble in *that*," Old Man Warner said stoutly. "Pack of young fools."

35 "Martin." And Bobby Martin watched his father go forward. "Overdyke. . . . Percy."

"I wish they'd hurry," Mrs. Dunbar said to her older son. "I wish they'd hurry."

"They're almost through," her son said.

"You get ready to run tell Dad," Mrs. Dunbar said.

Mr. Summers called his own name and then stepped forward precisely and selected a slip from the box. Then he called, "Warner."

40 "Seventy-seventh year I been in the lottery," Old Man Warner said as he went through the crowd. "Seventy-seventh time."

"Watson." The tall boy came awkwardly through the crowd. Someone said, "Don't be nervous, Jack," and Mr. Summers said, "Take your time, son."

"Zanini."

After that, there was a long pause, a breathless pause, until Mr. Summers, holding his slip of paper in the air, said, "All right, fellows." For a minute, no one moved, and then all the slips of paper were opened. Suddenly, all the women began to speak at once, saying, "Who is it?" "Who's got it?" "Is it the Dunbars?" "Is it the Watsons?" Then the voices began to say, "It's Hutchinson. It's Bill," "Bill Hutchinson's got it."

"Go tell your father," Mrs. Dunbar said to her older son.

45 People began to look around to see the Hutchinsons. Bill Hutchinson was standing quiet, staring down at the paper in his hand. Suddenly, Tessie Hutchinson shouted to Mr. Summers, "You didn't give him time enough to take any paper he wanted. I saw you. It wasn't fair!"

"Be a good sport, Tessie," Mrs. Delacroix called, and Mrs. Graves said, "All of us took the same chance."

"Shut up, Tessie," Bill Hutchinson said.

"Well, everyone," Mr. Summers said, "that was done pretty fast, and now we've got to be hurrying a little more to get done in time." He consulted his next list. "Bill," he said, "you draw for the Hutchinson family. You got any other households in the Hutchinsons?"

"There's Don and Eva," Mrs. Hutchinson yelled. "Make *them* take their chance!"

50 "Daughters draw with their husbands' families, Tessie," Mr. Summers said gently. "You know that as well as anyone else."

"It wasn't *fair*," Tessie said.

"I guess not, Joe," Bill Hutchinson said regretfully. "My daughter draws with her husband's family, that's only fair. And I've got no other family except the kids."

"Then, as far as drawing for families is concerned, it's you," Mr. Summers said in explanation, "and as far as drawing for households is concerned, that's you, too. Right?"

"Right," Bill Hutchinson said.

55 "How many kids, Bill?" Mr. Summers asked formally.

"Three," Bill Hutchinson said. "There's Bill, Jr., and Nancy, and little Dave. And Tessie and me."

"All right, then," Mr. Summers said. "Harry, you got their tickets back?"

Mr. Graves nodded and held up the slips of paper. "Put them in the box, then," Mr. Summers directed. "Take Bill's and put it in."

"I think we ought to start over," Mrs. Hutchinson said, as quietly as she could. "I tell you it wasn't *fair*. You didn't give him time enough to choose. *Every*body saw that."

60 Mr. Graves had selected the five slips and put them in the box, and he dropped all the papers but those onto the ground, where the breeze caught them and lifted them off.

"Listen, everybody," Mrs. Hutchinson was saying to the people around her.

"Ready, Bill?" Mr. Summers asked, and Bill Hutchinson, with one quick glance around at his wife and children, nodded.

"Remember," Mr. Summers said, "take the slips and keep them folded until each person has taken one. Harry, you help little Dave." Mr. Graves took the hand of the little boy, who came willingly with him up to the box. "Take a paper out of the box, Davy," Mr. Summers said. Davy put his hand into the box and laughed. "Take just *one* paper," Mr. Summers said. "Harry, you hold it for him." Mr. Graves took the child's hand and removed the folded paper from the tight fist and held it while little Dave stood next to him and looked up at him wonderingly.

"Nancy next," Mr. Summers said. Nancy was twelve, and her school friends breathed heavily as she went forward, switching her skirt, and took a slip daintily from the box. "Bill, Jr.," Mr. Summers said, and Billy, his face red and his feet over-large, nearly knocked the box over as he got a paper out. "Tessie," Mr. Summers said. She hesitated for a minute, looking around defiantly, and then set her lips and went up to the box. She snatched a paper out and held it behind her.

"Bill," Mr. Summers said, and Bill Hutchinson reached into the box and felt around,        65 bringing his hand out at last with the slip of paper in it.

The crowd was quiet. A girl whispered, "I hope it's not Nancy," and the sound of the whisper reached the edges of the crowd.

"It's not the way it used to be," Old Man Warner said clearly. "People ain't the way they used to be."

"All right," Mr. Summers said. "Open the papers. Harry, you open little Dave's."

Mr. Graves opened the slip of paper and there was a general sigh through the crowd as he held it up and everyone could see that it was blank. Nancy and Bill, Jr., opened theirs at the same time, and both beamed and laughed, turning around to the crowd and holding their slips of paper above their heads.

"Tessie," Mr. Summers said. There was a pause, and then Mr. Summers looked at Bill        70 Hutchinson, and Bill unfolded his paper and showed it. It was blank.

"It's Tessie," Mr. Summers said, and his voice was hushed. "Show us her paper, Bill."

Bill Hutchinson went over to his wife and forced the slip of paper out of her hand. It had a black spot on it, the black spot Mr. Summers had made the night before with the heavy pencil in the coal-company office. Bill Hutchinson held it up, and there was a stir in the crowd.

"All right, folks," Mr. Summers said. "Let's finish quickly."

Although the villagers had forgotten the ritual and lost the original black box, they still remembered to use stones. The pile of stones the boys had made earlier was ready; there were stones on the ground with the blowing scraps of paper that had come out of the box. Mrs. Delacroix selected a stone so large she had to pick it up with both hands and turned to Mrs. Dunbar. "Come on," she said. "Hurry up."

Mrs. Dunbar had small stones in both hands, and she said, gasping for breath, "I can't        75 run at all. You'll have to go ahead and I'll catch up with you."

The children had stones already, and someone gave little Davy Hutchinson a few pebbles.

Tessie Hutchinson was in the center of a cleared space by now, and she held her hands out desperately as the villagers moved in on her. "It isn't fair," she said. A stone hit her on the side of the head.

Old Man Warner was saying, "Come on, come on, everyone." Steve Adams was in the front of the crowd of villagers with Mrs. Graves beside him.

"It isn't fair, it isn't right," Mrs. Hutchinson screamed, and then they were upon her.

## Katherine Mansfield (1888–1923)

## *Miss Brill* (1920)

Although it was so brilliantly fine—the blue sky powdered with gold and great spots of light like white wine splashed over the Jardins Publiques°—Miss Brill* was glad that she had decided on her fur. The air was motionless, but when you opened your mouth there was just a faint chill, like a chill from a glass of iced water before you sip, and now and again a leaf came drifting—from nowhere, from the sky. Miss Brill put up her hand and touched her fur. Dear little thing! It was nice to feel it again. She had taken it out of its box that afternoon, shaken out the moth-powder, given it a good brush, and rubbed the life back into the dim little eyes. "What has been happening to me?" said the sad little eyes. Oh, how sweet it was to see them snap at her again from the red eiderdown! . . . But the nose, which was of some black composition, wasn't at all firm. It must have had a knock, somehow. Never mind—a little dab of black sealing-wax when the time came—when it was absolutely necessary. . . . Little rogue! Yes, she really felt like that about it. Little rogue biting its tail just by her left ear. She could have taken it off and laid it on her lap and stroked it. She felt a tingling in her hands and arms, but that came from walking, she supposed. And when she breathed, something light and sad—no, not sad, exactly—something gentle seemed to move in her bosom.

There were a number of people out this afternoon, far more than last Sunday. And the band sounded louder and gayer. That was because the Season had begun. For although the band played all the year round on Sundays, out of season it was never the same. It was like some one playing with only the family to listen; it didn't care how it played if there weren't any strangers present. Wasn't the conductor wearing a new coat, too? She was sure it was new. He scraped with his foot and flapped his arms like a rooster about to crow, and the bandsmen sitting in the green rotunda blew out their cheeks and glared at the music. Now there came a little "flutey" bit—very pretty!—a little chain of bright drops. She was sure it would be repeated. It was; she lifted her head and smiled.

Only two people shared her "special" seat: a fine old man in a velvet coat, his hands clasped over a huge carved walking-stick, and a big old woman, sitting upright, with a roll of knitting on her embroidered apron. They did not speak. This was disappointing, for Miss Brill always looked forward to the conversation. She had become really quite expert, she thought, at listening as though she didn't listen, at sitting in other people's lives just for a minute while they talked round her.

She glanced, sideways, at the old couple. Perhaps they would go soon. Last Sunday, too, hadn't been as interesting as usual. An Englishman and his wife, he wearing a dreadful Panama hat and she button boots. And she'd gone on the whole time about how she ought to wear spectacles; she knew she needed them; but that it was no good getting any; they'd be sure to break and they'd never keep on. And he'd been so patient. He'd suggested everything—gold rims, the kind that curved round your ears, little pads inside the bridge. No, nothing would please her. "They'll always be sliding down my nose!" Miss Brill had wanted to shake her.

---

°*Jardins Publiques:* public gardens or park. The setting of the story is apparently a French seaside town.   *Miss Brill:* Brill is the name of a common deep-sea flatfish.

The old people sat on the bench, still as statues. Never mind, there was always the crowd to watch. To and fro, in front of the flower-beds and the band rotunda, the couples and groups paraded, stopped to talk, to greet, to buy a handful of flowers from the old beggar who had his tray fixed to the railings. Little children ran among them, swooping and laughing; little boys with big white silk bows under their chins, little girls, little French dolls, dressed up in velvet and lace. And sometimes a tiny staggerer came suddenly rocking into the open from under the trees, stopped, stared, as suddenly sat down "flop," until its small high-stepping mother, like a young hen, rushed scolding to its rescue. Other people sat on the benches and green chairs, but they were nearly always the same, Sunday after Sunday, and—Miss Brill had often noticed—there was something funny about nearly all of them. They were odd, silent, nearly all old, and from the way they stared they looked as though they'd just come from dark little rooms or even—even cupboards!

Behind the rotunda the slender trees with yellow leaves down drooping, and through them just a line of sea, and beyond the blue sky with gold-veined clouds.

Tum-tum-tum tiddle-um! tiddle-um! tum tiddle-um tum ta! blew the band.

Two young girls in red came by and two young soldiers in blue met them, and they laughed and paired and went off arm-in-arm. Two peasant women with funny straw hats passed, gravely, leading beautiful smoke-coloured donkeys. A cold, pale nun hurried by. A beautiful woman came along and dropped her bunch of violets, and a little boy ran after to hand them to her, and she took them and threw them away as if they'd been poisoned. Dear me! Miss Brill didn't know whether to admire that or not! And now an ermine toque° and a gentleman in grey met just in front of her. He was tall, stiff, dignified, and she was wearing the ermine toque she'd bought when her hair was yellow. Now everything, her hair, her face, even her eyes, was the same colour as the shabby ermine, and her hand, in its cleaned glove, lifted to dab her lips, was a tiny yellowish paw. Oh, she was so pleased to see him—delighted! She rather thought they were going to meet that afternoon. She described where she'd been—everywhere, here, there, along by the sea. The day was so charming—didn't he agree? And wouldn't he, perhaps? . . . But he shook his head, lighted a cigarette, slowly breathed a great deep puff into her face, and, even while she was still talking and laughing, flicked the match away and walked on. The ermine toque was alone; she smiled more brightly than ever. But even the band seemed to know what she was feeling and played more softly, played tenderly, and the drum beat, "The Brute! The Brute!" over and over. What would she do? What was going to happen now? But as Miss Brill wondered, the ermine toque turned, raised her hand as though she'd seen some one else, much nicer, just over there, and pattered away. And the band changed again and played more quickly, more gaily than ever, and the old couple on Miss Brill's seat got up and marched away, and such a funny old man with long whiskers hobbled along in time to the music and was nearly knocked over by four girls walking abreast.

Oh, how fascinating it was! How she enjoyed it! How she loved sitting here, watching it all! It was like a play. It was exactly like a play. Who could believe the sky at the back wasn't painted? But it wasn't till a little brown dog trotted on solemn and then slowly trotted off, like a little "theatre" dog, a little dog that had been drugged, that Miss Brill discovered what it was that made it so exciting. They were all on the stage. They weren't only the

---

°*ermine toque:* close-fitting hat made of the white fur of an ermine; here the phrase stands for the woman wearing the hat.

audience, not only looking on; they were acting. Even she had a part and came every Sunday. No doubt somebody would have noticed if she hadn't been there; she was part of the performance after all. How strange she'd never thought of it like that before! And yet it explained why she made such a point of starting from home at just the same time each week—so as not to be late for the performance—and it also explained why she had quite a queer, shy feeling at telling her English pupils how she spent her Sunday afternoons. No wonder! Miss Brill nearly laughed out loud. She was on the stage. She thought of the old invalid gentleman to whom she read the newspaper four afternoons a week while he slept in the garden. She had got quite used to the frail head on the cotton pillow, the hollowed eyes, the open mouth and the high pinched nose. If he'd been dead she mightn't have noticed for weeks; she wouldn't have minded. But suddenly he knew he was having the paper read to him by an actress! "An actress!" The old head lifted; two points of light quivered in the old eyes. "An actress—are ye?" And Miss Brill smoothed the newspaper as though it were the manuscript of her part and said gently: "Yes, I have been an actress for a long time."

10      The band had been having a rest. Now they started again. And what they played was warm, sunny, yet there was just a faint chill—a something, what was it?—not sadness—no, not sadness—a something that made you want to sing. The tune lifted, lifted, the light shone; and it seemed to Miss Brill that in another moment all of them, all the whole company, would begin singing. The young ones, the laughing ones who were moving together, they would begin, and the men's voices, very resolute and brave, would join them. And then she too, she too, and the others on the benches—they would come in with a kind of accompaniment—something low, that scarcely rose or fell, something so beautiful—moving. . . . And Miss Brill's eyes filled with tears and she looked smiling at all the other members of the company. Yes, we understand, we understand, she thought—though what they understood she didn't know.

Just at that moment a boy and girl came and sat down where the old couple had been. They were beautifully dressed; they were in love. The hero and heroine, of course, just arrived from his father's yacht. And still soundlessly singing, still with that trembling smile, Miss Brill prepared to listen.

"No, not now," said the girl, "Not here, I can't."

"But why? Because of that stupid old thing at the end there?" asked the boy. "Why does she come here at all—who wants her? Why doesn't she keep her silly old mug at home?"

"It's her fu-fur which is so funny," giggled the girl. "It's exactly like a fried whiting."

15      "Ah, be off with you!" said the boy in an angry whisper. Then: "Tell me, ma petite chérie—"

"No, not here," said the girl. "Not *yet*."

On her way home she usually bought a slice of honeycake at the baker's. It was her Sunday treat. Sometimes there was an almond in her slice, sometimes not. It made a great difference. If there was an almond it was like carrying home a tiny present—a surprise—something that might very well not have been there. She hurried on the almond Sundays and struck the match for the kettle in quite a dashing way.

But to-day she passed the baker's by, climbed the stairs, went into the little dark room—her room like a cupboard—and sat down on the red eiderdown. She sat there for a long time. The box that the fur came out of was on the bed. She unclasped the necklet quickly; quickly, without looking, laid it inside. But when she put the lid on she thought she heard something crying.

Frank O'Connor (1903–1966)

*First Confession* (1951)

All the trouble began when my grandfather died and my grandmother—my father's mother—came to live with us. Relations in the one house are a strain at the best of times, but, to make matters worse, my grandmother was a real old countrywoman and quite unsuited to the life in town. She had a fat, wrinkled old face, and, to Mother's great indignation, went round the house in bare feet—the boots had her crippled, she said. For dinner she had a jug of porter° and a pot of potatoes with—sometimes—a bit of salt fish, and she poured out the potatoes on the table and ate them slowly, with great relish, using her fingers by way of a fork.

Now, girls are supposed to be fastidious, but I was the one who suffered most from this. Nora, my sister, just sucked up to the old woman for the penny she got every Friday out of the old-age pension, a thing I could not do. I was too honest, that was my trouble; and when I was playing with Bill Connell, the sergeant-major's son, and saw my grandmother steering up the path with the jug of porter sticking out from beneath her shawl I was mortified. I made excuses not to let him come into the house, because I could never be sure what she would be up to when we went in.

When Mother was at work and my grandmother made the dinner I wouldn't touch it. Nora once tried to make me, but I hid under the table from her and took the bread-knife with me for protection. Nora let on to be very indignant (she wasn't, of course, but she knew Mother saw through her, so she sided with Gran) and came after me. I lashed out at her with the bread-knife, and after that she left me alone. I stayed there till Mother came in from work and made my dinner, but when Father came in later Nora said in a shocked voice: "Oh, Dadda, do you know what Jackie did at dinner time?" Then, of course, it all came out; Father gave me a flaking; Mother interfered, and for days after that he didn't speak to me and Mother barely spoke to Nora. And all because of that old woman! God knows, I was heart-scalded.

Then, to crown my misfortune, I had to make my first confession and communion. It was an old woman called Ryan who prepared us for these. She was about the one age with Gran; she was well-to-do, lived in a big house on Montenotte, wore a black cloak and bonnet, and came every day to school at three o'clock when we should have been going home, and talked to us of hell. She may have mentioned the other place as well, but that could only have been by accident, for hell had the first place in her heart.

She lit a candle, took out a new half-crown, and offered it to the first boy who would    5
hold one finger—only one finger!—in the flame for five minutes by the school clock. Being always very ambitious I was tempted to volunteer, but I thought it might look greedy. Then she asked were we afraid of holding one finger—only one finger!—in a little candle flame for five minutes and not be afraid of burning all over in roasting hot furnaces for all eternity. "All eternity! Just think of that! A whole lifetime goes by and it's nothing, not even a drop in the ocean of your sufferings." The woman was really interesting about hell, but my attention was all fixed on the half-crown. At the end of the lesson she put it back in her

---

°*porter:* a dark-brown beer.

purse. It was a great disappointment; a religious woman like that, you wouldn't think she'd bother about a thing like a half-crown.

Another day she said she knew a priest who woke one night to find a fellow he didn't recognize leaning over the end of his bed. The priest was a bit frightened—naturally enough—but he asked the fellow what he wanted, and the fellow said in a deep, husky voice that he wanted to go to confession. The priest said it was an awkward time and wouldn't it do in the morning, but the fellow said that last time he went to confession, there was one sin he kept back, being ashamed to mention it, and now it was always on his mind. Then the priest knew it was a bad case, because the fellow was after making a bad confession and committing a mortal sin. He got up to dress, and just then the cock crew in the yard outside, and—lo and behold!—when the priest looked round there was no sign of the fellow, only a smell of burning timber, and when the priest looked at his bed didn't he see the print of two hands burned in it? That was because the fellow had made a bad confession. This story made a shocking impression on me.

But the worst of all was when she showed us how to examine our conscience. Did we take the name of the Lord, our God, in vain? Did we honour our father and our mother? (I asked her did this include grandmothers and she said it did.) Did we love our neighbours as ourselves? Did we covet our neighbour's goods? (I thought of the way I felt about the penny that Nora got every Friday.) I decided that, between one thing and another, I must have broken the whole ten commandments, all on account of that old woman, and so far as I could see, so long as she remained in the house I had no hope of ever doing anything else.

I was scared to death of confession. The day the whole class went I let on to have a toothache, hoping my absence wouldn't be noticed; but at three o'clock, just as I was feeling safe, along comes a chap with a message from Mrs. Ryan that I was to go to confession myself on Saturday and be at the chapel for communion with the rest. To make it worse, Mother couldn't come with me and sent Nora instead.

Now, that girl had ways of tormenting me that Mother never knew of. She held my hand as we went down the hill, smiling sadly and saying how sorry she was for me, as if she were bringing me to the hospital for an operation.

10      "Oh, God help us!" she moaned. "Isn't it a terrible pity you weren't a good boy? Oh, Jackie, my heart bleeds for you! How will you ever think of all your sins? Don't forget you have to tell him about the time you kicked Gran on the shin."

"Lemme go!" I said, trying to drag myself free of her. "I don't want to go to confession at all."

"But sure, you'll have to go to confession, Jackie," she replied in the same regretful tone. "Sure, if you didn't the parish priest would be up to the house, looking for you. 'Tisn't, God knows, that I'm not sorry for you. Do you remember the time you tried to kill me with the bread-knife under the table? And the language you used to me? I don't know what he'll do with you at all, Jackie. He might have to send you up to the bishop."

I remember thinking bitterly that she didn't know the half of what I had to tell—if I told it. I knew I couldn't tell it, and understood perfectly why the fellow in Mrs. Ryan's story made a bad confession; it seemed to me a great shame that people wouldn't stop criticizing him. I remember that steep hill down to the church, and the sunlit hillsides beyond the valley of the river, which I saw in the gaps between the houses like Adam's last glimpse of Paradise.°

---

°*Adam's last glimpse of Paradise:* Genesis 3:23–24.

Then, when she had maneuvered me down the long flight of steps to the chapel yard, Nora suddenly changed her tone. She became the raging malicious devil she really was.

"There you are!" she said with a yelp of triumph, hurling me through the church door. 15 "And I hope he'll give you the penitential psalms, you dirty little caffler."

I knew then I was lost, given up to eternal justice. The door with the coloured-glass panels swung shut behind me, the sunlight went out and gave place to deep shadow, and the wind whistled outside so that the silence within seemed to crackle like ice under my feet. Nora sat in front of me by the confession box. There were a couple of old women ahead of her, and then a miserable-looking poor devil came and wedged me in at the other side, so that I couldn't escape even if I had the courage. He joined his hands and rolled his eyes in the direction of the roof, muttering aspirations in an anguished tone, and I wondered had he a grandmother too. Only a grandmother could account for a fellow behaving in that heartbroken way, but he was better off than I, for he at least could go and confess his sins; while I would make a bad confession and then die in the night and be continually coming back and burning people's furniture.

Nora's turn came, and I heard the sound of something slamming, and then her voice as if butter wouldn't melt in her mouth, and then another slam, and out she came. God, the hypocrisy of women! Her eyes were lowered, her head was bowed, and her hands were joined very low down on her stomach, and she walked up the aisle to the side altar looking like a saint. You never saw such an exhibition of devotion, and I remembered the devilish malice with which she had tormented me all the way from our door, and wondered were all religious people like that, really. It was my turn now. With the fear of damnation in my soul I went in, and the confessional door closed of itself behind me.

It was pitch-dark and I couldn't see the priest or anything else. Then I really began to be frightened. In the darkness it was a matter between God and me, and He had all the odds. He knew what my intentions were before I even started; I had no chance. All I had ever been told about confession got mixed up in my mind, and I knelt to one wall and said: "Bless me, father, for I have sinned; this is my first confession." I waited for a few minutes, but nothing happened, so I tried it on the other wall. Nothing happened there either. He had me spotted all right.

It must have been then that I noticed the shelf at about one height with my head. It was really a place for grown-up people to rest their elbows, but in my distracted state I thought it was probably the place you were supposed to kneel. Of course, it was on the high side and not very deep, but I was always good at climbing and managed to get up all right. Staying up was the trouble. There was room only for my knees, and nothing you could get a grip on but a sort of wooden moulding a bit above it. I held on to the moulding and repeated the words a little louder, and this time something happened all right. A slide was slammed back; a little light entered the box, and a man's voice said: "Who's there?"

"'Tis me, father," I said for fear he mightn't see me and go away again. I couldn't see 20 him at all. The place the voice came from was under the moulding, about level with my knees, so I took a good grip of the moulding and swung myself down till I saw the astonished face of a young priest looking up at me. He had to put his head on one side to see me, and I had to put mine on one side to see him, so we were more or less talking to one another upside-down. It struck me as a queer way of hearing confessions, but I didn't feel it my place to criticize.

"Bless me, father, for I have sinned; this is my first confession," I rattled off all in one breath, and swung myself down the least shade more to make it easier for him.

"What are you doing up there?" he shouted in an angry voice, and the strain the politeness was putting on my hold of the moulding, and the shock of being addressed in such an uncivil tone, were too much for me. I lost my grip, tumbled, and hit the door an unmerciful wallop before I found myself flat on my back in the middle of the aisle. The people who had been waiting stood up with their mouths open. The priest opened the door of the middle box and came out, pushing his biretta back from his forehead; he looked something terrible. Then Nora came scampering down the aisle.

"Oh, you dirty little caffler!" she said. "I might have known you'd do it. I might have known you'd disgrace me. I can't leave you out of my sight for one minute."

Before I could even get to my feet to defend myself she bent down and gave me a clip across the ear. This reminded me that I was so stunned I had even forgotten to cry, so that people might think I wasn't hurt at all, when in fact I was probably maimed for life. I gave a roar out of me.

25    "What's all this about?" the priest hissed, getting angrier than ever and pushing Nora off me. "How dare you hit the child like that, you little vixen?"

"But I can't do my penance with him, father," Nora cried, cocking an outraged eye up to him.

"Well, go and do it, or I'll give you some more to do," he said, giving me a hand up. "Was it coming to confession you were, my poor man?" he asked me.

"'Twas, father," said I with a sob.

"Oh," he said respectfully, "a big hefty fellow like you must have terrible sins. Is this your first?"

30    "'Tis, father," said I.

"Worse and worse," he said gloomily. "The crimes of a lifetime. I don't know will I get rid of you at all today. You'd better wait now till I'm finished with these old ones. You can see by the looks of them they haven't much to tell."

"I will, father," I said with something approaching joy.

The relief of it was really enormous. Nora stuck out her tongue at me from behind his back, but I couldn't even be bothered retorting. I knew from the very moment that man opened his mouth that he was intelligent above the ordinary. When I had time to think, I saw how right I was. It only stood to reason that a fellow confessing after seven years would have more to tell than people that went every week. The crimes of a lifetime, exactly as he said. It was only what he expected, and the rest was the cackle of old women and girls with their talk of hell, the bishop, and the penitential psalms. That was all they knew. I started to make my examination of conscience, and barring the one bad business of my grandmother it didn't seem so bad.

The next time, the priest steered me into the confession box himself and left the shutter back the way I could see him get in and sit down at the further side of the grille from me.

35    "Well, now," he said, "what do they call you?"

"Jackie, father," said I.

"And what's a-trouble to you, Jackie?"

"Father," I said, feeling I might as well get it over while I had him in good humour, "I had it all arranged to kill my grandmother."

He seemed a bit shaken by that, all right, because he said nothing for quite a while.

40    "My goodness," he said at last, "that'd be a shocking thing to do. What put that into your head?"

"Father," I said, feeling very sorry for myself, "she's an awful woman."

"Is she?" he asked. "What way is she awful?"

"She takes porter, father," I said, knowing well from the way Mother talked of it that this was a mortal sin, and hoping it would make the priest take a more favourable view of my case.

"Oh, my!" he said, and I could see he was impressed.

"And snuff, father," said I. 45

"That's a bad case, sure enough, Jackie," he said.

"And she goes round in her bare feet, father," I went on in a rush of self-pity, "and she knows I don't like her, and she gives pennies to Nora and none to me, and my da sides with her and flakes me, and one night I was so heartscalded I made up my mind I'd have to kill her."

"And what would you do with the body?" he asked with great interest.

"I was thinking I could chop that up and carry it away in a barrow I have," I said.

"Begor, Jackie," he said, "do you know you're a terrible child?" 50

"I know, father," I said, for I was just thinking the same thing myself. "I tried to kill Nora too with a bread-knife under the table, only I missed her."

"Is that the little girl that was beating you just now?" he asked.

"'Tis, father."

"Someone will go for her with a bread-knife one day, and he won't miss her," he said rather cryptically. "You must have great courage. Between ourselves, there's a lot of people I'd like to do the same to but I'd never have the nerve. Hanging is an awful death."

"Is it, father?" I asked with the deepest interest—I was always very keen on hanging. 55 "Did you ever see a fellow hanged?"

"Dozens of them," he said solemnly. "And they all died roaring."

"Jay!" I said.

"Oh, a horrible death!" he said with great satisfaction. "Lots of fellows I saw killed their grandmothers too, but they all said 'twas never worth it."

He had me there for a full ten minutes talking, and then walked out the chapel yard with me. I was genuinely sorry to part with him, because he was the most entertaining character I'd ever met in the religious line. Outside, after the shadow of the church, the sunlight was like the roaring of waves on a beach; it dazzled me; and when the frozen silence melted and I heard the screech of trams on the road my heart soared. I knew now I wouldn't die in the night and come back, leaving marks on my mother's furniture. It would be a great worry to her, and the poor soul had enough.

Nora was sitting on the railing, waiting for me, and she put on a very sour puss when 60 she saw the priest with me. She was made jealous because a priest had never come out of the church with her.

"Well," she asked coldly, after he left me, "what did he give you?"

"Three Hail Marys," I said.

"Three Hail Marys," she repeated incredulously. "You mustn't have told him anything."

"I told him everything," I said confidently.

"About Gran and all?" 65

"About Gran and all."

(All she wanted was to be able to go home and say I'd made a bad confession.)

"Did you tell him you went for me with the bread-knife?" she asked with a frown.

"I did to be sure."

"And he only gave you three Hail Marys?" 70

"That's all."

She slowly got down from the railing with a baffled air. Clearly, this was beyond her. As we mounted the steps back to the main road she looked at me suspiciously.

"What are you sucking?" she asked.

"Bullseyes."

"Was it the priest gave them to you?" 75

""'Twas.''

"Lord God," she wailed bitterly, "some people have all the luck! 'Tis no advantage to anybody trying to be good. I might just as well be a sinner like you."

# Edgar Allan Poe (1809–1849)

## *The Cask of Amontillado* (1846)

The thousand injuries of Fortunato I had borne as I best could; but when he ventured upon insult, I vowed revenge. You, who so well know the nature of my soul, will not suppose, however, that I gave utterance to a threat. *At length* I would be avenged; this was a point definitively settled—but the very definitiveness with which it was resolved, precluded the idea of risk. I must not only punish, but punish with impunity. A wrong is unredressed when retribution overtakes its redresser. It is equally unredressed when the avenger fails to make himself felt as such to him who has done the wrong.

It must be understood, that neither by word nor deed had I given Fortunato cause to doubt my good will. I continued, as was my wont, to smile in his face, and he did not perceive that my smile *now* was at the thought of his immolation.

He had a weak point—this Fortunato—although in other regards he was a man to be respected and even feared. He prided himself on his connoisseurship in wine. Few Italians have the true virtuoso spirit. For the most part their enthusiasm is adopted to suit the time and opportunity—to practice imposture upon the British and Austrian *millionaires*. In painting and gemmary, Fortunato, like his countrymen, was a quack—but in the matter of old wines he was sincere. In this respect I did not differ from him materially: I was skilful in the Italian vintages myself, and bought largely whenever I could.

It was about dusk, one evening during the supreme madness of the carnival season, that I encountered my friend. He accosted me with excessive warmth, for he had been drinking much. The man wore motley. He had on a tight-fitting parti-striped dress, and his head was surmounted by the conical cap and bells. I was so pleased to see him, that I thought I should never have done wringing his hand.

5  I said to him—"My dear Fortunato, you are luckily met. How remarkably well you are looking to-day! But I have received a pipe of what passes for Amontillado, and I have my doubts."

"How?" said he. "Amontillado? A pipe? Impossible! And in the middle of the carnival!"

"I have my doubts," I replied; "and I was silly enough to pay the full Amontillado price without consulting you in the matter. You were not to be found, and I was fearful of losing a bargain."

"Amontillado!"

"I have my doubts."

10  "Amontillado!"

"And I must satisfy them."

"Amontillado!"

"As you are engaged, I am on my way to Luchesi. If any one has a critical turn, it is he. He will tell me—"

"Luchesi cannot tell Amontillado from Sherry."

15  "And yet some fools will have it that his taste is a match for your own."

"Come, let us go."

"Whither?"

"To your vaults."

"My friend, no; I will not impose upon your good nature. I perceive you have an engagement. Luchesi—"

"I have no engagement;—come."　　　　　　　　　　　　　　　　20

"My friend, no. It is not the engagement, but the severe cold with which I perceive you are afflicted. The vaults are insufferably damp. They are encrusted with nitre."

"Let us go, nevertheless. The cold is merely nothing. Amontillado! You have been imposed upon. And as for Luchesi, he cannot distinguish Sherry from Amontillado."

Thus speaking, Fortunato possessed himself of my arm. Putting on a mask of black silk, and drawing a *roquelaire*° closely about my person, I suffered him to hurry me to my palazzo.

There were no attendants at home; they had absconded to make merry in honor of the time. I had told them that I should not return until the morning, and had given them explicit orders not to stir from the house. These orders were sufficient, I well knew, to insure their immediate disappearance, one and all, as soon as my back was turned.

I took from their sconces two flambeaux, and giving one to Fortunato, bowed him　25 through several suites of rooms to the archway that led into the vaults. I passed down a long and winding staircase, requesting him to be cautious as he followed. We came at length to the foot of the descent, and stood together on the damp ground of the catacombs of the Montresors.

The gait of my friend was unsteady, and the bells upon his cap jingled as he strode.

"The pipe," said he.

"It is farther on," said I; "but observe the white web-work which gleams from these cavern walls."

He turned towards me, and looked into my eyes with two filmy orbs that distilled the rheum of intoxication.

"Nitre?" he asked, at length.　　　　　　　　　　　　　　　　　　30

"Nitre," I replied. "How long have you had that cough?"

"Ugh! ugh! ugh!—ugh! ugh! ugh!—ugh! ugh! ugh!—ugh! ugh! ugh!—ugh! ugh! ugh!"

My poor friend found it impossible to reply for many minutes.

"It is nothing," he said, at last.

"Come," I said, with decision, "we will go back; your health is precious. You are rich, re-　35 spected, admired, beloved; you are happy, as once I was. You are a man to be missed. For me it is no matter. We will go back; you will be ill, and I cannot be responsible. Besides, there is Luchesi—"

"Enough," he said; "the cough is a mere nothing; it will not kill me. I shall not die of a cough."

"True—true," I replied; "and, indeed, I had no intention of alarming you unnecessarily—but you should use all proper caution. A draught of this Medoc will defend us from the damps."

Here I knocked off the neck of a bottle which I drew from a long row of its fellows that lay upon the mould.

"Drink," I said, presenting him the wine.

---

°*roquelaire:* a type of cloak.

40    He raised it to his lips with a leer. He paused and nodded to me familiarly, while his bells jingled.

"I drink," he said, "to the buried that repose around us."

"And I to your long life."

He again took my arm, and we proceeded.

"These vaults," he said, "are extensive."

45    "The Montresors," I replied, "were a great and numerous family."

"I forget your arms."

"A huge human foot d'or, in a field azure; the foot crushes a serpent rampant whose fangs are imbedded in the heel."

"And the motto?"

*"Nemo me impune lacessit."*°

50    "Good!" he said.

The wine sparkled in his eyes and the bells jingled. My own fancy grew warm with the Medoc. We had passed through walls of piled bones, with casks and puncheons intermingling, into the inmost recesses of the catacombs. I paused again, and this time I made bold to seize Fortunato by an arm above the elbow.

"The nitre!" I said: "see, it increases. It hangs like moss upon the vaults. We are below the river's bed. The drops of moisture trickle among the bones. Come, we will go back ere it is too late. Your cough—"

"It is nothing," he said; "let us go on. But first, another draught of the Medoc."

I broke and reached him a flagon of De Grave. He emptied it at a breath. His eyes flashed with a fierce light. He laughed and threw the bottle upwards with a gesticulation I did not understand.

55    I looked at him in surprise. He repeated the movement—a grotesque one.

"You do not comprehend?" he said.

"Not I," I replied.

"Then you are not of the brotherhood."

"How?"

60    "You are not of the masons."

"Yes, yes," I said, "yes, yes."

"You? Impossible! A mason?"

"A mason," I replied.

"A sign," he said.

65    "It is this," I answered, producing a trowel from beneath the folds of my *roquelaire.*

"You jest," he exclaimed, recoiling a few paces. "But let us proceed to the Amontillado."

"Be it so," I said, replacing the tool beneath the cloak, and again offering him my arm. He leaned upon it heavily. We continued our route in search of the Amontillado. We passed through a range of low arches, descended, passed on, and descending again, arrived at a deep crypt, in which the foulness of the air caused our flambeaux rather to glow than flame.

At the most remote end of the crypt there appeared another less spacious. Its walls had been lined with human remains, piled to the vault overhead, in the fashion of the great catacombs of Paris. Three sides of this interior crypt were still ornamented in this manner. From the fourth the bones had been thrown down, and lay promiscuously upon the earth,

---

°*Nemo me impune lacessit:* No one attacks me with impunity.

forming at one point a mound of some size. Within the wall thus exposed by the displacing of the bones, we perceived a still interior recess, in depth about four feet, in width three, in height six or seven. It seemed to have been constructed for no especial use in itself, but formed merely the interval between two of the colossal supports of the roof of the catacombs, and was backed by one of their circumscribing walls of solid granite.

It was in vain that Fortunato, uplifting his dull torch, endeavored to pry into the depths of the recess. Its termination the feeble light did not enable us to see.

"Proceed," I said; "herein is the Amontillado. As for Luchesi—"                    70

"He is an ignoramus," interrupted my friend, as he stepped unsteadily forward, while I followed immediately at his heels. In an instant he had reached the extremity of the niche, and finding his progress arrested by the rock, stood stupidly bewildered. A moment more and I had fettered him to the granite. In its surface were two iron staples, distant from each other about two feet, horizontally. From one of these depended a short chain, from the other a padlock. Throwing the links about his waist, it was but the work of a few seconds to secure it. He was too much astounded to resist. Withdrawing the key I stepped back from the recess.

"Pass your hand," I said, "over the wall; you cannot help feeling the nitre. Indeed it is *very damp. Once more let me implore* you to return. No? Then I must positively leave you. But I must first render you all the little attentions in my power."

"The Amontillado!" ejaculated my friend, not yet recovered from his astonishment.

"True," I replied; "the Amontillado."

As I said these words I busied myself among the pile of bones of which I have before spo-   75
ken. Throwing them aside, I soon uncovered a quantity of building stone and mortar. With these materials and with the aid of my trowel, I began vigorously to wall up the entrance of the niche.

I had scarcely laid the first tier of my masonry when I discovered that the intoxication of Fortunato had in a great measure worn off. The earliest indication I had of this was a low moaning cry from the depth of the recess. It was *not* the cry of a drunken man. There was then a long and obstinate silence. I laid the second tier, and the third, and the fourth; and then I heard the furious vibrations of the chain. The noise lasted for several minutes, during which, that I might hearken to it with the more satisfaction, I ceased my labors and sat down upon the bones. When at last the clanking subsided, I resumed the trowel, and finished without interruption the fifth, the sixth, and the seventh tier. The wall was now nearly upon a level with my breast. I again paused, and holding the flambeaux over the mason-work, threw a few feeble rays upon the figure within.

A succession of loud and shrill screams, bursting suddenly from the throat of the chained form, seemed to thrust me violently back. For a brief moment I hesitated—I trembled. Unsheathing my rapier, I began to grope with it about the recess: but the thought of an instant reassured me. I placed my hand upon the solid fabric of the catacombs, and felt satisfied. I reapproached the wall. I replied to the yells of him who clamored. I re-echoed—I aided—I surpassed them in volume and in strength. I did this, and the clamorer grew still.

It was now midnight, and my task was drawing to a close. I had completed the eighth, the ninth, and the tenth tier. I had finished a portion of the last and the eleventh; there remained but a single stone to be fitted and plastered in. I struggled with its weight; I placed it partially in its destined position. But now there came from out the niche a low laugh that erected the hairs upon my head. It was succeeded by a sad voice, which I had difficulty in recognizing as that of the noble Fortunato. The voice said—

"Ha! ha! ha!—he! he!—a very good joke indeed—an excellent jest. We will have many a rich laugh about it at the palazzo—he! he! he!—over our wine—he! he! he!"

80    "The Amontillado!" I said.

"He! he! he!—he! he! he!—yes, the Amontillado. But is it not getting late? Will not they be awaiting us at the palazzo, the Lady Fortunato and the rest? Let us be gone."

"Yes," I said, "let us be gone."

*"For the love of God, Montresor!"*

"Yes," I said, "for the love of God!"

85    But to these words I hearkened in vain for a reply. I grew impatient. I called aloud—

"Fortunato!"

No answer. I called again—

"Fortunato!"

No answer still. I thrust a torch through the remaining aperture and let it fall within. There came forth in return only a jingling of the bells. My heart grew sick—on account of the dampness of the catacombs. I hastened to make an end of my labor. I forced the last stone into its position; I plastered it up. Against the new masonry I re-erected the old rampart of bones. For the half of a century no mortal has disturbed them. *In pace requiescat!*°

# Mark Twain (1835–1910)

## *Luck** (1891)

It was at a banquet in London in honor of one of the two or three conspicuously illustrious English military names of this generation. For reasons which will presently appear, I will withhold his real name and titles and call him Lieutenant-General Lord Arthur Scoresby, Y.C., K.C.B., etc., etc. What a fascination there is in a renowned name! There sat the man, in actual flesh, whom I had heard of so many thousands of times since that day, thirty years before, when his name shot suddenly to the zenith from a Crimean battlefield to remain forever celebrated. It was food and drink to me to look, and look, and look at that demigod; scanning, searching, noting: the quietness, the reserve, the noble gravity of his countenance; the simple honesty that expressed itself all over him; the sweet unconsciousness of his greatness—unconsciousness of the hundreds of admiring eyes fastened upon him, unconsciousness of the deep, loving, sincere worship welling out of the breasts of those people and flowing toward him.

The clergyman at my left was an old acquaintance of mine—clergyman now, but had spent the first half of his life in the camp and field and as an instructor in the military school at Woolwich. Just at the moment I have been talking about a veiled and singular light glimmered in his eyes and he leaned down and muttered confidentially to me—indicating the hero of the banquet with a gesture:

"Privately—he's an absolute fool."

This verdict was a great surprise to me. If its subject had been Napoleon, or Socrates, or Solomon, my astonishment could not have been greater. Two things I was well aware of: that the Reverend was a man of strict veracity and that his judgment of men was good.

---

°*In pace requiescat:* May he rest in peace.

*This is not a fancy sketch. I got it from a clergyman who was an instructor at Woolwich forty years ago, and who vouched for its truth. [Twain's note.]

Therefore I knew, beyond doubt or question, that the world was mistaken about this hero: he *was* a fool. So I meant to find out, at a convenient moment, how the Reverend, all solitary and alone, had discovered the secret.

Some days later the opportunity came, and this is what the Reverend told me:                    5

About forty years ago I was an instructor in the military academy at Woolwich. I was present in one of the sections when young Scoresby underwent his preliminary examination. I was touched to the quick with pity, for the rest of the class answered up brightly and handsomely, while he—why, dear me, he didn't know *anything*, so to speak. He was evidently good, and sweet, and lovable, and guileless; and so it was exceedingly painful to see him stand there, as serene as a graven image, and deliver himself of answers which were veritably miraculous for stupidity and ignorance. All the compassion in me was aroused in his behalf. I said to myself, when he comes to be examined again he will be flung over, of course; so it will be simply a harmless act of charity to ease his fall as much as I can. I took him aside and found that he knew a little of Caesar's history; and as he didn't know anything else, I went to work and drilled him like a galley-slave on a certain line of stock questions concerning Caesar which I knew would be used. If you'll believe me, he went through with flying colors on examination day! He went through on that purely superficial "cram," and got compliments too, while others, who knew a thousand times more than he, got plucked. By some strangely lucky accident—an accident not likely to happen twice in a century—he was asked no question outside of the narrow limits of his drill.

It was stupefying. Well, all through his course I stood by him, with something of the sentiment which a mother feels for a crippled child; and he always saved himself—just by miracle, apparently.

Now, of course, the thing that would expose him and kill him at last was mathematics. I resolved to make his death as easy as I could; so I drilled him and crammed him, and crammed him and drilled him, just on the line of questions which the examiners would be most likely to use, and then launched him on his fate. Well, sir, try to conceive of the result: to my consternation, he took the first prize! And with it he got a perfect ovation in the way of compliments.

Sleep? There was no more sleep for me for a week. My conscience tortured me day and night. What I had done I had done purely through charity, and only to ease the poor youth's fall. I never had dreamed of any such preposterous results as the thing that had happened. I felt as guilty and miserable as Frankenstein. Here was a wooden-head whom I had put in the way of glittering promotions and prodigious responsibilities, and but one thing could happen: He and his responsibilities would all go to ruin together at the first opportunity.

The Crimean War° had just broken out. Of course there had to be a war, I said to myself. We couldn't have peace and give this donkey a chance to die before he is found out. I    10
waited for the earthquake. It came. And it made me reel when it did come. He was actually gazetted to a captaincy in a marching regiment! Better men grow old and gray in the service before they climb to a sublimity like that. And who could ever have foreseen that they would go and put such a load of responsibility on such green and inadequate shoulders? I could just barely have stood it if they had made him a cornet; but a captain—think of it! I thought my hair would turn white.

Consider what I did—I who so loved repose and inaction. I said to myself, I am responsible to the country for this, and I must go along with him and protect the country

---

°*Crimean War:* In the Crimean War (1853–1856), England was one of the allies that fought against Russia.

against him as far as I can. So I took my poor little capital that I had saved up through years of work and grinding economy, and went with a sigh and bought a cornetcy in his regiment, and away we went to the field.

And there—oh, dear, it was awful. Blunders?—why he never did anything but blunder. But, you see, nobody was in the fellow's secret. Everybody had him focused wrong, and necessarily misinterpreted his performance every time. Consequently they took his idiotic blunders for inspirations of genius. They did, honestly! His mildest blunders were enough to make a man in his right mind cry; and they did make me cry—and rage and rave, too, privately. And the thing that kept me always in a sweat of apprehension was the fact that every fresh blunder he made increased the luster of his reputation! I kept saying to myself, he'll get so high that when discovery does finally come it will be like the sun falling out of the sky.

He went right along, up from grade to grade, over the dead bodies of his superiors, until at last, in the hottest moment of the battle of———down went our colonel, and my heart jumped into my mouth, for Scoresby was next in rank! Now for it, said I: we'll all land in Sheol in ten minutes, sure.

The battle was awfully hot; the allies were steadily giving way all over the field. Our regiment occupied a position that was vital; a blunder now must be destruction. At this crucial moment, what does this immortal fool do but detach the regiment from its place and order a charge over a neighboring hill where there wasn't a suggestion of an enemy! "There you go!" I said to myself; "This is the end at last."

15    And away we did go, and were over the shoulder of the hill before the insane movement could be discovered and stopped. And what did we find? An entire and unsuspected Russian army in reserve! And what happened? We were eaten up? That is necessarily what would have happened in ninety-nine cases out of a hundred. But no; those Russians argued that no single regiment would come browsing around there at such a time. It must be the entire English army, and that the sly Russian game was detected and blocked, so they turned tail, and away they went, pell-mell, over the hill and down into the field, in wild confusion, and we after them; they themselves broke the solid Russian center in the field, and tore through, and in no time there was the most tremendous rout you ever saw, and the defeat of the allies was turned into a sweeping and splendid victory! Marshall Canrobert looked on, dizzy with astonishment, admiration, and delight; and sent right off for Scoresby, and hugged him, and decorated him on the field in presence of all the armies!

And what was Scoresby's blunder that time? Merely the mistaking his right hand for his left—that was all. An order had come to him to fall back and support our right; and, instead, he fell *forward* and went over the hill to the left. But the name he won that day as a marvelous military genius filled the world with his glory, and that glory will never fade while history books last.

He is just as good and sweet and lovable and unpretending as a man can be, but he doesn't know enough to come in when it rains. Now that is absolutely true. He is the supremest ass in the universe; and until half an hour ago nobody knew it but himself and me. He has been pursued, day by day and year by year, by a most phenomenal astonishing luckiness. He has been a shining soldier in all our wars for a generation; he has littered his whole military life with blunders, and yet has never committed one that didn't make him a knight or a baronet or a lord or something. Look at his breast; why, he is just clothed in domestic and foreign decorations. Well, sir, every one of them is the record of some shouting stupidity or other; and, taken together, they are proof that the very best thing in all this world that can befall a man is to be born lucky. I say again, as I said at the banquet, Scoresby's an absolute fool.

# Eudora Welty (1909–2001)

## *A Worn Path* (1941)

It was December—a bright frozen day in the early morning. Far out in the country there was an old Negro woman with her head tied in a red rag, coming along a path through the pinewoods. Her name was Phoenix Jackson. She was very old and small and she walked slowly in the dark pine shadows, moving a little from side to side in her steps, with the balanced heaviness and lightness of a pendulum in a grandfather clock. She carried a thin, small cane made from an umbrella, and with this she kept tapping the frozen earth in front of her. This made a grave and persistent noise in the still air, that seemed meditative like the chirping of a solitary little bird.

She wore a dark striped dress reaching down to her shoe tops, and an equally long apron of bleached sugar sacks, with a full pocket: all neat and tidy, but every time she took a step she might have fallen over her shoelaces, which dragged from her unlaced shoes. She looked straight ahead. Her eyes were blue with age. Her skin had a pattern all its own of numberless branching wrinkles and as though a whole little tree stood in the middle of her forehead, but a golden color ran underneath, and the two knobs of her cheeks were illuminated by a yellow burning under the dark. Under the rag her hair came down on her neck in the frailest of ringlets, still black, and with an odor like copper.

Now and then there was a quivering in the thicket. Old Phoenix said, "Out of my way, all you foxes, owls, beetles, jack rabbits, coons and wild animals! . . . Keep out from under these feet, little bob-whites. . . . Keep the big wild hogs out of my path. Don't let none of those come running my direction. I got a long way." Under her small black-freckled hand her cane, limber as a buggy whip, would switch at the brush as if to rouse up any hiding things.

On she went. The woods were deep and still. The sun made the pine needles almost too bright to look at, up where the wind rocked. The cones dropped as light as feathers. Down in the hollow was the mourning dove—it was not too late for him.

The path ran up a hill. "Seem like there is chains about my feet, time I get this far," she said, in the voice of argument old people keep to use with themselves. "Something always take a hold of me on this hill—pleads I should stay."                                    5

After she got to the top she turned and gave a full, severe look behind her where she had come. "Up through pines," she said at length. "Now down through oaks."

Her eyes opened their widest, and she started down gently. But before she got to the bottom of the hill a bush caught her dress.

Her fingers were busy and intent, but her skirts were full and long, so that before she could pull them free in one place they were caught in another. It was not possible to allow the dress to tear. "I in the thorny bush," she said. "Thorns, you doing your appointed work. Never want to let folks pass, no sir. Old eyes thought you was a pretty little *green* bush."

Finally, trembling all over, she stood free, and after a moment dared to stoop for her cane.

"Sun so high!" she cried, leaning back and looking, while the thick tears went over her eyes. "The time getting all gone here."                                               10

At the foot of this hill was a place where a log was laid across the creek.

"Now comes the trial," said Phoenix.

Putting her right foot out, she mounted the log and shut her eyes. Lifting her skirt, leveling her cane fiercely before her, like a festival figure in some parade, she began to march across. Then she opened her eyes and she was safe on the other side.

"I wasn't as old as I thought," she said.

15     But she sat down to rest. She spread her skirts on the bank around her and folded her hands over her knees. Up above her was a tree in a pearly cloud of mistletoe. She did not dare to close her eyes, and when a little boy brought her a plate with a slice of marble-cake on it she spoke to him. "That would be acceptable," she said. But when she went to take it there was just her own hand in the air.

So she left that tree, and had to go through a barbed-wire fence. There she had to creep and crawl, spreading her knees and stretching her fingers like a baby trying to climb the steps. But she talked loudly to herself: she could not let her dress be torn now, so late in the day, and she could not pay for having her arm or leg sawed off if she got caught fast where she was.

At last she was safe through the fence and risen up out in the clearing. Big dead trees, like black men with one arm, were standing in the purple stalks of the withered cotton field. There sat a buzzard.

"Who you watching?"

In the furrow she made her way along.

20     "Glad this is not the season for bulls," she said, looking sideways, "and the good Lord made his snakes to curl up and sleep in the winter. A pleasure I don't see no two-headed snake coming around that tree, where it come once. It took a while to get by him, back in the summer."

She passed through the old cotton and went into a field of dead corn. It whispered and shook and was taller than her head. "Through the maze now," she said, for there was no path.

Then there was something tall, black, and skinny there, moving before her.

At first she took it for a man. It could have been a man dancing in the field. But she stood still and listened, and it did not make a sound. It was as silent as a ghost.

"Ghost," she said sharply, "who be you the ghost of? For I have heard of nary death close by."

25     But there was no answer—only the ragged dancing in the wind.

She shut her eyes, reached out her hand, and touched a sleeve. She found a coat and inside that an emptiness, cold as ice.

"You scarecrow," she said. Her face lighted. "I ought to be shut up for good," she said with laughter. "My senses is gone. I too old, I the oldest people I ever know. Dance, old scarecrow," she said, "while I dancing with you."

She kicked her foot over the furrow, and with mouth drawn down, shook her head once or twice in a little strutting way. Some husks blew down and whirled in steamers about her skirts.

Then she went on, parting her way from side to side with the cane, through the whispering field. At last she came to the end, to a wagon track where the silver grass blew between the red ruts. The quail were walking around like pullets, seeming all dainty and unseen.

30     "Walk pretty," she said. "This is the easy place. This the easy going."

She followed the track, swaying through the quiet bare fields, through the little strings of trees silver in their dead leaves, past cabins silver from weather, with the doors and windows boarded shut, all like old women under a spell sitting there. "I walking in their sleep," she said, nodding her head vigorously.

In a ravine she went where a spring was silently flowing through a hollow log. Old Phoenix bent and drank. "Sweet-gum makes the water sweet," she said, and drank more. "Nobody know who made this well, for it was here when I was born."

The track crossed a swampy part where the moss hung as white as lace from every limb. "Sleep on, alligators, and blow your bubbles." Then the track went into the road.

Deep, deep the road went down between the high green-colored banks. Overhead the live-oaks met, and it was as dark as a cave.

A black dog with a lolling tongue came up out of the weeds by the ditch. She was med- 35 itating, and not ready, and when he came at her she only hit him a little with her cane. Over she went in the ditch, like a little puff of milkweed.

Down there, her sense drifted away. A dream visited her, and she reached her hand up, but nothing reached down and gave her a pull. So she lay there and presently went to talking. "Old woman," she said to herself, "that black dog come up out of the weeds to stall you off, and now there he sitting on his fine tail smiling at you."

A white man finally came along and found her—a hunter, a young man, with his dog on a chain.

"Well, Granny!" he laughed. "What are you doing there?"

"Lying on my back like a June-bug waiting to be turned over, mister," she said, reaching up her hand.

He lifted her up, gave her a swing in the air, and set her down. "Anything broken, 40 Granny?"

"No sir, them old dead weeds is springy enough," said Phoenix, when she had got her breath. "I thank you for your trouble."

"Where do you live, Granny?" he asked, while the two dogs were growling at each other.

"Away back yonder, sir, behind the ridge. You can't even see it from here."

"On your way home?"

"No sir, I goin to town." 45

"Why, that's too far! That's as far as I walk when I come out myself, and I get something for my trouble." He patted the stuffed bag he carried, and there hung down a little closed claw. It was one of the bob-whites, with its beak hooked bitterly to show it was dead. "Now you go on home, Granny!"

"I bound to go to town, mister," said Phoenix. "The time come around."

He gave another laugh, filling the whole landscape. "I know you old colored people! Wouldn't miss going to town to see Santa Claus!"

But something held old Phoenix very still. The deep lines in her face went into a fierce and different radiation. Without warning, she had seen with her own eyes a flashing nickel fall out of the man's pocket onto the ground.

"How old are you, Granny?" he was saying. 50

"There is no telling, mister," she said, "no telling."

Then she gave a little cry and clapped her hands and said, "Git on away from here, dog! Look! Look at that dog!" She laughed as if in admiration. "He ain't scared of nobody. He a big black dog." She whispered, "Sic him!"

"Watch me get rid of that cur," said the man. "Sic him, Pete! Sic him!"

Phoenix heard the dogs fighting, and heard the man running and throwing sticks. She even heard a gunshot. But she was slowly bending forward by that time, further and further forward, the lids stretched down over her eyes, as if she were doing this in her sleep. Her chin was lowered almost to her knees. The yellow palm of her hand came out from the fold of her apron. Her fingers slid down and along the ground under the piece of money with the grace and care they would have in lifting an egg from under a setting hen. Then she slowly straightened up, she stood erect, and the nickel was in her apron pocket. A bird flew by. Her lips moved. "God watching me the whole time. I come to stealing."

55    The man came back, and his own dog panted about them. "Well, I scared him off that time," he said, and then he laughed and lifted his gun and pointed it at Phoenix.

She stood straight and faced him.

"Doesn't the gun scare you?" he said, still pointing it.

"No sir. I seen plenty go off closer by, in my day, and for less than what I done," she said, holding utterly still.

He smiled, and shouldered the gun. "Well, Granny," he said, "you must be a hundred years old, and scared of nothing. I'd give you a dime if I had any money with me. But you take my advice and stay home, and nothing will happen to you."

60    "I bound to go on my way, mister," said Phoenix. She inclined her head in the red rag. Then they went in different directions, but she could hear the gun shooting again and again over the hill.

She walked on. The shadows hung from the oak trees to the road like curtains. Then she smelled wood-smoke, and smelled the river, and she saw a steeple and the cabins on their steep steps. Dozens of little black children whirled around her. There ahead was Natchez shining. Bells were ringing. She walked on.

In the paved city it was Christmas time. There were red and green electric lights strung and crisscrossed everywhere, and all turned on in the daytime. Old Phoenix would have been lost if she had not distrusted her eyesight and depended on her feet to know where to take her.

She paused quietly on the sidewalk where people were passing by. A lady came along in the crowd, carrying an armful of red-, green-, and silver-wrapped presents; she gave off perfume like the red roses in hot summer, and Phoenix stopped her.

"Please, missy, will you lace up my shoe?" She held up her foot.

65    "What do you want, Grandma?"

"See my shoe," said Phoenix. "Do all right for out in the country, but wouldn't look right to go in a big building."

"Stand still then, Grandma," said the lady. She put her packages down on the sidewalk beside her and laced and tied both shoes tightly.

"Can't lace 'em with a cane," said Phoenix. "Thank you, missy. I doesn't mind asking a nice lady to tie up my shoe, when I gets out on the street."

Moving slowly and from side to side, she went into the big building, and into a tower of steps, where she walked up and around and around until her feet knew to stop.

70    She entered a door, and there she saw nailed up on the wall the document that had been stamped with the gold seal and framed in the gold frame, which matched the dream that was hung up in her head.

"Here I be," she said. There was a fixed and ceremonial stiffness over her body.

"A charity case, I suppose," said an attendant who sat at the desk before her.

But Phoenix only looked above her head. There was sweat on her face, the wrinkles in her skin shone like a bright net.

"Speak up, Grandma," the woman said, "What's your name? We must have your history, you know. Have you been here before? What seems to be the trouble with you?"

75    Old Phoenix only gave a twitch to her face as if a fly were bothering her.

"Are you deaf?" cried the attendant.

But then the nurse came in.

"Oh, that's just old Aunt Phoenix," she said. "She doesn't come for herself—she has a little grandson. She makes these trips just as regular as clockwork. She lives away back off the Old Natchez Trace." She bent down. "Well, Aunt Phoenix, why don't you just take a seat? We won't keep you standing after your long trip." She pointed.

The old woman sat down, bolt upright in the chair.

"Now, how is the boy?" asked the nurse.                              80

Old Phoenix did not speak.

"I said, how is the boy?"

But Phoenix only waited and stared straight ahead, her face very solemn and withdrawn into rigidity.

"Is his throat any better?" asked the nurse. "Aunt Phoenix, don't you hear me? Is your grandson's throat any better since the last time you came for the medicine?"

With her hands on her knees, the old woman waited, silent, erect, and motionless, just   85
as if she were in armor.

"You mustn't take up our time this way, Aunt Phoenix," the nurse said. "Tell us quickly about your grandson, and get it over. He isn't dead, is he?"

At last there came a flicker and then a flame of comprehension across her face, and she spoke.

"My grandson. It was my memory had left me. There I sat and forgot why I made my long trip."

"Forgot?" the nurse frowned. "After you came so far?"

Then Phoenix was like an old woman begging a dignified forgiveness for waking up   90
frightened in the night. "I never did go to school, I was too old at the Surrender," she said in a soft voice. "I'm an old woman without an education. It was my memory fail me. My little grandson, he is just the same, and I forgot it in the coming."

"Throat never heals, does it?" said the nurse, speaking in a loud, sure voice to old Phoenix. By now she had a card with something written on it, a little list. "Yes. Swallowed lye. When was it—January—two, three years ago—"

Phoenix spoke unasked now. "No missy, he not dead, he just the same. Every little while his throat begin to close up again, and he not able to swallow. He not get his breath. He not able to help himself. So the time come around, and I go on another trip for the soothing medicine."

"All right. The doctor said as long as you came to get it, you could have it," said the nurse. "But it's an obstinate case."

"My little grandson, he sit up there in the house all wrapped up, waiting by himself," Phoenix went on. "We is the only two left in the world. He suffer and it don't seem to put him back at all. He got a sweet look. He going to last. He wear a little patch quilt and peep out holding his mouth open like a little bird. I remembers so plain now. I not going to forget him again, no, the whole enduring time. I could tell him from all the others in creation."

"All right." The nurse was trying to hush her now. She brought her a bottle of medicine.   95
"Charity," she said, making a check mark in a book.

Old Phoenix held the bottle close to her eyes, and then carefully put it into her pocket.

"I thank you," she said.

"It's Christmas time, Grandma," said the attendant. "Could I give you a few pennies out of my purse?"

"Five pennies is a nickel," said Phoenix stiffly.

"Here's a nickel," said the attendant.                              100

Phoenix rose carefully and held out her hand. She received the nickel and then fished the other nickel out of her pocket and laid it beside the new one. She stared at her palm closely, with her head on one side.

Then she gave a tap with her cane on the floor.

"This is what come to me to do," she said, "I going to the store and buy my child a little windmill they sells, made out of paper. He going to find it hard to believe there such a thing in the world. I'll march myself back where he waiting, holding it straight up in this hand."

She lifted her free hand, gave a little nod, turned around, and walked out of the doctor's office. Then her slow step began on the stairs, going down.

**POEMS**

## Matthew Arnold (1822–1888)

### *Dover Beach* (1849)

The sea is calm tonight.
The tide is full, the moon lies fair
Upon the straits:—on the French coast the light
Gleams and is gone; the cliffs of England stand,
Glimmering and vast, out in the tranquil bay.     5
Come to the window, sweet is the night air!
Only, from the long line of spray
Where the sea meets the moon-blanched land,
Listen! You can hear the grating roar
Of pebbles which the waves draw back, and fling,     10
At their return, up the high strand,
Begin, and cease, and then again begin,
With tremulous cadence slow, and bring
The eternal note of sadness in.

Sophocles long ago     15
Heard it on the Ægean, and it brought
Into his mind the turbid ebb and flow
Of human misery; we
Find also in the sound a thought,
Hearing it by this distant northern sea.     20
The Sea of Faith
Was once, too, at the full, and round earth's shore
Lay like the folds of a bright girdle furled.
But now I only hear
Its melancholy, long, withdrawing roar,     25
Retreating, to the breath
Of the night wind, down the vast edges drear
And naked shingles of the world.

Ah, love, let us be true
To one another! for the world, which seems     30

To lie before us like a land of dreams,
So various, so beautiful, so new,
Hath really neither joy, nor love, nor light,
Nor certitude, nor peace, nor help for pain;
And we are here as on a darkling plain                    35
Swept with confused alarms of struggle and flight
Where ignorant armies clash by night.

## William Blake (1757–1827)

### *The Tyger*° (1794)

Tyger! Tyger! burning bright
In the forests of the night,
What immortal hand or eye
Could frame thy fearful symmetry?

In what distant deeps or skies                             5
Burnt the fire of thine eyes?
On what wings dare he aspire?
What the hand, dare seize the fire?

And what shoulder, & what art,
Could twist the sinews of thy heart?                       10
And when thy heart began to beat,
What dread hand? & what dread feet?

What the hammer? what the chain?
In what furnace was thy brain?
What the anvil? what dread grasp                           15
Dare its deadly terrors clasp?

When the stars threw down their spears,
And water'd heaven with their tears,
Did he smile his work to see?
Did he who made the Lamb make thee?                        20

Tyger! Tyger! burning bright
In the forests of the night,
What immortal hand or eye
Dare frame thy fearful symmetry?

---

°*Tyger:* Tyger here means not only a tiger but also a lion or similarly large and ferocious cat.

# Gwendolyn Brooks (1917–2000)

## *We Real Cool* (1959)

### The Pool Players.
### Seven at the Golden Shovel.

We real cool. We
Left school. We

Lurk late. We
Strike straight. We

Sing sin. We                                                    5
Thin gin. We

Jazz June. We
Die soon.

# Robert Browning (1812–1889)

## *My Last Duchess* (1842)

That's my last Duchess painted on the wall,
Looking as if she were alive. I call
That piece a wonder, now: Frà Pandolf's° hands
Worked busily a day, and there she stands.
Will't please you sit and look at her? I said          5
"Frà Pandolf" by design, for never read
Strangers like you that pictured countenance,
The depth and passion of its earnest glance,
But to myself they turned (since none puts by
The curtain I have drawn for you, but I)               10
And seemed as they would ask me, if they durst,*
How such a glance came there; so, not the first
Are you to turn and ask thus. Sir, 'twas not
Her husband's presence only, called that spot
Of joy into the Duchess' cheek: perhaps               15
Frà Pandolf chanced to say "Her mantle laps

---

°*Frà Pandolf:* an imaginary painter and a monk.    **durst:* dared.

Over my lady's wrist too much," or "Paint
Must never hope to reproduce the faint
Half-flush that dies along her throat": such stuff
Was courtesy, she thought, and cause enough                    20
For calling up that spot of joy. She had
A heart—how shall I say?—too soon made glad,
Too easily impressed; she liked whate'er
She looked on, and her looks went everywhere.
Sir, 'twas all one! My favor at her breast,                    25
The dropping of the daylight in the West,
The bough of cherries some officious fool
Broke in the orchard for her, the white mule
She rode with round the terrace—all and each
Would draw from her alike the approving speech,                    30
Or blush, at least. She thanked men—good! But thanked
Somehow—I know not how—as if she ranked
My gift of a nine-hundred-years-old name
With anybody's gift. Who'd stoop to blame
This sort of trifling? Even had you skill                    35
In speech—(which I have not)—to make your will
Quite clear to such a one, and say, "Just this
Or that in you disgusts me; here you miss,
Or there exceed the mark"—and if she let
Herself be lessoned so, nor plainly set                    40
Her wits to yours, forsooth, and made excuse
—E'en then would be some stooping; and I choose
Never to stoop. Oh sir, she smiled, no doubt,
Whene'er I passed her; but who passed without
Much the same smile? This grew, I gave commands;                    45
Then all smiles stopped together. There she stands
As if alive. Will't please you rise? We'll meet
The company below, then. I repeat,
The Count your master's known munificence
Is ample warrant that no just pretense                    50
Of mine for dowry will be disallowed;
Though his fair daughter's self, as I avowed
At starting, is my object. Nay, we'll go
Together down, sir. Notice Neptune,° though,
Taming a sea horse, thought a rarity,                    55
Which Claus of Innsbruck* cast in bronze for me!

---

°*Neptune:* statue of the Roman Sea God.    \**Claus of Innsbrook:* an imaginary sculptor.

# Samuel Taylor Coleridge (1772–1834)

## *Kubla Khan* (1816)

In Xanadu did Kubla Kahn  
A stately pleasure dome decree:  
Where Alph, the sacred river, ran  
Through caverns measureless to man  
    Down to a sunless sea.                          5  
So twice five miles of fertile ground  
With walls and towers were girdled round:  
And there were gardens bright with sinuous rills,  
Where blossomed many an incense-bearing tree;  
And here were forests ancient as the hills,              10  
Enfolding sunny spots of greenery.  

But oh! that deep romantic chasm which slanted  
Down the green hill athwart a cedarn cover!  
A savage place! as holy and enchanted  
As e'er beneath a waning moon was haunted           15  
By woman wailing for her demon lover!  
And from this chasm, with ceaseless turmoil seething,  
As if this earth in fast thick pants were breathing,  
A mighty fountain momently was forced:  
Amid whose swift half-intermitted burst              20  
Huge fragments vaulted like rebounding hail,  
Or chaffy grain beneath the thresher's flail;  
And 'mid these dancing rocks at once and ever  
It flung up momently the sacred river.  
Five miles meandering with a mazy motion          25  
Through wood and dale the sacred river ran,  
Then reached the caverns measureless to man,  
And sank in tumult to a lifeless ocean:  
And 'mid this tumult Kubla heard from far  
Ancestral voices prophesying war!                30  
    The shadow of the dome of pleasure  
    Floated midway on the waves;  
    Where was heard the mingled measure  
    From the fountain and the caves.  
It was a miracle of rare device,                35  
A sunny pleasure dome with caves of ice!  
    A damsel with a dulcimer  
    In a vision once I saw:  
    It was an Abyssinian maid,  
    And on her dulcimer she played,          40  
    Singing of Mount Abora.

Could I revive within me
Her symphony and song,
To such a deep delight 'twould win me,
That with music loud and long,                                    45
I would build that dome in air,
That sunny dome! those caves of ice!
And all who heard should see them there,
And all should cry, Beware! Beware!
His flashing eyes, his floating hair!                             50
Weave a circle round him thrice,
And close your eyes with holy dread,
For he on honeydew hath fed,
And drunk the milk of Paradise.

# John Donne (1572–1631)

## *Holy Sonnet 10: Death Be Not Proud* (1633)

Death, be not proud, though some have callèd thee
Mighty and dreadful, for thou art not so;
For those whom thou think'st thou dost overthrow
Die not, poor Death, nor yet canst thou kill me.
From rest and sleep, which but thy pictures° be,                  5
Much pleasure; then from thee much more must flow,
And soonest our best men with thee do go,
Rest of their bones, and soul's delivery.
Thou art slave to fate, chance, kings, and desperate men,
And dost with poison, war, and sickness dwell,                    10
And poppy* or charms can make us sleep as well
And better than thy stroke; why swell'st† thou then?
One short sleep past, we wake eternally°°
And death shall be no more; death, thou shalt die.

# Robert Frost (1875–1963)

## *Desert Places* (1936)

Snow falling and night falling fast, oh, fast
In a field I looked into going past,
And the ground almost covered smooth in snow,
But a few weeds and stubble showing last.

---

°*pictures*: imitations.   **poppy*: opium.   †*swell'st*: puff up with pride.   °°*we wake eternally*: we will live eternally.

The woods around it have it—it is theirs.                    5
All animals are smothered in their lairs.
I am too absent-spirited to count;
The loneliness includes me unawares.

And lonely as it is that loneliness
Will be more lonely ere it will be less—                    10
A blanker whiteness of benighted snow
With no expression, nothing to express.

They cannot scare me with their empty spaces
Between stars—on stars where no human race is.
I have it in me so much nearer home                         15
To scare myself with my own desert places.

### *The Road Not Taken* (1915)

Two roads diverged in a yellow wood,
And sorry I could not travel both
And be one traveler, long I stood
And looked down one as far as I could
To where it bent in the undergrowth;                        5

Then took the other, as just as fair,
And having perhaps the better claim,
Because it was grassy and wanted wear;
Though as for that the passing there
Had worn them really about the same,                        10

And both that morning equally lay
In leaves no step had trodden black.
Oh, I kept the first for another day!
Yet knowing how way leads into way,
I doubted if I should ever come back.                       15

I shall be telling this with a sigh
Somewhere ages and ages hence:
Two roads diverged in a wood, and I—
I took the one less traveled by,
And that has made all the difference.                       20

## Thomas Hardy (1840–1928)

### *Channel Firing* (1914)

That night your great guns unawares,
Shook all our coffins as we lay,

And broke the chancel window squares.
We thought it was the Judgment-day

And sat upright. While drearisome                                    5
Arose the howl of wakened hounds:
The mouse let fall the altar-crumb,
The worms drew back into the mounds.

The glebe° cow drooled. Till God called, "No;
It's gunnery practice out at sea                                    10
Just as before you went below;
The world is as it used to be:

"All nations striving strong to make
Red war yet redder. Mad as hatters
They do no more for Christés sake                                   15
Than you who are helpless in such matters.

"That this is not the judgment-hour
For some of them's a blessed thing,
For if it were they'd have to scour
Hell's floor for so much threatening . . .                         20

"Ha, ha. It will be warmer when
I blow the trumpet (if indeed
I ever do; for you are men,
And rest eternal sorely need)."

So down we lay again. "I wonder,                                    25
Will the world ever saner be,"
Said one, "than when He sent us under
In our indifferent century!"

And many a skeleton shook his head.
"Instead of preaching forty year,"                                 30
My neighbor Parson Thirdly said,
"I wish I had stuck to pipes and beer."

Again the guns disturbed the hour,
Roaring their readiness to avenge,
As far inland as Stourton Tower,                                   35
And Camelot, and starlit Stonehenge.*

---

°*glebe:* the land and cemetery surrounding and belonging to a church. Cows were kept there to keep the grass short.   *\*Stourton Tower . . . Stonehenge:* places in the south of England associated with ancient Druids and also with the mythical King Arthur.

## The Man He Killed (1902)

"Had he and I but met
By some old ancient inn,
We should have sat us down to wet
Right many a nipperkin!°

"But ranged as infantry,                                              5
And staring face to face,
I shot at him as he at me,
And killed him in his place.

"I shot him dead because—
Because he was my foe.                                                10
Just so: my foe of course he was;
That's clear enough; although

"He thought he'd 'list,* perhaps,
Off-hand like—just as I—
Was out of work—had sold his traps†                                  15
No other reason why.

"Yes; quaint and curious war is!
You shoot a fellow down
You'd treat if met where any bar is
Or help to half-a-crown."°°                                          20


## John Keats (1795–1821)

### Bright Star (1819)

Bright star! would I were steadfast as thou art—
    Not in lone splendor hung aloft the night,
And watching, with eternal lids apart,
    Like Nature's patient, sleepless eremite,**
The moving waters at their priestlike task                           5
    Of pure ablution round earth's human shores,
Or gazing on the new soft-fallen mask
    Of snow upon the mountains and the moors;

---

°*nipperkin:* a half-pint of ale.   *'list:* enlist.   †*traps:* personal possessions.   °°*half-a-crown:* perhaps as much as $10 or $20.   **\**eremite:* hermit.

No—yet still steadfast, still unchangeable,
  Pillowed upon my fair love's ripening breast,      10
To feel forever its soft fall and swell,
  Awake forever in a sweet unrest,
Still, still to hear her tender-taken breath,
And so live ever—or else swoon to death.

## Irving Layton (1912–2006)

### *Rhine Boat Trip*° (1977)

The castles on the Rhine
are all haunted
by the ghosts of Jewish mothers
looking for their ghostly children

And the clusters of grapes      5
in the sloping vineyards
are myriads of blinded eyes
staring at the blind sun

The tireless Lorelei*
can never comb from their hair      10
the crimson beards
of murdered rabbis

However sweetly they sing
one hears only
the low wailing of cattle-cars†      15
moving invisibly across the land

## Amy Lowell (1874–1925)

### *Patterns* (1916)

I walk down the garden paths,
And all the daffodils
Are blowing, and the bright blue squills.

---

°*Rhine Boat Trip:* The Rhine, Germany's best-known river, is virtually synonymous with German national history.   *Lorelei:* mythical shore nymphs who lured passing rivermen to their doom; subject of a famous poem by Heinrich Heine (1797–1856).   †*cattle-cars:* During the Holocaust in World War II, the Nazis crowded their victims together into cattle-cars and transported them by rail to concentration and extermination camps in Germany and neighboring countries.

I walk down the patterned garden-paths
In my stiff, brocaded gown.                                                                    5
With my powdered hair and jewelled fan,
I too am a rare
Pattern. As I wander down
The garden paths.

My dress is richly figured,                                                                    10
And the train
Makes a pink and silver stain
On the gravel, and the thrift
Of the borders.
Just a plate of current fashion                                                                15
Tripping by in high-heeled, ribboned shoes.
Not a softness anywhere about me,
Only whalebone° and brocade.
And I sink on a seat in the shade

Of a lime tree. For my passion                                                                 20
Wars against the stiff brocade.
The daffodils and squills
Flutter in the breeze
As they please.
And I weep;                                                                                    25
For the lime-tree is in blossom
And one small flower has dropped upon my bosom.

And the plashing of waterdrops
In the marble fountain
Comes down the garden-paths.                                                                   30
The dripping never stops.
Underneath my stiffened gown
Is the softness of a woman bathing in a marble basin,
A basin in the midst of hedges grown
So thick, she cannot see her lover hiding.                                                     35
But she guesses he is near,

And the sliding of the water
Seems the stroking of a dear
Hand upon her.
What is Summer in a fine brocaded gown!                                                        40

---

°*whalebone:* Baleen from whales was used to make corsets for women because it was strong and flexible, like an early plastic.

I should like to see it lying in a heap upon the ground.
All the pink and silver crumpled up on the ground.
I would be the pink and silver as I ran along the paths,
And he would stumble after,
Bewildered by my laughter. 45
I should see the sun flashing from his sword-hilt and buckles on his shoes.
I would choose
To lead him in a maze along the patterned paths,
A bright and laughing maze for my heavy-booted lover.
Till he caught me in the shade, 50
And the buttons of his waistcoat bruised my body as he clasped me,
Aching, melting, unafraid.
With the shadows of the leaves and the sundrops,
And the plopping of the waterdrops,
All about us in the open afternoon— 55
I am very like to swoon
With the weight of this brocade,
For the sun sifts through the shade.

Underneath the fallen blossom
In my bosom, 60
Is a letter I have hid.
It was brought to me this morning by a rider from the Duke.
Madam, we regret to inform you that Lord Hartwell
Died in action Thursday se'nnight.°
As I read it in the white, morning sunlight, 65
The letters squirmed like snakes.
"Any answer, Madam," said my footman.
"No," I told him.
"See that the messenger takes some refreshment.

No, no answer." 70
And I walked into the garden.
Up and down the patterned paths,
In my stiff, correct brocade.
The blue and yellow flowers stood up proudly in the sun,
Each one. 75
I stood upright too,
Held rigid to the pattern
By the stiffness of my gown.
Up and down I walked.
Up and down. 80

---

°*se'nnight:* on a Thursday, seven days before last Thursday.

In a month he would have been my husband.
In a month, here, underneath this lime,
We would have broken the pattern;
He for me, and I for him,
He as Colonel, I as Lady,                                85
On this shady seat.
He had a whim
That sunlight carried blessing.
And I answered, "It shall be as you have said."
Now he is dead.                                        90

In Summer and in Winter I shall walk
Up and down
The patterned garden-paths
In my stiff, brocaded gown.
The squills and daffodils                             95
Will give place to pillared roses, and to asters, and to snow.
I shall go
Up and down,
In my gown.
Gorgeously arrayed,                                100
Boned and stayed.
And the softness of my body will be guarded from embrace
By each button, hook, and lace.
For the man who should loose me is dead,
Fighting with the Duke in Flanders,°                      105
In a pattern called a war.
Christ! What are patterns for?


## John Masefield (1878–1967)

### *Cargoes* (1902)

Quinquereme* of Nineveh† from distant Ophir,°°
Rowing home to haven in sunny Palestine,
With a cargo of ivory,

---

°*Flanders:* a place of frequent warfare in Belgium (e.g., the Duke of Marlborough's Flanders campaigns of 1702–1710; The Battle of Waterloo, 1815, under the Duke of Wellington; battles with the Germans during World War I, 1914–1915).   *quinquereme:* largest of the ancient ships, with three tiers of oars operated by five men at each vertical oar station.   †*Nineveh:* the capital of ancient Assyria.   °°*Ophir:* Ophir, known for its gold, probably was in Africa.

　　　And apes and peacocks,°
　　　Sandalwood, cedarwood,* and sweet white wine.　　　　　　5

　　　Stately Spanish galleon coming from the Isthmus,†
　　　Dipping through the Tropics by the palm-green shores,
　　　With a cargo of diamonds,
　　　Emeralds, amethysts,
　　　Topazes, and cinnamon, and gold moidores.°°　　　　　　10

　　　Dirty British coaster with a salt-caked smoke-stack,
　　　Butting through the Channel in the mad March days,
　　　With a cargo of Tyne coal,**
　　　Road-rails, pig-lead,
　　　Firewood, iron-ware, and cheap tin trays.　　　　　　15

## Wilfred Owen (1893–1918)

### Anthem for Doomed Youth (1920)

　　　What passing-bells†† for these who die as cattle?
　　　Only the monstrous anger of the guns.
　　　Only the stuttering rifles' rapid rattle
　　　Can patter out their hasty orisons.°°°

　　　No mockeries for them from prayers or bells,　　　　　　5
　　　Nor any voice of mourning save the choirs—
　　　The shrill, demented choirs of wailing shells;
　　　And bugles calling for them from sad shires.***

　　　What candles may be held to speed them all?
　　　Not in the hands of boys, but in their eyes　　　　　　10
　　　Shall shine the holy glimmers of good-byes.
　　　The pallor of girls' brows shall be their pall;

　　　Their flowers the tenderness of patient minds,
　　　And each slow dusk a drawing-down of blinds.

---

°*apes and peacocks:* 1 Kings 10:22 and 2 Chronicles 9:21.　 *cedarwood:* 1 Kings 9:11.　 †Isthmus: the Isthmus of Panama.　 °°*moidores:* coins (in Portugal and Brazil).　 **Tyne coal:* coal from Newcastle upon Tyne, England.　 ††*passing-bells:* church bells that are tolled at the entry of a funeral cortege into a church cemetery.　 °°°*orisons:* prayers.　 ***shires:* British counties.

## Dudley Randall (1914–2000)

### *Ballad of Birmingham*° (1966)

"Mother dear, may I go downtown
    Instead of out to play,
And march the streets of Birmingham
    In a Freedom March today?"

"No, baby, no, you may not go,                              5
    For the dogs are fierce and wild,
And clubs and hoses, guns and jails
    Aren't good for a little child."

"But, mother, I won't be alone,
    Other children will go with me,               10
And march in the streets of Birmingham
    To make our country free."

"No, baby, no, you may not go,
    For I fear those guns will fire.
But you may go to church instead                            15
    And sing in the children's choir."

She has combed and brushed her night-dark hair,
    And bathed rose petal sweet,
And drawn white gloves on her small brown hands,
    And white shoes on her feet.                  20

The mother smiled to know her child
    Was in the sacred place,
But that smile was the last smile
    To come upon her face.

For when she heard the explosion                            25
    Her eyes grew wet and wild.
She raced through the streets of Birmingham
    Calling for her child.

---

°Four black children were killed when the Sixteenth Street Baptist Church in Birmingham, Alabama, was bombed in 1963. It was not until May 2002, thirty-nine years later, that the last of the four bombers was convicted of the crime.

She clawed through bits of glass and brick,
   Then lifted out a shoe                       30
"Oh, here's the shoe my baby wore,
   But, baby, where are you?"


## Christina Rossetti (1830–1894)

### *Echo* (1854)

Come to me in the silence of the night;
   Come in the speaking silence of a dream;
Come with soft rounded cheeks and eyes as bright
   As sunlight on a stream
      Come back in tears,                    5
      O memory, hope, love of finished years.

O dream how sweet, too sweet, too bitter sweet,
   Whose wakening should have been in paradise,
Where souls brimful of love abide and meet;
   Where thirsty longing eyes               10
      Watch the slow door
      That opening, letting in, lets out no more.

Yet come to me in dreams, that I may live
   My very life again though cold in death;
Come back to me in dreams, that I may give       15
   Pulse for pulse, breath for breath:
      Speak low, lean low,
      As long ago, my love, how long ago!


## Luis Omar Salinas (1937–2008)

### *In a Farmhouse* (1973)

Fifteen miles
out of Robstown
with the Texas sun
fading in the distance
I sit in the bedroom                  5
profoundly,

animated by the day's work
in the cottonfields.

I made two dollars and
thirty cents today                                               10
I am eight years old
and I wonder
how the rest of the Mestizos°
do not go hungry
and if one were to die                                           15
of hunger
what an odd way
to leave for heaven.

## Shelly Wagner (b. 1950)

### *The Boxes* (1991)

When I told the police I couldn't find you,
they began a search that included everything—
even the boxes in the house:
the footlockers of clothes in the attic,
the hamper in the bathroom,                                       5
and the Chinese lacquered trunk by the sofa.
They made me raise every lid.
I told them you would never stay in a box,
not with all the commotion.
You would have jumped out,                                        10
found your flashlight
and joined the search.

Poor Thomas, taking these men
who don't know us
through our neighbors' garages                                    15
where you never played,
hoping they were right
and we were wrong
and he would find you and
snatch you home by the hand                                       20

so the police cars could
get out of our driveway
and the divers would

---

°*Mestizos:* persons of mixed Spanish and Amerindian ancestry.

get out of our river
because it was certainly 25
past our bedtime.
We would double-bolt our doors
like always,
say longer prayers than usual
and go to bed. But during the night 30
I would have sat till morning
beside my sleeping boys.

But that's not what happened.
Thomas is still here, now older.
I still go to his room 35
when he is sleeping
just to look at him.
I still visit the cemetery,
not as often,
but the urge is the same: 40
to lie down on the grass,
put my arm around the hump of ground
and tell you, "Get out of this box!
Put a stop to this commotion. Come home.
You should be in bed." 45

## Walt Whitman (1819–1892)

### *Reconciliation* (1865, 1881)

Word over all, beautiful as the sky,
Beautiful that war and all its deeds of carnage must in time be utterly lost,
That the hands of the sisters Death and Night incessantly softly wash again, and ever
    again, this soiled world;
For my enemy is dead, a man divine as myself is dead, 5
I look where he lies white-faced and still in the coffin—I draw near,
Bend down and touch lightly with my lips the white face in the coffin.

## William Wordsworth (1770–1850)

### *Lines Written in Early Spring* (1798)

I heard a thousand blended notes,
While in a grove I sat reclined,
In that sweet mood when pleasant thoughts
Bring sad thoughts to the mind.

To her fair works did Nature link                                          5
The human soul that through me ran;
And much it grieved my heart to think
What man has made of man.

Through primrose tufts, in that green bower,
The periwinkle trailed its wreaths;                                        10
And 'tis my faith that every flower
Enjoys the air it breathes.

The birds around me hopped and played,
Their thoughts I cannot measure—
But the least motion which they made,                                      15
It seemed a thrill of pleasure.

The budding twigs spread out their fan,
To catch the breezy air;
And I must think, do all I can,
That there was pleasure there.                                             20

If this belief from heaven be sent,
If such be Nature's holy plan,
Have I not reason to lament
What man has made of man?

# William Butler Yeats (1865–1939)

## *The Second Coming°* (1920)

Turning and turning in the widening gyre*
The falcon cannot hear the falconer;
Things fall apart; the center cannot hold;
Mere anarchy is loosed upon the world.
The blood-dimmed tide[†] is loosed, and everywhere                         5

---

°*Second Coming:* the return of Jesus Christ for the salvation of believers, as described in the Book of Revelation, which foretold that Christ's return would be preceded by famine, epidemics, war, and civil disturbances. Yeats believed that human history could be measured in cycles of 2,000 years (approx.) and that Jesus's birth ended the Greco-Roman cycle. In 1919 when Yeats wrote "The Second Coming," he thought the Christian period was ending. The New Testament expectation was that Jesus would reappear, but Yeats held that the disruptions of the twentieth century were preceding a takeover by the forces of evil.   *gyre:* a radiating spiral, cone, or vortex. Yeats refers to the intersection of two of these shapes as a visual symbol of his cyclic theory. As one gyre spiraled, widened, and disintegrated, a period of history would be ending. At the same time a new gyre would be beginning a reverse spiral:

The falcon is at the broadest, centrifugal point of the old gyre, symbolizing the end of a historic cycle. The desert birds "reel" in a tighter circle, symbolizing the beginning of the new age in the new gyre.   [†]*Blood-dimmed tide:* See Shakespeare's *Macbeth,* 2.2.60–63.

The ceremony of innocence is drowned;
The best lack all conviction, while the worst
Are full of passionate intensity.
Surely some revelation is at hand;

Surely the Second Coming is at hand.                                    10
The Second Coming! Hardly are those words out
When a vast image out of *Spiritus Mundi*°
Troubles my sight; somewhere in sands of the desert
A shape with lion body and the head of a man,\*
A gaze blank and pitiless as the sun,                                   15
Is moving its slow thighs, while all about it
Reel shadows of the indignant desert birds.
The darkness drops again; but now I know

That twenty centuries of stony sleep
Were vexed to nightmare by a rocking cradle,                            20
And what rough beast, its hour come round at last
Slouches towards Bethlehem to be born?

**PLAYS**

## Anton Chekhov (1860–1904)

## *The Bear: A Joke in One Act* (1888)

### Cast of Characters

Mrs. Popov. *A widow of seven months,* MRS. POPOV *is small and pretty, with dimples. She is a landowner. At the start of the play, she is pining away in memory of her dead husband.*

Grigory Stepanovich Smirnov. *Easily angered and loud,* SMIRNOV *is older. He is a landowner, too, and a man of substance.*

Luka. LUKA *is* MRS. POPOV'S *footman (a servant whose main tasks were to wait table and attend the carriages, in addition to general duties). He is old enough to feel secure in telling* MRS. POPOV *what he thinks.*

Gardener, Coachman, Workmen, *who enter at the end.*

SCENE. *The drawing room of* MRS. POPOV'S *country home.*

[MRS. POPOV, in deep mourning, does not remove her eyes from a photograph.]

---

°*Spiritus Mundi:* "the spirit of the world," a collective human consciousness that furnished a common fund of images and symbols; Yeats referred to it as "a great memory passing on from generation to generation."
\**lion body and the head of a man:* a description of an Egyptian sphinx, which symbolized the Pharaoh as a sun spirit. Here the sphinx represents a monstrous satanic figure.

LUKA. It isn't right, madam . . . you're only destroying yourself. . . . The chambermaid and the cook have gone off berry picking; every living being is rejoicing; even the cat knows how to be content, walking around the yard catching birds, and you sit in your room all day as if it were a convent, and you don't take pleasure in anything. Yes, really! Almost a year has passed since you've gone out of the house!

MRS. POPOV. And I shall never go out. . . . What for? My life is already ended. *He* lies in his grave; I have buried myself in these four walls . . . we are both dead.

LUKA. There you go again! Your husband is dead, that's as it was meant to be, it's the will of God, may he rest in peace. . . . You've done your mourning and that will do. You can't go on weeping and mourning forever. My wife died when her time came, too. . . . Well? I grieved, I wept for a month, and that was enough for her; the old lady wasn't worth a second more. [*Sighs.*] You've forgotten all your neighbors. You don't go anywhere or accept any calls. We live, so to speak, like spiders. We never see the light. The mice have eaten my uniform. It isn't as if there weren't any nice neighbors—the district is full of them . . . there's a regiment stationed at Riblov, such officers—they're like candy—you'll never get your fill of them! And in the barracks, never a Friday goes by without a dance; and, if you please, the military band plays music every day. . . . Yes, madam, my dear lady: you're young, beautiful, in the full bloom of youth—if only you took a little pleasure in life . . . Beauty doesn't last forever, you know! In ten years' time, you'll be wanting to wave your fanny in front of the officers—and it will be too late.

MRS. POPOV. [*Determined.*] I must ask you never to talk to me like that! You know that when Mr. Popov died, life lost all its salt for me. It may seem to you that I am alive, but that's only conjecture! I vowed to wear mourning to my grave and not to see the light of day. . . . Do you hear me? May his departed spirit see how much I love him. . . . Yes, I know, it's no mystery to you that he was often mean to me, cruel . . . and even unfaithful, but I shall remain true to the grave and show him I know how to love. There, beyond the grave, he will see me as I was before his death. . . .

5    LUKA. Instead of talking like that, you should be taking a walk in the garden or have Toby or Giant harnessed and go visit some of the neighbors. . . .

MRS. POPOV. Ai! [*She weeps.*]

LUKA. Madam! Dear lady! What's the matter with you! Christ be with you!

MRS. POPOV. Oh, how he loved Toby! He always used to ride on him to visit the Korchagins or the Vlasovs. How wonderfully he rode! How graceful he was when he pulled at the reins with all his strength! Do you remember? Toby, Toby! Tell them to give him an extra bag of oats today.

LUKA. Yes, madam.

[*Sound of loud ringing.*]

10    MRS. POPOV. [*Shudders.*] Who's that? Tell them I'm not at home!

LUKA. Of course, madam. [*He exits.*]

MRS. POPOV. [*Alone. Looks at the photograph.*] You will see, Nikolai, how much I can love and forgive . . . my love will die only when I do, when my poor heart stops beating. [*Laughing through her tears.*] Have you no shame? I'm a good girl, a virtuous little wife. I've locked myself in and I'll be true to you to the grave, and you . . . aren't you ashamed, you chubby cheeks? You deceived me, you made scenes, for weeks on end you left me alone. . . .

LUKA. [*Enters, alarmed.*] Madam, somebody is asking for you. He wants to see you. . . .

MRS. POPOV. But didn't you tell them that since the death of my husband, I don't see anybody?

15    LUKA. I did, but he didn't want to listen; he spoke about some very important business.

MRS. POPOV. I am *not at home!*

LUKA. That's what I told him . . . but . . . the devil . . . he cursed and pushed past me right into the room . . . he's in the dining room right now.

MRS. POPOV. [*Losing her temper.*] Very well, let him come in . . . such manners! [*Luka goes out.*] How difficult these people are! What does he want from me? Why should he disturb my peace? [*Sighs.*] But it's obvious I'll have to go live in a convent. . . . [*Thoughtfully.*] Yes, a convent. . . .

SMIRNOV. [*Enters while speaking to LUKA.*] You idiot, you talk too much. . . . Ass! [*Sees MRS. POPOV and changes to dignified speech.*] Madam, may I introduce myself: retired lieutenant of the artillery and landowner, Grigory Stepanovich Smirnov! I feel the necessity of troubling you about a highly important matter. . . .

MRS. POPOV. [*Refusing her hand.*] What do you want?                                                    20

SMIRNOV. Your late husband, whom I had the pleasure of knowing, has remained in my debt for two twelve-hundred-ruble notes. Since I must pay the interest at the agricultural bank tomorrow, I have come to ask you, madam, to pay me the money today.

MRS. POPOV. One thousand two hundred. . . . And why was my husband in debt to you?

SMIRNOV. He used to buy oats from me.

MRS. POPOV. [*Sighing, to LUKA.*] So, Luka, don't you forget to tell them to give Toby an extra bag of oats.

[*LUKA goes out.*]

[*To SMIRNOV.*] If Nikolai, my husband, was in debt to you, then it goes without saying that I'll pay; but please excuse me today. I haven't any spare cash. The day after tomorrow, my steward will be back from town and I will give him instructions to pay you what is owed; until then I cannot comply with your wishes. . . . Besides, today is the anniversary—exactly seven months ago my husband died, and I'm in such a mood that I'm not quite disposed to occupy myself with money matters.

SMIRNOV. And I'm in such a mood that if I don't pay the interest tomorrow, I'll be owing     25 so much that my troubles will drown me. They'll take away my estate!

MRS. POPOV. You'll receive your money the day after tomorrow.

SMIRNOV. I don't want the money the day after tomorrow. I want it today.

MRS. POPOV. You must excuse me. I can't pay you today.

SMIRNOV. And I can't wait until after tomorrow.

MRS. POPOV. What can I do, if I don't have it now?                                                      30

SMIRNOV. You mean to say you can't pay?

MRS. POPOV. I can't pay. . . .

SMIRNOV. Hm! Is that your last word?

MRS. POPOV. That is my last word.

SMIRNOV. Positively the last?                                                                          35

MRS. POPOV. Positively.

SMIRNOV. Thank you very much. We'll make a note of that. [*Shrugs his shoulders.*] And people want me to be calm and collected! Just now, on the way here, I met a tax officer and he asked me: why are you always so angry, Grigory Stepanovich? Goodness' sake, how can I be anything but angry? I need money desperately . . . I rode out yesterday early in the morning, at daybreak, and went to see all my debtors; and if only one of them had paid his debt . . . I was dog-tired, spent the night God knows where—a Jewish tavern beside a barrel of vodka. . . . Finally I got here, fifty miles from home, hoping to be paid, and you treat me to a "mood." How can I help being angry?

MRS. POPOV. It seems to me that I clearly said: My steward will return from the country and then you will be paid.

SMIRNOV. I didn't come to your steward, but to you! What the hell, if you'll pardon the expression, would I do with your steward?

40     MRS. POPOV. Excuse me, my dear sir, I am not accustomed to such profane expressions nor to such a tone. I'm not listening to you any more. [*Goes out quickly.*]

SMIRNOV. [*Alone.*] Well, how do you like that? "A mood.". . . "Husband died seven months ago"! Must I pay the interest or mustn't I? I ask you: Must I pay, or must I not? So, your husband's dead, and you're in a mood and all that finicky stuff . . . and your steward's away somewhere; may he drop dead. What do you want me to do? Do you think I can fly away from my creditors in a balloon or something? Or should I run and bash my head against the wall? I go to Gruzdev—and he's not at home; Yaroshevich is hiding, with Kuritsin it's a quarrel to the death and I almost throw him out the window; Mazutov has diarrhea, and this one is in a "mood." Not one of these swine wants to pay me! And all because I'm too nice to them. I'm a sniveling idiot, I'm spineless, I'm an old lady! I'm too delicate with them! So, just you wait! You'll find out what I'm like! I won't let you play around with me, you devils! I'll stay and stick it out until she pays. Rrr! . . . How furious I am today, how furious! I'm shaking inside from rage and I can hardly catch my breath. . . . Damn it! My God, I even feel sick! [*He shouts.*] Hey, you!

LUKA. [*Enters.*] What do you want?

SMIRNOV. Give me some beer or some water! [*LUKA exits.*] What logic is there in this! A man needs money desperately, it's like a noose around his neck—and she won't pay because, you see, she's not disposed to occupy herself with money matters! . . . That's the logic of a woman! That's why I never did like and do not like to talk to women. I'd rather sit on a keg of gunpowder than talk to a woman. Brr! . . . I even have goose pimples, this broad has put me in such a rage! All I have to do is see one of those spoiled bitches from a distance, and I get so angry it gives me a cramp in the leg. I just want to shout for help.

LUKA. [*Entering with water.*] Madam is sick and won't see anyone.

45     SMIRNOV. Get out! [*LUKA goes.*] Sick and won't see anyone! No need to see me . . . I'll stay and sit here until you give me the money. You can stay sick for a week, and I'll stay for a week. . . . If you're sick for a year, I'll stay a year. I'll get my own back, dear lady! You can't impress me with your widow's weeds and your dimpled cheeks . . . we know all about those dimples! [*Shouts through the window.*] Semyon, unharness the horses! We're not going away quite yet! I'm staying here! Tell them in the stable to give the horses some oats! You brute, you let the horse on the left side get all tangled up in the reins again! [*Teasing.*] "Never mind" . . . I'll give you a never mind! [*Goes away from the window.*] Shit! The heat is unbearable and nobody pays up. I slept badly last night and on top of everything else this broad in mourning is "in a mood" . . . my head aches . . . [*Drinks, and grimaces.*] Shit! This is water! What I need is a drink! [*Shouts.*] Hey, you!

LUKA. [*Enters.*] What is it?

SMIRNOV. Give me a glass of vodka. [*LUKA goes out.*] Oaf! [*Sits down and examines himself.*] Nobody would say I was looking well! Dusty all over, boots dirty, unwashed, unkept, straw on my waistcoat. . . . The dear lady probably took me for a robber. [*Yawns.*] It's not very polite to present myself in a drawing room looking like this; oh well; who cares? . . . I'm not here as a visitor but as a creditor, and there's no official costume for creditors.

LUKA. [*Enters with vodka.*] You're taking liberties, my good man. . . .

SMIRNOV. [*Angrily.*] What?

50     LUKA. I . . . nothing . . . I only . . .

SMIRNOV. Who are you talking to? Shut up!

LUKA. [*Aside.*] The devil sent this leech. An ill wind brought him. . . . [*LUKA goes out.*]

SMIRNOV. Oh how furious I am! I'm so mad I could crush the whole world into a powder! I even feel faint! [*Shouts.*] Hey, you!

MRS. POPOV. [*Enters, eyes downcast.*] My dear sir, in my solitude, I have long ago grown unaccustomed to the masculine voice and I cannot bear shouting. I must request you not to disturb my peace and quiet!

SMIRNOV. Pay me my money and I'll go. 55

MRS. POPOV. I told you in plain language: I haven't any spare cash now; wait until the day after tomorrow.

SMIRNOV. And I also told you respectfully, in plain language: I don't need the money the day after tomorrow, but today. If you don't pay me today, then tomorrow I'll have to hang myself.

MRS. POPOV. But what can I do if I don't have the money? You're so strange!

SMIRNOV. Then you won't pay me now? No?

MRS. POPOV. I can't. . . . 60

SMIRNOV. In that case, I can stay here and wait until you pay. . . . [*Sits down.*] You'll pay the day after tomorrow? Excellent! In that case I'll stay here until the day after tomorrow. I'll sit here all that time . . . [*Jumps up.*] I ask you: Have I got to pay the interest tomorrow, or not? Or do you think I'm joking?

MRS. POPOV. My dear sir, I ask you not to shout! This isn't a stable!

SMIRNOV. I wasn't asking you about a stable but about this: Do I have to pay the interest tomorrow or not?

MRS. POPOV. You don't know how to behave in the company of a lady!

SMIRNOV. No, I don't know how to behave in the company of a lady! 65

MRS. POPOV. No, you don't! You are an ill-bred, rude man! Respectable people don't talk to a woman like that!

SMIRNOV. Ach, it's astonishing! How would you like me to talk to you? In French, perhaps? [*Lisps in anger.*] *Madame, je vous prie*° . . . how happy I am that you're not paying me the money. . . . Ah, pardon, I've made you uneasy! Such lovely weather we're having today! And you look so becoming in your mourning dress. [*Bows and scrapes.*]

MRS. POPOV. That's rude and not very clever!

SMIRNOV. [*Teasing.*] Rude and not very clever! I don't know how to behave in the company of ladies. Madam, in my time I've seen far more women than you've seen sparrows. Three times I've fought duels over women; I've jilted twelve women, nine have jilted me! Yes! There was a time when I played the fool; I became sentimental over women, used honeyed words, fawned on them, bowed and scraped. . . . I loved, suffered, sighed at the moon; I became limp, melted, shivered. . . . I loved passionately, madly, every which way, devil take me, I chattered away like a magpie about the emancipation of women, ran through half my fortune as a result of my tender feelings; but now, if you will excuse me, I'm on to your ways! I've had enough! Dark eyes, passionate eyes, ruby lips, dimpled cheeks; the moon, whispers, bated breath—for all that I wouldn't give a good goddamn. Present company excepted, of course, but all women, young and old alike, are affected clowns, gossips, hateful, consummate liars to the marrow of their bones, vain, trivial, ruthless, outrageously illogical, and as far as this is concerned [*taps on his forehead.*], well, excuse my frankness, any sparrow could give pointers to a philosopher in petticoats! Look at one of those romantic creatures: muslin, ethereal demigoddess, a thousand raptures, and you look into her soul—a common crocodile! [*Grips the back of a chair; the chair cracks and breaks.*] But the most revolting part of it all is that this crocodile imagines that she has, above everything, her own privilege, a monopoly on tender feelings. The hell with it—you can hang me upside down by that nail

---

°*Madame, je vous prie:* Madam, I beg you.

if a woman is capable of loving anything besides a lapdog. All she can do when she's in love is slobber! While the man suffers and sacrifices, all her love is expressed in playing with her skirt and trying to lead him around firmly by the nose. You have the misfortune of being a woman, you know yourself what the nature of a woman is like. Tell me honestly: Have you ever in your life seen a woman who is sincere, faithful, and constant? You never have! Only old and ugly ladies are faithful and constant! You're more liable to meet a horned cat or a white woodcock than a faithful woman!

70   MRS. POPOV. Pardon me, but in your opinion, who is faithful and constant in love? The man? SMIRNOV. Yes, the man!

MRS. POPOV. The man! [*Malicious laugh.*] Men are faithful and constant in love! That's news! [*Heatedly.*] What right have you to say that? Men are faithful and constant! For that matter, as far as I know, of all the men I have known and now know, my late husband was the best. . . . I loved him passionately, with all my being, as only a young intellectual woman can love; I gave him my youth, my happiness, my life, my fortune; he was my life's breath; I worshipped him as if I were a heathen, and . . . and, what good did it do—this best of men himself deceived me shamelessly at every step of the way. After his death, I found his desk full of love letters; and when he was alive—it's terrible to remember—he used to leave me alone for weeks at a time, and before my eyes he flirted with other women and deceived me. He squandered my money, made a mockery of my feelings . . . and, in spite of all that, I loved him and was true to him . . . and besides, now that he is dead, I am still faithful and constant. I have shut myself up in these four walls forever and I won't remove these widow's weeds until my dying day. . . .

SMIRNOV. [*Laughs contemptuously.*] Widow's weeds! . . . I don't know what you take me for! As if I didn't know why you wear that black outfit and bury yourself in these four walls! Well, well! It's no secret, so romantic! When some fool of a poet passes by this country house, he'll look up at your window and think: "Here lives the mysterious Tamara, who, for the love of her husband, buried herself in these four walls." We know these tricks!

MRS. POPOV. [*Flaring.*] What? How dare you say that to me?

75   SMIRNOV. You may have buried yourself alive, but you haven't forgotten to powder yourself!

MRS. POPOV. How dare you use such expressions with me?

SMIRNOV. Please don't shout. I'm not your steward! You must allow me to call a spade a spade. I'm not a woman and I'm used to saying what's on my mind! Don't you shout at me!

MRS. POPOV. I'm not shouting, you are! Please leave me in peace!

SMIRNOV. Pay me my money and I'll go.

80   MRS. POPOV. I won't give you any money!

SMIRNOV. Yes, you will.

MRS. POPOV. To spite you, I won't pay you anything. You can leave me in peace!

SMIRNOV. I don't have the pleasure of being either your husband or your fiancé, so please don't make scenes! [*Sits down.*] I don't like it.

MRS. POPOV. [*Choking with rage.*] You're sitting down?

85   SMIRNOV. Yes, I am.

MRS. POPOV. I ask you to get out!

SMIRNOV. Give me my money . . . [*Aside.*] Oh, I'm so furious! Furious!

MRS. POPOV. I don't want to talk to impudent people! Get out of here! [*Pause.*] You're not going? No?

SMIRNOV. No.

90   MRS. POPOV. No?

SMIRNOV. No!

MRS. POPOV. We'll see about that. [*Rings.*]

[*LUKA enters.*]

Luka, show the gentleman out.

LUKA. [*Goes up to SMIRNOV.*] Sir, will you please leave, as you have been asked. You mustn't . . .

SMIRNOV. [*Jumping up.*] Shut up! Who do you think you're talking to? I'll make mincemeat out of you!

LUKA. [*His hand to his heart.*] Oh my God! Saints above! [*Falls into chair.*] Oh, I feel ill!   95
I feel ill! I can't catch my breath!

MRS. POPOV. Where's Dasha? Dasha! [*She shouts.*] Dasha! Pelagea! Dasha! [*She rings.*]

LUKA. Oh! They've all gone berry picking . . . there's nobody at home . . . I'm ill! Water!

MRS. POPOV. Will you please get out!

SMIRNOV. Will you please be more polite?

MRS. POPOV. [*Clenches her fist and stamps her feet.*] You're nothing but a crude bear! A   100
brute! A monster!

SMIRNOV. What? What did you say?

MRS. POPOV. I said that you were a bear, a monster!

SMIRNOV. [*Advancing toward her.*] Excuse me, but what right do you have to insult me?

MRS. POPOV. Yes, I am insulting you . . . so what? Do you think I'm afraid of you?

SMIRNOV. And do you think just because you're one of those romantic creations, that you   105
have the right to insult me with impunity? Yes? I challenge you!

LUKA. Lord in Heaven! Saints above! . . . Water!

SMIRNOV. Pistols!

MRS. POPOV. Do you think just because you have big fists and you can bellow like a bull, that I'm afraid of you? You're such a bully!

SMIRNOV. I challenge you! I'm not going to let anybody insult me, and I don't care if you are a woman, a delicate creature!

MRS. POPOV. [*Trying to get a word in edgewise.*] Bear! Bear! Bear!   110

SMIRNOV. It's about time we got rid of the prejudice that only men must pay for their insults! Devil take it, if women want to be equal, they should behave as equals! Let's fight!

MRS. POPOV. You want to fight! By all means!

SMIRNOV. This minute!

MRS. POPOV. This minute! My husband had some pistols. . . . I'll go and get them right away. [*Goes out hurriedly and then returns.*] What pleasure I'll have putting a bullet through that thick head of yours! The hell with you! [*She goes out.*]

SMIRNOV. I'll shoot her down like a chicken! I'm not a little boy or a sentimental puppy.   115
I don't care if she is delicate and fragile.

LUKA. Kind sir! Holy father! [*kneels.*] Have pity on a poor old man and go away from here! You've frightened her to death and now you're going to shoot her?

SMIRNOV. [*Not listening to him.*] If she fights, then it means she believes in equality of rights and emancipation of women. Here the sexes are equal! I'll shoot her like a chicken! But what a woman! [*Imitates her.*] "The hell with you! . . . I'll put a bullet through that thick head of yours! . . ." What a woman! How she blushed, her eyes shone . . . she accepted my challenge! To tell the truth, it was the first time in my life I've seen a woman like that. . . .

LUKA. Dear sir, please go away! I'll pray to God on your behalf as long as I live!

SMIRNOV. That's a woman for you! A woman like that I can understand! A real woman! Not a sour-faced nincompoop but fiery, gunpowder! Fireworks! I'm even sorry to have to kill her!

120   LUKA. [*Weeps.*] Dear sir . . . go away!

SMIRNOV. I positively like her! Positively! Even though she has dimpled cheeks, I like her! I'm almost ready to forget about the debt. . . . My fury has diminished. Wonderful woman!

MRS. POPOV. [*Enters with pistols.*] Here they are, the pistols. Before we fight, you must show me how to fire. . . . I've never had a pistol in my hands before . . .

LUKA. Oh dear Lord, for pity's sake. . . . I'll go and find the gardener and the coachman. . . . What did we do to deserve such trouble? [*Exit.*]

SMIRNOV. [*Examining the pistols.*] You see, there are several sorts of pistols . . . there are special dueling pistols, the Mortimer with primers. Then there are Smith and Wesson revolvers, triple action with extractors . . . excellent pistols! . . . they cost a minimum of ninety rubles a pair. . . . You must hold the revolver like this . . . [*Aside.*] What eyes, what eyes! A woman to set you on fire!

125   MRS. POPOV. Like this?

SMIRNOV. Yes, like this . . . then you cock the pistol . . . take aim . . . put your head back a little . . . stretch your arm out all the way . . . that's right . . . then with this finger press on this little piece of goods . . . and that's all there is to do . . . but the most important thing is not to get excited and aim without hurrying . . . try to keep your arm from shaking.

MRS. POPOV. Good . . . it's not comfortable to shoot indoors. Let's go into the garden.

SMIRNOV. Let's go. But I'm giving you advance notice that I'm going to fire into the air.

MRS. POPOV. That's the last straw! Why?

130   SMIRNOV. Why? . . . Why . . . because it's my business, that's why.

MRS. POPOV. Are you afraid? Yes? Aahhh! No, sir. You're not going to get out of it that easily! Be so good as to follow me! I will not rest until I've put a hole through your forehead . . . that forehead I hate so much! Are you afraid?

SMIRNOV. Yes. I'm afraid.

MRS. POPOV. You're lying! Why don't you want to fight?

SMIRNOV. Because . . . because you . . . because I like you.

135   MRS. POPOV. [*Laughs angrily.*] He likes me! He dares say that he likes me! [*Points to the door.*] Out!

SMIRNOV. [*Loads the revolver in silence, takes cap and goes; at the door, stops for half a minute while they look at each other in silence; then he approaches MRS. POPOV hesitantly.*] Listen. . . . Are you still angry? I'm extremely irritated, but, do you understand me, how can I express it . . . the fact is, that, you see, strictly speaking . . . [*He shouts.*] Is it my fault, really, for liking you? [*Grabs the back of a chair, which cracks and breaks.*] Why the hell do you have such fragile furniture! I like you! Do you understand? I . . . I'm almost in love with you!

MRS. POPOV. Get away from me—I hate you!

SMIRNOV. God, what a woman! I've never in my life seen anything like her! I'm lost! I'm done for! I'm caught like a mouse in a trap!

MRS. POPOV. Stand back or I'll shoot!

140   SMIRNOV. Shoot! You could never understand what happiness it would be to die under the gaze of those wonderful eyes, to be shot by a revolver which was held by those little velvet hands. . . . I've gone out of my mind! Think about it and decide right away, because if I leave here, then we'll never see each other again! Decide . . . I'm a nobleman, a respectable gentleman, of good family. I have an income of ten thousand a year. . . . I can put a bullet through a coin tossed in the air . . . I have some fine horses. . . . Will you be my wife?

Mrs. Popov. [*Indignantly brandishes her revolver.*] Let's fight! I challenge you!

Smirnov. I'm out of my mind . . . I don't understand anything . . . [*Shouts.*] Hey, you, water!

Mrs. Popov. [*Shouts.*] Let's fight!

Smirnov. I've gone out of my mind. I'm in love like a boy, like an idiot! [*He grabs her hand, she screams with pain.*] I love you! [*Kneels.*] I love you as I've never loved before! I've jilted twelve women, nine women have jilted me, but I've never loved one of them as I love you. . . . I'm weak, I'm a limp rag. . . . I'm on my knees like a fool, offering you my hand. . . . Shame, shame! I haven't been in love for five years, I vowed I wouldn't; and suddenly I'm in love, like a fish out of water. I'm offering my hand in marriage. Yes or no? You don't want to? You don't need to! [*Gets up and quickly goes to the door.*]

Mrs. Popov. Wait!                                                                              145

Smirnov. [*Stops.*] Well?

Mrs. Popov. Nothing . . . you can go . . . go away . . . wait . . . No, get out, get out! I hate you! But—don't go! Oh, if you only knew how furious I am, how angry! [*Throws revolver on table.*] My fingers are swollen from that nasty thing. . . . [*Tears her handkerchief furiously.*] What are you waiting for? Get out!

Smirnov. Farewell!

Mrs. Popov. Yes, yes, go away! [*Shouts.*] Where are you going? Stop. . . . Oh, go away! Oh, how furious I am! Don't come near me! Don't come near me!

Smirnov. [*Approaching her.*] How angry I am with myself! I'm in love like a student. I've  150 been on my knees. . . . It gives me the shivers. [*Rudely.*] I love you! A lot of good it will do me to fall in love with you! Tomorrow I've got to pay the interest, begin the mowing of the hay. [*Puts his arm around her waist.*] I'll never forgive myself for this. . . .

Mrs. Popov. Get away from me! Get your hands away! I . . . hate you! I . . . challenge you!

[*Prolonged kiss,* Luka *enters with an ax, the* Gardener *with a rake, the* Coachman *with a pitchfork, and* Workmen *with cudgels.*]

Luka. [*Catches sight of the pair kissing.*] Lord in heaven! [*Pause.*]

Mrs. Popov. [*Lowering her eyes.*] Luka, tell them in the stable not to give Toby any oats today.

CURTAIN


## Susan Glaspell (1882–1948)

### *Trifles* (1916)

#### Cast of Characters

George Henderson, county attorney

Henry Peters, sheriff

Lewis Hale, a neighboring farmer

Mrs. Peters Mrs. Hale

Scene. *The kitchen in the now abandoned farmhouse of* John Wright, *a gloomy kitchen, and left without having been put in order—unwashed pans under the sink, a loaf of bread outside the breadbox, a dish-towel on the table—other signs of incompleted work. At the rear the outer door opens and the* Sheriff *comes in followed by the* County Attorney *and* Hale. *The* Sheriff *and* Hale *are men in middle life, the* County Attorney *is a young man; all are much bundled up and go at once to the stove. They are followed by the two women—the* sheriff's *wife first; she is a slight wiry woman, a thin nervous face.* Mrs. Hale *is larger and would ordinarily be called more comfortable looking, but she is disturbed now and looks fearfully about as she enters. The women have come in slowly, and stand close together near the door.*

County Attorney. [*Rubbing his hands.*] This feels good. Come up to the fire, ladies.

Mrs. Peters. [*After taking a step forward.*] I'm not—cold.

Sheriff. [*Unbuttoning his overcoat and stepping away from the stove as if to mark the beginning of official business.*] Now, Mr. Hale, before we move things about, you explain to Mr. Henderson just what you saw when you came here yesterday morning.

County Attorney. By the way, has anything been moved? Are things just as you left them yesterday?

5    Sheriff. [*Looking about.*] It's just the same. When it dropped below zero last night I thought I'd better send Frank out this morning to make a fire for us—no use getting pneumonia with a big case on, but I told him not to touch anything except the stove—and you know Frank.

County Attorney. Somebody should have been left here yesterday.

Sheriff. Oh—yesterday. When I had to send Frank to Morris Center for that man who went crazy—I want you to know I had my hands full yesterday. I knew you could get back from Omaha by today and as long as I went over everything here myself—

County Attorney. Well, Mr. Hale, tell just what happened when you came here yesterday morning.

Hale. Harry and I had started to town with a load of potatoes. We came along the road from my place and as I got here I said, "I'm going to see if I can't get John Wright to go in with me on a party telephone." I spoke to Wright about it once before and he put me off, saying folks talked too much anyway, and all he asked was peace and quiet—I guess you know about how much he talked himself; but I thought maybe if I went to the house and talked about it before his wife, though I said to Harry that I didn't know as what his wife wanted made much difference to John—

10   County Attorney. Let's talk about that later, Mr. Hale. I do want to talk about that, but tell now just what happened when you got to the house.

Hale. I didn't hear or see anything; I knocked at the door, and still it was all quiet inside. I knew they must be up, it was past eight o'clock. So I knocked again, and I thought I heard somebody say, "Come in." I wasn't sure, I'm not sure yet, but I opened the door—this door [*Indicating the door by which the two women are still standing.*] and there in that rocker—[*Pointing to it.*] sat Mrs. Wright.

[*They all look at the rocker.*]

County Attorney. What—was she doing?

Hale. She was rockin' back and forth. She had her apron in her hand and was kind of—pleating it.

County Attorney. And how did she—look?

15   Hale. Well, she looked queer.

County Attorney. How do you mean—queer?

Hale. Well, as if she didn't know what she was going to do next. And kind of done up.

County Attorney. How did she seem to feel about your coming?

Hale. Why, I don't think she minded—one way or other. She didn't pay much attention. I said, "How do, Mrs. Wright, it's cold, ain't it?" And she said, "Is it?"—and went on kind of pleating at her apron. Well, I was surprised; she didn't ask me to come up to the stove, or to set down, but just sat there, not even looking at me, so I said, "I want to see John." And then she—laughed. I guess you would call it a laugh. I thought of Harry and the team outside, so I said a little sharp: "Can't I see John?" "No," she says, kind o' dull like. "Ain't he home?" says I. "Yes," says she, "he's home." "Then why can't I see him?" I asked her, out of patience. "'Cause he's dead," says she. "*Dead?*" says I. She just nodded her head, not getting a bit excited, but rockin' back and forth. "Why—where is he?" says I, not knowing what to say. She just pointed upstairs—like that. [*Himself pointing to the room above.*] I got up, with the idea of going up there. I walked from there to here—then I says, "What did he die of?" "He died of a rope round his neck," says she, and just went on pleatin' at her apron. Well, I went out and called Harry. I thought I might—need help. We went upstairs and there he was lyin'—

County Attorney. I think I'd rather have you go into that upstairs, where you can point    20
it all out. Just go on now with the rest of the story.

Hale. Well, my first thought was to get that rope off. It looked . . . [*Stops, his face twitches.*] . . . but Harry, he went up to him, and he said, "No, he's dead all right, and we'd better not touch anything." So we went back downstairs. She was still sitting that same way. "Has anybody been notified?" I asked. "No," says she, unconcerned. "Who did this, Mrs. Wright?" said Harry. He said it businesslike—and she stopped pleatin' of her apron. "I don't know," she says. "You don't *know?*" says Harry. "No," says she. "Weren't you sleepin' in the bed with him?" says Harry. "Yes," says she, "but I was on the inside." "Somebody slipped a rope round his neck and strangled him and you didn't wake up?" says Harry. "I didn't wake up," she said after him. We must 'a looked as if we didn't see how that could be, for after a minute she said, "I sleep sound." Harry was going to ask her more questions but I said maybe we ought to let her tell her story first to the coroner, or the sheriff, so Harry went fast as he could to Rivers' place, where there's a telephone.

County Attorney. And what did Mrs. Wright do when she knew that you had gone for the coroner?

Hale. She moved from that chair to this one over here [*Pointing to a small chair in the corner.*] and just sat there with her hands held together and looking down. I got a feeling that I ought to make some conversation, so I said I had come in to see if John wanted to put in a telephone, and at that she started to laugh, and then she stopped and looked at me—scared. [*The* County Attorney, *who has had his notebook out, makes a note.*] I dunno, maybe it wasn't scared. I wouldn't like to say it was. Soon Harry got back, and then Dr. Lloyd came, and you, Mr. Peters, and so I guess that's all I know that you don't.

County Attorney. [*Looking around.*] I guess we'll go upstairs first—and then out to the barn and around there. [*To the* Sheriff.] You're convinced that there was nothing important here—nothing that would point to any motive.

Sheriff. Nothing here but kitchen things.    25

[*The* County Attorney, *after again looking around the kitchen, opens the door of a cupboard closet. He gets up on a chair and looks on a shelf. Pulls his hand away, sticky.*]

County Attorney. Here's a nice mess.

[*The women draw nearer.*]

Mrs. Peters. [*To the other woman.*] Oh, her fruit; it did freeze. [*To the* Lawyer.] She worried about that when it turned so cold. She said the fire'd go out and her jars would break.

Sheriff. Well, can you beat the women! Held for murder and worryin' about her preserves.

COUNTY ATTORNEY. I guess before we're through she may have something more serious than preserves to worry about.

30     HALE. Well, women are used to worrying over trifles.

[*The two women move a little closer together.*]

COUNTY ATTORNEY. [*With the gallantry of a young politician.*] And yet, for all their worries, what would we do without the ladies? [*The women do not unbend. He goes to the sink, takes a dipperful of water from the pail and pouring it into a basin, washes his hands. Starts to wipe them on the roller-towel, turns it for a cleaner place.*] Dirty towels! [*Kicks his foot against the pans under the sink.*] Not much of a housekeeper, would you say, ladies?

MRS. HALE. [*Stiffly.*] There's a great deal of work to be done on a farm.

COUNTY ATTORNEY. To be sure. And yet [*With a little bow to her.*] I know there are some Dickson county farmhouses which do not have such roller towels.

[*He gives it a pull to expose its full length again.*]

MRS. HALE. Those towels get dirty awful quick. Men's hands aren't always as clean as they might be.

35     COUNTY ATTORNEY. Ah, loyal to your sex, I see. But you and Mrs. Wright were neighbors. I suppose you were friends, too.

MRS. HALE. [*Shaking her head.*] I've not seen much of her of late years. I've not been in this house—it's more than a year.

COUNTY ATTORNEY. And why was that? You didn't like her?

MRS. HALE. I liked her all well enough. Farmers' wives have their hands full, Mr. Henderson. And then—

COUNTY ATTORNEY. Yes?

40     MRS. HALE. [*Looking about.*] It never seemed a very cheerful place.

COUNTY ATTORNEY. No—it's not cheerful. I shouldn't say she had the homemaking instinct.

MRS. HALE. Well, I don't know as Wright had, either.

COUNTY ATTORNEY. You mean that they didn't get on very well?

MRS. HALE. No, I don't mean anything. But I don't think a place'd be any cheerfuller for John Wright's being in it.

45     COUNTY ATTORNEY. I'd like to talk more of that a little later. I want to get the lay of things upstairs now.

[*He goes to the left, where three steps lead to a stair door.*]

SHERIFF. I suppose anything Mrs. Peters does'll be all right. She was to take in some clothes for her, you know, and a few little things. We left in such a hurry yesterday.

COUNTY ATTORNEY. Yes, but I would like to see what you take, Mrs. Peters, and keep an eye out for anything that might be of use to us.

MRS. PETERS. Yes, Mr. Henderson.

[*The women listen to the men's steps on the stairs, then look about the kitchen.*]

MRS. HALE. I'd hate to have men coming into my kitchen, snooping around and criticizing.

[*She arranges the pans under the sink which the LAWYER had shoved out of place.*]

50     MRS. PETERS. Of course it's no more than their duty.

MRS. HALE. Duty's all right, but I guess that deputy sheriff that came out to make the fire might have got a little of this on. [*Gives the roller towel a pull.*] Wish I'd thought of that sooner. Seems mean to talk about her for not having things slicked up when she had to come away in such a hurry.

MRS. PETERS. [*Who had gone to a small table in the left rear corner of the room, and lifted one end of a towel that covers a pan.*] She had bread set.

[*Stands still.*]

MRS. HALE. [*Eyes fixed on a loaf of bread beside the breadbox, which is on a low shelf at the other side of the room. Moves slowly toward it.*] She was going to put this in there. [*Picks up loaf, then abruptly drops it. In a manner of returning to familiar things.*] It's a shame about her fruit. I wonder if it's all gone. [*Gets up on the chair and looks.*] I think there's some here that's all right, Mrs. Peters. Yes—here; [*Holding it toward the window.*] this is cherries, too. [*Looking again.*] I declare I believe that's the only one. [*Gets down, bottle in her hand. Goes to the sink and wipes it off on the outside.*] She'll feel awful bad after all her hard work in the hot weather. I remember the afternoon I put up my cherries last summer.

[*She puts the bottle on the big kitchen table, center of the room. With a sigh, is about to sit down in the rocking-chair. Before she is seated realizes what chair it is; with a slow look at it, steps back. The chair which she has touched rocks back and forth.*]

MRS. PETERS. Well, I must get those things from the front room closet. [*She goes to the door at the right, but after looking into the other room, steps back.*] You coming with me, Mrs. Hale? You could help me carry them.

[*They go in the other room; reappear, MRS. PETERS carrying a dress and skirt, MRS. HALE following with a pair of shoes.*]

MRS. PETERS. My, it's cold in there.                                                                              55

[*She puts the clothes on the big table, and hurries to the stove.*]

MRS. HALE. [*Examining the skirt.*] Wright was close. I think maybe that's why she kept so much to herself. She didn't even belong to the Ladies Aid. I suppose she felt she couldn't do her part, and then you don't enjoy things when you feel shabby. She used to wear pretty clothes and be lively, when she was Minnie Foster, one of the town girls singing in the choir. But that—oh, that was thirty years ago. This all you was to take in?

MRS. PETERS. She said she wanted an apron. Funny thing to want, for there isn't much to get you dirty in jail, goodness knows. But I suppose just to make her feel more natural. She said they was in the top drawer in this cupboard. Yes, here. And then her little shawl that always hung behind the door. [*Opens stair door and looks.*] Yes, here it is.

[*Quickly shuts door leading upstairs.*]

MRS. HALE. [*Abruptly moving toward her.*] Mrs. Peters?

MRS. PETERS. Yes, Mrs. Hale?

MRS. HALE. Do you think she did it?                                                                               60

MRS. PETERS. [*In a frightened voice.*] Oh, I don't know.

MRS. HALE. Well, I don't think she did. Asking for an apron and her little shawl. Worrying about her fruit.

MRS. PETERS. [*Starts to speak, glances up, where footsteps are heard in the room above. In a low voice.*] Mr. Peters says it looks bad for her. Mr. Henderson is awful sarcastic in a speech and he'll make fun of her sayin' she didn't wake up.

MRS. HALE. Well, I guess John Wright didn't wake when they was slipping that rope under his neck.

MRS. PETERS. No, it's strange. It must have been done awful crafty and still. They say it     65
was such a—funny way to kill a man, rigging it all up like that.

MRS. HALE. That's just what Mr. Hale said. There was a gun in the house. He says that's what he can't understand.

MRS. PETERS. Mr. Henderson said coming out that what was needed for the case was a motive; something to show anger, or—sudden feeling.

MRS. HALE. [*Who is standing by the table.*] Well, I don't see any signs of anger around here. [*She puts her hand on the dish towel which lies on the table, stands looking down at table, one half of which is clean, the other half messy.*] It's wiped to here. [*Makes a move as if to finish work, then turns and looks at loaf of bread outside the breadbox. Drops towel. In that voice of coming back to familiar things.*] Wonder how they are finding things upstairs. I hope she had it a little more red-up° up there. You know, it seems kind of *sneaking*. Locking her up in town and then coming out here and trying to get her own house to turn against her!

MRS. PETERS. But Mrs. Hale, the law is the law.

70      MRS. HALE. I s'pose 'tis. [*Unbuttoning her coat.*] Better loosen up your things, Mrs. Peters. You won't feel them when you go out.

[*MRS. PETERS takes off her fur tippet,* goes to hang it on hook at back of room, stands looking at the under part of the small corner table.*]

MRS. PETERS. She was piecing a quilt.

[*She brings the large sewing basket and they look at the bright pieces.*]

MRS. HALE. It's a log cabin pattern. Pretty, isn't it? I wonder if she was goin' to quilt it or just knot it?

[*Footsteps have been heard coming down the stairs. The SHERIFF enters followed by HALE and the COUNTY ATTORNEY.*]

SHERIFF. They wonder if she was going to quilt it or just knot it!

[*The men laugh; the women look abashed.*]

COUNTY ATTORNEY. [*Rubbing his hands over the stove.*] Frank's fire didn't do much up there, did it? Well, let's go out to the barn and get that cleared up.

[*The men go outside.*]

75      MRS. HALE. [*Resentfully.*] I don't know as there's anything so strange, our takin' up our time with little things while we're waiting for them to get the evidence. [*She sits down at the big table smoothing out a block with decision.*] I don't see as it's anything to laugh about.

MRS. PETERS. [*Apologetically.*] Of course they've got awful important things on their minds.

[*Pulls up a chair and joins MRS. HALE at the table.*]

MRS. HALE. [*Examining another block.*] Mrs. Peters, look at this one. Here. This is the one she was working on, and look at the sewing! All the rest of it has been so nice and even. And look at this! It's all over the place! Why, it looks as if she didn't know what she was about!

[*After she has said this they look at each other, then start to glance back at the door. After an instant MRS. HALE has pulled at a knot and ripped the sewing.*]

MRS. PETERS. Oh, what are you doing, Mrs. Hale?

MRS. HALE. [*Mildly.*] Just pulling out a stitch or two that's not sewed very good. [*Threading a needle.*] Bad sewing always made me fidgety.

80      MRS. PETERS. [*Nervously.*] I don't think we ought to touch things.

---

°*red-up:* neat, arranged in order.     \**tippet:* scarf-like garment of fur or wool for the neck and shoulders.

MRS. HALE. I'll just finish up this end. [*Suddenly stopping and leaning forward.*] Mrs. Peters?

MRS. PETERS. Yes, Mrs. Hale?

MRS. HALE. What do you suppose she was so nervous about?

MRS. PETERS. Oh—I don't know. I don't know as she was nervous. I sometimes sew awful queer when I'm just tired. [*MRS. HALE starts to say something, looks at MRS. PETERS, then goes on sewing.*] Well I must get these things wrapped up. They may be through sooner than we think. [*Putting apron and other things together.*] I wonder where I can find a piece of paper, and string.

MRS. HALE. In that cupboard, maybe. 85

MRS. PETERS. [*Looking in cupboard.*] Why, here's a birdcage. [*Holds it up.*] Did she have a bird, Mrs. Hale?

MRS. HALE. Why, I don't know whether she did or not—I've not been here for so long. There was a man around last year selling canaries cheap, but I don't know as she took one; maybe she did. She used to sing real pretty herself.

MRS. PETERS. [*Glancing around.*] Seems funny to think of a bird here. But she must have had one, or why would she have a cage? I wonder what happened to it.

MRS. HALE. I s'pose maybe the cat got it.

MRS. PETERS. No, she didn't have a cat. She's got that feeling some people have about 90 cats—being afraid of them. My cat got in her room and she was real upset and asked me to take it out.

MRS. HALE. My sister Bessie was like that. Queer, ain't it?

MRS. PETERS. [*Examining the cage.*] Why, look at this door. It's broke. One hinge is pulled apart.

MRS. HALE. [*Looking too.*] Looks as if someone must have been rough with it.

MRS. PETERS. Why, yes.

[*She brings the cage forward and puts it on the table.*]

MRS. HALE. I wish if they're going to find any evidence they'd be about it. I don't like this 95 place.

MRS. PETERS. But I'm awful glad you came with me, Mrs. Hale. It would be lonesome for me sitting here alone.

MRS. HALE. It would, wouldn't it? [*Dropping her sewing.*] But I tell you what I do wish, Mrs. Peters. I wish I had come over sometimes when *she* was here. I—[*Looking around the room.*] I—wish I had.

MRS. PETERS. But of course you were awful busy, Mrs. Hale—your house and your children.

MRS. HALE. I could've come. I stayed away because it weren't cheerful—and that's why I ought to have come. I—I've never liked this place. Maybe because it's down in a hollow and you don't see the road. I dunno what it is, but it's a lonesome place and always was. I wish I had come over to see Minnie Foster sometimes. I can see now—

[*Shakes her head.*]

MRS. PETERS. Well, you mustn't reproach yourself, Mrs. Hale. Somehow we just don't see 100 how it is with other folks until—something comes up.

MRS. HALE. Not having children makes less work—but it makes a quiet house, and Wright out to work all day, and no company when he did come in. Did you know John Wright, Mrs. Peters?

MRS. PETERS. Not to know him; I've seen him in town. They say he was a good man.

MRS. HALE. Yes—good; he didn't drink, and kept his word as well as most, I guess, and paid his debts. But he was a hard man, Mrs. Peters. Just to pass the time of day with him—[*Shivers.*]

Like a raw wind that gets to the bone. [*Pauses, her eye falling on the cage.*] I should think she would 'a wanted a bird. But what do you suppose went with it?

MRS. PETERS. I don't know, unless it got sick and died.

[*She reaches over and swings the broken door, swings it again, both women watch it.*]

105     MRS. HALE. You weren't raised round here, were you? [*MRS. PETERS shakes her head.*] You didn't know—her?

MRS. PETERS. Not till they brought her yesterday,

MRS. HALE. She—come to think of it, she was kind of like a bird herself—real sweet and pretty, but kind of timid and—fluttery. How—she—did—change. [*Silence; then as if struck by a happy thought and relieved to get back to everyday things.*] Tell you what, Mrs. Peters, why don't you take the quilt in with you? It might take up her mind.

MRS. PETERS. Why, I think that's a real nice idea, Mrs. Hale. There couldn't possibly be any objection to it, could there? Now, just what would I take? I wonder if her patches are in here—and her things.

[*They look in the sewing basket.*]

MRS. HALE. Here's some red. I expect this has got sewing things in it. [*Brings out a fancy box.*] What a pretty box. Looks like something somebody would give you. Maybe her scissors are in here. [*Opens box. Suddenly puts her hand to her nose.*] Why—[*MRS. PETERS bends nearer, then turns her face away.*] There's something wrapped up in this piece of silk.

110     MRS. PETERS. Why, this isn't her scissors.

MRS. HALE. [*Lifting the silk.*] Oh, Mrs. Peters—it's—

[*MRS. PETERS bends closer.*]

MRS. PETERS. It's the bird.

MRS. HALE. [*Jumping up.*] But, Mrs. Peters—look at it! Its neck! Look at its neck! It's all—other side *to*.

MRS. PETERS. Somebody—wrung—its—neck.

[*Their eyes meet. A look of growing comprehension, of horror. Steps are heard outside. MRS. HALE slips box under quilt pieces, and sinks into her chair. Enter SHERIFF and COUNTY ATTORNEY. MRS. PETERS rises.*]

115     COUNTY ATTORNEY. [*As one turning from serious things to little pleasantries.*] Well, ladies, have you decided whether she was going to quilt it or knot it?

MRS. PETERS. We think she was going to—knot it.

COUNTY ATTORNEY. Well, that's interesting, I'm sure. [*Seeing the bird-cage.*] Has the bird flown?

MRS. HALE. [*Putting more quilt pieces over the box.*] We think the—cat got it.

COUNTY ATTORNEY. [*Preoccupied.*] Is there a cat?

[*MRS. HALE glances in a quick covert way at MRS. PETERS.*]

120     MRS. PETERS. Well, not *now*. They're superstitious, you know. They leave.

COUNTY ATTORNEY. [*To SHERIFF PETERS, continuing an interrupted conversation.*] No sign at all of anyone having come from the outside. Their own rope. Now let's go up again and go over it piece by piece. [*They start upstairs.*] It would have to have been someone who knew just the—

[*MRS. PETERS sits down. The two women sit there not looking at one another, but as if peering into something and at the same time holding back. When they talk now it is in the manner of feeling their way over strange ground, as if afraid of what they are saying, but as if they cannot help saying it.*]

MRS. HALE. She liked the bird. She was going to bury it in that pretty box.

MRS. PETERS. [*In a whisper.*] When I was a girl—my kitten—there was a boy took a hatchet, and before my eyes—and before I could get there—[*Covers her face an instant.*] If they hadn't held me back I would have—[*Catches herself, looks upstairs where steps are heard, falters weakly.*]—hurt him.

MRS. HALE. [*With a slow look around her.*] I wonder how it would seem never to have had any children around. [*Pause.*] No, Wright wouldn't like the bird—a thing that sang. She used to sing. He killed that, too.

MRS. PETERS. [*Moving uneasily.*] We don't know who killed the bird.                    125

MRS. HALE. I knew John Wright.

MRS. PETERS. It was an awful thing was done in this house that night, Mrs. Hale. Killing a man while he slept, slipping a rope around his neck that choked the life out of him.

MRS. HALE. His neck. Choked the life out of him.

[*Her hand goes out and rests on the birdcage.*]

MRS. PETERS. [*With rising voice.*] We don't know who killed him. We don't know.

MRS. HALE. [*Her own feeling not interrupted.*] If there'd been years and years of noth-    130
ing, then a bird to sing to you, it would be awful—still, after the bird was still.

MRS. PETERS. [*Something within her speaking.*] I know what stillness is. When we homesteaded in Dakota, and my first baby died—after he was two years old, and me with no other then—

MRS. HALE. [*Moving.*] How soon do you suppose they'll be through, looking for the evidence?

MRS. PETERS. I know what stillness is. [*Pulling herself back.*] The law has got to punish crime, Mrs. Hale.

MRS. HALE. [*Not as if answering that.*] I wish you'd seen Minnie Foster when she wore a white dress with blue ribbons and stood up there in the choir and sang. [*A look around the room.*] Oh, I wish I'd come over here once in a while! That was a crime! That was a crime! Who's going to punish that?

MRS. PETERS. [*Looking upstairs.*] We mustn't—take on.                                 135

MRS. HALE. I might have known she needed help! I know how things can be—for women. I tell you, it's queer, Mrs. Peters. We live close together and we live far apart. We all go through the same things—it's all just a different kind of the same thing. [*Brushes her eyes; noticing the bottle of fruit, reaches out for it.*] If I was you I wouldn't tell her her fruit was gone. Tell her it ain't. Tell her it's all right. Take this in to prove it to her. She—she may never know whether it was broke or not.

MRS. PETERS. [*Takes the bottle, looks about for something to wrap it in; takes petticoat from the clothes brought from the other room, very nervously begins winding this around the bottle. In a false voice.*] My, it's a good thing the men couldn't hear us. Wouldn't they just laugh! Getting all stirred up over a little thing like a—dead canary. As if that could have anything to do with—with—wouldn't they *laugh*!

[*The men are heard coming down stairs.*]

MRS. HALE. [*Under her breath.*] Maybe they would—maybe they wouldn't.

COUNTY ATTORNEY. No, Peters, it's all perfectly clear except a reason for doing it. But you know juries when it comes to women. If there was some definite thing. Something to show—something to make a story about—a thing that would connect up with this strange way of doing it—

[*The women's eyes meet for an instant. Enter HALE from outer door.*]

140      HALE. Well, I've got the team around. Pretty cold out there.

COUNTY ATTORNEY. I'm going to stay here a while by myself. [*To the* SHERIFF.] You can send Frank out for me, can't you? I want to go over everything. I'm not satisfied that we can't do better.

SHERIFF. Do you want to see what Mrs. Peters is going to take in?

[*The* COUNTY ATTORNEY *goes to the table, picks up the apron, laughs.*]

COUNTY ATTORNEY. Oh, I guess they're not very dangerous things the ladies have picked out. [*Moves a few things about, disturbing the quilt pieces which cover the box. Steps back.*] No, Mrs. Peters doesn't need supervising. For that matter, a sheriff's wife is married to the law. Ever think of it that way, Mrs. Peters?

MRS. PETERS. Not—just that way.

145      SHERIFF. [*Chuckling.*] Married to the law. [*Moves toward the other room.*] I just want you to come in here a minute, George. We ought to take a look at these windows.

COUNTY ATTORNEY. [*Scoffingly.*] Oh, windows!

SHERIFF. We'll be right out, Mr. Hale.

[HALE *goes outside. The* SHERIFF *follows the* COUNTY ATTORNEY *into the other room. Then* MRS. HALE *rises, hands tight together, looking intensely at* MRS. PETERS, *whose eyes make a slow turn, finally meeting* MRS. HALE'S. *A moment* MRS. HALE *holds her, then her own eyes point the way to where the box is concealed. Suddenly* MRS. PETERS *throws back quilt pieces and tries to put the box in the bag she is wearing. It is too big. She opens box, starts to take bird out, cannot touch it, goes to pieces, stands there helpless. Sound of a knob turning in the other room.* MRS. HALE *snatches the box and puts it in the pocket of her big coat. Enter* COUNTY ATTORNEY *and* SHERIFF.]

COUNTY ATTORNEY. [*Facetiously.*] Well, Henry, at least we found out that she was not going to quilt it. She was going to—what is it you call it, ladies?

MRS. HALE. [*Her hand against her pocket.*] We call it—knot it, Mr. Henderson.

### CURTAIN

# A Glossary of Important Literary Terms

This glossary presents brief definitions of terms that are boldfaced in the text. Page references indicate where readers may find additional detail and illustration, together with discussions about how the concepts may be used in writing about literature.

**accent,** or **beat**    The heavy stresses or accents in lines of poetry. Because heavy stresses are paired with *light stresses* to compose metrical *feet*, the numbers of accents or beats in a line usually govern the meter of the line (five feet in a *pentameter* line, four in a *tetrameter* line, etc.). (191)

**accented rhyme**    See *heavy-stress rhyme.*

**accented syllable**    A syllable receiving a major, or heavy, *stress.* (191)

**actions**    The major activities and events in a work of narrative fiction. (2)

**acute accent**    In some forms of poetic scansion, the prime mark (´) indicating a heavy *stress.* (191)

**allegory**    A complete narrative that may also be applied to a parallel set of moral, philosophical, political, religious, or social situations. (Ch. 11: 157)

**alliteration**    The repetition of identical consonant sounds in close proximity, most often, but not always, the sounds beginning words (e.g., "*s*omewhere *s*afe to *s*ea," "*g*racious, *g*olden, *g*littering *g*leams," "And *d*eath once *d*ead, there's no more *d*ying then," "While *p*ensive *p*oets *p*ainful vigils kee*p*"). (198)

**allusion**    Unacknowledged references and quotations that authors make while assuming that readers will recognize the original sources and relate their meanings to the new context. Allusions are hence compliments that authors pay to readers for their perceptiveness, knowledge, and awareness. (162)

**amphibrach**    A three-syllable foot consisting of a light, heavy, and light stress, as in "*I'm SING-ing.*" (195)

**amphimacer,** or **cretic**    A three-syllable foot consisting of a heavy, light, and heavy stress, as in *SING-ing SONGS.* (195)

**analytical sentence outline**    A scheme or plan for an essay, arranged according to topics (A, B, C, etc.) and with the topics expressed in sentences. (31)

**analyzed rhyme**    See *inexact rhyme.*

**anapest**    Sometimes spelled **anapaest.** A three-syllable foot consisting of two light stresses and a heavy stress, as in *and bright STARS* and *ear-ly LIGHT.* (194)

**antagonist**    (i.e., One who struggles against.) The person, idea, force, or general set of circumstances opposing the *protagonist*; an essential element of *plot.* (87)

**anticipation**    See *procatalepsis.*

**archetypal/symbolic/mythic critical approach**    An interpretive literary approach explaining literature in terms of archetypal patterns (e.g., God's creation of human beings, the sacrifice of a hero, the search for paradise, the initiation or "test" of a young person). (313)

**argument**    The development of a pattern of interpretation or thought with an intent to persuade. In most writing about literature, the persuasive situation is to show the validity of a particular idea or circumstance in a story, poem, or play. More broadly, the term *argument* applies to any situation about which there may be disagreement. Although sometimes *argumentative* discourse may become disputatious, one should never forget that true arguments should stem from the logical and reasonable interpretation of correct and accurate data. (20, 27, 36, 40, 216)

**assertion**   A sentence putting an idea or argument (the subject) into operation (the predicate); necessary for both developing and understanding the idea. (123)

**assonance**   The repetition of identical vowel sounds in different words in close proximity, as in the *deep green sea*. (198)

**atmosphere,** or **mood**   The emotional aura invoked by a work. (116)

**auditory images**   References to sounds. (138)

**authorial symbol**   See *contextual symbol.*

**authorial voice**   The *voice* or *persona* used by authors when seemingly speaking for themselves. The use of the term makes it possible to discuss a narration or presentation without identifying the ideas absolutely with those of the author. See also *speaker, point of view,* and *third-person point of view.* (71, 126)

**Bacchius** or **Bacchic**   A three-syllable foot consisting of a light stress followed by two heavy stresses, as in *a NEW SONG* and *the OLD WAYS.* (195)

**ballad, ballad measure**   A narrative poem, originally a popular form, composed of quatrains in *ballad measure*—that is, a pattern of iambic tetrameter alternating with iambic trimeter and rhyming *x-a-x-a.* (3, 203)

**beast fable**   A narrative or poem attributing human characteristics to animals, including powers of thought and speech. (161)

**beat**   See *accent.*

**blank verse**   Unrhymed iambic pentameter. Most of the poetry in Shakespeare's plays is blank verse, as is the poetry of Milton's *Paradise Lost* and many of Wordsworth's longer poems. (3)

**brainstorming**   The exploration and discovery of details to be developed in a composition. (18)

**breve**   In traditional poetic scansion, a mark in the shape of a bowl-like half circle (˘) to indicate a light stress or lightly accented syllable. (191)

**cacophony**   Meaning "bad sound"—but by no means bad—*cacophony* refers to words combining sharp sounds and heavy accents, as in Pope's "When Ajax strives some rock's vast weight to throw," and Coleridge's "And from this chasm, with ceaseless turmoil seething, / As if this earth in fast thick pants were breathing." Cacophony is contrasted with *euphony* (good sound). See *euphony.* (199)

**cadence group**   A coherent word group spoken as a single rhythmical unit, such as a noun phrase ("our sacred honor") or prepositional phrase ("of human events"). (196)

**caesura,** (plural **caesurae**)   The pause(s) or juncture(s) separating words and phrases within lines of poetry, as in Pope's line "Trees, where you sit, shall crowd into a shade" (Second Pastoral, "Summer," line 74), in which there is a caesura after "Trees" and also after "sit." In poetic *scansion,* the caesura is marked by a double *virgule* (//). The control of caesurae is a vital aspect of poetic *rhythm.* (197)

**catalexis**   See *imperfect foot.*

**central idea, central argument,** or **central statement**   The thesis or main idea of an essay; the *theme* of a literary work. (27)

**character**   An extended verbal representation of a human being, the inner self that determines thought, speech, and behavior. (Ch. 4: 83)

**choree**   See *trochee.*

**chronology** (the "logic of time")   The sequence of events in a work, with emphasis on the intertwining of cause and effect. (95)

**cliché rhyme**   A rhyme that is typically easy and unoriginal, such as the word "breeze" followed by "trees." (200)

**climax (Greek for "ladder")**   The high point of *conflict* and tension preceding the resolution of a story or play; the point of decision, of inevitability and no return. The climax is sometimes merged with the *crisis* in the consideration of dramatic and narrative structure. (103)

**close reading**   The detailed study of a poem or passage, designed to explain characters, motivations, situations, ideas, style, organization, word selections, settings, similarities and contrasts of sound, and so on. (Ch. 2: 52–64)

**comparison-contrast analysis**   A technique of analyzing two or more works in order to determine similarities and differences in topic, treatment, and quality. (Ch. 15: 224)

**complication**   A stage of narrative and dramatic structure in which the major *conflicts* are brought out; the rising action of a *drama*. (102)

**conflict**   The opposition between two characters, between large groups of people, or between *protagonists* and larger forces such as natural objects, ideas, modes of behavior, public opinion, and the like. Conflict may also be internal and psychological, involving choices facing a *protagonist*. The resolution of conflict is the essence of *plot*. (95)

**consonant sounds,** or **consonant segments**   Consonant sounds (i.e., sounds that accompany ["con"= "with"] the sound ["sonant," = vowel sounds]). They are produced as a result of the touching or close proximity of the tongue or the lips in relation to the teeth or palate (e.g., *m, n, p, f, sh, ch*); to be compared and contrasted with *vowel sounds, q.v.* (189)

**contextual, private,** or **authorial symbol**   A symbol that is derived not from common historical, cultural, or religious materials, but that is developed within the context of an individual work. See also *cultural,* or *universal, symbol.* (158, 163)

**cosmic irony (irony of fate)**   Situational irony that reveals a fatalistic or pessimistic view of life. Although individual characters may struggle with great tenacity, their efforts are doomed right from the start (plans cannot be carried out; sickness occurs unexpectedly; friends go back on their words; promises are not kept; meanings are misunderstood; false tales are told, etc). See *irony.* (179)

**couplet**   Two lines that may be unified by rhyme or, in biblical poetry, by content. (3)

**creative nonfiction**   A type of literature that is technically nonfiction, such as diaries, journals, and news features, but which nevertheless exhibits high degrees of imaginative and literary skill. (3)

**cretic**   See *amphimacer.*

**crisis**   The point of uncertainty and tension—the turning point—that results from the *conflicts* and difficulties brought about through the *complications* of the plot. The crisis leads to the *climax*— that is, to the attempts made by the protagonist to resolve the conflict. Sometimes the crisis and the climax are considered as two elements of the same stage of *plot* development. (103)

**cultural context**   See *historical context.*

**cultural,** or **universal, symbol**   A symbol that is recognized and shared as a result of a common political, social, and cultural heritage. See also *contextual, private,* or *authorial, symbol.* (158)

**dactyl**   A three-syllable foot consisting of a heavy stress followed by two light stresses, as in the words *hap-pi-ness, ev-i-dent,* and *lib-er-ty.* (194)

**dactylic rhyme**   Rhyming dactyls, such as *spillable* and *syllable* or *mortify* and *fortify.* Also called *triple rhyme.* (201)

**deconstructionist critical approach**   An interpretive literary approach that rejects absolute interpretations and stresses ambiguities and contradictions. (314)

**dénouement (untying),** or **resolution**   The final stage of plot development, in which mysteries are explained, characters find their destinies, lovers are united, sanity is restored, and the work is completed. Usually the dénouement is done as speedily as possible, because it occurs after all conflicts are ended and little that is new can be introduced to hold the interest of readers. (103)

**dilemma**   A situation presenting a character with two choices, each one of which is unacceptable, dangerous, or even lethal. (96)

**dimeter**   A poetic line of two metrical *feet.* (192)

**dipody, dipodic foot,** or **syzygy**   A strong beat that creates a single foot out of two normal feet—usually iambs or trochees—so that a "galloping" or "rollicking" rhythm results. (195)

**documentation**   Granting recognition to the ideas and words of others, whether through textual, parenthetical, or footnote references. (273)

**double entendre (French for "double meaning")**   Deliberate ambiguity, usually humorous, and often sexual. (179)

**double rhyme**   See *trochaic rhyme.*

**drama**   An individual play; also plays considered as a group. One of the three major genres of *imaginative literature.* (3)

**dramatic irony**    A special kind of *situational irony* in which a character is ignorant of his true plight, or may perceive it in a limited way, whereas readers and the audience—and perhaps one or more of the other characters—understand it fully. (180)

**dramatic,** or **objective, point of view**    A *third-person narration* reporting speech and action but excluding commentary about the actions and thoughts of the characters. (71)

**dying rhyme**    See *falling rhyme.*

**dynamic character**    A character who tries to assert control by recognition, adjustment, and change. Dynamic changes may be shown in (1) an action or actions, (2) the realization of new strength and therefore the affirmation of previous decisions, (3) the acceptance of new conditions and the need for making changes and improvements, (4) the discovery of unrecognized truths, or (5) the reconciliation of the character with adverse conditions. In a *short story*, there is usually only one dynamic character, whereas in a *novel* there may be many. Compare with a *static character, q.v.* (87)

**echoic**    Refers to words that (very likely) originated as imitations or echoes of the objects or actions they describe, such as *bounding, buzz, flutter, pop, slap, stammer,* and *yodel.* Echoic words are essential to the device of *onomatopoeia.* (199)

**economic determinist/Marxist critical approach**    An interpretive literary approach based on the theories of Karl Marx (1818–1883), stressing that literature is to be judged from the perspective of economic and social class inequality and oppression. (311)

**elegy**    A poem of lamentation about a death. Often an elegy takes the form of a pastoral poem. (3)

**enclosing setting**    See *framing setting.*

**end-stopped (line)**    A poetic line ending in a full pause, usually indicated with a period or semicolon. (197)

**enjambement,** or **run-on line**    A line having no end punctuation but running over to the next line. (197)

**epic**    A long narrative poem elevating character, speech, and action. Some of the earliest surviving literary works are epics about the exploits of Gilgamesh, the wrath of Achilles, and the wanderings of Odysseus (3)

**essay**    In writing about literature, an essay is a short and tightly organized written composition dealing with a topic such as character, a major idea, or point of view. Broadly, essays also deal with any and all conceivable topics. (15, passim)

**euphony ("good sound")**    Word groups containing consonants and vowels together that encourage speakers to utter an easy and pleasant flow of spoken sound. To describe a passage as euphonious is highly subjective—more so, probably, than to declare something cacophonous. Shakespeare's Hamlet tells his friends from the visiting acting company to speak their speeches "trippingly on the tongue" so that they may give their lines "smoothness" (*Hamlet,* Act 3, Scene 2). Here he seems to be describing euphony. See also *cacophony.* (199)

**exact rhyme**    Also sometimes called *perfect rhyme.* Exact rhyme is the placement of rhyming words or syllables in which both the vowel and concluding consonant sounds, if any, are identical, as in *done* and *run,* and *see* and *be.* It is important to judge rhymes on the basis of *sound* rather than spelling, as in these examples. Words do not have to be spelled the same way to be exact rhymes. (199)

**examination**    A written or oral test or inquiry designed to discover a person's understanding and capacity to deal successfully with a particular topic or set of topics. (Ch. 19: 293–302)

**exposition**    The stage of dramatic or narrative structure that introduces all things necessary for the development of the plot. (102)

**eye rhyme,** or **sight rhyme**    Words that seem to rhyme because parts of them are spelled identically even though they are pronounced differently (e.g., *bear, fear; fury, bury; shove, stove; wonder, yonder; clover, hover*). (202)

**fable**    A brief *story* illustrating a moral truth, most often associated with the ancient Greek writer Aesop. See also *beast fable.* (161)

**falling rhyme**    Trochaic rhymes, such as *dying* and *crying,* and also multisyllabic rhymes, such as *flattery* and *battery* and *listening* and *glistening.* See *trochee.* (201)

**feet**   See *foot.*

**feminist critical approach**   An interpretive literary approach designed to raise consciousness about the importance and unique nature of women in literature. (309)

**fiction**   *Narratives* based in the imagination of the author, not in literal, reportorial, or historical facts; one of the three major genres of imaginative literature (2)

**figurative devices**   See *figurative language.*

**figurative language**   An organized pattern of comparison that deepens, broadens, extends, illuminates, and emphasizes meaning, and also that conforms to particular patterns or forms such as parallelism, *metaphor*, and *simile*. (146)

**figures**   See *figurative language.*

**figures of speech**   See *figurative language.*

**first-person point of view**   The use of an "I," or first-person, speaker or narrator who tells about things that he or she has seen, done, spoken, heard, thought, and also learned about in other ways. (68, 74)

**flashback**   Also called *selective recollection*. A method of *narration* in which past events are introduced into a present action. (104)

**flat character**   A character, usually minor, who is not individual but useful and structural, static and unchanging; distinguished from *round character, q.v.* (87)

**foot, feet**   A poetic foot consists of the measured combination of heavy and light *stresses*, such as the *iamb*, which contains a light stress followed by a heavy stress (e.g., "*of YEAR*"). In poetic scansion, the feet are separated by a *virgule* or single slash mark (/), as in the first line of Shakespeare's Sonnet 73: "That TIME / of YEAR / thou MAY'ST / in ME / be – HOLD." (191)

**formal substitution**   See *substitution.*

**formalist critical approach**   See *New Critical/formalist critical approach.*

**framing (enclosing) setting**   The same features of topic or setting used at both the beginning and ending of a work so as to "frame" or "enclose" the work. (115)

**free verse**   Poetry based on the natural rhythms of phrases and normal pauses, not metrical feet. (3)

**freewriting**   See *brainstorming.*

**genre**   One of the types of literature, such as *fiction* and *poetry*. Also, a type of work, such as detective fiction, comedy, epic poetry, or tragedy. (2)

**graph, graphics (spelling)**   The appearance of words on a page, as opposed to their actual sounds; spelling. Thus, the *sh* sound may be graphed (spelled) in many different ways, such as "*ship*," "*nation*," "*ocean*," "*fission*," and "Fu*chsia*." (191)

**guidelines for reading**   Systematic procedures for recording responses and ideas during the reading process. An essential step toward the development of analytical thought. (13)

**gustatory images**   References to sensations and impressions of taste. (138)

**haiku**   A poetic form derived from Japanese literature, traditionally containing three lines of five, seven, and five syllables, in that order, and treating topics generally derived from nature. (3)

**half rhyme**   See *inexact rhyme.*

**heavy-stress rhyme, rising rhyme,** or **accented rhyme**   A rhyme, such as rhyming iambs or anapests, ending with a strong stress. The rhymes may be produced with one-syllable words, like *earth* and *dearth,* or with multisyllabic words in which the accent falls on the final syllable, such as *decline* and *confine*. (191, 201)

**heptameter,** or **septenary**   A line consisting of seven metrical feet. (192)

**hero, heroine**   The major male and female *protagonists* in a narrative or drama. The terms are often used to describe leading characters in adventures and romances. (87)

**hexameter**   A poetic line consisting of six metrical feet. (192)

**historical context** (also **cultural context** and **intellectual context**)   The historical time when a work was written, together with the intellectual and cultural ideas of this period. To study a work of literature in this perspective is to determine the degree to which the work spoke not only to people of its own time but continues to speak to people of the present time (and perhaps to people of all time). (Ch. 16: 242)

**historical critical approach**   See *topical/historical critical approach.*

**hovering accent**   See *spondee.*

**humor**   The feature or features of a situation or expression designed to provoke laughter and amusement. (177, 182)

**hymn**   A religious song, consisting usually of a number of replicating stanzas, designed for religious services. (3)

**hyperbole,** or **overstatement**   A rhetorical figure in which emphasis is achieved through exaggeration. (179)

**iamb**   A two-syllable *foot* consisting of a light stress followed by a heavy stress (e.g., *the WINDS, have FELT, of MAY*). The iamb is the most common metrical foot in English poetry inasmuch as it closely resembles natural speech but is also determined by measured poetic accents. (192)

**iambic rhyme**   A *heavy-stress rhyme* that is built from rhyming *iambs* such as *the WEST* and *in REST*, or from rhyming two-syllable words such as "ad - MIRE" and "de - SIRE." (201)

**idea,** or **theme**   A concept, thought, opinion, or belief; in literature, a unifying, centralizing conception or theme. (Ch. 8: 123, 182)

**identical rhyme**   The use of the same words in rhyming positions, such as *veil* and *veil*, or *stone* and *stone.* (202)

**image, imagery**   Images are references that trigger the mind to fuse together memories of sights (*visual*), sounds (*auditory*), tastes (*gustatory*), smells (*olfactory*), and sensations of touch (*tactile*). "Image" refers to a single mental creation. "Imagery" refers to images throughout a work or throughout the works of a writer or group of writers. Images may be *literal* (descriptive and pictorial) or *metaphorical* (figurative and suggestive), or both. (3, Ch. 9: 136)

**imaginative literature**   *Literature* based in the imagination of the writer. The genres of imaginative literature are *fiction, poetry,* and *drama.* (1, *passim*)

**imperfect foot**   A metrical *foot* consisting of a single heavily or lightly stressed syllable, such as the *ing* in *at the TWI - light's last GLEAM - ing.* There is nothing imperfect about an imperfect foot. It is so named because, having only one syllable, it does not fit into the patterns of the other poetic feet. Some analysts of prosody use the term *catalexis* (Greek for "leave off") rather than *imperfect foot,* to indicate that a syllable is lacking in the foot in question. (194)

**incidents**   See *actions.*

**incongruity**   A discrepancy between what is ordinarily or normally expected and what is actually experienced. The resulting gap is a major cause of amusement. (177)

**inexact rhyme**   Rhymes that are created from words with similar but not identical sounds. In most of these instances, either the vowel segments are different while the consonants are the same, or vice versa. This type of rhyme is variously called *slant rhyme, near rhyme, half rhyme, off rhyme, analyzed rhyme,* or *suspended rhyme.* (202)

**intellectual context**   See *historical context.*

**intellectual critical approach**   See *moral/intellectual critical approach.*

**internal rhyme**   The occurrence of rhyming words within a single line of verse, as with Poe's "Can ever dissever" in *Annabel Lee.* (200)

**irony**   A major aspect of literary tone, based on the proposition that even the simplest events in human life may be seen in multiple ways. Irony therefore deals with contradictions and ambiguities—the shadows underlying human existence. It is conveyed through indirection both in situations and in language. See *cosmic irony, dramatic irony, situational irony,* and *verbal irony.* (178)

**irony of fate**   See *cosmic irony.*

**irony of situation**   See *situational irony.*

**journal**   A notebook or word-processor file for recording responses and observations that, for purposes of writing, may be used in the development of essays. (12)

**kinesthetic images**   Words describing human or animal motion and activity. (139)

**kinetic images**   Words describing general motion. (139)

**light stress**   In speech and in metrical scansion, the less emphasized syllables, as in Shakespeare's Sonnet 30, "WHEN to/the SESS -/ions of/SWEET SI -/lent THOUGHT" in which *to, the, ions, of,* and *lent* are pronounced less strongly than *WHEN, SESS, SWEET, SI-,* and *THOUGHT.* See *accent.* (191)

**limited point of view, limited third-person point of view,** or **limited-omniscient point of view** A third-person narration in which the actions, thoughts, and speeches of the protagonist are the primary focus of attention. (71)

**line** The basic unit of length of a poem, appearing as a row of words on a page, or sometimes as a single word or even part of a word making up the line, and cohering grammatically through phrases and sentences. Lines in closed-form poetry are composed of determinable numbers of metrical feet, such as five, four, or three. Lines in open-form poetry are variable, changing with the poet's subject matter and rhythmical speech patterns. (191)

**literary devices** See *figurative language.*

**literary research** See *research.*

**literature** Written or oral compositions that tell stories, dramatize situations, express emotions, analyze and advocate ideas, and express ideals. Literature is designed to engage readers emotionally as well as intellectually, with the major genres being *fiction, poetry, drama,* and *nonfiction prose* and with many separate subforms. (1, *passim*)

**lyric** A short and concentrated poem or song, usually meditative, often personal, and sometimes philosophical. Traditional lyrics follow a fixed stanzaic form, having been originally intended for a musical setting, such as hymns or texts of dramatic arias. The lyrics of many modern poets, however, are comparatively free and unrestricted, and many modern lyrics are designed not for music at all, but rather for silent reading or spoken delivery. (3)

**major mover** A primary participant in a work's action who either causes things to happen or who is the subject of major events. If the first-person narrator is also a major mover, such as the *protagonist,* that fact gives first-hand authenticity to the narration. (66)

**malapropism** The comic use of an improperly pronounced word so that what comes out is a real but also an incorrect word. Examples are *odorous* for *odious* (Shakespeare) or *pineapple* for *pinnacle* (Sheridan). The new word must be close enough to the correct word so that the resemblance is immediately recognized, along with the error. (177)

**Marxist critical approach** See *economic determinist/Marxist critical approach.*

**mechanics of verse** See *prosody.*

**metaphor ("carrying out a change")** *Figurative language* that describes something as though it actually were something else, thereby enhancing understanding and insight. (Ch. 10: 146)

**metaphorical language** See *figurative language.*

**meter** The number of feet within a line of traditional verse, such as *iambic pentameter* referring to a line containing five *iambs.* (192)

**metrical foot** See *foot.*

**metrics** See *prosody.*

**monometer** A line consisting of one metrical foot. (192)

**mood** See *atmosphere.*

**moral/intellectual critical approach** An interpretive literary approach that is concerned primarily with content and values. (304)

**music of poetry** See *prosody.*

**myth, mythology, mythos** A *myth* is a story that deals with the relationships of gods to humanity or with battles among heroes. A myth may also be a set of beliefs or assumptions among societies. *Mythology* refers collectively to the stories and beliefs either of a single group or number of groups. A system of beliefs and religious or historical doctrine is a *mythos.* (161)

**mythic critical approach** See *archetypal/symbolic/mythic critical approach.*

**narration, narrative fiction** The relating or recounting of a sequence of events or actions. Whereas a narration may be reportorial and historical, *narrative fiction* is primarily creative and imaginative. See also *prose fiction* and *creative nonfiction.* (2, 65, 69)

**narrative fiction** See *prose fiction.*

**narrator** See *speaker.*

**nasal consonants**   Continuant consonants in which the consonant position is held while the sound is released through the nose. The three English nasal consonants are *n*, *m*, and *ng*, as in ta*n*, ta*m*, and ta*ng*,

**near rhyme**   See *inexact rhyme*.

**New Critical/formalist critical approach**   An interpretive literary approach based on the French method of *explication de texte* (the [detailed] explanation of a text), stressing the form, details, and meanings of literary works. (306)

**New Historicism**   A type of literary criticism that treats literature as a functional and integrated part of culture and history. (305)

**nonfiction prose**   A *genre* consisting of essays, articles, and books about real as opposed to fictional occurrences and objects; one of the major *genres* of literature. (3)

**novel**   A long work of prose fiction. (2)

**objective point of view**   See *dramatic point of view*.

**octameter**   A line of eight metrical *feet*. (192)

**ode**   A stanzaic poem with varying line lengths and often intricate rhyme schemes that contrast it with *songs* and *hymns*. (3)

**off rhyme**   See *inexact rhyme*.

**olfactory imagery**   Images referring to impressions of smell. (138)

**omniscient point of view**   A *third-person narrative* in which the *speaker* or *narrator*, with no apparent limitations, may describe intentions, actions, reactions, locations, and speeches of any or all of the characters and may also describe their innermost thoughts (when necessary). (72)

**onomatopoeia**   A blending of consonant and vowel sounds designed to imitate or suggest the object or activity being described, as in line 357 of Pope's *An Essay on Criticism*: "That like a wounded Snake, drags its slow length along." (199)

**outline**   See *analytical sentence outline*.

**overstatement**   See *hyperbole*.

**parable**   A short *allegory* designed to illustrate a religious truth, most often associated with Jesus as recorded in the Gospels. (161)

**pastoral**   A traditional poetic form with topical material drawn from the idealized lives and vocabularies of rural and shepherd life. Famous English pastorals are Matthew Arnold's *Thyrsis* (1867), John Milton's *Lycidas* (1637), Alexander Pope's *Pastorals* (1709), and Edmund Spenser's *The Shepheardes Calendar* (1579).

**pentameter**   A poetic line of five metrical *feet*. (192)

**perfect rhyme**   See *exact rhyme*.

**persona**   See *speaker*.

**phonetic, phonetics**   The actual pronunciation of sounds, as distinguished from spelling or *graphics*. Thus, *bear*, *eat*, and *ear* are each spelled or graphed with an *ea* vowel combination, but phonetically the words are pronounced differently. (191)

**plagiarism**   A writer's use of the language and ideas of another writer or writers without proper acknowledgment. Plagiarism is an exceedingly serious breach of academic honor; some call it intellectual theft, and others call it an academic crime. (266, 278)

**plausibility**   See *probability*.

**plot**   The plan or groundwork for a story or a play, with the actions resulting from believable and authentic human responses to a *conflict*. It is causality, conflict, response, opposition, and interaction that make a plot out of a series of actions. Aristotle's word for plot was *muthos*, from which our modern English word *myth* was derived. (Ch. 5: 95)

**poem, poet, poetry**   Poetry is a variable literary genre which is, foremost, characterized by the rhythmical qualities of language. Whereas poems may be short (including *haiku* of just a few lines) or long (*epics* of thousands of lines), the essence of poetry is compression, economy, and force, in contrast with the expansiveness and logic of prose. There is no bar to the topics that poets may consider, and poems may range from the personal and lyric to the public and discursive. A *poem* is one poetic work. A *poet* is a person who writes poems. *Poetry* may refer to the poems of one writer, to poems of a number of writers, to all poems generally, or to the aesthetics of poetry considered as an art. (3, *passim*)

**point of view**    The *speaker, voice, narrator,* or *persona* of a work; the position from which details are perceived and related; a centralizing mind or intelligence; not to be confused with opinion or belief. (Ch. 3: 65)

**point-of-view character**    The central figure or *protagonist* in a *limited-point-of-view narration,* the character about whom events turn, the focus of attention in the narration. (72)

**private,** or **contextual, symbol**    See *cultural symbol.*

**probability** or **plausibility**    The standard that literature should be concerned with what is likely, common, normal, and usual. (88)

**problem**    A question or issue about the interpretation or understanding of a work. (Ch. 14: 214)

**procatalepsis,** or **anticipation**    A rhetorical strategy whereby the writer raises an objection and then answers it; the idea is to strengthen an argument by anticipating and thereby forestalling objections. Also called a figure of *presumptousness* or *presupposal.* (216)

**prose fiction**    *Imaginative* prose narratives (*short stories* and *novels*) that focus on one or a few characters who undergo a change or development as they interact with other characters and deal with their problems. (2, 54)

**prosody**    Metrics and versification; the sounds, rhythms, rhymes, and general qualities of poetic technique; the relationships between content and sound in poetry. (Ch. 13: 188–213)

**protagonist**    The central character and focus of interest in a narrative or drama. (87)

**psychological/psychoanalytic critical approach**    An interpretive literary approach stressing how psychology may be used in the explanation of both authors and their works. (312)

**pyrrhic**    A substitute metrical foot consisting of two unaccented syllables, as in the words "on their" in the following line from Pope's *Pastorals* ("Winter," line 5): "Now SLEEP - / ing FLOCKS / on their /SOFT FLEE - / ces LIE." (193)

**quatrain**    (1) A four-line stanza or poetic unit. (2) In an English or Shakespearean sonnet, a group of four lines united by rhyme. (203)

**queer theory**    An interpretive literary approach based on the idea that sexual orientation is partly ideological and partly social. A number of queer theorists see the heterosexual/homosexual divide as less distinct than has traditionally been understood. The application of the theory is the discovery, often previously ignored, that many works contain either obvious or submerged homosexual elements. (309)

**reader-response critical approach**    An interpretive literary approach based on the proposition that literary works are not fully created until readers make transactions with them by actualizing them in the light of their particular knowledge and experience. (315)

**realism,** or **verisimilitude**    The use of true, lifelike, or probable situations and concerns. Also, the theory underlying the depiction of reality in literature. (88, 114)

**reliable narrator**    A speaker who is untainted by self-interest or other limitations, who therefore has no reason to hide details and make misstatements. This speaker's narration is therefore to be accepted at face value; contrasted with an *unreliable narrator,* q.v. (70)

**representative character**    A *flat character* with the qualities of all other members of a group (i.e., clerks, cowboys, detectives, etc.); a *stereotype.* (88)

**research, literary**    The systematic use of primary and secondary sources for assistance in studying and writing about a literary *problem.* (Ch. 18: 259)

**resolution**    See *dénouement.*

**response**    A reader's intellectual and emotional reactions to a literary work. (3)

**review**    A free-ranging essay on a literary work. Reviews may be designed for general readers and also for readers with specific fields of interest (i.e., politics, religion, history, science, family life, etc.). (Ch. 17: 253)

**rhetorical figures**    See *figurative language.*

**rhetorical substitution**    See *substitution.*

**rhyme**    The repetition of identical or closely related sounds in the syllables of different words, usually in concluding syllables at the ends of lines, such as Shakespeare's *day* and *away* ("Sonnet 18") and Swinburne's *forever* and *never* ("The Garden of Proserpine"). See *internal rhyme.* (199, 201, 202)

**rhyme scheme**   A pattern of *rhyme*, usually indicated by the assignment of a letter of the alphabet to each rhyming sound, as in *a b b a* as the rhyming pattern of the first quatrain of an Italian or Petrarchan sonnet. (203)

**rhythm**   The varying speed, intensity, elevation, pitch, loudness, and expressiveness of speech, especially poetry. (205)

**rising rhyme**   See *heavy-stress rhyme.*

**romance**   (1) Lengthy Spanish and French stories of the sixteenth and seventeenth centuries. (2) Modern formulaic stories describing the growth of an impulsive, passionate, and powerful love relationship. (2)

**round character**   A literary character, usually but not necessarily the *protagonist* of a story or play, who is three-dimensional, rounded, authentic, memorable, original, and true to life. A round character is the center of our attention and is both individual and unpredictable. The round character also profits from experience and, in the course of a story or play, undergoes change or development. See *dynamic character.* (86)

**run-on line**   See *enjambement.*

**scan, scansion**   The determination of the prevailing *rhythm* and poetic characteristics of a poem. (191)

**second-person point of view**   A narration in which a second-person listener ("you") is the protagonist and the speaker is someone (e.g., doctor, parent, rejected lover) with knowledge that the protagonist does not possess or understand about his or her own actions. Sometimes the "you" of the second person is used popularly and vaguely to signify persons in a general audience, including the speaker. (70, 74, 75)

**segment**   The smallest meaningful unit of sound, such as the *l, uh,* and *v* sounds making up the word *love.* Segments are to be distinguished from spellings. Thus, the *oo* sound may be spelled as *ui* in *fruit, u* in *flute, oo* in *foolish, o* in *lose, uu* in *vacuum,* or *ou* in *troupe.* (190, 206)

**selective recollection**   See *flashback.*

**semivowel sounds**   Meaningful semivowel sounds occupy a pronunciation area between vowels and consonants. They either (1) begin in an initiating vowel position, and then conclude in a terminating vowel position, or (2) begin, with breath added, and end in the same vowel position, as with *h.* The semivowels are *w* (wake, wend), *y* (yellow, union) and *h* (heart, happy). (189)

**septenary**   See *heptameter.*

**setting**   The natural, manufactured, and cultural environment in which characters live and move, including all their possessions, homes, ways of life, and assumptions. (Ch. 7: 113)

**short story**   A compact, concentrated work of *narrative fiction* that may also contain description, dialogue, and commentary. Poe used the term "brief prose tale" for the short story, and emphasized that it should create a powerful and unified impact. (2)

**sight rhyme**   See *eye rhyme.*

**simile**   A figure of comparison, using "like" with nouns and "as" with clauses, as in "the trees were bent by the wind *like actors bowing after a performance*," (Ch. 10: 147)

**situational irony,** or **irony of situation**   A type of *irony* emphasizing that particular characters are enmeshed in forces that greatly exceed their perception, comprehension, and control. See *irony.* (179)

**slant rhyme**   A *near rhyme* in which the concluding consonant sounds (but not the vowels) are identical, as in *should* and *food, slim* and *ham.* See also *inexact rhyme.* (202)

**song**   See *lyric.*

**sound**   The phonetics of language, separately and collectively considered. See also *prosody.* (190)

**speaker**   The *narrator* of a story or poem, the *point of view,* often an independent character who is completely imagined and consistently maintained by the author. In addition to narrating the essential events of the work (justifying the status of narrator), the speaker may also introduce other aspects of his or her knowledge and may express judgments and opinions. Often the character of the speaker is of as much interest in the story as the *actions* or *incidents.* 65

**spondee**   A two-syllable *foot* consisting of successive, equally heavy *accents* (e.g., *SLOW TIME, MEN'S EYES, BLAZE UP*). (193)

**sprung rhythm**   A poetic line, associated with Gerard Manley Hopkins (1844–1889), in which the accents are "sprung" forth by the close juxtaposition of one-syllable stressed words, often characterized by both rhyme and alliteration. (196)

**stanza**   A group of poetic lines corresponding to paragraphs in prose; stanzaic meters and rhymes are usually repeating and systematic. (203)

**static character**   A character who undergoes no change, a *flat character*; contrasted with a *dynamic character* or *round character*. (87)

**stereotype**   A character who is so ordinary and unoriginal that he or she seems to have been cast in a mold; a *representative* character. (88)

**stock character**   A *flat character* in a standard role with standard *traits*, such as the irate police captain, the bored hotel clerk, or the sadistic criminal; a *stereotype*. (87)

**stop sounds,** also called **plosives** or **check consonants**   Consonant sounds that in an initial position require a momentary stoppage of breath, and then a quick release, thus making a noticeable burst of air (i.e., small "explosion") before moving to the following vowel. In medial and concluding positions, the stops do not demand the same burst of air, and often they are hardly released at all. The three voiceless stops are *p* (*present*, Phili*p*), *t* (*tele*phone, i*t*), and *k* (*keep*, stic*k*). The voiced stops are *b* (*bunch*, tu*b*e), *d* (*dense*, le*d*), and *g* (*golly*, lu*g*). (189)

**story**   A *narrative*, usually fictional, and usually centering on a major character and rendering a complete action. (2)

**stress**   The emphasis given to a syllable, either strong or light. See also *accent*. (191)

**strong-stress rhythm**   See *sprung rhythm*.

**structuralist critical approach**   An interpretive literary approach attempting to find relationships and similarities among elements that appear to be separate and discrete. (307)

**structure**   The arrangement and placement of materials in a work. (Ch. 6: 102–112)

**substitution**   In prosody, the presence of a variant poetic *foot* within a poem in which a particular metrical foot is dominant. *Formal substitution* is the use of an actual variant foot within a line, such as an *anapest* being used in place of an *iamb*. *Rhetorical substitution* is the manipulation of the *caesura* to create the effect of a series of differing feet. (194)

**suspended rhyme**   See *inexact rhyme*.

**syllable**   A meaningful and separately pronounced part of a word (e.g., the *sing* and *ing* parts of *singing*; the *sub*, *sti*, *tu*, and *tion* parts of *substitution*). Some words consist of only one syllable (e.g., *a, an, boy, girl, the, when, screeched*). Many other words contain many syllables (e.g. antidisestablishmentarianism). (190)

**symbol, symbolism**   A specific word, idea, or object that may stand for ideas, values, persons, or ways of life. (Ch. 11: 157)

**symbolic literary approach**   See *archetypal/symbolic/mythic critical approach*.

**syzygy**   See *dipody*.

**tactile imagery**   *Images* of touch and responses to touch. (138)

**tenor**   The ideas conveyed in a *metaphor* or *simile*. See also *vehicle*. (150)

**tense**   Besides embodying reports of actions and circumstances, verbs possess altering forms—*tenses*—that signify the times when things occur, whether past, present, or future. Perfect and progressive tenses indicate completed or continuing activities. Tense is an important aspect of *point of view* because the notation of time influences the way in which events are perceived and expressed. Narratives are usually told in the past tense, but many recent writers of fiction prefer the present tense for conveying a sense of immediacy. No matter when a sequence of actions is presumed to have taken place, the introduction of dialogue changes the action to the present. See *point of view*. (32, 73, 76)

**tetrameter**   A line of four metrical *feet*. (192)

**tercet** or **triplet**   A three-line unit or stanza of poetry, usually rhyming aaa, bbb, bcb, cdc, etc. (3)

**theme**   (1) The major or central idea of a work. (2) An essay, a short composition developing an interpretation or advancing an argument. (3) The main point or idea that a writer of an essay asserts and illustrates. (124)

**thesis sentence,** or **thesis statement**    An introductory sentence that names the topics to be developed in the body of an essay. (28)

**third-person point of view**    A third-person method of *narration* (i.e., *she, he, it, they, them,* etc.) in which the *speaker* or *narrator* is not a part of the story, unlike the involvement of the narrator of a *first-person point of view.* Because the third-person speaker may exhibit great knowledge and understanding, together with other qualities of character, he or she is often virtually identified with the author, but this identification is not easily decided. See also *authorial voice, omniscient point of view.* (71, 74)

**third-person objective point of view**    See *dramatic point of view.*

**tone**    The techniques and modes of presentation that reveal or create attitudes. (Ch. 12: 175)

**topic sentence**    The sentence determining or introducing the subject matter of a paragraph. (29)

**topical/historical critical approach**    An interpretive literary approach that stresses the relationship of literature to its historical period. (305)

**trait, traits**    A typical mode of behavior; the study of major traits provides a guide to the description of *character.* (83)

**trimeter**    A line of three metrical *feet.* (192)

**triple rhyme**    See *dactylic rhyme.*

**trochaic (double) rhyme**    Rhyming trochees such as *FLOW-er* and *TOW-er.* (201)

**trochee, trochaic**    A two-syllable foot consisting of a heavy stress followed by a light stress (e.g., *RUN-ning, SING-ing, EAT-ing*). (193)

**unaccented syllable**    A syllable receiving a light stress. See *light stress.* (191)

**understatement**    Rhetorically, the deliberate underplaying or undervaluing of an assertion or idea to create emphasis; a form of *irony.* (179)

**universal symbol**    See *cultural symbol.*

**unreliable narrator**    A speaker who through ignorance, self-interest, deviousness, or lack of capacity may tell lies and otherwise distort truth. For the reader to locate truth in the unreliable narrator's story requires careful judgment and not inconsiderable skepticism. See also *reliable narrator.* (70)

**unstressed syllable**    See *light stress.*

**value, values**    The attachment of worth, significance, and desirability to an *idea* so that the idea is judged not only for its significance as thought but also for its importance as a goal, ideal, or standard. (124)

**vehicle**    The image or reference of figures of speech, such as a *metaphor* or *simile*; it is the vehicle that carries or embodies the *tenor.* See also *tenor.* (150)

**verbal irony**    Language stressing the importance of an idea by stating the opposite of what is meant. Verbal irony may convey humor, but as often as not it also reflects serious criticism and even bitterness and mockery of particular facets of life and the universe. See *irony.* (178)

**verisimilitude ("like truth")**    A characteristic whereby the setting, circumstances, characters, dialogue, actions, and outcomes in a work are designed to seem true, lifelike, real, plausible, and probable. See also *realism.* (88)

**versification**    See *prosody.*

**villanelle**    A poem of nineteen lines, composed of five *tercets* and a concluding *quatrain.* The form requires that whole lines be repeated in a specific order and that only two rhyming sounds occur throughout. (3)

**virgule**    A slash mark (/) used in poetic *scansion* to mark the boundaries of poetic *feet.* A double virgule (//) is commonly used to indicate the placement of a *caesura.* See *caesura.* (192)

**visual image**    Language describing visible objects and situations. (137)

**voice**    See *speaker.*

**voiced, voiceless sounds**    Consonant sounds that either are voiced (as with the *v* in the word *voiced*) or unvoiced (as with the concluding *s* and *t* sounds concluding the same word, *voiced* [i.e., voist]). (189).

**vowel sounds,** or **vowel segments**    Meaningful sounds produced by the continuant resonation of the voice in the space between the tongue and the top of the mouth, such as the *ay* in *pray,* the *ee* in *feel,* the *i* in *fine,* the *oh* in *flow,* and the *oo* in *cool.* (188)

# Credits

# Index of Authors and Titles, Topics, References, and Chapter Titles

Authors are listed alphabetically, followed by the titles of their works. In some instances, such as the *Oxford Companions*, the titles are listed separately. Anonymous works are indexed under the titles. For brief definitions of important terms and concepts used in the text, please consult the preceding Glossary on pages 401–412.